THE GOOD GARDENS GUIDE

NINETEENTH EDITION

THE GOOD GARDENS GUIDE

Edited by Peter King & Katherine Lambert
Associate Editor: Anne Gatti

supported by

Part of the Garden Writers' Guild

FRANCES LINCOLN LIMITED

PUBLISHERS

Frances Lincoln Ltd
4 Torriano Mews
Torriano Avenue
London NW5 2RZ
www.franceslincoln.com

The Good Gardens Guide
Nineteenth Edition
Copyright © Frances Lincoln 2008
Text copyright © Peter King 2008
Photographs copyright © See page 552

First Frances Lincoln edition: 2008

Administrators and Disk Editors:
  Anita Owen and Mala Rohling
Design: Keith Rigley
Maps: Linda M. Dawes,
  Belvoir Cartographics & Design
Index: Angie Hipkin

A catalogue record for this book is
available from the British Library.

ISBN: 978-0-7112-2744-6

Printed and bound in Singapore

9 8 7 6 5 4 3 2 1

CONTENTS

THE GARDENS

A GUIDE TO THE *GUIDE*

The Good Gardens Guide, first published in 1990 by Peter King and the late Graham Rose and now in its nineteenth year, is dedicated to encouraging its readers to visit gardens, private estates, public parks and green spaces in every corner of the British Isles. They number over 1160 and range from the twin walled gardens at Dunbeath Castle in northernmost Scotland to Barbara Hepworth's sculpture garden in the toe of Cornwall, from the cottage garden created by three sisters at Plas-yn-Rhiw on the windswept Lleyn Peninsula to the formal layout of Walmer Castle, one of the Cinque Ports guarding the approach to Kent. Not forgetting, of course, gardens in Ireland and on our offshore islands – the Isle of Wight, Guernsey and Jersey, the Scilly Isles, and Skye, Mull and others that pepper the sea off the western coast of Scotland.

Each year a certain number of these drop out or are dropped, which provides the opportunity to seek out new gardens, with suggestions coming from the *Guide*'s inspectors, from garden designers and photographers, journalists and horticulturists, friends, readers and the garden owners themselves. This year there are 45. Among them are gardens made to complement historic houses (Aiket Castle in Scotland, Weston Park in Herefordshire and Hindringham Hall in Norfolk); gardens of wit and imagination (Wyckhurst in Kent, Yews Farm in Somerset and 29 West Hill in London); and those that combine passionate plantsmanship and good design (23 Docklands Avenue in Essex, Poppy Cottage in Cornwall and Crossbills in Suffolk). Two gardens in Buckinghamshire are indelibly associated with their previous owners – Gipsy House with Roald Dahl, The Old Thatch with Enid Blyton.

The *Guide* is arranged by UK counties, followed by Northern Ireland, the Republic of Ireland, Scotland, Wales and the Channel Islands. Entries appear alphabetically. Some have postal addresses in one county and are physically located in another, so if a garden seems to be missing, it is worth consulting the index. London, exceptionally, has been divided into public spaces and private gardens. At the end of each county or region are Other Recommended Gardens, where the entries have been made briefer; this may be because they are very small, because they are rarely open or because their distinct quality can be set down to advantage in a few carefully chosen words.

The entries are written by a team of independent inspectors, who generally choose to visit anonymously to ensure objectivity. Due to the size of certain counties or regions, and the sheer number of gardens included, it is not possible for them to evaluate every garden on an annual basis, so visits are organised as part of a rolling programme.

To help readers, the inspectors and editors have devised a starring system for the gardens. Over 100 have been marked ★★, indicating that in our opinion these are the finest in Britain and Ireland in terms of design and planting; a few rank among the finest in the world. Many are of historic importance, others are of recent origin. Readers will appreciate that direct comparisons cannot be made between a vast estate like Chatsworth and a tiny plantsman's garden behind a terraced house, although both may be excellent of their kind. (A list of two-starred gardens appears on p xvi.) Other gardens of exceptional quality have a single ★. The bulk of gardens in the *Guide* are not given a mark of distinction, but all have considerable merit and are worthy of a visit when in the region, while some have distinctive features of design or plant content, given in the description, which will justify making a special journey.

All the information needed for an enjoyable garden visit is given in the column adjoining the main text. It is the best available to us, but in the interim changes do occur: properties are sold or ownership varied, or limitations imposed on opening times, entry charges increased. When owners open for the National Gardens Scheme, this is indicated, and visitors should consult the Yellow Book for details. Otherwise, specific dates and times apply to 2008 only. When making a special or long-distance journey, it may be wise anyway to telephone in advance or consult the website. The dates and times given are inclusive – 'May to Sept' means that the garden is open from 1st May to 30th Sept inclusive, and 2 – 5pm means that visits will be effective between those times, although you should aim to arrive at least half an hour before closing time.

At the end of the book is a listing of nurseries with attractive gardens attached, where plants on sale are often to be found growing in special display area or in the owner's own adjacent garden. Many of these are of a quality that merits their own entry, but a further 100 have separate entries in this section.

Finally, there are 24 pages of maps.

The following symbols are used to give additional information at a glance:

NEW New garden this year

○, ◑, ◐, ● **Opening times** These symbols indicate gardens are open as follows: ○ throughout the year; ◑ most of the year; ◐ more or less throughout the season from Easter to October for several days (i.e. more than two or three) each week; and ● open on a certain number of days and/or by appointment.

♨, ✗, 🧺 **Refreshments** Where ♨ is given, tea or light refreshments are usually available. ✗ indicates that meals are served. 🧺 means that picnics are permitted, although probably in certain areas only.

WC, **WC** **Toilet facilities** WC indicates that access to a toilet or toilets is provided, while **WC** means that the toilet facilities are also suitable for disabled visitors. Where neither symbol is given, no specific toilets are available and enquiries will have to be directed to staff or owners.

♿ **Wheelchair suitability** Owners and inspectors have told us where they believe a garden is partly or wholly negotiable by someone in a wheelchair. This symbol refers to the garden only; if a house or other building is also open, it may or may not be suitable for wheelchairs.

🐕 **Dogs** They are allowed in the property on leads (although often in restricted areas).

🌿 **Plants for sale** These are often propagated on site, but may also be bought in from a commercial source for re-sale.

🏚 **Shop** A sales outlet on the premises, such as National Trust shops, those selling souvenirs, etc.

🎪 **Events** These range from large-scale and national to low-key and local, and may be held during, or in addition to, normal garden opening times. Those wishing to participate in (or to avoid) events should check before travelling.

⚲ **Children-friendly** Some owners pay particular attention to expanding the attractions for the whole family, while other gardens are intriguing to children by their very design and content.

B&B **Bed and breakfast** An increasing number of owners offer accommodation – a fine way for visitors to become acquainted with a garden.

No symbol means either that a certain facility is not available at a garden or that we have not been notified of it. However, details of partial availability and other helpful information specific to particular gardens may be listed above the symbols.

NOTES ON GREAT GARDENERS

Sir Charles Barry (1795–1860) A highly successful architect (Houses of Parliament etc), he popularised the formal Italian style of gardening in the mid-nineteenth century, creating impressive designs which incorporated terraces, flights of steps, balustrading, urns, fountains and loggias. His most notable gardens were at Trentham, Dunrobin, Cliveden, Shrubland Park and Harewood House.

Christopher Bradley-Hole (b. 1955) He worked first on a range of architectural projects before moving over to landscapes and gardens. He can claim to be among the earliest of British minimalists to practise the art of garden design. Winner of five gold medals at Chelsea, he works chiefly for private clients, although the London garden he designed at 82 Wood Vale may be visited.

Charles Bridgeman (d. 1738) Famous for the way in which he exploited the outstanding features of the sites which he chose to create as gardens, he became the link between the rigid formality of much seventeenth-century garden design and the apparent freedom of the landscape movement pioneered by William Kent and `Capability' Brown. While retaining features such as geometric parterres close to the house and straight allées, he also incorporated wilderness and meadow areas linked by meandering paths. By his use of the ha-ha, he made vistas of the surrounding landscape an integral part of his designs. Apart from work for royal patrons in gardens such as Richmond and Kensington Gardens, he carried out important works at Blenheim, Claremont, Rousham, Cliveden and Stowe.

John Brookes (b. 1933) Designer of over 700 gardens here and abroad, he is in Jane Brown's estimation 'the most talented Modernist who has worked in Britain since the war'. His Mondrianesque garden for Penguin Books in Harmondsworth is his most elegant modern garden, Denmans his best-known.

Lancelot 'Capability' Brown (1716–83) Having worked as head gardener and clerk of works at Stowe early in his career, Brown became familiar with the work of Bridgeman and Vanbrugh and helped to execute the designs of William Kent and James Gibbs. However, he was more radical than any of them, discarding formality when creating natural-looking landscapes with large stretches of water and impressive clumps of native trees, and confining flowering plants and vegetables to walled gardens well away from the house. Examples of his work in the *Guide* are: Audley End, Berrington, Blenheim, Bowood, Burghley, Cadland House, Chatsworth, Claremont, Croome Park, Harewood, Highclere, Holkham, Leeds Castle, Longleat, Petworth, Sheffield Park, Sledmere, Syon, Temple Newsam, Trentham, Warwick Castle, Weston House, Wimpole Hall and Wrest Park.

Brenda Colvin (1897–1981) A highly influential landscape architect who worked at both ends of the scale – large projects such as land reclamation schemes and new towns, and small gardens for private clients. She helped to found the Landscape Institute, serving as its President from 1951 to 1953, and her *Land and Landscape* became a prime reference book for the profession.

Dame Sylvia Crowe (1901–98) She was responsible for many large-scale projects for a crop of new towns and became an acknowledged expert on the sympathetic integration of development schemes, such as the construction of power stations, with the surrounding landscape. She was President of the Landscape Institute from 1957 to 1959. Examples of her work may be seen at Blenheim, Cottesbrooke and Lexham Hall.

Margery Fish (1888–1969) An informed plantswoman and influential lecturer and author, a partisan of William Robinson's naturalistic approach to gardening. This she developed in her own garden at East Lambrook, which became a haven for endangered garden plants. Her style of mixing semi-formal features with traditional planting has been influential.

Henk Gerritsen (b. 1948) One of a famous group of Dutch garden designers, he has been involved in turning the 40-acre garden at Waltham Place into a wholly organic garden.

Isabelle Van Groeningen (b. 1965) She arrived in the UK in 1983 from Belgium to train at Wisley and Kew, and in 1992 formed the Land Art practice with the German landscape architect Gabriella Pape. Together they have tackled a range of projects both in Europe and elsewhere — historic gardens, new private gardens, public parks and commercial sites. Examples of their work in the *Guide* are at Eltham Palace, Cliveden, Ryton Organic Garden and The London Wetland Centre.

Charles Hamilton (1704–86) Under the influence of William Kent between 1738 and 1773, when he was obliged to sell the estate at Painshill Park in Surrey to pay his debts, Hamilton created one of Britain's most picturesque landscape gardens. As well as being a talented designer, he was an exemplary plantsman, incorporating many exotics in his schemes. He also designed a cascade and grotto at Bowood in Wiltshire and advised on work at Holland Park in London and Stourhead.

Ian Hamilton Finlay (1925–2006) A calligrapher and sculptor of the highest order, he will be remembered above all for his home in Lanarkshire, Little Sparta, which has been described by Sir Roy Strong as 'the most original contemporary garden in the country'. This is modernism at its most elegant and refined, and a showcase for a lifetime of his own work.

Gertrude Jekyll (1843–1932) Both by her writing and her planting (much of it accomplished in partnership with the architect Sir Edwin Lutyens), she has probably had as much influence on the appearance of British gardens as any other designer. Her great strength was in carefully considered and subtle use of plant colour. Finding inspiration in the informality of cottage gardens, she created large interwoven swathes of plants rather than confining them to precise `spotty' patterns. One of the best examples of her work with Lutyens is Hestercombe; others are Barrington Court, Castle Drogo, Folly Farm, Goddards, Hatchlands, Knebworth, Upton Grey Manor House, Munstead Wood, Tylney Hall, Vann and Yalding.

Sir Geoffrey Jellicoe (1900–96) Shortly after becoming an architect, he made an extensive study of Italian gardens with J.C. Shepherd, which led in 1925 to their classic book, *Italian Gardens of the Renaissance*. The publication of *Gardens and Design* in 1927 helped to bring him interesting commissions, such as the design of a large formal garden at Ditchley Park in Oxfordshire, giving scope for the strongly architectural quality of his work. After World War II he was given much public work, including the Cathedral Close in Exeter, the Kennedy Memorial at Runnymede and a large theme park at Galveston in Texas. Among his work for private clients, the gardens at Sutton Place and Shute House are notable. His work may also be seen at Cliveden, Cottesbrooke, Mottisfont and Sandringham.

Charles Jencks (b. 1939) An American academic long resident in the UK, he is best known for his re-landscaping of the garden at Portrack in the Scottish Borders with his wife Maggie Keswick. The principal landscape elements, monumental earthworks, echo the Land Art movement of the 1960s. Since his wife's death he has created the Garden of Cosmic Speculation (a scientific theme park) at Portrack, and the Landform Ueda for the Scottish Gallery of Modern Art in Edinburgh.

Lawrence Johnston (1871–1948) One of the most outstandingly stylish twentieth-century gardeners, he was an American who spent much of his youth in Paris and built two great gardens in Europe which influenced the design of a great many others, including Sissinghurst. In 1905 he began to make the garden at Hidcote, where he pioneered the creation of a series of sheltered and interconnected garden rooms, each of which surprised by its different content and treatment.

William Kent (1685–1748) The former apprentice coach painter from Hull twice made the Grand Tour of Italy with his most influential patron, Lord Burlington. Heavily influenced by the paintings of Claude and Salvator Rosa, he later tried to introduce the type of romantic landscape encountered in their canvases into his gardens, freeing them from much of the formality which had dominated previous British gardening. His work at Rousham, Holkham, Chiswick House, Claremont and Stowe had a great influence on `Capability' Brown, Charles Hamilton and Henry Hoare of Stourhead.

Arabella Lennox-Boyd (b. 1938) Italian by birth and upbringing, she has designed some 300 gardens – in Europe, Barbados, Canada, the United States and Mexico. She is renowned for the clarity and elegance of her designs and planting, and is a Chelsea gold medallist five times over. Examples of her work may be seen at Stanbridge Mill, Eaton Hall, Ascott, Whitfield House and in her own garden, Gresgarth in Lancashire.

Christopher Lloyd (1921–2006) The doyen of twentieth-century garden-makers and one of the most stimulating of garden writers. He was the son of Nathaniel Lloyd, the architectural writer, who commissioned Edwin Lutyens to extend his house at Great Dixter and to design the garden. Christopher Lloyd brought to it his great skill as a plantsman and an almost iconoclastic approach to Lutyens' planting.

Sir Edwin Lutyens (1869–1944) A fine architect who between 1893 and 1912 created approximately 70 gardens in partnership with Gertrude Jekyll. Her subtle planting always softened and complemented the strong architectural nature of his garden designs, and they in their turn splendidly integrated the house with the garden and its site. A fine example is at Hestercombe; others are at Abbotswood, Ammerdown, Castle Drogo, Folly Farm, Goddards, Heywood, Knebworth, Misarden, Munstead Wood and Parc Floral des Moutiers.

Thomas H. Mawson (1861–1933) A Lancastrian who trained in London and set up a landscape practice in Windermere in 1885, his reputation quickly grew and he was chosen by many of the rich northern industrialists to landscape the gardens of their Lakeland holiday homes. Examples of his work may be seen at Brockhole, Dyffryn, Graythwaite, The Hill Garden, Holker, Rivington Terraced Garden and Wightwick.

Hal Moggridge (b. 1936) He trained as an architect before working for Geoffrey Jellicoe. He started his own practice in 1967 after advising the GLC on suitable sites for new towns, then two years later joined Brenda Colvin in practice as Colvin and Moggridge. As a firm they have designed industrial landscapes, public gardens and private parks, landscaped the National Botanic Garden of Wales and planted William Morris's diminutive garden at Kelmscott.

William E. Nesfield (1793–1881) Working often in partnership with the architect Salvin, his style was eclectic, usually reflecting that of the houses they surrounded; he was responsible for the reintroduction of the parterre (a good example is at Holkham) as a garden feature. He worked also at Alton, Blickling, Cliveden, Dorfold Hall, Holkham, Kew, Rode Hall, Shugborough, Somerleyton and Trentham.

Piet Oudolf (b. 1944) One of the best-known proponents of naturalistic planting with perennials and grasses, the celebrated Dutchman is a nurseryman as well as a garden designer. He has done some of his best work in Britain – at Wisley, Bury Court, Pensthorpe and Scampston. His latest grand projet is in collaboration with Tom Stuart-Smith at Trentham.

Russell Page (1906–85) Trained as a painter, he quickly became absorbed by garden design, working for several years in association with Jellicoe. After the war he secured many commissions in Europe and America, including the garden at the Frick in New York and the Battersea Festival Gardens in London. He encapsulated many of his ideas about garden design in *The Education of a Gardener*, first published in 1962. Examples of his work are at Longleat and Port Lympne.

Sir Joseph Paxton (1803–65) Gardener at Chatsworth for 32 years from 1826, where he made the great fountain and the pioneering conservatory. One of the early designers of public parks, including those at Birkenhead and Halifax, he was also influential as a writer and a founder of *The Gardener's Chronicle*. Other examples of his work are at Birkenhead, Capesthorne, Somerleyton and Tatton.

Dan Pearson (b. 1964) He began his professional career in 1987, and has completed a wide range of private and public sector commissions. He was responsible for re-landscaping the grounds of Althorp and for the landscape design surrounding the Millennium Dome. He is also well known as an author, a columnist and a TV presenter.

Harold Peto (1854–1933) A talented architect working for the partnership which later employed the young Lutyens, who undoubtedly influenced his style. A lover of Italianate formal gardens, one of his best-known works was his own garden at Iford Manor, but the canal garden at Buscot Park and the Casita garden at Ilnacullin are also notable achievements. Other examples are at Easton Lodge, Greathed Manor, Heale House, Wayford Manor and West Dean.

Humphry Repton (1752–1818) The most influential eighteenth-century landscaper after the death of Lancelot Brown, he was a great protagonist of Brown's ideas but tended to favour denser planting, and his parkland buildings were rustic rather than classical. He restored formality to gardens with terracing, flights of steps and balustrading. He produced over 400 of his famous 'before and after' Red Books and worked tireleslly on such fine estates as Holkham, Sheffield Park, Woburn and Sheringham. Other examples in the *Guide* are at Ashridge, Attingham, Corsham, Hatchlands, Kenwood, Longleat, Rode Hall and Ston Easton.

William Robinson (1838–1935) An Irishman who settled in England and became one of the most prolific writers and influential designers of his epoch. By his teaching and example he liberated gardeners from the prim rigidity which had begun to dominate garden design in the mid-nineteenth century, advocating a free and natural attitude towards the creation of herbaceous and mixed beds. His planting philosophy early inspired Gertrude Jekyll. He founded a weekly journal, *The Garden*, and wrote the best-selling *The English Flower Garden*. Examples of his work are at Gravetye Manor, High Beeches, Killerton and Leckhampton College in Cambridge.

Lanning Roper (1912–83) A Harvard graduate from New Jersey who adopted Britain as his home and became one of the most popular landscapers in the 30 years after World War II. His best schemes, such as that at Glenveagh Castle, involved a subtle handling of plants combined with interesting formal features. One of his most controversial designs is the ornamental canal in the RHS garden at Wisley. Other examples of his work are at Anglesey Abbey, Broughton Castle, Fairfield House and Orford Old Rectory.

Vita Sackville-West (1892–1962) With her husband, Harold Nicolson, she made the famous garden at Sissinghurst Castle, begun in 1932. The couple were friendly with and influenced by Lawrence Johnston. Another example of her work may be seen at Alderley Grange. Although she was the propagandist of the pair, some think that her husband's conception of structure made a great contribution to twentieth-century garden design.

Tom Stuart-Smith (b. 1960) A superb plantsman and a perennial Chelsea gold medallist. He aims to create 'informal and wild' gardens, and indeed his gardens are becoming increasingly naturalistic. Although most of his work is for private clients such as his beautiful and exciting design for the walled garden at Broughton Grange, he has also created gardens at Wisley and Rosemoor, another at Windsor Castle, and is currently a key player in the vast restoration project at Trentham.

Sir John Vanbrugh (1644–1726) A considerable dramatist and spectacular architect of palaces like Blenheim in Oxfordshire and Castle Howard in Yorkshire. Although he did not generally design landscapes, he ensured that his houses were magnificently sited and often created buildings for their gardens, such as the bridge at Blenheim, and for landscapes made by other designers such as Stowe and Claremont.

Rosemary Verey (1918–2001) A renowned plantswoman who created a famous garden at Barnsley House, and designed others for private clients. Other examples of her work are at Holdenby House and The Old Rectory in Sudborough. She was also an inspiring lecturer and one of England's foremost gardening writers, author of 17 books.

Kim Wilkie (b. 1955) A landscape architect, urban designer and an environmental planner, expert at introducing modern designs into historic landscapes. Responsible for the Thames Landscape Strategy, he threaded together the eighteenth-century waterside villas and landscape and made the administrative authorities along the Thames look anew at their heritage. He has helped to revive the cult of earth sculpting with his grass terraces at Great Fosters and Heveningham Hall. His new garden at the V&A in London is restrained, practical and elegant.

GLOSSARY OF GARDEN TERMS

Arbour Any sheltered covered area open to one side which usually contains a seat. Often surrounded by masonry, hedging or trelliswork covered with climbing plants.

Allée **or alley** A path either cut through a thick shrubbery or woodland or closely flanked by a hedge or wall.

Auricula theatre A shelter rising in tiers housing a collection of auriculas – an early-nineteenth-century collectors' craze.

Bath house A rectangular sunken pool for cold-water bathing, with seating approached by steps.

Bosquet or bosket A block of closely planted trees with allées between.

Canal An ornamental water basin made in the form of an elongated rectangle. It can either be excavated into the ground or confined above ground within masonry walls.

Clair-voie **or** *clair-voyée* A gap in a wall or hedge which extends the view by allowing a glimpse of the surrounding countryside; also an openwork gate, fence or grille at the end of an allée.

Cottage orné A deliberately picturesque rustic dwelling designed to ornament a park.

Crinkle-crankle wall A serpentine wall sheltering fruit trees within its walls.

Exedra An area of turf within a semi-circular hedge which is commonly used to display ornaments or to locate a semi-circular seat; or the seat itself.

Eye-catcher A building such as a tower, temple, obelisk, etc., or sometimes merely a bench, large urn or outstanding long-lived plant designed to beckon the eye towards a particularly rewarding view.

Finial An ornament such as an urn or a pointed sculptural form used to cap features like gateposts, the tops of spires, the top corners of buildings, etc.

Folly A decorative building with no serious function except perhaps to lure attention along a vista or to improve the composition of the garden 'picture'.

Gazebo Dog latin for 'I will gaze', used to describe a building usually sited on a high terrace from which the surrounding countryside can be enjoyed.

Grotto/Nymphaeum An artificial garden feature made to simulate an underground cavern and usually dimly lit from a single small natural light source such as the cave mouth or an oval occulus pierced through the roof or wall. But when formally shaped and lined with statuary and a sophisticated encrustation of shellwork, a grotto can become a nymphaeum.

Ha-ha A deep ditch separating the garden from the landscape beyond. It allows the unscreened view to be enjoyed from the house but is profiled in such a way that livestock cannot enter the garden.

Hermitage A rustic building popularised in the eighteenth century, supposedly as a hermit's retreat.

Knot garden Geometric patterns of low-growing hedge plants such as box or shrubby germander which are made to appear as though they intertwine like knotted cord. The areas between the hedges are filled with plants or decorative gravel.

Moon door or gate A circular opening in a door or wall.

Mount An artificial hill usually surmounted by an arbour from which landscapes both inside and beyond the garden can be enjoyed from a different perspective.

Obelisk A tall, thin vertical column diminishing in width as it rises, and frequently tapered to a pyramid. Large-scale examples have been built to commemorate great events or notable people and often to act as eye-catchers in great landscape schemes. Smaller treillage versions have been used to beckon for attention in smaller gardens or to act as vertical frames for climbing plants.

Pagoda A feature in a few great landscape gardens based on Buddhist multi-storey towers of spiritual significance. In Britain they were first introduced during the eighteenth-century craze for things Chinese.

Palladian bridge A bridge with a classical superstructure, usually open-sided with columns supporting a roof.

Parterre An intricately patterned formal garden which usually includes other features such as statuary, water basins and fountains; much larger than a knot garden.

Patte d'oie Literally 'goose foot'; a series of usually three formal paths or grand avenues leading fan-wise from a single point through densely planted trees.

Pergola A framework of columns supporting beams, usually clad with climbing plants such as roses, clematis or wisteria.

Pleaching Training the branches of a line of trees horizontally by pruning and attaching them to wires, so that the remainder can be intertwined as they grow to form a screen of foliage.

Quincunx A pattern (sometimes a repeat-pattern) of four trees at the corners of a square and one at the centre.

Red Book Bound books of proposals including 'flap' overlays, drawn by Humphry Repton for his clients.

Rotunda Strictly, circle of classical columns on a raised circular plinth supporting a domed roof. Instead of a solid dome it may be topped with an open ironwork dome. Sometimes loosely called a kiosk.

Rustic work Garden features, such as garden houses, fences or seats, made from unbarked tree branches, and frequently embellished with such decoration as patterns made from sectioned pine cones.

Souterrain An underground chamber, usually in a grotto.

Stumpery Roots and stumps arranged upside down and covered with trailing plants.

Stilt hedge Clipped trees, such as limes, which have all their branches removed for several feet above the ground to reveal a line of bare trunks like stilts.

Théâtre de verdure Similar to but usually more spacious than an exedra, a turf 'stage' with a backcloth of trimmed hedge and sometimes other hedges disposed like the wings of a theatre.

Treillage Architectural features such as arbours, obelisks or ambitious screens made out of trellis.

Trompe-l'oeil A feature designed to deceive the eye, such as a path which narrows as it recedes from a viewpoint to exaggerate the perspective and make the garden seem larger.

Wilderness A bosquet, grove or wood traversed by paths.

TWO-STARRED GARDENS IN THE *GUIDE*

Buckinghamshire
Ascott; Cliveden; The Manor House, Bledlow;
Stowe Landscape Garden; Waddesdon Manor;
West Wycombe Park

Cambridgeshire
Anglesey Abbey

Cheshire
Ness Botanic Gardens; Tatton Park

Cornwall
Caerhays; Heligan; Trebah; Tresco Abbey;
Trewithen

Cumbria & Isle of Man
Holehird; Holker Hall; Levens Hall

Derbyshire
Chatsworth

Devon
Castle Drogo; Knightshayes; RHS Rosemoor

Dorset
Cranborne Manor; Forde Abbey; Mapperton

Essex
Beth Chatto Garden

Gloucestershire
Abbotswood; Daylesford; Hidcote; Kiftsgate;
National Arboretum Westonbirt; Sezincote

Hampshire & Isle of Wight
Exbury; Longstock Park; Mottisfont; The Sir
Harold Hillier Gardens; West Green

Herefordshire
Brockhampton Cottage

Hertfordshire
Benington Lordship; Hatfield

Kent
Goodnestone Park; Hever Castle; Sissinghurst

Lancashire
Gresgarth Hall; The Old Zoo Garden

London
Chiswick House; Hampton Court Palace; Royal
Botanic Gardens Kew

Norfolk
East Ruston Old Vicarage; Houghton Hall

Northamptonshire
Coton Manor; Cottesbrooke Hall

Northumberland
Belsay Hall

Oxfordshire
Blenheim Palace; Broughton Grange; Pettifers;
Rousham; University of Oxford Botanic Garden;
Westwell

Shropshire
Hodnet Hall; Wollerton Old Hall

Somerset
Cothay Manor; Greencombe; Lady Farm

Staffordshire
Biddulph Grange

Suffolk
Helmingham Hall; Somerleyton Hall

Surrey
Painshill; RHS Garden Wisley; Savill Garden;
Valley Gardens

East Sussex
Great Dixter

West Sussex
Leonardslee; Nymans; Wakehurst Place

Wiltshire
Iford Manor; Stourhead

North & East Yorkshire
Castle Howard; Newby Hall; Scampston Hall;
Studley Royal & Fountains Abbey

Northern Ireland
Annesley Gardens; Mount Stewart; Rowallane

Republic of Ireland
Dillon Garden; Mount Congreve; Mount Usher

Scotland
Arduaine; Benmore Botanic Garden; Castle
Kennedy; Crarae Garden; Crathes Castle;
Culzean Castle; Drummond Castle; Garden of
Cosmic Speculation; Inverewe Garden; Little
Sparta; Logan Botanic Garden; Manderston;
Mount Stuart; Pitmuies Garden; Royal Botanic
Garden Edinburgh

Wales
Bodnant; Powis Castle

BEDFORDSHIRE

For further information about how to use the *Guide*
and for an explanation of the symbols, see pages vi–viii.
Specific dates and times are those given to us by garden owners for 2008.
For 2009 dates, check with the individual properties.
For opening dates under the National Gardens Scheme,
readers should consult *The Yellow Book* or www.ngs.org.uk.
Maps are to be found at the end of the *Guide*.

THE MANOR HOUSE ★

Kathy Brown

Church Road, Stevington, Bedford
· MK43 7QB. Tel: 01234 822064;
www.kathybrownsgarden.homestead.com

5m NW of Bedford off A428, through
Bromham. In Stevington, turn right at
crossroads; garden is on left after 0.25m

Open 3rd and 10th Feb, 12 noon –
4pm; 25th May, 22nd June (for NGS)
and 27th July, 2 – 6pm; and for parties
by appt

Entrance: £4, children free

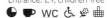

The Manor House

A garden of exuberant imagination, atmospheric and brimful of ideas, with a strong emphasis on garden art. Each of the twenty distinct areas within its 4.5 acres is completely different in atmosphere. The summer garden planted around the old fish pond is colourful and strongly Mediterranean, with a variety of succulents and imposing echiums followed by a fine display of aeoniums, agaves and dasylirions. Beautifully understated by contrast is the avenue of *Betula utilis* var. *jacquemontii* 'Grayswood Ghost' underplanted with acanthus. It leads to a flowery meadow through beds of grasses (dressed with pebbles or slate) which prolong the attraction into autumn and winter. The French garden is an essay in formal design; the yew hedges that back the box parterres commemorate Fouquet's famous 1661 trial with 12 'jurors' clipped into shape. Moving swiftly forward in time, the visitor

comes to a 'Rothko room' glowing with purple beech, berberis and prunus, and an airy 'Hepworth room' of grasses mingling with herbaceous plants. Major collections of late spring and summer bulbs, clematis and roses are dotted around the garden.

SEAL POINT ★

Mrs Danae Johnston

7 Wendover Way, Luton LU2 7LS.
Tel: (01582) 611567

In NE of Luton. Turn N off Stockingstone Road into Felstead Way and take second turning on left

Open by appt

Entrance: £3.50

◐ ☕ WC & ◈

This sloping one-acre town garden with a Japanese theme goes from good to better, with interesting plants and gorgeous colour schemes from spring right through the summer. A hardy standard fuchsia is now over three metres high, and 20 or more different grasses are integrated into the borders. There is something unusual at every turn: a wildlife copse, a tiny bonsai garden, three pools (one with a waterfall), yin and yang beds, amusing topiary, original ornaments, and much more. The garden is run organically, and with log piles, ladybird lodges, bumble bee nests and nectar plants the accent everywhere is on nurturing wildlife.

TODDINGTON MANOR ★

Sir Neville and Lady Bowman-Shaw

Park Rd, Toddington LU5 6HJ.
Tel: (01525) 872576;
www.toddingtonmanor.co.uk

8m NW of Luton, 1m NW of Toddington, 1m W of M1 junction 12

Open 26th May, 11am – 5pm; May to July, Tues, 1 – 5pm; and for parties by appt

Entrance: £4

Other information:
Vintage tractor collection

◐ 🍴 <u>WC</u> ⟨🐕⟩ ◈ ⛪ ☕ B&B

The six-acre garden is maintained to the highest standards but the shrubs and plants are allowed to grow and flower and seed in abundance. Each area is themed individually. The pleached lime walk – a most successful *allée* – is paved and surrounded by large herbaceous borders displaying an exuberance of hostas with many variations of leaf, blue delphiniums, white astilbes and hellebores, euphorbias and angelicas. Inside the walled garden are borders with dramatic sweeps of delphiniums, peonies, clematis and grasses, backed by shrubs. In the rose garden the air is scented by yellow and white floribunda roses and philadelphus, with eremurus growing through; under the roses violas have spread in sheets. A stream flows through and feeds the ponds and the fountain. There is a good herb garden and greenhouse, and beyond the walls a wildflower meadow, orchards and 20 acres of woodland contribute to a fine display of natural beauty.

TOFTE MANOR

Mrs C. Castleman

Souldrop Road, Sharnbrook MK44 1HH.
Tel: (01234) 781425;
www.toftelabyrinth.co.uk

Off A6 between Bedford and Rushden. Exit at roundabout signed to Sharnbrook, and go through village towards Souldrop. At Y-junction take right fork; house is 400 yards ahead on left

Open May to July and Sept, alternate Suns (telephone or check website for details), for NGS, and for parties by appt

Entrance: £3.50, children (under 10) free

◑ ☕ WC & ⛪ ☕ ℗ B&B

In 1995 the present owners moved into the 1613 manor house and began to landscape the flat five-acre site, creating a large sunken garden with a central arbour and an unusual water feature. Already well furnished with magnificent cedars and other mature trees, there are now spring bulbs in profusion, colour-themed herbaceous borders, wild areas and a parterre garden with modern statues. The main feature is a large and heavily symbolic circular grass labyrinth based on the famous one at Chartres Cathedral. It is set in a double pentagram, with water running under the grass pathways in 600m of copper piping and a smoky quartz crystal buried at its heart. Visitors in search of a still moment can walk its sacred geometry and drink from its waters.

WOBURN ABBEY

(Historic Garden Grade I)

Early in the seventeenth century, Woburn was established as the principal seat of the 4th Earl of Bedford, who extended the abbey buildings and commissioned Isaac de Caus to build a grotto in the new north wing. At the Restoration, a series of enclosed gardens was laid out to the west of the house and woodland planted with rides cut through. By 1714, the park had been extended and George London's Bason Pond created as an integral part of his grand Baroque west approach, and by 1738 Charles Bridgeman had largely removed all the formal gardens around the house. In 1780 Holland designed a greenhouse (later a sculpture gallery) and the Chinese dairy overlooking a small lake with a covered walk. At the same time informal gardens were created and enclosed to the east and south. The 6th Duke then employed Humphry Repton to draw up a landscape scheme for the park as a whole, and by 1805 the result was Repton's finest Red Book. His proposals were a triumph, and he was able to claim that 'The improvements I have had the honour to suggest have nowhere been so fully realised as at Woburn Abbey.' These comprised the creation of a group of linked yet separate areas of garden: an American and a Chinese garden, a rosery, a menagerie and an aviary. He also reshaped the lakes westwards from the abbey and rerouted the southern approach drive. In the 1930s the gardens were redeveloped by Percy Cane, and the 42 acres today are those made in the twentieth century. The park is still a deer park (with 10 species of deer), largely pasture, and surrounds the gardens and pleasure grounds of the past. The private gardens, which are rarely open to the public, contain a large hornbeam maze, formal gardens and good herbaceous borders.

The Duke of Bedford and Trustees of Bedford Estates

Woburn MK17 9WA.
Tel: (01525) 290333;
www.discoverwoburn.co.uk

11m NW of Luton between A5 and M1 (follow signs from junctions 12 or 13)

Open Easter to Sept, daily, 11am – 4pm (telephone or consult website)

Entrance: House and garden £10.50, OAPs £9.50, children £6, plus additional £2 per person parking

WREST PARK

(Historic Garden Grade I)

One of the few places in England where it is possible to see a Baroque formal garden of the early eighteenth century. The Long Water – a canal flanked by hedges – dominates the 'Great Garden' and provides the main axis of the grounds, cutting through thick blocks of woodland. At its head stands the Banqueting House, a beautiful domed Thomas Archer pavilion with strong echoes of a similar garden building designed by Daniel Marot, only recently discovered. 'Capability' Brown worked here later, creating a naturalistic river to surround the grounds at their perimeter. The woods on either side of the Long Water are intersected by avenues and dotted with 'incidents of delight', including a delicate Chinese pavilion and giant urns set in grassy glades by Thomas Acres. The 1770 Bath House was built as a romantic classical ruin. Water catches the eye in every direction. The 1830s

English Heritage

Silsoe, Bedford MK45 4HS.
Tel: (01525) 860152;
www.englishheritage.org.uk

10m S of Bedford,
0.75m E of Silsoe off A6

Open April to Sept, Sat, Sun and Bank Holiday Mons, 10am – 6pm; Oct, Sat and Sun only, 10am – 5pm (last admission 1 hour before closing). Advisable to check times before travelling

Entrance: £4.70, OAPs £3.50, children (5–15) £2.40, family £11.80

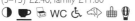

Wrest Park

house (not open) was built in the French style, fronted by terraces and box-edged parterres tightly packed with vibrant annuals. The large orangery was designed by Cléphane.

OTHER RECOMMENDED GARDENS

STOCKWOOD PARK

Farley Hill, Luton LU1 4BH (01582 738714; www.luton.gov.uk/museums). Open April to Oct, daily except Mon (but open Bank Holiday Mons), 10am – 5pm; Nov to March, Sat and Sun, 10am – 4pm

A series of period gardens within the walls of an old house, and in the park a landscape garden with sculpture by the late Ian Hamilton Finlay, combine to suggest the 18th-century ideal of a harmonious blend of parkland, planting, architecture and sculpture. The Stockwood Discovery Centre opens in July 2008. 10 acres.

THE SWISS GARDEN

The Swiss Garden, Old Warden Park, Biggleswade SG18 9ER (01767 627666; www.shuttleworth.org). Open all year, daily, 10am – 5pm (closes 4pm Nov to March)

A distinctive 10-acre landscape garden conceived in the 1820s as a pleasure ground complete with a rustic thatched cottage, a grotto, canals and a fernery. Some remarkable trees survive. (Listed Grade II*)

BERKSHIRE

For further information about how to use the *Guide*
and for an explanation of the symbols, see pages vi–viii.
Specific dates and times are those given to us by garden owners for 2008.
For 2009 dates, check with the individual properties.
For opening dates under the National Gardens Scheme,
readers should consult *The Yellow Book* or www.ngs.org.uk.
Maps are to be found at the end of the *Guide*.

ENGLEFIELD HOUSE ★

(Historic Garden Grade II)

There has been a garden here since the seventeenth century, and today its nine acres have achieved a rare and successful balance between the formal and informal. Stone-balustraded terracing provides an appropriately grand setting for the house and a place to view the surrounding deer park descending to the lake. On the terraces box-edged and less formal borders set against stone walls are planted with climbers, shrubs, perennials and annuals. An informal touch is added by swathes of meadow grass spangled with bulbs beneath trees within an area of formal lawn. The ground rises steeply behind the terraces into tree-covered slopes underplanted with thickets of colourful shrubs – the glory of this garden. A stream edged with candelabra primulas, ferns and bog plants winds below a slope covered with azaleas and maples; a flint- and rock-faced grotto, its interior lined with a mosaic of fir cones, stands at the top of the stream, and a place has been found for a carved wooden bear and an imaginative children's garden.

Sir William and Lady Benyon

Englefield, Theale, Reading RG7 5EN.
Tel: (0118) 930 2221;
www.englefield.co.uk

5m W of Reading. Entrance on A340, near Theale

Open all year, Mon; plus April to Nov, Tues – Thurs; all 10am – 6pm

Entrance: £3, children free

FROGMORE GARDENS

(Historic Garden Grade I)

The 35 acres of landscaped gardens are set within the home park of Windsor Castle. In 1792 the estate was purchased for Queen Charlotte, who lavished large sums of money on the gardens, introducing rare plants and developing the landscape in Picturesque style. From the nineteenth century come James Wyatt's delightful wisteria-festooned Gothick ruin overlooking the lake, the Duchess of Kent's mausoleum, and other commemorative and architectural features, including Queen Victoria's tea house, an exquisite white marble Indian kiosk, and the royal couple's imposing mausoleum. The feeling of harmony and tranquillity which prompted them to choose this site for their final resting place still prevails – the lake and meandering canal, and the fine mature trees casting their shadows over immaculate swathes of lawn contribute to the sense of Victorian peace and plenty.

H.M. The Queen

Windsor SL4 2JG.
www.royalcollection.org.uk

At Windsor Castle. Entrance via signed car park on B3021 between Datchet and Old Windsor. Pedestrian access only from Long Walk

House open as garden, in Aug only

Garden usually open several days in late May and Aug – telephone (020) 7766 7305 for information

Entrance: house, gardens and mausoleum £6, OAPs £5, children under 17 £4 (2007 prices)

Inholmes

Lady Williams
Woodlands St Mary RG17 7SY.
Tel: (07855) 392628

3m SE of Lambourn off A338. Take
B4000 towards Lambourn; signed

Open for NGS, and by appt

Entrance: £3.50, children free

Other information: Teas on NGS open
days only

NEW WC

INHOLMES

The 10-acre gardens are set within parkland and woodland where swathes of bluebells flower in the spring; there are has wonderful views over the park, particularly from the terrace which is planted out in blocks of lavender. The walled gardens and formal areas around the house are distinguished by a strong sense of individuality and contemporary planting. The main walled garden, named after the famous racing driver Piers Courage, is reached by a traditional gate given a modern look by a coat of pink paint, and a bench in the same garden is painted a light lime green. The centrepiece is a bronze statue of a giant cockerel; formal lawns and gravel paths edged with clumps of santolina contrast with the wild and airy feel to the planting in the borders. The cutting and vegetable garden nearby is a rich mix of plants in box-hedged enclosures with pathways running under tunnels of willow. This is a garden still being developed but with much to enjoy at present.

Anthony and Fenja Anderson

Mariners Lane, Bradfield RG7 6HU.
Tel: (0118) 974 5226

10m W of Reading. From M4 junction
12 take A4 W; at roundabout take A340
signed to Pangbourne, then turn left
(after 350m) signed to Bradfield. After
1m turn left again signed to Bradfield
Southend then after 1m turn right
opposite signpost to Tutts Clump; house
is on left at bottom of hill

Open for NGS, and 16th June to 15th
July by appt

MARINERS ★

The present owners have consulted the genius of their sloping 1.5-acre site with intelligence and imagination. On the bank above the broad terrace two borders have been contoured so that the colour and texture of imaginatively chosen flowers and foliage may be enjoyed at close quarters; one is planted in a predominantly wine and red colour theme, the other in soft blues, creams and yellows. The main herbaceous border and the bank border opposite, which incorporates a bog garden, forms the backbone. Lawns planted with unusual trees link the various areas and lead the eye upwards to the highest level, where there is an orchard, a sundial garden, a border of grasses and a hexagonal arbour supporting vines and clematis.

Mariners

Beyond is a one-acre wildflower meadow with a charming 'borrowed' tower terminating the view. The most atmospheric part of the garden is the sunken rose garden, a fabulous sight in June and gloriously scented by many old varieties of shrub roses underplanted with herbaceous perennials; an arbour and moon gate are festooned with clematis and rambling roses. From there a path leads down under trees to a streamside walk.

Entrance: £3.50, children under 16 free

Other information: Plants for sale on charity day only. Wheelchair access limited due to slopes. No dogs please

Other information: Refreshments for parties by arrangement

 WC &

THE OLD RECTORY, FARNBOROUGH
(see Oxfordshire)

POTASH ★

The five acre garden is continually being enriched with fresh plants and new areas of interest, such as the Mediterranean planting on the banks above the recessed tennis court. Mr Mooney was a forester by profession, and so the character of the place is dominated by mature and handsome trees, many of them unusual. The site sweeps down from lawns and shrubberies to a winding stream crossed by a wooden Japanese bridge. A large pond has a richly planted bog area, and the rising ground beyond is edged with a dense cordon of specimen shrubs blending into carefully planned young woodland. At the start of the year a spectacular show of snowdrops fringes the banks of the pool and stream, followed by early spring bulbs and daffodils in their thousands. Early-flowering shrubs and trees provide points of interest throughout, with roses and a herbaceous border for summer colour and autumn leaves to complete the cycle.

Mr and Mrs J.W. C. Mooney

Potash, Mariners Lane, Southend Bradfield, Reading RG7 6HU. Tel: (0118) 974 4264

10m W of Reading. From M4 junction 12 take A4 W; at roundabout take A340 signed to Pangbourne, then turn left after 350 metres signed to Bradfield. After 1m turn left again signed to Bradfield Southend; turn right opposite sign, and garden is 370 metres on left by beech hedge

Open all year by appt

Entrance: £3, children free

The Payne family

Cockpole Green, Wargrave, Reading
RG10 8QP. Tel: (01628) 822648

4m E of Henley-on-Thames, off A4 at
Knowl Hill, halfway between Warren
Row and Cockpole Green

Open for various charities, and by appt

Entrance: £3, children free

Other information: Picnics permitted on
Cockpole Green

SCOTLANDS ★

The five-acre garden, created since 1980, uses slopes and undulations of its landscape to great effect. In the dip of a valley a small lake scooped out of a wet and boggy area reflects the surrounding trees and waterside plants. Water is also a feature of the meticulously tended woodland garden beyond the summer house and lake. Here are rivulets, channels, still pools and a waterfall, all surrounded by specimen trees, well-chosen shrubs and a rich variety of waterside plants. The ground rises steeply from the lake to the small formal gardens clustering round the chalk-and-flint house. The original seventeenth-century low-walled kitchen garden, which has criss-crossing pathways punctuated by clipped box and pots, with a handsome architectural brick and flint tool shed of eighteenth-century design in one corner, is planted with roses mixed with cottage-garden plants, herbs and cardoons. Herbaceous borders edge the path leading to the oval swimming pool enclosed by yew hedging west of the house, and on to a spacious shady area of trees and grass overlooked by an arbour surrounded by shrub roses.

Mr and Mrs N. F. Oppenheimer

Waltham Place, White Waltham,
Maidenhead SL6 3JH.
Tel: (01628) 825517;
www.walthamplace.com

3.5m S of Maidenhead. From M4
junction 8/9 take A404M and follow
signs to White Waltham. Turn left to
Windsor and Paley Street. Parking
signposted at top of hill

Open for NGS May to Sept, Wed,
10am – 4pm; guided tours with head
gardener Fri, 11am-2pm; Tues and Thurs
by appt.

Entrance: £3.50, children £1
(2007 prices)

Other information: Organic farm shop

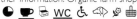

WALTHAM PLACE ★

The ornamental gardens lie within a walled enclosure of mellow brick, the oldest dating from the seventeenth century; substantial brick-pillared pergolas support an abundance of roses and climbers and provide shady walks. In striking contrast to this traditional formality are the naturalistic plantings created by the Dutch designer Henk Gerritsen. He has filled one small enclosed garden mainly with plants to attract butterflies, another with herbs and native species. The Square Garden combines lawns and generous sweeps of gravel, dotted with a variety of grasses, in a freely drawn design separated by box hedges. A large area of rich herbaceous planting holds some surprises, such as that familiar invader, ground elder, introduced deliberately for its striking

Waltham Place

leaves and subtle flowers. Beyond the potager, knot garden and Japanese garden are long, densely packed herbaceous borders, where newly planted beech alcoves shelter beds of tall weeds, including our native bindweed and stipa grasses. The original formal yew hedges have been transformed into billowing shapes, as if by a creative giant with hedge cutters. Within these 40 acres are other gardens, a lake and woodlands, and a maze cut through long grass – all part of the 170-acre estate, which also includes an organic farm.

OTHER RECOMMENDED GARDENS

ASHDOWN HOUSE

Lambourn, Newbury RG16 7RE (01488 72584; www.nationaltrust.org.uk). Open April to Oct, Wed and Sat, 2 – 5pm. Woodlands open all year, Sat –Thurs, dawn – dusk. Parties must pre-book. NT

The exquisite hunting lodge built by Lord Craven for Elizabeth of Bohemia and set in a hauntingly beautiful valley may have lost its large formal park, but is perfectly framed by two lime avenues and an intricate parterre in front of the house. Spring sees the mass flowering of snowdrops along the avenues and in woodland. (Listed Grade II*)

CHIEVELEY MANOR

Mr and Mrs C.J. Spence, Chieveley, Newbury RG20 8UT (01635 248208). Open for NGS

The mellow, self-confident 3-acre garden of generous lawns, fine trees, sophisticated borders and a fabulous display of roses, is the perfect foil for the Tudor brick manor house. Secluded areas include a sunken terrace, a walled garden and a swimming-pool garden with a Mediterranean atmosphere.

THE LIVING RAINFOREST

Hampstead Norreys, Nr Newbury RG18 0TN (01635 202444; www.livingrainforest.org). Open all year, daily except 25th and 26th Dec, 10am – 5.15pm (last admission 4.30pm)

This remarkable 1-acre glasshouse contains a splendidly grown and imaginatively displayed collection of exotic plants native to the world's rainforests. Look out for free-roaming animals, butterflies and birds.

SANDLEFORD PLACE

Mr and Mrs Alan Gatward, Newtown, Newbury RG20 9AY (01635 40726). Open for NGS, and by appt

The 5-acre garden is the creation of an innovative plantswoman who is always exploring new colour and plant combinations – particularly successful is the walled garden, where borders are planted with a bold and exuberant mixture of shrubs, climbers and perennials. Elsewhere are fine mature trees and shrubs giving year-round interest, a long herbaceous border flanking a wildflower meadow and a tiny woodland walk. The unspoilt charm of the River Enborne, its banks spangled with wild flowers, can be viewed from a decked terrace overlooking the flow of water.

The Living Rainforest

BIRMINGHAM AREA

For further information about how to use the *Guide*
and for an explanation of the symbols, see pages vi–viii.
Specific dates and times are those given to us by garden owners for 2008.
For 2009 dates, check with the individual properties.
For opening dates under the National Gardens Scheme,
readers should consult *The Yellow Book* or www.ngs.org.uk.
Maps are to be found at the end of the *Guide*.

ASHOVER

Mr and Mrs Martin Harvey

25 Burnett Road, Streetly B74 3EL.
Tel: (0121) 353 0547

8m N of Birmingham. Take A452
towards Streetly, then B4138 alongside
Sutton Park. Turn left at shops

Open for NGS and by appt

Entrance: £3, children free

Other information: Plants on NGS open
days only

● WC

This is a garden for all who love colour – a third of an acre
cleverly planted for year-round interest, from bulbs and
azaleas in the spring through roses, clematis, lilies and
herbaceous plants, both traditional and unusual, in summer
and autumn, with a 'hot' border making its impact in July and
August. Colour-themed beds and an attractive water feature
catch the eye and close planting constantly challenges the
interest of the discerning visitor. Surprises at every turn make
the garden appear larger than it actually is and a luxuriant
atmosphere is generated by the sheer variety, quality and
quantity of plants amassed here.

THE BIRMINGHAM BOTANICAL GARDENS AND GLASSHOUSES ★
(Historic Garden Grade II*)

Westbourne Road, Edgbaston B15 3TR.
Tel: (0121) 454 1860;
www.birminghambotanicalgardens.org.uk

2m SW of city centre. Approach from
Hagley Road or Calthorpe Road,
following tourist signs

Open all year, daily, 9am – 7pm, or dusk
if earlier (opens 10am on Sun)

Entrance: £6.50, OAPs, disabled, students
and children £4, family £19

Other information: Manual and electric
wheelchairs available free of charge

○ ● ⬛ WC ⬤ ⚲ ⯗ ⬤ ⚲

This 15-acre ornamental garden will appeal both to the keen
plantsperson and to the everyday gardener. In addition to the
unusual plants in the tropical and Mediterranean houses, there

The Birmingham Botanical Gardens
and Glasshouses

is a sub-tropical house and an arid house, a small display of carnivorous plants, aviaries with parrots and macaws, peacocks and a waterfowl enclosure. Less rarefied gardeners will enjoy the beautiful old trees, the border devoted to E.H. Wilson plants, the raised alpine bed and the sunken rose garden beside the Lawn Aviary. The rock garden contains a wide variety of alpine plants, primulas, astilbes and azaleas. There are also herbaceous borders, a quaint cottage-style garden, a herb garden and model historic and organic gardens, plus a trials area and a sculpture trail, where many of the exhibits are for sale. An attractive courtyard houses a National Collection of bonsai, and a Japanese garden is intended to create a mood of harmony, reflection and relaxation. The alpine yard has examples of the many ways to grow plants in raised beds and containers. An imaginative children's discovery garden, a playground and adventure trail make this a pleasant place for a family outing. Bands play on summer Sundays and Bank Holidays, and there are events throughout the year to suit all ages.

CASTLE BROMWICH HALL GARDENS ★

(Historic Garden Grade II*)

The hall (not open) was built at the end of the sixteenth century and sold to Sir John Bridgeman in 1657. His wife, with expert help from Captain William Winde, George London and Henry Wise, created a garden famous in its time. It fell into decay, but now has a series of formal connecting gardens – 10 acres in all contained within a west-facing slope – which have gradually been restored by a dedicated team of volunteers to give them the appearance and content of a garden of 1680–1740. They contain a large collection of rare period plants and a nineteenth-century holly maze. An elegant greenhouse and summerhouse stand at each end of a broad holly walk. In the formal parterre, re-created to a 1728 design and bordered by culinary and medicinal herbs, several heritage vegetables are grown, such as skirrets, scorzonera, orache, cardoons and salsify. Fruit trees have been planted in orchards and along paths.

Castle Bromwich Hall Gardens Trust

Chester Road, Castle Bromwich B36 9BT. Tel: (0121) 749 4100; www.cbhgt.org.uk

4m E of city centre, 1m from junction 5 of M6 northbound; southbound leave M6 at junction 6 and follow A38 and A452. Signposted

Open April to Oct, Tues – Fri, 11am – 4pm (closes 3.30pm Fri), Sat, Sun and Bank Holiday Mons, 1.30 – 5.30pm; Nov to March, Wed – Fri, 11.30am – 3.30pm.

Entrance: £3.50, concessions £3, children 50p (2007 prices)

WINTERBOURNE BOTANIC GARDEN

The six-acre Arts-and-Crafts garden has been owned by the University of Birmingham since 1944. Many of the original features survive, such as the sunken rock and water garden where drifts of gunnera fringe the water's edge and a Japanese bridge arches over a trickling stream. The walled garden contains a National Collection of historic European roses, colour-themed borders and a fully restored Edwardian glasshouse stocked with plants from Madeira. Among the interesting trees are dawn redwoods, a Japanese pagoda tree, a handkerchief tree and many more, while a nut walk provides

University of Birmingham

58 Edgbaston Road, Edgbaston B15 2RT. Tel: (0121) 414 3832; www.botanic.bham.ac.uk

2m SW of city centre, 0.5m off A38 Bristol road. Follow brown tourist-signs

Open Jan to March, Oct to Dec, Mon – Fri, 12 noon – 3.30pm; April to Sept, Mon – Fri, 11am – 4pm, Sun, 1 – 5pm

Entrance: £3, children £1.50 (under 5 free)

Winterbourne Botanic Garden

Other information: Guided tours available

a handkerchief tree and many more, while a nut walk provides a cool retreat in summer and an interesting framework in winter. The garden has undergone a major restoration programme since 2004, and new areas have also been added, including a winter border and a Mediterranean bed.

OTHER RECOMMENDED GARDENS

CITY CENTRE GARDENS

Cambridge Street B1 2NP. Open all year, daily, during daylight hours

A 0.5-acre garden for all seasons created from a demolished building site. The layout is formal, the planting skilful, varied and exuberant.

WIGHTWICK MANOR

Wightwick Bank, Wolverhampton WV6 8EE (01902 761400; www.nationaltrust.org.uk). Open March to Dec, Wed – Sat, plus Bank Holiday Suns and Mons, and other weekdays by appt. NT

The 17.5-acre garden designed by Alfred Parsons and Thomas Mawson to surround the neo-Tudor house has most of the traditional late-Victorian accoutrements: fine trees, a rose garden, herbaceous borders, pools and an orchard, plus a magnificent octagonal arbour and Mathematical Bridge. A pelargonium display takes place on Spring Bank Holiday. (Listed Grade II)

BRISTOL AREA

For further information about how to use the *Guide*
and for an explanation of the symbols, see pages vi–viii.
Specific dates and times are those given to us by garden owners for 2008.
For 2009 dates, check with the individual properties.
For opening dates under the National Gardens Scheme,
readers should consult *The Yellow Book* or www.ngs.org.uk.
Maps are to be found at the end of the *Guide*.

ASHTON COURT ESTATE
(Historic Park Grade II*)

The Ashton estate is an astonishing survival to find on the edge of a major city. It has two deer parks, and its 850 acres include many ancient oaks. The house itself is fifteenth-century with a handsome seventeenth-century wing. The park was first landscaped in the 1600s; two hundred years later it was redesigned with advice from Humphry Repton. The year 2004 saw the start of major restoration to the deer enclosures, buildings and woodland with help from the Heritage Lottery Fund.

Bristol City Council

Long Ashton BS41 9JN.
Tel: (0117) 963 9174;
www.bristol-city.gov.uk

SW of city off A369

Open all year, daily, 8am – dusk

Entrance: free

BLAISE CASTLE HOUSE MUSEUM ★
(Historic Garden Grade II*)

Blaise Hamlet, a picturesque village owned by the National Trust, is laid out in the form of a green surrounded by nine cottages with private gardens, designed by John Nash with George and John Repton in 1809 for the pensioners of John Harford's estate. The village pump and sundial of 1812 remain. Jasmines, ivies and honeysuckles were planted around the cottages to reflect their picturesque names ('Jessamine', 'Rose Briar'), with ornamental shrubs added to the woodland setting. A spectacular drive can be taken from Henbury Hill to the entrance lodge of Blaise Castle House – another charming *cottage orné* is half-way. The driveway into the gorge and up to the house passes a Robber's Cave and Lovers' Leap. Near the house are the ornamental dairy and elegant orangery, both by Nash.

Henbury BS10 7QS.

Tel: (0117) 903 9818 (Museum);
(0117) 353 2266 (Estate Office);
www.bristol-city.gov.uk

4m N of city, W of Henbury,
N of B4057

Museum open all year, Sat – Wed,
10am – 5pm (booking advisable for
parties)

Entrance: free

Other information: Visitors requested
not to picnic or invade privacy of
cottage owners

GOLDNEY HALL
(Historic Garden Grade II*)

The eighteenth-century garden is a thrilling discovery in the middle of the city. Perched on a hillside, it is full of surprises, not least the small formal canal with an orangery at its head. From the largely nineteenth-century house the visitor is led through the shadows of an *allée* of yews to a dark grotto

University of Bristol

Lower Clifton Hill, Clifton BS8 1BH.
Tel: (0117) 903 4873/4880;
www.goldneyhall.com

In city centre at top of Constitution Hill

Open 27th April, 2 – 6pm; check
website for other open days

Goldney Hall

Entrance: £3, concessions £1.50, children under 5 free.

entrance, the facade of which is a striking example of early but sophisticated Gothick. The grotto itself is astonishingly elaborate: water really gushes through it and the walls are liberally encrusted with shells and minerals. Passing through the grotto and out by narrow labyrinthine passages, suddenly there is a terrace, a broad airy grass walk with magnificent views over the old docks. At the far end of the terrace is a Gothick gazebo, and towering above the other end a castellated tower. Goldney also has follies, a parterre and a herb garden packed into its 10 acres.

UNIVERSITY BOTANIC GARDEN

University of Bristol

The Holmes, Stoke Park Road, Stoke Bishop, Bristol. Tel: (0117) 331 4912; www.bris.ac.uk/Depts/BotanicGardens

From city centre, take A4108 north to end of Whiteladies Rd, turn left at roundabout into Stoke Rd, then 2nd right into Stoke Park Rd. Garden is opposite Churchill Hall of Residence

Open 21st March to 2nd Nov, Wed – Fri and Sun. 10am – 4.30pm

Entrance: £3

The new four-acre botanic garden designed by Land Use Consultants (of Eden Project fame) is a happy marriage of education and contemporary design. The relaxed and fluid layout is focused on a lake surrounded by groups of local flora and threatened native plants. A sunken dell is connected by

University Botanic Garden

paths that meander through formal and informal plantings charting the seminal stages of the evolution of plants on our planet, from primitive liverworts and tree ferns to a spectacular flowering of magnolias. The fine collection of Mediterranean plants built up at the botanic garden's former home has been relocated here, and the Chinese medicinal herb collection flourishes now in the shadow of a splendid mature ginkgo.

OTHER RECOMMENDED GARDENS

ASHLEY VALE ALLOTMENTS

Ashley Down, Bristol BS7 9BP (0117 942 9323). Open by appt

Extending over 11 acres on a steep hillside in north Bristol is an intricate grid of allotments teeming with energy – 110 in all, rescued and presided over by Bernard Coote and his wife Jenny. Their own 4 acres, planted for the benefit of wildlife and for the education of young visitors, is a companionable riot of fruit trees, vegetables, wild flowers and many unusual native and tropical species.

BRISTOL ZOO GARDENS

Clifton BS8 3HA (0117 974 7399; www.bristolzoo.org.uk). Open all year, daily except 25th Dec, 9am – 5.30pm (closes 4.30pm in winter)

The gardens were in their day (1835) the very model of Victorian gardening, with vibrantly colourful bedding, herbaceous borders, rock and rose gardens. 170 years later, they retain the same period charm.

EMMAUS HOUSE

Retreat and Conference Centre, Sisters of La Retraite, Clifton Hill, Clifton BS8 1BN (0117 907 9950; www.emmaushouse.org.uk).Open by appt for NGS

Hidden behind two 18th-century merchants' houses, a succession of separate gardens is set on different levels and linked together, with extensive views towards Bristol harbour. Within the 1.5 acres clusters a diversity of well-planted spaces ranging from a Victorian kitchen garden to a Zen garden, from a wild area to a secret garden where old apples trees are underplanted with spring bulbs.

THE RED LODGE

Park Row BS1 5LJ (0117 921 1360; www.bristol.gov.uk/museums). House and garden open, all year, Sat – Wed, 10am – 5pm (garden may be closed for refurbishment in early 2008 but may be viewed from house)

A careful reconstruction of the small garden surrounding a merchant's town house of the 16th century, borrowing interior details to create a knot garden and copying early trelliswork to enclose the garden.

BUCKINGHAMSHIRE

For further information about how to use the *Guide*
and for an explanation of the symbols, see pages vi–viii.
Specific dates and times are those given to us by garden owners for 2008.
For 2009 dates, check with the individual properties.
For opening dates under the National Gardens Scheme,
readers should consult *The Yellow Book* or www.ngs.org.uk.
Maps are to be found at the end of the *Guide*.

ASCOTT ★★
(Historic Garden Grade II*)

The National Trust

Wing, Leighton Buzzard, Bedfordshire
LU7 0PS. Tel: (01296) 688242;
www.ascottestate.co.uk

7m NE of Aylesbury, 0.5m E of Wing,
S of A418

House and gardens open 25th March to
27th April, 29th July to 12th Sept, daily
except Mon; 29th April to 24th July,
Tues – Thurs ; all 2 – 6pm

Entrance: £4, children £2 (house and
garden £8, children £4)

Other information: Parking 220 metres
from house

◑ <u>WC</u> ♿

Ascott began life as a farmhouse in the seventeenth century;
acquired by Baron Meyer de Rothschild in 1873, it was
progressively transformed by his nephew Leopold into the
'palace-like cottage' we see today. The garden is thirty acres of
Victorian designs and planting at their best, laid out with the
aid of Veitch and overlaid with more recent schemes. It is
notable for its collection of mature trees set in rolling lawns.
Interesting topiary includes an evergreen sundial with a yew
gnomon and the inscription 'Light and shade by turn but love
always' in golden yew. Wide lawns slope away to magnificent
views across the Vale of Aylesbury, glimpsed between
towering cedars. Formal gardens include the Madeira Walk
with sheltered flower borders, and the bedded-out Dutch
garden. The Long Walk leading to the lily pond has been
imaginatively reconstructed by Arabella Lennox-Boyd as a
serpentine walk with beech hedging, and a wild garden
planted in Coronation Grove. Two stately fountains were
sculpted by Thomas Waldo Story in the nineteenth century.
Spring gardens feature massed carpets of bulbs.

Ascott

CHENIES MANOR HOUSE ★

The fine linked gardens, highly decorative and maintained to the highest standards, are in perfect keeping with the fifteenth- and sixteenth-century brick manor house. Planted for a long season of colour, spring sees the mass flowering of tulips in the sunken garden, followed by vibrant annual bedding that is matched by colourful herbaceous plantings; old-fashioned roses and cottage plants are favoured too. There is always something to enjoy here: formal topiary in the white garden, collections of medicinal and poisonous plants in a physic garden, a parterre, an historic turf maze, an intricate yew maze over two metres high, and a highly productive kitchen garden. On her visits here, Queen Elizabeth I had a favourite tree and the 'Royal Oak' survives. Ten acres in all.

Mrs MacLeod Matthews

Chenies, Rickmansworth WD3 6ER. Tel: (01494) 762888; www.cheniesmanorhouse.co.uk

3m E of Amersham off A404

House and garden open April to Oct, Wed, Thurs and Bank Holiday Mons, 2 – 5pm

Entrance: £4, children £2 (house and garden £5.50, children £3)

Other information: Plant and garden fair 20th July, 10am – 5pm

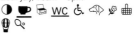

CLIVEDEN ★★

(Historic Garden Grade I)

The setting of the house is one of the most beautiful in Britain. The flamboyant Duke of Buckingham found it and William Winde exploited it, taking the raw material – 'a cliffy ground as hanging over the Tamise and sum Busshis groinge on it' and creating, by excavation and earth-moving, a platform for the house and a terrace for access. John Evelyn's verdict was that 'the house stands somewhat like Frascati on the platform . . . a circular view of the uttmost verge of the Horison, which with the serpenting of the Thames is admirably surprising . . . The Cloisters, Descents, Gardens, & avenue through the wood august and stately.' The present house (now an hotel), designed by Sir Charles Barry, incorporates a terrace with a balustrade brought by the 1st Viscount Astor from the Villa Borghese in Rome in the 1890s. There is an attractive water garden, a secret garden and herbaceous borders, formal gardens below the house, the Long Garden, and fountains, temples and statuary galore. Among famous designers who have worked on the 376-acre grounds are Bridgeman (walks and amphitheatre), Leoni (Octagon Temple) and John Fleming (parterre). From the ilex grove a shaded path leads through a gate to the Secret Garden, planted originally by the 3rd Lord Astor in the 1950s to the designs of Geoffrey Jellicoe. Once a rose garden, it has been planted anew by Isabelle Van Groeningen with a mixture of perennials and grasses to give year-round interest.

The National Trust

Taplow, Maidenhead, Berkshire SL6 0JA. Tel: (01628) 605069; www.nationaltrust.org.uk

6m NW of Slough, 2m N of Taplow off A4094

House open April to Oct, Thurs and Sun, 3 – 5.30pm

Estate and gardens open March to 23rd Dec, daily, 11am – 6pm (closes 4pm Nov and Dec)

Woodlands open all year, daily except 24th Dec to 3rd Jan, 11am – 5.30pm (closes 4pm Nov to March)

Entrance: £7.50, children £3.70, family £18.70 (house £1 extra, entry by timed ticket)

Other information: Refreshments in Conservatory Restaurant, March to Oct, daily. Dogs allowed in specified woodlands only

GIPSY HOUSE

Fans of Roald Dahl may be surprised – and perhaps even a little disappointed – that the one-acre garden enfolding the appealing Georgian farmhouse in which he lived and wrote for 36 years until his death in 1990 does not display the inspired anarchy to be found in his books. Rather the reverse: it is grown-up and highly sophisticated. Set in unspoilt countryside, it is divided into a sequence of spaces protected

Mrs Felicity Dahl

Whitefield Lane, Great Missenden HP16 0BP. Tel: (01494) 890465; www.roalddahlfoundation.org

Gipsy House

5m NW of Amersham on A4128, off A413. From High Street in Great Missenden turn into Whitefield Lane and continue under railway bridge to small Georgian house on right. Parking in field opposite

Open for NGS and for The Roald Dahl Foundation

Entrance: charge

NEW

by tall hedges or walls. Four large *Quercus ilex* lollipops in the Sundial Garden, raised beds outlined by sturdy railway sleepers in the terraced kitchen garden, an avenue of pleached limes luxuriantly underplanted with alliums and hostas, an airy gazebo guarded by two stone eagles – these and other details are handsome and self-confident, softened by planting schemes that change in mood and colour from pale and delicate to dark and hot. There are a few Dahl footprints, however: his little white writing hut with its bright yellow door, a low maze in which the Yorkstone slabs are carved with extracts of his writings, and the gaily painted gipsy caravan that spawned *Danny Champion of the World*. Beyond, a wildflower meadow merges into the surrounding landscape.

THE MANOR HOUSE ★★

Lord and Lady Carrington

Bledlow, Princes Risborough HP27 9PE

8m NW of High Wycombe, 0.5m E of B4009 in middle of Bledlow

Manor House Garden open for NGS, and May to Sept for parties by written appt. Lyde Garden open all year, daily

Entrance: Manor House Garden £4.50, children free. Lyde Garden free

Manor House Garden: ◑ ঐ
Lyde Garden: ○ ঐ

With the help of landscape architect Robert Adams, Lord and Lady Carrington have created an elegant English garden of an exceptionally high standard. The productive and colourful walled vegetable garden has York-stone paths and a central gazebo. Formal areas are enclosed by tall yew and beech hedges; in the centre of one is a water feature by William Pye. Mixed flower and shrub borders feature many roses and herbaceous plants around immaculately manicured lawns. Another garden, approached through a yew and brick parterre, was planned around existing mature trees on a contoured and upward-sloping site with open views. It is now thoroughly established, with its trees and lawns fulfilling the original landscaping design, and incorporates several modern sculptures including a second water feature by Barry Mason and two works by Peter Randall Page. *The Lyde Garden*, across the lane, is a magnificent wild water garden of great beauty and tranquillity. Note: children do need watching here.

OLD THATCH ★

The characterful seventeenth-century thatched house, once the home of Enid Blyton, has been enlivened with a series of vibrant and informal gardens, some traditional, others revealing the present owner's unusual and skilful approach to design and planting. Moving from the formal garden running the length of the house, and the pretty rose and clematis walk, the garden becomes ever more intriguing as it fans outwards. In the water garden the many small beds that surround the satisfyingly large pool and fountain are enfolded by large borders in shades of turquoise, blue, silver and bronze. Elsewhere is a circular garden with a tapestry bed, two shady secret spaces, and a bed bouncing with balls of *Lonicera nitida* 'Baggesen's Gold' and architectural foliage plants. The central part of the house has been made into an attractive tea room, fronted by a hot gravelled enclosure brimming with an informal and sometimes self-seeded mixture of grasses and flowers. Two enclosures are modern and free-spirited. One has small groups of acers and malus planted among herbaceous perennials in rectangular, brick-lined beds flanking grassy rectangles pierced by slivers of orange bamboo. The other, lined by eight standard *Prunus* 'Chanticleer', is charmingly light-hearted: the eye is led from a bold squiggle of colour created by bright pink geraniums up to three tall wooden 'crayons' tipped with pink. Throughout the garden, tall perimeter trees give enviable seclusion and swirling grass paths make a graceful link between the different spaces.

Jacky and David Hawthorn

Coldmoorholme Lane, Well End, Bourne End SL8 5PS. Tel: (01628) 527518; www.jackyhawthorne.co.uk

3m E of Marlow, 1m NW of Bourne End off A4155. Turn left down Coldmoorholme Lane; house is on left just before Spade Oak pub, car park 100 yds further on

Open for NGS, and June to Aug, Sat and Sun, 2 – 5.30pm – 5pm, and by appt for parties of 15 or more

Entrance: £3, children £1

NEW

STOWE LANDSCAPE GARDENS ★★

(Historic Garden Grade I)

This is garden restoration on an heroic scale. Stowe has had enormous influence on garden design from the mid seventeenth century onwards under a succession of distinguished designers, including the owner, Viscount Cobham: Vanbrugh, Bridgeman, Kent, 'Capability' Brown, and then the new owner Lord Temple, who thinned out Brown's plantings after 1750. What remains today is a *locus classicus* of eighteenth-century landscaping, with a nineteenth-century overlay diversifying the landscape into distinct 'scenes', each with its own character. The aim over the last twenty years has been to reinstate them. The concept of the restoration was brilliantly planned, using the Trust's considerable management and computer resources to reinstate lost plantings and remove recent irrelevant additions. There are two ways of visiting. One is just to wander through the gardens enjoying the wonderful views, the water, the splendid trees and autumn colour and the historic buildings – Stowe has more than twice as many listed garden buildings as any in England – and its statuary. The other approach is to step back in time and try to understand what was meant by the political and philosophical programme that fashioned the landscape movement. In the

The National Trust

Buckingham MK18 5EH.
Tel: (01280) 822850;
www.nationaltrust.org.uk

3m NW of Buckingham via Stowe Avenue off A422 Buckingham – Brackley road

House (Stowe School) open – telephone (01280) 818166 for details

Garden open 5th Jan to 2nd March, 8th Nov to Dec, Sat, Sun and Bank Holiday Mons, 10.30am – 3.30pm; 5th March to 2nd Nov, Wed – Sun and Bank Holiday Mons, 10.30am – 5.30pm (last admission 90 mins before closing)

Entrance: £6.90, children £3.50, family £17.10 (all parties must pre-book)

Other information: Refreshments for parties must be pre-booked through Group Bookings Co-ordinator. Self-drive powered 2-seater batricars available, must be prebooked (telephone 01280 818825)

past decade land has been bought back – 320 acres including the home farm and deer park, which included the Wolfe obelisk, the Gothic umbrello and a superb set of 1790s farm buildings. The Chinese house has been returned from Ireland, six of the seven Saxon deities have reappeared, and the Corinthian Arch has been restored. What is staggering is that the Trust has restored 70 per cent of the listed buildings at Stowe and Cobham is back on his column. Heroic indeed.

TURN END ★

Mr and Mrs P. Aldington

Townside, Haddenham, Aylesbury
HP17 8BG. Tel: (01844) 291383/291817

7m SW of Aylesbury. From A418 turn to Haddenham. From Thame Road turn at Rising Sun pub into Townside; garden is 250 metres on left

Open for NGS, and for parties of 10 or more by appt

Entrance: charge

Other information: No parking at garden
● 🗄 WC ♿ ⟨⟩ 🐾

Peter Aldington's RIBA-award-winning development of three linked houses (now listed) is surrounded by a series of garden rooms of less than an acre which have evolved since the 1960s. A sequence of spaces, each of individual character, provides focal points at every turn. There is a fishpond courtyard, a shady court, a formal box court, an alpine garden, hot and dry raised beds and climbing roses, all contrasting with lawns, borders and glades. A wide range of plants is displayed to good effect against a framework of mature trees, and spring and early summer are the best seasons to visit.

Turn End

WADDESDON MANOR ★★
(Historic Garden Grade I)

Baron Ferdinand de Rothschild's grandiloquent château (built 1874–89) is set in 165 acres of appropriately grand grounds with fountains, vistas, terraces and walks laid out by Elie Lainé, his landscape designer, with an extensive collection of Italian, French and Dutch statuary. The extensive parterre and fountains to the south require over 100,000 plants in the main summer display alone; the theme changes every year. To the west of the parterre, an ornate, semi-circular aviary of eighteenth-century French Rococo style, erected in 1889, provides a distinguished home for many exotic birds. It also acts as an exedra, focusing on the pleasure grounds and the expansive views of the landscape beyond. The area in front of it has been restored to its original bedding-plant scheme. The gardens undergo changes almost annually, with old features being restored and new ones added. Wildflower Valley has daffodils in spring, and in summer wild flowers, including cowslips, ox-eye daisies and a range of orchids, which are encouraged to seed. Close by, over 20,000 camassias, colchicums, lilies-of-the valley and wild garlic have been naturalised in grassland and in the woodland garden.

The National Trust

Waddesdon, Aylesbury HP18 0JH.
Tel: (01296) 653226, for advance bookings with charge, garden tours and events; or visit website
www.waddesdon.org.uk

6m NW of Aylesbury, 11m SE of Bicester on A41. Entrance in Waddesdon village

House (inc. wine cellars) open 19th March to 23rd Dec, Wed – Sun and Bank Holiday Mons, 12 noon – 4pm;

Grounds open 5th Jan to 16th March, Sat and Sun; then 19th March to Dec, Wed – Sun and Bank Holiday Mons; all 10am – 5pm. Closed 24th to 26th Dec

Entrance: £7, children £3.50, family £17.50 (house and grounds £15, children £11) (high season rates)

Other information: Parking for disabled. Guide dogs only. Many special events

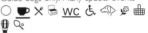

Waddesdon Manor

The National Trust

West Wycombe HP14 3AJ.
Tel: (01494) 513569;
www.nationaltrust.org.uk

2m W of High Wycombe, at W end of
West Wycombe, S of A40 Oxford road

House open as garden but June to Aug
(weekday entry by guided tour)

Grounds open April to Aug,
Sun – Thurs, 2 – 6pm
(last admission 5.15pm)

Entrance: £3.15, children £1.60 (house
and grounds £6.30, children £3.15,
family £15.75)

WEST WYCOMBE PARK ★★
(Historic Garden Grade I)

The 60-acre park was largely created by the second Sir Francis Dashwood and was influenced by his experiences on the Grand Tour, which included visits to Asia Minor and Russia. The first phase involved the creation of the lake with meandering walks, completed by 1739. Numerous classical temples and statues were added subsequently, as well as the delightful little flint and wooden bridges which span the streams. Later still, in the 1770s, the park was enlarged; Nicholas Revett was employed to design yet more temples and follies, including a particularly fine music temple on one of the three islands. Thomas Cook, a pupil of 'Capability' Brown, was entrusted with the planting of trees and alterations to the landscape. There are splendid vistas, especially towards the swan-shaped lake.

OTHER RECOMMENDED GARDENS

BLOSSOMS

Dr and Mrs Frank Hytten, Cobblers Hill, Great Missenden HP16 9PW (01494 863140). Open for NGS by appt

A garden of 5 acres which is likely to appeal to dendrologists and plantsmen alike, overlooking the Misbourne Valley. Good herbaceous borders, extensive woodland and two water gardens.

HUGHENDEN MANOR

High Wycombe HP14 4LA (01494 755573; www.nationaltrust.org.uk). Open March to 2nd Nov, Wed – Sun and Bank Holiday Mons, 11am – 5pm. NT

Recently restored by the Trust, the High Victorian terraced garden of woodland, orchard, lawns and vibrant annual bedding schemes was the creation of Benjamin Disraeli's wife Mary Anne. 4.75 acres. (Listed Grade II)

NETHER WINCHENDON HOUSE

Mr and Mrs R. Spencer Bernard, Nether Winchendon, Nr Aylesbury HP18 0DY (01844 290101); www.netherwinchendonhouse.com. Open for NGS and by appt

The romantic brick-and-stone Tudor manor has an attractive 5-acre country-house garden dominated by a legacy of magnificent trees planted by the Spencer Bernard family over the centuries.

WOTTON HOUSE

Mrs April Gladstone, Wotton Underwood, Aylesbury HP18 0SB. Open mid-April to mid-Sept, Wed, 2–5pm, and for parties by written appt.

A remarkable 200-acre landscape with twin double avenues planted by George London and a third by 'Capability' Brown, aggrandising a magnificent Baroque pile – part seventeenth-century and part Soanesque. There are many follies and garden buildings, gradually being rescued and restored. (Listed Grade II*)

CAMBRIDGESHIRE

For further information about how to use the *Guide*
and for an explanation of the symbols, see pages vi–viii.
Specific dates and times are those given to us by garden owners for 2008.
For 2009 dates, check with the individual properties.
For opening dates under the National Gardens Scheme,
readers should consult *The Yellow Book* or www.ngs.org.uk.
Maps are to be found at the end of the *Guide*.
A few gardens with Peterborough postcodes are to be found
in the Northamptonshire section.

ABBOTS RIPTON HALL ★
(Historic Garden Grade II)

A superb eight-acre garden in which many of the great twentieth-century gardeners have had a hand. In the 1950s Humphrey Waterfield designed a ring of historic roses with a circular lawn at its centre and planted a grey border with alpines and sun-loving perennials. His dedicated work ended abruptly in 1971 when he was killed in a car crash. At the foot of a memorial urn is the inscription: 'Remember Humphrey Waterfield who made this garden anew'. Between 1960 and 1970 Lanning Roper also advised on planting and design. The follies – the work of Peter Foster, Surveyor of the Fabric at Westminster Abbey – range from two large Gothic screens in the spectacular herbaceous borders stretching from the eighteenth-century house, which are backed by columns of yew and philadelphus, to the Chinese pagoda at the end of the lake. Jim Russell advised on trees and added a plantation along the earth bank to protect the garden from the noise of traffic, and Peter Coates and Tony Venison also worked here. The present Lady De Ramsey is a keen gardener, and with Peter Beales has replanted the rose circle and many of the borders. With her husband she has started a collection of rare oaks from acorns collected all over the world.

Lord and Lady De Ramsey

Abbots Ripton, Huntingdon PE28 2PQ.
Tel: (01487) 773555
www.abbotsriptonhall.co.uk

2m N of Huntingdon, approached from B1090

Open 21st and 22nd June,
10am – 6pm; and by appt

Entrance: £3 on charity days; £8 (including plant guide) for parties of 12 or more

ANGLESEY ABBEY GARDENS AND LODE MILL ★★
(Historic Garden Grade II*)

This is a National Trust garden of repute, noted for its fine collection of statues, urns and columns; it provides an excellent afternoon in the country for visitors to Cambridge. To help bring the scale of the 114 acres into perspective, it should be split into three. The formal gardens around the house would have been part of the original 1860s layout; the 1st Lord Fairhaven designed the present formal gardens and added the statuary in the 1930s; and the mile-long winter

The National Trust

Lode, Cambridge CB5 9EJ.
Tel: (01223) 810080;
www.nationaltrust.org.uk

6m NE of Cambridge off A14, on B1102

House open 19th March to 2nd Nov;
Wed – Sun and Bank Holiday Mons,
1 – 5pm
Garden open 19th March to 2nd Nov,
Wed – Sun and Bank Holiday Mons,
10.30am – 5.30pm (last admission 4.30pm).

Anglesey
Abbey
Gardens

Winter garden open 5th Nov to 15th March, Wed – Sun, 10.30am – 4:30pm. Closed 22nd to 30th Dec

Entrance: £4.95, children £2.50 (house, garden and Lode Mill £8.80, children £4.40). Charge made for tours with Head Gardener

Other information: Electric buggies available. Mill machinery working first and third Sat of month

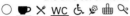

walk was added by the Trust in 1998. For wildlife interest, visit the new Hoe Fen wildlife discovery area. Bulbs – snowdrops, hyacinths, narcissi and leucojums – appear in their thousands, equalled in density and diversity by the wild flowers in the meadows. Later the huge curving herbaceous borders and gardens filled with modern bush roses and dahlias keep the garden alive as a delightful splash of *Amaryllis belladonna* against the grey stone walls ushers in the autumn, and the arboretum trees turn red and gold. Then it is the turn of white-stemmed birches and black-stemmed *Cornus alba* 'Kesselringii' in the winter walk to make a final flourish before the snowdrops begin the year again.

CHIPPENHAM PARK ★

Mr and Mrs Eustace Crawley

Chippenham Park, Ely CB7 5PT. Tel: (01638) 720221/721991. www.chippenhamparkgardens.info; and www.chippenhamcambs.info.

5m NE of Newmarket, 1m off A11

Open possibly Feb to Sept, Thurs – Sat, 11am – 5pm (check websites), and for parties of 20 or more by appt

Entrance: £4, parties with guided tour £6

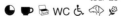

One of the county's most original gardens. The perimeter drive and tadpole-shaped lake and island were created by William Emes, known both as a landscaper and an enthusiast for garden flowers. As a designer he was sensitive, retaining many of the original features; at Chippenham the old formal water garden was allowed to remain, also the trees planted by Admiral Russell in the seventeenth century to echo the formation of the ships drawn up at the battle of La Hogue. The present owners have created a 15-acre garden within the 350-acre park, embellishing Emes's work with distinction. The great canal has been strengthened by the introduction of a glowing copper beech avenue, and in Adrian's Walk (named after a still-serving gardener of 53 years) the colourful plantings are reflected in the waters of the lake. The long south border grows peonies and alliums to perfection, while the Victorian box walk preserves an air of mystery at the entrance to the woodland garden. The old vegetable garden, divided into four, includes a mound and a quince garden, a Spanish garden with olive trees and a green theatre, and a memorial garden to Admiral Russell planted around the magnificent statue of a sitting hare. With over 750 rose bushes and a wide selection of acers and rarer trees, this garden never gives the feeling of being too large or too busy to comprehend. The daffodils are in period with the 1895 house, and the spires of eremurus in season reflect the grandeur of its gables.

CLARE COLLEGE FELLOWS' GARDENS
(Historic Garden Grade II)

Reached by crossing the oldest bridge over the Cam from the college itself, or from Queens Road by walking along the avenue laid out in 1690, two gardens, totalling three acres, lie between the college buildings and the bridge. To the north is the private Master's Garden and to the south the Scholars' Garden, where the planting relies on silver, blue, purple and white. Professor E.N. Willmer designed the present planting scheme for the Fellows' Garden; the fine trees are mainly the legacy of his predecessors. At the garden's heart, concealed by hedges, is a formal pool; adjoining this and enclosed by shrubs is a new sub-tropical planting of bananas, canna lilies and plants for foliage effect. The double herbaceous borders have a yellow and blue theme, while along the northern boundary is a ribbon of silver with a mass of white flowers, including some that show up well against walls and hedges. Summer bedding is used to insert oranges and reds in island beds by the river. Robert Myers has prepared a master plan for development over the next decade.

Trinity Lane, Cambridge CB2 1TL.
Tel: (01223) 333200;
www.clare.cam.ac.uk
In city centre. Entry from Queens Road and Trinity Lane
Open April to Sept, daily, 10:30am – 4.30pm. Closed on graduation, May Ball and special events days
Entrance: College and garden £2.50

CROSSING HOUSE GARDEN ★

Highly recommended, a delightful, eccentric place which proves that plantsmanship is alive and well in Cambridgeshire. A small garden, started by the present owners in 1967, it is crammed full of plants and is an eye-opener about what can be achieved in a small space. There two pools, excellent dwarf box edging, an arbour in clipped yew, rockeries and a lawn,

Mr and Mrs Douglas Fuller
78 Meldreth Road, Shepreth, Royston, Hertfordshire SG8 6PS.
Tel: (01763) 261071
8m SW of Cambridge, 0.5m W of A10
Entrance: free

Crossing House Garden

and two tiny glasshouses full of orchids and alpines. There are thousands of different plants here, so a visit at any time of year will be rewarding. Docwra's Manor (see below) is about 250 metres away.

Docwra's Manor (see below)

DOCWRA'S MANOR

Mrs John Raven

2 Meldreth Road, Shepreth, Royston, Hertfordshire SG8 6PS. Tel: (01763) 260677; www.docwrasmanorgarden.co.uk

8m SW of Cambridge, 0.5m W of A10. Opposite war memorial

Open all year, Wed and Fri, 10am – 4pm; first Suns of March to Oct, 2 – 5pm; and at other times by appt. Parties welcome

Entrance: £4, accompanied children under 16 free. Extra charge for guided and out-of-hours parties

Other information: Park in village hall car park

 WC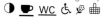

'Simply a garden as reasonably varied as could be' – that was John and Faith Raven's original intention when they bought the manor house with 2.5 acres of land in 1954, and this they achieved. Divided into unexpected compartments by buildings, walls and hedges, it contains many choice plants. The effect is wild in parts; other areas are more formal, with hosts of roses, spurges, clematis, eryngiums and philadelphus. Few gardens arouse so many mixed emotions in visitors – some consider that its romantic atmosphere of *temps perdu* makes it one of the greatest of East Anglian gardens, others find the casual emergence of chance seedlings an irritation. It is best viewed perhaps as the creation of cultured minds — John Raven was a classicist and an eminent field botanist, and his book, *A Botanist's Garden* (1971; reissued) describes the plants he and his wife grew together here.

ELGOOD'S BREWERY

Elgood's Brewery

North Brink, Wisbech PE13 1LN. Tel: (01945) 583160; www.elgoods-brewery.co.uk

In Wisbech, at W end of North Brink

Brewery open as garden for tours, Tues – Thurs, 2pm (£6.50 inc. tasting)

Garden open May to Sept, Tues – Thurs, 11.30am – 4.30pm

Entrance: £3, OAPs and children £2.50

Other information: Guide dogs only

Wisbech is an elegant market town and among its delights are several splendid Georgian terraces. North Brink, along the River Nene, is arguably the most spectacular. Peckover House (see entry) is near the eastern end of the Brink, and some of the brewery's magnificent trees were a gift from the Peckover family in the nineteenth century. They now give grace and dignity to a four-acre garden that is one of the county's most original. As features, herbaceous borders, lake and herb garden are traditional enough, but here they have been given delightful touches of modern artifice. Unusual and attractive too are the thuja and laurel maze and the sensory garden planted with aromatic plants and grasses set in gravel and enlivened by water emerging from stainless steel shapes.

ELTON HALL

Sir William and Lady Proby

Peterborough PE8 6SH. Tel: (01832) 280468 (office hours); www.eltonhall.com

8m W of Peterborough in Elton, just off A605

Hall open as garden

Garden open 25th and 26th May; June, Wed; July and Aug, Wed, Thurs, Sun and Bank Holiday Mon; all 2 – 5pm. Also open for tours by appt April to Sept

(Historic Garden Grade II*)

Steps cloaked in aubrietia and lavender, guarded by two sphinxes, ascend to the low castellated house, parts of which date from 1475. Beside the steps is a knot garden in box, elegantly wrought, and in front a smooth lawn rises to meet the surrounding parterre. A sunken pool, enveloped in a billow of whites and blues with some purple, is the first feature visitors see as they pass under an archway into the main garden. A gravel path encircles the lawn, which has an ornamental well-head offset in the middle, and immaculately clipped low yew hedges, emphasised by clumps of golden yew, lead into the rose garden, re-designed by Xa Tollemache.

The planting is designed to reflect the history of the place, and gives high summer a delightful accent. The distant sound of water will eventually beckon you on, across a hornbeam-lined avenue punctuated by pyramids of box, to the millennium orangery situated beneath a graceful paulownia. The tea room is some 500 yards from the house, in the centre of a well designed and carefully-kept garden centre. Eight acres in all.

Entrance: £5, OAPs £4.50 (hall and garden £7.50, OAPs £6.50, accompanied children under 16 free)

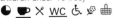

ISLAND HALL

The eighteenth-century house and its three-acre garden, returned to the Vane Percy family by the present owners in 1984, is in two parts, separated by a mill-race yet linked by an award-winning Chinese-style wooden bridge erected in 1988. The Island was the pleasure garden in Victorian times – today it has tall trees, mainly horse-chestnuts, underneath which cow parsley and other wild flowers are being encouraged. The Mill Garden introduces visitors to the semi-formal, eighteenth-century style of the gardens around the house: here are hornbeams and a sundial ensconced in a box parterre spilling over with white shrubby cinquefoil, white Scotch roses and columbines. There are lovely views across the River Ouse to Portholme Meadow. Beyond the croquet lawn, another formal parterre with clipped variegated box hedges, box spirals and yew pyramids anchors the house handsomely into its surroundings.

Mr Christopher and Lady Linda Vane Percy

Post Street, Godmanchester PE29 2BA. Tel: (01480) 459676

2m S of Huntingdon, in centre of Godmanchester

Open for NGS, and May to July and Sept for parties by appt

Entrance: £3

21 LODE ROAD ★

The owner is the well-known retired head gardener from Anglesey Abbey, and his years there are reflected in his accomplished use of foliage – golden, feathery, silvery, opulent– in his own small garden. All the plants are placed to their best advantage, the colours blending delightfully without too much emphasis on any particular individual. The satisfying design of small island beds, and the garden is being further added to by a well-chosen selection of herbaceous plants. Although the climbing rose 'Erinnerung an Brod' dominates the entrance, the garden is not over-rosed. There are modern water features and a row of tubs showing how delightful hostas can be if they are well grown and kept free of slugs.

Richard Ayres

Lode, Cambridge CB25 9ER. Tel: (01223) 811873

6m NE of Cambridge. From A14 take B1102 to Lode

Open for NGS and by appt

Entrance: £3

Other information: Parking facilities at village hall. Possible for wheelchairs but narrow paths

MADINGLEY HALL

The hall was built in 1543 by Sir John Hynde and remained in the family until 1871, and the eight acres of garden embrace three main periods of activity. The Kip engraving of c.1705 reveals elaborate formal Dutch gardens laid out around the house; these were swept away by 'Capability' Brown after 1756 when he refashioned the landscape as parkland, built a new coach road and created an S-shaped pond. When Colonel Walter Harding bought the estate in 1905, he introduced terraces and symmetry on the north side; his son contributed yew hedges and topiary and a rose garden. In

University of Cambridge

Madingley, Cambridge CB3 8AQ. Tel: (01954) 280272; www.cont-ed.cam.ac.uk

3m W of Cambridge in village of Madingley. Accessible from M11, A14 and A428

Open 5th April, 17th May and 16th Aug for parties of 10–20 (1 party on each day – telephone to book), and for NGS

Entrance: charge

Other information: NCCPG plant sale 7th Sept, 2.30 – 5.30pm. Refreshments available if booked in advance

 WC

1948 the estate passed to the University, and since the mid-1980s the eight acres surrounding the house have been restored and developed with sense and sensitivity. The atmosphere is not that of an institutional garden but of an English country house. The delightful ornamental walled gardens to the south of the stable courtyard, filled with a wide range of hardy plants, alpines and medicinal herbs, include a rose pergola and a nut walk to give height and shade, while the Alberni Border in the formal garden is planted for year-long colour and interest. The hall (not open) is listed Grade 1 by English Heritage, and the twelfth-century parish church beside the entrance bridge is well worth a visit.

Diana Boston

Hemingford Grey, Huntingdon PE28 9BN. Tel: (01480) 463134; www.greenknowe.co.uk

4m SE of Huntingdon off A14. Access off river tow path

House open by appt

Garden open all year, daily, 11am – 5pm (closes dusk in winter)

Entrance: £3 (main season), children free (house £6, OAPs £4.50, children £2)

THE MANOR

The moated Norman manor (c.1130) is one of the oldest inhabited houses in the country and the childhood home of those fabled eighteenth-century beauties, the Gunning sisters. Lucy Boston, author of the *Greene Knowe* stories, moved here in 1939 and created a delightful 4.5-acre garden which is perfectly in keeping with the charm of the house; the topiary deer so important in the story survives. Graham Stuart Thomas advised her on the planting of a collection of old roses and the very best of Sir Cedric Morris's irises were included in her schemes. These are interwoven with beds of delightful old English garden plants.

Timothy Clark

Tanner's Lane, Soham, Ely CB7 5AB. Tel: (01353) 720269

6m SE of Ely on A142; pass church and war memorial and take second road on left. From Newmarket turn right in Soham at second road after cemetery

Open for NGS, and for parties of 10 or more by appt

Entrance: £2

NETHERHALL MANOR

An elegant garden, touched with antiquity, and full of old-fashioned plants; indeed the owner's avowed intention is to present historic plants to the general public. In spring it blazes with Victorian hyacinths, old daffodils, crown imperials and old primroses, followed by a display of florists' tulips and florists' ranunculus. The rare double-flowered white Turk's cap lily (which originated here) and the very rare rose 'Jules Margottin' mentioned in *Mary's Meadow*, both flower here, as does Gertrude Jekyll's favourite dahlia, 'White Aster'. Entering through a courtyard with box-edged beds and a handsome fountain, visitors first glimpse the formal aconite garden (later filled with old fuchsias); behind is the organic vegetable garden. To the right runs a colonnade of lichen-encrusted columns linked by a balustrade on which pots of seasonal flowers are displayed; summer is represented by gold and silver tricolour pelargoniums, yellow and golden-brown calceolarias, heliotropes and double lobelias, and a few of the first dahlia cultivars. Notable too are the old apples, specimen trees, clumps of violets and hepatica and, most remarkably, the double-flowered ornamental blackberry (*Rubus ulmifolius* 'Bellidiflorus') trained against the gable wall. 3m SW of Soham is the *Wicken Fen National Nature Reserve*, one of the wild treasures of Cambridgeshire, and the simple effective garden of *Fen Cottage* (National Trust) is open April to October on Sundays and Bank Holiday Mondays, 2 – 5pm.

PECKOVER HOUSE

(Historic Garden Grade II)

The red-brick town house, located on the banks of the River Nene in a splendidly elegant Georgian terrace, is set off by a fine example of a late-Victorian garden with mature trees and shrubberies, a croquet lawn, bedding plants and roses, a formal pool and clipped topiary shapes. The two wide borders designed by Graham Stuart Thomas in the 1960s may be at variance with all this period charm, but the gardeners work hard to keep the structure of the Victorian features, including the recently restored propagation house and fernery, intact and attractive. The house contains mementoes of the Peckover and Clarkson families, in the forefront of the battle for the abolition of slavery.

The National Trust

North Brink, Wisbech PE13 1JR.
Tel: (01945) 583463;
www.nationaltrust.org.uk

In centre of Wisbech on N bank of River Nene

House open as garden, but 1 – 4.30pm

Garden open 15th March to 2nd Nov, Sat – Wed, plus Bank Holiday Mons and Good Fri, 12 noon – 5pm

Entrance: £3.50, children £1.75 (house and garden £5.50, children £2.75, family £14)

UNIVERSITY BOTANIC GARDEN ★

(Historic Garden Grade II)

This diverse and impressive garden covers 40 acres, and admirably fulfils its three purposes – research, education and amenity. Even in winter a visit is worthwhile to see the red,

University of Cambridge

Bateman Street, Cambridge CB2 1JF.
Tel: (01223) 336265;
www.botanic.cam.ac.uk

In S of city, on E side of A1309
(Trumpington Road). Entrance off
Bateman Street

Open all year except 2th Dec to 1st
Jan, 10am – 6pm (closes 5pm in spring
and autumn, 4pm in winter)

Entrance: £4, OAPS and students £3.50,
children under 17 free

black, green and yellow-ochre stems of the dogwoods contrasting with *Rubus biflorus* and the stunning pale pink trunk of *Betula albo-sinensis* var. *septentrionalis*. The garden has the best collection of trees in the east of England, with limes, chestnuts, willows and conifers featuring prominently. Exotic trees include pawpaw and good specimens of madrona, black walnut and dawn redwood. The historic systematic beds display the hardy representatives of 90 families of flowering plants, and there are both limestone and sandstone rock gardens. The glasshouse range has recently been restored and replanted to highlight the drama of plant diversity under conditions ranging from tropical rainforest to arid desert. In the alpine house, plants are changed regularly as they come into flower. The Dry Garden investigates how design and plant selection can eliminate the need for watering in a typical city garden. Local habitats are displayed nearby, including a major fenland display. The Genetic Garden shows how the huge variety of flowering plants results from genetic variation due to mutation, while the figure of 'Healthy Herbie' and a display about compost and compost-making highlight current concerns about chemicals, drugs, recycling and sustainable living. In the new Cambridge Border a mixed shrub and herbaceous planting highlights species which originated in the Botanic Garden, including *Rosa* 'Cantabrigiensis' and *Epimedium* x *cantabrigiensis*, together with prize-winning garden stalwarts like *Viburnum* x *bodnantense* 'Dawn' and *Mahonia* x *media* 'Lionel Fortescue'.

WIMPOLE HALL
(Historic Garden Grade I)

The National Trust

Arrington, Royston SG8 0BW.
Tel: (01223) 206000; www.wimpole.org

7m SW of Cambridge, signed off A603 at
New Wimpole

House open

Garden open Jan to 16th July, Sept to 24th
Dec, Sat – Wed, 10.30am – 5pm
(11am – 4pm Jan to mid-March, Nov and
Dec); 19th July to Aug, Sat – Thurs,
10.30am – 5pm. Open Good Fri, closed
Christmas period. Park walks open all year

Entrance: £3.50, children £1.85 (hall and
garden £8.40, children £4.70, family £24)

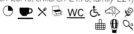

Historically this is the most important garden in Cambridgeshire: the vast landscape park has features by Bridgeman (1720s), 'Capability' Brown (1760s) and the little-known but widely admired William Emes (1790s). The Trust has lavished money on this property and it shows. The rebuilt greenhouses in the walled garden are matched in quality by the planting surrounding them, and restoration continues. The parterre on the north front is decorated with some modern sculpture which may astonish the viewer. Vast avenues lead to the cardinal points of the compass, past lakes, bridges and a splendid 1770 folly – soothing the eye from the shock of the parterre. Fine trees embellish the walk to the folly which takes an hour to reach (a leaflet is available for an alternative tour). The home farm contains a remarkable collection of rare breeds of cattle and sheep.

OTHER RECOMMENDED GARDENS

CAMBRIDGE COLLEGE GARDENS

Most colleges are helpful about access, although the Master's or Fellows' Gardens are often private or rarely open. The best course is to ask at the porter's lodge of each college, or to telephone in advance. The following are among those of particular interest: Downing, Emmanuel, Jesus, King's, Leckhampton, Magdalene, Pembroke, Peterhouse, Robinson, St John's and Trinity..

CHILDERLEY HALL

Mr and Mrs John Jenkins, Dry Drayton CB3 8BB (01954 210271). Open mid-May to mid-July by appt

The structure of the 4-acre garden – moat, raised grass walks and circular mounts – originally complemented the Elizabethan house. The planting today is based around an extensive collection of shrub and species roses flourishing in mixed borders, accessed by paths winding through trees and shrubs. A remote and tranquil place. (Listed Grade II*)

HARDWICKE HOUSE

John Drake, High Ditch Road, Fen Ditton, Cambridge CB5 8TF (01223 292246). Open by appt

In this inventive and original 2-acre garden, a host of unusual species shelter in compartments created by towering hedges. It is full of interest at every season, with a National Collection of aquilegias flowering from late spring to midsummer.

THORPE HALL

Longthorpe, Peterborough PE3 6LW (01733 330060). Open all year, Mon – Fri, except Good Fri, Bank Holiday Mons, 25th and 26th Dec, 10am – 5pm

An L-shaped garden comprising a series of architectural parterres, colourful borders and rose gardens. Three listed pavilions and ancient trees give echoes of past grandeur. (Listed Grade II*)

WEAVER'S COTTAGE

Miss Sylvia Norton. Weaver's Cottage, 35 Streetly End, West Wickham CB21 4RP. Tel: (01223) 892399. Open by appt April to July

Foxgloves are the owner's particular enthusiasm, and she has blended them skilfully into the delightful and fragrant garden surrounding the charming early-18th century cottage. There is an exuberance in the planting of spring bulbs, shrubs and old roses that makes the garden appear larger than its 0.5 acre. A National Collection of lathyrus is held here.

WYTCHWOOD

Mr David Cox, Owl End, Stukeley, Huntingdon PE28 4AQ (01480 454835). Open for NGS, and by appt May to July

The 2-acre garden starts with an explosion of perennials and bedding plants and becomes wilder and wilder as it recedes from the house, ending with an inspired series of meadow islands and a spinney of native trees underplanted with ferns, hostas, foxgloves and spring bulbs. Insects, butterflies and dragonflies abound. Springtime and June are the best times to visit.

Wytchwood

CHESHIRE

For further information about how to use the *Guide*
and for an explanation of the symbols, see pages vi–viii.
Specific dates and times are those given to us by garden owners for 2008.
For 2009 dates, check with the individual properties.
For opening dates under the National Gardens Scheme,
readers should consult *The Yellow Book* or www.ngs.org.uk.
Maps are to be found at the end of the *Guide*.
We have included some gardens with Cheshire postal addresses in the Manchester
Area for convenience. So before planning a day out in Cheshire it is worthwhile
consulting pages 236–239.

The Viscount Ashbrook

Arley, Great Budworth, Northwich
CW9 6NA. Tel: (01565) 777353;
www.arleyhallandgardens.com

5m W of Knutsford off A50, 7m SE of
Warrington off A559. Signed from M6
junctions 19 and 20 and M56 junctions
9 and 10

Hall open as garden, but Tues and Sun

Garden open 21st March to Sept,
Tues – Sun and Bank Holiday Mons;
Oct, Sat and Sun; all 11am – 5pm

Entrance: £5, OAPs £4.50, children
£2.50 (Hall extra)

Other information: Arley Garden
Festival 28th and 29th June,
10am – 5pm

◑ ☕ ✕ 🛍 <u>WC</u> ♿ ⌖ 🌿 ▦
🔦 ⚲

ARLEY HALL AND GARDENS ★

(Historic Garden Grade II*)

Stretching over 23 acres, the gardens consist of many distinct areas, each with its own character and charm, but it is for its superb herbaceous border that Arley is most famed; dating from before 1846, it is reputed to be the earliest of its kind in England. A watercolour by George Elgood of 1889 shows it looking much as it does today, with a broad grass walk and clipped yew buttresses. At one end a classical pavilion provides a focal point framed by chess-piece topiary, and a little to one side is a fine wrought-iron gate. The large range of perennials includes some varieties used here a century ago. Designed to give colour from June to September, the

Arley Hall and Gardens

season begins with soft yellows, blues and silvers before the spires of delphiniums and aconitums make their impact along with the softer forms of gypsophila and achillea; towards the end of the year the hotter colours of sedum, helianthus and crocosmia come to the fore. There is plenty of interest elsewhere too: the walled garden has perennials and shrubs grown in attractive combinations, and in the walled kitchen garden is a vinery containing a good collection of tender plants and a fine border with climbing roses and clematis, irises and peonies. Some areas, such as the flag garden and herb garden, are intimate in scale, while others have wide open vistas. Topiary, mellow brickwork and stone ornaments contribute to the structure and character throughout. Away from the more formal areas an extensive woodland garden has been created by the present Viscount Ashbrook, where 300 varieties of rhododendron grow amongst a collection of rare trees and shrubs in a delightfully tranquil setting. Attached to the gardens is a good nursery selling hardy and tender herbaceous perennials and other plants to be seen in the gardens.

BLUEBELL COTTAGE GARDENS
(Lodge Lane Nursery)

The present owner, who won the BBC Garden of the Year competition in 2006, has many changes planned for these well-known gardens and nursery. The 1.5 acres on a south-west-facing slope include large informal beds of shrubs, small trees and an impressive range of perennials. Areas of shade and others in sun are all suitably planted, and the intention is to increase the planting further while creating vistas through the gardens. There are also six acres of bluebell woods and wildflower meadow. The nursery stocks a large range of perennials, including many rare varieties.

Sue and David Beesley

Lodge Lane, Dutton, Nr Warrington WA4 4HP. Tel: (01928) 713718; www.lodgelane.co.uk

4m SE of Runcorn, 6m NW of Northwich, S of M56 and A533. Signposted

Gardens and nursery open 21st March to 28th Sept, Wed – Sun, 10am – 5pm

Entrance: £3, children free

BRIDGEMERE GARDEN WORLD ★

The 25-acre garden centre has some 5000 different plants for sale including several rare and unusual varieties. There are also six acres of display gardens, some modern in style and others more traditional. They change with the seasons and are constantly being altered. One is Mediterranean in feel with an area of terracotta, a fine stout pergola and many plants with striking foliage; another has mock ruins overlooking a moat and an area devoted to moisture lovers. A rockery and a pool (filled with water lilies and surrounded by varieties of iris and astilbe) are backed by a collection of pines; close by is a bed of euphorbias that reminds one just how many fine varieties of this plant there are. The displays of tulips are particularly impressive, and a good selection of azaleas and rhododendrons grows around the mound, which gives a fine view across the whole garden. Statuary, trellises, grottoes and garden ornaments are used to good effect throughout.

Bridgemere, Nantwich CW5 7QB. Tel: (01270) 521100; www.bridgemere.co.uk

On A51 7m SE of Nantwich. Signed from M6 junctions 15 and 16

Open all year, daily except 25th and 26th Dec, 9am – 7pm (closes 6pm in winter)

Entrance: free

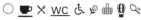

CAPESTHORNE HALL AND GARDENS

Mr W.A. Bromley Davenport
Macclesfield SK11 9JY.
Tel: (01625) 861221;
www.capesthorne.co.uk

7m S of Wilmslow, 1m S of Monks
Heath on A34

House open as gardens but
1.30 – 3.30pm

Gardens open April to Oct, Sun, Mon
and Bank Holidays, 12 noon – 5pm

Entrance: gardens, hall and chapel £6.50,
OAPs £5.50, children (5–18) £3

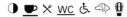

Set within a 1000-acre estate, the gardens have something of a quiet majesty about them and include fine architectural features. The surrounding parkland was laid out in the seventeenth and eighteenth centuries with three lakes forming the southern perimeter. Vernon Russell-Smith designed the formal lakeside garden in the 1960s to replace the large kitchen gardens. It is mainly laid to lawn, but also has herbaceous borders containing a good variety of plants and a wonderful set of Rococo Milanese gates. There is a serene view from here across the lake with its attractive brick bridge and memorial garden alongside. The mellow brickwork of the eighteenth-century chapel sets off the glossy foliage of the *Magnolia grandiflora*, camellias and cherry trees in the small garden which surrounds it. On the north side the old rock garden has been replanted with ferns and tree ferns, and there are many new artefacts. Azaleas and rhododendrons lead to the 'Millennium Dome' in the arboretum, which includes two enormous sweet chestnuts, some giant redwoods and a more recently planted selection of maples. The surrounding park and woodland offer excellent walks.

CHOLMONDELEY CASTLE GARDENS ★
(Historic Garden Grade II)

The Marquess of Cholmondeley
Malpas SY14 8AH.
Tel: (01829) 720383

7m W of Nantwich, 6m N of Whitchurch
on A49

Open April to Sept, Wed, Thurs, Sun
and Bank Holiday Mons, plus 7th and
21st Oct; all 11.30am – 5pm. Also
open on other days by appt for
parties of 20 or more

Entrance: £4, children £2

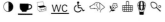

Of the great formal garden laid out by George London in 1690 no trace remains. Instead, set in idyllic parkland and blessed with a most extensive range of mainly acid-loving trees and shrubs, the present gardens are designed to take advantage of spectacular views. The early nineteenth-century castle perches majestically on a hill overlooking the estate, which includes two lakes and a superbly sited cricket pitch. The lawns which slope up to the castle are covered with bulbs in spring. The gardens to the west have some of the most interesting plants. In the glade, sheltered by large trees, are varieties of magnolia and cornus, an *Abutilon vitifolium*, a *Davidia involucrata*, species rhododendrons and a large liquidambar. On a lower level are primulas, narcissi and cyclamens. The rose garden is one of the few formal areas: a pleasant layout of beds divided by stone-flagged paths, with a fine *Magnolia sieboldii* standing at the entrance. Most impressive of all is the temple garden, where the landscaping and architecture give a classical feel – a Claude painting contrived by a horticulturist. Around a pool with its two grassed islands are some attractive combinations of shrubs and trees, good use being made of purple, gold and blue foliage. Tower Hill is a wilder area, where mature woodland of beech, oak and sweet chestnut is underplanted with camellias, more magnolias, azaleas, cornus and rhododendrons. Another water garden, known as the Duckery, has recently been restored and planted with rhododendrons, shrubs and trees; a collection of ferns surrounds the two Victorian waterfalls. 40 acres.

Dunge Valley Hidden Gardens

DUNGE VALLEY HIDDEN GARDENS ★

A superbly sited garden nestling in a small valley high in the Pennines; the location is so remote that often only the song of the lark or the cry of the curlew can be heard. Walks wind across and around the rocky valley, disclosing wonderful views over the garden and into the rugged landscape beyond. It is a superb natural setting for many rhododendrons, camellias, acers and magnolias, with shrub and species roses providing interest later in the season. When the garden was begun in 1983, pine, larch and hemlock were planted as shelter belts and now, even at an altitude of 300 metres, some surprisingly tender specimens survive. Rodgersias, rheums, primulas and other moisture-lovers cluster around the stream that runs through the valley, and close to the stone farmhouse are cultivated pockets of choice plants, including collections of meconopsis and peonies. The expanding *Hardy Plant Nursery* now has one of the best collections of hybrid and species rhododendrons in the North of England, plus meconopsis grown from seed collected by the owners in Nepal and Arunachal Pradesh (plants may be bought when the garden is closed – telephone for an appointment). The garden has increased to eight acres with over 600 new trees and shrubs added.

David and Elizabeth Ketley

Windgather Rocks, Kettleshulme, Whaley Bridge, High Peak SK23 7RF. Tel: (01663) 733787; www.dungevalley.co.uk

6m NE of Macclesfield, 12m SE of Stockport in Kettleshulme. Signed from B5470 Macclesfield – Whaley Bridge road

Open March to June, Thurs – Sun; July and Aug, Sat, Sun and Bank Holiday Mons; all 10.30am – 5pm

Entrance: £3.50, children £1

Other information: Mini-buses up to 30 seats only.

EATON HALL ★
(Historic Garden Grade II*)

The 88 acres of gardens and parkland surrounding the modern hall are vast. There are several fine features, including well-kept herbaceous beds and many stone statues and urns. A long, narrow greenhouse contains camellias, and a deep bed

The Duke of Westminster

Eccleston, Chester CH4 9ET. Tel: (01244) 684400; www.eeo.co.uk

4m S of Chester off A483

Open 23rd March, 25th May and 24th Aug, 1.30 – 5.30pm

Entrance: £4, children £1

backing against the walled garden is planted for dramatic effect with hot-coloured perennials, cotinus and dark-flowering dahlias. There is also a large lake and a small Gothic-style cottage with stone and brick paths set within its own small herb garden. Close to the house is the imposing Italian garden surrounded by a high yew hedge; a large dragon fountain stands at the centre of a pool, and there are beds of annuals and more statues. Arabella Lennox-Boyd has been working on the garden since 1990.

The National Trust

Hare Hill, Over Alderley, Macclesfield SK10 4QB. Tel: (01625) 584412; www.nationaltrust.org.uk

5m NW of Macclesfield, N of B5087 between Alderley Edge and Prestbury

Open 21st March; then 12th May to 2nd June daily; 3rd June to Oct, Wed, Thurs, Sat, Sun and Bank Holiday Mons; all 10am – 5pm.

Parties by written appt

Entrance: £3.20, children £150. £1.80 per car refundable on entry to garden

HARE HILL GARDENS

Hybrid and species rhododendrons, some of enormous size, are the main attraction in the 12 acres here. Other acid-lovers – azaleas, magnolias, acers and tree-like pieris – thrive in the damp, lush setting and sheltering canopy of beech and oak. A pool at the heart of the wood gives a break in the trees, and the colours of the rhododendrons are reflected in its waters; rustic timber bridges cross to a central island. There is also a walled garden, once used for growing vegetables but now laid mainly to lawn with beds of roses and some good climbers. Along the drive to the south, majestic conifers and pines tower above rhododendrons and azaleas. Although at its peak in spring and early summer, the rolling countryside surrounding the garden and the views of the Pennines to the east make it a good centre for walks at any time of the year.

Mr S. Z. de Ferranti

Macclesfield SK11 9PJ.

2m W of Macclesfield on A537

Open for NGS

Entrance: £5, children £1

HENBURY HALL ★

The hall, modelled on the Villa Rotunda, sits confidently on a gentle eminence at the heart of parkland. The remarkable 12-acre *giardino segreto* is skilfully hidden from the park by a backcloth of trees. The main garden to the north-east, centred around a lake with a high jet, has steep banks planted with rhododendrons, azaleas and small trees such as acers, laburnums and birches, which give it something of the aura of Stourhead (see entry in Wiltshire); around the

Henbury Hall

margins are beds of hostas, candelabra primulas, gunneras, irises and royal ferns. The garden buildings here include a Chinese bridge, a small Chinese summerhouse and a Gothick folly. There is also a productive walled garden and a double herbaceous border. The tennis court is discreetly hidden, as is the swimming pool which is sited within a conservatory. At the entrance to the house is a small sunken garden with a round pool and a fountain and quadripartite lawns edged with miniature box. Three fine statues by Simon Verity are placed around the garden.

LITTLE MORETON HALL

The extraordinary timber-framed house, built between c.1504 and c.1610, is undoubtedly the magnet for visitors, but its quiet, contemplative one-acre garden plays its part in establishing the aura of the place. Designed to frame the building in suitable style, it is actually a modern creation. The most outstanding feature, the knot garden, was laid out by Graham Stuart Thomas using a simple geometric seventeenth-century pattern of gravel, lawn and box edging enclosed by a high yew hedge. There is also a yew tunnel and four beds of period herbs and vegetables, and a small orchard set within a lawn. The perimeter of the garden is defined by a moat, its clear waters filled with golden orfe and overhung by trees, including a fine old willow. A gravel walk follows the moat, giving views back across the garden to the unforgettable hall.

The National Trust

Congleton CW12 4SD.
Tel: (01260) 272018;
www.nationaltrust.org.uk

4m SE of Congleton on E side of A34

Open 1st to 16th March, 8th Nov to 21st Dec, Sat and Sun, 11.30am – 4pm; 19th March to 2nd Nov, Wed – Sun, 11.30am – 5pm. Open Bank Holiday Mons

Entrance: £6.40, children £3.20, family £14.90 (hall and gardens).

Other information: Wheelchair for loan. Guide dogs and hearing dogs only

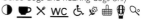

MELLORS GARDENS

(Historic Garden Grade II)

Where can you pass through the Valley of the Shadow of Death, climb Jacob's Ladder, see the Mouth of Hell and visit the Celestial City, all within the space of ten minutes? Here, at the heart of a valley in a rugged but attractive part of the Peak District, during the second half of the nineteenth century, James Mellor, much influenced by Swedenborg, designed a unique allegorical garden of two acres, which attempts to re-create the journey of Christian in Bunyan's The Pilgrim's Progress. There are many small stone houses and other ornaments to represent features of the journey. Most areas are grassed, with stone paths running throughout; at one end a large pond is overlooked by an octagonal summerhouse. Excellent guide book.

Mr and Mrs A. Rigby

Hough Hole House, Sugar Lane, Rainow, Macclesfield SK10 5UW.
Tel: (01625) 573251

From Macclesfield take B5470 Whaley Bridge road. In Rainow turn off to N opposite church into Round Meadow, then turn first left into Sugar Lane and follow road down to garden

Open 26th May and 25th Aug, 2 – 5pm, and for parties of 10 or more by appt

Entrance: £1.50, children free

THE MOUNT

The two-acre garden, originally planted in the 1920s but enlarged, improved and replanted by the present owners, is a fine setting for the Regency house. Each distinct area has its own individual style. The terrace garden has an Italian feel, with a swimming pool, many architectural features and brightly planted terracotta pots. The shade garden is more informal, with rhododendrons, azaleas and camellias underplanted with

Mr and Mrs Nicholas Payne

Andertons Lane, Whirley, Henbury, Macclesfield SK11 9PB.

2m W of Macclesfield off A537. Turn into Pepper Street opposite Blacksmith's Arms, and left into Church Lane which becomes Andertons Lane. Garden is 200 metres further on. Signposted

Open for NGS, and by written appt at other times for parties of 10 or more

Entrance: £5 (£6 for private visits), children free

Other information: Plants for sale on NGS day only

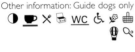

University of Liverpool

Neston Road, Ness, Wirral CH64 4AY. Tel: (0151) 353 0123; www.nessgardens.org.uk

10m NW of Chester, 2m off A540 between Ness and Burton

Open, all year, daily except 25th Dec, 9.30am – 5pm (closes 4pm Nov to Jan)

Entrance: charge

Other information: Guide dogs only

The Norton Priory Museum Trust

Tudor Road, Manor Park, Runcorn WA7 1SX. Tel: (01928) 569895; www.nortonpriory.org

2m E of Runcorn. From M56 junction 11 turn for Warrington and follow signs. From all other directions follow signs to Runcorn, then Norton Priory

Open all year, daily, 12 noon – 5pm (closes 6pm Sat, Sun and Bank Holiday Mons; 4pm Nov to March). Walled garden open April to Oct, daily, 1.30 – 4.30pm

Entrance: £4.50, concessions £3.25, family £12

Other information: Museum open. Teas and snacks in museum

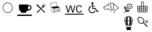

hostas and other shade-lovers. An area of lawn has a pair of herbaceous borders; opposite is another small border planted entirely with astilbes, and a conservatory containing a climbing pelargonium. In one corner of the garden an area of grass has been cut to different heights, forming patterns and paths leading to an obelisk looking across the Cheshire plain towards Wales. May and early June are perhaps the most colourful times to visit.

NESS BOTANIC GARDENS ★★

(Historic Garden Grade II)

Arthur Kilpin Bulley, a Liverpool cotton broker, began gardening on this site in 1898, using seeds from plants collected for him by George Forrest, the noted plant hunter. The gardens extend to 64 acres, and those who have experience of the north-west winds blowing off the Irish Sea will marvel at the variety and exotic nature of the plant life. The secret is in trees planted as shelter belts. The aim has been to provide interest from spring onwards, through the herbaceous garden of summer to the heather and sorbus collections of autumn. There are in addition areas of specialist interest, such as the Pinewood and adjacent areas, home to the best collection of rhododendrons and azaleas in the north-west of England. A National Collection of sorbus is held here.

NORTON PRIORY MUSEUM AND GARDENS ★

The woodland garden, covering 30 acres and containing many fine mature trees, surrounds the remains of the twelfth-century Augustinian priory. The stream glade is the most attractive area, planted with azaleas and candelabra primulas; a water-lily tank has a statue of Coventina (goddess of wells and streams) at its centre. There are many modern sculptures dotted around both parts of the garden. At some distance to the north is the clearly signposted walled garden, built in the mid-eighteenth century and now redesigned on more ornamental lines with a rose walk running down the centre and two broad borders planted with a variety of shrub roses. It also contains an orchard of pears, plums, greengages and quinces (a National Collection of *Cydonia oblonga*, the tree quince, is held here), a vegetable garden and a distinctive herb garden. Along the south-facing wall a series of brick arches, covered with vines and honeysuckles and sheltering two large figs, is fronted by beds of perennials, strongly planted with kniphofias, euphorbias, salvias and geums. Indeed the walled garden is a good illustration of the twin strengths of the garden as a whole – a bold, coherent design and a great variety of plants.

ONE HOUSE NURSERY

There are two very different gardens to visit in this 1.5-acre plot. The first is the one attached to the nursery where the owner grows the plants that clearly interest her so much. One area in full sun has a newly created pool where gunneras and rodgersias contrast with tall sword-leaved irises, and a raised bed containing a large range of alpines. Away from the nursery and close to large trees is a shaded area ideal for her collection of hostas and other perennials, including geraniums and meconopsis. Candelabra primulas surround a second pool, while fine shrub roses, a rockery and a hornbeam arbour occupy a brighter area. A short walk from the nursery is an early-eighteenth-century walled garden on a steep south-facing slope, originally built to supply vegetables for the long-demolished One House. Hidden away and abandoned for sixty years, a restoration project has brought it back to life and filled it once again with a broad range of vegetables and fruit, including many old varieties. At one end of the garden is an old bothy with an open fire – this provides a welcome shelter for the volunteers against the unpredictable weather, for the garden is perched high on the edge of the Pennines with dramatic views over the Cheshire plain.

Louise Baylis

Buxton New Road, Macclesfield SK11 0AD. Tel: (01625) 427087; www.onehousenursery.co.uk

2.5m NE of Macclesfield on A537 to Buxton

Open 10th to 26th May, 9am – 5.30pm, and by appt at other times

Entrance: £3, children free

WC

THE QUINTA ★

Sir Bernard Lovell began planting this garden in 1948 to satisfy his love of trees. It now contains a large variety of trees and shrubs. There are National Collections of pine and ash, good collections of birch and oak, five of the six varieties of wingnut and an Oriental plane directly descended from the Hippocratic tree on the island of Cos. Most areas are informally planted and interspersed with grassed glades; several avenues pass up and down the garden, including one of red-twigged limes planted in 1958 to commemorate Sir Bernard's Reith lectures, and one of *Populus nigra* to celebrate his knighthood; to mark his 90th birthday collections of camellias, rhododendrons, primulas and malus were assembled. To the west of the garden a walk taking in some marvellous views across the Dane Valley (SSSI) leads to the 39 steps that descend into the wooded valley of a small brook (one mile from the car park and back). 36 acres in all.

Tatton Garden Society with Cheshire Wildlife Trust

Swettenham, Congleton CW12 2LF. www.tattongardensociety.co.uk

5m NW of Congleton, E of A535 Holmes Chapel – Alderley Edge road, near Twemlow Green. Follow signs for Swettenham Village; arboretum is next to Swettenham Arms

Open all year, daily except 25th Dec, 9am – sunset, and for parties by appt

Entrance: £2.50

RODE HALL
(Historic Garden Grade II)

A long drive leads through parkland to an attractive red-brick house with fine stable buildings. A small Italian garden has been created here in the ruins of the old tenants' hall, with a fountain, Italian pines and olive trees. The 10-acre gardens lie to the north and east, with many areas remaining as planned by Repton in 1790. The rose garden and formal areas were designed by Nesfield in 1860; these are mainly laid to lawn, with gravel paths and clipped yews, and there are good views

Sir Richard and Lady Baker Wilbraham

Church Lane, Scholar Green ST7 3QP. Tel: (01270) 882961; www.rodehall.co.uk

5m SW of Congleton between A34 and A50

House open

Garden open Feb (for snowdrops), daily except Mon, 12 noon – 4pm; April to Sept, Tues – Thurs and Bank Holiday Mons, 2 – 5pm; and for parties by appt

39

Entrance: £3, OAPs £2.50 (house and garden £5, OAPs £4)

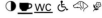

from here of the surrounding countryside and Repton's lake. In a dell to the west is a woodland garden with hellebores and flowering shrubs, rhododendrons, azaleas and some fine climbing roses. Old stone steps ascend the opposite side of the dell to a grotto and early-nineteenth-century terraced rock garden. A small stream is dammed at the open end of the dell with the resulting pond surrounded by marginals; a path leads from here to the lake. Snowdrops, daffodils and bluebells light up the early months, while the two-acre Georgian walled kitchen garden is at its best from June to August. The ice-house in the park is also worth a visit.

Mr R.G.A. Davies

London Road, Stapeley, Nantwich CW5 7LH. Tel: (01270) 623868; www.stapeleywg.com

1m SE of Nantwich on A51. Signed from M6 junction 16

Open all year, daily except 25th Dec. Opening and closing times vary from 9am – 10am and 4pm – 8pm

Entrance: Display gardens free. The Palms Tropical Oasis £4.45, OAPs £3.95, children £2.60 (2007 prices)

Other information: Wheelchairs available

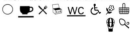

STAPELEY WATER GARDENS

Two acres of garden shopping under cover. Within it, a few areas are attractive gardens in their own right. At the back are many pools containing a National Collection of water lilies; the land around is landscaped with lawns and shrub borders. Another area has small demonstration gardens. Across the car park is The Palms Tropical Oasis. This huge greenhouse has none of the architectural merit of a Victorian palm house, but the main hall is impressive, with a long rectangular pool flanked by huge palm trees, the Jungle Floor (a variety of exotic plants and animals), and other exhibits. Those with an interest in water gardens might comment that this is a bleak description – think of the giant *Victoria amazonica* water lily from Brazil, the rare breeding sting-rays, the *Nymphaea gigantea* from Australia. There is also an angling centre for the non-horticultural.

Cheshire County Council/ The National Trust

Knutsford WA16 6QN. Tel: (01625) 374400; www.tattonpark.org.uk

3m N of Knutsford, signed from M6 and M56

House open 15th March to 28th Sept, daily except Mon, 12 noon – 4pm

Gardens open all year, daily except Mon, 10am – 7pm (11am – 4pm Oct to March) (last admission 1 hour before closing). Closed 25th Dec

Entrance: £3.50, children £2, family £9, park £4.50 per car

Other information: RHS Flower Show here 23rd to 27th July

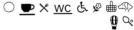

TATTON PARK ★★
(Historic Garden Grade II*)

Tatton Park was, throughout four centuries, the home of the Egertons, an immensely rich family who could indulge their every whim on their vast estate. The 50 acres of gardens here are among the finest in Britain and contain some unique features created by the best designers in the country. Repton made a Red Book in 1791, and much of his work is still visible in the wonderful rolling parkland that surrounds the gardens. When Lewis Wyatt completed his work on the house in 1815 he was asked to design the kidney-shaped flower garden and the elegant orangery. From 1859 Paxton was at work, and his fernery was built to take the collection of plants made by Lord Egerton's brother; it now houses New Zealand tree ferns. Also by Paxton is the Italian garden, the grandest and most formal part of the gardens: an arrangement of terraces spaciously laid out with an ornate design of clipped hedges and beds. They are overlooked by the south-facing portico of the house and fine views stretch out across the parkland from here. The garden constructed in 1910 by Japanese workmen and recently restored has a wholly different feel. Set in a small valley, the contrasting textures of mounds of moss, delicate

Tatton Park

acer leaves, large stones and a gently flowing stream give this garden its particular charm, while large conifers provide a backdrop and lend it intimacy. Tatton has much more besides: pools and lakes, huge numbers of rhododendrons and azaleas, a rose garden that has something of the feel of Lutyens about it, a maze and an arboretum with especially fine pines. With the help of Heritage Lottery Funding, a huge project is underway to restore the walled gardens to their former working glory, with areas of fruit and vegetables and large greenhouses, including a pinery for forcing pineapples.

WEEPING ASH

This two-acre garden has been created by a retired nurseryman, so it is only to be expected that a great variety of plants is found here: an extensive collection of small trees, particularly sorbus, shrubs, roses, and a large range of perennials, including a selection of snowdrops and hellebores and many bulbs; one large bed is devoted to lilies. But it is his ideas on design that bring so much to the garden. The herbaceous border is 90 metres long. Broad grass paths snake around the mixed beds, small offshoot paths give interesting glimpses back into the main areas, and there are views over the whole garden from a ruined Doric temple on a mound. Many structures have been created as hosts to climbing plants, the best being a rustic gazebo built entirely from scrapwood, which is now covered by a passion flower and a golden hop.

John Bent

Glazebury, Warrington Road, Warrington WA3 5NT. Tel: (01942) 266303 (Bents Garden Centre); www.bents.co.uk

14m W of Manchester. Turn S off A580 at Greyhound Hotel roundabout onto A574 to Culcheth. Garden is 0.25m further on left

Open Jan to Nov, 3rd Sun in each month, 11am – 5pm

Entrance: £2, children free

Other information: Amenities at adjacent garden centre

OTHER RECOMMENDED GARDENS

ADLINGTON HALL

Mrs C.J.C. Legh, Macclesfield SK10 4LF (01625) 829206; www.adlingtonhall.com). Open July, Sun – Wed, 2 – 5pm, and for parties Mon – Fri by appt at other times

The hall – a hunting lodge which gradually became a manor house – and the estate have been in the unbroken ownership of the Legh family since 1315. Near the house formal gardens have been re-created and a parterre and a yew maze planted. The ancient deer park developed over the centuries into an impressive wooded landscape, gaining in the 18th century several handsome garden buildings. 30 acres. (Listed Grade II*)

BRAMALL HALL

Bramhall Park, Bramhall, Stockport SK7 3NX (08458 330974; www.bramallhall.org.uk). Hall open – telephone for details. Park open all year, daily, during daylight hours

Although the puny plantings surrounding the magnificent timber-framed house are a missed opportunity, the 66-acre park is another matter, with broad areas of grassland encircling a number of small lakes, wildflower banks and mature woodland trees blanking out the suburbia beyond.

DORFOLD HALL

Mr R. Roundell, Acton, Nr Nantwich CW5 8LD (01270 625245). Open April to Oct, Tues and Bank Holiday Mons, 2 – 5pm, and for NGS.

An 18-acre garden for all seasons. The steeply sloping woodland garden is especially attractive in spring, and colourful rose and herbaceous borders are a fine setting for the historic Jacobean house. (Listed Grade II)

GAWSWORTH HALL

Mr and Mrs T. Richards, Macclesfield SK11 9RN (01260 223456; www.gawsworthhall.com). Open Easter to Sept, Sun – Wed, mid-June to Aug, daily; all 2 – 5pm

The impressive half-timbered manor house, complete with a tilt yard and the bones of an unfinished late-17th-century garden, is approached by two rhododendron-fringed lakes and surrounded by colourful formal gardens, including one of modern roses edged with bright annuals. (Listed Grade II*)

73 HILL TOP AVENUE

Mr and Mrs Martin Land, Cheadle Hulme SK8 7HZ (0161 486 0055). Open for NGS and by appt

Perennials – camellias, crocosmias, phlox and much more – are the mainstay of this small suburban garden, and the variety is huge, topped up by shrubs, roses and climbers. It is much more than an impressive plant collection, however, for the planting has been planned for its aesthetic effect.

JODRELL BANK ARBORETUM

Macclesfield SK11 9DL (01477 571339; www.jb.man.ac.uk/scicen). Open mid-March to Oct, daily, 10.30am – 5.30pm; Nov to mid-March, Tues – Sun, 11am – 4pm. Closed several days over Christmas and New Year

Sir Bernard Lovell started planting an arboretum in 1972 to counter the effect of a flat landscape dominated by a massive radiotelescope. His fine collection of shrubs and trees, including National Collections of malus and sorbus, now covers 35 acres.

PEOVER HALL GARDENS

Mr R. Brooks, Over Peover, Knutsford WA16 9HW. Open May to Aug, Mon and Thurs, 2 – 5pm, and for NGS.

Set within a large early-18th-century park are 15 acres of mainly Edwardian gardens. Around the Elizabethan house formal gardens with distinctive and ornate topiary combine perfectly with old brick walls and stone path; to the west is a wooded area with an attractive flowery dell. (Listed Grade II)

QUEEN'S PARK

Victoria Avenue, Wistaston Road, Crewe CW2 7SE (01270 537882; www.crewe-nantwich.gov.uk). Open all year, daily, 9am – sunset

The 45-acre park opened in 1887. Perfectly oval in shape, it was well landscaped and furnished with fine trees, lakes, woodland and a typically Victorian set-piece of clock tower and twin lodges. This impressive public space is currently being restored with lottery funds. (Listed Grade II)

REASEHEATH COLLEGE

Reaseheath, Nantwich CW5 6DF (01270 625131; www.reaseheath.ac.uk). Open 18th May (College Festival and Open Day), 11am – 5pm; then 21st, 22nd, 28th and 29th May, 1 – 5pm

Many areas of horticultural interest in the 12 acres here – a lake stocked with aquatic plants, a woodland with fine trees, heather and rock gardens, herb and gravel gardens, island beds, glasshouses and a nursery.

WALTON HALL GARDENS

Walton Lea Road, Higher Walton, Warrington WA4 6SN (01925 601617; www.warrington.gov.uk/waltongardens). Open all year, daily, 8am – dusk

Dominated by the dark brick Victorian mansion with its distinctive clock tower, the 20-acre gardens respond in kind with a large pool, an impressive rockery, mighty beech trees and a series of flower-filled formal gardens separated by yew hedges.

THE WELL HOUSE

Mrs S.H. French-Greenslade, Tilston, Malpas SY14 7DP (01829 250332). Open for NGS and March to July by appt

A 2-acre garden with a great variety of plants, a natural stream flowing through and a new wildflower meadow. Various water features enhance the steeply sloping site in a cleverly integrated design – an inspiration for those with small gardens.

CORNWALL

For further information about how to use the *Guide*
and for an explanation of the symbols, see pages vi–viii.
Specific dates and times are those given to us by garden owners for 2008.
For 2009 dates, check with the individual properties.
For opening dates under the National Gardens Scheme,
readers should consult *The Yellow Book* or www.ngs.org.uk.
Maps are to be found at the end of the *Guide*.

ANTONY ★
(Historic Garden Grade II*)

Antony is a little off the beaten track, but it is well worth the effort to visit one of the country's finest early-eighteenth century houses in its magnificent natural setting. The house and adjacent formal gardens now belong to the National Trust, while the woodland gardens, which lie between the parkland and the River Lynher and are also open, belong to a family trust. The formal gardens, with a terrace round the house, wide lawns, extensive vistas, yew hedges and old walls, are of the highest quality. A water feature by William Pye on the west lawn mirrors the yew topiary nearby. Eighteenth century statues, modern sculpture and topiary are features of the yew walk and of the formal compartments of the summer garden; the latter includes a pleached lime hedge, mixed shrub and herbaceous borders with roses, and a knot garden. The woodland gardens, also known as the wilderness – the central section – include Jupiter Hill and a late-Georgian bath house and are planted with superb camellias, magnolias and rhododendrons, with scented rhododendrons outstanding in May. A standing stone of Cornish granite has been erected on top of Jupiter Hill in memory of the present owner's parents, who created the woodland gardens. In the neighbouring woodland walk is a ruined fifteenth-century dovecote and Richard Carew's sixteenth-century Fishful Pond, and there are fine walks along the river banks. Two National Collections are held here: hemerocallis (610 cultivars) and *Camellia japonica* (300 cultivars).

The National Trust/
Trustees of Carew Pole Garden Trust

Torpoint PL11 2QA.
Tel: (01752) 812364;
www.nationaltrust.org.uk

2m W of Torpoint on A374, 16m SE of Liskeard. From Plymouth use Torpoint car ferry

House open as formal gardens

Formal gardens open Easter to Oct, Tues – Thurs and Bank Holiday Mons; also 3rd June to Aug, Sun; all 1.30 – 5.30pm (last admission 4.45pm).

Woodland gardens open March to Oct, Tues – Thurs, Sat, Sun and Bank Holiday Mons, 11am – 5.30pm

Entrance: £4 (house and formal gardens £5.80, children £2.90, family £14.50) (2007 prices)

Other information: Separate car parks for formal and woodland gardens

BARBARA HEPWORTH MUSEUM AND SCULPTURE GARDEN ★
(Historic Garden Grade II)

The wonderful collection of Hepworth's own sculptures combines superbly with the architectural planting of her garden as a permanent testimonial to her importance. The house and half-acre sloping garden are kept as they were in her lifetime. The strong vertical and other architectural

Administered by The Tate Gallery

Barnoon Hill, St Ives TR26 1AD.
Tel: (01736) 796226;
www.tate.org.uk/stives

In centre of St Ives. Signposted

Opposite: Antony

Barbara Hepworth Sculpture Garden

Open March to Oct, daily,
10am – 5.20pm; Nov to Feb, daily
except Mon, 10am – 4.20pm

Entrance: museum and sculpture garden
£4.75, concessions £2.75, OAPs and
children free (2007 prices)

○ WC &

statements and the soft underplanting occlude views outside
and provide a soft contrasting background for the sculptures.
Trees shade the upper part of the garden and give transient
light effects in the sun. They include *Cordyline australis*,
bamboos and a metasequoia on the back wall, and below
them *Magnolia grandiflora*, a ginkgo, and a row of *Prunus*
'Amanogawa' providing cover for a small but important pond
and separating the upper garden from the small open lawn
which forms the lower part. Below are herbaceous beds and
a silver-grey path. The garden is within walking distance of the
Tate St Ives; the small but attractive *Trewyn Garden*, well
planted and with an immaculate lawn, adjoins, and nearby is
Tregenna Castle Hotel, with a small sub-tropical walled garden
and an attractive waterfall [both open all year, daily, during
daylight hours].

Mr and Mrs A.D.G. Fortescue

The Estate Office, Boconnoc, Lostwithiel
PL22 0RG. Tel: (01208) 872507;
www.boconnocenterprises.co.uk

Between Lostwithiel and Liskeard,
S of A390

Gardens open 13th, 20th and 27th
April, 4th, 11th, 18th and 25th May, and
1st June, 2 – 5pm; also for NGS and for
parties of 10 or more by appt

Entrance: £4.50, children free

Other information: Guided tours of
house, garden, church and estate, with
refreshments, by prior arrangement.

BOCONNOC

(Historic Garden Grade II*)

The superb parkland was first laid out by Thomas Pitt, Lord
Camelford (grandfather of Pitt the Elder), in the eighteenth
century. With its sweeping views and enormous hardwoods, it
is a fine example of the Picturesque landscape and makes a
wonderful backdrop for the 20-acre garden. Along the drive
rhododendrons, azaleas and camellias thrive on a carpet of
bluebells; on the lawns around the house are camellias and
large clumps of *luteum* and 'Cornish Red' rhododendrons. A
Golden Jubilee walk around the lake has been planted with
daffodils. The magnificent woodland garden, covering some 20
acres, contains fine flowering shrubs and many large and

unusual trees. Using the original 1840 list, the circular pinetum is being replanted into sections based on the points of the compass: the Americas, Europe and Asia, with 'play' areas for Chile and New Zealand.

BONYTHON ESTATE GARDENS ★

This is a major new and exciting garden of 20 acres which is still being developed. The owners started in 1999 with an old walled garden, a few ornamental trees and shrubs, background trees and essential shelter belts (now extended by another 15,000 trees!). In a courtyard of the 1780s house a complex water feature, planted with grasses, herbs and bamboos, is adjoined by a herb parterre. The lawn is surrounded by rhododendrons and azaleas. The large walled garden consists of an upper part where herbaceous and shrub borders surround a swimming pool themed with changing blues and purples, and below it a newly designed potager in shades of pink and burgundy. The areas below the walled garden are more sheltered. An orchard with wild flowers beneath the trees slopes down to Lake Joy against a background of specimen trees and shrubs, while the sunny bank which dams it boldly displays South African and Mediterranean plants, and camassias cluster beside the water course. Below this Lake Sue, planted since 2001 but now mature, is surrounded by masses of ornamental grasses and hot red colours for late summer. From here a stream trickles through the woodland dell, where a path flanked by hellebores leads among dense plantings of dicksonias, young rhododendrons and other spring shrubs to the newly enlarged Quarry Lake backed by vertical cliffs.

BOSAHAN

The 100-year-old garden, with fine views from its top of the Helford River and the sea, runs from the house down to an attractive stream and pond fringed with moisture-loving plants in the first of its two valleys. Its five acres contain mature conifers and rhododendrons as well as camellias, magnolias, tree ferns and other specimens, with palms throughout the garden. Beyond the main garden a mature wooded valley, where tree ferns grow, shadows the stream down to the Helford River. Christine Graham-Vivian is a garden designer, and her sure touch is evident throughout.

BOSVIGO ★

An immaculately maintained garden of great artistry and imagination. The two acres surrounding the Georgian house consist of several delightful enclosed and walled areas. The hot garden displays red, yellow and orange flowers, the Vean Garden white and yellow, and the walled garden is planted in blues, lavenders and mauves. Flowers and foliage are grouped with boldness or subtlety to enchanting effect. Though not a

Holiday accommodation available

● ● ✕ WC ⑤ ⬠ ⬥ B&B

Mr and Mrs R. Nathan

Cury Cross Lanes, Helston TR12 7BA.
Tel: (01326) 240234;
www.bonythonmanor.co.uk

5m S of Helston on A3083. Turn left at Cury Cross Lanes (Wheel Inn), and take entrance on right signposted 'Bonython Estate'

Open April to Sept, Tues – Fri,
10am – 4.30pm (closed Good Fri),
and for parties of 10 or more by appt

Entrance: £6, children £2

 ◐ ● WC ⑤ ⬥

Mr and Mrs R.J. Graham-Vivian

Bosahan, Manaccan, Helston TR12 6JL.
Tel: (01326) 231351

10m SE of Helston, 1m NE of Manaccan

Open 24th March to 20th June,
Mon – Fri, 11am – 4.30pm (closed all Bank Hols)

Entrance: £4, OAPs £3

◐ WC ⬠ ⬥

Wendy Perry

Bosvigo Lane, Truro TR1 3NH.
Tel: (01872) 275774; www.bosvigo.com

0.75m W of Truro. From A390, turn into Dobbs Lane next to Aldi sign, just W of Sainsbury roundabout. Entrance is 500 metres down lane on left, just after sharp left bend

Open March to Sept, Thurs and Fri,
11am – 6pm

Entrance: £4, children £1, under 5 free

typical Cornish garden (rhododendrons and camellias do not play a major part), there is a wonderful spring section with a woodland walk containing many treasures such as hellebores, epimediums and erythroniums. The garden as a whole, however, is at its best in summer when the mainly herbaceous plants start their display. A good selection of rare and unusual plants is on offer in the nursery.

Mr F.J. Williams

Caerhays, Gorran, St Austell PL26 6LY.
Tel: (01872) 501310;
www.caerhays.co.uk

10m S of St Austell, on coast by Porthluney Cove between Dodman Point and Nare Head

House open 10th March to May, Mon – Fri, 12.15 – 4pm

Garden open 18th Feb to 1st June, daily, 10am – 5pm

Entrance: £5.50, children under 16 £2.50 (under 5 free) (house and garden £9.50, children under 16 £3.50)

Other information: Car park by beach; short walk to garden entrance

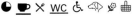

CAERHAYS CASTLE GARDEN ★★
(Historic Garden Grade II*)

Caerhays, unsurpassed as a spring garden and one of the greatest of all Cornish and British gardens, fully deserves its international reputation. Principally a woodland garden, it stretches up and around the extensive hillside above the romantic early-nineteenth-century castle. It can claim its collection of camellias and rhododendrons to be amongst the finest and its magnolias to be unrivalled. All of these, as well as many other fine shrubs and trees, are not only huge themselves but bear flowers of a remarkable size and depth of colour. The extensive replanting in the higher garden after the storm of 1990 has matured with great effect, while the felling of a stand of mature beech trees for safety reasons has revealed wonderful new views looking down on many of the most spectacular magnolias. A large number of plants are raised from material brought back by famous plant hunters or sent recently from China, and it was at Caerhays that the famous x williamsii camellias were originally propagated. 60 acres.

Mr and Mrs H.A.E. Rogers

Mawnan Smith, Falmouth TR11 5JA.
Tel: (01326) 250258;
www.carwinion.com

5m SW of Falmouth. From Mawnan Smith take left road by Red Lion. 500 metres up hill on right is white gate marked 'Carwinion'

Open all year, daily, 10am – 5.30pm

Entrance: £4, children free

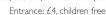

CARWINION
The garden is notable for its bamboos – the Bamboo Society's reference collection is held here. They are planted intensively in the walled section and, accompanied by camellias, rhododendrons and other shrubs, in other parts of the garden. Among these is a fine *Michelia doltsopa* and a good *Drimys winteri*. The lawn below the house is adorned with shrubs and bamboos, and a series of small valleys with an attractive high-level path converges to form ponds and a bog of gunnera. This leads past the open lawns of the new quarry garden through woodland sheltering tree ferns and hellebores, and on down to the Helford river. Much impressive clearing and replanting has taken place in the 14 acres here since 1998.

Mr N. Holman

Zelah, Truro TR4 9HD.
Tel: (01872) 540324

8m NE of Redruth, 1m W of Zelah on A30. At end of bypass, turn N at Marazanvose; entrance is 0.5m on right

CHYVERTON ★
(Historic Garden Grade II)

Chyverton contains a series of plantings of national importance, surrounding the 1730s house and stretching into woodland at the bottom of the adjacent valley, where new views are being opened up. In all, 20 acres of gardens are set in 120 acres of woodland. Eighty years of unbroken planting has resulted in one of the greatest collections of magnolias in Britain, together with fine rhododendrons, camellias and ferns and many other shrubs and trees, both hardwoods and conifers. Such are the renown and the growing conditions of the place that collectors and botanical institutions send their rarities there to ensure their survival. Until recently it has been maintained virtually single-handed by the owner and had become somewhat overgrown, being described by him as a 'magic jungle'. However, clearance on the ground and removal of damaged trees is being put in hand – all the more necessary due to the twin afflictions of *Phytophthera ramorum*, which has devastated historic rhododendrons and large swathes of viburnums, and of damaging storms in early 2007.

Open March to May by appt

Entrance: £6

 WC

COTEHELE ★
(Historic Garden Grade II*)

There are two separate parts to this 19-acre garden, which lies in especially beautiful countryside. The upper gardens around the romantic, largely sixteenth-century house are largely formal, with courts, herbaceous borders, walls, yew hedges, fine lawns, a pool and a formally planted terrace falling away from the east front of the house. There is also a daffodil and wildflower meadow, a grove of acers and an orchard. The woodland valley garden, with a medieval dovecot and stewpond at its heart, lies in the view below the formal terrace. Here large conifers and hardwoods have been given a striking and thickly planted understorey of ornamental trees, rhododendrons, azaleas and other shrubs, and beneath all spreads a carpet of spring bulbs. The valley tumbles down towards the River Tamar, and from a hilltop behind the house the Prospect Tower offers fine views. Spring and early summer are the times to visit.

The National Trust

St Dominick, Saltash PL12 6TA.
Tel: (01579) 351346;
www.nationaltrust.org.uk

12m NE of Liskeard, 8m SW of Tavistock. Turn S off A390 at St Anne's Chapel

House open daily, 10.30am – dusk

Garden open all year

Mill open Jan to June, Sept to Dec, daily except Fri (but open Good Fri); July and Aug, daily; all 1pm – 5pm

Entrance: garden and mill £4.40 (house, garden and mill £8) (2007 prices)

Other information: Holiday cottages available

CREED HOUSE

The five-acre garden, which has been devotedly restored and developed by its present owners, plantaholics both, surrounds a fine Georgian rectory and has views of the countryside through mature trees. The beautiful trees and shrubs include camellias, magnolias and rhododendrons. A most enjoyable concealed walk leads through the shrubs surrounding the lawn. Below the lawn the pond is a focus, while herbaceous borders in the walled garden behind the house and elsewhere give particular summer interest. For maximum enjoyment, use the garden guide to be found beside the front door and view the historical photographic montage in the stable-block garage.

Mr and Mrs W.R. Croggon

Creed, Grampound TR2 4SL.
Tel: (01872) 530372

Mid-way between St Austell and Truro. Take A390 to Grampound, then road in main street signed to Creed. After 1m, opposite Creed church, turn left; entrance to house and garden is on left

Open all year, daily, 10am – 5.30pm.

Open for NGS.

Entrance: £3.50, children free

 B&B

The National Trust

Mawnan Smith, Falmouth TR11 5JZ.
Tel: (01326) 250906;
www.nationaltrust.org.uk

4m SW of Falmouth, 0.5m SW
of Mawnan Smith on road to
Helford Passage

Open 9th Feb to 1st Nov, Tues – Sat
and Bank Holiday Mons,
10.30am – 5.30pm (last admission
4.30pm). Closed 21st March

Entrance: £6, children £3

GLENDURGAN GARDEN ★
(Historic Garden Grade II)

Set, like nearby Trebah (see entry), in a ravine with a fine view of the Helford River and the surrounding countryside, Glendurgan is predominantly a springtime garden and in part a sub-tropical one. Established by the Fox family in the 1820s, it contains many fine mature trees and shrubs, including rhododendrons, and camellias in variety, a vast 150-year-old liriodendron and a large michelia. An attractive pond graces the lower valley, together with tree ferns, gunneras, hydrangeas and bamboos. There is also a camellia avenue, a 1833 maze of cherry laurel, and a Giant Stride for children. The upkeep of the 25 acres is immaculate.

The Lost Gardens of Heligan

Pentewan, St Austell PL26 6EN.
Tel: (01726) 845100; www.heligan.com

5.5m S of St Austell off A390.
Take B3273 signed to Mevagissey past
Pentewan

Open all year, daily except
24th and 25th Dec, 10am – 6pm
(closes 5pm in winter) (last admission
4.30pm in summer, 3.30pm in winter).

Guided tours by arrangement

HELIGAN ★★
(Historic Garden Grade II)

Started in the late eighteenth century but neglected since 1914, the renaissance of this 200-acre garden is, rightly, a well-known story. The restored productive gardens to the north of the house, a superb demonstration of horticultural archaeology (the pineapple pits are particularly fascinating), are surrounded by Victorian pleasure grounds laid out as a series of secluded enclosures with fountains and a sundial. Massive, mainly 'Cornish Red' rhododendrons enclose the large lawn; some were collected by Sir Joseph Hooker. The Jungle, some fifteen minutes' walk away, is a wild, beautiful

Heligan

valley where rhododendrons, bamboos, tree ferns and Chusan palms flourish. Further on, magical woodland walks can be taken in the Lost Valley. The Steward's House has a well-planted young garden with magnolias, and beyond that a pioneering wildlife conservation project is being developed. Like the Eden Project, Heligan is a busy tourist target; plan your visit carefully, especially at holiday times.

Entrance: £8.50, OAPs £7.50, children (5–16) £5, family £23.50

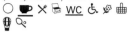

INCE CASTLE

Nine acres of formal and informal gardens are knit together here by strong design and the personalities of its two generations of creators. The formal areas and lawns, enhanced by statues and planted with summer flowers, are set round the castle, with dramatic views over the Lynher River and a background of mature trees. Daffodils and other bulbs create colour early in the year, while the woodland areas, with paths and an elliptical open space, contain camellias, rhododendrons, azaleas and other fine shrubs. The summerhouse is decorated internally with shells collected during the 1960s. The castle itself is romantic and stands at the end of a very long lane.

The Viscount and Viscountess Boyd of Merton

Saltash PL12 4QZ. Tel: (01752) 842672

3m SW of Saltash off A38 at Stoketon Cross. Turn at sign for Trematon and then for Elmgate

Open for NGS, and for parties by appt

Entrance: £3, children under 14 free

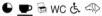

LAMORRAN HOUSE ★

This 4.5-acre garden on a south-facing slope above the sea enjoys a most favoured microclimate that supports wonderful collections of plants from the southern hemisphere, sub-tropical plants flourishing in the lower sections of the garden, temperate plants higher up. The latter include rhododendrons, evergreen azaleas and camellias. The garden has a fine collection of palms (over 30 varieties) and tree ferns, including varieties of cyathea. Paths in an intricate pattern zigzag down the steep hillside between enclosed compartments, some designed in Japanese or Italian style, and all with fine views over the sea to St Anthony's Head. There are many imaginative neo-classical statues and columns, and streams and pools permeate the whole slope. The planting is so dense and comprehensive that the paths, though there is often little space between them, are well screened from each other and so appear to magnify the total area. The immaculate upkeep of the garden enhances the overall effect. Nearby, in the grounds of *St Mawes Castle*, is another sub-tropical garden, with good views.

Mr and Mrs R. Dudley-Cooke

Upper Castle Road, St Mawes TR2 5BZ. Tel: (01326) 270800; www.lamorrangardens.co.uk

Above St Mawes turn right at garage. Signposted at castle. Continue for 0.5m, and house is on left set behind line of pine trees

Open April to Sept, Wed and Fri, 10.30am – 5pm, and at other times by appt

Entrance: £5.50, children free (2007 price)

Other information: Coaches by prior appt only

LANHYDROCK ★
(Historic Garden Grade II*)

Although the collection of trees was started as early as 1634, the bones of this superb 30-acre garden, in a dramatic woodland and parkland setting, were put in place in 1857 by the first Baron Robartes. The architect of his choice was George Gilbert Scott, who had been brought in to restore

The National Trust

Bodmin PL30 5AD. Tel: (01208) 265950; www.nationaltrust.org.uk

2.5m SE of Bodmin off A38 and A30, or off B3268

House open 15th March to 2nd Nov, Tues – Sun and Bank Holiday Mons, 11am – 5.30pm (closes 5pm Oct)

Lanhydrock

Garden open all year, daily, 10am – 6pm (closes 5pm Oct)

Entrance: garden and grounds £5.60, children £2.80 (house, garden and grounds £9.90, children £4.95, family £24.75)

Other information: Parking 550 metres from garden but disabled may park next to garden

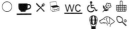

and extend the seventeenth-century house and to redesign the garden. The formal gardens remain largely as he conceived them. Behind the original seventeenth-century gatehouse is a formal lawn with 29 topiary yews in the shape of truncated cones and with rose beds in between, and, beside the house, a Victorian parterre flanked by six similar yews has spring and summer bedding plants. The herbaceous circle is planted for both spring and autumn. A shady stream fringed by water-loving plants runs off the hill behind the house. The Higher Garden, planted with large groups of 'Cornish Red' and other rhododendrons, many camellias, azaleas, magnolias and *Viburnum plicatum*, has a new border planted with perennials. The hillside woods have fine walks beneath mature trees underplanted with large-leaved rhododendrons and bluebells, although for some visitors the heavily gravelled paths introduce a somewhat artificial note. 900 acres in all.

Mrs Judith Stephens

St Andrew's Road, Par PL24 2LU. Tel: (01726) 815920 www.marshvillagardens.co.uk

5m E of St Austell. Leave A390 at St Blazey traffic lights, then take first left; garden is 700 metres on left

Open April to Sept, Sun – Wed, 10am – 6pm

Entrance: £4, children free

MARSH VILLA GARDENS

This magical garden has been created since 1986 from a poorly drained meadow. Although it is worth visiting at any time, the herbaceous plantings ensure that it is at its best in summer. A hornbeam avenue forms the main axis of the garden, with sinuous paths of gravel and grass leading off to areas of varying character and interest. The formal herbaceous garden is enclosed by an escallonia hedge; there are many mixed borders and underplanted woodland areas, and a large natural pond overlooked by a capacious summerhouse. New features include a long trellis planted with roses and clematis, and an everglade-like bog garden. Beyond the main garden of three acres lie 14 more of wild garden and marshland, where native irises, willows and alders thrive.

MOUNT EDGCUMBE HOUSE AND COUNTRY PARK ★

(Historic Garden Grade I)

The gardens and Grade-I landscaped park created by the Edgcumbe family in the eighteenth century were praised by William Kent and Humphry Repton. There are three main areas of interest. Surrounding the house is the Victorian Earl's Garden, with a fine formal east lawn containing flower beds, statues and urns, and with superb views down the wide hardwood avenue to the formal gardens below. In the landscaped woodland above and beside the house a National Collection of camellias (1000 cultivars), currently semi-mature, is developing attractively. The entrance to the formal gardens, best reached from below, has a fine view of the house. With a background of holm oaks and other mature trees, they include a formal Italian garden with orange trees, less formal English and French gardens, and two commemorating the Edgcumbe family's connection with America and New Zealand. In the centre of these is the 2002 Jubilee Garden. Rhododendrons and azaleas make late spring an attractive time to visit, and a rose garden gives summer interest. 865 acres in all.

Cornwall County Council and Plymouth City Council

Cremyll, Torpoint PL10 1HZ. Tel: (01752) 822236; www.mountedgcumbe.gov.uk

0.5m S of Torpoint via A374 and B3247. Signposted from Antony village and Trulefort Roundabout on A38. Access also by ferry from Plymouth

House open as Earl's Garden

Park and formal gardens open all year, daily, 8am – dusk. Earl's Garden open April to Sept, Sun – Thurs, 11am – 4.30pm

Entrance: park and formal gardens free. Earl's Garden and house £5, concessions £4, children £2.50. family £11.50

Other information: Coaches must pre-book

PENCARROW ★

(Historic Garden Grade II*)

The magnificent Palladian mansion lies at the end of an impressive one-mile drive, planted with flowering shrubs, conifers and hardwoods. The setting is superb, with formal gardens on two sides, a rock garden above, and wide and beautiful lawns in front of mature trees; these include an open beech grove. The trees are underplanted with shrubs, including azaleas and huge mounds of 'Cornish Red' and other rhododendrons. There is a fine view over the formal garden with its circular lawn from the main facade of the house. The park and woodland, which extends to 50 acres, contain many rhododendrons and camellias, and a woodland walk leads to a lake and ice-house. A memorial garden has been planted to fill the gap between the peak time in spring and later in the year.

The Molesworth-St Aubyn family

Washaway, Bodmin PL30 3AG. Tel: (01208) 841369; www.pencarrow.co.uk

4m NW of Bodmin. Signed from A389 and from B3266 at Washaway

House open 23rd March to 19th Oct, Sun – Thurs, 11am – 3:30pm

Garden open March to Oct, daily, 9am – 5.30pm

Entrance: £4, children £1 (house and garden £8, children £4)

Other information: Craft gallery/shop

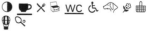

PENWARNE

This magical 12-acre spring garden, originally planted in the 1860s, has been much restored and combines conservation of mature trees and shrubs with new plantings. The approach to the eighteenth-century Palladian house is marked by plantations of azaleas, and from the sweeping front lawn fine

Mr and Mrs S. Sawyer

Mawnan Smith, Falmouth TR11 5PH. Tel: (01326) 250129

3m SW of Falmouth, 1m N of Mawnan Smith

Open two days in late March and late
April for charity, and for specialist
gardening parties of 15 or more by appt

Entrance: charge

NEW WC &

views look towards Falmouth Bay. Large mounds of 'Cornish
Red' and other rhododendrons cluster around the house and
below the lawn. In the area beside the lawn and in the
adjacent dell are old hardwoods, including a fine copper
beech, an enormous *Rhododendron luteum*, camellias and tree
ferns, together with younger rhododendrons, azaleas,
hydrangeas and magnolias. At the top of the dell a duck pond
is overlooked by a stone water tower reputed to have been
constructed from the stones of a former chapel. The
traditional walled garden houses an extensive collection of
roses and a newly restored vegetable garden. Beside and
above the main garden are younger plantings, which include
rhododendrons, azaleas and camellias.

Mr and Mrs R. Clemo

Holmbush, St Austell PL25 3RQ.
Tel: (01726) 73500;
www.pine-lodge.co.uk

Just E of St Austell off A390 between
Holmbush and turning for Tregrehan.
Signposted

Open all year, except 24th to 26th Dec,
daily, 10am – 6pm, and for NGS

Entrance: £6.50, children £3

PINE LODGE GARDEN AND NURSERY ★

Assembled in this immaculately maintained 30-acre garden is
a wide-ranging collection of over 6000 different plants, all of
them labelled. In the formal gardens, many less familiar shrubs
from around the world complement the magnolias, camellias,
rhododendrons and azaleas surrounding the perfect lawns,
adding to the year-round interest from spring bulbs to
herbaceous perennials and autumn stalwarts. There are
statues, too, and several ponds, including separate ones for koi
carp, newts and frogs. Beyond is a tightly planted arboretum
with tidily mown grass, flanked on one side by a four-acre
pinetum with its collection of 80 different conifers and on the
other by parkland leading down to the lake, where an island
is home to black swans and many waterfowl. A Japanese
garden has recently been added, a bell tower sited in a
wildflower meadow, and a three-acre winter garden is in the

Pine Lodge
Garden and
Nursery

making. A National Collection of grevilleas is held here, and plants for sale in the extensive nursery include some raised from seed collected on annual expeditions.

POPPY COTTAGE

This is a wonderful plantsman's garden covering a little less than one acre, separated into different but linked visual areas. Such is the design and ingenuity of form and layout that is appears vastly larger – an object lesson to any garden lover in the intensive use of space. The owners expanded their small plot by the purchase of a field three feet higher than the original garden, and linked the two with steps and a retaining wall. From the woodchip path at higher level visitors wander through many unusual shrubs, all underplanted with ground cover, to look down or across over the informal sequence of gardens, each one hidden from the next. Drifts of spring bulbs are woven through the beds, and rare, beautiful and unusual trees, shrubs and herbaceous plants flower in succession to ensure colour and interest right through to autumn. There are garden seats in many positions with a variety of viewpoints from which to appreciate both the planting and the design.

Tina Pritchard and David Primmer

Ruan High Lanes, Truro TR2 5JR
Tel: (01872) 501411

On Roseland Peninsula, 1m NW of Veryan, 4m SW of Tregony, on A3078 St Mawes Road

Open March to Sept, Tues – Thurs and Sun, 2 – 5.30pm

Entrance: £2.50, children free

NEW ◑

ST MICHAEL'S MOUNT ★
(Historic Garden Grade II)

It is the private eighteenth-century walled garden belonging to the St Aubyn family that is important here. Rising in terraces from just above sea level at the south-eastern corner of the castle to the foot of its southern wall, such is the microclimate that, despite constant exposure to salt spray and gales, many tender and exotic sub-tropical plants thrive within the shelter belt of Monterey pines and evergreen oaks. Escallonia hedges also provide some shelter, and much of the planting is amongst granite boulders. The private garden, laid out on several terraces near the top, is approached along an informal avenue of kniphofia across rough grass. Both here and above are groups of striking plants: *Agave americanum*, aeoniums, succulents, *Euphorbia mellifera* and yuccas. Visitors who make the rough, steep climb up to the castle walls will be rewarded with an outstanding view.

The National Trust

Marazion, Penzance TR17 0EF.
Tel: (01736) 710507;
www.nationaltrust.org.uk

0.5m from shore at Marazion, 0.5m S of A394. Access by motor boat (summer only) or pedestrian across causeway

Castle open 16th March to 2nd Nov, daily except Sat; winter for guided tours (telephone for availability)

Garden open 16th March to June, Mon – Fri; July to 2nd Nov, Thurs and Fri; all 10.30am – 5pm (last admission 4.15pm – allow sufficient time for travel from mainland)

Entrance: £3, children £1 (castle £6.60, children £3.30, family £16.50)

TREBAH ★★
(Historic Garden Grade II)

The most remarkable feature of Trebah – apart from its fascinating history of fame and fortune, decline and fall, and rejuvenation – is the spectacular view over the massive clumps of rhododendrons, tree ferns and bamboos and into the ravine, which runs between towering trees, including the tallest Chusan palms in the country, down to the Helford River. The garden is about 25 acres in all and contains many beautiful mature trees and shrubs. April is the winning month

Trebah Garden Trust

Mawnan Smith, Falmouth TR11 5JZ.
Tel: (01326) 252200;
www.trebah-garden.co.uk

4m SW of Falmouth. Signed from A39/A394 junction at Treliever Cross roundabout, 500 metres W of Glendurgan Garden

Open all year, daily, 10.30am – 5pm (or dusk if earlier)

Trebah

Entrance: £7, OAPs £6, disabled £3.25, children (5–15) £2, RHS and NT members free Nov to Feb

Other information: Powered wheelchairs available; paths steep in places

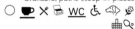

by a short head, but there is colour and interest at every season. An extensive collection of sub-tropical Mediterranean plants, a stream and some carp ponds occupy the upper reaches, while in the lower parts is a lake, a vast plantation of gunnera, and acres of blue and white hydrangeas giving summer colour. Superbly maintained throughout, but in no way over-manicured.

The Carlyon Estate/Mr T. Hudson Par PL24 2SJ. Tel: (01726) 814389

2m E of St Austell, on A390 Lostwithiel – St Austell road. Entrance opposite Britannia Inn 1m W of St Blazey

Open 15th March to May, Wed – Sun and Bank Holiday Mons, 10.30am – 5pm; 4th June to 27th Aug, Wed, 2 – 5pm

Entrance: £4.50, children free. Guided tours for groups by prior arrangement;

Other information: holiday cottages available

TREGREHAN ★
(Historic Garden Grade II*)

A wonderful spring garden, much restored since 1989 by the new owner. Its 20 acres are mainly planted woodlands, but there is a nineteenth-century walled garden which contains a magnificent, newly restored Victorian glasshouse range, an arch of *Acer palmatum* and interesting spring- and summer-flowering climbers. A formal yew walk, dark in itself, effectively frames the upper gardens. The woodland dell is furnished with huge and interesting conifers and native hardwoods. The near, steep side features very fine rhododendrons and camellias, whilst in the newly cleared areas beside the stream at the bottom and on the opposite bank – beautifully light on a sunny day – are young and rare shrubs and trees from the southern hemisphere. A bluebell walk is magical in spring. The views into the dell are magnificent, ranking with the best in any Cornish garden. Open for the first time, with the aid of an English Heritage grant, is the eighteenth-century wooded driveway and restored pond and waterfall, planted up with many species from South-East Asia [Open to parties by appt; the £10 charge includes entrance to the main garden.]

TRELISSICK ★
(Historic Garden Grade II*)

Trelissick ranks among the most beautiful of Cornish spring gardens, and also has many summer-flowering shrubs. It covers 40 acres, set in the middle of 400 acres of park and farm land, and offers panoramic views down Carrick Roads to the open sea. It is young compared to many similar gardens, with plantings and layout dating only from 1937. It has fine open lawns, particularly in the area known as the Carcaddon, and is known both for its collection of hydrangeas, camellias, magnolias and rhododendrons in the spring, and for its large collection of other tender and exotic plants. One area is devoted to aromatic plants, another houses a collection of fruit trees. An orchard of Cornish apples was planted in 2003. The woodland walks, surrounded by shrubs, have attractive views across the River Fal in the distance below.

The National Trust

Feock, Truro TR3 6QL.
Tel: (01872) 862090;
www.nationaltrust.org.uk

4m S of Truro on B3289 above west end of King Harry Ferry (boat services from Falmouth, Truro and St Mawes, April to Sept)

Open 11th Feb to Oct, daily, 10.30am – 5.30pm; telephone for winter opening times

Entrance: £6.60, children £3.30, family £16.50. Parking charge £3.50 (refundable)

Other information: Wheelchairs and batricar available

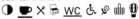

TRENGWAINTON GARDEN ★
(Historic Garden Grade II*)

The 27 acres enjoy a particularly benign climate, and the drive, broad and sweeping uphill, is unsurpassed for its grandeur and planting. Near the entrance an old walled garden is divided into five primary bays containing huge and impressive magnolias as well as tender and exotic shrubs and plants of the greatest interest. Beyond this, on the right, a shrub garden with many camellias under mature hardwoods leads to open lawns studded with ornamental trees and divided by shrub beds. On the left of the drive, beyond a narrow lawn, is a small stream fringed colourfully with astilbes, primulas, arisaemas, lilies and lysichitons. At the top of the garden magnificent rhododendrons and azaleas surround the ponds and lawn, and breathtaking views stretch across Mounts Bay and the Lizard.

The National Trust

Madron, Penzance TR20 8RZ.
Tel: (01736) 363148;
www.nationaltrust.org.uk

2m NW of Penzance on B3312, 0.5m N of A3071

Open 10th Feb to 2nd Nov, Sun – Thurs (but open Good Friday), 10.30am – 5pm

Entrance: £5.50, children £2.70, family £13.70

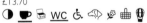

TRESCO ABBEY ★★
(Historic Garden Grade I)

Tresco, located in the Scilly Isles 28 miles off Land's End and in the full Gulf Stream, is a unique sub-tropical garden of the very highest quality. Within a formal framework of paths, steps, the ruined walls of the old abbey and high hedges is a lush profusion of flourishing exotic plants that soften the outlines and provide striking colour and contrasting shapes and textures. Set on a south-sloping hillside with horizontal walks, the gardens are visually quite self-contained. From the top terrace views slant downwards to the sea, revealing the wonderful plantings below, especially those in the more open areas such as the pond, where four Mediterranean cypresses form strong verticals. Myrtles and notably various metrosideros, are set amongst the background trees. Aeoniums, cacti, puyas, proteas and huge agaves (some with

Mr R.A. Dorrien-Smith

Tresco, Isles of Scilly TR24 0PU.
Tel: (01720) 424105 (Garden Curator: Mike Nelhams); www.tresco.co.uk

On island of Tresco. Travel by helicopter from Penzance heliport to Tresco heliport (reservations (01736) 363871 and (01720) 422970) or from St Mary's by launch

Open all year, daily, 10am – 4pm

Entrance: £9, children free, weekly tickets (7 days) £15

Tresco Abbey

Other information: Possible for wheelchairs but some paths very steep. Wheelchairs available at gate.

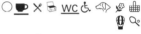

leaves 46 cms wide) stand out, and callistemons, banksias, agapanthus, and *Geranium maderenese* play a major part. Just five gardeners plus some student help maintain the 25 acres. The gardens are probably at their peak from March to the autumn, and at their most colourful from late April to the end of June.

Mr M. Sagin and Mr N. Helsby

Trevarno Manor, Helston TR13 0RU.
Tel: (01326) 574274; www.trevano.co.uk

3m NW of Helston off A394 or B3302

Open all year, daily except 25th and 26th Dec, 10.30am – 5pm

Entrance: £6.40, OAPs £5.50, concessions £3, children (5 – 14) £2.10 (2007 prices)

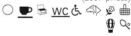

TREVARNO ESTATE AND GARDENS ★

Great and continuing restoration has taken place on the estate and in the 3.5-acre gardens, which combine formal and less formal elements. The lawn, with a splendid avenue of Japanese cherries to one side, leads to the formal Italian garden; from here a woodland walk descends to the lake, which sports a Victorian boathouse and a cascade at its top end and a fine rhododendron rockery beyond. Above this is the pinetum underplanted with shrubs, and the Georgian walled gardens and glasshouses. With rhododendrons, Japanese cherries, camellias and bluebells in the woodlands, it is probably at its best in the spring. The National Museum of Gardening is located near the entrance, and there are interesting craft workshops nearby.

Bolitho Estates

Buryas Bridge, Penzance TR20 8TT.
Tel: (01736) 363021
www.trewiddengarden.co.uk

2m W of Penzance on A30

Open 13th Feb to 5th Oct, Wed – Sun and Bank Holiday Mons, 10.30am – 4.30pm

Entrance: £4.50, under 16 free

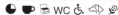

TREWIDDEN ★

Until 2002 this wonderful sub-tropical spring garden, created by the Bolitho family in the nineteenth century, was only rarely open to the public; now, following recent restoration after storm damage and pruning of over-mature camellias, it is essential visiting for serious gardeners. It covers 12 acres, including the separate South Garden, and consists mostly of informal woodland paths, some leading to an attractive pond with a Japanese lantern and a whale-tail sculpture. Although chiefly renowned for its camellias, of which there are over 300 varieties from India, China and other parts of the Far East, equally fine are the early-flowering magnolias, which shine forth above the other shrubs throughout. These include huge specimens of *M.* x *veitchii* 'Peter Veitch' and *M. hypoleuca*, as well as outstanding examples of *M.* 'Trewidden Belle', *M. sargentiana* and varieties of *M. campbellii*. There is also a magnificent stand of tree ferns set in the remains of an early open-cast tin mine. The south-facing walled garden is under restoration, with an emphasis on summer-flowering plants and artefacts from the tin industry.

TREWITHEN ★★
(Historic Garden Grade II*)

Trewithen is one of the greatest of all Cornish gardens. It covers 30 acres, mainly of woodland, and is known internationally for its collections, often formed from the wild, of magnolias, camellias and rhododendrons, as well as of many other rare trees and shrubs. Mid-March to mid-June are fine times to visit. The most striking feature is the long lawn in front of the 1730s house, flanked by sinuous borders of mature rhododendrons, magnolias, acers and other shrubs and ornamental trees, and backed by mature hardwoods. The enormous size of many of the rhododendrons and magnolias is particularly exciting. To the west the shrub beds and paths are sheltered by beech and other woodland trees. To the south-west is the main camellia collection, with specimens noticeable for their huge flowers, and many other wonderful shrubs. Three viewing platforms have been erected to give a new perspective of the camellias from canopy level. A deep sunken garden contains tree ferns as well as acers and camellias, and a *camera obscura* has been sited in one of the glades. Herbaceous plantings have been developed in the Deer Park Garden. The eighteenth-century walled garden (not always open) is laid out as a herb and rose garden with herbaceous borders; it has a fish pond, an old summerhouse and a wisteria-clad pergola. Many hybrid rhododendrons and camellias originated at Trewithen, some of them named by George Johnstone, the garden's creator, after members of his family. The inspiration for Tom Leaper's magnolia fountain derived from the great specimens to be found here. A well-stocked nursery adjoins.

Mr and Mrs A.M.J. Galsworthy

Grampound Road, Truro TR2 4DD.
Tel: (01726) 883647;
www.trewithengardens.co.uk

On A390 between Truro and St Austell
House open April to July, Mon and Tues,
2 – 4pm

Gardens open March to Sept,
Mon – Sat, 10am – 4.30pm (also Suns in
March to May)

Entrance: £5, parties of 20 or more
£4.50 per person (house and garden
£10)

OTHER RECOMMENDED GARDENS

BURNCOOSE GARDENS

Gwennap, Redruth TR16 6BJ (01209 860316;
www.burncoose.co.uk). Open all year, daily except
25th Dec, 8.30am – 5pm (opens 11am Suns)

The 30-acre woodland garden, threaded by a network of paths, sparkles with colour from a fine collection of camellias, magnolias, rhododendrons, acers and other spring-flowering shrubs and ornamental trees. Many are also on offer in the extensive nursery.

EDEN PROJECT

Bodelva, St Austell PL24 2SG (01726 811911;
www.edenproject.com). Open all year daily except 24th
and 25th Dec, 10am – 6pm (closes 4.30pm Nov to March)

Not so much a garden, more a spectacular educational theme park of botany and ecology. The two huge transparent geodesic domes covering 8 acres on their own and landscaped into a disused china clay pit are famous the world over. 34 acres in all.

FOX ROSEHILL GARDENS

Melville Road, Falmouth TR11 4DB (01872 224400).
Open all year, daily, 8am – dusk

A remarkable 2-acre park famous for its many exotic trees and shrubs, all set among paths and lawns. A delight for all visitors and of special interest to plant lovers.

HEADLAND

Jean Hill, Battery Lane, Polruan-by-Fowey PL23 1PW (01726 870243; www.headlandgarden.co.uk).
Open May to 28th Aug, Thurs, 2 – 6pm

Set on a steep cliff face with fine sea views, this 1.5-acre garden has tremendous character and a colourful collection of temperate, alpine, antipodean and sub-tropical plants has been amassed in the teeth of salt spray and gales.

KEN CARO

Mr and Mrs K.R. Willcock, Bicton, St. Ives, Liskeard PL14 5RF (01579 362446). Open 25th Feb to Sept, daily, 10am – 6pm

Two separate gardens here: a series of small enclosed spaces filled with shrubs, conifers, rhododendrons and herbaceous plants, and a more open area of beds, borders and ponds with pleasant views to the surrounding landscape. There is also a meadow and a woodland walk. 12 acres in all.

LADOCK HOUSE

Holborow Family, Ladock, Nr Truro TR2 4PL (01726 882274). Open for NGS, and for parties by appt

The Georgian rectory is set in 8 acres of spacious lawns, camellias, rhododendrons and azaleas in individual gardens fringed by woodland, all reclaimed and planted since the 1970s – a serene and charming ensemble.

MORRAB SUBTROPICAL GARDEN

Penzance (01736 336621; www.penwith.gov.uk).
Open all year, daily, dawn – dusk

A stylish sub-tropical garden of 2.5 acres, beautifully maintained, in the centre of town; and boasting two ponds, a fountain and a fine bandstand as well. (Listed Grade II)

THE OLD MILL HERBARY

Brenda and Robert Whurr, Helland Bridge, Bodmin PL30 4QR (01208 841206; www.oldmillherbary.co.uk).
Open April to Sept, daily except Wed, 10am – 5pm

The tranquil 5-acre garden on the banks of the River Camel has intriguing original features, including a trio of sizeable islands supporting mature woodland trees, a semi-wild garden designed in a pattern of horizontal paths and borders, and some unusual statuary. Something of interest and colour at every season, and an abundance of wildlife.

PENJERRICK

Mrs M. Morin, Budock, Falmouth TR11 5ED (01872 870105; www.penjerrick.co.uk). Open March to Sept, Wed, Fri and Sun, 1.30 – 4.30pm

This wonderfully wild and romantic 10-acre garden, overgrown in parts, is famous as the home of the rhododendron hybrids 'Penjerrick' and 'Barclayi'. Other species are outstanding too, matched by fine large camellias and trees magnolias. (Listed Grade II)

TREWOOFE HOUSE

Mr and Mrs H.M. Pigott, Lamorna, Penzance TR19 6PA (01736 810269). Open May to July, Wed and Sun, 2 – 5pm, and for parties by appt

The 2-acre garden at the head of the Lamorna valley is on two levels, linked by bridges over the ancient mill leat. A bog garden with a wide range of moisture-lovers thriving in this environment is at its peak in May and June, and everywhere the colourful shrub and herbaceous plantings are informal and relaxed.

Trewoofe House

CUMBRIA

For further information about how to use the *Guide*
and for an explanation of the symbols, see pages vi–viii.
Specific dates and times are those given to us by garden owners for 2008.
For 2009 dates, check with the individual properties.
For opening dates under the National Gardens Scheme,
readers should consult *The Yellow Book* or www.ngs.org.uk.
Maps are to be found at the end of the *Guide*.

BRANTWOOD

A superb site with wonderful views, atmosphere and history. The rocky hillside behind the house is threaded with a wandering network of paths created by John Ruskin to delight the eye and please the mind. A succession of eight small, individual gardens threads the landscape, exploring themes that fascinated the artist and visionary social reformer. This 'living laboratory' of ideas is being revived by Sally Beamish and her small team, and Ruskin's own Professor's Garden, the woodland pond and harbour walk are maturing well. An extensive collection of British native ferns surrounds an icehouse and several waterfalls. There is a British herb garden, and the allegorical Zig-zaggy depicting the levels of Purgatory found in Dante's *Divine Comedy* is now complete. The High Walk, actually a Victorian viewing platform, encourages contemplation of the magnificent Lakeland scenery beyond the garden. The high points of the year here are spring and autumn. In all, 250 acres.

Brantwood Trust

Coniston LA21 8AD.
Tel: (01539) 441396;
www.brantwood.org.uk

On E side of Coniston Water off B5285, signposted. Regular boat services

House open as garden

Garden open 17th March to 16th Nov, daily, 11am – 6pm; winter season Wed – Sun, 11am – 4.30pm (closed 25th and 26th Dec)

Entrance: £4 (house and garden £5.95, students £4.50, children under 16 £1.20)

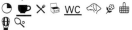

DALEMAIN HISTORIC HOUSE AND GARDENS ★

(Historic Garden Grade II*)

Dalemain has evolved in the most natural way from a twelfth-century pele tower with its kitchen garden and herbs. The Tudor-walled knot garden remains, as do the Stuart terrace (1680s) and the walled orchard where apple trees like 'Nonsuch' and 'Keswick Codling', planted in 1728, still bear fruit. The gardens were re-established by the late Mrs Sylvia McCosh during the 1960s and '70s with shrubs, a collection of over 100 old-fashioned roses, and other rarities, together with richly planted herbaceous borders along the terraces and around the orchard; maintained and developed by her daughter-in-law, they continue to improve. The wild garden on the lower ground features an outstanding display of Himalayan blue poppies in early summer and a walk past the Tudor gazebo into thoughtfully planted woodland overlooking the Dacre Beck. A plantsman's garden with an artist's appreciation of form, texture and colour.

Mr and Mrs R.B. Hasell-McCosh

Dalemain Estate Office, Penrith CA11 0HB. Tel: (01768) 486450; www.dalemain.com

On A592 3m W of Penrith on Ullswater road

House open as garden, but 23rd March to 23rd Oct only, 11.15am – 4pm

Garden open 5th Feb to mid-Dec, Sun – Thurs, 10.30am – 5pm (11am – 4pm in winter)

Entrance: £3.50, children free (house and garden £6.50, children free)

Other information: Wheelchair and electric scooter available by prior arrangement.

Dogs outside garden only, on lead

High
Cleabarrow

Mr and Mrs R.T. Brown

Windermere LA23 3ND.
Tel: (01539) 442808;
www.highcleabarrow.com

3m SE of Windermere off B5284
(opposite Windermere Golf Course)

Open for parties of 8 or more by appt,
April to Oct

Entrance: £3.50, children under 12 free

Other information: Teas by prior
arrangement

HIGH CLEABARROW ★

A two-acre plantswoman's garden of restful charm and year-long interest, created by the owners since 1990. Set over 200 metres above sea level in a shallow bowl sloping gently to a pond with waterside planting, a wealth of shrubs and hardy perennials, many of them unusual and rare, is to be found in island beds and in a wide border running the length of the garden. Large collections of hellebores, hardy geraniums, roses, clematis, hostas, hydrangeas, rhododendrons and azaleas give interest at all times. A knot garden filled with old-fashioned roses underplanted with violas, geraniums and campanulas is a fragrant summer secret concealed behind a beech hedge. At the rim the garden is sheltered by woodland, but also includes a large rocky outcrop 24 metres high. Bracken and brambles have been cleared, pathways struck, a glade of azaleas planted, terracing furnished with dwarf rhododendrons and more azaleas, a raised bed planted with alpines and a cobble bed created for succulents and grasses. For the owners the challenges go on and on, but visitors can relax in the summerhouse, from which fine views of the surrounding countryside open up.

Linda Orchant

Bridge Lane, Troutbeck LA23 1LA
Tel: (015394 88521

HIGH CROSS LODGE

Linda Orchant has created an exotic garden on a one-acre slope which would be remarkable in Cornwall, never mind Lakeland, although fortunately it is protected to the north by columns of conifers 30 metres tall. Tree ferns, some thirty in all, are a highlight, luxuriating in the generous rainfall. Yuccas, phormiums and bamboos mingle with architectural plants such as euphorbias, *Melianthus major*, alliums, eucomis and palms such as *Chamaerops humilis and Trachycarpus fortunei*, with *Cordyline australis* lending further evergreen structure. This is acid-soil country, so rhododendrons, azaleas and acers make an appearance too, and also waterfall country – a delightful stream fed by a nearby pond on the fells weaves its way under various bridges before disappearing into the beck below the garden. The sound of trickling water adds to the peaceful atmosphere, which can be enjoyed from the delightful summerhouse at the highest level.

2.5m N of Windemere off A591. From Windermere, turn right after Lakes School into Bridge Lane next to YHA

Open May to Aug for parties by appt

Entrance: £3

HOLEHIRD ★★

Managed by a charity dedicated to promoting and developing the science, practice and art of horticulture with special reference to the conditions in Lakeland, this garden is maintained to an exceptionally high standard by its members, who are all volunteers. It lies on a splendid hillside site alongside the house with a natural water course and rocky banks looking over Windermere to the Langdale Pikes. The Society has 10 acres of attractive gardens and trial areas. Much of the earlier planting has been preserved, including many fine specimen trees, together with acid-loving plants that do well in the free-draining soil. Highlights are the summer-autumn heathers, winter- and spring-flowering shrubs, alpines and

Lakeland Horticultural Society

Patterdale Road, Windermere LA23 1NP.
Tel: (01539) 446008;
www.holehirdgardens.org.uk

1m N of Windermere on A592 Patterdale road

Open all year, daily, sunrise – sunset. Wardens available to advise April to Oct, 11am – 5pm, and for parties by appt

Entrance: by donation (min. £3 appreciated)

Holehird

Other information: Annual plant sale
1st Sat in May in local school

National Collections of astilbes, hydrangeas and polystichum ferns. The walled garden, now accessible for wheelchairs, has fine herbaceous borders, herbs and climbers, and with the additional of dahlias and other late-flowering perennials has achieved a much longer season of interest. The site has expanded to encompass the lower Victorian terrace of the estate and includes original period features, such as the restored greenhouses. The views of the fells from the garden are breathtaking.

Lord and Lady Cavendish

Cark-in-Cartmel, Grange-over-Sands
LA11 7PL. Tel: (01539) 558328;
www.holker-hall.co.uk

4.5m W of Grange-over-Sands,
4m S of Haverthwaite on B5278

House open

Garden open 3rd Feb to 23rd Dec, daily
except Sat, 10.30am – 5pm

Entrance: wide variety of entrance
prices depending on visitor
requirements

Further information: Garden Festival
30th May and 1st June

HOLKER HALL ★★

(Historic Garden Grade II)

Essentially a spring garden, the 25 acres of woodland walks and formal gardens, set in 125 acres of parkland, loe close to Morecambe Bay – of which there are magical glimpses from the woodland – and enjoy a beguilingly mild west-coast climate. The have been cared for by the present innovative and knowledgeable owners since the late 1970s. Some mighty rhododendrons, so fashionable once, survive from the original planting, dominating the garden in spring and early summer; the magnolias are also stunning. The range of shade-loving shrubs has been extended with a National Collection of styracaceae, and massive eucryphias play a major role in the woodland from mid- to late summer. The woods now contain many rare and beautiful trees, most of them tagged and chronicled in the excellent guide to the garden walks. There is another side to Holker: varied formal gardens near the house have been created and developed to great effect over the years, although the herbaceous borders run slightly out of steam as the season progresses. The cascade, echoing the more famous one at Chatsworth, is evocative of the Villa d'Este. The garden is also home to the huge Holker lime – one of the 50 trees selected as part of Her Majesty's Jubilee celebrations. Paramount, however, is the welcoming and informal atmosphere here, developed over the years in a seemingly effortless style. The annual festival has become a leading celebration of gardening and the countryside in the north-west.

Lord and Lady Inglewood

Penrith CA11 9TH. Tel: (01768) 484449;
www.hutton-in-the-forest.co.uk

6m NW of Penrith on B5305
(M6 junction 41)

House open

Garden open 20th April to Oct, daily
except Sat, 11am – 5pm, and for private
parties by appt

Entrance: £3.50, children £1 (house and
garden £6, children £3, family £15)

HUTTON-IN-THE-FOREST

(Historic Garden Grade II)

This garden, a compelling setting for an intriguing house which ranges across the centuries from a thirteenth-century pele tower to Salvin's handsome alterations, is itself a mixture of features from the seventeenth to the twentieth centuries. It has great visual appeal, with a magnificent view from the seventeenth-century terraces embellished with Victorian topiary. The beautiful walled garden, dating from the 1730s, is divided into compartments and has excellent herbaceous borders, trained fruit trees and roses. The backdrop of the house, the surrounding yew hedges and compartments and well-filled herbaceous borders combine to make a dramatic composition. Some of the mature woodland trees were planted in the early eighteenth century. Other features include a seventeenth-century dovecot, an eighteenth-century lake and a cascade.

LEVENS HALL ★★
(Historic Garden Grade I)

No serious garden visitor can afford to miss the topiary gardens here. Designed by James II's gardener, Guillaume Beaumont, in 1694, it is a rare example of an intact formal garden. As well as being a time-capsule, the garden has benefited from having only 10 head gardeners in over 300 years creating a great feeling of tradition and continuity. But Levens can never be accused of sitting on its laurels. The current head gardener, Chris Crowder, has been a source of innovation and inspiration since the late 1980s. The garden repays repeat visits to see the explosion of tulips in spring and the sweeping carpets of yellow antirrhinums and *Verbena rigida* in summer. Astonishing all year are the enormous topiary specimens which, having established their individual characters over the years, lean and bend like weird, giant chesspieces, unmindful of the constant hum of traffic on the A6, just over the wall (the 1994 tercentenary fountain garden helps to offset this). Elsewhere paths lead through ancient and gnarled beech hedges, past beech roundels (at their best in spring when sheets of wild garlic flower at their feet) along herbaceous borders to imaginative vegetable gardens and a nuttery.

Other information: Electric scooter available for disabled. Refreshments when house open; meals on request

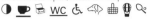

Mr C.H. Bagot

Kendal LA8 0PD. Tel: (01539) 560321; www.levenshall.co.uk

5m S of Kendal on A6 (M6 junction 36)

House open as garden, but 12 noon – 4pm

Garden open Easter period, then April to mid-Oct, Sun – Thurs, 10am – 5pm

Entrance: £6.50, children £3.50, family £18.50 (house and garden £9.50, children £4.50, family £24) (2007 prices)

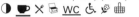

Levens Hall

The National Trust

Ambleside LA22 0HE.
Tel: (01539) 446027

0.5m S of Ambleside on A591

Open April to June, daily,
10am – 6.30pm, July to Oct by appt
(s.a.e. to NT Property Office,
St Catherine's, Patterdale Road,
Windermere LA23 1NH)

Entrance: £2.50, children free

STAGSHAW

Set on a west-facing hillside of oak trees with splendid views looking out over the head of Lake Windermere is a little gem of a garden, beautifully planted and maintained. Azaleas and rhododendrons have been carefully blended among camellias, magnolias and other fine shrubs with unusual underplanting, and another area is massed with pink erythroniums. Rather difficult of access, with the volume of traffic on A591 making the exit especially tricky, but worth the effort. In his book on the gardens of the National Trust, Stephen Lacey has described Stagshaw as 'sheer perfection in woodland gardening'.

David and Diane Kinsman

Crook Road, Windermere LA23 3JA.
Tel: (01539) 446238

1m S of Bowness-on-Windermere, on B5284. Turn up Linthwaite Hotel driveway

Open for NGS, 10am – 5pm,
and by appt

Entrance: £3

WINDY HALL

Four of the most cherished acres around Windermere are worked around a row of early-seventeenth-century terraced cottages converted into a single house, which hunkers down into the thin and stony hillside to avoid the teeth of the wind. The rear garden stretches up the steep slope, becoming woodland at the highest level. A deserted quarry area carpeted with moss has all the calm and simplicity of a Japanese garden, and other international influences crop up throughout the garden. Most of the plants have been chosen because they are all-rounders – offering evergreen foliage and scent in addition to flowers and colour. The owners' scientific backgrounds have led to the cultivation of National Collections of aruncus and filipendulas (not herded into trial ground beds, but integrated within the garden), and to the active encouragement of wildlife, with one pond dedicated as an 'insect factory'. A fruit and vegetable garden has been carved out within a sloping walled enclosure; a colony of ornamental wildfowl and a flock of Hebridean sheep add to the liveliness of the scene. There are twenty-five years of good gardening practice to be learned from a visit here – prepare to be inspired.

Jonathan Denby

Hampsfell Road, Grange-over-Sands LA11 6BE. Tel: (01539) 532469;
www.yewbarrowhouse.co.uk

15m SW of Kendal off A590. Take B5277 to Grange-over-Sands, continue up main street past railway station to mini roundabout and turn right. At crossroads turn right, then left up Hampsfell Road. Road narrows and goes into woodland; pass cottage on left, take left fork at footpath signed to Yewbarrow Wood, then left again up narrow unmade road to entrance gates

YEWBARROW HOUSE ★

This interesting 4.5-acre fellside garden with a breathtaking view over Morecambe Bay has been redesigned by the owner with help from Christopher Holliday. It is on the site of a Victorian garden which, except for the kitchen garden, had mostly reverted to woodland; the mild west-coast climate, shelter from the prevailing wind by boundary trees, well-drained soil and an almost frost-free microclimate enable exotica from all over the world to flower and survive. Individual gardens are divided by attractive limestone walls: Mediterranean and gravel gardens, ferns in woodland, a Japanese garden with a swimming pool disguised as a hot spring pool and a tea house, flower terraces and a rhododendron area. Included in the mix are olive trees bearing flowers and some ripe fruit, phormiums, palms, yuccas,

Yewbarrow House

Magnolia grandiflora, Paulownia tomentosa, cannas and much more. The owner's aim is to have something in flower throughout the year alongside evergreen plants providing colour and structure, although late summer and autumn are probably the best times to visit. This is surely a Lakeland garden with a difference.

Open for NGS, and by appt

Entrance: £3

 WC

OTHER RECOMMENDED GARDENS

ACORN BANK

Temple Sowerby, Penrith CA10 1SP (01768 361893; www.nationaltrust.org.uk). Open in March for snowdrops (telephone for details), then 15th March to 2nd Nov, Wed – Sun and Bank Holiday Mons, 10am – 5pm. NT

This is primarily a woodland garden, carpeted with a succession of snowdrops, daffodils, narcissi and Lenten lilies, but the walled gardens shelter spring blossoms and bulbs, colourful herbaceous borders, and the largest collection of culinary and medicinal plants in the North. 2.5 acres.

BROCKHOLE

Lake District Visitor Centre, Windermere LA23 1LJ (01539 446601). Open all year, daily, 10am – dusk

Skilfully exploiting a series of ornamental and floriferous terraces as a magnificent viewing platform focusing on Lake Windermere and the Langdale Pikes, this is Thomas Mawson at his most imaginative, aided by his architect colleague Dan Gibson. 30 acres in all, divided between formal gardens, grassland and woodland. (Listed Grade II)

COPT HOWE

Professor R.N. Hazeldine, Chapel Stile, Great Langdale, Ambleside LA22 9JR (01539 437685). Open for NGS; plus 7th, 11th, 26th and 28th April; 8th, 12th, 16th, 20th, 23rd and 27th May; 2nd, 4th, 9th, 13th, 16th and 20th June. Also open for private visits and parties by appt – telephone for recorded weekly information

This plantsman's fellside woodland 2-acre garden, with magnificent views of the Langdale Pikes, has an exceptionally wide range of rare acid-loving plants from many mountainous countries, including meconopsis, cardiocrinums, trilliums, hellebores, nomocharis, orchids, hepaticas, camellias, acers and alpines. Varied plantings and dramatic colours from spring through to autumn.

GRAYTHWAITE HALL

Ulverston, Graythwaite LA12 8BA (01539 531248; www.graythwaitehall.co.uk). Open April to Aug, daily, 10am – 6pm

A serene spring garden of 12 acres in a beautiful parkland and woodland setting. Thomas Mawson's billowy plantings and hallmark yew topiary clipped into globes and battlements are complemented by Dan Gibson's finely wrought gate and sundials. A fine example of this late Victorian partnership.

HALECAT

Mrs M. Stanley, Witherslack, Grange-over-Sands LA11 6RU (01539 552536 – Mrs K. Willard). Open all year, daily, 10am – 5pm (opens 12.30pm Sun)

A pleasing, personal garden of 2 acres created as a series of terraces and squares, surrounded by woodland and with fine distant views. Interesting mixed borders, a wildflower meadow, a damson orchard and a gazebo designed by the architect Francis Johnson.

MUNCASTER CASTLE

Mr and Mrs Gordon Duff-Pennington, Ravenglass CA18 1RQ (01229 717614; www.muncaster.co.uk). Open Feb to Dec, daily, 10.30am – 6pm (or dusk if earlier)

Described by Ruskin as the 'Gateway to Paradise', the spectacular views are the backdrop to rare and unusual plants in the Himalayan garden, the Georgian terrace and Church Wood, home to a collection of Japanese maples. The 77-acre landscaped gardens, first planted in the 1780s, are also home to hundreds of rhododendrons. (Listed Grade II*)

RYDAL MOUNT

Ambleside LA22 9LU (01539 433002; www.rydalmount.co.uk). Open March to Oct, daily, 9.30am – 5pm; Nov to Feb, daily except Tues, 10am – 4pm. Closed 25th and 26th Dec and Jan

The 4.5-acre garden is Wordsworth's memorial, and the 'sloping terrace', lawns and winding shady paths reflect his tenets that a garden should be informal, in harmony with its landscape and protective of its views. Masses of spring bulbs, good herbaceous borders, interesting summer-flowering shrubs and unusual trees. (Listed Grade II)

SIZERGH CASTLE

Kendal LA8 8AE (01539 560951; www.nationaltrust.org.uk). Open 17th March to 2nd Nov, 11am – 5pm. NT

The 14th-century tower of the castle vies with the remarkable 1926 rock garden terraced within a dell, and is surrounded by 16 acres of varied gardens, especially good in early summer and autumn. What stays in the memory, however, is the rolling parkland and Howgill hills looming in the distance. (Listed Grade II)

DERBYSHIRE

For further information about how to use the *Guide*
and for an explanation of the symbols, see pages vi–viii.
Specific dates and times are those given to us by garden owners for 2008.
For 2009 dates, check with the individual properties.
For opening dates under the National Gardens Scheme,
readers should consult *The Yellow Book* or www.ngs.org.uk.
Maps are to be found at the end of the *Guide*.

The National Trust

Ticknall DE73 7LE. Tel: (01332) 863822;
www.nationaltrust.org.uk

10m S of Derby, off A514 at Ticknall

House open as garden, but 12:30 – 5pm

Garden open 15th Mar to Oct,
Sat – Wed; 3rd July to Aug, daily; all
11am – 5pm. Park open all year, daily
except 25th Dec

Entrance: £5.30, children £2.70, family
£13.30. £3.80 vehicle charge for entry
to park

Other information: Dogs and picnics in
park only

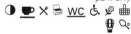

CALKE ABBEY ★
(Historic Garden Grade II*)

Previously owned by the Harpur Crewe family, Calke has a long history punctuated by neglect; the Trust has slowly and sensitively brought the garden back from the brink of decay. The vinery in the physic garden has been restored, as have the tomato house, frames, pits, backsheds and the only early nineteenth-century auricula theatre left in England; in summer pelargoniums replace the auriculas on its shelves. The gardeners are growing flowers, fruit and old varieties of vegetables in the two walled compartments formerly kept for flowers and herbs. The third compartment is the kitchen garden, which is overlooked by an orangery and a recently restored peach house and houses a head gardener's office of 1777. An orchard of old local apple varieties is of particular interest. 20 acres in all.

The Duke and Duchess of Devonshire
and the Chatsworth House Trust

Bakewell DE45 1PP. Tel: (01246) 582204;
www.chatsworth.org

4m E of Bakewell, 10m W of
Chesterfield on B6012, off A619 and A6

House open

Garden open mid-March to mid-Dec,
daily, 11am – 6pm

Entrance: £6.75, OAPs and students
£5.25, children £3.25, family £15
(2007 prices). Parking charge for cars
only £1.50

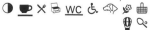

CHATSWORTH ★★
(Historic Garden Grade I)

One of Britain's greatest gardens. The 105 acres have developed over 400 years and still reflect the fashions of each century. The seventeenth-century gardens of London and Wise remain only as the cascade, the canal pond to the south and the copper 'willow tree' with water pouring from its branches. During the eighteenth century 'Capability' Brown destroyed much of the formal gardens to create a landscaped woodland park; notable is the vista he created from the Salisbury Lawn to the horizon, which remains unchanged, as does the lawn itself since no liming or fertilisers are used, allowing many varieties of wild flowers, grasses, moss and sedges to thrive. Paxton's work still gives pleasure, including some rare conifers and the magnificent 84-metre water jet from the Emperor Fountain. Although his Great Conservatory was a casualty of the 1914–18 war (metre-wide stone walls in the old conservatory garden are all that remain to give an idea of its size), damaged areas of Paxton's giant rockeries were rebuilt in 2003. From the twentieth century come the

Chatsworth

orange and blue-and-white borders, the terrace, the display greenhouse, the rose garden, the old conservatory garden with its lupin, dahlia and Michaelmas daisy beds, and a yew maze planted in 1963. In the arboretum and pinetum the suffocating rhododendrons, laurels and sycamores have been removed and many new trees planted. The double rows of pleached red-twigged limes and serpentine beech hedge, both planted in the 1950s, are now rewarding features. The epitome of a cottage garden has two striking neighbours: a flight of yew stairs leading to a 'bedroom' where the four-poster is of ivy and the dressing-table of privet, and a sensory garden. The kitchen garden has been resited and redesigned – it has been called 'indelibly British'. The first major piece of garden statuary to be placed in the garden for 150 years, 'War Horse' by Dame Elisabeth Frink, is sited at the south end of the canal, and her 'Walking Madonna' is a new and important presence. *The Garden at Chatsworth* by The Duchess of Devonshire, with photographs by Gary Rogers, was published by Frances Lincoln in 1999.

DAM FARM HOUSE ★

Mrs Jean Player

Yeldersley Lane, Ednaston, Ashbourne DE6 3BA. Tel: (01335) 360291

8m NW of Derby, 5m SE of Ashbourne on A52. Opposite Ednaston village turn, gate is 500 metres on right

Open Mon, Tues and Fri, and by appt. Groups and coach parties welcome

Entrance: £4, children free

This wonderful garden, created from a field, owes its existence to the inspiration of the owner, whose knowledgeable eye for good plants of all kinds – trees, perennials, shrubs and roses – is evident throughout. Climbers are used abundantly for clothing walls, pergolas, even spilling down over high retaining walls. It is the overall quality of the planting that gives the garden, including the vegetable garden, its special character. Garden rooms span outwards from the house, mostly enclosed by high beech and yew hedges; an evergreen tapestry hedge divides the arboretum from the main garden. The scree has a selection of choice alpines, and the stone troughs in the farmyard are also filled with plants. One of the best gardens in Derbyshire, maturing after decades of collecting and intermittent planting. Many rare trees, shrubs and plants are propagated for sale.

Other information: Tea, coffee and biscuits available by arrangement

DERBY ARBORETUM

(Historic Garden Grade II*)

The first specifically designed urban arboretum in Britain, this was commissioned in 1839 from John Claudius Loudon, whose original plans involved the planting of 1000 trees. A useful leaflet now lists 40 varieties, many from around the world, all individually numbered, and also describes other parks in Derby, including the well-known *Markeaton Park*. While in the city, try to visit the refurbished market place, where there is a splendid water sculpture by William Pye of free-falling water over a bronze cascade — it will give you the sensation of walking behind a waterfall.

Derby City Council

Arboretum Square, Derby DE23 8FN. Tel: (01332) 716518

Between Reginald Street and Arboretum Square

Open all year, daily, 8am – 8pm (closes 9pm June and Aug, 6pm Nov to March)

Entrance: free

DOVE COTTAGE

It is only to be expected that this richly stocked 0.5-acre cottage garden is above the average, for it has had the benefit of being developed and nurtured by an owner who is a qualified horticulturist. The visiting season starts in April with a spectacular daffodil display, and these are followed by the colourful flowers of several hardy plant collections, including alliums, campanulas, euphorbias, geraniums and a number of variegated plants; hardy perennials are being nurtured in a dry woodland area. A pleasant walk leads between a flower bed and the River Dove, where kingfishers may sometimes be spotted.

Mr and Mrs S. G. Liverman

Clifton, Ashbourne DE6 2JQ. Tel: (01335) 343545

1.5m SW of Ashbourne off A515. In Clifton turn right at crossroads then first left down lane (signed 'Mayfield Yarns')

Open by appt for parties, and certain Suns April to July for charity, 1 – 5pm

Entrance: £4 (£3 on charity open days), children free

ELVASTON CASTLE COUNTRY PARK ★

(Historic Garden Grade II*)

The 200-acre gardens were designed by William Barron in the early nineteenth century for the 4th Earl of Harrington and include Italian, parterre and Old English gardens, all enclosed within 11 miles of hedges. It is probable that these were the first garden rooms, which influenced others when, twenty years after their establishment, they were opened to the public. Discover the extensive topiary, tree-lined avenues and large ornamental lake, search out the golden gates, boat house and Moorish temple, and wonder at the distinctive cedars of Lebanon. Barron transplanted mature trees as high as 13 metres from as early as 1831, using his unique transplanting machines, one of which is housed at the Royal Botanic Gardens, Kew. For those who find a park out of scale with their own smaller gardens, a tiny 'romantic' garden nearby, *White Gate* at Arleston Meadows, is recommended, and Mrs Judy Beba-Thompson welcomes private visits and small parties by prior appointment (Tel: (01332) 763653).

Derbyshire County Council

Borrowash Road, Elvaston DE72 3EP. Tel: (01332) 571342; www.derbyshire.gov.uk

2m SE of Derby on B5010 between Borrowash (A6005) and Thulston (A6). Signed from A6 and A52

Open all year, daily, 9am – 5pm

Entrance: free, but parking charge
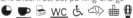

FANSHAWE GATE HALL

Mr and Mrs John Ramsden

Holmesfield S18 7WA.
Tel: (0114) 289 0391; www.fgh.org.uk

6m NW of Chesterfield, 6m SW of
Sheffield, 1m E of Holmesfield. Follow
B6054 and turn first right after Penny
Acres School

Open for NGS, and June and July for
parties of 10 or more by appt

Entrance: £2.50

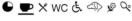

This is a fabulous location with stunning views over the countryside, and on open days makes a pleasant day out with plant stalls, teas and spacious lawns on which to sit and admire the mellowed stone of the 700-year-old hall, while listening to the soothing sound of the courtyard cascade. A knot garden is historically in keeping, and an attractive dovecot and roaming chickens add to the atmosphere. The two-acre garden is in the traditional English country house style, epitomised by the timeless picture of twin borders of nepeta and luxuriously scented yellow standard roses flanking the drive, which retains its original stone posts. In recent years the orchard has been renovated and a wildlife pool now teems with dragonflies, newts and frogs.

HADDON HALL
(Historic Garden Grade I)

Lord Edward Manners

Bakewell DE45 1LA.
Tel: (01629) 812855;
www.haddonhall.co.uk

2m SE of Bakewell, 6.5m N of
Matlock on A6

House open

Garden open: telephone or consult
website for dates and times

Entrance: hall and gardens £8.50,
OAPs £7.50, children £4.50, family £22
(2007 prices). Parking charge for
cars £1, coaches free

The castellated hall, medieval in origin and owned by the Manners family for 800 years, is the main attraction here. To reach it, visitors walk over a bridge crossing the beautiful River Wye and up a steep slope. One of the most interesting parts of the six-acre garden is the private area by the old stables, where giant topiary cut in the shape of a nesting peacock and a boar's head dominate the small cottage. The accessible part behind the hall is on two open terraces which make the most of the views from the highly buttressed garden walls across the valley to woods and fields. The design is simple: a fountain and small pool, many stone steps, lawns surrounded by rose beds, yews and a knot garden. A bed of delphiniums occupies the house wall and there are some unusual perennials in a narrow bed against a large limestone retaining wall. The best time to visit is for the flowering of the roses in June and July.

HARDWICK HALL ★
(Historic Garden Grade I)

The National Trust

Doe Lea, Chesterfield S44 5QJ
Tel: (01246) 850430;
www.nationaltrust.org.uk

9.5m SE of Chesterfield, 6.5m NW of
Mansfield. From M1 junction 29
take A6175

House open March to Oct, Wed, Thurs,
Sat, Sun, Bank Holiday Mons and Good
Friday, 12 noon – 4.30pm

Garden open March to Oct, Wed – Sun,
11am – 5.30pm. Country park open all
year, daily, 8am – 6pm

Entrance: £4.50, children £2.25, family
£11.25 (house and garden £9, children
£4.50, family £22.50) (2007 prices)

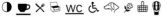

This famous Elizabethan mansion was built by Bess of Hardwick and designed by Robert Smythson in the late sixteenth century. Mature yew hedges and stone walls provide necessary protection in an otherwise exposed escarpment site. The borders of the south court have shrubs and herbaceous planting to give structure and extend the flowering period, while the west court's herbaceous borders are planted in strong, hot colours graduating to soft hues, with the peak flowering season in late summer and autumn. The herb garden is outstanding. In the south-east quarter is an orchard, with varieties of apples, pears, plums, gages and damsons, and the north-east orchard has been progressively replanted with old varieties such as crab apples, with the grass left long for naturalised daffodils and wild flowers. 17.5 acres.

Horsleygate
Hall

HORSLEYGATE HALL

When the present owners arrived in 1989, the two-acre garden was a wilderness. They set to with a will, and have completed much of the work themselves. There are few level areas; the garden works with the slope, with grass and bark paths winding around small lawns and shady corners. Interesting and eccentric artefacts, furniture and structures abound, often made out of recycled materials and all in keeping with the characterful part-Victorian, part-Georgian house. A wooden bridge and a small pool, pergolas, sculptures carved out of ash or Kilkenny limestone, lots of seats and tables, a gazebo and a couple of breeze houses, beckon around corners or punctuate the view. The garden itself, immaculately cared for, is as interesting for its plantsmanship as for its design. Unusual shrubs and trees are a particular passion, but there are perennials in variety too. The contents of the large walled kitchen garden proclaim a keen interest in good food, destined for the family and B&B and holiday cottage guests, while guinea fowl and a splendid Welsomer cockerel and his harem peck politely about the orchard.

Margaret and Robert Ford

Horsleygate Lane, Holmesfield
S18 7WD.
Tel: (0114) 289 0333

8m SW of Sheffield, 8m NW of Chesterfield off B6051. Take B6051 to Millthorpe; Horsleygate Lane 1 mile on right

Open for NGS, and by appt

Entrance: £3

🌑 ☕ WC ✂ ♿ ✂ B&B

KEDLESTON HALL ★
(Historic Garden Grade I)

The extensive gardens are not in competition with the neoclassical Robert Adam palace – the ancient home of the Curzon family – but are of mature parkland where the eye is always drawn to the house. The rhododendrons when in flower are worth seeing in their own right, otherwise visit

The National Trust

Kedleston, Derby DE22 5JH.
Tel: (01332) 842191;
www.nationaltrust.org.uk

4.5m NW of Derby on Derby – Hulland road between A6 and A52. Signposted

DERBYSHIRE

Kedleston Hall

Hall open as garden but Sat – Wed
12 noon – 4.30pm

Garden open 10th March to Oct, daily,
10am – 6pm. Park open all year, daily,
10am – 6pm (closes 4pm in winter).
Closed 25th and 26th Dec

Entrance: park and garden £3.80, children
£1.90, family £9.60 (hall, park and garden
£8.50, children £4.20, family £21.50)
(2007 prices)

Other information: Consult Property
Administrator for information about group
visits and disabled access

Lord Ralph Kerr

Melbourne DE73 8EN. Tel: (01332) 862502;
www.melbournehall.com

8m S of Derby between A514 and A453,
off B587 in Melbourne

House open Aug, daily except 4th, 11th
and 18th, 2 – 5pm (last admission 4.15pm)

Garden open April to Sept, Wed, Sat, Sun
and Bank Holiday Mons, 1.30 – 5.30pm, and
in Aug as house

Entrance: £3.50, OAPs and children £2.50
(house and gardens £5.50, OAPs £4.50,
children £3.50)

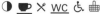

the gardens as a pleasurable way to view not only Adam's
magnificent south front but also the hexagonal-domed
summerhouse, the orangery, the Venetian-windowed fishing
house, the bridge across the lake, the aviary and
slaughterhouse (now a loggia) and the main gateway. The
formal gardens have a sunken rose garden. The Sulphur Bath
House, one of the earliest eighteenth-century landscape park
features, where a small spa used to operate, has been
restored but is not accessible to the public.

MELBOURNE HALL GARDENS ★
(Historic Garden Grade I)

There has been little alteration to Thomas Coke's formal plan,
so this is a visual record of a complete late seventeenth-/early
eighteenth-century design laid out by London and Wise in the
style of Le Nôtre. It is in immaculate condition with some
unusual magnolias flowering in early April. Avenues culminate
in exquisite statuary and fountains, including a lead urn of The
Four Seasons by van Nost, whose other lead statuary stands
in niches of yew. A series of terraces runs down to a lake, the
Great Basin, and a grotto has an inscription by George Lamb.
Unique in English gardens is the Birdcage iron arbour of 1706,
which can be seen from the house along a long walk hedged
with yews.

RENISHAW HALL ★
(Historic Garden Grade II*)

For nearly twenty years Renishaw had 'the most northerly vineyard in western Europe'. Also astonishing to see at this northerly latitude and on top of a hill are enormous specimens of rare and slightly tender shrubs. Sir George Sitwell spent much of his life in Italy and this is the style he re-created at Renishaw a century ago. Within a framework of vistas, walks and topiary, plants riot in ordered confusion in the sheltered gardens to the south of the house. Statues, terraces and the sound of splashing water enhance the Italianate atmosphere, and the present incumbents have added a stupendous water jet to increase the effect. They have also increased the number of different gardens (10 in all), divided and protected by yew hedges and columns, enlarged the borders, introduced innovative planting, and linked the garden to the wood with new planting and paths. At the end of the lime avenue on the top lawn stands Sir Hamo Thornycroft's statue of the Angel of Fame, regilded by Lady Sitwell. Beyond the brick wall is a greenhouse that contains the National Collection of yuccas, and below that winds a spinney that badgers now share with a statue walk. A nature trail leads to an avenue of camellias, on to a bluebell wood – an azure carpet in early May – and on still further to the classic temple, Gothick lodge, old sawmill, cave and lakes. Five acres in all.

Sir Reresby and Lady Sitwell

Renishaw, Sheffield S21 3WB.
Tel: (01246) 432310; www.sitwell.co.uk

6m SE of Sheffield, 5m NE of Chesterfield on A6135. From M1 at junction 30, take A616 towards Sheffield for 3m through Renishaw

Open 20th March to 28th Sept, Thurs – Sun and Bank Holidays, 10.30am – 4.30pm

Entrance: £5, concessions £4.20, children under 10 free

Other information: Museums and galleries open

OTHER RECOMMENDED GARDENS

FIR CROFT

Dr S.B. Furness, Froggatt Road, Calver, Hope Valley S32 3ZD (www.alpineplantcentre.co.uk). Open for NGS

One of the largest and most eclectic collections of alpines in Britain, created since 1985 by a botanist-cum-botanical photographer. 1 acre.

LEA GARDENS

Mr and Mrs Tye, Long Lane, Lea, Matlock DE4 5GH (01629 534380; www.leagarden.co.uk). Open 20th March to 30th June, daily, 10am – 5pm, and by appt

The 4.5 acres are notable for the comprehensive collection of rhododendrons, azaleas, alpines and conifers brought together after 1935 by John Marsden Smedley, and now increased and expanded within its beautiful woodland setting. The nursery sells unusual rhododendrons, azaleas and alpines.

PAVILION GARDENS

St John's Road, Buxton SK17 6XN (01298 23114; www.paviliongardens.co.uk). Open, all year, daily, from 10am

A Victorian landscaped park, woodland and ornamental lakes spanning 23 acres, laid out in 1871 by Edward Milner, Paxton's chief assistant at Crystal Palace, together with an octagon, a well-stocked conservatory and vibrant bedding schemes. Plant and garden design fairs are held in the octagon.

DEVON

For further information about how to use the *Guide*
and for an explanation of the symbols, see pages vi–viii.
Specific dates and times are those given to us by garden owners for 2008.
For 2009 dates, check with the individual properties.
For opening dates under the National Gardens Scheme,
readers should consult *The Yellow Book* or www.ngs.org.uk.
Maps are to be found at the end of the *Guide*.

Mr and Mrs John Tremlett

Kenn, Exeter EX6 7XL.
Tel: (01392) 832671

6m S of Exeter on A38 before junction
with A380. Leave dual carriageway at
Kennford Services and follow signs to
Kenn, then take first right and follow lane
for 0.75m to end of no-through road

Open for NGS, and at other times
by appt

Entrance: £3.50, children free

BICKHAM HOUSE ★

The eight acres of garden in a peaceful wooded valley
overlook a small lake. The house has been in the family since
it was built in 1682, but the garden has been extensively
remodelled over the last few years, and new features are still
being added. There are lawns and fine trees, spring-flowering
shrubs and many naturalised bulbs, and a box-hedged
parterre around a lily pond; banks around the main lawn are
left uncut to encourage butterflies. In the mixed borders great
attention is paid to colour co-ordination. The one-acre walled
garden (the oldest part) is divided into rose beds, a formal
herb garden and a highly productive flower and vegetable
section, all full of colour and interest throughout the year; an
avenue of palm trees leads to the millennium summerhouse.
There is a colourful small water garden and a spinney full of
cowslips and naturalised aquilegias. The Edwardian
conservatory opens onto an enclosed cobbled area with
raised beds and a wall fountain.

Bicton Park

East Budleigh, Budleigh Salterton
EX9 7BJ.
Tel: (01395) 568465;
www.bictongardens.co.uk

2m N of Budleigh Salterton on B3178

Open daily except 25th and 26th Dec,
10am – 6pm (closes 5pm in winter)

Entrance: £6.95, concessions and children
(3–15) £5.95, family £22.95

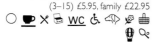

BICTON PARK BOTANICAL GARDENS ★

(Historic Garden Grade I)

There is much to see in these 64 acres. The formal and
informal gardens date from c.1735, largely landscaped in the
style of Le Nôtre. There is a stream garden with a 150-year
old mulberry, azaleas, camellias and flowering cherries,
herbaceous borders against magnolia-clad walls, an American
garden established in the 1830s, and a hermitage garden with
a lake and water garden. The pinetum, first planted in 1839
and extended in 1910 to take the collection of the famous
botanist and explorer 'Chinese' Wilson, has some rare
conifers, including the tallest Grecian fir ever recorded (41
metres). Perhaps Bicton's greatest glory is the palm house,
built between 1825 and 1830 and one of the oldest in the
country. There are also arid and temperate houses, and a
tropical house for orchids, bananas, bromeliads, figs and
bougainvilleas. The Countryside Museum, one of the largest in
the West Country, houses a collection of farm machinery,

gardening tools and craft exhibits, reflecting changes in rural life since the 1700s. There is a display of cacti and other succulents in a naturalistic desert-like landscape in the arid house, and one of Britain's earliest Victorian ferneries has been re-established among the rocks around the shell house. Next door, the gardens of *Bicton College* have considerable horticultural interest, with many unusual plants, fine herbaceous borders and an arboretum (open all year – telephone 01395 562427 for seasonal details).

BLACKPOOL GARDENS

Facing south and rising steeply, this engrossing secret garden overlooks the perfect crescent of Blackpool Sands. This chunk of Devon's Heritage Coast has been in the same family since the late eighteenth century, but the landscaping of the three-acre woodland garden was begun in 1896. Four wide parallel paths run the length of the garden, joined by further paths and steps to climb upwards in a gentle zig-zag. The hillside between is filled with a wide variety of sub-tropical, temperate and antipodean trees and shrubs, some of great age, others introduced more recently. An 1848 Monterey pine and an 1896 avenue of cork oaks with venerably pitted bark survive from the earliest period. The award of a European grant in 2000 enabled the present owner to start regenerating the landscaping and rejuvenating the plantings, and a water garden is planned, centred on an existing pond garden above the terraces. Enjoy the stunning view fading away to distant Start Point, then make your way back to the beach below to enjoy a swim, hire a kayak, and return to the real holiday world.

Sir Geoffrey Newman, Bt

Blackpool Sands, Blackpool, Dartmouth TQ6 0RG. Tel: (01803) 770606; www.blackpoolsands.co.uk

3m S of Dartmouth on A379. Parking by beachside cafe. Entrance through Blackpool Sands car park

Open Easter to Sept, daily (subject to weather), 10am – 4pm, and to private and school parties by appt

Entrance: £2.50 (tickets available at Blackpool Sands ticket office), children free

Other information: Refreshments and toilets available at Blackpool Sands

 ◑ ☕ ✕ 📷 <u>WC</u>

BURROW FARM GARDENS ★

The 10-acre gardens, created from pasture land, are the inspiration of Mary Benger and her family. Foliage effect has been admirably achieved with a colourful array of azaleas and

Mr and Mrs John Benger

Dalwood, Axminster EX13 7ET. Tel: (01404) 831285; www.burrowfarmgardens.co.uk

Burrow Farm

4m W of Axminster off A35 Honiton road. After 3.5m turn N near Shute garage onto Stockland road. Garden is 0.5m on right

Open April to Sept, daily, 10am – 7pm

Entrance: £4.50, children 50p, parties (discount rate) by appt

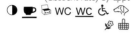

rhododendrons. A former Roman clay pit is graded from top to bottom through mature trees and shrubs to an extensive bog garden with a marvellous show of candelabra primulas and native wild flowers during the early part of the season. In summer the pergola walk, with its old-fashioned roses and herbaceous borders, is a picture, and a courtyard garden and a terraced garden feature late-flowering herbaceous plants. The rill garden has ponds, a classical summerhouse and a ha-ha laid out in a formal design, luxuriantly and informally planted. An azalea glade looks down past a thatched summerhouse towards the lake rich in wildlife and surrounded by a subtle blend of cultivated and wild flowers. The setting and sense of grandeur are more typical of gardens of greater repute, and the views are magnificent. The attached nursery specialises in moisture- and shade-loving plants and in those with ornamental foliage.

The National Trust

Drewsteignton EX6 6PB.
Tel: (01647) 433306;
www.nationaltrust.org.uk

5m S of A30 or 4m NW of Moretonhampstead on A382; follow signs from Sandy Park

Castle open as garden but 11am – 5pm

Garden open 15th March to 2nd Nov, Wed – Mon, 10.30am – 5pm (open daily at half-term and during school holidays)

Entrance: £5, children £2.75 (house and garden £7.80, children £3.90, family £19.50) (reduced rates in winter)

Other information: Disabled parking. Access for wheelchairs by arrangement

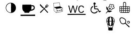

CASTLE DROGO ★★
(Historic Garden Grade II*)

The 12 acres at Drogo, the last castle to be built in England and at 800 feet the National Trust's highest garden, are a testament to the vision of George Dillistone, whose planting skills and stately shelter belts enabled him to create one of the South-West's most spectacular formal gardens. At the lower end the view from the rose garden (at this altitude, a considerable achievement in itself) provides the unusual sight of herbaceous borders raised to eye level on top of local-granite walls. Curved paths, influenced by the castle's architect Sir Edwin Lutyens, wind between extensively planted beds, while in each corner imposing arbours roofed with *Parrotia persica* are peaceful and secluded. Graceful stone steps and neat gravel paths lead through wisterias, unusually planted as a screen, and along borders of maples and spring-flowering shrubs up to the spectacular round lawn, large enough for four croquet courts and surrounded by an immaculate tall yew hedge. Beneath the castle, perched on the top of the precipitously steep Teign gorge, rhododendrons, azaleas, magnolias, cornus and native woodland tumble down from the massive stone ramparts, from where there are fine uninterrupted views of the distant moor.

The Earl and Countess of Arran

Filleigh, Barnstaple EX32 ORQ.
Tel: (01598) 760336 Ext.4;
www.castlehilldevon.co.uk

7m SE of Barnstaple, 19m NW of Tiverton off A361. Leave A361 at roundabout after South Molton, heading for Filleigh. Take second right, then after 2.5m turn right into drive at yellow lodge

CASTLE HILL ★
(Historic Garden Grade I)

The eighteenth-century landscape garden and park, leading away from the magnificent Palladian house, were created by the 1st Lord Fortescue in 1730 with temples, follies, ponds, and across the valley a triumphal arch. At the top of the hill above the house is a castle (complete with cannons) from which Dartmoor, Exmoor and Lundy Island are visible on a clear day. The woodland garden shelters magnolias, camellias,

Castle Hill

rhododendrons, azaleas, a two-acre daffodil wood, thousands of bulbs, and there are also some renowned trees in the Easter Close. As if this were not enough, the millennium garden designed by Xa Tollemache has herbaceous borders planted with lilies, agapanthus, phlox and penstemons edged with box and lavender in gentle curves lining gravel paths. There is an avenue of formal clipped *Quercus ilex* underplanted with *Viburnum tinus* and a spectacular water sculpture by Giles Rayner. The unique feature of this landscape is its beautiful valley with steep, rounded hills swooping down to a winding river and up to the castellated folly (complete with cannons) from which on a clear day Exmoor, Dartmoor and Lundy are visible. Visiting these 40 acres could well occupy the best part of a day – take a picnic.

Open Feb to Sept, daily except Sat, plus Suns all year, 11am – 5pm. Closed 25th Dec

Entrance: £4

Other Information: Refreshments on Suns and Bank Holiday Mons, May to Aug

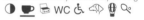

THE CIDER HOUSE

The three-acre garden is a congenial setting for the medieval house. Clipped box and berberis hedges define the formal terraced areas, giving way to relaxed areas of woodland and herbaceous planting. The hot border, vibrant in colour all year round, marks the boundary, with rolling Devon farmland beyond. The walls of the ancient cloisters form an impressive backdrop for climbing plants and the kitchen garden, once part of the monks' larger walled garden, is now restored and fully productive for vegetables and cut flowers. There is colour and interest in the garden from May to September, and the kitchen garden comes into its own from mid-June. The garden also blends harmoniously with its neighbour, the Cistercian

Michael and Sarah Stone

Buckland Abbey, Yelverton PL20 6EZ. Tel: (01822) 853285

8m N of Plymouth. From A386, follow signs to Buckland Abbey. At crossroads before Abbey, turn N signed to Buckland Monachorum. Drive is 180 metres on left

Open for NGS, and by appt

Entrance £3, children free

monastery *Buckland Abbey* (National Trust); its garden, also largely a twentieth-century creation, has a herb parterre and an Elizabethan garden, delightful estate walks and splendid views. [Open 25th March to 29th Oct, daily except Thurs, 10.30am – 5.30pm; off-season, weekends only, 12.30 – 5pm. Closed 21st Dec to 20th Feb.]

The National Trust

Brownstone Road, Kingswear, Dartmouth TQ6 0EQ. Tel: (01803) 752466; www.nationaltrust.org.uk

3m E of Dartmouth, 3m S of Brixham off B3205. 2.5m from Kingswear, take Lower Ferry Road and turn off at toll house

House and garden open 15th March to 20th July, 3rd Sept to 2nd Nov, Wed – Sun; 21st July to Aug, daily except Tues; all 10.30am – 5pm

Entrance: £6.10, children £3.10 (house and garden £6.60, children, £3.30, family £16.50)

Other information: Holiday cottages available

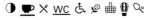

COLETON FISHACRE GARDEN ★
(Historic Garden Grade II*)

Oswald Milne, a pupil of Edwin Lutyens, designed the house and the architectural features of this 30-acre garden for Rupert and Lady D'Oyly Carte; the house was completed and the garden begun in 1926. The exceptionally mild setting is a Devon combe, sloping steeply to the cliff tops and the sea, and sheltered by belts of Monterey pines and holm oaks. The streams and ponds make a humid atmosphere for moisture-loving and sub-tropical plants. There is a collection of unusual trees like dawn redwood, swamp cypress and Chilean myrtle, and dominating all a tall tulip tree and a tree of heaven (*Ailanthus altissima*) the same age as the house. The Paddock Woodland Walk runs from the Gazebo Walk near the house through woodland to a main viewing area. Formal walls and terraces create a framework round the house for a large number of sun-loving tender plants. There are various water features, notably a stone-edged rill and a circular pool in the herbaceous-bordered walled garden.

Dartington Hall Trust

Dartington, Totnes TQ9 6EL. Tel: (01803) 862367; www.dartingtonhall.com

2m NW of Totnes, E of A384. In Dartington, turn left past church (from London and north) or right before church (from west)

Open all year, daily, dawn – dusk. Parties by appt only

Entrance: by donation £2, guided tours by arrangement £6

Other information: Coaches by appt

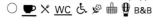

DARTINGTON HALL ★
(Historic Garden Grade II*)

In 1925, Leonard and Dorothy Elmhirst purchased the ancient and dying estate in order to launch their great experiment in rural regeneration. The hall is one of the most beautiful medieval manor houses in Devon. Standing at the crest of its sheltering combe and commanding a green tiltyard, the 28-acre garden is an astonishing piece of theatre. Twelve Irish yews in apostolic procession face a wall of tall and narrow turfed terraces, crowned by a line of chestnut trees and a majestic Henry Moore 'Reclining Figure' in Hornton stone. Low, clipped yew screens loosely close the triangle, and Percy Cane's grand stone staircase leads to the upper level. Cane also planted a glade and an azalea dell, while the American Beatrix Farrand transformed the courtyard and opened up the woodland walkways. There are three walks, each using yew and holly as background plantings for collections of camellias, magnolias and rhododendrons. More recently, Preben Jacobsen redesigned the sunny herbaceous border in quiet shades of cream, blue and purple, Philip Booth laid out a Japanese garden and Georgie Wolton rationalised the forecourt entrance. Over the seasons, the spotlight of colour sweeps around the garden, but the overall effect is strongly

Dartington Hall

architectural, with the tiltyard and terraces at its heart. Arguably the best view of these is from the top of the new wheelchair-accessible path, signalled by Peter Randal-Page's 'Jacob's Pillow'.

DOCTON MILL GARDENS ★

The nine-acre garden and the water mill of Saxon origin were rescued from dereliction in 1980. The mill was restored, the ponds, leats and smaller streams were cleared, a bog garden was created and a vast number of trees planted. The millennium saw another burst of activity with the planting of

Mr and Mrs J. Borrett

Lymebridge, Hartland EX39 6EA.
Tel: (01237) 441369;
www.doctonmill.co.uk

14m W of Bideford, 12m N of Bude off A39. From north Devon travel via Hartland to Stoke or from north Cornwall to West Country Inn, then turn left signed to Elmscott towards Lymebridge in Spekes Valley

Open March to Oct, daily, 10am – 6pm

Entrance: £4, OAPs £3.75, children under 16 free

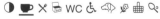

Docton Mill Gardens

81

a woodland garden and the transformation of the old donkey paddock into a magnolia garden with large herbaceous borders. The intention is to blend the garden into the natural landscape of valley and water. In spring there are displays of narcissi, primulas, camellias, rhododendrons and azaleas, with bluebells carpeting the woods; in summer the garden abounds in roses, including a bank of 'Felicia' and 'Pax', and the adjacent herbaceous border is in full flower.

THE GARDEN HOUSE ★

The Fortescue Garden Trust

Buckland Monachorum, Yelverton PL20 7LQ. Tel: (01822) 854769; www.thegardenhouse.org.uk

10m N of Plymouth, 2m W of Yelverton off A386

Open March to Oct, daily, 10.30am – 5pm

Entrance: £5.50, concessions £5, children £2

Originally restricted to a two-acre walled garden centred around the romantic ruins of a medieval vicarage, the garden was first developed in the 1940s by Lionel Fortescue. He breathed life into its then-derelict terraces, selecting and combining a diverse range of plants and introducing a number of his own varieties of rhododendrons and mahonias. From 1978 Keith Wiley continued its development, creating from six acres of adjacent pasture the Long Walk, a garden laid out with winding paths around spectacular vistas. Within this are South African and quarry gardens, a cottage garden and meadow, an acer glade, a birch wood and a bulb meadow. The pioneering planting style known as new naturalism is inspired by natural plant communities in the UK and further afield and features choice trees and shrubs underplanted with thousands of perennials and bulbs. The ongoing evolution of the garden is now in the hands of Matt Bishop, head gardener since 2003, who has instigated a programme of replanting and refurbishment which began with the front lawns and South African garden, and now continues in the walled garden and Long Walk. The plant centre offers a wide range of plants to seen growing in the garden.

GIDLEIGH PARK

Andrew and Christina Brownsword

Chagford TQ13 8HH. Tel: (01647) 432367; www.gidleigh.com

Off A382 11m SE of Okehampton. In Chagford Square turn right into Mill Street by Lloyds TSB. After 150 metres fork right (virtually straight across junction), and go to end of road – about 2m

Open all year Mon – Fri (but closed Bank Holiday Mons)

Entrance: £6 (inc. full afternoon tea; advance booking essential)

Other information: Lunches and teas served in hotel

The acclaimed hotel and restaurant is set in 54 acres of magnificent and secluded grounds on the north bank of the North Teign River, within Dartmoor National Park. The woodland garden and parkland were created between 1850 and 1930. Since 1980 the owners have undertaken an extensive programme of restoration. Among the many interesting features is a delightful water garden, rebuilt and planted in 1986 and extended significantly into the woodland in 1997. Visitors can take this in on their way round the Boundary Walk – a 45-minute stroll through natural mixed woodland, underplanted with azaleas and rhododendrons. The river is never far away, tumbling over granite boulders, past spring displays of rhododendrons. The mock-Tudor house gives way to a terrace resplendent with summer colour, while a parterre and a herb garden add a touch of formality. An avenue of young pleached limes stands adjacent to the front lawn, and the croquet lawns, the very upmarket golf 'putting garden' and the pavilion create the final decadent flourishes.

GREENWAY

The ancient 30-acre Devon estate is set high on the curving bank of the tree-lined Dart river with beautiful woodland walks, and enclosed flower gardens near the barn and stables and beyond the sizeable kitchen garden. The Trust's researches indicate that Repton may have worked here. There are so many indigenous trees over 150 years old, that in high summer the river is completely hidden from the house, and even from Dittisham on the opposite bank the house is barely visible. This natural paradise is gorgeous at every season, starting with camellias, rhododendrons, magnolias, davidias and michelias underplanted with narcissus, cyclamen, primroses and bluebells, followed by paulownias, embothriums and *Cornus capitata* with their understorey of campions, foxgloves and ferns. The camellia and fernery gardens and the vinery have been restored, the border in the top garden redeveloped. Interesting trees and shrubs from around the world, especially South America. The house (Agatha Christie's holiday home for many years) and the area immediately around it are not open.

The National Trust

Greenway Road, Galmpton, Churston Ferrers, Brixham TQ5 0ES.
Tel: (01803) 842382;
www.nationaltrust.org.uk

4m W of Brixham. From A3022 Paignton – Brixham road, take road to Galmpton, then towards Greenway quay and ferry. Vehicles strictly regulated, and no parking allowed in lanes outside property. Parking spaces for minicoaches (up to 27) must be pre-booked. Visitors should park at Dartmouth park-and-ride, then take river cruise to Greenway (ferry service (01803) 844010). Ferries also from Torquay and Brixham. Allow 4 hours

Open March to 12th Oct, Wed – Sun, 10.30am – 4.30pm

Entrance: £5, children £2.50 (extra charge for car)

HARTLAND ABBEY

Once an Augustinian monastery, the abbey has belonged to the Stucley family for many generations. It is set across a narrow sheltered valley. Due to Atlantic gales, gardens were not created around the house – although a row of 100-year-old bay trees survives – but were planted either side of the valley with azaleas, rhododendrons, camellias, hydrangeas, gunneras and many other shrubs and trees. Some paths in the bog garden were designed by Gertrude Jekyll, who used to be a guest at the abbey, and the Victorian fernery, also thought to be by her, has been replanted. The walk to the Atlantic, a mile away, is carpeted in spring with bluebells, primroses and violets; a newly-restored nineteenth-century gazebo faces out to sea. A series of eighteenth-century walled gardens, set in a south-facing, gently sloping valley five minutes' walk away, is filled with vegetables, herbaceous plants, roses, climbers and tender perennials – *Echium pininana* thrives here. Within the 20 acres, peacocks roam free in the garden, and donkeys and black Welsh Mountain sheep graze in the old deer park.

Sir Hugh and Lady Stucley

Bideford EX39 6DT.
Tel: (01237) 441264/441234;
www.hartlandabbey.com

15m SW of Bideford off A39. Follow signs to Hartland; drive through village, take road to Hartland Quay. Signposted

House open 21st March to 26th May, Wed, Thurs, Sun and Bank Holiday Mons; 27th May to 5th Oct, Sun – Thurs; all 12 noon – 5pm

Garden and grounds open 10th and 17th Feb for snowdrops; 21st March to 5th Oct, daily except Sat, 12 noon – 5pm; and by appt at other times

Entrance: £5, children £1.50 (house, gardens and grounds £8.50, children £2.50)

Other information: Shop open as house

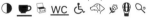

HEDDON HALL

Nestling in a valley with views of Exmoor, the four-acre Georgian rectory garden was renovated in the mid-1980s by Jane Keatley, a keen plantswoman, and is full of horticultural delights. Through the cobbled courtyard lies a walled garden with an elaborate formal design of box hedges and cordon fruit trees designed by Penelope Hobhouse; the imaginative combination of flowers, fruit, herbs and vegetables between the intricate hedges is the work of Carol Klein. Next door, in

Juliet and Fred de Falbe

Parracombe EX31 4QL.
Tel: (01598) 763541;
www.heddonhallgardens.co.uk

10m NE of Barnstaple off A39. Follow A39 towards Lynton, around Parracombe (avoiding village centre), then turn left towards village; entrance 200 yards on left

Heddon Hall

Open Feb, Sun, 10am – 5pm for hellebores and snowdrops; then May to July, Wed and Sun, 10 – 5.30pm, and for parties by appt all year

Entrance: £4, children free

the rose garden, cordoned and pleached limes line colour-themed beds planted with unusual herbaceous plants brought back from various seed-collecting trips. On the steeply sloped Himalayan bank bulbs and shade loving plants, including many unusual epimediums, flower beneath an abundance of rhododendrons, azaleas, camellias and acers. The young River Heddon flows first through the water garden and then into three ancient stew ponds separated by cascades. A rhododendron tunnel has been planted alongside, and a further bed of rhododendrons includes *R. sinogrande* and *R. rex* subsp. *fictolacteum*. Snowdrops and hellebores start the gardening year, followed by magnolias, rhododendrons, new English and shrub roses, going out in a blaze of foliage colour from the large collection of specimen acers in the arboretum.

Mr and Mrs D. R. A. Quicke

Lustleigh, Newton Abbot TQ13 9SP.
Tel: (01647) 277275

13m NW of Torquay, 8m NW of Newton Abbot, 3m NW of Bovey Tracey on A382 towards Moretonhampsted. After 2.5m, turn left at Kelly Cross for Lustleigh; after 0.25m left then right at Brookfield along Knowle Road; after 0.25m turn down steep drive on left

Open for NGS, and March to May, Sun and Bank Holiday Mons, 11am – 6pm, and by appt between these dates

Entrance: £2.50, children free

HIGHER KNOWLE

A three-acre woodland spring garden surrounds the romantic 1914 Lutyens-style house, constructed of local grit stone and granite, in an elevated position with spectacular views towards the River Bovey and Dartmoor to the south-west. It is sheltered from the north and east and tends to shed frosts, providing excellent conditions for tender plants. Numerous well-rounded granite boulders add natural sculpture to the old oak woodland, which is carpeted with primroses, bluebells and other wild flowers. Collections of mature camellias, magnolias, rhododendrons and other acid-loving shrubs and trees such as embothriums, eucryphias and tree ferns thrive here; all are labelled. A wildlife pond with fountain adds interest to this lovely garden.

Holbrook
Garden

HOLBROOK GARDEN

The owners of this two-acre garden work closely with nature to create a riot of colour and a haven for wildlife. The year starts with wildflower plantings of cowslips and fritillaries, with primulas and irises to follow. Midsummer brings a blaze of Mediterranean colour, autumn a tapestry of oranges, blues and purples. Tons of pebbles and naturalistic planting have created a stone garden, which is filled with drought-tolerant plants. The garden houses a National Collection of heleniums and the adjacent nursery stocks an interesting range of unusual plants.

Martin Hughes-Jones and Susan Proud

Sampford Peverell, Tiverton EX16 7EN.
Tel: (01884) 821164;
www.holbrookgarden.com

1m NW from M25 junction 27, follow brown signs to Minnows camping site. Garden 300 metres up Holbrook Hill

Open April to Oct, Tues – Sat, 9 – 5pm

Entrance: £3, children free

◑ 🪑 WC 🐾

KILLERTON ★

(Historic Garden Grade II*)

Surrounded by 6000 acres of woodland, parkland and farmland, the 18-acre hillside garden was created by John Veitch in the late eighteenth century. It will provide pleasure and interest to all, particularly to tree and shrub enthusiasts. Besides the avenue of beeches, there are Wellingtonias (the first plantings in England), Lawson cypresses, oaks, maples and many other fine broad-leaved trees. Trees and shrubs introduced by Veitch are now reaching an imposing size. Terraced beds and extensive herbaceous borders provide summer colour. The rhododendron collection numbers 95 different species, many brought back from China and Japan. There is also an early-nineteenth-century summerhouse, the

The National Trust

Broadclyst, Exeter EX5 3LE.
Tel: (01392) 881345;
www.nationaltrust.org.uk

7m NE of Exeter on W side of B3181

House and costume museum open March to Oct, daily except Tues, 11am – 5.30pm

Park and garden open all year, daily, 10.30am – dusk

Entrance: £5.70, children £2.80

Other information: Tea room limited opening in winter. Motorised buggies with drivers available for disabled

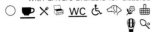

The National Trust

Bolham, Tiverton EX16 7RQ. Tel: (01884) 254665 (Property Manager); (01884) 253264 (Garden Office); www.nationaltrust.org.uk

16m N of Exeter, 2m N of Tiverton. Turn off A396 at Bolham

House open

Garden open 16th to 24th Feb, 1st, 2nd, 8th and 9th March, all 11am – 4pm; 15th March to 2nd Nov, daily, 11am – 5pm

Entrance: £6.50, children £3.10, (house and garden £7.80, children £3.90, family £19.50)

Other information: Dogs on lead in park and Impey Walk only

Mr & Mrs J. Howell

Harford, Ivybridge PL21 0JF. Tel: (01752) 691749/893390; www.lukesland.co.uk

1.5m N of Ivybridge off A38, on Harford road

Open for NGS, and by appt

Entrance: £4, children free

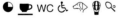

Bear's Hut, an icehouse and a rock garden. The handsome Victorian chapel has its own three-acre grounds containing many other fine trees, notably an enormous tulip tree. Peat-free plants for sale in the plant centre have been propagated at the nursery on the estate.

KNIGHTSHAYES ★★
(Historic Garden Grade II*)

The garden and landscaping were originally planned by Edward Kemp in the late 1870s when the house was being completed. It remained essentially unchanged until Sir John and Lady Amory began replanting in the 1950s. The most memorable part of Knightshayes is the Garden in the Wood – an extensive and magical woodland sheltering magnolias, rhododendrons, cornus, hydrangeas and other rare and tender plants, some grown in raised peat blocks; drifts of pink erythroniums, white foxgloves and cyclamen appear in their seasons. Near the house the terraces are planted with shrub roses, tree peonies and herbaceous plants in soft colours and silvers. Yew encloses a paved garden in shades of pink, purple and grey with two standard wisterias. Battlemented hedges frame the pool garden with a backdrop of *Acer pseudoplatanus* 'Brilliantissimum', and topiary hounds endlessly chase a fox on a lower terrace. The Victorian walled kitchen garden, constructed in tiers with a central ornamental pool, provides organic vegetables, fruit and cut flowers.

LUKESLAND

More a botanical park than a garden – entering the grounds you could be forgiven for believing you were in the foothills of the Himalayas. Lying on the hem of Dartmoor, Lukesland is Victorian in both origin and taste. The house was built in 1862 in the Victorian Gothic style by W.E. Matthews. The delightfully secluded valley of Addicombe Brook is the setting for 24 acres of flowering shrubs, trees and carpets of wild flowers – a gem of its kind. Although recent planting has ensured a greater variety of all-year interest, it is in spring that the profusion of rhododendrons, camellias and azaleas show the garden at its resplendent best, while fiery autumn colours give the garden a second spectacular season. The magnificent *Magnolia campbellii*, with a spread of over 100 feet, is registered as a champion tree, and the handkerchief tree planted in 1936 is also one of the largest in the country. The brook, which tumbles and gurgles its way over ponds and waterfalls, is criss-crossed by a series of delightful bridges which enable the visitor to wander at leisure amid scenes of great tranquillity. James McAndrew undertook the first major landscaping of the garden in the 1880s. The late owner and his family have carried out further planting, including a fine pinetum, and the construction of more ponds and bridges, all in the spirit of the original.

MARWOOD HILL ★

While the number and range of rare and unusual species amassed in the 20 acres here by the late Dr Snowdon will be of special interest to the connoisseur, the impressive trees and delightful setting cannot fail to give pleasure to any visitor. Five thousand different varieties of plants cover collections of willows, ferns, magnolias, eucryphias, rhododendrons and hebes, plus a fine collection of camellias in a glasshouse. There is also a large planting of eucalyptus and betulas. Other features include a pergola draped with 12 varieties of wisteria, raised alpine scree beds, three small lakes with an extensive bog garden and National Collections of astilbes, clematis, *Iris ensata* and tulbaghias. The garden continues to evolve; new prairie-style plantings of herbaceous perennials, grasses and wild flowers are being developed in a further few acres. To keep a place of such size and planting density at a permanently high level of upkeep is a heroic labour, but some overcrowding and loss of vistas are a small price to pay for the continued existence of this visionary and much-loved garden.

Patricia Stout

Marwood, Barnstaple EX3 4EB.
Tel: (01271) 342528;
www.marwoodhillgarden.co.uk

4m NW of Barnstaple off A361.
Signposted

Open all year, daily except 25th Dec, 9.30am – 5.30pm, and for parties by appt

Entrance: £4.50, accompanied children under 12 free

Other information: garden tearoom and plant sales

OVERBECK'S MUSEUM AND GARDEN ★
(Historic Garden Grade II*)

Palms stand in this exotic seven-acre garden high above the Salcombe estuary, giving a strongly Mediterranean atmosphere. The mild maritime climate enables it to be filled with exotics such as myrtles, daturas, agaves and the rare example of a camphor tree, *Cinnamomum camphora*. The *Magnolia campbellii* 'Overbeck's', over 100 years old and 12 metres high and wide, is a sight to see in February and March. The steep terraces were built in 1901 and lead down through fuchsia trees, huge fruiting banana palms and ginger lilies to a wonderful *Cornus kousa*. In the centre of the garden four beds packed with herbaceous perennials, many of them rare and tender, are spectacular from July through to September. The parterre of classical design is enlivened in season by orange and lemon trees. The range of unusual and exotic plants is being extended and some of the more hidden areas at the perimeters of the garden made more accessible.

The National Trust

Sharpitor, Salcombe TQ8 8LW.
Tel: (01548) 842893;
www.nationaltrust.org.uk

1.5m S of Salcombe, SW of South Sands

Museum open 18th March to 28th Oct – telephone for details

Garden open all year, daily except Sat, 10am – 5:30pm

Entrance: £6

Other information: No coaches

RHS GARDEN ROSEMOOR ★★

Lady Anne Berry created the garden here and the original eight acres contain over 3500 plants from all over the world, many of them collected by her. Rosemoor was the Society's first regional garden, second in importance only to Wisley, with which it has a certain stylistic affinity. The 65 acres include a new formal garden with 2000 roses in 200 varieties, colour-themed gardens, a herb garden, a potager, cottage, foliage and winter gardens, an alpine terrace, three model gardens and extensive herbaceous borders. The new garden designed by Tom Stuart-Smith displays a range of plants grown mainly for their leaves, particularly grasses. The eighteenth-century

The Royal Horticultural Society Garden Rosemoor

Great Torrington EX38 8PH.
Tel: (01805) 624067; www.rhs.org.uk

7m SE of Bideford, 1m SE of Great Torrington on A3124

Open all year, daily except 25th Dec, 10am – 6pm (closes 5pm Oct to March)

Entrance: £6, children £2 (2007 prices)

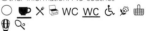

RHS Garden Rosemoor

gazebo from the grounds of Palmer House in Great Torrington has been reconstructed in the south arboretum, giving fine views across the garden and the valley. Elsewhere are stream and bog gardens and a large walled fruit and vegetable garden. National Collections of ilex (over 100 kinds) and cornus are planted throughout. Lectures, talks, garden walks and demonstrations are held all year; there are also many events.

SALTRAM HOUSE

(Historic Garden Grade II*)

The National Trust

Plympton, Plymouth PL7 1UH.
Tel: (01752) 333500;
www.nationaltrust.org.uk

3m E of Plymouth. From A379 turn N to Billacombe and after 1m turn left to Saltram

House open

Park open all year, daily, dawn – dusk

Garden and gallery open all year, daily except Fri, (but open Good Fri), 11am – 4pm. Closed 22nd to 1st Jan

Entrance: £4.20, children £2.10

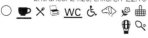

The original garden dates from the 1740s, with Victorian and twentieth-century overlays. There are three eighteenth-century buildings – a castle or folly, an orangery (home to orange and lemon trees during the winter months) and a classical garden house named Fanny's Bower after Fanny Burney, who came here in 1789 in the entourage of George III. A long lime avenue is underplanted with narcissi in spring and *Cyclamen hederifolium* in autumn, and a central glade has specimen trees like the stone pine and Himalayan spruce. Set against rolling lawns are several walks with magnolias, camellias, rhododendrons and Japanese maples which, with other trees, make for dramatic autumn colour; the Serpentine Walk now has a prairie planting and areas of long grass to encourage the flowering of wildflowers in mid- to late summer. The restored Graham Stuart Thomas border provides colour through the summer months, as do a wide variety of hydrangeas. Many areas of long grass abound with wild flowers throughout the spring and early summer. In all, 21 acres.

Sherwood

SHERWOOD ★

This is a masterpiece of a garden, created by the present owners, plant enthusiasts whose passion for learning, meticulous attention to detail and assured use of colour permeate the 15 acres. It sits astride two narrow valleys which provide a spectacular setting; woodland paths winding along the hillsides give unusual perspectives both above and across the valleys. For forty years, initially guided by Lionel Fortescue of The Garden House (see entry), they have sensitively and knowledgeably planted a profusion of woodland plants, including over 500 rhododendrons and National Collections of Knap Hill azaleas, magnolias and berberis, to cascade in their hundreds down the steep hillside. Collections of camellias, buddleias, cotoneasters, hydrangeas, cornus, acers, over 1000 heathers and swathes of wild daffodils help to ensure interest from spring through to autumn. After extensive clearance of overgrown laurels, another steep area further down the valley has been planted with epimediums and numerous other shade-loving woodland perennials beneath a canopy of ash and oak.

Sir John and Lady Quicke

Newton St Cyres, Exeter EX5 5BT.
Tel: (01392) 851216

2m SE of Crediton, off A377 Exeter – Barnstaple road. Signposted after 0.75m on Crediton side of village

Open all year, Sun, 2 – 5pm, and for NGS

Entrance: £3

○

TAPELEY PARK
(Historic Garden Grade II*)

The mellow red-brick William and Mary house bestrides the narrow estuary of the River Torridge, and the nobility of this elevated setting inspired the architect John Belcher in the early twentieth century to create a triple cascade of Italian terraces; these were replanted by Mary Keen. The structure of the garden is of great interest, with giant beeches, oaks and palm trees and characterful garden buildings as important

Hector Christie

Instow EX39 4NT.
Tel: (01271) 342558

2m N of Bideford S of A39 Barnstaple – Bideford road

House open for pre-booked parties (additional £2.50 per person)

Gardens open late-March to Oct, daily except Sat, 10am – 5pm

Entrance: £4, OAPs £3.50, children
£2.50 (2007 prices)

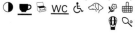

incidents in the landscape. It is varied too, including woodland, an ornamental lake, an ilex tunnel and a wild garden. The present owner is at the forefront of the sustainability movement, so the eighteenth-century walled kitchen garden and new organic garden are both thriving, but the Edwardian character is less powerful, the sharp edges of the layout less crisp than they once were. The Christie family also own *Glyndebourne* in Sussex, where the gardens, well-known to operatic picnickers, have been revived by Mary Keen, the late Christopher Lloyd and the present head gardener.

University of Exeter

Streatham Estate, Prince of Wales Road,
Exeter EX4 4PX.
Tel: (01392) 263059;
www.ex.ac.uk

On N outskirts of Exeter on A396, turn
E onto B3183. Signposted

Garden open all year, daily

Entrance: free

Other information: Coaches by
appt only

UNIVERSITY OF EXETER ★

High above Exeter with views over the city, the 300-acre university campus contains an impressive collection of unusual trees and shrubs from the temperate regions of the world – all credit to the authorities for the sensitivity with which they have woven the modern buildings into this mature arboretum. In the 1860s, an East India merchant who had inherited a fortune made by blockade-running in the Napoleonic wars employed the Exeter firm of Veitch to lay out the original 15-acre garden. Veitch's plant collectors, among them E.H. Wilson and the Lobb brothers, brought back numerous species from around the globe; many, such as the wingnut tree (*Pterocarya stenoptera*) and one of the first Wellingtonias to be planted in this country, are still flourishing. The sheltered site is perfect for tender plants, including hardy bananas, podocarpus and callistemons, and for a large range of magnolias, rhododendrons and camellias growing in woodland. A stream has been dammed to create three ponds, and this contrasts with the formal bedded area and the scented garden on the site of the original orangery. The garden holds a National Collection of azaras. A sculpture walk includes works by Barbara Hepworth.

OTHER RECOMMENDED GARDENS

ARLINGTON COURT

Arlington, Barnstaple EX31 4LP (01271 850296; www.nationaltrust.org.uk). Open 16th March to 2nd Nov, daily except Sat (but open Bank Holiday Sats), 11am – 5pm. NT

An intriguing amalgam of mature parkland and substantial estate (2700 acres in total), the Georgian house is set in a mature 30-acre garden of appealing informality. A symmetrical Victorian terraced garden, a handsome conservatory and a walled kitchen garden give an element of structure and formality. [Listed Grade II*]

CLOVELLY COURT

The Hon. John Rous, Clovelly, Nr Bideford EX39 5SZ (01237 431200; www.clovelly.co.uk). Open March to Oct, daily, 10am – 4pm

New life has been breathed into the 1.5-acre gardens here, especially the classic Victorian kitchen garden with its five greenhouses, fan-trained fruit trees and exuberant herbaceous borders, and the formal garden with terraced lawns and a magnificent view of Lundy Island.

CONNAUGHT GARDENS

Sidmouth, Peak Road, Sidmouth (01395 516551).
Open daily, dawn – dusk

The superlative municipal 8.5-acre gardens
include 2.5 acres devoted to traditional bedding
displays, unusual and tender shrubs and plants
and imaginative herbaceous borders. There are
breathtaking views across the bay from a
clifftop walk.

HAMBLYN'S COOMBE

Bridget McCrum, Dittisham TQ6 0HE
(01803 722228). Open by appt

The garden has a superb setting in a spectacular
wooded valley of the River Dart. The sculptor's
sensitively positioned works mingle with
camellias, wild flowers and tree ferns among
gently sloping woodland paths leading down to
the shore. Topiary and clipped hedges planted
by Mrs McCrum and her late husband are a
perfect foil for the bronze and stone sculptures.

Hamblyn's Coombe

HILL HOUSE

Mr and Mrs Raymond Hubbard and Mr Matthew
Hubbard, Landscove, Ashburton, Newton Abbot
TA13 7LY (01803 762273; www.hillhousenursery.co.uk).
Open all year, daily, 11am – 5pm. Closed 19th Dec to
5th Jan

The 3-acre garden is known by enthusiasts for
the garden created by that great plantsman
Edward Hyams. Since the 1980s it has been
restored as a private garden. The Hubbards'
family-run nursery adjoining sells a mouth-
watering range of rare and unusual plants,
including tender and exotic species.

LEE FORD

Mr and Mrs N. Lindsay-Fynn, Budleigh Salterton
EX9 7AJ (01395 445894). Open for charity for parties
of 20 or more by appt

An extensive spring-flowering woodland garden
of 40 acres in development since the 1950s,
including masses of mature rhododendrons,
azaleas and camellias. Formal lawns, a Victorian
walled vegetable garden, and rose, herb and bog
gardens contribute to the fine setting.

PAIGNTON ZOO
ENVIRONMENTAL PARK

Totnes Road, Paignton TQ4 7EU (01803 697500;
www.paigntonzoo.org.uk). Open all year, daily except
25th Dec, from 10am (closing times vary seasonally)

The first zoo in the country to combine animals
and a botanic garden, 80 years ago. There are five
habitat areas, and garden areas are themed
geographically and botanically. A large glasshouse,
a tropical area and a garden of tender plants. It's
all here, spread over 80 acres.

DORSET

For further information about how to use the *Guide*
and for an explanation of the symbols, see pages vi–viii.
Specific dates and times are those given to us by garden owners for 2008.
For 2009 dates, check with the individual properties.
For opening dates under the National Gardens Scheme,
readers should consult *The Yellow Book* or www.ngs.org.uk.
Maps are to be found at the end of the *Guide*.

Ilchester Estates

Abbotsbury, Weymouth DT3 4LA.
Tel: (01305) 871387;
www.abbotsbury-tourism.co.uk

9m NW of Weymouth, 9m SW of
Dorchester off B3157

Open March to Oct, daily, 10am – 6pm;
Nov to Feb, daily except Christmas and
New Year period (telephone to check),
10am – dusk

Entrance: £8, OAPs £7.50, children £4.50

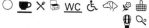

ABBOTSBURY SUBTROPICAL GARDENS★

(Historic Garden Grade I)

The walled garden was established by the 1st Countess of
Ilchester in 1765 as a kitchen garden for the nearby castle,
which burned down in 1913. It forms the nucleus of these
famous gardens, which contain a rich selection of plants from
the Mediterranean – proximity to the sea and shelter from
the north create the microclimate that has turned the area
into a botanical treasure trove. A Mediterranean bank grows
exotics from Australia, South Africa and Mexico, including
proteas, banksias, agaves and olive trees. In 1899 a catalogue
of 5000 plants was produced; today there must be many
more within the 30-acre site, which has been extensively
restored and replanted over the last two decades. Rare trees
abound. Bamboo groves, bog gardens, bananas from Ethiopia,
masses of hydrangeas, azaleas, hostas and much else besides
are all to be seen on the well-marked woodland walk, where
peacocks, golden pheasants and other exotic birds may be
spotted among the trees. A lush waterside planting of
primulas, hostas, rogersias and other moisture-lovers is
maturing well. A new magnolia walk, 250 metres long, leads

Abbotsbury Subtropical Gardens

out of the garden up to a high point giving spectacular views of the World Heritage Jurassic coast. The nearby swannery at the eastern end of the village should not be missed.

ARNMORE HOUSE

A one-acre garden of considerable personality, created by a composer who also has a strong feeling for Chinese art. His planting is tactile and shape, colour and texture all matter – hence the unusual specimen trees, the topiary against walls and the patterned paving. The formal parterre is a striking composition of diagonals, with *Buxus sempervirens* accompanied by clipped balls of *B.s. Aureovariegata*'. Trees and shrubs chosen for year-round colour are all around, some in pots and many pruned and trained to give exactly the desired effect. Ease of maintenance has also been a priority as Mrs Hellewell is disabled.

Mr and Mrs David Hellewell

57 Lansdowne Road, Bournemouth BH1 1RN. Tel: (01202) 551440; www.mdmusic.com/arnmore

On B3064 just S of hospital

Open all year by appt

Entrance: £2, children free

ATHELHAMPTON HOUSE AND GARDENS ★

(Historic Garden Grade I)

The four gardens and two pavilions of the Tudor manor house were designed for Alfred Cart de La Fontaine in 1891 by F. Inigo Thomas, and the garden was extended with great sensitivity during the 1960s and '70s by the present owner's father; it extends now over 15 acres. Courts and walls follow the original plan with beautiful stone and brickwork arches. Visitors will take away with them an abiding memory of some of the most stylish architectural topiary in England, and of the River Piddle, girdling the garden in its own right and busily harnessed within it to service pools, fountains and a long canal studded with water lilies. Major features are a fifteenth-century circular dovecot on the lawn facing the west wing of the house, and the circular pleached lime behind the Pyramid Garden. Here, twelve massive yews are fashioned to echo the obelisks on the raised terrace walk, which has a matching pair of charming pavilions standing at each end. The toll house to the south has been restored, and a new raised boardwalk extends over 200 metres along the River Piddle. The planting,

Patrick Cooke

Athelhampton House, Athelhampton Dorchester DT2 7LG. Tel: (01305) 848363; www.athelhampton.co.uk

5m NE of Dorchester, 1m E of Puddletown off A35 at Northbrook junction

House open as garden but from 11am

Gardens open March to 1st Nov, Sun – Thurs, 10.30am – 5pm; Nov to Feb, Sun, 10.30am – dusk

Entrance: house and garden £8, OAPs £7.50, children free, parties of 12 or more £5.50 per person (2007 prices)

Other information: Picnics in riverside area only. Self-catering accommodation available

Athelhampton House Gardens

including tulips, rambling roses, clematis and jasmine, is big-boned, low-key and sophisticated. A remarkable, unforgettably atmospheric interpretation of the late-medieval ideal.

CHIDEOCK MANOR

Mr and Mrs Howard Coates

Chideock, Bridport DT6 6LF.
Tel: (01297) 489890

2m W of Bridport on A35. In centre of village turn right by church; entrance to house on right along narrow lane

Open for NGS, and Sat and Sun by appt

Entrance: £3.50

The attractive driveway leads through downland and woodland and over a stream to the imposing Regency mansion (not open), home from 1803 to 1996 to the Weld family; the adjoining chapel was added in 1879. They left a legacy of magnificent mature trees, an imposing yew walk, a walled kitchen garden and several fine statues, but the five-acre garden seen today is largely the creation of the present owners. The layout is formal in parts, and the statues collected by the Welds have taken their place in the new scheme, relocated as focal points in the Lady Gardens, the lime walk and other distinctive areas. There is colour in the garden from the flowering of spring bulbs through camellias, rhododendrons, roses and herbaceous perennials. From the knot garden with its whorls of santolina, paths lead to the old yew walk and on to woodland, where masses of *Zantedeschia aethiopica* grace the extensive bog garden in summer. More developments are promised; meanwhile, visitors can sit in the stone belvedere and admire the fine views.

CHIFFCHAFFS ★

Mr and Mrs K. R. Potts

Chaffeymoor, Bourton, Gillingham SP8 5BY. Tel: (01747) 840841

7m NW of Shaftesbury, 3m E of Wincanton. Leave A303 (Bourton bypass) signed to Bourton and continue to end of village

Open for NGS, April to Oct, Wed and Thurs; and other Suns March to Sept; all 2 – 5pm; also open by appt

Entrance: £3, children £1

Other information: Refreshments and toilet facilities for parties only

An impressive avenue of flowering cherries, the beautiful *Prunus* 'Shirotae', leads to the 400-year-old cottage and its three immaculately maintained acres of cottage garden, with an invitation to more pleasures at each turn of the path. The terraces and viewpoints afford glimpses of open countryside, and the varied and colourful beds and borders are filled with a noteworthy collection of dwarf bulbs, dwarf rhododendrons, old-fashioned roses and a wide range of herbaceous plants. Ornamental trees and shrubs populate the sloping woodland garden beyond the house. Mr Potts' well-stocked nursery has a wide variety of healthy-looking plants on offer.

Chiffchaffs

CORSCOMBE HOUSE

High yew hedges in this well-planned two-acre garden create shady, well-ordered rooms punctuated by vivid hot and cool herbaceous plantings; there is also a walled kitchen garden. Yew topiary, an avenue of fruit and crab trees and box parterres planted with white flowers are attractive touches, and a new formal secret garden in the Persian style has a central fountain, lemon trees in pots and other Mediterranean planting. A wildflower meadow and subtle green spaces blend effortlessly into the countryside and sheltering hills.

Jim Bartos

Corscombe DT2 0NU.
Tel: (01935) 891288

7m SW of Crewkerne off A356. Take 2nd turn left to Corscombe, then right signed to church; house is next to church

Open for NGS, and by appt

Entrance: £3.50, children free

NEW ☾

CRANBORNE MANOR GARDEN ★★

(Historic Garden Grade II*)

Tradescant established the basic framework of the garden in the early seventeenth century, but little remains. Neglected for a long time, the last four generations have left their mark by developing certain parts, changing others, replanting and creating new vistas whilst always keeping the secrecy and quiet charm of this most beautiful garden. Clipped yew hedges surround formal beds and a large croquet lawn to the west, and the walled north garden is planted with white flowers and shrubs. The high-walled entrance courtyard to the south is approached through two Jacobean gatehouses (sometimes closed). A circular lawn on which an Angela Connor fountain sits, surrounded on all four sides by shrubs and old-fashioned flowers, provides the perfect introduction to what has been called 'the most magical house in Dorset'. The long grass on either side of the south drive contains a thriving collection of orchids throughout the early part of summer and leads through three more yew-lined rooms to the garden centre and car park. The excellent nursery specialises in traditional rose varieties and carries a wide selection of clematis, herbaceous perennials and flowering shrubs. Another garden with an interesting historical pedigree, but an entirely different experience, is to be found at nearby *Ashley Park Farm*, Damerham. Created by a dedicated conservationist, there are unusual trees and shrubs in attractive woodland walks, ponds and a wildflower meadow, a farm and wild fowl and rare sheep. [Open by appt. Tel: (01725) 518200.]

Viscount Cranborne

Cranborne, Wimborne Minster BH21 5PP. Tel: (01725) 517248; www.cranborne.co.uk

10m N of Wimborne on B3078. Entrance via garden centre

Open March to Sept, Wed, 9am – 5pm (last admission 4pm), for NGS, and some weekends for charity – telephone to check dates

Entrance: £4, OAPs £3.50, children 50p

Other information: Garden centre and tearoom open all year, daily

FORDE ABBEY ★★

(Historic Garden Grade II*)

This unique and fascinating former Cistercian abbey, inhabited as a private house since acquiring a castellated face-lift in 1649, is set in a varied and most attractive garden. An early-eighteenth-century canal at the end of the long and stately range of abbey buildings, lime and walnut avenues and a large lake some distance away, are major features of the garden, which extends over 30 acres. Old walls and colourful

Mr M. Roper

Chard, Somerset TA20 4LU.
Tel: (01460) 221290;
www.fordeabbey.co.uk

8m NW of Beaminster, 7m W of Crewkerne, 4m SE of Chard off A30

House open 18 th March to Oct, Tues – Fri, Sun and Bank Holiday Mons, 12 noon – 4pm

Garden open all year, daily,
10am – 4.30pm

Entrance: £5.50, OAPs £5, children
under 15 free (house and garden £7.50,
OAPs £7, children under 15 free)

Other information: Parties of 20
or more telephone (01460) 220231
for bookings

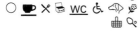

borders, sloping lawns, cascades and ponds (don't miss the unusual pleached beech pavilion overlooking the Great Pond), graceful statuary and enormous mature trees combine to create an atmosphere of timeless elegance. A 50-metre fountain celebrates the Roper family's 100 years at Forde Abbey. There is something here for every gardener to appreciate: the bog garden (at its peak in July) displays a large collection of primulas and other Asiatic plants; the shrubbery contains a variety of magnolias, rhododendrons and other delightful specimens. The rock garden was revolutionised by the late Jack Drake, and a fine arboretum has been built up since 1947. At the back of the abbey is an extensive walled kitchen garden and a nursery selling rare and unusual plants.

Richard and Jo Earle

Ryme Intrinseca, Sherborne DT9 6JT.
Tel: (01935) 872304

Just off A37 Yeovil – Dorchester road.
3m S of Yeovil turn left; garden is
0.25m on left

Open for NGS, and by appt

Entrance: £2.50, children free

FRANKHAM FARM

In spring and early summer, visitors to this charming garden can be assured of plenty of colour. Developed since the 1960s, the flat site of over three acres includes extensive plantings of roses and clematis. Well-stocked herbaceous borders frame a fine view of adjacent fields, with grass walks meandering through woodland and a wild garden planted with spring bulbs and shrubs making a pleasing contrast. Farm buildings form an attractive backdrop as a striking group of *Cornus kousa* with white foxgloves under eucalyptus leads from the neat and productive kitchen garden into a small plantation of unusual trees, including the Chilean firebush (*Embothrium coccineum*) and *Aesculus pavia*, alongside rhododendrons, azaleas and camellias. Many of the plants and trees have been grown from seed.

Mr and Mrs David Ashcroft

Beaminster DT8 3HB.
Tel: (01308) 862212

1.5m N of Beaminster on A3066
on left before tunnel

Open for NGS, and April to Oct,
Tues – Thurs, by appt

Entrance: £3.50

Other information: Teas by prior
arrangement

HORN PARK

Although the impressive house designed by Lawrence Dale, a pupil of Lutyens, dates from 1910, the garden is based partly on features discovered as the work progressed. A drive through parkland leads to the wide gravel sweep before the entrance porch, with terraced lawns to the front of the house and a panoramic view towards Beaminster and the distant coast. Other features include rock areas, herbaceous and rose borders, unusual plants and shrubs, a water garden beneath a steep azalea bank, ponds, a woodland garden and walks among wild flowers, including orchids and bluebells in spring. The natural wildflower meadow, with over 160 different flowers and grasses, is listed as a site of nature conservation interest.

Anne and Alan Stevens

Aller Lane, Lower Ansty, Dorchester
DT2 7PX. Tel: (01258) 880053

IVY COTTAGE ★

Mrs Stevens trained and worked as a professional gardener before coming to her cottage in 1964. Although chalk underlies the surrounding land, this 1.75-acre informal cottage garden is actually on greensand; it has springs and a stream that keep it well watered and is therefore an ideal home for plants such as primulas, irises, gunneras, and in particular trollius and moisture-loving lobelias. Other delights are a thriving and ordered kitchen garden (which hardly ever needs a hose), large herbaceous borders giving colour all year round, drifts of bulbs and other spring plants surrounding specimen trees and shrubs, and three most interesting raised beds for alpines. The new roof garden on the garage can be seen from a high path nearby. Wildlife is actively encouraged.

12m NE of Dorchester, 10m W of Blandford in centre of triangle between A352, A354 and A3030. Take turning near Fox Inn, Ansty

Open May to Sept, last Thurs in month, 11am – 5pm, and at other times for parties by appt

Entrance: £3, children free

 WC

KINGSTON LACY ★
(Historic Garden Grade II)

This 32-acre formal garden, with nine acres of lawn, also has a wonderful lime avenue planted in 1668, which leads to the Nursery Wood containing a fine collection of rhododendrons and azaleas. The terrace displays urns, vases and lions in bronze and marble, and there are interesting marble wellheads and tubs for bay trees; also an Egyptian obelisk and a sarcophagus. The parterre was laid out in 1899 for Henrietta Bankes in memory of her husband and is still planted in the seasonal bedding schemes designed for her. The Victorian fernery, planted with 25 different types of fern and a National Collection of *Anemone nemorosa*, leads to the once-fine cedar walk, where one of the trees was planted by the Duke of Wellington in 1827 and others by visiting royalty. Snowdrops, daffodils and bluebells abound, and in summer the spectacular display of roses includes 'Bonica', 'Cardinal Hume', 'Nozomi' and 'Amber Queen'. The restored Japanese gardens lie in 7.5 acres of the southern shelter belt. Originally laid out by Henrietta Bankes *c.* 1910, they are the largest of their kind in England and include a formal tea garden complete with a stone 'stream', a tea house and a waiting arbour. The garden holds National Collections of convallarias and anemones, and in spring, many areas are covered in snowdrops, daffodils and bluebells. There is a circular woodland walk, including a children's playground.

The National Trust

Wimborne Minster BH21 4EA.
Tel: (01202) 883402;
www.nationaltrust.org.uk

1.5m NW of Wimborne on B3082

House open 15th March to 2nd Nov, Wed – Sun, 11am – 5pm (last admission 4pm)

Park and garden open Feb, Sat and Sun, 10.30am – 4pm; 15th March to 2nd Nov, daily, 10.30am – 5.30pm; 5th Nov to 21st Dec, Fri – Sun, 10.30am – 4pm. Additional opening for snowdrops – telephone for details

Entrance: garden and park: £5, children £2.50, family £12.50 (house, garden and park £10, children £5, family £25)

Other information: Volunteer-driven buggy on house open days

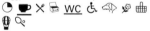

KINGSTON MAURWARD GARDENS ★
(Historic Garden Grade II*)

Three distinct periods coexist harmoniously here. In 1720 the handsome house was built, dignified by a contemporary landscape park with 50 acres of fine trees, water and woodland. Then, between 1918 and 1920, the formal gardens to the west of the mansion were laid out by the Hanbury family, who also owned the celebrated La Mortola in Italy. Within splendid stone terraces, balustrading, steps and yew hedges, they made a series of intimate enclosures, including water features, topiary, a yew maze, and other requisites of a grand Edwardian garden. Positioned on a steep hillside overlooking the eight-acre lake, the views are outstanding. The

Kingston Maurward Gardens

Dorchester DT2 8PY.
Tel: (01305) 215003;
www.kmc.ac.uk/gardens

E of Dorchester off A35. Turn off at roundabout at end of bypass

Open all year, daily, 10am – 5.30pm. Closed 21st Dec to 4th Jan. Guided tours by appt

Entrance: £5, children £3, under 3 free. Family season tickets available to gardens and farm animal park

most recent phase has been their determined restoration since 1990 by the present incumbents, the staff and students of Kingston Maurward College. Their utilitarian training facilities might occupy the perimeter, but the formal gardens are resplendent once more. National Collections of penstemons and salvias are held here, together with a large collection of herbaceous perennials; in spring drifts of bulbs occupy the sweeping lawns and the margins of the lake. Of particular interest is the statuary on long loan from the Palace of Westminster and the restored Grecian temple at the lake's edge. There is also a Japanese-style garden with Chusan palms, bamboos and maples, a tree trail with 65 different species to discover, and an animal park for children. *Hardy's Cottage*, a National Trust property with a small colourful garden, is nearby.

Mr Neil Lucas

Hampreston, Wimborne Minster BH21 7ND. Tel: (01202) 873931; www.knollgardens.co.uk

Between Wimborne and Ferndown, off Ham Lane (B3073). Leave A31 at Canford Bottom roundabout. Signed after 1.5m

Open Dec to April, Wed – Sun and Bank Holiday Mons, 10am – 4pm; May to Nov, Tues – Sun and Bank Holiday Mons, 10am – 5pm. Closed 21st Dec to 31st Jan

Entrance: £4.75, concessions £4.25, children (4–14) £3.25

KNOLL GARDENS ★

Twenty-five years ago this was a private botanic garden, but it is now laid out in an informal English setting with mature specimen trees and shrubs creating a relaxed and intimate atmosphere. Although only a little over four acres, the many different areas, winding pathways and constantly changing views give an impression of a much larger area. The owners continue to develop the garden. The summer garden has a collection of exotic-looking tender perennials, the water garden several waterfalls, the Dragon Garden boasts a nationally acclaimed collection of modern perennials and grasses, displayed to their best effect, and a naturalistic border was planted in 2004 with over 800 grasses and hardy perennials. There are areas planted for dry shade and for moisture and a newly extended gravel garden for drought-tolerant plants. National Collections of deciduous ceanothus,

Knoll
Gardens

phygelius and pennisetums are held here, and the nursery specialises in hardy perennials and grasses. Christopher Bradley-Hole's amphitheatre garden at *Portland Castle* is 12 miles away.

LANGEBRIDE HOUSE

A 2.75-acre garden with many desirable features: a 200-year-old copper beech rising from wide, lush lawns, underplanted with carpets of spring bulbs; a thriving enclosed vegetable garden of manageable size; a sloping grass area with colourful mixed borders along the tile-topped walls; a mixed wild woodland behind; a formal yew-lined lawn with a pond and old stone features, from which steps descend through sloping shrubberies towards the front of the house. A miniature area of greensand allows a patch of acid-loving plants to provide contrast. A long line of pleached limes runs parallel with the bi-colour beech hedge along the road, and a tall rockery, planted with alpines, acts as a viewing point and sun-trap. There are also beds and borders, trellises for climbing plants and low stone walls for those that prefer to hang, and all around, thousands of bulbs hide in waiting for the spring explosion which, in the owner's opinion, is the best season to visit.

Mrs J. Greener

Long Bredy, Dorchester DT2 9HU.
Tel: (01308) 482257

8m W of Dorchester off A35
Dorchester – Bridport road. Turn S to
Long Bredy

Open Feb to June by appt

Entrance: £3

◑ WC ⅊

MAPPERTON ★★
(Historic Garden Grade II*)

Dorset's combes are famously intriguing, and Mapperton offers one of the county's most atmospheric gardens: 15 acres set into a unique stepped valley. This is garden-as-opera-set, beginning on the first of three levels with the courtyard garden at the front of the charming sixteenth- and seventeenth-century manor house which introduces a cast of old roses and clematis. To the east, beyond the seventeenth-century house and below the main lawn, the drama quickens as the land falls to the Fountain Court with its sculptured topiary and Italianate features. Pools of water, carved stone steps, a pergola and foaming Mediterranean borders face the classical orangery built by the current owner's father in 1968. A golden hamstone wall shows off a living wallpaper of pink *Erigeron karvinskianus* and a tree poppy, *Romneya coulteri*. The Baroque-inspired fountain, beautifully restored, is surrounded by box and yew to evoke the original 1920s' design (probably by Pike, a local architect) for the then owner, Mrs Labouchère. Below are deep fishponds reflecting 'walls' of yew and the tower house above. These yew walls repay attention, for their niches display evocative statuary. Down on the third level – the floor of the valley – is a small arboretum of species trees and shrubs, which opens into the 'wild' countryside beyond with cattle looming. There is flower and leaf interest throughout the visiting season from the first magnificent pink flowers of *Magnolia campbellii* to the fruits and berries

The Earl and Countess of Sandwich

Beaminster DT8 3NR.
Tel: (01308) 862645;
www.mapperton.com

5m NE of Bridport, 2m SE of
Beaminster between A356 and A3066

House open 23rd June to 1st Aug,
Mon – Fri and Bank Holiday Mons,
2 – 4.30pm

Garden open March to Oct, daily
except Sat, 11am – 5pm

Entrance: £4.50, children (5–18) £2,
under 5 free. Garden tours by appt,
£2 extra

Mapperton

appearing among the tints in the valley garden. Mapperton is a draw for garden lovers and for photographers and watercolourists in particular, because of the play of light across the planes of this extraordinary north-south valley.

Mrs T. Lewis
Melplash, Bridport DT6 3UH
5m N of Bridport on A3066
Open for NGS, and by written appt
Entrance: £5

MELPLASH COURT

The elegant sixteenth-century house, set among the Dorset hills with the sea over the horizon, is approached through an avenue of mature chestnut and lime trees. The owners respected plans for the garden as laid out by a previous owner, Lady Diana Tiarks, but have extensively restored and extended the area so that new planting is a feature without disturbing the general concept. On the whole, muted colours are preferred and expressed in a wonderful variety of foliage, particularly on the banks of the stream garden. Each section, including the outstanding Japanese garden, is a surprise as the visitor progresses via walled areas into carefully planned bedding that dramatises the sloping contours. A walled kitchen garden features knots where again leaf shape, in the form of rhubarb, leek, cabbage and angelica, creates attractive patterns. Herbaceous borders have recently been planted on the croquet lawn stretching out from the house. Maintenance is first-class. 36 acres in all.

The Hon Mr and Mrs Henry Digby
Minterne Magna, Dorchester DT2 7AU.
Tel: (01300) 341370;
www.minterne.co.uk
9m N of Dorchester, 2m N of Cerne Abbas on A352
Open March to Oct, daily, 10am – 6pm
Entrance: £4, accompanied children free

MINTERNE ★
(Historic Garden Grade II)

Minterne is a grand house in a magnificent setting. There are many rare trees, and one and a half miles of walks with palm trees, cedars, beeches, etc giving spectacular spring and autumn colour. At the lower end of the valley the stream with its waterfalls and lakes adorned by water lilies is surrounded by splendid tall trees, among which the paths wind back towards the house. The garden has an interesting collection of Himalayan rhododendrons and azaleas, spring bulbs, cherries and maples. A restful and attractive atmosphere — the informative and personally written labels will encourage visitors to linger.

THE OLD RECTORY, LITTON CHENEY

Within its five-acre garden, the house rests comfortably below the church and is approached by a gravel drive which circles a small lawn; a thatched summerhouse stands to one side like a massive beehive. The small walled garden has outhouses and a large barn on two sides and borders around three, prolifically stocked with well-chosen and favourite plants in specific colour bands, including many roses. A steep path leads down into the four acres of natural woodland, a surprisingly extensive area of mature trees with many springs, streams and ponds. This area was reclaimed by the current owners, who are adding new young trees and shrubs as well as successfully encouraging many spring-flowering plant colonies, mostly native. Climbing back above the house, the visitor arrives at the belvedere giving views over trees to farmland on the other side of the valley. Spring and autumn are the best times to see this garden, from which Reynolds Stone, the wood engraver, drew inspiration. In the same village, *Tithe Barn House* in Chalk Pit Lane has a charming small garden with a wealth of plants and pots, a reflecting pool and sweeping valley views. [Open for NGS, and for parties of 10 or more by appointment — telephone Mr and Mrs Antony Longland on (01308) 482219.]

Mr and Mrs Hugh Lindsay

Litton Cheney, Dorchester DT2 9AH.
Tel: (01308) 482383

9m W of Dorchester, 1m S of A35

Open probably during Feb for snowdrops (see local press), for NGS, and at other times by appt

Entrance: £4, children free

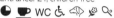

THE OLD RECTORY, NETHERBURY ★

The garden-makers here are the present owners, who since 1994 have transformed a five-acre pine forest into a marvellous amalgam of formal and wild spaces, sparing only

Simon and Amanda Mehigan

Netherbury DT6 5NB.
Tel: (01308) 488757

The Old Rectory, Netherbury

6m N of Bridport, 3m SW of
Beaminster off A3066, next to
parish church

Open for NGS, and mid-May to mid-
June for parties of 10 or more by appt

Entrance: £3.50 (for charity),
children free

Other information: Teas available by
arrangement

some majestic oaks, a splendid ginkgo and other mature trees. They have divided up the flat land beyond the house into a series of small gardens. From an enclosed courtyard with box-edged beds and a central fountain, a series of walks runs out, creating a processional way - a rose arch, four pairs of yew pyramids and a taller yew *allée*. To give variety and a change of rhythm, the central path changes from patterned cobbles to mown grass and back again. Blocks of *Geranium clarkei* 'Kashmir White', ribbons of *Iris pallida* var. *dalmatica* and other herbaceous perennials are used tellingly to add colour and lightness to each enclosure. To the side of this formal lay-out the land drops sharply to the left, opening out to a bog garden threaded by a wandering stream, where irises, primulas, hostas and arum lilies carpet the ground, revelling in the moist conditions; a pointed-roofed summerhouse marks the transition to a wildflower meadow. To the east of the house is a well-stocked kitchen garden with a castellated hedge leading the eye to the church tower at the far end.

The Wingfield Digby family

Sherborne DT9 5NR.
Tel: (01935) 813182 (Estate Office);
(01935) 812072 (Castle);
www.sherbornecastle.com

Signed from Sherborne

Castle and garden open 22nd March to
30th Oct, Tues – Thurs, Sat, Sun and
Bank Holiday Mons, 11am – 4.30pm
(castle interior opens 2pm Sat)

Entrance: £4, children free (castle and
grounds £8.50, OAPs £8, children free)
(2007 prices)

SHERBORNE CASTLE ★
(Historic Park Grade II*)

As they are seen today, the 30-acre castle grounds are based on landscaping undertaken in the late eighteenth century by 'Capability' Brown for the 6th Lord Digby, when the lake was created out of the then-flowing River Yeo, and the famous hanging gardens enjoyed by Sir Walter Raleigh and his wife Bess a century earlier were lost forever. Sweeping acres of deer park surround the impressive castle, and masonry salvaged from the crumbling ruin of the old castle, destroyed during the Civil War in 1645, gave rise to fine stable blocks, courtyards and nearby Castleton Church. The gardens on the north side of the lake have been extended to the east of the ruins to take in the late-eighteenth-century Dry Grounds Walk, an eight-acre avenue with many fine specimen trees and a serpentine trail of original pathways. A charming walled flower garden has been designed within one of the courtyards near the orangery, but the main attraction lies surely in the site's unique history, the colourful scene of water against graceful sloping lawns, and the ancient ruin visible across the lake. The delightful and comprehensive *Castle Gardens Plant Centre*, established in the original walled kitchen garden of the castle and accessible from the main road, is worth a detour.

Mr and Mrs John Lewis

Donhead St Mary, Shaftesbury
SP7 9DG. Tel: (01935) 814389

5m NE of Shaftesbury, off A30. Near
Donhead St Mary church

Open all year, Mon – Fri, by appt only,
for parties of 20 to 40

SHUTE HOUSE ★

The handsome early-eighteenth-century house (originally a fifteenth-century pilgrims' inn) stands at the edge of the estate close to the road, surrounded by a garden of many springs and ponds – the source of a river. The marvellous site faces south, overlooking a slope to farmland. Behind, mysterious shrubberies have a magical hold on the visitor, who is led by paths through groves of camellias and rhododendrons into knot gardens and borders and by placid pools and canals. The late Sir Geoffrey Jellicoe designed the musical cascade that tumbles down the slope over projecting copper Vs set in concrete – a 1972 flashback to his earlier involvement in the Modern Movement. This famous feature has been revived and replanted, while other structural features are being created by the present owners, who are respecting Jellicoe's overall design 'while introducing their own sense of fun'.

STANBRIDGE MILL ★

Designed in its initial stages by Arabella Lennox-Boyd with sensitive later additions by the present owner and head gardener, the 50-acre site greets the summer visitor with clouds of white ox-eye daisies either side of the drive. This wild theme is paramount throughout. Extensive water meadows, managed as a nature reserve, attract an abundance of bird life and wild flowers; grass drives meander alongside streams towards an elegant thatched summerhouse – an ideal point from which to view this pleasing profusion. The house itself, once a water mill, is surrounded by more formal areas, although the millstream remains a key part of the design. A particular feature is the Mound Garden, from where tiers of hedges – ranging from diminutive box through yew and beech to pleached lime – lead up to a higher level with a magnificent swimming pool and a pavilion. All is rectangular, with clever planting edged by neat box. A striking white-flowered *allée* lies beneath a series of iron archways and the ensuing wisteria walk with herbaceous borders stretches for some 60 metres. Everything is well maintained and shown off to perfection by paving and steps created in patterns by up-ended tiles, flints and bricks.

Entrance: charge

Other information: Teas by arrangement

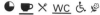

James Fairfax

Gussage All Saints BH21 5EP.
Tel: (01258) 841067

7m N of Wimborne on B3078
Cranborne road

Open for NGS, and for parties by written appt

Entrance: £5, children under 14 free

 WC &

Stanbridge Mill

276 Wimborne Road West,
Stapehill, Nr Wimborne BH21 2EB.
Tel: (01202) 861686

On old A31 Wimborne – Ferndown
road, 0.5m E of Canford Bottom
roundabout

Telephone for opening times and prices

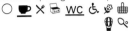

STAPEHILL ABBEY AND GARDENS

Formerly home for 200 years to Cistercian nuns, the lovely old abbey has now been restored and the grounds transformed into award-winning gardens, including a Victorian cottage garden, a wisteria walk, a tropical house, a lake, a woodland walk and picnic area, a large rock garden with waterfall and pools, and a Japanese garden. Craft shops in the abbey offer demonstrations of traditional crafts on most days. The restaurant is in the former refectory, off a walled terrace so that one can eat out of doors in summer. The Country World museum has a good collection of tractors etc., and overlooks the farmyard.

Julian Cotterell
Nr Wareham BH20 5PA.
Tel: (01929) 480709

5m S of Wareham, 1m N of
Kimmeridge off A351

Open by written appt only

Entrance: £5

STEEPLE MANOR ★

Set in a remote valley and surrounding a historic house of Purbeck stone and slate, the 5.5-acre gardens were designed in 1923 by Brenda Colvin, pioneer landscape architect and author of the seminal *Land and Landscape* (1947). It is one of three complete gardens by her to have survived. Colvin's practicality and aesthetic sensibility are shown from the start as two high curved beech hedges embrace the parking circle and hide all vehicles from view. Streams from the bog garden drop to a rill in the formal lily pond garden with its *allée* of pleached limes backed by escallonia hedges, and from there to a meadow with ponds and trees, and to the countryside beyond. The walled garden to the south has a terrace crammed with pots and urns of tender plants, and steps through a gate to a theatrical space where lawn is bordered by a crescent of yew backed by a taller hedge of beech, giving the layered effect beloved by today's *fashionistas*. By extending the garden, the present owners have combined Colvin's rigour and sense of drama with generous and varied plantings of their own. The west borders are planted in shades of blue and white, while the raised grass terrace is punctuated by five pillar cypresses. Primulas and irises are followed by the roses and clematis and later by *viticella* clematis, dahlias of all kinds and colours, buddleias and much more, and the wall borders are filled with cistus, helianthemums, rosemary and salvias. The adjacent church has connections with George Washington.

Mr and Mrs E. A.W. Bullock
Buckhorn Weston, Gillingham SP8 5HG.
Tel: (01963) 371005

4m W of Gillingham, 4m SE of
Wincanton. From A30 turn N to
Kington Magna, continue towards
Buckhorn Weston and after railway
bridge take left towards Wincanton.
House is second on left

Open April to July by appt

WESTON HOUSE

Although centred around an exceptional collection of old-fashioned and English roses – currently 95 varieties, all clearly labelled – this is not merely a rose garden. Near the house stone walls are enveloped in 'Paul Lédé', 'Aloha', 'White Cockade' roses and many clematis, and to one side is a small, fragrant garden enclosed by mellow stone walls, with a great variety of roses and other climbers and skilfully chosen companion plants. Elsewhere, hot colours, a herb collection and buddlejas attract the butterflies. Borders of *Nepeta* 'Six Hills Giant' and *Rosa* 'Polar Star' standards lead through an arch smothered in ramblers to the main area of roses. More borders fan out at the sides of the extensive lawn, which reaches outwards to the meadows and trees of the Blackmore Vale. Part of an adjoining natural hayfield has been added to the garden and seeded with additional wild flowers. Around the perimeter there is more to explore: a plantation of old-fashioned roses, an area of perennials and grasses leading down to woodland and a wildlife pond – a delightful shady contrast much enjoyed by children. 1.5 acres.

Entrance: £3, children free

Other information: Teas by arrangement

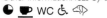

OTHER RECOMMENDED GARDENS

CHETTLE HOUSE

Mr and Mrs Peter Bourke, Chettle, Blandford Forum DT11 8DB (01258 830858). Open 23rd March, then first Sun of each month to Oct, 11am – 5pm

The 5-acre garden, approached through mature trees, is above all the setting for the unusual and impressive Queen Anne house designed by the Baroque architect Thomas Archer. Wide lawns, vistas and lavish herbaceous borders are all appropriate in scale and period.

CITY FARMHOUSE

Nigel and Angela Shaw, Sydling St Nicholas, Dorchester DT2 9NX (01300 341593). Open 25th and 26th May, 2 – 6pm, with other village gardens

Located in a beautiful, unspoilt village, the planting of this 0.5-acre cottage garden is colourful, informal and intermingled (70 different roses, for a start). A trout stream borders the spacious lawn, and an immaculate grass tennis court is surrounded by a tall topiary hedge.

DEAN'S COURT

Sir Michael and Lady Hanham, Wimborne Minster BH21 1EE (Tel: 01202 886116). Open for NGS

The centuries have left their mark on house, park and garden, from the monastic Saxon stewpond to the serpentine-walled kitchen garden built by Napoleonic prisoners-of-war, where organic produce is usually for sale. Fine trees, a courtyard massed with herbs, and a landscaped rose garden add to the interest. 13 acres in all.

DOMINEY'S YARD

Mr and Mrs William Gueterbock, Buckland Newton DT2 7BS (01300 345295; www.domineys.com) Open for NGS, and by appt

A rich seasonal display of bulbs, herbaceous plants, shrubs and trees surrounds the 16th-century thatched cottage, and vegetables, fruit and arboretum trees all prosper amazingly in the fertile and adaptable greensand of this charmingly rural part of Dorset. 5 acres.

EDMONDSHAM HOUSE

Mrs J. Smith, Edmondsham, Cranborne, Wimborne Minster BH21 5RE (01725 517207). House open April and Oct, Wed, 2 – 5pm. Garden open April to Oct, Wed and Sun, 2 – 5pm, and by appt

The charismatic house, ranging in date from the 16th to the 18th centuries, and its attractive dairy are matched in interest by the 1-acre walled garden with its deep and colourful herbaceous borders and succulent displays of vegetables and fruit, all managed organically. Fine trees and an interesting early 'cockpit' in the surrounding 6 acres.

MORETON GARDENS

Tom and Debra Penny, Moreton DT2 8RF (01929 405084). Open all year, daily, 10am – 5pm, and by appt for evening parties

The 3-acre garden shows the influence of Jekyll in the design of paved roundels, pergolas and long views, softened by a profusion of roses, herbaceous borders and a woodland area abounding in hostas, azaleas and lilies. Some original trees remain, and a stream flows through the grounds. A new garden is centred around a replica of the font in the famous local church.

THE OLD RECTORY, PULHAM

Mr and Mrs N. Elliott, Pulham, Dorchester DT2 7EA
(01258 817595). Open for NGS and by appt for
parties

Surrounding the fine 18th-century house are
well-maintained and formal gardens attractively
planted with flower-filled parterres and
ecclesiastical borders, sheltered by yew hedges,
pleached hornbeams and mature trees. Beyond
lie woodland and a shrubbery, two ponds and a
small arboretum. Superb views. 14 acres
including two woods.

THE PRIEST'S HOUSE MUSEUM

23-27 High Street, Wimborne Minster BH21 1HR
(01202 882533; www.priest-house.co.uk). Open April
to Oct, Mon – Sat, 10am – 4.30pm. Advisable to check
in advance

The 100-metre-long walled garden behind the
museum (itself well worth a visit) has an
appealing lay-out of lawn, herbaceous and herb
borders, and some formal beds, well cared for
by a team of helpful volunteers.

SNAPE COTTAGE

Ian and Angela Whinfield, Chaffeymoor, Bourton
SP8 5BZ (01747 840330; www.snapestakes.com).
Open Feb to Aug, last 2 Suns in month; May to Aug,
Thurs; all 10.30am – 5pm. Also open parties by appt

The 0.6-acre garden is planted with a profusion
of old-fashioned and uncommon perennials,
from snowdrops to asters. Summer borders are
designed in a naturalistic cottage-garden style,
and the main themes are wildlife conservation
and plants with a history.

Snape Cottage

DURHAM

For further information about how to use the *Guide*
and for an explanation of the symbols, see pages vi–viii.
Specific dates and times are those given to us by garden owners for 2008.
For 2009 dates, check with the individual properties.
For opening dates under the National Gardens Scheme,
readers should consult *The Yellow Book* or www.ngs.org.uk.
Maps are to be found at the end of the *Guide*.
Some gardens have postal addresses in one county and are physically situated in
another. If in doubt, check the index.

BEDBURN HALL GARDENS

A 10-acre terraced garden, largely developed by the present owner, beautifully situated by Hamsterley Forest. It is dominated by a lake with associated rhododendrons and bamboos. A 17-metre lavender bed and a fruit cage of similar size are recent additions. A well-established conservatory contains passion flowers and other exotics. Lilies and fuchsias are a speciality, and azaleas and rhododendrons, roses, lilies, fuchsias and autumn-tinted leaves give a long season of colour and interest.

Mr I. Bonas

Hamsterley, Bishop Auckland DL13 3NN.
Tel: (01388) 4888231

9m NW of Bishop Auckland, W of A68,
3m SE of Wolsingham off B6293

Open for NGS, and by appt at other times

Entrance: £3, children 50p

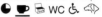

THE BOWES MUSEUM GARDEN

(Historic Garden Grade II)

In front of the museum to the south, beneath a stone balustrade, a traditional herbaceous border announces a formal parterre, redesigned in 1982 to complement the style of the building designed in 1869 by Jules Pellechet for John Bowes. The raised beds of the parterre are edged with box, which if laid out would stretch for over one and a half miles. There are 23 acres of grounds, planted with 56 different tree species. A double avenue starts behind the east lodge and follows the park perimeter; the trees mark a carriageway which once led from the main gate to the first site of the Bowes chapel. The low terrace wall and enclosed garden and tennis courts are on the site of the chapel, also now a picnic area, and the yews survive from this scheme. (The chapel itself was moved to a new site near the main gates.) The trees continue as a windbreak round the whole of the northern edge of the grounds, with exotics such as Wellingtonias and a monkey puzzle planted in front of the native species. The mound behind the car park has been designed as a retreat, with shrubs and statues.

The Bowes Museum

Barnard Castle DL12 8NP.
Tel: (01833) 690606;
www.thebowesmuseum.org.uk

In Barnard Castle

Museum open all year, daily except
25th and 26th Dec, and 1st Jan,
10am – 5pm (closes 4pm in winter)

Garden and park open all year, daily,
dawn – dusk.

Entrance: free (museum £7, OAPs £6,
children under 16 free)

Crook Hall and
Gardens

Mr and Mrs K. Bell

Sidegate, Durham City DH1 5SZ.
Tel: (0191) 384 8028;
www.crookhallgardens.co.uk

In centre of Durham, near Millburn Gate

House and gardens open 21st to 24th
March, then 6th April to 28th Sept,
Sun – Thurs, 11am – 5pm

Entrance: £5.50, concessions £5, children
£4.50, family £16

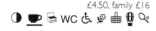

CROOK HALL AND GARDENS

The medieval manor house is surrounded by six acres of romantic themed gardens. These include secret walled gardens where venerable fruit trees are clothed with 'Rambling Rector' and 'Wedding Day' roses, a Shakespeare garden with Elizabethan plants and aromatic herbs, and the Cathedral Garden where the flower beds have been designed to represent the stained-glass windows of the cathedral. There are magnificent views of both cathedral and castle from many parts of the garden. There is also a moat pool, a wildflower meadow and a maze. An attractive, peaceful place and a must for visitors to Durham, especially in June.

Gordon Long and Malcolm Hockham

Eggleston, Barnard Castle DL12 0AG.
Tel/Answerphone: (01833) 650115;
www.egglestonhallgardens.co.uk

EGGLESTON HALL GARDENS

The early-nineteenth-century house and its lodge were designed by Ignatius Bonomi, and the four acres of walled gardens include many plants of note – *Syringa emodi*, veratrums, epimediums, fritillaries, meconopsis and a host of rare perennials. The signature plant here is *Celmisia spectabilis* 'Eggleston Silver' from New Zealand. The winding paths within the main garden hold much excitement, rounding corners to reveal colourful vistas that change with the seasons. The old churchyard, with gravestones dating from the seventeenth century, has been lovingly restored, and there are interesting plantings among the re-erected gravestones and within the sheltered, roofless area inside the church walls. Three Victorian greenhouses are still in working order and everyday use, and a good range of usual and unusual plants is for sale in the nursery.

5m NW of Barnard Castle on B6278

Open all year, daily except 25th Dec to 27th Dec, 10am – 5pm

Entrance: £1

Other information: Catering and guided tours for parties by arrangement

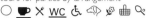

GIBSIDE

(Historic Garden Grade I)

Gibside was once one of the finest designed landscapes in England of the eighteenth century, created by a Whig MP, George Bowes of the Bowes Lyon family, another of whom fashioned St Paul's Walden Bury (see entry in Hertfordshire). In 1729, amongst wooded slopes cut through with radiating avenues, he commissioned and positioned a series of buildings – an early, more formal version of Stowe (see entry in Buckinghamshire). Each one was admirably sited, and all were constituents of a harmonious plan. Employing various architects, he built a Gothick banqueting house, a Palladian chapel and stables. The landscape *pièce de résistance* was a grand terrace with a statue to British Liberty – on a column taller than Nelson's in London – at one end and the architectural masterpiece, James Paine's stately Palladian chapel, at the other. The Trust, assisted by the National Heritage Memorial Fund, has acquired 354 acres to secure the future of this great landscape garden and to protect the chapel's setting. Well-marked walks have been opened up with views to the ruined hall, orangery and other estate buildings in the grounds. Restoration of the ruined buildings and removal of the Forestry Commission's intrusive tree planting is ongoing. Bowes also made a walled garden, part of which is now the car park and part devoted to varieties of heritage vegetables, fruit and flowers grown up to 1874.

The National Trust

Burnopfield, Gateshead NE16 6BG.
Tel: (01207) 541820;
www.nationaltrust.org.uk

6m SW of Gateshead, 20m NW of Durham from B6314, off A694 at Rowlands Gill. Signed from A1(M)

Open all year, daily except 25th to 27th Dec and 31st Dec to 2nd Jan, 10am – 4.30pm

Entrance: £5, children £3

Other information: Chapel open, service first Sun each month

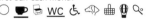

RABY CASTLE GARDENS

(Historic Garden Grade II*)

One of the country's most impressive medieval castles, once the seat of the Nevills and home to Lord Barnard's family for 380 years, is set in a 250-acre deer park and has an interesting walled garden. This formal garden, dating from the mid-eighteenth century, was designed by Thomas Wright (the Wizard of Durham) for the 2nd Earl of Darlington and has a wide array of trees, shrubs and herbaceous plants; the borders in late June are colourful and impressive. Thomas

The Rt Hon. The Lord Barnard

Staindrop, Darlington DL2 3AH.
Tel: (01833) 660202;
www.rabycastle.co.uk

1m N of Staindrop on A688 Barnard Castle – Bishop Auckland road

House open as garden but 1 – 5pm

Garden open 7th to 9th April; May, June and Sept, Sun – Wed; July and Aug, daily except Sat; plus Bank Holidays; all 11am – 5.30pm

Entrance: £5, OAPs/students £3.50, children £2.50 (12-15yrs), under 12 free

Other information:
Annual orchid show in Aug

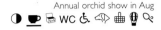

White advised on the landscaping along with Joseph Spence. The garden walls built from locally hand-made bricks have flues which used to enable sub-tropical fruits to be grown on the south terrace. The famous white Ischia fig tree, brought to Raby in 1786, still survives. Rose garden, shrub borders, original yew hedges, lakes and ornamental pond – all exceptionally well maintained.

OTHER RECOMMENDED GARDENS

AUCKLAND CASTLE DEER PARK

Bishop Auckland DL14 7NR. (01325 462966 – Smiths-Gore Chartered Surveyors; www.auckland-castle.co.uk). Open all year, daily, 7.30am – dusk

The River Gaunless traces its meandering course around precipitous bluffs and craggy outcrops of the 160-acre inner and outer parkland. Canals, avenues and groves of trees and a remarkable deer house (a scheduled monument) reveal a flurry of 18th-century landscaping activity echoing the architectural remodelling of the medieval castle. (Listed Grade II*)

MOWBRAY WINTER GARDENS

Burdon Road, Sunderland, Tyne and Wear SR1 1PP (0191 553 2323; www.twmuseums.org.uk). Open all year, daily: park, 7am – dusk, winter gardens, 10am – 5pm (opens 2pm Sun)

Restored to its former Victorian splendour, the 24-acre park is awash with colour from bedding, roses and shrubs; the southern end is more naturalistic, with a quarry garden and limestone crag. The winter gardens attached to the museum are dominated by an amazing glass and steel structure housing exotic plants and a torrential William Pye water sculpture. (Listed Grade II)

ESSEX

For further information about how to use the *Guide*
and for an explanation of the symbols, see pages vi–viii.
Specific dates and times are those given to us by garden owners for 2008.
For 2009 dates, check with the individual properties.
For opening dates under the National Gardens Scheme,
readers should consult *The Yellow Book* or www.ngs.org.uk.
Maps are to be found at the end of the *Guide*.

AUDLEY END

(Historic Garden Grade I*)

The house has long been a fascinating relic of an extraordinary Jacobean pile. Now visitors can enjoy an early version of the parterre garden, restored to the plans developed by the 3rd Lord Braybrooke and his wife *c.* 1830, advised by William Sawrey Gilpin. The design was inspired by classic seventeenth-century French parterres but with sheltering shrubberies to relate to the contemporary (1830) interiors. English Heritage has introduced the whole repertory of the flower garden of the period – irises, martagon lilies, roses, peonies and astrantias, violas, hypericums along with spring and summer bedding – all planted in some 170 beds. The herbaceous borders leading into the parterre have recently been planted out with a wide variety of perennials. The restoration has taken ten years and has been completed without interfering with the surrounding 'Capability' Brown landscape. The park buildings included a circular temple, a bridge, Lady Portsmouth's Column by Robert Adam, and a cascade constructed in the same year on the site of an ancient mill dam. There are fine planes, oaks and tulip trees, and a pond garden, laid out in 1868, containing many scented old roses and sub-tropical bedding, with a Pulhamite rock garden at one end. Everything is immaculately maintained. The walled kitchen garden, which includes a 52-metre-long vine house, a full set of service buildings, a gardeners' bothy and an orchard house, has been developed into a working organic kitchen garden laid out in the Victorian style, including fruit trees on the walls and a splendid variety of period vegetables, which are also for sale in season.

THE BETH CHATTO GARDENS ★★

Beth Chatto designed these gardens, seven acres of which are open to the public, in the 1960s from a neglected hollow which was either boggy and soggy or exceedingly dry. She, more than anyone else, has influenced gardeners by her choice of plants for any situation, and her ability to show them

English Heritage

Saffron Walden CB11 4JF.
Tel: (01799) 522399;
www.english-heritage.org.uk

1m W of Saffron Walden on B1383

House open as grounds, but different opening and closing times

Garden open April to Sept, Wed – Sun, 10am – 6pm; March and Oct, Sat and Sun, 10am – 5pm (last admission 1 hour before closing)

Entrance: £5, OAPs £3.80, children under 16 £2.50, family £12.50 (house and grounds £9.20, OAPs £6.90, children under 16 £5, family £23)

Other information: Snowdrop walks in spring (Sat and Sun only) – telephone for details.

Mrs Beth Chatto

Elmstead Market, Colchester CO7 7DB.
Tel: (01206) 822007;
www.bethchatto.co.uk

3m E of Colchester, 0.25m E of Elmstead Market on A133

The Beth Chatto Gardens

Open March to Oct, Mon – Sat, 9am – 5pm; Nov to Feb, Mon – Fri, 9am – 4pm, and for parties by appt

Entrance: £4.50, accompanied children under 14 free

off to perfection. Her planting is a lesson to every gardener on how to use both leaf and flower to best advantage. The large gravel garden which she planted to replace the old car park is maturing well as a home for beautiful plants which can thrive in very dry conditions. In the last few years some of the earliest borders have been renewed, and part of the Mediterranean garden has been given over to scree beds – a setting for the smaller plants in the form of five irregular islands. The other major change has taken time to evolve: the creation of five large ponds, each slightly lower than the other, at the heart of the garden. On the perimeter of the garden, a patch of woodland garden nurtures shade-loving plants. The beautifully designed and photographed handbook (£3) includes a fully descriptive catalogue. Adjoining is the excellent *Unusual Plants Nursery.*

Mr and Mrs T. Chamberlain

Great Yeldham CO9 4PT.
Tel: (01787) 237370

10m N of Braintree, on A1017 between Halstead and Haverhill

Open by appt

Entrance: by donation to collecting box

CRACKNELLS ★

Mr Chamberlain started contouring this 12-acre plot even before he started building his house. The landscape rolls away down to the lake, also excavated at the start. This is not a garden in the accepted sense but 'a garden picture painted with trees', to use his own words. He has gathered together an impressive collection from all over the country. Here is the rare cut-leaf beech, *Fagus sylvatica* var. *heterophylla*, and its purple- and pink-leaved forms, 'Rohanii' and 'Purpurea Tricolor', as well as the variegated tulip tree, *Liriodendron tulipifera* 'Aureomarginatum'. There are also collections of birches, acers, sorbus and oaks. If you are a lover of trees, make your pilgrimage.

23 DOCKLANDS AVENUE

This is a real plantsman's garden: one acre with large themed rooms, a copse of tree ferns and cardiocrinums underplanted with arisaemas and hostas, and a natural pond fringed by candelabra primulas. At the height of the season, in late spring and early summer, it is an extravaganza of colour, carefully planned with a sure eye for design and the most effective combination of plants. Many different varieties of agapanthus, alstroemeria, delphinium (more than 20 varieties), hemerocallis (in excess of 40 varieties), iris, penstemons and phlox catch the eye at the lower levels, while clematis (at least 100 varieties), eremurus and roses add yet more colour, and height, to this vibrant garden. There is also an orchid house.

Doreen and Paul Crowder

Ingatestone CM4 9DS.
Tel: (01277) 352815

6 miles SW of Chelmsford off A414. From Margaretting take B1002 to Ingatestone; turn left at village sign opposite playing field

Open for NGS, and May to July for parties of 12 or more by appt

Entrance: £3, children free

NEW ● 💵 WC ♿

GLEN CHANTRY ★

The present owners started laying out their garden on a gently sloping three-acre site in 1976, and it is now at the peak of its maturity, magnificent and impeccably maintained. The design is both elegant and rather informal, with lawns swooping around beds massed with the rare and the unusual. Plants with different requirements thrive in a variety of carefully cultivated habitats, and the enviably wide range that results is maintained throughout the year. Spring sees an abundance of bulbs, woodland plants and early alpines, and in early summer the beds are beautifully planted with many euphorbias, plants with variegated foliage, grasses lightened by groups of *Allium sieboldii* and *A. christophii*, some very pretty irises, and much more. And so on, to autumn colour, seed heads and berries, and the brave flowers of winter. Two pools patterned with water lilies are densely fringed with moisture-lovers, and large tufa rock gardens have areas of shingle planted with alpines and scree-loving plants. The adjoining nursery sells a wide variety of plants – some are old favourites, others uncommon or more of a challenge to grow.

Wol and Sue Staines

Wickham Bishops, Witham CM8 3LG.
Tel: (01621) 891342;
www.glenchantry.demon.co.uk

9m NE of Chelmsford off A12, 2m SE of Witham. Turn left off B1018 towards Wickham Bishops. Pass golf course, cross River Blackwater bridge and turn left up Ishams Chase by Blue Mills

Open 4th April to 30th Aug, Fri and Sat, 10am – 4pm. Coaches by appt

Entrance: £3.50, children 50p

◑ 💵 🍽 WC ♿ 🐾

Glen Chantry

HILL HOUSE

Mr and Mrs R. Mason

Chappel, Colchester CO6 2DX.
Tel: (01787) 222428

8m W of Colchester on A1124 between Colchester and Earls Colne

Open by appt

Entrance: by donation to charity

The 4.5-acre garden was designed by the owners on formal lines, using yew hedging and walls to create vistas, and with a lime avenue sited to lead the eye out into the country. A mixed planting of tough native trees like sorbus and hawthorn has been established as a windbreak. A small courtyard with a raised pool, reminiscent of a London plot, is planted with green-leaved plants and white flowers only. Another feature is a pond with two black swans. The bones of the garden are in place including urns, statues and seats, and all the colour and secondary planting has now been introduced. Further land has been acquired giving a fine view over the Colne Valley and Chappel Viaduct, and hedges and trees are being established here. May and June are recommended months to visit.

LANGTHORNS PLANTERY

The Cannon family

High Cross Lane West, Little Canfield, Dunmow CM6 1TD.
Tel: (01371) 872611;
www.langthorns.com

3m W of Great Dunmow, 5m E of M11 junction 8, on A120

Plantery open daily, 10am – 5pm

Garden open by appt

Entrance: free

The owners are well known as avid collectors of unusual plants, which they propagate in the nursery. Their six-acre garden is a good place to appreciate an impressive number of plants in combination; it has now been revamped and is open to the public on a limited basis. The nursery itself stocks one of the widest ranges of good-quality plants in the country, including trees, shrubs, conservatory plants, alpines and herbaceous perennials. There are also a good collection of clematis and honeysuckles, and many unusual forms of tricyrtis, geraniums and salvias.

THE MAGNOLIAS

Mr and Mrs R. A. Hammond

18 St John's Avenue, Brentwood CM14 5DF. Tel: (01277) 220019;
www.themagnolias.co.uk

From A1023 turn S to A128. After 300 metres turn right at traffic lights, over railway bridge. St John's Avenue is third on right

Open several days a year (telephone or consult website for details); also open by appt

Entrance: £1.50, children 50p

The garden may be a bit of a jungle, but it is a plantsman's delight, with 70 different magnolias, camellias, hostas, bamboos and epimediums. The open days are spaced over eight months so that visitors can catch the seasonal highlights. The front garden (7.5 × 6 metres) has impressive trees and shrubs – *Carpenteria californica* with white-flowered *Solanum jasminoides* growing through it, *Cercis canadensis* 'Forest Pansy', *Sophora microphylla* and *Cytisus battandieri*. A shady path leads to a long narrow garden with seven ponds, and mature trees and plantings, including trilliums, *Embothrium coccineum* (Chilean firebush), a *Magnolia campbellii* which did its first reasonable flowering twenty-five years after planting, in time for the owners' silver wedding anniversary, and several flowering cornus including 'Norman Hadden'.

MARKS HALL ★

The Thomas Phillips Price Trust

Coggeshall CO6 1TG
Tel: (01376) 563796;
www.markshall.org.uk

1.5 m N of Coggeshall on B1024. Signposted from Coggeshall by-pass

The Trust was formed in 1971 to oversee the restoration of the then-derelict grounds and gardens. They made an inspired choice in selecting Brita Schoenaich in 1999 to redesign the wonderful walled garden. With eighteenth-century brick walls on three sides, the garden slopes down and is open to the lake on its fourth side. This creates a micro-climate that enables unusual and exotic plants such as giant echiums and

Marks Hall

oleanders to be grown. Dominated by a towering *Magnolia grandiflora*, the walled garden contains five exciting and unusual areas, including an earth sculpture in the shape of a tilted slab of soil like a giant's footprint. A pittosporum hedge, stone walling and slate paths run like threads uniting the different areas, where the planting is sometimes dense and feathery, sometimes simple and strong-boned, and the colour schemes vary between dazzlingly pure and dazzlingly complex. Along the top runs the 160-metre long border, the longest in East Anglia, combining contemporary and traditional plants, grey grasses and a succession of flowering plants and shrubs. The walled garden is at the centre of the 200-acre arboretum, planted on a geographical basis representing the world's temperate zones; three woodland walks wind among and around often-unfamiliar trees and shrubs. The landscaping is always changing and new projects are constantly being developed; there are already two lakes, a taxodium swamp inhabited by many amphibians and insects, a millennium walk planted for winter colour and scent, and a 0.75-mile avenue where some 200-year-old oaks survive.

Open Jan to March, Nov to Dec, Fri – Sun, 10am – 4pm; April to Oct, Tues – Sun, 10.30am – 5pm. Closed over Christmas period

Entrance: £3, children (5–15) £1

OLIVERS

This is a wonderfully atmospheric garden surrounded by woodland originally planted in the seventeenth century with rides cut through; many fine old trees survive. The Georgian-fronted house is sited on a hill with a fine view of the gardens and woodland. In spring the borders on the generous Yorkstone terrace in front of the house blossom into a spectacular display of tapestry bedding, with tulips, white myosotis and wallflowers planted closely together. Wicker fighting-cock baskets used as frost protectors make an amusing feature early in the year. Yew hedges divide the well-planted borders below the terrace into small sections, each with a different colour theme; *Ceanothus repens* is a wonderful

Mr and Mrs David Edwards

Olivers Lane, Colchester CO2 0HJ. Tel: (01206) 330575

3m SW of Colchester off B1022 Maldon road. Follow signs to Colchester Zoo. From zoo continue 0.75m towards Colchester and at round-about turn right. After 0.25m turn right again into Olivers Lane. From Colchester pass Shrub End church and Leather Bottle pub then turn left at second roundabout

Open by appt

Entrance: £3, children free

sight in full bloom. A 'willow pattern' bridge crosses the first of a succession of pools dropping down to an ancient fish pond, with *Taxodium distichum*, metasequoia, ginkgo and tree ferns flourishing by the waterside. Beyond, an orchard and a collection of quinces and medlars merge into a natural meadow – cut only to encourage wild flowers and grasses – which spreads out to the trees bordering the river. There is also a delightful woodland walk, where mature native trees shelter rhododendrons, azaleas and shrub roses in the rides.

RHS GARDEN HYDE HALL ★

The Royal Horticultural Society

Rettendon, Chelmsford CM3 8ET.
Tel: (01245) 400256; www.rhs.org.uk

7m SE of Chelmsford, signed from A130

Open all year, daily except 25th Dec,
10am – 6pm (last admission 5pm),
(closes dusk Oct to March)

Entrance: £5, children (5–16) £1.50

Other information: Guide dogs only

Within a total holding of 360 acres, the cultivated area of the garden – in excess of 24 acres – is perched above the East Anglian wheatfields in a truly Tuscanesque manner. Very low rainfall and the exposed nature of the site combine to make it a challenging place to garden in, but by choosing the right plants for the right places the RHS has demonstrated that it is possible even in adverse conditions to create a garden of beauty. Overall, great efforts have been made to give Hyde Hall year-round colour and interest, with over 300,000 bulbs alone planted during the past few years. The garden demonstrates an eclectic range of horticultural styles, from the formality of clipped hedges in the Hilltop Garden to the naturalistic planting of perennials and grasses on Clover Hill. The now-famous dry garden boasts many thousands of healthy-looking plants in hundreds of varieties. The original rose garden contains a number of species roses interplanted with naturalised *Eremurus robustus*, while the newer rose beds, surrounded by low yew hedging, are given added height by tall obelisks supporting climbing roses. The colour-themed herbaceous borders are at their best in late summer, and the gardens hold a National Collection of viburnums. The two-acre Robinson Garden, completed in 2007 in memory of Helen and Dick Robinson, who bequeathed the land and their own flourishing garden to the Society in 1993, is a dell garden planted with over 150 different perennials as well as numerous shrubs. The heavy stone walls are clad in ferns and ivy, and two fine bridges made of English oak enable visitors to look down into the garden and over a lake, parkland and farmland. Also new in 2007 were the vegetable plots, each one different, either demonstrating alternative systems of cultivation and growing (for example the 'no dig system') or showcasing a selection of vegetables from various parts of the world. Five hectares of wildflower meadow will be sown in 2008.

R. AND R. SAGGERS ★

R. and R. Saggers

Waterloo House, High Street, Newport,
Saffron Walden CB11 3PG.
Tel: (01799) 540858;
www.randrsaggers.co.uk

This small, immaculately kept nursery has a charming 0.25-acre town garden running down between flint walls to a stream where an amusing clipped box character in a hat carries under his arm a vase overflowing with running water. Old-fashioned roses and many rare and unusual trees and plants are propagated and grown *in situ*, and there is a new trend towards Mediterranean species such as the hardy *Poncirus trifoliata* with its white flowers and plentiful crop of oranges, olive trees, bananas and others that require some winter protection. Early June sees the garden at its peak, but a good range of statues, urns, Whichford pots and armillary sundials may be bought all year.

6m S of Saffron Walden on B1383 through Newport

Open all year, daily except Mon (but open Bank Holiday Mons), 10am – 5pm (closed Suns, Jan to March)

Entrance: free

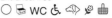

SALING HALL
(Historic Garden Grade II)

Hugh Johnson's wonderful garden is clearly the work of a tree lover – a rare example of a picturesque landscape created by a very wide-ranging dendrological collection. The whole garden is planned as a succession of vistas given definition and mood by the choice of trees. When the huge elms of Saling died, he turned the 12 acres of chalky boulder clay into an arboretum of genera that thrive on alkaline clay or gravel. A collection of pines, quercus, sorbus, aesculus, acers, prunus, tilias, fraxinus, fagus, salix and betulas leads the eye to a classical Temple of Pisces. There are many rarities like *Carpinus fangiana*, *Tilia oliveri*, *Toona sinensis*, *Staphylea colchica*, weeping Chinese juniper, incense cedars from Oregon seed, and unusual pines. Japanese maples have also been a striking success. In the south-west facing walled garden apple trees are trimmed into parasol shapes to provide shade on parallel lawns between beds and borders planted informally and generously with roses, shrubs and perennials. There is also a vegetable garden, a Japanese garden, a water garden, a secret garden and a strange menhir in its private yew-hedged 'chapel'. The old moat with its cascade is home to some substantial carp.

Mr and Mrs Hugh Johnson

Great Saling, Braintree CM7 5DT

6m NW of Braintree, halfway between Braintree and Dunmow on B1256; turn N at Blake End

Open May to July, Wed, 2 – 5pm and for parties by written appt, Mon – Fri

Entrance: £3, children free

WOOLARD'S ASH

The seventeenth-century house (not open) started life as a humble farmhouse and has now grown to comfortable proportions. The estate covers nearly 30 acres, and since retiring in 1995, the owner has spent much of his time designing and redesigning the three-acre garden; there are now five distinct rooms bounded by neatly clipped yew and beech hedging. The vegetable garden is screened by a hedge of colourful and sweetly scented *Rosa mundi*, and the main garden, with the aid of the ha-ha, has a beautiful view of the borrowed landscape. His favourite garden is Sissinghurst, reflected here in the many soft colours of the sumptuous mixed borders, which reach their peak when the roses are in full bloom; further plantings soften the swimming pool and tennis court and extend into the paddock. In every part of the garden visitors will have a sense of tranquillity and intimacy, no more so than in the wild meadow, where time seems to stand still as the seed-heads of the grasses sway to and fro in the breeze. A flock of chocolate-brown Castlemilk Morit sheep, peacocks, guinea fowl and bantams add to the atmosphere.

Michael and Judy Herbert

Hatfield Broad Oak CM22 7JY.
Tel: (01279) 718284

5m SE of Bishops Stortford between A120 and A1060. From Hatfield Broad Oak follow B183 N, signed to Takeley; after 0.75m take 1st right, signed to Taverners Green and Broomshawbury, then 2nd right to Woolards Ash. From Takeley take B183 S, signed to towards Hatfield Broad Oak; after 0.75m take 1st left, signed to Canfield and High Roding, then 2nd left to Woolards Ash

Open for NGS, and May to July for parties by appt

Entry £3.50

Other information: Refreshments by arrangement

NEW ☾ WC

OTHER RECOMMENDED GARDENS

THE ECHO GARDEN

Oaklands Park, Moulsham Street, Chelmsford
CM2 9AQ. Open all year, daily, 7am – dusk

An imaginative dry garden of 0.25 acres
created by Bella D'Arcy with the enthusiastic
cooperation of local primary-school children.
The peripatetic nymph Echo is the theme, the
planting distinctively Mediterranean, and three
sculptures by Tom Grimsey relate to echoes,
vibration and repetition. A worthwhile and
attractive community project.

THE ELEMENTS GARDEN

Boleyn Gardens, White Hart Lane, Chelmsford
CM2 5PA. Open all year, daily, 7.30am – dusk

Another stylish space designed by Bella D'Arcy
within an attractive local park. It is a
contemporary garden with a mass of
herbaceous and exotic flowers for late summer
and autumn, planted with the aid of local
children. In the centre, a swirling concrete path
set in lawns focuses on a forceful sculpture –
the Sphere of Wind and Fire.

THE GIBBERD GARDEN

Marsh Lane, Gilden Way, Harlow CM17 0NA
(01279 442112; www.thegibberdgarden.co.uk).
Open Feb for snowdrops and Oct for autumn festival
(telephone for details); then April to Sept ,Wed, Sat,
Sun and Bank Holiday Mons, 2 – 6pm

The architect and art collector Sir Frederick
Gibberd's design for his own 7-acre garden was
a pioneering attempt at creating an episodic

garden defined by sculpture. Dramatic and
tranquil by turns, it has been lauded by Hugh
Johnson as 'one of the most important gardens
in the history of the twentieth century'. (Listed
Grade II)

INGATESTONE HALL

Lord Petre, Ingatestone CM4 9NR (01277 353 5010).
Open Easter to July, plus Sept, Sat, Sun and Bank
Holiday Mons; Aug, Wed – Sun and Bank Holiday
Mons; all 1 – 6pm

The garden framing the Elizabethan house
(itself well worth a visit) is evocative of its long
history, complete with a gunnera-fringed
stewpond, a rose-filled walled garden, shaded
walks, immaculate lawns and an eclectic choice
of specimen trees. 7 acres including woodland.

PERRYMANS

Mr and Mrs R Human, Dedham Road, Boxted,
Colchester CO4 5SL (01206 272297). Open by appt

The 10-acre garden was spurred into being by
a Beth Chatto visit in 1973; lakes were dug, 3
acres of woodland planted, many climbing roses
added and vegetable and contemporary
gardens laid out. Colourful and interesting all
year, especially from March to July.

TYE FARM

Mrs A. Gooch, Colchester Road, Elmstead Market,
Colchester CO7 7AX (01206 822400). Open by appt

The 1-acre garden has been cleverly
compartmented by hedges to fend off the
prevailing winds. The varied and different areas
– an abundance of roses, a yellow-themed
walled garden, a formal layout in front of a
well-stocked conservatory – are planted with
knowledgeable flair so that the seasons
merge colourfully.

The Gibberd Garden

GLOUCESTERSHIRE

For further information about how to use the *Guide*
and for an explanation of the symbols, see pages vi–viii.
Specific dates and times are those given to us by garden owners for 2008.
For 2009 dates, check with the individual properties.
For opening dates under the National Gardens Scheme,
readers should consult *The Yellow Book* or www.ngs.org.uk.
Maps are to be found at the end of the *Guide*.
Some gardens have postal addresses in one county and are physically situated in
another. If in doubt, check the index.

ABBOTSWOOD ★★
(Historic Garden Grade II*)

In this most beautiful of Cotswold settings the 20-acre garden retains its Edwardian charm, merging gently into the landscape with descending streams, surrounding woodland and pastoral views. The elegant formal gardens around the house were originally designed by Lutyens with a spectacular fountain, a terraced lawn, a sunken garden, a lily pond and a rose garden, all planted in harmonious Jekyll style. The box-edged blue garden, with its deep blue forget-me-nots and later *Salvia farinacea*, is particularly attractive. Herbaceous borders are full of interest and colour, and there are extensive heather beds, flowering shrubs, specimen trees and, artfully framed by dense foliage, luscious rhododendrons in shades of pink (no shrieking oranges here). In spring fritillaries yield to spotted orchids in the wild garden beside the stream that meanders down into the wooded ravine, its slopes massed with bulbs, and into the Dikler river, widened to form a lake in the field beside the drive. The prolific and immaculate walled garden, usually open later in the season, is well worth the short walk.

Dikler Farming Co
Stow-on-the-Wold GL54 1EN.
Tel: (01451) 830173

1m W of Stow on B4077

Open 13th April, 11th May, 1st June, 6th July, 3rd Aug and 14th Sept, 1.30 – 6pm

Entrance: £4, children free

Other information: Coaches must drop passengers at top gate and park in Stow

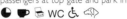

ALDERLEY GRANGE
(Historic Garden Grade II)

A two-acre garden of character and charm in a tranquil walled setting, renowned for its collection of aromatic plants and scented flowers. Designed by the late Alvilde Lees-Milne, it is believed to be the last garden in which Vita Sackville-West had a hand. The fine house and a mulberry tree date from the seventeenth century; a pleached and arched lime walk leads to a series of enclosed gardens. There is a notable hexagonal herb garden with many delightful perspectives of clipped, trained or potted shrubs and trees, and abundant plantings of old roses, tender and unusual plants.

Mr Guy and The Hon. Mrs Acloque
Alderley GL12 7QT.
Tel: (01453) 842161

6m N of Chipping Sodbury, 2m S of Wotton-under-Edge. Turn NW off A46 Bath – Stroud road at Dunkirk

Open June by appt

Entrance: £3.50, children free

119

BARNSLEY HOUSE ★

Rupert Pendered and Tim Haigh

Barnsley, Nr Cirencester GL7 5EE.
Tel: (01285) 740000

4m NE of Cirencester on B4425

Open for NGS, 17th and 29th
May, 11am – 5pm, and for small
parties throughout the year,
strictly by prior appt

Entrance: £5

Other information: Coaches on open
days only by prior appt. Refreshments
available at Village Pub opposite house

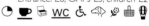 X WC & B&B

This was a highly influential garden in its day, comprising many garden styles from the past, carefully blended by Rosemary and David Verey after 1951. The 1697 Cotswold stone house (now a country-house hotel and restaurant) is set in the middle of the four-acre garden, surrounded on three sides by a 1770 stone wall. Borders create vistas and divide the garden into areas of distinct and individual character, and great attention is paid to colour and texture. The laburnum, allium and wisteria walk and the potager with its numerous small beds were renowned in their day; the latter has been enlarged into the adjacent field to meet the demands made upon it by the hotel kitchen. The thought is bound to surface that a living replica cannot be preserved indefinitely – will the cunningly concealed sauna take precedence over the garden? However, Barnsley will remain both her creation and her memorial.

BATSFORD ARBORETUM ★
(Historic Garden Grade I)

The Batsford Foundation

Batsford Park, Moreton-in-Marsh
GL56 9QB. Tel: (01386) 701441;
www.batsarb.co.uk

1.5m NW of Moreton-in-Marsh
on A44 to Evesham

Open all year, daily, 10am – 5pm
(times may vary Dec and Jan)

Entrance: £6, OAPs £5, children £2

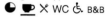 WC &

From 1886 Algernon Mitford (the first Lord Redesdale), grandfather of the celebrated social and literary sisterhood, started to assemble in the 56 acres surrounding this newly built mansion a collection of Chinese and Japanese trees and shrubs, with bamboos a special interest and bronze statues an additional decorative element. Some of the major specimens survive from this time, together with rockeries, water features and a hermit's cave created by the Pulham brothers; a 'swampery' is an unusual combination of bog and stumpery. In 1916 the property passed to the first Lord Dulverton, likewise a horticultural enthusiast, and his son continued to preserve and extend the collection, which is now managed by a charitable trust. Every season has its highlights: aconites and snowdrops, daffodils and bluebells, magnolias and a National Collection of Japanese cherries, through to the autumn colours of prunus, sorbus and acers and the skeletal allure of winter. While dendrologists will appreciate the rarities, every visitor will derive pleasure from the varied walks, westward among towering woodland trees, eastward through the water garden to the little church and Batsford village, passing magnificent views onto the house and the wider landscape. The adjoining nursery is noted for its rare trees and shrubs.

BOURTON HOUSE ★

Mr and Mrs R. Paice

Bourton-on-the-Hill, Moreton-in-Marsh
GL56 9AE. Tel: (01386) 700754;
www.bourtonhouse.com

2m W of Moreton-in-Marsh on A44

Open 28th May to Aug, Wed – Fri;
Sept to Oct, Thurs and Fri; plus 25th
and 26th May, 24th and 25th Aug; and
for NGS; all 10am – 5pm

The handsome eighteenth-century Baroque Cotswold house with fine views is enhanced by its 10-acre garden which is an inspiring alternative to traditional country-house acres. The diminutive geometrical potager is a particular delight. Well-kept lawns, quiet fountains, a knot garden and Cotswold stone walls are set off by a number of herbaceous borders which make skilful use of current fashions in garden design. The colours and choice of plants are bold and sophisticated,

Bourton House

mixing spiky, semi-tropical, traditional and unusual species in a versatile display. Each year there are new interests – a raised pond in the top garden, a topiary walk, and long terraces on the main lawn planted with low-growing shrubs, perennials and roses. The plantation in the field opposite is a pleasure to roam, and a gallery of local arts, crafts and design has opened in the tithe barn. The cocoon-like shade-house is a flourishing environment for novel shade-loving plants. Many of the plants may be unfamiliar to visitors; labels would be welcome.

Entrance: £5.50, OAPs £5, children free

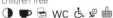

CERNEY HOUSE GARDENS ★

Around the house remodelled by Decimus Burton in 1791, goats, sheep and horses graze and wild flowers flourish in their meadow. The 10-acre garden laid out in a sheltered hollow surrounded by woodland is a dream. The walled garden, filled with vegetables, riotous herbaceous borders, old-fashioned roses and clematis, occupies 3.5 acres. As you enjoy the view down the gazebo walk you may, if you are lucky, see the resident peacock in full display framed by roses at the far end. In May masses of tulips flower in informal groups among the herbaceous plants and formally in beds and pots. The woodland walk is carpeted with snowdrops and bluebells, with abundant spring bulbs all around. The rockery, geranium and thyme bank and pink border beside the swimming pool are well established, the herb garden richly stocked. A genera

Sir Michael and Lady Angus

North Cerney, Cirencester GL7 7BX.
Tel: (01285) 831300/831205;
www.cerneygardens.com

3.5m N of Cirencester off A435 Cheltenham road. Turn left opposite Bathurst Arms, follow road up hill past church, signed to Bagendon, and turn in through gates on right

Open April to July, Tues, Wed, Fri and Sun, 10am – 5pm, and for parties by appt at other times

Entrance: £4, children £1

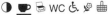

garden leads down to a pond and a tree trail. The happy and unrestrained plants include a National Collection of tradescantias. Informative labelling is a bonus, including those in the new beds to the side of the house telling the stories of plant-hunters and famous nurserymen. The locality is rich in history, with *Chedworth Roman Villa* a few miles away (note the attractive Roman snails meandering along the paths). The beautiful twelfth-century church nearby is well worth a visit.

COLESBOURNE PARK ★

Henry and Carolyn Elwes

Near Cheltenham GL53 9NP.
Tel: (01242) 870264;
www.colesbournegardens.org.uk

6m S of Cheltenham on A435

Open 26th Jan to 24th Feb, Sat and Sun,
for snowdrops; then 24th March,
27th and 28th Sept; all 1 – 4.30pm;
and for parties by appt, Mon – Fri

Entrance: £6, children free

One of the joys of late winter and early spring in the Cotswolds is a visit to the famous snowdrop collection at Colesbourne Park, and the season has now been extended by a restoration project to celebrate the great days of that celebrated Victorian plantsman and collector, Henry John Elwes. Then the garden was world-famous for its trees as well as its bulbs, and now early-flowering scented shrubs and many thousands of small-flowered daffodils have been planted to sparkle in meadow and lakeside, and a superb collection of hellebores is flourishing among other bulbs in woodland. But the glory of the garden is still the snowdrops – great swathes and drifts spreading in variety through the woods and beside the lake, and some 250 rare and beautiful cultivars displayed in the Spring Garden and in raised beds near the house, where formal beds open onto wide lawns with vistas and gentle prospects across the surrounding parkland.

Colesbourne Park

COTSWOLD FARM

A mature four-acre garden of the classic English country house kind, planted by succeeding generations of the family, and sustained with sensitive artistry, surrounding a fine Arts and Crafts house in a traditional Cotswold setting. The attractive terrace was designed by Norman Jewson in 1938. The formal walled gardens have a pool and are planted with shrub, bush and climbing roses, alpines, lavender and a collection of scented flowers. There are also established plantings of shrubs, herbaceous perennials and many small treasures; including a collection of snowdrops, overlooking the mercifully still unspoilt wooded valley.

Mrs Mark Birchall

Duntisbourne Abbots, Cirencester GL7 7JS. Tel: (01285) 821857

5m NW of Cirencester off A417. Turn left signed to Duntisbourne Abbots, then right, right again after 270 metres, under dual carriageway, and house drive is opposite

Open for NGS, 10th and 11th Feb for Red Cross; all 2 – 6pm; and by appt

Entrance: £4

DAYLESFORD HOUSE ★★

Warren Hastings, the first Governor-General of Bengal, bought the estate in 1788 and commissioned Samuel Pepys Cockerell to design a house in the Anglo-Indian style then becoming fashionable. Hastings, a keen gardener, employed John Davenport to create the overall layout of the garden, including the splendid Gothick orangery, walled garden and lakes. Since 1988 the present owners have gradually restored and re-created the original combination of semi-natural parkland, with particular emphasis on naturalised plantings that contrast with the more formal areas. In its strikingly beautiful setting, with sweeping lawns, lakes and woodland, every aspect is a delight. The orangery has a sensational display of blue *Salvia guarantica* along the south-facing wall, as well as a collection of citrus in huge clay pots and in a central bed underplanted with box. Behind is the sheltered Secret Garden designed by Rupert Golby with tender exotics, a pavilion and a pool presided over by a seventeenth-century Neptune; his blue-and-white planting schemes continue into the border outside. Above the orangery shrubs and climbing roses have been planted in meadowland. From the top lake a waterfall cascades into the dell, the stream flowing over a series of falls designed by Colvin and Moggridge in a scheme close to the original before emptying into the bottom lake. A scented walk and stumpery lead to the two-acre walled garden designed by Mary Keen and Lady Bamford with peach and orchid houses, an impressive potager and a series of yew-hedged areas, with a cut-flower garden and quince lawn leading to the raised rose garden. Topiary echoes the Anglo-Indian theme of the house. Inspiring and immaculately maintained, the whole is run organically.

Sir Anthony and Lady Bamford

Daylesford Estate Office, Moreton in Marsh GL56 0YH. Tel: (01608) 658888

Off A436 between Stow-on-the-Wold and Chipping Norton

Open for NGS, and occasional charity events (contact Estate Office for details)

Entrance: £4, children free (NGS charge)

DYRHAM PARK
(Historic Garden Grade II*)

Only a tiny fragment of the extensive London and Wise Baroque garden shown in the view by Kip in 1710 survives to the east of the house. The terraces were all smoothed out in the late eighteenth century to form an 'English' landscape

The National Trust

Chippenham SN14 8ER.
Tel: (0117) 937 2501;
www.nationaltrust.org.uk

8m N of Bath, 12m E of Bristol on A46. Take M4 junction 18 towards Bath

Dyrham Park

House open as garden, Fri – Tues,
11am – 4.30pm

Garden open 14th March to 2nd Nov,
daily, 11am – 5pm. Park open all year, daily
except 25th Dec, 11am – 5pm or dusk if
earlier

Entrance: park and garden £4, children £2,
family £8.90, park only (Wed and Thurs)
£2.60, children £1.30, family £5.80 (house,
park and garden £10, children £5, family
£25)

Garden:

Park: ○ 🖼 ℃

with a fine sweeping drive bringing the visitor in from the
new entrance. Avenues of elms survived until the mid-1970s;
they have since been replaced by limes. The cascade in the
garden on the west side of the house is still working and one
can make out the form of the original garden. The west
garden is being redeveloped to combine the formal
boundaries of the eighteenth century with lush Victorian
planting and contemporary elements. Talman's great orangery
rekindles the former sense of splendour that the water
gardens must have achieved in their heyday. The views
towards Bristol and the elegance of the 'natural' landscape,
with the house and church tucked into the hillside, make this
an outstanding example of English landscape gardening. In all,
263 acres of ancient parkland.

EASTLEACH HOUSE ★

Mrs David Richards

Eastleach Martin, Cirencester GL7 3NW.
www.eastleachhouse.com

6m SW of Burford off A361 Lechlade
road or off A40 via Westwell and
Eastleach Turville. House opposite church
gates, up steep drive

Open for NGS, and guided tours by
owner for parties of 10 or more at other
times. Requests in writing please

Entrance £5, accompanied children free

Other information: Limited parking at
house for infirm or disabled. Coaches
must drop visitors at gate and park
outside village

A beautiful and relatively unknown 14-acre garden created
since 1983. The owner interweaves plants and combines
colours and textures with skill and sensitivity, handles
changes of level with panache, and creates interlocking
spaces and outdoor rooms to form a coherent flow. The
early-twentieth-century house, sitting on the top of a hill and
facing the four points of the compass, has become the
reference point, the fulcrum of the design. The rear facade
looks out across lawn to the countryside through a pair of
wrought-iron gates decorated with clematis. Beyond, a newly
planted lime avenue leads to a yew roundel encircling the
statue of a stag. A meandering path through the miniature
arboretum brings the visitor to the edge of the croquet
lawn; ascend the broad steps and opposite is an arbour and
a tapestry border of shrubs. In the walled garden roses climb
through clematis and around fastigiate Irish yews. Stand at
the west end of the house, look down onto the rill and have
your eye caught by the perfectly shaped balls of Sorbus aria
'Lutescens' beyond the borders of perennials embracing the
entire colour spectrum. Only one secret is hidden from the
house – the sunken wildlife pond beyond the walled garden.
This is a garden of sheer delight, especially in the heady days
of summer.

FRAMPTON COURT

(Historic Park & Garden Grade I)

Home of the remarkable Clifford family of female artists, who created the *Frampton Flora* (1830-1860), the elegant 1730s house stands on land owned by the family since the twelfth century. It was possibly designed by John Strahan in the style of Vanbrugh; the interior has exquisite woodwork and furnishings. The park overlooks a lake and the five-acre garden, with fine trees and a formal water garden of Dutch design. The Strawberry Hill Gothick orangery of 1750 (not always open but available for holiday letting), where the ladies are believed to have executed their work, stands reflected in the still water, planted with lilies and flanked by a mixed border. The walled garden at the orangery is now home to *Pan Global Plants*, a rare plant nursery. (Telephone (01452) 741641 for details of opening times). Visitors to the garden at Frampton Court may also be able to see that of *Frampton Manor*, also occupied by Cliffords, where a boldly planted walled garden with many unusual plants and old roses is set off splendidly by a fine fifteenth-century timbered house. (Open 24th April to 25th July, Thurs and Fri, 2.30 – 5pm).

Mr and Mrs Rollo Clifford

Frampton-on-Severn GL2 7EU.
Tel: (01452) 740268
www.framptoncourtestate.co.uk

SW of Gloucester, 2m from M5 junction 13, signposted. On left-hand side of village green through gates in long wall
House open all year for parties of 10 or more by appt

Garden open all year by appt

Entrance: £3 (house £6)

Other information: Refreshments by arrangement

 WC ♿ B&B

HIDCOTE MANOR GARDEN ★★

(Historic Garden Grade I)

One of the most famous gardens in Britain, 10.5 acres in extent, which combines a strongly architectural framework, with miles of sculptured hedges delineating a bewildering number of formal outdoor rooms. Some of these – the Pillar Garden, the Long Walk and Bathing Pool Garden – are Italianate in feeling, and many are filled with wonderfully dramatic and diverse plantings. This Arts-and-Crafts *tour de force* was created in the early years of the twentieth century by Lawrence Johnston, an American with a strong sense of design and great planting skills; although he imbibed the taste of such designers as Jekyll, Lutyens, Alfred Parsons and Norah Lindsay, he had a uniquely idiosyncratic way of combining plants. He made many new introductions and rediscovered many forgotten species, some of which he collected himself; several varieties now bear the Hidcote name. Since acquiring the garden in 1948, the Trust has done its best to retain the spirit of the original, but some parts have become overgrown in time, and recently uncovered evidence confirmed that his planting legacy was steadily eroded over the years. Thanks to a £1.6m grant in 2006, the 12-year plan is focused on making a gradual return to Johnston's own stated vision of 'a wild garden in a formal setting'. His plant house has been re-created and the East Court Gardens and Rock Bank restored. As always, a garden to watch. *The Garden at Hidcote* by Fred Whitsey, photographs by Tony Lord, is published by Frances Lincoln.

The National Trust

Hidcote Bartrim, Chipping Campden
GL55 6LR.Tel: (01386) 438333;
www.nationaltrust.org.uk

3m NE of Chipping Campden.
Signposted

Open 15th March to 2nd Nov,
Sat – Wed, plus Fri, July and Aug,
10am – 6pm (closes 5pm Oct).
Parties by written appt only. On fine weekends and Bank Holidays garden less crowded after 3pm

Entrance: £8.50, children £4.25, family £21.20

Other information: Coaches by appt only

Mr and Mrs T. K. Marshall

North Nibley, Dursley GL11 6DZ.
Tel: (01453) 547440

1.5m SW of Dursley, 2m NW of
Wotton-under-Edge near North Nibley.
Turn E off B4060 in Nibley at Black
Horse Inn and fork left after 0.25m

Open all year except Aug, Tues – Sat
and Bank Holiday Mons,
9am – 12.30pm, 1.45pm – 5pm, and
some Suns for NGS, 2 – 6pm. Closed
21st March and 25th Dec to 2nd Jan

Entrance: £3, children free

Other information: Teas on Suns only

HUNTS COURT

A must for those with a love of old roses. June sees in excess of 400 varieties – species, climbing and shrub – filling the borders, cascading over rails, pergolas and trees and spilling out over the informal grass paths which weave a passage through rare shrubs and herbaceous perennials. Summer is inevitably dominated by roses, but this is not to deny interest in other seasons, from spring-flowering shrubs to trees with good autumn colour. A more formal sundial garden with beds intersected by gravel paths provides a home for hardy geraniums, penstemons and diascias. In another area mown paths draw the eye towards the Cotswold escarpment which commands the eastern landscape. An arboretum has been added with acers and other more unusual trees and shrubs. 2.5 acres. In the adjoining nursery roses and many of the other plants growing in the garden are for sale, and the owner is on hand with advice.

Mr and Mrs J. G. Chambers

Chipping Campden GL55 6LN.
Tel: (01386) 438777; www.kiftsgate.co.uk

3m NE of Chipping Campden and near
Mickleton, very close to Hidcote, which
is signposted

Open 23rd March to April, Aug and
Sept, Sun, Mon, Wed, 2 – 6pm; May to
July, Sat – Wed, 12 noon – 6pm
(Note: opening times not identical
to Hidcote's)

Entrance: £6, children £1.50

Other information: Coaches by appt
only

KIFTSGATE COURT ★★

(Historic Garden Grade II*)

The house was built in the late nineteenth century on a magnificent six-acre site surrounded by three steep banks, and the four-acre garden was largely created by the present owner's grandmother after World War I. Her work was carried on by her daughter, Diany Binny, who made a few alterations but followed the same colour schemes in the borders, and by her grand-daughter Anne Chambers, who continues to perfect her vision. In spring, the white sunken garden is covered with bulbs, and there is a fine show of daffodils along the drive. June and July are the peak months for colour and scent, but the magnificent old and species roses are the glory of this garden, home of *Rosa filipes* 'Kiftsgate'. Notable too are perennial geraniums, a mighty wisteria and many species of hydrangea, some very large. In autumn, Japanese maples glow in the bluebell wood. Unusual plants are sometimes amongst those available for sale. Most visitors had thought of Kiftsgate as trapped in a charming time warp, when, lo and behold, the owners add a serenely simple flower-free water garden – flower-free, that is, apart from Simon Allison's inspired foliage sculpture reflected in the black water of the pool. Note: young children and the elderly should take care on the steep, uneven and sometimes slippery paths.

The Viscount Bledisloe

Lydney GL15 6BU.
Tel: (01594) 842844/842922

20m SW of Gloucester. N of A48
between Lydney and Aylburton

Open late March to early June, Wed,
Sun and Bank Holiday Mons, 10am –
5pm. Parties and guided tours by appt

LYDNEY PARK GARDENS

The park dates from the seventeenth century, and although it has been in the hands of one family since 1723, a new house was built in 1875 and the old one demolished. An area near the house has an interesting collection of magnolias, and a picturesque sight is the bank of daffodils and cherries, splendid in season. From 1955 a woodland garden was developed in the wooded valley behind and below the house, with the aim of achieving bold colour at different times between March and June. Near the entrance to the main part of the gardens is a small pool surrounded by azaleas and a collection of acers. From here the route passes through carefully planted groups of rhododendrons and past a folly, brought from Venice, which overlooks a valley and bog garden. Criss-crossing the hillside are rare and fine rhododendrons and azaleas, including an area planted with unnamed seedlings. Enormous effort has gone into the plant design, colour combination and general landscaping. Nearby is the Roman camp and museum containing the famous bronze Lydney dog, while the park has a fine collection of trees and herds of fallow deer. Eight acres.

Entrance: £4 (£3 on Weds), accompanied children 50p (2007 prices)

Other information: Picnics in deer park. Iron Age fort, Roman temple site and New Zealand museum

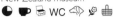

MISARDEN PARK GARDENS ★

(Historic Garden Grade II*)

This lovely, timeless English garden, which commands spectacular views over the Golden Valley, has most of the features to be expected of a garden started in the seventeenth century. Notable are the extensive yew hedges and yew walk, the York-stone terrace, the Lutyens loggia overhung with wisteria, and a good specimen of *Magnolia* × *soulangeana*. The south lawn supports splendid grass steps and a fine, ancient mulberry. West of the house the ground ascends in a series of lawns, terraces and shrubberies. Within the walled garden the long double herbaceous borders have been reconstructed with mixed plantings; themed colours link the beds. The former rose walk has been replanted as a mixed border in shades of apricot and grey, echoing the neighbouring parterre which contains hebes, lavender, tulips, alliums and 'Chanelle' roses. A rill with a fountain and a summerhouse were added as a feature to mark the millennium. Beneath the house, blue 'Rozanne' geraniums, asters and agapanthus, together with golden rubus, *Populus richardii* and gleditsia lead the eye to a venerable cedar in the deer park below. There are many fine specimen trees and the spring show of blossom and bulbs is spectacular. A good nursery (open daily except Monday) adjourns.

Major M.T. N. H. Wills

Miserden, Stroud GL6 7JA. Tel: (01285) 821303

6m NW of Cirencester, 3m off A417. Signposted

Open April to Sept, Tues – Thurs, 10am – 5pm, and for parties by appt

Entrance: £4 (inc. printed guide), children free. Guided tour extra

THE NATIONAL ARBORETUM, WESTONBIRT ★★

(Historic Arboretum Grade I)

This is perhaps the finest arboretum in Britain – 600 acres in all. Started in 1829 by Robert Stayner Holford, it was expanded and improved by successive generations of the same family until it was taken over by the Forestry Commission in 1956. Numerous grass rides divide the trees into glades used for special plantings. Westonbirt is noted for its vast range of stunning mature specimen trees. A short walk from the original arboretum is Silkwood, with collections of native, Asian and American species that in spring are carpeted

The Forestry Commission

Westonbirt, Tetbury GL8 8QS. Tel: (01666) 880220; www.forestry.gov.uk/westonbirt

3m SW of Tetbury on A433, 5m NE of A46 junction

Open all year, daily; 9am – 8pm or dusk if earlier (opens 8am Sat and Sun, closes 5pm Nov to March)

Entrance: Charges vary seasonally –
maximum for individuals £8, OAPs £7,
children £3, (reduced rates for disabled,
educational, and parties) (2007 prices)

with primroses, wood anemones and bluebells. There are in excess of 17,000 numbered trees, including an exceptional National Collection of Japanese maples, extended in 2006 by the newly planted Rotary Glade. Colour is best in May (rhododendrons, magnolias, etc.) and October (Japanese maples, Persian ironwoods, katsuras, etc.). From early December until Christmas the Enchanted Wood is illuminated at weekends with a wonderful festive display, and many champion trees are floodlit. Although it does not keep big stocks of plants, the plant centre offers some rare and interesting shrubs and trees, especially Japanese maples, conifers and specimen trees. Just across the road the fine and spacious Victorian grounds of *Westonbirt School* open for the NGS, and may also be visited at certain times during school holidays (telephone (01666) 880333 for details, or consult www.westonbirt.gloucs.sch.uk)

Charles and Mary Keen

Duntisbourne Rouse, Daglingworth,
Cirencester GL7 7AP

3m NW of Cirencester off A417. From Daglingworth take narrow valley road for the Duntisbournes. After 1m house is on right before church

Open for NGS, and for parties of 10 or more by written appt

Entrance: charge

THE OLD RECTORY, DUNTISBOURNE ROUSE ★

Since 1983 the garden writer and designer Mary Keen has created an intimate and inspiring 1.5-acre garden full of colour, variety and interest at every season. House and garden nestle among softly wooded Cotswold hills beside a tiny, unspoilt Saxon church. The garden has been designed with its exceptional setting in mind, its views drawing the eye towards the surrounding countryside. Visitors should start their tour by taking themselves up to the former schoolroom and browsing through the latest collection of cuttings and comments about the garden, giving themselves time to take in the peaceful atmosphere. It is divided into many different areas of changing levels and moods, separated by yew or box hedges. The initial calm expanse of lawn at the front of the house gives way to sunken areas of exuberant colour, an auricula house, a winter garden and a dark reflective pool. A partially hidden pathway lined with snowdrops leads to a shrub dell carpeted by wood anemones and more snowdrops. Behind the house, steps lead up through seasonally changing borders past the restored schoolhouse, to a greenhouse filled with special treasures, a gooseberry garden, a wildflower orchard with a hazel walk and mown pathways, and on into the vegetable garden and borders facing the churchyard.

Michael Stone

Ozleworth, Wotton-under-Edge
GL12 7QA. Tel: (01453) 845591

5m S of Dursley off A4135
Tetbury – Dursley road. At junction with B4058, turn S on single-track lane signed to Ozleworth, and follow signs for 2m

Open for NGS, and one day for charity

OZLEWORTH PARK ★

The garden surrounding the handsome house is quite simply magnificent: in the generosity of its spaces, the scale and sophistication of its plantings and the artistry of its design, carried out by Antony Young, Jane Fearnley-Whittingstall, Charles Hornby and the head gardener Colin Durber. Behind the house three venerable cedars stand on a huge lawn sweeping to a quarter-mile-long ha-ha. The stable courtyard to the east is substantial too, and the octagonal-towered Norman church is drawn into the assembly of

Ozleworth Park

outbuildings. There is space here only to hint at a few of the multiple enclosures laid out within yew hedges or beautiful old walls: a stepped rill with slabs of stone and square ponds, rising up a steep hillside to a wild area at the top; an espaliered pear pergola underplanted with alliums and agapanthus reached by a green yew corridor; an 1806 bath house encircled by a walkway; wide and deep borders planted with a subtle, exuberant range of shrubs and perennials; a rose garden that really is given over to roses; a little stream crossed by a wooden bridge and thickly planted with moisture-lovers. One of the most successful spaces is the water garden, tucked away at the perimeter, where two long rectangular pools studded with water lilies and separated by a bronze statue of Diana the huntress are flanked by a plump lavender hedge and a low yew hedge. Plus greenhouses, and a cutting garden, and a vast vegetable garden. Twelve acres in all, this is a twenty-first-century garden restored to its original Victorian splendour.

PAINSWICK ROCOCO GARDEN ★
(Historic Garden Grade II*)

A great deal of time, money and effort is going into the continuing restoration (almost complete redevelopment) of this rare Rococo survival. Much of the work is now completed, with new plantings becoming established. At present, the best features are the eighteenth-century garden buildings, the views into beautiful surrounding countryside, and the marvellous snowdrop wood spanning a stream that flows from a pond at the lower end. This must be one of the best displays of naturalised snowdrops in England. There are some splendid beech woods and older specimen trees. Wild

Painswick Rococo Garden Trust
Painswick GL6 6TH.
Tel: (01452) 813204;
www.rococogarden.org.uk

0.5m from Painswick on B4073. Signposted

Open 10th Jan to Oct, daily, 11am – 5pm

Entrance: £5.50, OAPs £4.50, children £2.50

Other information: Coaches by appt

flowers are allowed complete freedom. Rococo gardening was an eighteenth-century combination of formal geometric features with winding woodland paths, revealing sudden incidents and vistas – in essence, a softening of the formal French style, apparent from about 1715 onwards in all forms of art. The basis for Painswick's present restoration is a painting of 1748 by Thomas Robins (1716–78) for Benjamin Hyett, who created the garden in the grounds of the house built by his father in 1735. To celebrate the 250 years of its existence, Painswick's owners have planted a maze, designed by Angela Newing, in adjoining farmland. Visitors (who should be fit for some steep inclines) must allow three-quarters of an hour even for a brisk walk round the many beauties to be found within the 10 acres.

ROCKCLIFFE ★

Mr and Mrs Simon Keswick
Lower Swell, Stow-on-the-Wold
GL54 2JW
3m W of Stow-on-the-Wold on B4068
Open June, Wed, 10am – 5pm
Entrance: £4.50, children under 15 free
● WC ⟨

The house was built in the late nineteenth century for the dowagers of Eyford Park, the estate that marches with it, and looks due west towards a glorious stretch of unspoilt country enclosed by a curving shelter belt of mature park trees. Two elegant pavilions added by Nicky Johnson to the house pull the whole composition together and create a generous forecourt. This is the start of the seven-acre garden. On the stone slabs is a series of geometric beds planted with 'Sawyers' lavender, with a centrepiece in the form of a box-

Rockcliffe

edged spoked wheel with a stone wellhead in the centre; the paving froths lime-green with *Alchemilla mollis*. From the forecourt the view is of beech obelisks stalking up the broad grass ride towards the new ha-ha and beyond to open countryside. Between the terrace and the tree-lined boundary to the north is a shady enclosure where a stone-edged pool is overhung by six elegant *Cornus controversa* 'Variegata'. This lower-level garden leads to another where two simple canals of reflective water are framed by York-stone paving. In this placid green space are parallel lines of pleached hornbeams; a deep herbaceous border in pastel shades is relegated to a supporting role. Then come three flower-filled *boîtes* – two yew-edged rooms, richly planted in shades of white and purple-blue, and a scented swimming-pool garden with four huge standard bay trees and a pool-house covered with *Rosa* 'Zéphirine Drouhin'. The walled kitchen garden is productive and pretty, but on the other side of the kitchen garden is the *pièce de résistance*: topiary yew birds perching in pairs on the slope leading through the orchard to a handsome octagonal stone dovecote.

RODMARTON MANOR ★
(Historic Garden Grade II*)

The manor and its eight-acre garden, designed by Ernest Barnsley for the Biddulphs from 1909, is an excellent example of the English Arts and Crafts Movement at its best. The drive lies between impeccably clipped tapestry hedges, and the garden, which retains virtually all its original features, comprises a series of outdoor rooms, each with its own character, bordered by the fine hedges of yew, beech, holly and box for which it is famous. In front of the house is the terrace and topiary garden, the recently replanted trough garden, the sunken garden and white borders leading to the cherry orchard, which has a wide variety of snowdrops in early spring as well as shrubs and roses. There is a good rockery, a wild garden with a hornbeam avenue, and many attractive vistas. The large kitchen garden features both culinary and ornamental plants, old apple arches, a collection of old-fashioned and scented roses, and a row of sinks. Several areas have been replanted since 1991 when the present generation moved into the manor; they include parts of the leisure garden, where plants billow gentle over the paving, and the four large herbaceous borders continue to develop. The shrubbery has also been renovated.

Mr and Mrs Simon Biddulph

Rodmarton, Cirencester GL7 6PF.
Tel: (01285) 841253;
www.rodmarton-manor.co.uk

6m SW of Cirencester, 4m NE of Tetbury off A433, halfway between Cirencester and Tetbury

House open as garden

Garden open 10th, 14th and 17th Feb for snowdrops, 1.30pm – dusk; 24th March, 2 – 5pm; then May to Sept, Wed, Sat and Bank Holiday Mons, 2 – 5pm

Entrance: £4, accompanied children (5-15) £1 (house and garden £7, children £3.50)

Other information: Coaches use holly (west) drive

 WC &

SEZINCOTE ★★
(Historic Garden Grade I)

The entrance to Sezincote is up a long dark avenue of holm oaks that opens into the most English of parks, with a distinct Reptonian feeling – fine trees and distant views of Cotswold

Mr and Mrs E. Peake

Moreton-in-Marsh GL56 9AW;
www.sezincote.co.uk

1.5m W of Moreton-in-Marsh on A44 just before Bourton-on-the-Hill

House open May to Sept, Thurs, Fri,
2.30 – 6pm (no children in house)

Garden open Jan to Nov, Thurs, Fri and
Bank Holiday Mons, 2 – 6pm
(or dusk if earlier); and for NGS

Entrance: £5, children £1.50, under 5
free (house and garden £7)

Other information: Teas on NGS open
day only

hills. Turning the last corner is the surprise, for there is that fascinating rarity, an English country house built in the Moghul architectural style by Samuel Pepys Cockerell. The form of the garden has not changed since Repton's time, but the more recent planting was carried out by Lady Kleinwort with help from Graham Stuart Thomas, and on her return from India in 1968 she laid out the Paradise Garden in the south garden with canals and Irish yews. Behind this is the curved orangery, home to many tender climbing plants. The house is sheltered by great copper beeches, cedars, yews and limes, which provide a fine backdrop for the exotic shrubs. Streams and pools are lined with great clumps of bog-loving plants, and the stream is crossed by an Indian bridge adorned with Brahmin bulls. Planted for year-round interest, the garden is particularly strong on autumn colours. Graham Stuart Thomas's instructive guidebook is highly recommended.

The National Trust

Broadway WR12 7JU. Tel: (01386) 852410;
www.nationaltrust.org.uk

2.5m SW of Broadway off A44

House open as garden, but 12 noon – 5pm

Garden open 19th March to 2nd Nov,
Wed – Sun and Bank Holiday Mons,
11am – 5.30pm

Entrance: £4.40, children £2.20, family
£11.10 (house and garden £8.10, children
£4.10, family £20.60)

Other information: Motorised buggy
available

SNOWSHILL MANOR ★

(Historic Garden Grade II)

From a design by the Arts and Crafts architect M.H. Baillie-Scott, Charles Wade transformed a 'wilderness of chaos' on a Cotswold hillside into an interconnecting series of outdoor rooms from the 1920s onwards. Wade was a believer in the Arts and Crafts rustic ideal and the two-acre garden, like the house, expresses his eccentricities. Seats and woodwork are painted 'Wade blue', a powdery dark blue with touches of turquoise which goes well with the Cotswold stone walls. The simple cottage style conceals careful planting in shades of blue, mauve and purple, with bright accents from such traditional favourites as Oriental poppies, lupins and foxgloves. Organic gardening is employed here.

Derry Watkins

Greenways Lane, Cold Ashton,
Chippenham SN14 8LA.
Tel: (01225) 891686;
www.specialplants.net

7m N of Bath just S of junction A46 and
A420. Turn into Greenways Lane (signed
to nursery)

Open July to Sept, Wed, 11am – 5pm,
for NGS, and for parties by appt

Entrance: £4 (incl. plant list)

Other information: Lectures and courses
in autumn and winter; telephone for
details

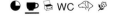

SPECIAL PLANTS NURSERY

Set high on the Cotswold Way is the one-acre garden of Derry Watkins, owner of the adjacent Special Plants Nursery. The structure and imaginative modern design are the work of her architect husband, Peter Clegg, while she has employed her discerning eye for colour and knowledge of a vast range of unusual perennials to produce a dramatic and brilliant display rising to a climax in late summer. The steepness of the south-facing site, mercifully sheltered by mature willows, ash and horse chestnut, enables many borderline tender plants and shrubs to flourish and grow to immense size in deep gravel terraces and richly planted borders. Bold shapes in gravel, water and grass echo the outlines of the magnificent surrounding scenery, and there are superb colour associations, such as the deep crimson/almost black border and the shades of apricot edging the new gravel garden. The garden is still developing – the productive vegetable garden and a peaceful woodland walk are new features. The nursery

Special Plants Nursery

outstanding, selling a wide range of beautifully grown and well displayed perennials, both hardy and tender, and many new introductions.

STANCOMBE PARK ★
(Historic Garden Grade I)

This must be the most curious park and garden south of Biddulph Grange (see entry in Staffordshire), constructed in the first half of the nineteenth century. Set on the Cotswold escarpment, it has all the ingredients of a Gothick best-seller. A narrow path drops into a dark glen, roots from enormous oaks, copper beeches and chestnuts trip your feet, ferns brush your face, walls drip water, and ammonites and fossils loom in the gloom. Rocks erupt with moss, Egyptian tombs trap the unwary, tunnels turn into grottoes. Even plants live in wire cages. But it is not a place of gloom; indeed the secret garden can be light and friendly when it is not raining. A millennium folly with a peace motif, placed at the head of a small pond, has reused the facade of a ruined chapel found in the woods; a bog garden has been planted behind. The upper garden around the house has a pattern border, created by the owner and the designer Nada Jennett. In all, 20 acres.

Mrs Gerda Barlow

Stancombe, Dursley GL11 6AU.
Tel: (01453) 542815

Between Wotton-under-Edge and Dursley on B4060

Open for parties by appt

Entrance: £3

 WC

STANWAY HOUSE ★
(Historic Garden Grade I)

Stanway is a honey-coloured Cotswold village with a Jacobean great house which has changed hands just once since AD 715. The garden rises in a series of dramatic terraced lawns and a rare, picturesque grasswork to the pyramid, which in the eighteenth century stood at the head of a 190-metre-long cascade descending to a formal canal on a terrace above the house. This was probably designed by Charles Bridgeman, and

Lord Neidpath

Winchcombe, Cheltenham GL54 5PQ.
Tel: (01386) 584469;
www.stanwayfountain.co.uk

1m E of B4632 Cheltenham – Broadway road, 4m NE of Winchcombe

House open as garden but closed Sat

Garden open June, Tues and Thurs; July and Aug, Tues, Thurs and Sat; all 2 – 5pm

Entrance: £4, children £1 (house and garden £6, OAPs £4.50, children £1.50)

exceeded in length and height (36 metres) its famous rival at Chatsworth (see entry in Derbyshire). Inside the house is a fascinating painting recording the cascade as it looked in the eighteenth century. The canal, the upper pond behind the pyramid, a short section of the cascade, and the upper fall below the pyramid were restored in 1998, and a 100-metre-high single-jet fountain (the tallest garden fountain in the world) added in the middle of the canal. The medieval pond in the Lower Garden, recently restored, has enhanced the beauty of the fourteenth-century tithe barn. It is hoped soon to restore the upper cascade – a series of pools and waterfalls – on the hillside east of the pyramid, from which magnificent views of the cascades, canal, fountain, house and Vale of the Severn open up. A high walk along the hillside above the cascade reveals the splendid park trees. In all, 23 acres.

Mr and Mrs Andrew Lukas

Wyck Rissington GL54 2PN.
Tel: (01451) 810337

1.5m S of Stow-on-the-Wold off A429 just NE of Bourton-on-the-Water. Last house in village, past church on opposite side of road

Open for NGS, and by appt

Entrance: £4

Other information: Refreshments by prior arrangement. Plant fairs 7th March, 10am – 1pm, 18th April, 10am – 1pm, 26th May, 10am – 2pm, 16th Sept, 10am – 3pm

STONE HOUSE ★

This enviable garden radiates stylish simplicity in both design and planting, while avoiding horticultural clichés all year round – note, for example, the bold use of euphorbias. The 2.5 acres are filled with unusual bulbs, shrubs and herbaceous perennials, including an abundance of aquilegias and hostas. There is a crab-apple walk, rose borders and a herb garden, and fritillaries are naturalising in the meadow walk. A spring-fed stream flowing into the River Dikler bubbles throughout; the area of sloping, box-edged lawns leading down from a terrace via rounded Lutyensesque brick steps to the water's edge is especially charming. The overall design makes full and sensitive use of the sloping site and the views out across a ha ha to unspoilt countryside; major elements such as a swimming pool and tennis court are cunningly concealed. It is worth visiting the unusual village church with a fine tower, where Gustav Holst was organist for a period.

The Lord and Lady Vestey

Northleach GL54 3LE.
Tel: (01285) 720610 (head gardener)

8m NE of Cirencester, 2m SW of Northleach off A429. Drive entrance is on right after long stone wall

Open for NGS

Entrance: £4, children free

Other information: Teas on open days only, plant sale on May opening

NEW ☾ WC

STOWELL PARK ★

(Historic Park Grade II)

The original Elizabethan house was enlarged for the Earl of Eldon in the 1880s by Sir John Belcher and used as a shooting lodge. The setting is exceptionally beautiful. The original eight-acre garden is thought to have been laid out in the 1870s, but since 1981 Lady Vestey and head gardener Neil Hewertson have been introducing new ideas and plantings sympathetically complementing its traditional Cotswold character. A pleached lime approach leads to immaculate lawned terraces with herbaceous borders, old-fashioned roses and magnificent unspoilt views over the Coln Valley towards Chedworth woods. The huge walled garden is cleverly divided into wide colour-themed borders, sections for cut-flower sections, fruit and vegetables, and a long rose pergola lined with box edging – an original touch. In the little orchard a rose-circle centrepiece is balanced by a circular fruit cage beyond a hedge interwoven with climbing roses, honeysuckles and clematis. There are extensive peach and vine houses, and a splendid array of pot plants in the greenhouse. Woodland and shrubberies continue to develop.

SUDELEY CASTLE AND GARDENS ★
(Historic Garden Grade II*)

There has been a house on this magnificent site, with views of the surrounding Cotswold hills at every turn, for over 1000 years; today the emphasis is on tourism. The extensive grounds contain ten integrated but individual gardens, notably the Queen's Garden with its outstanding collection of old-fashioned roses, surrounded by immaculately clipped double yew hedges. These were laid out in the nineteenth century by an ancestor of the present owners on the site of the original Tudor parterre. In recent years Jane Fearnley-Whittingstall guided the restoration of this area, as well as designing the knot garden and a newly planted buddleja walk featuring 23 different varieties. The gardens surrounding the ruins of the banqueting hall and the tithe barn with its carp pond are exceptionally lovely, with old climbing roses and (should you be lucky enough to avoid the coachloads) a romantic atmosphere. There is a white garden, a secret garden replanted by Charles Chesshire, and a tree peony garden. The Victorian kitchen garden is managed in collaboration with Garden Organic (see entry in Warwickshire). The July-to-October exhibition of modern sculpture seems set to continue.

Lady Ashcombe, Henry and Mollie Dent-Brocklehurst

Winchcombe, Cheltenham GL54 5JD. Tel: (01242) 602308; www.sudeleycastle.co.uk

8m NE of Cheltenham off B4632 at Winchcombe

Castle and gardens open main season – telephone or check website for details. Private guided tours by arrangement

Entrance: castle and gardens £7.20, concessions £6.20, children £4.20, family £20.80 (2007 prices)

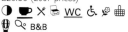

TEMPLE GUITING MANOR

The Tudor manor farm and its clutch of fourteenth-century ancillary buildings and barns have, after a long period of disuse and decay, been rescued and endowed with a remarkable and cerebral modern garden. The transformation is so complete that it is almost impossible to imagine the expanse of sloping, sheep-shorn grass that once surrounded the house, nor the vigorous laurel hedge that dominated and concealed the stream coursing through the precipitous valley below. With a generous budget, garden designer Jinny Blom has created a new linear flow for the garden, stretching out longitudinally from the side of the house. Visitors entering the garden from the other end pass through a solid oak gate and find themselves in a beautifully planted rhomboidal ante-garden where each bed has curvilinear sides and overflows with grasses, achilleas, *Verbena bonariensis* and many other summer flowers. The higher terraced lawn is aligned with an elegant 30-metre-long canal at a lower level, and also gives access to the Granary Walk, frothing with the lavender, silver and white of perovskias and roses. From here a gnarled ivy arch leads into a tennis court where a series of clipped box plants serve as spectators to the action. Framing the canal is a double

Mr S. Collins

Temple Guiting, nr Stow-on-the-Wold GL54 5RP

7m from Stow-on-the-Wold on B4077

Open for NGS

Entrance: £3, children free

screen of pleached hornbeams underplanted with cardoons, agapanthus, lilies and white delphiniums. The designer's brilliant use of colour in Granary Walk is echoed with its blue and white scheme, and contains the entire spectrum of mauve and purple shades. The terrace below the canal is subdivided into varied compartments which include yew, box, lavender and roses, and opens up the view over a beautiful drystone retaining wall, for which Gilbert Sterling Lee, Jinny Blom and Ptolemy Dean were joint winners of the Pinnacle Award in 2006. The land then slopes to the valley below, with a path running down to a lake and stream. From the simple expanse of lawn in front of the manor the drop is vertiginous.

THROUGHAM COURT ★

Dr Christine Facer

Througham GL6 7HG;
www.christinefacer.com

8m W of Cirencester. From Birdlip, follow B4070 until left turn signed to The Camp; after The Camp take first left signed to Througham. Take second left turn down hill; house immediately on right

Open May to Sept by appt: parties of more than 20 welcome (with lecture tour: fee negotiable)

● ☕ WC

Througham Court

The intriguing house – a Jacobean, eighteenth-century and Arts-and-Crafts hybrid, listed Grade II* – lies at the heart of the three-acre garden, and the garden acts as a viewing platform for the landscape beyond. It is a fascinating amalgam of the traditional (garden compartments, topiary, courtyards and terraces) and the contemporary (a wild grass meadow, a magical black bamboo maze, a mound planted with late perennials). Science has been a deep inspiration on both the design and the details: reminders of the cosmos are expressed in stone, statuary and in a host of allusive names such as the Cosmic Evolution Garden, Fibonacci Jumps, Entry Into Chaos Gate, Molecule Seat. It comes as no surprise that the owner,

a scientist turned landscape designer, has worked closely with Charles Jencks. There are witty and light-hearted touches too: a rippling photinia hedge as background to a series of sculptured slate shards cascading down a slope; steps covered with a surprising red astroturf 'carpet', shimmering banners by Shona Watt. High-quality is the workmanship of the complex stainless-steel gates, perfectly formed and engraved Ancaster stone balls and slate starburst linked to a black reflective pool and a rill. The planting shows the same fine eye for colour and a talent for blending and juxtaposing plants in subtle or startling groups. A new viewing terrace is planned for 2008 with inspiration from chiral or mirror molecules – expect many reflective elements. A remarkable contemporary garden, still in the making.

TUDOR HOUSE

Located near the village green in a Cotswold hamlet off the well-beaten Cirencester-to-Tetbury track, the two-acre garden has been refashioned by the present owner since 2001. Calling on the services of Tim Rees, he discovered that the designer had worked on the garden a decade earlier. Together they have pared down the design and planting so that the bones stand out with elegant simplicity, clothed with an ample sufficiency of flowers and foliage. The garden in front of the mainly sixteenth-century house is framed by a double line of yews, and the pleached hornbeams on the boundary wall give it the calm of a cloister. Beyond a beech hedge to the side of the house is the garden proper, laid out as a series of spaces and enclosures – a knot garden set in lawn; herbaceous borders planted largely in shades of blue, purple and white; a characterful gazebo; a terrace looking out over 'borrowed' fields and woodland. The land then slopes steeply down to the boundary wall, and the garden, spreading out longitudinally, takes on a new and wilder feel. Sorbus, Turkish hazels and other specimen trees trace the lines of paths mown through a meadow flowering in summer with geraniums, centaureas, *Knautia macedonica*, ox-eye daisies, and those two wonderful wild roses: *R. omeiensis* with its wicked-looking thorns, and *R. roxburghii*, the plump-hipped chestnut rose. Strategically placed modern sculpture is the final *leitmotif* of this restful and exciting garden.

Richard Szpiro

Cherington GL8 8SW.
Tel: (01285) 841286/(020) 7727 9757

9m SW of Cirencester, 5m NE of Tetbury off A433

Open April to Oct, Fri – Mon, by appt

Entrance: free

UPTON WOLD ★★

Hidden away in a hollow and seemingly remote, two things have combined to make this a most intriguing and rewarding garden – the rolling lie of the land and the intellectual creativity of the present owners. Starting in 1976 with a barren and neglected estate, they called in the late Brenda Colvin to fill sumptuous curving borders graded by height and colour, Hal Moggridge to lay out a network of hedges sheltering various garden rooms, and Anthony Archer-Wills to

Mr and Mrs I. R. S. Bond

Northwick Estate, Moreton-in-Marsh GL56 9TR. Tel: (01386) 700667

5m NW of Moreton-in-Marsh on A44. Pass Batsford, Sezincote and Bourton House, continue up Bourton hill, pass Troopers Lodge Garage at A424 junction, and drive is 1m further on right

Upton
Wold

Open for NGS, and May to July
by appt, 10am – 6pm
Entrance: NGS openings £5, children
free; May to July openings £6

construct a canal and fountain garden overlooking the broad
view at the rear of the early-seventeenth-century house. This
all inclines to the formal and quintessentially English style, and
ambitious fruit and vegetable gardens, rose gardens,
hornbeam *allées*, wildflower meadows and suchlike are by no
means unusual in this prosperous part of the Cotswolds. The
nine acres here, however, are imbued with an energy and
unconventionality at every rise, fall and occasional flat plane of
the complicated site. Thus, to give just a few examples, to one
side of Colvin's borders is an immensely long and narrow
herbaceous border sandwiched between a wall and a tall yew
hedge with elongated 'windows' cut through; the intimate
Hidden Garden is a sloping, triangular wedge filled with
unusual magnolias and other fine specimen trees,
underplanted with herbaceous perennials and a froth of
Queen Anne's lace; a patterned pathway leads down to a
sloping tunnel of *Malus* 'John Downie' flanked by a clipped
'higgledy-piggledy' hedge; an arboretum of 200 walnut trees in
14 different species, set high on a hill, has a collection of
sculpted nuts cast on the ground beneath. Caroline Bond is an
intuitive and skilful plantswoman, while Ian Bond's passions are
for trees and water; everywhere rare and unusual plants
abound, with smaller-scale treasures woven into borders and
important specimen trees placed at strategic points as eye-
catchers. The garden reaches a crescendo during its short
summer opening season: allow several hours to do it justice.

OTHER RECOMMENDED GARDENS

CONDERTON MANOR

Mr and Mrs William Carr, Conderton, Tewkesbury GL20 7PR (01386 725389); village website: www.overbury.org. Open by appt

Enhanced by impressive recent tree planting, the relaxed and informal 11-acre garden and arboretum surrounding the 17th-century manor makes the most of its spectacular views. These command admiration throughout – from the low and subtle parterre near the house and the old walled rose garden, from grassy paths and secret winding walks.

THE ERNEST WILSON MEMORIAL GARDEN

Leasbourne, High Street, Chipping Campden (01386 840529 – Ann Taylor). Open all year, daily except 25th Dec, 9am – dusk

Backed by a beautiful church tower, a 0.75-acre memorial garden created in memory of Ernest 'Chinese' Wilson, who was born in the town. *Acer griseum*, *Davidia involucrata* and *Lilium regale* are just a representative few of the 1200 species of trees and shrubs he introduced to Britain.

GRANGE FARM

Evenlode, Nr Moreton-in-Marsh GL56 0NT (01608 650607). Open for NGS, and May to Aug by appt

A charming, traditional English country garden of 2 acres which melds into the surrounding Evenlode valley. Subtly planted herbaceous borders are timed for summer perfection, the water garden is sensational in May, roses flower *en masse* in June, and the vegetable garden remains immaculate throughout the open season.

KELMSCOTT MANOR

Kelmscott, Lechlade GL7 3HJ (01367 252486; www.kelmscottmanor.co.uk). House and garden open April to Sept, Wed, 11am – 5pm, plus certain Sats (telephone for details); garden only open June to Sept, Thurs, 2 – 5pm; and for parties by appt Thurs and Fri

The romantic 3.5-acre garden that weaves its way round the charming cluster of farm buildings and the manor once owned by

William Morris has been re-created with great subtlety by Hal Moggridge. Morris himself described in *News From Nowhere* in 1892 how 'the roses were rolling over one another with that delicious superabundance of small, well-tended gardens'. (Listed Grade II)

MILL DENE

Mr and Mrs B. S. Dare, Blockley, Moreton-in-Marsh GL56 9HU (01386 700457; milldenegarden.co.uk). Open April to Oct, Tues – Fri and Bank Holiday Mons (except Easter and 24th to 27th July), 10am – 5pm, and by appt

The 2.5-acre garden, characterised by the owner's sense of fun, climbs up in steep terraces, each with its own character and colour scheme. First comes a rose walk, then a cricket lawn, and at the topmost level a potager and fruit garden, a herb garden with rills and a fountain, and a summerhouse giving splendid village views. Beside the house attractive plantings surround the mill pond and stream.

MOOR WOOD

Mr and Mrs Henry Robinson, Woodmancote, Cirencester GL7 7EB (01285 831397). Open for NGS 24th June and 1st July, 2 – 6pm, and by appt

With its attractive valley setting, this is the perfect home for a National Collection of rambler roses – 140 in all – clambering over every available wall and support within the 2 acres of diverse gardens. The wildflower planting in the old walled garden contributes to a delightfully natural atmosphere.

NEWARK PARK

Ozleworth, Wotton-under-Edge GL12 7PZ (01453 842644; www.nationaltrust.org.uk). Open April and May, Wed and Thurs; June to Oct, Wed, Thur, Sat, Sun and Bank Holiday Mons; plus Easter Mon – Fri; all 11am – 5pm. NT

The house, originally known as 'the new works', was a Tudor hunting lodge built as a retreat from court life. The east front looks out onto the private garden, and a deer park was added from farmland to the west of the house. No lover of the English landscape should miss a visit to Newark with its majestic panoramic views. 14 acres in all. (Listed Grade II)

THE OLD BARN

Dawn and Jamie Adams, Upper Dowdeswell,
Cheltenham GL54 4LT (01242 820858).
Open by appt

Garden designer Dawn Adams has brought
style and naturalistic planting to this beautifully
kept 1.75-acre hillside garden. Immaculate
beech and yew hedges and stone walls form
the framework for borders, lawns, fruit trees
and a white garden, all planted for year-round
appeal with many unusual species.

THE OLD RECTORY, QUENINGTON

Mr and Mrs D. Abel Smith, Quenington, Nr Fairford,
Cirencester GL7 5BN (01285 750358;
www.freshairart.org). Open for NGS, and by appt

The River Coln meandering through the 5-acre
garden and the set-piece mill race make this a
superb natural setting for the owners' fine, and
increasing, sculpture collection. An international
selling exhibition is held on alternate years
(next in 2009).

TRULL HOUSE

Caroline and Simon Mitchell, Trull, Tetbury GL8 8SQ
(01285 841255; www.trullhouse.co.uk). Open 27th
April to Aug, Wed, Sat (but closed 31st May), and most
Suns, 11am – 5pm. Also open for parties by appt.

The 8-acre gardens laid out at the beginning of
20th century are in the best English tradition:
expansive, lush and mature. Herbaceous
borders overflow, a sunken lily pond, rockery
and spectacular walled garden evoke the grand
Edwardian days.

WESTBURY COURT GARDEN

Westbury on Severn GL14 1PD (01452 760461;
www.nationaltrust.org). Open 12th March to June,
3rd Sept to 26th Oct, Wed – Sun and Bank Holiday
Mons; July and Aug, daily; all 10am – 5.30pm. NT

The remarkable 17th-century Dutch water
garden, unique in Britain, is an exquisite
ensemble of *allée*, canal, *clairvoyée* and vista.
Although beset by a debilitating combination of
traffic noise, unaesthetic neighbouring houses
and seemingly incurable yew disease, its status
as a national treasure will not be eclipsed. 2
acres. (Listed Grade II*)

HAMPSHIRE & THE ISLE OF WIGHT

For further information about how to use the *Guide*
and for an explanation of the symbols, see pages vi–viii.
Specific dates and times are those given to us by garden owners for 2008.
For 2009 dates, check with the individual properties.
For opening dates under the National Gardens Scheme,
readers should consult *The Yellow Book* or www.ngs.org.uk.
Maps are to be found at the end of the *Guide*.
Gardens on the Isle of Wight will be found at the end of the Hampshire section.

ABBEY COTTAGE

A series of vistas linked by steps, slopes and hedge corridors leads the visitor into this 1.5-acre organic garden with varied levels and enclosures. The framework of yew and other hedging makes a satisfying foil to shrubs and perennials, while an oval window cut through the hedge of one garden gives glimpses into the next, of a pond and an immaculate box bench with box cushions. Walls are covered with unusual species clematis and the perennial climber *Malvastrum lateritium*; among many striking plants are *Magnolia* x *loebneri* 'Merril', flowering against the yew hedge in spring, *Cornus alternifolia* 'Argentea' and ancient, well-groomed apple trees. One meadow is planted with spring bulbs and young specimen trees, another with late-summer wild flowers, and at the highest point in the garden there is a young plantation containing native trees.

Col. Patrick Daniell

Rectory Lane, Itchen Abbas, Winchester SO21 1BN. Tel: (01962) 779575; www.abbeycottage.net

2m W of New Alresford on B3047, 1m E of Itchen Abbas

Open for NGS, and by appt

Entrance: £3

● ☕ 🍽 WC ও

APPLE COURT ★

The 1.3-acre garden is a showcase for a National Collection of hostas and hemerocallis. The daylily garden, with a frothy rectangle of ornamental grasses at its centre, is at its peak in July and August, when the flowers are mixed with agapanthus, crocosmias, kniphofias and phormiums. The white garden has a different drama – a square of yew hedging contains an oval border of white flowers and silvery-leaved grasses viewed through an inner oval of pleached hornbeams which frames them like a series of lit pictures. The effect is architectural, like entering a square with a circular colonnade. Three rectangular ponds are connected by cascading rills, and a Japanese garden with a Koi pond was added in 2004. A fern path, large herbaceous borders lined with rose-covered rope swags, and a grass display garden are other quite unusual features. Many of these delights are for sale in the nursery.

Charles and Angela Meads

Hordle Lane, Hordle, Lymington SO41 0HU. Tel: (01590) 642130; www.applecourt.com

200 metres N of A337 between Lymington and New Milton along Hordle Lane opposite Royal Oak

Open March to Oct, Fri – Sun and Bank Holiday Mons, 10am – 5pm

Entrance: £3

Other information: Plants for sale in adjoining nursery

🕐 🍽 WC ও ⚘ ✎

Bramdean House

Mr and Mrs H.Wakefield

Bramdean, Alresford SO24 0JU.
Tel: (01962) 771214

9m E of Winchester, 5m SE of New
Alresford on A272 in middle of
Bramdean

Open for NGS, and by appt at
other times

Entrance: NGS days £3.50, other days
£4.50, children free

 WC &

BRAMDEAN HOUSE ★
(Historic Garden Grade II)

Very much a traditional garden worked in the old style, with many interesting plants, this will give particular inspiration to anyone wondering what to grow on thin chalk soil. The fine eighteenth-century red-brick house is protected from the road by a large cloud hedge of yew and box, and the five-acre garden slopes up behind. It is divided into three parts linked by an axial path which leads from a circular pond through mirror-image herbaceous borders – given over in June largely to blues, with nepetas, geraniums, tradescantias, *Clematis* × *diversifolia* 'Hendersonii' and galegas, followed by yellows and then the russets of late summer. Surrounding beds are packed with plants, including white standard abutilons and a handsome *Cornus alternifolia* 'Argentea'. The path, lined with dianthus and roses, proceeds via wrought-iron gates into the walled kitchen garden with its abundance of fruit and vegetables, old-fashioned sweet peas and a mass of herbaceous flowers. Beyond a second wrought-iron gate is an orchard with a curving tapestry hedge of alternating box and yew, fruit trees underplanted with daffodils, flowering cherries and beehives. The path is terminated by a striking apple house and belfry. Trees on the eastern side include *Ginkgo biloba*, *Maytenus boaria*, *Liriodendron tulipifera* and *Davidia involucrata*, magnolias and fine specimens of *Staphylea colchica*. Spring brings to the garden carpets of aconites, snowdrops, crocuses and other early bulbs, autumn a large collection of tender and hardy nerines.

Mr and Mrs M. Baron

Brandy Mount, Alresford SO24 9EG.
Tel: (01962) 732189;
www.brandymount.co.uk

BRANDY MOUNT HOUSE

This informal 1.25-acre garden of trees, shrubs, beds and grass is very much for the plantsman, with unusual species and varieties to be discovered at every turn. Michael Baron is on hand to guide visitors through his National Collections of snowdrops (at least 220 named varieties) and daphnes (over 70 varieties). A raised trial bed for some 90 special snowdrops is an interesting feature. There are woodland plants by the pond, and good displays of hellebores, ferns, trilliums, pulmonarias and erythroniums. The alpine house houses dwarf narcissi and alpine primulas, a delight on cold spring days, and the potager is packed with vegetables. Alresford seems to have more than its fair share of attractive and interesting gardens – don't miss this one, which is worth revisiting periodically to see what new rarities have been assembled.

In town centre, first right in East Street

Open early Feb, 11am – 4pm, for snowdrops (telephone or consult website for details); and for NGS

Entrance: £3, children free

Other information: No vehicular access. Parking in station car park and Broad Street. Children must be supervised

BURY COURT

This 1.5-acre plantsman's garden incorporates designs by two leading contemporary masters of the art. The walled garden, entered through three oast houses, is the work of Piet Oudolf and displays both his naturalism and his characteristic use of grasses. It opens onto a swirling tapestry of asymmetrical beds, dominated by robust perennials and grasses, clipped hedges, two mirror pools and an outstanding gravel bed with mounds of silver-leaved Mediterranean species. At the front of the main house is a modernist grid design by Christopher Bradley-Hole, using geometric raised beds edged with rusted steel and planted with drifts of grasses shot through with accents of colour from unusual varieties of perennials.

John Coke

Bentley, Farnham, Surrey GU10 5LZ.
Tel: (07989) 300703

6m NE of Alton, 5m SW of Farnham, 1.5m N of Bentley on road signed to Crondall

Open for parties by appt

Entrance: £3

CADLAND GARDENS ★
(Historic Garden Grade II*)

The landscape garden of eight acres, laid out for the banker Robert Drummond in 1775, is 'Capability' Brown's smallest surviving pleasure ground. It has been restored to the original plan, using plants available before 1780. A path with tiered shrubs underplanted with wild flowers winds from the modern house (encapsulating the original thatched *cottage orné* designed by Brown and Henry Holland), along the Solent shore and back through a lime walk and a Georgian flower border. Broad vistas alternate with carefully orchestrated views of the sea. There is a kitchen garden with fruit houses and a gravel garden. A second walled garden has a red border, a cool grey border and rare plants – *Astelia chathamica, Pileostegia viburnoides*, tender acacias and leptospermums.

Mr and Mrs Maldwin Drummond

Fawley, Southampton SO45 1AA.
16m SE of Southampton off A326/B3053

House open by appt

Garden open May to July, Sept and Oct, by written appt for parties of 20 or more

Entrance: £5

Other information: Teas by arrangement.

CONHOLT PARK ★

Surrounding the Regency house is an imaginative 10-acre garden created over the past few years. Spacious lawns, towering cedars and fine views are grace-notes providing a dignified setting for a variety of individual spaces, including rose, secret, winter and Shakespeare gardens, an Edwardian Ladies' Walk and a laurel millennium maze, in the shape of a foot and possibly the longest in the country. The walled

Professor Caroline Tisdall

Chute, Nr Andover SP11 9HA.
Tel: (07803) 021208

5m NW of Andover off A342. Turn N at Weyhill church and continue 5m through Clanville and Tangley Bottom. Turn left for Conholt; house is 0.5m on right just off Chute causeway

Open for NGS

Entrance: £3, children free

Mr E. L. de Rothschild

Exbury, Southampton SO45 1AZ.
Tel: (023) 8089 1203; www.exbury.co.uk

15m S of Southampton. From M27 west
junction 2 take A326 then B3054. 2.5m
SE of Beaulieu, after 1m turn right for
Exbury. Signposted

Open early March to mid Nov, daily,
10am – 5.30pm (or dusk if earlier),
plus limited winter opening
(check for details)

Entrance: high-season £7.50, OAPs £7,
children (3–15) £1.50, family £17.50.
Seasonal discounts (2007 prices)

kitchen garden has good glasshouses, a sunken pool and tunnels of runner beans, herbs and flowers. Future plans include a meadow rose garden with the roses allowed free growth through an existing meadow – something which has been done in France but rarely over here.

EXBURY GARDENS ★★
(Historic Garden Grade II*)

Established between the wars by Lionel de Rothschild, these 200-acre gardens of rhododendrons and azaleas are the most outstanding of their kind in the south. Winding paths meander over 200 acres and proceed under a light canopy of trees, mostly oak and pine, over a bridge and beside ponds to the Beaulieu River. Many rhododendrons and azaleas, such as *R. yakushimanum* and *R.* (Hawk Group) 'Crest', were introduced here and are to be found growing beside purple Japanese maples and candelabra primulas. At times the colour associations seem brash – harsh orange beside blush, metallic magenta beside pale blue – but a glade of towering white blooms, pink in bud, more than makes up for this. In March early rhododendrons, camellias and the daffodil meadow flower; in April the rock garden, miniature mountain scenery with screes and valleys, is at its peak with alpine rhododendrons flowering among 'Skyrocket' junipers. May is the high season. In summer the herbaceous and grass garden is a mass of colour and variety, while the recently planted exotic garden is full of unusual plants. For autumn interest there is a superb collection of deciduous trees, shrubs, notably acers, which exhibit fiery hues next to the ponds. The Summer Lane Garden, planted in a contemporary design inspired by Piet Oudolf, combines huge swathes of herbaceous plants,

Exbury Gardens

grasses, bulbs and wild flowers, and includes an apple orchard, a pumpkin patch and a sunflower meadow. This is accessible via a steam railway which has opened up the south-east corner of the gardens, offering visitors a 20-minute journey in comfort. Then pay a visit to the wide-ranging plant centre.

FARLEIGH HOUSE ★

An exemplary modern garden of six acres in the classic tradition, designed by Georgia Langton, immaculately maintained and complementing the knapped-flint house. The large kitchen garden has a herbaceous border running with blue *Clematis durandii*, and culminates in a conservatory (with a pond), scented by various brugmansias, rare passion flowers and other choice plants. The quadripartite fountain garden, of roses, nepeta and alchemilla, is followed by an area of species roses with silver metallic seagulls wheeling overhead. A simple maze leads, via two topiary peacocks pecking at strawberries, to a rectangular waterlily garden; beyond, at the end of the Scots pine walk, wrought-iron gates open onto a 1.5-acre lake. Note the details: a huge smooth granite apple in woodland lit by a shaft of light …another pair of wrought-iron gates decorated with flowers and abstract geometrical patterns … hedges dipping to give glimpses of gardens beyond … the little barrel seat above the well-house. Good shrubs and trees, including a fine *Cornus controversa* 'Variegata'.

The Earl and Countess of Portsmouth

Farleigh Wallop, Basingstoke RG25 2HT.
Tel: (01256) 842684

3m SE of Basingstoke off B3046.
Leave M3 at junction 7 and follow signs from Dummer

Open for NGS, and for parties by appt

Entrance: £8

HEATHLANDS ★

The garden is approached along a roadside planted with a row of paulownias raised from seed by the owner. The sylvan setting is reinforced by the *Styrax japonicus*, sweet chestnut, camellias, embothriums and crinodendrons surrounding the lawn and by the woodland beyond. There are 1000 different plants in this one acre, with flowering interest maintained from bulbs and an acacia in early spring to hydrangeas and scented eucryphias in August. Notable are a gigantic flowering phormium, yuccas, a tree fern, *Abutilon megapotamicum* and many clematis. A splendid holly drum, over 10 feet high, becomes sculpture among the natural planting, and a yew hedge leading to the kitchen garden sports a topiary peacock, its tail in low relief against the hedge and its head and crown outlined above. Fine rhododendron hedges line a walk focused on an obelisk and delineate secret areas with ponds and ferns; they are cut through at intervals to give glimpses of the woodland beyond.

Dr John Burwell

47 Locks Road, Locks Heath,
Southampton SO31 6NS
Tel: (01489) 573598

5m W of Fareham. Leave M27 at junction 9. Locks Road runs due S from A27 at Park Gate

Open for NGS, and 4th May, 2 – 5.30pm, for Red Cross

Entrance: £3, children free

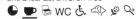

HINTON AMPNER ★

The garden was created by Ralph Dutton, later Lord Sherborne, who inherited the estate in 1935. The terraces below the Georgian-style house command fine views over downland. Their cross-axes, revealing glimpses of urns, statues or an obelisk, are almost Italianate in feel, but this is essentially

The National Trust

Hinton Ampner, Bramdean, Alresford
SO24 0LA. Tel: (01962) 771305

8m E of Winchester, 1m W of
Bramdean on A272

Hinton Ampner

House open

Garden open 17th March to Oct,
Sat – Wed, 11am – 5pm. Parties of 15
or more by appt

Entrance: £5.50, children (5–16) £2.75
(extra charge for house) (2007 prices)

Other information: Coaches must use
entrance through village

a classic English garden of lawns and avenues, deep borders and secret places. The yew and box hedging and topiary are dense and crisp, the giant yew mushrooms surreal in feel. Among the wide range of unusual plants are *Syringa* × *laciniata*, *Abelia triflora* and *A. floribunda* with raspberry tubes, *Amorpha fruticosa* and *Gymnocladus dioica* (the Kentucky coffee tree). The plants are unlabelled but the gardeners happy to identify. As befits a large formal house, the climbers, punctuated by pillars of yew and holly, are trained to reach high and grow wallpaper-tight with never an overlapping stem. The old walled kitchen garden is now laid out as a formal orchard. A rose garden has been planted, and interest extends to September and beyond with salvias and autumn crocuses, and the late-flowering *Heptacodium miconioides*. In all, 12 acres.

HOUGHTON LODGE

(Historic Garden Grade II*)

Mr and Mrs Martin Busk

Stockbridge SO20 6LQ.
Tel: (01264) 810912/810502;
www.houghtonlodge.co.uk

1.5m S of Stockbridge. Signposted

Open March to Sept, daily, 10am – 5pm
(Wed by appt only)

Telephone for winter opening times

Entrance: £5; meadow walks and alpacas
£2.50 extra. Children free

The early eighteenth-century *cottage orné* (some cottage!) is superbly sited on an eminence overlooking an open and gently curving stretch of the River Test, with lovely meadow and riverside walks. Its 18-acre garden is the centrepiece of a miniature 30-acre estate. Fine specimen trees stand on the ridge beyond the lawns, and topiary abounds, including a peacock garden with a patterned box parterre; in spring it is a mass of snowdrops, daffodils and the rare *Scilla bythinica*. A one-acre organic kitchen garden contained by chalk cob walls is divided in two by a central path; there is also a modern hydroponicum in which plants are cultivated without soil, and an orchid collection. Two alapacas, Tom and Dick, are the latest inhabitants.

53 LADYWOOD ★

Situated in the middle of Eastleigh, this immaculate garden on clay shows how many plants (over 1800 to date, each one named on an inconspicuous black label) can be grown in just 15 square metres. It is divided into rooms – among them water, scree and shade gardens – laid out beside a circular lawn. Over the years several shrubs like *Viburnum* 'Pink Beauty' have had their lower branches removed to show their legs and raise the canopy. The display begins with spring bulbs and ends with late-flowering *viticella* and other clematis. In between come alpines, alliums and early perennials like the small cut-leaved hybrids of *Paeonia tenuifolia*, followed by delphiniums, phlox and hardy geraniums galore, including the black-leaved *G. pratense* 'Midnight Reiter'. Mrs Ward's plants are like a vast orchestra beckoned to sound then fade according to season, and her love of carefully chosen variegated foliage – hostas, *Hacquetia epipactis* 'Thor Svantsen', *Actinidia kolomikta* 'Tricolor' and grasses like *Melica uniflora* – make this an entrancing garden at any time of year.

Mr and Mrs D. Ward

Eastleigh SO50 4RW.
Tel: (02380) 615389

Leave A33/M3 at junction 12 on A335 signed to Eastleigh, turn right at roundabout into Woodside Avenue, second right into Bosville, 5th right into Ladywood

Open for NGS, and by appt April to July, Tues, 2 –5.30pm

Entrance: £3, children £1

Other information: Parking in Bosville only

LAKE HOUSE

The tall and handsome walls of the old kitchen gardens of the ruined Grange make a pleasing contrast with the low modern house nearby. The walled garden has herbaceous borders and box-edged plots filled with old roses and perennials, as well as a vegetable and cutting area with espalier apples, a rose and wisteria pergola and an avenue of Irish yews leading to a moon gate. There are large areas of naturalised daffodils and a snakes'-head fritillary meadow. The house – surrounded by a conservatory, a terrace, a formal pond and pots – looks across lawns to the lake with a scenic walk which includes views of the neo-classical shell of the old house, a nineteenth-century cascade, ancient cedars, a castle folly and an arched flint bridge. The 20 acres of *The Grange* itself, designed by William Wilkins and formerly home of the Ashburton family, are now in the guardianship of English Heritage (Historic Park Grade II*) and may be visited at any time.

Lord Ashburton

Northington, Alresford SO24 9TG.

3m NW of Alresford off B3046. Follow English Heritage signs for Northington and The Grange, and turn sharp left before entrance to Grange

Open for NGS

Entrance: £4, children free (2007 price)

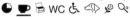

THE LITTLE COTTAGE

Drama is the essence of this tiny and splendidly over-the-top town garden divided into four rooms with a connecting corridor. Every path and vista is focused on an ornamental seat, door, arbour or urn, and exploring it is like walking through a series of stage sets. First comes the blue and yellow garden, where the path is lined with gold and green standard *Euonymus japonicus* 'Aureus' surrounded by flowers like morning glory and *Commelina tuberosa*; their blueness is echoed in vases, seats, balls and ceramic cats. The shady blue and white corridor leads to the courtyard garden with white flowers and ornamental doves. There are two side gates, one opening to a soft pastel garden, the other to a geometric black

Peter and Lyn Prior

Southampton Road, Lymington SO41 9GZ. Tel: (01590) 679395

On northern outskirts of Lymington on A337 opposite Toll House Inn

Open for NGS, and by appt

Entrance: £2

and white Gothick garden with glittering white chippings and black paving, black pots, seats and ceramic balls which Lyn Prior hopes will 'frighten the good-taste brigade'. Heaven and hell lie side by side. Among the black plants are chocolate cosmos and chocolate mint, the millet 'Purple Majesty', a ruffled black basil, *Persicaria microcephala* 'Red Dragon' and *Sambucus* 'Black Lace' contrasting with artemesias and other grey-leaved plants. In the New Forest area with its sandy acid soil it is refreshing to find a garden without a single rhododendron, and one that flourishes in late summer.

LITTLE COURT

Professor and Mrs Andrew Elkington

Crawley, near Winchester SO21 2PU. Tel: (01962) 776365

5m NW of Winchester off A272 or B3049, in Crawley village, 300 yards from either pond or church

Open for NGS, and for parties by appt

Entrance: £3.50, children free

Other information: Home-made teas on Suns only

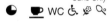

This is a quintessential country-house garden of three acres, filled with spring bulbs and a host of summer flowers. In early summer the borders flow with geraniums of many varieties, including the dissected-leaved G. 'Nimbus' and coral-coloured G. x *oxonianum* 'Wageningen', all set off by other large perennials including *Crambe cordifolia*, *Clematis recta* 'Lime Close', *Eremurus robustus*, and many alliums. Beyond this profusion is a succession of spaces and eye-catchers: a walled kitchen garden with bantams, an orchard which is pale lavender in late winter from a carpet of *Crocus tommasinianus*, climbing roses, a tree house for all ages, a spiralling grass path inspired by the labyrinth of Chartres Cathedral. There is an ancient yew standing above an ivy circle, and near the house a dark courtyard of hostas. At the far end of the garden a gap in a flint wall leads to a field with views of rolling chalk downland to the east and south.

LONGSTOCK PARK WATER GARDEN ★★

John Lewis Partnership (Leckford Estate)

Longstock, Stockbridge SO20 6EH. Tel: (01264) 810904; www.longstockpark.co.uk

5m S of Andover, 2m N of Stockbridge. From A30 turn N on A3057. Signposted

Open April to Sept, first and third Sun of each month, 2 – 5pm, and by appt for parties

Entrance: £5, children £1

Other information: Refreshments at nursery

The seven acres of these superb water gardens, created by John Spedan Lewis in 1948, are fed from the River Test and surrounded by acid-loving trees and shrubs. They form an archipelago connected by narrow bridges and causeways. Gunneras and swamp cypresses, surrounded by stilts, royal ferns and *Aralia elata* are just some of the plants reflected in the clear waters moving with gold carp, and a walk along the paths gives a succession of views followed by more intimate spaces. Aquatics include 48 different water lilies. Do not miss a visit to *Longstock Park Nursery* nearby (also open daily), which has a fine herbaceous border and an extensive collection of *viticella* clematis; a National Collection of buddlejas may be seen by request.

THE MANOR HOUSE ★
(Historic Garden Grade II*)

Mr and Mrs J. Wallinger

Upton Grey, Basingstoke RG25 2RD. Tel: (01256) 862827; www.gertrudejekyllgarden.co.uk

6m SE of Basingstoke in Upton Grey, on hill immediately above church

The five-acre garden has been meticulously restored since 1985 to the original 1908 Gertrude Jekyll planting plans, copies of which are on display, and the tender care invested makes it more than a unique museum piece. Here are formal beds with lilies, peonies and roses edged with lamb's ears; drystone walls clothed with plants; terraces, pergola and yew hedging; and her only surviving restored wild garden with a pond, daffodils and rambling roses. The garden is at its best from mid-May to the end of June. A living example of many Jekyll theories, it is worth noting her use of colour, with hot reds moving through yellows to distant greys and blues, the proportions of the steps, and the relation of the garden to the house (designed in grand vernacular style with hung tiles, etc by Ernest Newton for Charles Holme, founder and owner of *The Studio* magazine). This is claimed to be the most authentic Jekyll garden reconstruction, supported by a useful booklet and plant list.

Open May to Aug, Mon – Fri (but closed Bank Holiday Mons), by appt only

Entrance: £5

◑ ☕ WC ♿ ✿ ▦

MOTTISFONT ABBEY GARDEN ★★
(Historic Garden Grade II)

This famous collection of historic roses, based on the design and selection by Graham Stuart Thomas, was established in 1972 in the original walled kitchen garden, quartered with paths and box hedging – a formal design given additional interest by herbaceous borders, a central pond and a fountain. Here are the Albas, Damasks and Gallicas of the Middle Ages, cabbage and moss roses, and the earliest Chinas, Bourbons, hybrid perpetuals, French nineteenth-century Gallicas and Albas as well as Rugosas, and ramblers up walls, arches and stands – in all, a National Collection of 300 old-fashioned roses (also a few species and New English roses), now being renovated. The best time to visit is on midsummer evenings, when there are fewer visitors and the scent is at its strongest. Sweeping lawns around the house, cedars, the largest London plane tree in the country, a

The National Trust

Mottisfont, Romsey SO51 0LP.
Tel: (01794) 340757;
www.nationaltrust.org.uk

15m NW of Southampton, 4.25m NW of Romsey, 0.5m W of A3057

House open

Garden open 3rd to 28th Feb, Nov to 21st Dec, Sat and Sun, 11am – 4pm; March to Oct, Sat – Thurs, 11am – 5pm. Special rose openings 31st May to 23rd June, daily, 11am – 7.30pm (closes 5pm Sun)

Entrance: £7.50, children £3.80, family £18.80 (extra charge during rose openings, reduced winter rates) (2007 prices) Please see website for details of opening dates and special prices

Mottisfont Abbey Garden

Other information: Coaches must pre-book. Four-seater golf buggy available. No smoking in walled garden during rose season

magically deep and bubbling pool, and a spring running down to the River Test provide a tranquil contrast to the heady and scented delights of the roses. The simple but effective design of grass terraces, yew octagon and pollarded lime walk is the work of the late Sir Geoffrey Jellicoe, while Norah Lindsay contributed the small lavender- and box-edged parterre infilled with spring bulbs and summer annuals.

Lady Clark

Redenham, Nr Andover SP11 9AQ.
Tel: (01264) 772511

4m NW of Andover on A342

Open for parties by appt

Entrance: £5.50

Other information: Teas by arrangement

REDENHAM PARK ★

The perfect setting for a Jane Austen novel, this classic five-acre garden embraces its early-nineteenth-century ashlar-faced house. Views of parkland with sheep and cedars are followed by an enclosed paved rose garden with a circular pond (home to zantedeschias and white irises) and a fountain, then by herbaceous borders leading to a pleached lime walk and a moon gate. There are also fine borders, sculptural clipped yews, a tapestry hedge of copper- and green-leaved beech bordering a croquet lawn, and a low pear and apple espalier in a walled garden, where walls and paths drip in June with scented roses. The walled kitchen garden is immaculate, and exotic fowls roam free.

Lady Scott

East Tisted, Alton GU34 3QE.
Tel: (01420) 588207

4m S of Alton on A32

Open for NGS, and May and Sept for parties by appt

Entrance: £2.50, children free

ROTHERFIELD PARK

(Historic Garden Grade II*)

The Grade-I-listed house was built between 1815 and 1822 by the Scott family, with later additions in a medley of medieval and Tudor styles – note the laundry house chimney like Rapunzel's tower – and is an integral part of the 250-acre Picturesque landscape, looking to the church which was rebuilt as a *point de vue* complete with little tower. The quadripartite, one-acre walled garden is approached via splendid yew hedges supported by golden yew buttresses, and entered through magnificent wrought-iron gates, with a fine Victorian summerhouse terminating the vista. There is a fruit section with espalier apples and pears along the walls, standard shrub sections. In May the 60-acre pleasure ground is a haze of bluebells. Elsewhere, an orchard and maze, an ice-house and a ha-ha, and many fine trees and shrubs.

Mrs Rosemary Alexander

Rogate, Petersfield GU31 5HU.
Tel: (01730) 818373
www.rosemaryalexander.co.uk

4m E of Petersfield off A272. From crossroads in Rogate, take road signed to Nyewood and Harting. Follow road for 1m over small bridge; house is on right over cattle grid

Open for NGS, and by appt

Entrance: £3, children free

SANDHILL FARM HOUSE

Within the 1.5-acres are two gardens, lying either side of the house, and each is different in mood. The first – informal, shady and enclosed – is approached by an opening cut through a beech hedge underplanted with *Hedera helix* 'Maple Leaf'. Beyond is a woodland garden contoured by peat bricks, with gravel paths winding around trees and shrubs such as ginkgo, *Ilex aquifolium* 'Hascombensis', a fatshedera, the white-stemmed and golden-leaved *Rubus cockburnianus* 'Goldenvale' and two birches whose silky grey and pink barks are scrubbed every Easter Sunday. Beside the house are the rarely seen *Lyonothamnus floribundus* with its little white flowers appearing in early summer. The other garden is laid out in patterns with a potager and a tiny gazebo, herbaceous borders and a lawn overlooking the surrounding countryside. One border is planted in shades of red, yellow and orange; the other, complemented by a variegated Italian buckthorn, has mauves, delicate blues, greys and pinks. Vistas are carefully controlled.

THE SIR HAROLD HILLIER GARDENS ★★
(Historic Garden and Arboretum Grade II)

Administered by Hampshire County Council since 1977, this collection of hardy trees and shrubs, the largest in the world, was begun in 1953 by the late Sir Harold Hillier. It extends to 180 acres and includes approximately 12,000 different species and cultivars, with many rarities. Eleven National Collections, including quercus and hamamelis are held here, more than any other garden. Weekly lists of plants of current-season interest are produced, and lead the visitor to herbaceous, scree, heather and bog gardens. With a total of about 42,000 plants it is impossible at any time of year not to be impressed or learn something about what, where and how to plant. Notable among the trees are *Eucalyptus nitens* and *E. niphophila*, *Magnolia cylindrica* spp *zanthoxylum* (the prickly ash or toothache tree) as well as acers and sorbus. Among the shrubs is a wide range of rhododendrons, azaleas, camellias and hydrangeas. The winter garden specialises in plants at their best from November to March, and includes gold- and black-stemmed bamboos and the white-stemmed *Rubus thibetanus*.

Hampshire County Council

Jermyns Lane, Ampfield, Romsey
SO51 0QA. Tel: (01794) 369318;
www.hilliergardens.org.uk

2m NE of Romsey, 9m SW of Winchester, 0.75m W of A3090 along Jermyns Lane. Signed from A3090 and A3057

Open all year, daily, except 25th and 26th Dec, 10am – 6pm (or dusk if earlier)

Entrance: £7.50, concessions £6.50, children under 16 free

The Sir Harold Hillier Gardens

Much more than an arboretum, this attractively laid-out garden can be enjoyed at many levels. The visitor education pavilion is approached by a curved walk of *Metasequoia glyptostroboides*, and the visitor now approaches the arboretum with a view of rare trees merging with the Hampshire countryside beyond. Nearby at *Broadlands* there is a 'Capability' Brown landscape (Historic Park Grade II*). It is also worth the detour into Winchester to view *Queen Eleanor's Garden*, the re-creation of a small medieval plot designed by Dr Sylvia Landsberg behind the Great Hall of Winchester Castle.

SPINNERS ★

Mr P. G. G. Chappell

School Lane, Boldre, Lymington SO41 5QE. Tel: (01590) 673347

1.5m N of Lymington. Follow county signs on A337 between Brockenhurst and Lymington

Open April to mid-Sept, Tues – Sat, 10am – 5pm, and at other times by appt

Entrance: £2.50

This informal woodland garden on the acid soil of the New Forest is remarkable for its plant associations and the owner's careful choice of scale. Nothing is over-large or dwarfs the smaller pleasures. In spring the sun shines through the canopy of trees, lighting camellias and dwarf rhododendrons, exochordas, magnolias, *Cornus kousa* and the brilliant coral leaves of *Acer palmatum* 'Shishio Improved'. Many of the rarer magnolias and tree cornus have been planted recently, and the numbers of species and lace-cap hydrangeas increased to extend the flowering season. Admire at ground level the carpets of cyclamen, *Erythronium revolutum* like pale pink stars, and the white and strange maroon trilliums. Beside the spring near the house the yellow-greens of ferns and variegated iris synchronise with white and yellow skunk cabbage. Ferns, primulas and hostas thrive in the bog garden, and good autumn colouring comes from *Nyssa sinensis* and other trees. The nursery has an enticing collection of rare and unusual hardy trees, shrubs and plants, especially magnolias and trilliums.

TYLNEY HALL HOTEL ★
(Historic Garden Grade II*)

Rotherwick, Hook RG27 9AZ.

Tel: (01256) 764881;
www.tylneyhall.com

Access from M3 junction 5 (take A287 via Newnham) or from M4 junction 11 (take B3349 via Rotherwick)

Open for NGS, and for non-residents eating at hotel

Entrance: £3, children free

Other information: Refreshments and plants for sale on open days

An Edwardian period piece. The elaborate brick house with gardens stretching to 66 acres was built in 1900 by Seldon Wornum for Sir Lionel Phillips, a South African diamond merchant. Wornum and Robert Weir Schultz designed the gardens, with an Italian terrace and fountain overlooking the boathouse lake, a Dutch garden, a fine avenue with Wellingtonias and splendid vistas framed by trees to the north and south. Designs were obtained from Gertrude Jekyll for the wild water garden, where two rivulets fell from one lake to another. When the house became a school in 1946, hard tennis courts were built on the Italian terrace, the lakes became choked and balustrades and statuary were lost. It is now a hotel, and the gardens have been restored and replanted. A fountain plays again on the Italian terrace, the boathouse lake is cleared and its bridge rebuilt, the water gardens are restored with rivulets, lakes and bogside planting, the kitchen garden has regained its rose pergola, the orchards stock 20 varieties of apple, and the vistas with their mature trees now look better than in the photographs of earlier days. There are also fine specimen trees.

WEST GREEN HOUSE GARDEN ★★

Nestling in a wooded corner of Hampshire is a ravishingly attractive 1720s manor house, where busts of gods, emperors and dukes look down from the walls onto two major gardens. The inner gardens, enclosed by eighteenth-century walls, are all devoted to parterres. One is filled with water lilies, another is of classical design with box topiary, and a third enacts the whimsy of *Alice in Wonderland*. The main walled garden is planted in subtle hues of mauve, plum and blue, contained in beds that have been restored to their original outlines. Flamboyant groups of tulips echo the walled garden's imaginative colour schemes. A decorative potager is centred around berry-filled fruit cages where herbs, flowers and unusual vegetables are designed into colourful patterns that change every year. All this is surrounded by a second garden, a remarkable neo-classical park studded with follies, birdcages and monuments designed by Quinlan Terry. The entrance to the park is through a tunnel of hornbeams, pleached to direct the eye to two Chinese pagodas, where the Dragon Garden reveals two monsters devised by Nick Muscamp, surrounded by black-red peonies. Water is everywhere. A tree-fringed lake is especially attractive in spring with its drifts of fritillaries and other bulbs; and a grand water garden, the Nymphaeum, spills down rills and steps from a devil's mouth into serene ponds. Between the two lies a geometric parterre of moated trees and grass rectangles which seem to float above the water; lines of water play. A green theatre, a picturesque orangery and long green *allées* are other fine features. This exciting combination of dramatic restoration and new design has been undertaken by the well-known Australian gardener Marylyn Abbott.

Miss Marylyn Abbott

West Green, Hartley Wintney, Hook RG27 8JB. Tel: (01252) 844611; www.westgreenhouse.co.uk

10m NE of Basingstoke, 1m W of Hartley Wintney, 1m N of A30

Open 14th May to 10th Aug, Wed, Thurs, Sat, Sun and Bank Holiday Mons, 11am – 4.30pm, and May to 10th Aug for parties of 15–60 by appt.

Entrance: £5.50

Other information: Opera season 25th to 27th July

◑ ☕ WC ♿ 🐾 ♨ 🍷

West Green House Garden

OTHER RECOMMENDED GARDENS

AMPORT HOUSE

Amport, Andover SP11 8BG. Open by appt in writing to the Principal

The little-known garden of the Lutyens-Jekyll partnership surrounds a Jacobean-style house built in 1857 for the Marquis of Winchester, whose coat of arms adorns the parterre. Lutyens' big-boned terraces, steps and rilled water garden stand out, and although little remains of Jekyll's planting, the rock garden she designed survives. Fine driveway trees and cordon lime walks add to the historic atmosphere. 8 acres. (Listed Grade II)

FURZEY GARDENS

Minstead, Lyndhurst SO43 7GL (023 8081 2464; www.furzey-gardens.org). Open daily except 25th and 26th Dec, 10am – 5pm, gallery open March to Oct.

The informal 8-acre garden on acid soil was established in the 1920s, with a group of picturesque thatched buildings and narrow paths winding down to tree houses and a bog garden. Fine views look over colourful shrub plantings and woodland trees.

GILBERT WHITE'S HOUSE AND GARDEN

Selborne GU34 3JH (01420 511275; www.gilbertwhiteshouse.org.uk). Open all year, Tues –Sun and Bank Holiday Mons, plus Mons, June to Aug, all 11am – 5pm. Closed 25th to 31st Dec. Unusual plants fair 21st and 22nd June. NT

The 20-acre garden with its splendid views of the beech-clad hanging wood, is a living testament to the famous naturalist and author of *The Natural History of Selborne* (published

1788). Quincunx, sundial and ha-ha survive, beds and borders have been planted with contemporary favourites, and the pond and vegetable garden are also true to the spirit of the time.

HIGHCLERE CASTLE

The Earl and Countess of Carnarvon, Highclere, Newbury, Berkshire RG20 9RN (01635 253210; www.highclerecastle.co.uk). Open July and Aug, Sun – Thurs, 11am – 4:30pm (last entry 3.30pm), plus some Bank Holidays (telephone for details)

The Houses of Parliament look-alike created by Sir Charles Barry stands amid lawns and cedars in a gloriously simple 'Capability' Brown landscape. Three follies, a lakeside rotunda, a roofless temple and Heaven's Gate on a hill predate Brown's work, and tucked out of sight is the walled garden and the flower garden designed by the late James Russell. 600 acres in all. (Listed Grade I)

WEST SILCHESTER HALL

Mrs Jenny Jowett, Silchester RG7 2LX (0118 970 0278). Open for NGS, and for parties by appt

The 1.5-acre garden has been designed by a plantswoman and accomplished botanical artist, who has filled her curving borders with a mass of clematis, roses, unusual shrubs and herbaceous plants leading down to a waterlily pond; half-hardies include a large collection of salvias. There is also a self-supporting kitchen garden. The colour pairings are especially good, and one season seems to merge effortlessly into the next.

ISLE OF WIGHT

BARTON MANOR

Robert Stigwood

Whippingham, East Cowes PO32 6LB. Tel: (01983) 528989

From East Cowes take A3021, 500 metres beyond Osborne House on left

Open four days for charity – telephone or consult www.iwhospice.org for details

Entrance: £3, children £1

The Jacobean-style mansion was built in 1846 as an overflow for royal guests at Osborne House (see entry). Many of the fine trees from Prince Albert's original design have been felled by gales, but the terraces laid out by Edward VII remain, and balls of hypericum march either side of a path leading down to Queen Victoria's skating rink, now home to carp, black swans and waterfowl. On the far side lie a water garden laid out by Hilliers in 1968 and a hidden garden planted with azaleas and rhododendrons. A conifer maze with a dark castle at its heart may be viewed from a platform outside. Herbaceous borders include fine dahlias, and National Collections of kniphofias and watsonias are held here.

MOTTISTONE MANOR

The six-acre garden surrounding the beautiful L-shaped Elizabethan house (restored and enlarged with advice from Lutyens in 1927) lies in a sheltered valley. North of the house steps rise to a rose garden, then to a fine double herbaceous border at its peak in July, and beyond to an orchard planted with an avenue of flowering and fruiting trees. The path culminates at a seat backed by an elliptical yew hedge, with views of Brighstone Bay. The organic kitchen garden is a model of productivity, and an olive grove has been planted on the hillside above. A sunken walled garden to the south shelters a tulip tree, a holm oak, a black mulberry and slightly tender shrubs such as solanum, ceanothus, carpenteria and pittosporum, giving a Mediterranean feel to the planting.

OSBORNE HOUSE ★

(Historic Garden Grade II*)

Built by Queen Victoria in 1845–51 as a family retreat, the 20-acre gardens, designed jointly by the royal couple in the formal Italianate style, are now being restored and replanted to the original designs. Old cultivars have been used for the Victorian-style bedding on the terraces, and the borders have been replanted with plants of the period. The park and gardens are notable for their magnificent trees. The Swiss Cottage Garden, in what were the royal children's gardens, has nine plots, each with 14 beds, planted with old varieties of soft fruit, flowers and vegetables. The Swiss Cottage museum has

Other information: Coaches welcome. Guide dogs only

The National Trust

Mottistone PO30 4ED.
Tel: (01983) 741302;
www.nationaltrust.org.uk

2m W of Brighstone on B3399

House open 29th May only, 2 – 5.30pm (guided tours for NT members 10am – 12 noon)

Garden open 15th March to 2nd Nov, Sun to Thurs, 11am – 5.30pm

Entrance: £3.70, children £1.90, family £9.25

NEW

English Heritage

East Cowes PO32 6JY.
Tel: (01983) 200022;
www.english-heritage.org.uk

1m SE of East Cowes off A3021

House open as grounds, 10am – 5pm

Grounds open April to Oct, daily, 10am – 6pm (closes 4pm Oct). Telephone for winter opening times

Entrance: £5.90, concessions £4.40, children £3, family £14.80 (house and grounds £9.80, concessions £7.40, children £4.90, family £24.50

Osborne House

replicas of the royal children's individually named wheelbarrows, and other curiosities inlcude a mock fort and Queen Victoria's bathing machine. There is also a wildflower meadow and an orchard. The one-acre walled garden has been restored sympathetically by Rupert Golby using historic plants within a modern design. The usual wall-trained fruit – vines, figs, pears, plums and cherries – are complemented by olive, orange and lemon trees. Drifts of multiple plantings span the length and width of the garden, ensuring a continuous display of striking colour throughout the summer, and broad rows of herbaceous plants are offset by extensive plots of annually sown flowers, herbs and vegetables. The glasshouses commissioned by Prince Albert have been restored and house collections of plants from South Africa and those introduced to Britain during the Victorian period. The entwined V & A motifs to be seen in the furnishings of the house are also used here on ironwork arches, garden benches and terracotta pots.

OTHER RECOMMENDED GARDENS

BUTTERFLY WORLD

Staplers Road, Wootton PO33 4RW (01983 883430).
Open April to Oct, daily, 10am – 5.30pm

This under-cover garden, useful on rainy days, has more to recommend it than the wonderfully exotic butterflies floating over seas of impatiens and jungle greenery. There is also a very small Italian garden, an animated clown band, a quirky Japanese garden with carp, and a water garden with jets tossing from one pool into another and a water tunnel to walk through – enough to make Renaissance gardeners gawp. Kitsch and good fun.

MORTON MANOR

J. A. Trzebski, Brading, Sandown PO36 0EP
(01983 406168). Open 21st March to Oct, daily except Sat, 10am – 5.30pm (last admission 4.30pm)

The origins of Morton can be traced to the 13th century, the sunken garden is Elizabethan in origin, the terraces 19th-century. However, the show of spring bulbs, extensive herbaceous displays and parade of fine trees (100 different varieties of Japanese maple) give the garden far more than historical interest.

NUNWELL HOUSE

Col. And Mrs J. A. Aylmer, Coach Lane, Brading
PO36 0JQ (01983 407240). Open 25th and 26th May, 30th June to 3rd Sept, Mon – Wed, 1 – 5pm, and for parties by appt

The 5.5-acre garden surrounding the pretty 16th-century house is a tranquil place of walks and borders, with terrace views over a circular lily pond and across the countryside to Spithead. Near the house a steep lavender-bordered flight of steps leads to woodland. (Listed Grade II)

PITT HOUSE

L. J. Martin, Love Lane, Bembridge PO35 5NF.
Open June to Aug, Thurs, 2 – 5pm

The 4-acre garden is noted for its fine trees and Solent views. Water features, many intriguing sculptures and a Victorian greenhouse give added interest, and a shady dell is hidden at a lower level.

VENTNOR BOTANIC GARDEN

Undercliff Drive, Ventnor PO38 1UL (01983 855397).
Open all year daily, dawn – dusk, but 'Green' House and visitor centre have restricted openings

Originally planted by Sir Harold Hillier to house the tender trees and shrubs in his collection, the 22 acres feature exotics from China, the Americas, Japan, the Mediterranean, New Zealand and South Africa. A National Collection of pseudopanax is here, and the plant sales area has a range of unusual varieties on offer. (Listed Grade II)

HEREFORDSHIRE

For further information about how to use the *Guide*
and for an explanation of the symbols, see pages vi–viii.
Specific dates and times are those given to us by garden owners for 2008.
For 2009 dates, check with the individual properties.
For opening dates under the National Gardens Scheme,
readers should consult *The Yellow Book* or www.ngs.org.uk.
Maps are to be found at the end of the *Guide*.

ABBEY DORE COURT GARDENS ★

Only first-rate plants are allowed to grow here: flower, colour or shape – everything is in some way exemplary. The 10 acres, two of them left wild, incorporate part of the original Abbey Dore Court garden (laid out in 1858 but developing its present character and plantings since the late 1970s). A new area, designed around a delicate gazebo, is quickly becoming established. The purple, gold and silver borders, created at the suggestion of Graham Stuart Thomas, are eye-catching and retain year-round interest. They lead to a wild riverside walk, and across the River Dore a four-acre meadow is planted with rare trees and shrubs, intersected by mown paths. A walled Victorian garden with wide borders punctuated by white foxgloves and cimicifugas has been developed with a sure eye for colour and form. The fruit trees have now all gone and a wide path dissects the old orchard area. There is a wire seat at the end looking down to an original water feature, and in the west-facing corner a slate table raised by terracing catches the evening sun. Extravagant plantings, laid out with flair and imagination, delight the eye on every side. Hellebores, peonies, astrantias and clematis are specialities, and these and other herbaceous perennials are on offer in the nursery.

Mrs C.L. Ward

Abbey Dore Court, Hereford HR2 0AD.
Tel: (01981) 240419;
www.abbeydorecourt.co.uk
11m SW of Hereford off A465

Open April to Sept – visitors welcome any day but must telephone first; groups by appt

Entrance: £3.50, children £1

◑ WC ♿ ✾

BROCKHAMPTON COTTAGE ★★

In this marvellous three-acre garden, created since 2000, Tom Stuart-Smith and Peter Clay of the internet nursery Crocus have combined to anchor the plantings with dexterity within its stunning landscape. The strong but fairly restricted prairie-planting palette of 'bruised' colours – using such stalwarts as echinaceas, persicarias and dark-leaved sedums – blends well with the characterful dusky-pink stone house, while grasses in variety echo the crop plantings in the surrounding fields. Among the eye-catching plants are dwarf narcissi, *Anemone nemorosa* 'Robinsoniana', scillas and black-flowered tulips for spring, perlargoniums in pots for summer scent. On the west side eight topiaried beech trees stand sentinel between the raised York stone terrace and the perry pear orchard below. On the main garden front the slope is cleverly dealt with by

Peter and Ravida Clay

Brockhampton, Nr Hereford HR1 4TQ.
Tel: (01989) 740386

8m SW of Hereford, 5m N of Ross-on-Wye off B4224. In Brockhampton take road signed to Brockhampton Church, continue up hill for 0.5m; after set of farm buildings driveway is on left over cattle grid

Open for parties by appt

Entrance: charge

● ⬛WC ✾

means of a series of shallow stone-edged grass terraces flanked by a pair of generous herbaceous borders that give way to others sweeping outwards towards the view. Beyond, wildflower meadows drop to a large serpentine lake fringed by gunneras, *Iris sibirica* and many bulbs (a swathe of land was boldly scooped out to make the lake visible from the house) and a young arboretum planted largely with American species in a gesture of ancestral respect. Then the rolling panorama of woods and fields takes over.

EASTNOR CASTLE
(Historic Park Grade II*)

Eastnor Estate

Eastnor, Ledbury HR8 1RL.
Tel: (01531) 633160;
www.eastnorcastle.com

8m SW of Great Malvern, 2m E of
Ledbury on A438

Castle open

Garden open 20th to 24th March;
30th March to 28th Sept,
Bank Holiday Suns and Mons;
14th July to 29th Aug, daily except Sat;
all 11am – 4.30pm

Entrance: £4, OAPs £3, children £2
(house and garden £8, OAPs £7,
children £5, family £20)

The arboretum here contains some of the earliest plant-hunter collections of exotic trees in the country, especially of conifers. Roughly contemporary with Westonbirt (see entry in Gloucestershire), the main collection was established between 1840 and 1860, with seed being brought from around the world throughout the nineteenth century. A tree trail leads to the most important and interesting specimens, and to far-flung areas of the extensive grounds. A lakeside walk gives fine views back to the fairytale Gothick castle designed by Robert Smirke. Restoration is ongoing: new groves of cercidiphyllums and acers, for example, will add to the variety of colour and texture for all seasons. Near to the castle, the terraces have not been restored to their nineteenth-century character; instead, a long border is planted for mid- to late-summer colour, while the upper terrace has an iris border, together with lavenders, santolinas and other sun-loving shrubs. A cottage-style garden is being planted near the maturing yew maze. 90 acres in all.

HAMPTON COURT GARDENS ★

Hampton Court Gardens
(Herefordshire) Ltd

Nr. Hope under Dinmore, Leominster
HR6 0PN. Tel: (01568) 797777;
www.hamptoncourt.org.uk

5m S of Leominster, on A417
near junction with A49 between
Leominster and Hereford

Telephone for details of opening times
and prices

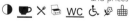

This fine garden has only been in creation since 1996, and its future continues to hang in the balance. Surrounding a fifteenth-century Grade-I-listed building (not open), with a conservatory designed by Paxton, the grounds were originally laid out on a suitably grand scale by Simon Dorrell. The

Hampton Court Gardens

decorative potager produces organic fruit and vegetables. The water garden is a large, geometrically laid-out walled enclosure, with a pair of octagonal pavilions surrounded by canals and ornamental water steps; the borders, lushly planted with lilies, lavenders, macleayas and cardoons, create an effective contrast to their crisp formality. It is worth puzzling your way through the intricate yew maze to reach the tower, from where a bird's eye view of the walled garden – like a medieval pleasaunce with the crenellated house beyond – is especially beguiling. From the tower a subterranean tunnel leads to a thatched hermitage beside a cascade and sunken pool. A nineteenth-century wisteria arch is magically sweet-smelling in flower, and leads to the calm tranquillity of a Dutch-inspired water garden. Wide lawns surround the house; the ha-ha allows a view of cattle grazing under magnificent trees in the park beyond.

HERGEST CROFT GARDENS ★
(Historic Garden Grade II*)

The varied garden, created over a period of 100 years by three generations of the Banks family, stretches over 50 acres. The design was much influenced by the writings of William Robinson, and is laid out in four sections: the plantings around the house itself, the kitchen garden, an azalea garden and Park Wood. The lawns and borders surrounding the Edwardian house are filled with a large collection of herbaceous plants and shrubs, backed by some outstanding specimen trees, including a huge sycamore planted c. 1800. The croquet lawn is like a restful, empty room amid all this fascinating variety, featuring only clipped yew hedges and large urns filled with lilies. The old-fashioned kitchen garden, containing a wide variety of unusual vegetables and fruit, has an avenue of ancient apple trees and double borders of spring flowers, underplanted with many coloured tulips and forget-me-nots – an ordinary enough combination, but somehow particularly pretty here. The double herbaceous borders blaze with colour in summer. The Azalea Garden is outstanding, shaded by many of the magnificent birches and maples that form part of National Collections. A grove of maples, designed by Elizabeth Banks and planted since 1985, includes many new or reintroduced species from China and elsewhere. The outer reaches of Park Wood are retained as natural beech and oak woodland, carpeted with anemones and bluebells in spring, but at its heart lies a secret valley of giant rhododendrons and exotic trees: a positively Himalayan scene. Rare trees and shrubs are on sale in the nursery.

KINGSTONE COTTAGES
The two-acre garden has only been in existence since 1976, but thanks to the owners' skilful use of reclaimed brick and stone it has the mellow atmosphere of a much older one. The

W.L. Banks

Kington HR5 3EG. Tel: (01544) 230160; www.hergest.co.uk

14m W of Leominster, 0.5m W of Kington off A44

Open March, Sat and Sun; April to Oct, daily; all 12 noon – 5.30pm

Entrance: £5.50, children under 16 free,

Other information: Flower fair 5th May, 10.30am – 5.30pm; autumn plant fair 12th Oct, 11am – 5:30pm

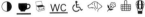

Michael and Sophie Hughes

Weston under Penyard, Nr Ross-on-Wye HR9 7PH. Tel: (01989) 565267/ (07792) 880684

2m E of Ross-on-Wye off A40. Turn left at Weston Cross public house signed to Bromsash, then left signed to Rudhall. Garden is 0.75m down this lane, on left

Open May to early July, daily except Sat, 10am – 5pm, and by appt

Entrance: £2, children free

Other information: Refreshments by arrangement for pre-booked parties

● 🍴 ♿ 🐾 B&B

Mr and Mrs Clive Richards

Ullingswick, Hereford HR1 3JF. Tel: (01432) 820557

7m NE of Hereford. At roundabout on A465 near Burley Gate take A417 towards Leominster. After 2m turn right, signed to Pencombe and Lower Hope; garden is 0.6m on left. Signposted

Open for NGS, plus 10th Aug, 2 – 5pm, and for parties by appt

Entrance: £3, children £1

Other information: Guide dogs only

● ☕ WC ♿ 🐾

planting is subtle and varied, well balanced between flowering plants and foliage. A pond full of bulrushes and water lilies is overhung by a cleverly constructed summerhouse, creating a magically secret spot. Other plantings frame fine views out to the Black Mountains. A grotto, a honeysuckle and clematis tunnel and a small formal water garden are other attractions, with a 'scrap-iron garden' adding a more surreal note. A special feature is a National Collection of old dianthus, with 140 varieties on show, and many of these and other unusual plants are for sale.

LOWER HOPE

Clive Richards has a Paxtonian passion for damming, diverting and pumping water with virtuoso inventiveness into streams, fountains and ponds. Visitors to the dazzlingly colourful and immaculately maintained eight-acre garden at Lower Hope will marvel at its many features. Indeed the map provided at the entrance is most helpful, especially in finding the woodland stream and bog gardens and the semi-circular lime walk to a small lake surrounded by wild flowers and young trees. From the entrance a white garden leads away from a shady tree-fern stumpery opening into lawns and colourfully planted island beds. Charming near-life-size sculptures of children are artfully placed beside a pond overhung with Japanese maples of striking colour and texture. The woodland bog and water gardens boast impressive gunneras and swathes of candelabra primulas, and a laburnum walk in the wood near the old tennis court is equally magnificent in early summer. Nearer the house a formal Mediterranean pool is convincing in style with its fountain, palms and quiet seclusion. Bananas, palms, melons, orchids and other exotic plants flourish in a fine glasshouse fronted by an enclosed garden of English roses and lavenders and a herb and vegetable garden. Prize-winning pedigree Hereford cattle and Suffolk sheep graze in the surrounding farmland.

Lower Hope

Lower Hopton Farm

LOWER HOPTON FARM

This is a gardener's garden in every sense. Mrs Cross (the garden designer Veronica Adams) had created from a five-acre field a formal Italianate garden reflecting her classic horticultural training, to which she has added, since 1992, a maze of secret places: an enclosure of topiary animals; a tangle of small, exquisite woodland areas planted with magnolias and shrub roses; an impressive collection of peonies and tree peonies of rare colour and variety. English borders, arbours of laburnum and robinia and a view across the lawn of a red Chinese bridge add to these delights. Rare plants abound: there are more than 100 named cultivars of snowdrops, and species of roses, magnolias and other unusual shrubs such as *Viburnum acerifolium* and the chestnut rose. On the moated island trilliums, hellebores, smilacinas and other shade-lovers thrive. One arbour is clothed by 'Debutante' roses, and there is another of white wisteria and Judas trees. A tall `Paul's Himalayan Musk' was a casualty when one of the cedars in the formal gardens blew down in winter, but the scars in this area have healed and *Ostrowskia magnifica* continues to flower happily. The most recent addition is a pretty summer house allowing a view up the stream to a quiet copse where *Cardiocrinum giganteum* make a superb display each year.

Mr and Mrs Giles Cross

Stoke Lacy, Bromyard HR7 4HX.
Tel: (01885) 490294

10m NE of Hereford off A465
Bromyard – Hereford road

Open for individuals and parties of 20 or more only, by personal introduction, to be confirmed in writing

Entrance: By donation – guideline £10 per person, parties of 45–50 £6 per person

THE OLD CORN MILL

Unlike the many Herefordshire gardens to be found perched on hilltops the better to soak up the rolling landscape, this one is hidden at the bottom of a little valley, surrounded by tall trees and threaded by the Rudhall Brook. The eighteenth-century mill house, beautifully modernised by the owner's architect son, is an important part of the scene. About 1.5 of the four acres is intensively gardened, and charmingly so,

Jill Hunter

Aston Crews HR9 7LW.
Tel: (01989) 750059

5m E of Ross-on-Wye. From A40, turn left at traffic lights at crossroads in Lea onto B4222 (signed to Newent); garden is 0.5m on left

Open for NGS, and by appt

Entrance: £2.50

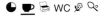

striking the difficult balance between naturalistic and ornamental planting – artistry without artificiality. The area in front of the house and the steep slope behind, traversed by paths of bark and grass, are filled with small bulbs, old roses, delicate perennials, ferns and grasses. Beyond lie the stream and woodland, and here the planting is simpler and wilder, with willows and alders luxuriating in the damp and fertile soil, and a small pond fringed with *Iris sibirica* and herb robert. A host of birds and insects, a family of rather raggedy willow ducks and a sculpture of a seated woman (intriguingly made of cement, fibreglass and paper) contribute to the atmosphere of this most attractive place.

G. Fenn and R. Treasure

Kimbolton, Leominster HR6 0HB.
Tel: (01568) 613432

1m NE of Leominster. From A49, turn right onto A4112 Kimbolton road. Garden is 300 metres on right. Signposted

Open April to Sept, Wed – Sun and Bank Holiday Mons, 12 noon – 5pm

Entrance: £4.50

Other information: Unsuitable for children

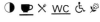

STOCKTON BURY GARDENS ★

Thoughtfully laid out over a four-acre site divided by stone and brick walls and yew hedges, this meticulously maintained garden is a feast for the plant-lover's eye. In a virtuoso display, climbing and herbaceous clematis in variety are grown through and under shrubs among an array of herbaceous plants of myriad shapes and colours. *Iris sibirica* surround The Dingle among hostas and primulas, producing vibrant clashes of orange, red and purple, and water lilies and zantedeschias are equally splendid and healthy. There are orchids and martagons in profusion, peonies and tree peonies, deutzias, viburnums and lilacs, and several unusual varieties of philadelphus flowering alongside the beautiful *P.* 'Belle Etoile'. A charming small, square rock garden planted with a choisya and daphnes provides a shaded seating area. Also interesting is the very large dovecote, left unoccupied so that the construction of the nesting boxes can be viewed from the inside – provided one can negotiate the Lilliputian door. The lawns are weed-free and perfectly edged. Many unusual plants, including trilliums, are for sale and reasonably priced. One can only wonder at the indefatigable energy and planting skills of Messrs Fenn and Treasure.

Mr Pelham and Miss Lucinda Aldrich-Blake

Weston-under-Penyard HR9 7NS.
Tel: (01989) 562597

1m E of Ross-on-Wye, 15m W of Gloucester on A40

Open for NGS, and for parties by appt

Entrance: £3.50, children free

NEW

WESTON HALL

This six-acre garden has been tended by the same family for four generations. Antique gates open onto the old drive leading to the sixteenth-century house built of weathered red sandstone; much of its southern facade is covered by a magnificent white-flowered wisteria. Lawns beside the house include mature specimens of *Sophora japonica*, magnolias, a ginkgo, cedars of Lebanon and a lovely lax *Rosa willmottiae*. A snowdrop tree, *Halesia carolina,* grows in the wide border against the high brick wall that forms one side of the walled garden, which is overlooked by a two-storey millennium folly echoing a Jacobean structure. The courtyard on the house side of the walled garden has been redesigned by Julian Dowle to appear square (it is not) with a central fountain of dolphins in the middle of four box-edged corner beds filled with white roses, lavenders, pinks, heucheras, geraniums and nicotianas. Within the walled garden the space is divided by low yew hedges interspersed with espaliered fruit trees, and among other delights in the long herbaceous borders are peonies, goldenrod, daylilies, kniphofias, romneyas and agapanthus, with *Gladioli byzantinus* romping through. On the far side of the house a small lake is surrounded by natural 'wild' planting of swamp cypresses, gunneras, water lilies and irises, while a juniper has a small island to itself. This is essentially a late spring and early summer garden, but in its antique setting it is beautiful at all seasons.

WESTONBURY MILL WATER GARDENS

This is a highly individual water garden of 3.5 acres with a broad collection of damp- and water-loving plants laid out around a maze of leats, channels, streams and in a bog criss-crossed by narrow paths. Views to the hills and across the old meadows surrounding the garden are emphasised by the planting, and an adjacent meadow with streamside walks to the weir is being developed as a wildflower area. The garden has been landscaped and planted by the owner, a retired hydro-geologist with a flair for quirky constructions. These include an African-style open hut, a willow tunnel and a stone tower with gargoyles spouting intermittent chutes of water – reminiscent of watery Renaissance jokes in Italian villas. A fern grotto has a domed roof made of wine bottles which glow in the sun like cathedral windows. Massed plantings include many irises – *Iris pseudacorus* var. *bastardii*, *I. laevigata* 'Snowdrift', *I. × robusta* 'Gerald Darby', *I. sibirica* 'Perry's Blue' – *Primula wilsonii*, *Ligularia × hessei*, *Rodgersia podophylla* and *Gunnera manicata*.

Richard and Sally Pim

Pembridge HR6 9HZ.
Tel: (01544) 388650;
www.westonburymillwatergardens.com

Off A44 between Leominster and Kington. From Pembridge take Kington road for 1.5m; garden is signed on left

Open 21st March to Sept, daily, 11am – 5pm

Entrance: £3.50, children £1

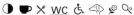

WHITFIELD HOUSE
(Historic Garden Grade II)

A splendid 15-acre garden surrounds the house, plus extensive woodland walks. The estate boasts some magnificent trees, including a stand of giant redwoods planted in the mid-nineteenth century and reputed to be the largest in Europe. The gardens adjacent to the house have been redesigned by Arabella Lennox-Boyd and are currently under construction; cubes of yew and pleached limes will add a crisp formality. A string of lakes leads away from the facade, where golden orfe fry turn the water in the Fountain Pool positively gold in early summer. Castle Pool has a folly island devised by the late owner, a rare creation in the twentieth century. A fernery, punctuated with martagon lilies, flourishes in the shade of a large copper beech, and there are some fine magnolias. An extensive walled garden is reached through the camellia house, with a classical portico; a vinery and a ginkgo tree with the greatest girth in the country are among its delights.

Mr and Mrs Edward Clive

Wormbridge HR2 9BA.
Tel: (01981) 570202

8m SW of Hereford on A465 Abergavenny road

Open for NGS, and by appt

Entrance: £3, children free

OTHER RECOMMENDED GARDENS

ARROW COTTAGE GARDEN

Mr and Mrs D. Martin. Ledgemoor, Weobley HR4 8RN (01544 318468; www.arrowcottagegarden.co.uk). Open May to Aug, Fri to Sun, 11am – 4pm

The clever layout of the garden designed originally by Lance Hattatt makes it seem much larger than 2 acres. A series of well-defined spaces, including one with a long rill and an elegant fountain, offers a cornucopia of contrasting shapes, colours and moods.

BERRINGTON HALL

Leominster HR6 0DW (01568 615721; www.nationaltrust.org.uk). Park & garden open 1st to 16th March, Sat and Sun; 17th March to 1st Nov, Sat – Wed (but open Good Fri); all 11am – 5pm. NT

'Capability' Brown's parkland retains its rolling 18th-century landscape and fine trees, and the colourful garden plantings closer to the red sandstone hall were mostly developed from the mid-18th century. Notable are the glowing, low-growing avenue of clipped yews leading from the Triumphal Arch and the walled garden refurnished with fruit trees and herbaceous borders. 11 acres of garden within a 4000-acre estate. (Listed Grade II*)

CROFT CASTLE

Leominster HR6 9PW (01568 780246). Open 1st to 16th March, Nov to 21st Dec, Sat and Sun; 19th March to Oct, Wed – Sun and Bank Holiday Mons; all 12 noon – 5pm; and for parties by written appt. NT

The 14th-century Welsh Marches castle, Gothicised in Victorian times, commands a spectacular landscape of mountains, parkland and woods. The sides of the Fishpool Valley are densely planted with trees above a stream and ponds, while the walled garden and castle surrounds are given over to fruit and flowers. A haunt of ancient peace with a domestic overlay. 1300 acres in all. (Listed Grade II*)

HOW CAPLE COURT

Mr and Mrs Roger Lee, How Caple, Hereford HR1 4SX (01989 740626; www.howcaplecourt.com). Open 19th March to 12th Oct, daily, 10am – 5pm, and for parties by appt

The 11-acre Arts-and-Crafts garden, gently decaying and unkempt in parts, is intensely romantic and full of surprises. As well as the usual rose and rock gardens, shrubberies and woodland, there are formal, stone-flagged terraces, a stunning Italianate water garden almost lost in woodland with a great rill at its heart, a viewing terrace with Tuscan columns. The views are magnificent.

THE LONG BARN

Roger and Fay Oates, Eastnor, Ledbury HR8 1EL (01531 632718; www.rogeroates.com). Open late May to mid-Sept, Wed – Fri, 10am – 5pm, and by appt at other times

The 0.25-acre garden sits contentedly in its handsome landscape, anchored by a strong, simple structure of walls, hedges and trellises festooned with climbers. Within square plots divided by grass and gravel paths the textile-designer owners have woven together a harmonious profusion of herbaceous plants, herbs and vegetables. The effect is loose, sometimes shaggy, and altogether delightful.

MONNINGTON COURT

John and Angela Bulmer, Monnington-on-Wye HR4 7NL (01981 500488; www.monnington-morgans.co.uk). Open 18th, 19th, 25th and 26th May, 10am – 5pm, and by appt

The 25 acres around the medieval house are a fine setting for many interesting figurative and abstract sculptures – Mrs Bulmer is the well-known sculptor Angela Conner. A mile-long avenue of pine and yew trees, a lovely man-made lake, a boundary formed by the River Wye, and (at 4pm) a display by the famous Morgan horses are powerful attractions on the few open days.

THE WEIR GARDEN

Swainshill, Hereford HR4 7QF (01981 590509; www.nationaltrust.org.uk). Open 19th, 20th, 26th and 27th Jan, 30th Jan to 24th Feb, 7th May to 26th Oct, Wed – Sun; 27th Feb to 6th May, daily; all 11am – 4pm (closes 4pm Jan and Feb). NT

This now essentially 'wild' woodland riverside garden is perhaps best visited in spring when bulbs carpet the ground beneath beeches, chestnuts and oaks. A steep descent from the top of the garden is thickly planted in terraces of laurel, lonicera, cotoneaster and hypericum, and criss-crossed by paths providing splendid views of the River Wye and the Black Mountains beyond.

HERTFORDSHIRE

For further information about how to use the *Guide*
and for an explanation of the symbols, see pages vi–viii.
Specific dates and times are those given to us by garden owners for 2008.
For 2009 dates, check with the individual properties.
For opening dates under the National Gardens Scheme,
readers should consult *The Yellow Book* or www.ngs.org.uk.
Maps are to be found at the end of the *Guide*.

THE ABBOT'S HOUSE

This 1.75-acre plantsman's garden is full of delights: *Crinodendron hookerianum*, *Itea ilicifolia*, *Hoheria sexstylosa* 'Stardust' and *Halesia carolina*, and many outstanding shrub and tree specimens,, some of which are tender. The sunken garden has plants thriving between the brickwork. There is also a Mediterranean semi-formal garden, a shrub border with contrasting foliage, borders of differing colour schemes, a wildflower meadow and a conservatory. A good range of interesting plants is for sale in the adjoining nursery.

Peter and Sue Tomson

10 High Street, Abbots Langley WD5 0AR. Tel: (01923) 264946

5m N of Watford, in Abbots Langley.

Open for NGS, and by appt

Entrance: £3.50, children free

BENINGTON LORDSHIP ★★
(Historic Garden Grade II)

Surrounding the manor house, Norman gatehouse and Victorian folly is a romantic hill-top seven-acre garden with fine views over the lake and open countryside. The massive and well-filled herbaceous double borders are designed with

Mr and Mrs R. R. A. Bott

Benington, Stevenage SG2 7BS.
Tel: (01438) 869668
www.beningtonlordship.co.uk

5m E of Stevenage

Open 2nd to 24th Feb, daily,
12 noon – 4pm, for snowdrops;
Easter and Bank Holiday weekends,
Suns, 2 – 5pm, Mons, 12 noon – 5pm.
Also open for NGS, and all year by appt

Entrance: £4 (Suns in Feb £4.50),
children free

Other information: Coaches must
pre-book. Refreshments on
open days only

 WC

Benington Lordship

a glorious feeling for texture and colour, backed by the kitchen garden wall and a sloping bank planted with an informal mixture of foliage and flowering plants. The old rock garden has been grassed over, and its original three pools now sit serenely among newly planted ornamental trees. A lavender-edged rose garden is set in a square in the centre of the old bowling green, and the kitchen garden has ornamental borders as well as functional rows of vegetables. In the moat and the surrounding grounds, the display of snowdrops followed by drifts of scillas is outstanding.

BROMLEY HALL

Julian and Edwina Robarts
Standon, Ware SG11 1NY.
Tel: (01279) 842422
6m W of Bishop's Stortford near A120 and A10 on Standon – Much Hadham road
Open for NGS, and for parties by appt
Entrance: £4, children free

The 4.5-acre garden, distinguished by its architectural qualities and its plantsmanship, has reached a wonderful maturity. The site is windy and exposed, and all possible use has been made of walls and hedges, including one of copper beech. The wide border flanking the drive flowers in early summer with a pleasing mixture of syringa, foxgloves, poppies and the lovely *Allium christophii*, and another startles with its bold mixture of red brooms, pink cistus and other hot-coloured flowers. A sculptural addition is an obelisk with a striking gilded pattern of intertwining leaves and lizards. The kitchen garden contains an array of mouth-watering produce, helped into immaculate growth by curly ornamental steel pea-sticks and terracotta rhubarb forcers. Vistas reveal glimpses of mown paths, rough grass, mature trees, and the countryside stretching out in the distance.

GREAT MUNDEN HOUSE

Mrs D. Wentworth-Stanley
Dane End, Ware SG11 1HU.
Tel: (01920) 438244
7m N of Ware off A10. Turn off W of Puckeridge bypass
Open April to June for small parties by appt
Entrance: £4 (inc. refreshments)

The charming three-acre garden, beautifully planned, immaculately kept and containing a great variety of plants, is situated down the side of a valley with a backdrop of wheat fields and trees. Beech hedges surrounding lawns act as necessary windbreaks against the wind funnelling down the valley. The mixed borders are imaginatively planted with shrubs, shrub roses, phlox and excellent foliage plants. Spring colour and interest come from bulbs and blossom, and the main border in May flowers blue, mauve and pink with early irises, alliums, aquilegias and perennial geraniums. A paved pond area is surrounded by silver plants and roses, with a *Juniperus virginiana* 'Skyrocket' in each corner, and climbing roses ramble through old apple trees. Primulas and hostas surround a small statue, and the herb garden is protected by a clipped *Lonicera nitida* hedge. A new border at the end of the croquet lawn has been planted with pink shrub roses. There is also an interesting small vegetable garden.

HANBURY MANOR HOTEL

Hanbury Manor Hotel
Ware SG12 0SD. Tel: (01920) 487722;
www.hanbury-manor.com

Edmund Hanbury inherited the property in 1884 and replaced the old house with a Jacobean-style mansion. The family were gifted horticulturists and the original gardens, now part of the hotel complex, were widely acclaimed for their species trees and orchid houses. Today, a colourful pre-Victorian walled garden with a listed moon gate has extensive herbaceous borders, a herb garden and fruit houses. The original pinetum with its centuries-old sequoias still stands, and major restoration work has seen the revival of the period rose gardens and bulb-planted orchard. The secret garden created in a woodland setting is also worth walking to see. On the outskirts of Ware, on A1170, is *Van Hage's Nursery*, superbly run with top-class plants and a wide range of garden furniture and accessories. [Open daily except Easter Sun, Christmas Day and Boxing Day, Mon – Sat, 10am – 6pm, Sun, 10.30am – 4.30pm.]

2m N of Ware off A10

Open all year

Entrance: free (charge on charity days)

Other information: Refreshments, toilet facilities and shop in hotel

HATFIELD HOUSE ★★
(Historic Garden Grade I)

Laid out originally in the early seventeenth century by Robert Cecil and planted by John Tradescant the Elder, the garden evolved over the centuries, particularly in the Victorian era and in the twentieth century at the hands of the Dowager Marchioness of Salisbury. There are many splendours here: a charming herb garden in the scented garden, the formal East Garden with its parterre, topiary, herbaceous borders and vegetable garden. The famous knot garden, filled with species used from the fifteenth to seventeenth centuries, adjoins the Old Palace where Elizabeth I spent much of her childhood. There is also a wild garden around the New Pond (originally formed in 1607). In the wilderness garden, delightful in spring

The 7th Marquess of Salisbury

Hatfield AL9 5NQ. Tel: (01707) 287010; www.hatfield-house.co.uk

2m from A1(M) junction 4 off A414 and A1000, opposite Hatfield railway station

House open

Park, West Garden, restaurant and shop open Easter Sat to Sept, daily, 11am – 5.30pm. East Garden open Thurs only

Entrance: park and West Garden £5, children £4; park only £2.50, children £1.50 (house, park and West Garden £9, OAPs £8.50, children £4)

Hatfield House

Other information: Many horticultural events – telephone or consult website for details

Aubrey Barker
Much Hadham SG10 6BU.
Tel: (01279) 842509; www.hopleys.co.uk

5m W of Bishop's Stortford off A120. In Much Hadham 50 metres N of Bull pub

Open March to Oct, Mon, Wed – Sat, 9am – 5pm, Sun, 2 – 5pm; on special days for charities; and by appt

Entrance: free (donations welcome)

Other information: Self-service refreshments

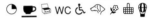

the wilderness garden, delightful in spring with bluebells and daffodils, up to 20,000 bulbs are planted each year, and the park has extensive walks and picnic areas. *The Gardens at Hatfield* by Sue Snell and The Dowager Marchioness of Salisbury was published by Frances Lincoln in 2005.

HOPLEYS ★

A remarkable five-acre garden and nursery with a most interesting structure and layout. The pool and bog garden are now well established, and developments continue: a gravel garden is established and a hornbeam avenue has been planted. There are some lovely mature trees, including mulberries and several different chestnuts, fine shrubs, choice perennials and much more. The extensive nursery sells many rarities. Much Hadham has two other properties of interest to gardeners. In Bourne Lane is the headquarters of *Andrew Crace* (Tel: (01279) 842685), who designs and sells a wide range of fine garden furniture and bronze and stone ornaments. *Dane Tree House* is the home of the Henry Moore Foundation and his collection, studios and workshops stand in parkland, with larger works placed in the surrounding fields. [Open April to Sept, Tues – Thurs, mornings only by appointment, or 2.30pm for tour. Tel: (01279) 843333.]

The Hon. Henry Lytton Cobbold
Knebworth, Nr Stevenage SG3 6PY.
Tel: (01438) 812661;
www.knebworthhouse.com

Signposted from A1(M) junction 7

House open as garden, but 12 noon – 5pm

Garden open 15th and 16th March, 12th April to 18th May, 7th to 29th June, 6th to 28th Sept, Sat, Sun and Bank Holiday Mons; 21st March to 6th April, 24th May to 1st June, 30th June to 2nd Sept, daily; all 10am – 5pm (last admission 4.15pm)

Entrance: £7.50, family £26 (house and gardens £9.50, OAPs and children £9, family £33)

KNEBWORTH HOUSE ★
(Historic Garden Grade II*)

The ancient home of the Lytton family has seen many alterations. The gardens evolved from a simple Tudor green and orchard to Sir Edward Bulwer Lytton's elaborate Jacobean-style design of the 1880s. In 1909 Edwin Lutyens, who married into the family, remodelled and simplified them in a scheme that included pollarded lime walks, rose gardens and pools. Beyond a tall yew hedge lie his Green Garden, Gold Garden and Brick Garden (with a blue and silver theme), and a pergola covered with clematis and roses. To one side is a pets' cemetery, to the other a crab-apple walk. The Victorian maze was replanted in 1995, and the herb garden, designed by Gertrude Jekyll in 1907, was laid out in 1982. The redeveloped walled garden has a collection of culinary herbs and vegetables. The Wilderness is a carpet of daffodils in spring followed by blue alkanet, foxgloves and other wild flowers; life-size dinosaurs are to be found grazing in three of its seven acres. In all there are 25 acres of garden to explore within the 250-acre park – a good day out for the whole family.

David and Celia Haselgrove
Brent Pelham, Buntingford SG9 0HH.
Tel: (01279) 777473

PELHAM HOUSE

The 3.5-acre garden was created from a cold and windswept field by the present owners. Beds were raised, tons of topsoil and mulch carted in, sheltering hedges of yew, beech and thuja planted. David Haselgrove is an excellent plantsman and grows rare and exotic varieties from seed, some of them collected by him from the wild: *Cornus capitata* is now a substantial tree, and exciting peonies come in many colours. Among the interesting trees is a cut-leaved oak, *Cornus* 'Eddie's White Wonder', and a good collection of birches. It is a lovely place to wander in spring among unusual hellebores, erythroniums, trilliums and many bulbs. A tufa garden holds a collection of daphnes, gentians and alpines, and there are fine statues by Antony Turner and Dominic Welch. Beside the church in the same village, and open on the same NGS days, is *Church Cottage*, an interesting and imaginative 0.75-acre cottage garden with delightful hidden corners, a winding pond and a bog garden.

7m NW of Bishop's Stortford, E of Brent Pelham on B1038 Buntingford – Newport Road

Open for NGS, 13th April for Red Cross, and by appt at other times

Entrance: £4

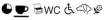

ST PAUL'S WALDEN BURY ★

(Historic Garden Grade I)

The formal 60-acre landscape garden laid out in 1730 is one of the few to survive; the Bowes Lyon family have lived at St Paul's Walden for more than 250 years and it was the childhood home of the late Queen Mother. The long mown rides or *allées* are lined with clipped beech hedges and fan out from the eighteenth-century house – the heart of the layout – through bosquets to temples, statues, ponds and a medieval church. In one of the bosquets is a green theatre. The lake, with its temple and wonderful vistas, is also not to be missed and there are fine seasonal displays of snowdrops, daffodils, rhododendrons, magnolias, banks of cowslips, and lilies. From the house the landscape is ravishing. The maintenance of a garden of this age and extent can never be an easy task.

Sir Simon Bowes Lyon and family

Whitwell, Hitchin SG4 8BP.
Tel: (01438) 871218

5m S of Hitchin, 0.5m N of Whitwell on B651

Open for NGS, plus 27th April and 21st May; all 2 – 7pm; and by appt at other times

Entrance: £3.50, children 50p, private visits £6 per person

VINEYARD MANOR

A garden of vivid imagination created by the present owners since 1995, and at its peak in high summer. Visitors enter up a slope planted with ferns, exciting hostas and other shade-loving plants under mature trees, past an amusing man's head with two clutching hands by Mark Hall and a tall bronze of fighting hares by Paul Jenkins. Behind the house a terrace with a wide border let into the hillside is planted in shades of gold, silver and bronze with good colour contrasts. This leads to a swimming pool surrounded by, and lined with, grey Chinese slate – a most ingenious solution. A secret garden with an old dew pond has been taken into the garden and planted in generous drifts of colour, with a mass of dark sedums, ligularias, geraniums, veronicas and monardas, *Rheum palmatum* and a highly scented *Telekia speciosa*, *Gunnera manicata* and tall grasses in variety.

Mr and Mrs H. Tee

Much Hadham SG10 6BS.
Tel: (01279) 843761

5m W of Bishop's Stortford off A120

Open May to Aug by appt

Entrance: £5

Other information: Teas by arrangement

OTHER RECOMMENDED GARDENS

ASHRIDGE BUSINESS SCHOOL

Berkhamsted HP4 1NS (01442 843491;
www.ashridge.com). Open for NGS, and Easter to
Sept, Sat. Sun and Bank Holiday Mons, 2 – 6pm

For the 7th Earl of Bridgwater's new 8-acre
pleasure grounds Humphry Repton came up
with a scheme of 15 different gardens,
producing a Red Book in 1813. Some of his
own invention survive, including the Monk's
Garden and the Rosary. In all, 90 acres of
considerable historical interest within a
5000-acre estate. (Listed Grade II)

Ashridge Business School

THE BEALE ARBORETUM

West Lodge Park Hotel, Cockfosters Road, Hadley
Wood EN4 0PY (020 8216 3900;
www.bealeshotels.co.uk). Open all year, daily, 2 – 5pm,
and for parties by appt

The knowledgeable dendrologist Edward Beale
bought the hotel in 1945 in order to enrich its
fine 18th-century park. Now this little-known
gem comprises 35 acres of arboretum, a lake
and 3 acres of more formal garden. The huge
strawberry tree in the park is said to have been
there when John Evelyn visited in 1675.

SOUTH FARM

Peter Paxman, Shingay, Royston SG8 0HR
(01223 207581; www.south-farm.co.uk). Open one
day for Red Cross, and April to Aug for parties by
appt

Familiar flowers abound in the main part of the
garden, enclosed and protected by a tall cypress
hedge. A pool terrace, a conservatory, a mosaic
of beds bursting with fruit and vegetables and a
wildflower meadow are some of the other
exuberant ingredients of this happy, not-too-tidy
8-acre garden.

KENT

For further information about how to use the *Guide*
and for an explanation of the symbols, see pages vi–viii.
Specific dates and times are those given to us by garden owners for 2008.
For 2009 dates, check with the individual properties.
For opening dates under the National Gardens Scheme,
readers should consult *The Yellow Book* or www.ngs.org.uk.
Maps are to be found at the end of the *Guide*.
We have included some gardens with Kent postal addresses in the London section
for convenience. So before planning a day out in Kent it is worthwhile consulting
pages 213–235.

ABBOTSMERRY BARN

The south-facing seven-acre garden with distant views towards Penshurst is an object lesson in how to exploit a challenging sloping site. The handsome converted Kentish barn, sheltered by mature trees and a stilted lime hedge, stands at the highest point. A sunny circular terrace, surrounding a large well, is filled with sun-loving plants, and impressive herbaceous borders in shades of purple and silver curve along the hillside towards bold groups of fragrant shrub roses. The latest area, planted with native trees, joins the existing woodland, with its shady dells and paths mown through grasses, and the wildflower meadow sweeping into the valley. Further exploration reveals a quarry with huge gnarled cherries, roses and foxgloves emerging from fissures in the sandstone, set around a tranquil oriental pool and a lush bog garden.

Mr and Mrs K. Wallis

Salmans Lane, Penshurst TN11 8DJ.
Tel: (01892) 870900;
www.abbotsmerry.co.uk

5m SW of Tonbridge off B2176 towards
Leigh. Turn left 180 metres N of
Penshurst; house is 1m down lane

Open for parties by appt

Entrance: £4, children free

 WC

BEDGEBURY NATIONAL PINETUM AND FOREST GARDENS ★

(Historic Arboretum Grade II*)

The modern 300-acre pinetum was founded in 1924, but some of the larger specimen trees dating from 1850 are still flourishing. The conifer collection has been listed as the best in the world by the International Dendrological Research Institute. In addition it has many deciduous trees, including rare oaks and maples, and a wide range of rhododendrons flowers from January to August. The pinetum holds five National Collections: Lawson and Leyland cypresses, junipers, yews and thujas.

Forestry Commission

Goudhurst, Cranbrook TN17 2SL.
Tel: (01580) 879820;
www.forestry.gov.uk/bedgebury

10m SE of Tunbridge Wells off A21, on
B2079 Goudhurst – Flimwell road

Pinetum open all year, daily, 8am – 8pm
(closes 5pm in winter)

Entrance: £6 per car, £20 per minibus,
£30 per coach (2007 prices)

Harris (Belmont) Charity

Belmont Park, Throwley, Faversham
ME13 0HH. Tel: (01795) 890202;
www.belmont-house.org

4m SW of Faversham, 1.5m W of A251
Faversham – Ashford road

House open April to Sept, Sat, Sun and
Bank Holiday Mons, 2 – 5pm

Garden open all year, daily, 10am – 6pm
(or dusk if earlier)

Entrance: £3, children £1 (house, clock
museum and gardens £6, concessions
£5.50, children £3) (2007 prices)

Other information: Teashop open Sat,
Sun and Bank Holiday Mon only,
from 3pm

BELMONT ★

(Historic Garden Grade II)

The distinctive eighteenth-century house designed by Samuel Wyatt commands fine views over rolling Kent countryside, and is surrounded by 40 acres of gardens and 150 acres of mature parkland. Since 2001, the charity formed by the 5th Lord Harris has sought to restore and regenerate the gardens. Bold herbaceous borders line the old walled garden, and a new nuttery, filled with wild flowers, leads to the two-acre Victorian kitchen garden where head gardener Graham Watts, working to a design by Arabella Lennox-Boyd, has created a striking scheme combining fruit, vegetables, herbaceous plants and herbs centred around a pool. Walls and pergolas support every type of fruit, and beyond a pleached pear hedge are arbours clothed in golden hops symbolic of local history. A *mandala*, a formal garden based on a Hindu design, reflects the family links with India, and a Coronation Walk of clipped yew planted in 1937 leads to a Gothic folly.

Mr and Mrs Peregrine Massey

Woodchurch, Ashford TN26 3RA.
Tel: (01233) 860302

7m SW of Ashford off A28. Turn left at
High Halden village green and second
right signed to Redbrook Street and
Woodchurch. Turn right down
unmarked lane, and after 0.5m right
again through brick entrance, past oast;
follow signs to car park

Open for NGS, and by appt

Entrance: £4, children free

NEW

BOLDSHAVES

The house, designed by a pupil of Lutyens, overlooks a quintessentially Kentish valley of sheep and distant oasts. The seven-acre gardens, sheltered by 'shaves' or bands of woodland, were taken on as a challenge by the present owner, a passionate gardener. From the house, broad grass terraces have been transformed with bold herbaceous borders planted in swathes of silver, blue and purple and backed by interesting shrubs, and the old tennis court is now grassed and furnished with specimen trees. New features are continually being developed: a border planted in fiery shades makes a telling contrast with the magnificent black weatherboarded barn, the old walled garden has been rescued from years of neglect to become a secluded secret garden, and the productive potager has been extended with a herb garden, linked to the lower lawns by a pergola swathed in roses and clematis. In the 30 acres of woodland more informal delights include walks through carpets of bluebells and a rush-fringed pond created from an old marl pit.

Mr and Mrs Bigwood

Westerham TN16 1PL.
Tel: (01732) 504556;
www.chartsedgegardens.co.uk

S of M25 and A25, 0.5m S of
Westerham on B2026 towards
Chartwell

Open mid-April to mid-Sept, Fri and
Sun, 2 – 4.30pm; for NGS; and for
parties of 5 or more by appt

CHART'S EDGE

The sweeping lawns are the start of a voyage of discovery through dells of magnificent azaleas and rhododendrons planted in mercifully subtle and harmonious colours, and on into intimate and exotic areas designed to make the most of the varying levels and vistas. The dell garden, filled with acers, tree ferns and hostas, leads to a flint-lined Victorian grotto adjoining a brick-lined room with a sunken bath. On the wide terraces cut into the valley side, water flows down through a series of gravel gardens; nearer the house colour comes from roses, a large and well-planted rockery and a bank of

Doddington Place
Gardens

Rhododendron yakushimanum. There is also a rill garden and a rainbow border, and new borders are being planted in 2008. Eight acres.

DODDINGTON PLACE GARDENS

(Historic Garden Grade II)

The theatrical quality of the 10-acre gardens where, appropriately, open-air opera is performed each year, is significantly heightened by newer features. The scale is intrinsically grand – smooth lawns are punctuated by towering specimen trees and enclosed by yew hedges pruned into amorphous, cloud-like shapes, and a Wellingtonia avenue planted in the mid-nineteenth century is contemporary with the house. A young *allée* of *Betula* 'Grayswood Ghost' accentuates the geometry of the Pond Walk, and a mirror-glass obelisk is the striking focus of the flower-filled grasses of the Spring Garden. A new brick-and-flint Gothick folly marks the transition between the formality of the Folly Walk and the wildness of the three-acre woodland garden beyond, where camellias, rhododendrons, acers and bulbs are spectacular in May and June. The formal sunken garden has imaginative modern planting schemes, the Edwardian rock garden is undergoing major restoration, and a formal box and peony garden is a new addition.

EDENBRIDGE HOUSE

This five-acre garden, originally made in the 1930s, is set on a south-facing slope. The part-sixteenth-century house is surrounded on three sides by a wide terrace on which a large variety of tender plants flourishes in pots. A walled courtyard to one side of the house contains a parterre filled with displays of annuals. Roses, *Itea ilicifolia*, *Clerodendrum bungei*, wisteria, jasmine and a *Magnolia grandiflora* drape the walls. Garden rooms are linked to the house by a lawn

Entrance: £3.50, children free

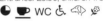

Richard and Amicia Oldfield

Doddington, Sittingbourne ME9 0BB.
Tel: (01795) 886101;
www.doddington-place-gardens.co.uk

6m S of Sittingbourne. From A20 turn N at Lenham, from A2 turn S at Teynham. Signposted

Refer to website for revised and additional opening dates. Also open for NGS, and by appt

Entrance: £4, children (over 5) £1

Mrs M.T. Lloyd

Main Road, Edenbridge TN8 6SJ.
Tel: (01732) 862122

1.5m N of Edenbridge on B2026

Open April to Sept, Tues – Thurs, 2 – 5pm, for NGS, and for parties by appt

Entrance: £3.50

containing a fountain pool guarded by elegant drum-shaped golden yews. A small stream, crossed by two wisteria-clad bridges, meanders down to a small lower pool; the banks of the stream are edged with rocks and planted with moisture-loving plants. There is a large kitchen garden, a soft-fruit cage and an apple and cherry orchard. Part of the kitchen garden has been turned into an arboretum and planted with a selection of trees and shrubs to give a wide range of colour, and there is a 21-metre-long peach house. A gravel garden has hostas, bamboos, various grasses, ferns, spiky agaves and palms. This is a plantsman's garden, with year-round interest provided by displays of early spring bulbs, colourful summer herbaceous borders and the foliage colours of autumn. The attached nursery specialises in alpines and hardy and half-hardy perennials.

EMMETTS GARDEN ★
(Historic Garden Grade II)

The National Trust

Ide Hill, Sevenoaks TN14 6AY.
Tel: (01732) 868381;
www.nationaltrust.org.uk

1.5m S of A25 and M25 junction 5,
1.5m N of Ide Hill off B2042

Open 15th March to 1st June, Tues – Sun and Bank Holiday Mons; 4th to 29th June, Wed – Sun; 2nd July to 2nd Nov, Wed, Sat and Sun; all 11am – 5pm (or dusk if earlier)

Entrance: £5.90, children £1.50, family £13.30

Other information: Buggy available

◐ ☕ 🥪 WC ♿ ⏴⏵ 🏛 🍴 ⚲

The garden gives a superb view over the Weald of Kent and provides an impressive setting for an eclectic collection of trees and shrubs. It is particularly fine in spring, with its bluebell woods and flowering shrubs. Noted especially for its rhododendrons and azaleas, the planting follows the late-nineteenth-century style of combining exotics with conifers to provide a 'wild' garden. A rose garden, a rock garden and a collection of acers planted for autumn colour extend the interest throughout the year. The enforced clearance of some trees and shrubs after the gales of 1987 has enabled new planting to keep the traditions of the garden and also to expand it – the rock garden in particular is becoming established. A splendid site and a fascinating garden.

GODINTON HOUSE
(Historic Garden Grade I)

The Godinton House Preservation Trust

Godinton Lane, Ashford TN23 3BP.
Tel: (01233) 620773;
www.godinton-house-gardens.co.uk

Off M20 junction 9, 1.5m NW of Ashford in Godinton Lane at Potter's Corner (opposite Hare and Hounds pub)

House open 21st March to 5th Oct, Fri – Sun, 2 – 5.30pm

Garden open 21st March to 27th Oct, Thurs – Mon, 2 – 5.30pm

Entrance: £4, children free (house and garden £7, children free)

Other information: Coaches by appt only

The 12-acre gardens surrounding the house have evolved over centuries, and in 1902 were redesigned by architect Reginald Blomfield, an exponent of the revival of the formal style of the seventeenth century. As restored, it is now in essence an elegant formal garden with a modern sensibility. Its stylish simplicity is evident in the entrance courtyard, where four *Acer pseudoplatanus* 'Brilliantissimum' glow against the great yew boundary hedge, cut to echo the Flemish gables of the house. Beyond, elegant terraces defined by topiary link different areas, such as the box-hedged Pan Garden and huge formal herbaceous borders leading to the lily pond, originally an Edwardian swimming pool. A redesigned rose garden burgeons with boldly underplanted fragrant shrub roses; another is filled with bulbs and wild flowers bordering an informal pond, while the intimate Italian Garden, approached via a classical colonnade, has been replanted with

Godinton House

Mediterranean plants. The major work-in-progress is in the walled kitchen garden, where gravel paths lined with espalier fruit have been restored and a Victorian glasshouse replaced. Borders maintained by the Delphinium Society line the walls, and new beds are being planted with decorative mix of cutting flowers and produce.

GOODNESTONE PARK ★★
(Historic Garden Grade II*)

Built in 1704, the Palladian-inspired house commands a panoramic view of eighteenth-century parkland, complete with estate cricket pitch. Since the 1960s, the 14 acres of garden surrounding the house have gradually been restored and expanded by Lady FitzWalter. Below the terrace, a box parterre marks the millennium, and rising from the porticoed west entrance a grass amphitheatre leads to a majestic lime walk. Mature woodland contains fine specimen trees underplanted with magnolias, cornus, hydrangeas and spring bulbs; beyond is the Golden Arboretum planted in 2001. The latest project is a gravel garden created by Graham Gough on the site of the old tennis court, where a shingle path curves between waving grasses and drought-tolerant perennials. The *pièce de résistance* is the walled garden, with an enchanting vista towards the Norman church through three profusely planted enclosures. The first includes old-

Garden tours available by prior arrangement. Refreshments available when house is open and for pre-booked parties

Lady FitzWalter

Goodnestone, Nr Wingham, Canterbury CT3 1PL. Tel: (01304) 840107; www.goodnestoneparkgardens.co.uk

5m E of Canterbury. Take A2 signed to Dover, turn left at junction B2046 for Wingham/Aylesham, then E after 1m

House open by appt for parties

Garden open 17th Feb to 16th March, Sun, 12 noon – 5pm; 19th March to May, Wed – Sun, 11am – 5pm (opens 12 noon Sat and Sun); June to 3rd Oct, Tues – Fri and Sun, 11am – 5pm (opens 12 noon Sun)

Entrance: £4.50, OAPs £4, children (6-16) £1, family £10

Other information: Gardening lectures spring and summer – telephone for details

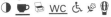

fashioned roses, clematis and early colour; the central room features mid- to late-summer flowering perennials; and beyond, fruit and vegetables mingle with flowers for cutting. The overall effect is spectacular.

GREAT COMP ★

Great Comp Charitable Trust

Comp Lane, Platt, Borough Green, Sevenoaks TN15 8QS. Tel: (01732) 886154; www.greatcomp.co.uk

From M20 junction 2, take A20 towards Maidstone. At Wrotham Heath take B2016. Signposted

Open April to Oct, daily, 11am – 5pm

Entrance: £4.50, children £1

A half-day may be required to do justice to this imaginatively planned seven-acre garden, which offers all-year interest. Although the setting for an early-seventeenth-century house, it was only created after 1957 out of the neglected earlier garden, rough woodland and paddock. Long grass walks intersect the beds and borders, providing ever-changing views to tempt visitors to stray from their intended route. Focal points and interest are given by statuary, a temple and ruins built from the tons of ironstone dug up over the years. There are woodland areas, herbaceous borders, a heather garden, a rose garden, formal lawns and an Italianate garden designed to set off a collection of Mediterranean plants. Hellebores are a feature, and the introduction of salvias, dahlias, kniphofias and crocosmias has given the garden a new exoticism. The *Taxus baccata* at the front of the house was planted in 1840. Other specimen trees include a *Metasequoia glyptostroboides* and a *Sequoia sempervirens* 'Cantab'. A music festival is held here each year, with recitals in the former stables.

GROOMBRIDGE PLACE ★
(Historic Garden Grade I*)

Groombridge, Tunbridge Wells TN3 9QG. Tel: (01892) 861444; www.groombridge.co.uk

4m SW of Tunbridge Wells. Take A264 towards East Grinstead, then after 2m B2110 to Groombridge

Half hidden in a broad wooded valley, the handsome moated manor house (not open) was built in 1662. Centuries have gone into the making of the gardens within the ancient walls of the original 1230 moated castle, but recently the

Groombridge Place

seventeenth-century formal gardens have been imaginatively restored. From a magnificent border on the highest terrace, a gravelled path leads between a striking double procession of 24 drum-shaped yews. On either side are garden rooms of differing character: the Oriental Garden inspired by the colours of an oriental rug, the Drunken Garden of misshapen junipers, the former kitchen garden now the White Rose Garden. A narrow canal feeds a tranquil lake, originally the village millpond, and there are newer features such as the Giant Chessboard, the Golden Key Maze and a knot garden. An exciting aerial walkway leads to the Enchanted Forest, created by land artist Ivan Hicks and designer Myles Challis, where extraordinary sculptures and mysterious pools provide imaginative challenges for children and adults.

Open April to Nov, daily, 10.30am – 5.30pm

Entrance: £8.95, OAPs and children (3–12) £7.45, family £29.95 (2007 prices)

Other information: Canal boat rides, birds of prey

HEVER CASTLE AND GARDENS ★★
(Historic Garden Grade I)

The gardens were laid out between 1904 and 1908 to William Waldorf Astor's designs. One thousand men were employed, 800 of whom dug out the 35-acre lake; steam engines shifted rock and soil to create apparently natural new features, and teams of horses moved mature trees from Ashdown Forest. Today the gardens have reached their maturity and are teeming with colour and interest throughout the year. Among the many superb features is an outstanding four-acre Italian garden, the setting for a large collection of classical statuary; opposite is a magnificent pergola supporting camellias, wisteria, crab apple, Virginia creeper and roses. It fuses into the hillside beyond, which has shaded grottoes of cool damp-loving species such as hostas, astilbes and polygonums. Less formal areas include the rhododendron walk, Anne Boleyn's orchard and her walk, which extends along the full length of the grounds. A Tudor herb garden has been added, and the Sunday Walk nearby runs beside a stream past newly created borders in mature woodland. The 110-metre herbaceous border has been re-created and the water maze on Sixteen-Acre Island, planted with a range of aquatic plants, offers walks down to the millennium fountain.

Broadlands Properties Ltd

Hever, Edenbridge TN8 7NG.
Tel: (01732) 865224;
www.hevercastle.co.uk

3m SE of Edenbridge off B2026, between Sevenoaks and East Grinstead

Castle open as gardens, but from 12 noon, plus 1st to 21st Dec

Gardens open March, Wed – Sun, 11am – 4pm; April to Oct, daily, 11am – 6pm; Nov, Thurs – Sun, 11am – 4pm (last admission 1 hour before closing)

Entrance: £9.30, OAPs £7.90, children (5–14) £6, family £24.60 (castle and gardens £11.50, OAPs £9.70, children (5–14) £6.30, family £29.30)

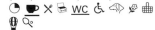

HOLE PARK

Majestic chestnut trees line the drive through beautiful parkland to the superb early-eighteenth-century house surrounded by 15 acres of tranquil and immaculate gardens. A series of formal garden spaces enclosed by yew hedges planted by the owner's great-grandfather contrasts with smooth lawns offset by towering specimen trees, topiary, classical statuary, and a theatrical wisteria-clad pergola. Around the house, elegant garden rooms are sheltered by old walls, where climbers and herbaceous plants are used to great effect, including a pool garden with sun-loving plants and shrubs. Further delights lie in the extensive woodland valley,

Mr and Mrs Edward Barham

Rolvenden, Cranbrook TN17 4JA.
Tel: (01580) 241344/241386;
www.holepark.com

4m W of Tenterden, on B2086 between Rolvenden and Benenden

Open 23rd March to Oct, Wed, Thurs, Sun and Bank Holiday Mons, 2 – 6pm; Bluebell and Spring Spectacular 13th April to 11th May, 11am – 6pm. Also open by appt

Entrance: £4.50, children (under 12) 50p

Other information:
Refreshments and plants on
Suns and Bank Holiday Mons only

where bulbs and ornamental trees lead through magnificent azaleas and rhododendrons to a stream and secret shady pool with lush marginal planting and fine autumn colour. The views towards Rolvenden postmill and the villages and landscape of the Weald of Kent are also rewarding.

LADHAM HOUSE ★

Goudhurst TN17 1DB.

8m E of Tunbridge Wells, NE of Goudhurst off A262

Open for NGS, and by written appt

Entrance: £3.50, children 50p, £4.50 for private visits

Other information: Teas must be pre-booked

The house, Georgian with additional French features, is surrounded by parkland and a 10-acre garden being restored and redeveloped on an impressive scale. It is interesting to see the bog garden replacing a leaking pond, and the arboretum replacing the old kitchen garden. The mixed shrub borders are attractive; notable are the magnolias – two *M.* x *wieseneri* over 10 metres tall and a deep-red-flowering 'Betty Jessel', a seedling from Darjeeling. Among other rarer trees and shrubs are *Cornus kousa*, embothriums, American oaks, *Aesculus parviflora*, *Carpenteria californica* and *Azara serrata*. The arboretum is maturing and has some unusual and interesting trees. The Fountain Garden has been completely reconstructed, the rock garden restored with a waterfall incorporated, a 200-metre-long Kentish ragstone ha-ha built to the north of the house, and a woodland walk down the side of the park opened up. A new garden close to the swimming pool uses tropical and hot-coloured plants.

LEEDS CASTLE ★

Leeds Castle Foundation

Maidstone ME17 1PL.
Tel: (01622) 765400;
www.leeds-castle.com

7m E of Maidstone on B2163 near M20 junction 8

(Historic Garden Grade II*)

Visit the castle and grounds for its romantic, wooded setting, covering some 500 acres; the woodland garden, with its old and new plantings of shrubs, is especially beautiful at daffodil time. The Culpeper Garden, in a secluded area beyond the castle, is not a herb garden as often thought, though a small area does include some herbs, but is named after a

Leeds Castle

seventeenth-century owner. Started in 1980 by Russell Page on a slope overlooking the River Len, and surrounded by high brick walls of stabling and old cottages, it consists of a simple pattern of paths lined with box containing old roses riotously underplanted with herbaceous perennials. The terraced Italian-style Lady Baillie Garden overlooking the Great Water has stunning architectural plants. Don't miss the spectacular grotto beneath the maze. The garden is complemented by some rare and attractive birds in the duckery and aviary, which are well placed amid numerous shrubs and small trees.

Grounds open all year, daily, from 10am, except for special ticketed events – telephone or consult website for details

Entrance: castle, park and gardens £14, concessions £11, children (4–15) £8.50 (2007 prices)

MARLE PLACE GARDENS AND GALLERY ★

The 10-acre garden, filled with interest, reflects the personality of its artistic owner (her studio is open to garden visitors). Close to the seventeenth-century house a small shady fern garden and a border of several varieties of cistus are set off by an old wall furnished with interesting climbers, and a double herbaceous border leads to an area of alliums and ornamental grasses. Near the house too is an old ornamental pool garden with a wildflower bank and aromatic plants, a croquet lawn and specimen trees. Within the yew-hedged kitchen garden are a box parterre and a raised-bed rose garden. Tapestry hedges are used to striking effect as a background to many of the borders. A red Chinese bridge leads over a boggy area backed by bamboos, and a mosaic terrace has been laid within a blue-and-yellow border. A five-acre arboretum is carpeted with buttercups and scented clover, and there are areas of wild flowers both within the garden and in the 10-acre wood of native trees. Along the woodland walk leading to two small lakes, visitors come upon a two-acre 'gallery wood', where they are invited to

Mr and Mrs G. Williams

Brenchley, Tonbridge TN12 7HS. Tel: (01892) 722304; www.marleplace.co.uk

9m E of Tunbridge Wells, 1m SW of Horsmonden, W of B2162. Follow brown tourist-signs from Forstal Farm roundabout on A21, and from Brenchley village.

Open 21st March to 6th Oct, Fri – Mon, 10am – 5.30pm, and by appt at other times

Entrance: £4.50, OAPs and children (4–12) £4, wheelchair users free

Other information: Art exhibitions in gallery throughout season

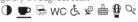

Marle Place Gardens

participate in creating artworks made from the natural objects surrounding them. Several large iron sculptures of horses and other work by varied artists, plus carved wooden furniture made by the owners' daughter, add to the eclectic charm of this stimulating garden.

MOUNT EPHRAIM

Mrs Mary Dawes and Mr and Mrs E.S. Dawes

Hernhill, Faversham ME13 9TX.
Tel: (01227) 751496;
www.mountephraimgardens.co.uk

6m W of Canterbury, 3m E of Faversham off A299. At Duke of Kent pub turn to Hernhill; garden is through village on left, signposted

Open April to Sept, Wed, Thurs, Sat, Sun and Bank Holiday Mons, all 1 – 5pm (Bank Holiday weekends 11am – 5pm)

Entrance: £4.50, children £2.50 (under 3 free), concessions £1

Other information: Craft shop open Sun afternoon only

(Historic Garden Grade II)

The fine 10-acre gardens surrounding the house mirror two centuries of changing horticultural fashions. From its eminent position, with far-flung views over fruit orchards to the Thames estuary, the house overlooks sweeping lawns, huge borders and magnificent specimen trees, including a sweet chestnut planted to commemorate the Battle of Waterloo. The steeply sloping site retains the original formal plan in the rose terrace, with flights of steps hedged in venerable yew, leading to the tranquil lake and a water garden. The restored Japanese-influenced rock gardens are a turn-of-the-century feature. In 1950 the indefatigable Mary Dawes and her husband began the restoration work, which continues today with the creation of an elegant millennium garden filled with fragrant new and old-fashioned roses. Nigel Lee Evans was responsible for its layout of the new rose garden, Sarah Morgan for its planting; she also carried out the design of the Ivan-Hicks-inspired grass maze on the side of the old vineyard. A long herbaceous border, skilfully planted and sheltered by old stable walls, lines the topiary garden with its idiosyncratic collection of birds, animals and First World War memorabilia in clipped yew. The arboretum was planted in 1995.

NETTLESTEAD PLACE ★

Mr and Mrs R.C. Tucker

Nettlestead, Maidstone ME18 5HA.
Tel: (01622) 812205;
www.nettlesteadplace.co.uk

6m SW of Maidstone off B2015. Next to church

Open for NGS, and at other times by appt

Entrance: £4

An avenue of Irish yews leads down from the early fourteenth-century gatehouse to the thirteenth-century manor house set in 10 acres on the banks of a tranquil stretch of the River Medway. A long gravel garden planted with rock plants and dwarf bulbs lies along the eastern side of the house, which is clothed with akebia, sophora, fremontodendron and Rosa 'Frances Lester'. A large sunken pond bounded by a ragstone wall provides a sheltered environment for tender plants, and a natural spring flowing down the hill in the glen garden is edged with damp- and shade-lovers. Beyond this a woodland garden sheltered by a steep bank leads through to a collection of bamboos. The astounding plantsman's collection continues throughout the garden – shrubs, hybrid tea and floribunda roses in the large rose garden, specialised trees and shrubs in a series of island beds, a comprehensive range of plants in the herbaceous garden, and a small, recently planted China rose garden. An arboretum containing over 30 different acers delights in spring with its interesting bark variations and in autumn with its vibrant foliage colours.

OLD BUCKHURST

In open country, paddock boundary hedges planted with carefully chosen native trees are the first line of defence against the wind for the two-acre gardens surrounding the fifteenth-century farmhouse. They too have been designed with shelter in mind: a series of interlocking spaces densely planted with shrubs, perennials and climbers creates a cottage-garden atmosphere and includes a walled garden burgeoning with soft pink and red perennials and silver foliage. Paths leading around the tile-hung house are bordered with harmonious planting and good texture, leading to a tiny, well-stocked nursery.

Jane and John Gladstone

Markbeech, Nr Edenbridge TN8 5PH. Tel: (01342) 850825; www.oldbuckhurst.co.uk

4m SE of Edenbridge via B2026. At Queen's Arms turn E to Markbeech; garden is first on right after leaving village

Open May to July, Wed and 1st and 4th Sats; and for NGS; all 11am – 5.30pm. Also open for parties by appt

Entrance: £3, children free

 WC

OLD PLACE FARM ★

The superb four-acre gardens surrounding the Tudor farmhouse are the result of the vision and enthusiasm of Ann Eker, who with the help of designer Anthony du Gard Pasley has created a series of stylish spaces, some enclosed and intimate, others opening into the wider pastoral landscape. Throughout, a strong sense of style confidently combines profuse planting and restrained decoration. Burgeoning herbaceous borders lead to a sheltered herb parterre and a charming cutting garden, where a decorative *potager* is screened by vines and roses. Hellebores, bulbs and lush ferns cluster under a striking avenue of topiary hawthorn, and the lake is overlooked by a delightful gazebo against a backdrop subtly planted in shades of blue, purple, cream, apricot and silver. Woodland areas, a philadelphus walk and meadow-fringed ponds contrast with the croquet lawn, near where the latest project, an imaginative and playful topiary garden, is taking shape. Inspirational.

Mr and Mrs Jeffrey Eker

High Halden, Ashford TN26 3JG. Tel: (01233) 850202

10m SW of Ashford. From A28, opposite Chequers pub in High Halden, take Woodchurch road and follow for 0.5m

Open by appt

Entrance: £4, guided tour £5 per person

Further information: Teas by arrangement

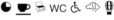

PENSHURST PLACE AND GARDENS ★

(Historic Garden Grade I)

The 600-year-old gardens, contemporary with the house, reflect their creation under the Tudor owner, Sir Henry Sidney, and their restoration over many decades. An example is the 640-metre double line of oaks, their planting completed in 1995 as part of a 15-year programme to re-create the historic parkland structure. The many separate enclosures, surrounded by trim and tall yew hedges, offer a wide variety of interesting planting, with continuous displays from spring to early autumn. Just inside the entrance is a garden for the blind, with raised beds of aromatic plants, a small wooden gazebo and the constant music of water splashing on pebbles. The Italian garden with its oval fountain and century-old ginkgo dominates the south front of the house. Herbaceous borders are teeming with colour. Note also the borders designed by Lanning Roper in the late 1960s and the blue and yellow border. Contrast is made by the nut trees and over a dozen different crab apples underplanted

Lord De L'Isle

Penshurst, Tonbridge TN11 8DG. Tel: (01892) 870307; www.penshurstplace.com

5m SW of Tonbridge on B2176, 7m N of Tunbridge Wells off A26

House open as gardens, but 12 noon – 4pm

Gardens open 1st to 16th March, Sat and Sun; 21st March to 2nd Nov, daily; all 10.30am – 6pm

Entrance: £7, children (5–16) £5, family £20 (house and gardens £8.50, children £5.50, family £23)

Other information: Tours available for parties of 15 or more. Guide dogs only

 WC

with daffodils, myosotis, tulips, bluebells, Lenten lilies, and a magnificent bed of peonies bordering the orchard. Even in late summer the rose garden is colourful with 'Anisley Dickson' and 'Anna Olivier', and their perfumes mingle with those of mature lavender bushes. A lake and woodland trail have been developed so that the style of design enjoyed here by Gertrude Jekyll and Beatrix Farrand is fully recaptured. Two medieval fish ponds have been reclaimed and stocked with fish. There is an imaginative play area for children.

RESTORATION HOUSE ★

Robert Tucker

17-19 Crow Lane, Rochester ME1 1RF. Tel: (01634) 848520; www.restorationhouse.co.uk

In centre of historic Rochester

House open

Garden open 30th May to 27th Sept, Thurs and Fri, plus 1st June, all 10am – 5pm

Entrance: £2.75, OAPs £2.50, children over 8 £1.50 (house and garden £5.50. OAPs £4.50, children (6-16) £2.50, family £12.50)

Other information: Teas on 1st Thurs of each month, plus 1st June

 WC

This immaculate 0.75-acre walled garden lies within the walls of the city of Rochester. The late-sixteenth/early-seventeenth century house had, as its name implies, strong Royalist connections, and was later immortalised by Dickens as Miss Havisham's doomed dwelling. In the garden the present owners have achieved an imaginative and skilful re-creation of what might have been. Divided longitudinally by a mellow brick wall, and on two levels, the way the different components have been blended is excellent. In the upper garden, the lawn near the house is edged with low box hedges and brick and stone paths – a feature of the garden as a whole – flanked by herbaceous borders. Roses and hydrangeas abound, together with many elegant box and yew topiary shapes, and an intricate central parterre replicates a Jacobean door in the house. The north side of the wall, pierced by substantial Gothic arches, drops to lawn and an ornamental pool. Beyond are prolific and well-stocked vegetable, fruit and cutting gardens; an elegant oak-framed greenhouse shelters against the wall at the end of the garden, while an ingeniously camouflaged potting shed is carefully incorporated into the main bisecting wall. Nothing jars the beauty of the whole. At the far end a mound overhung by a magnificent *Catalpa bignonioides* is the ideal spot from which to view this oasis of calm.

Restoration House

RIVER GARDEN NURSERIES

The sound of running water and rustling willows pervades the peaceful three-acre gardens encircled by the shallow waters of the little River Darent. The owner has not only created a series of stylish garden spaces with yew hedges and a box parterre, delicate planting and roses scrambling high into the trees, but has also established a successful topiary nursery. Here, cones, balls, obelisks, spirals and characterful birds, plus tiny knot gardens and window boxes, are all patiently trained and clipped from *Buxus sempervirens* and other varieties. Regular one-day topiary workshops are held in this delightful setting.

Jenny Alban Davies

Troutbeck, Otford, Sevenoaks TN14 5PH. Tel: (01959) 525588

In Otford High Street, turn down small drive opposite gates of Broughton Manor

Garden and nursery open by appt only

ROCK FARM ★

The Kentish farmhouse, set on an east-facing slope, is surrounded by a two-acre plantswoman's garden. The entrance is along a colourful iris border, and the best season is May to July when the large herbaceous border is at its peak. The soil is alkaline and there are excellent specimens of ceanothus, a huge *Solanum crispum*, a *Fremontodendron californicum* and a *Magnolia grandiflora*. Of special interest is the *Chionanthus virginicus* or fringe tree. Natural springs supply water for two ponds bordered by cupressus of various foliage colour and for a small stream whose banks are planted with primulas and other moisture-lovers. A *Catalpa bignonioides* 'Aurea' is cut annually to give huge golden leaves, and a *Sequoia sempervirens* is also pruned drastically, resulting in rarely seen new foliage of this coniferous forest tree.

Mrs P.A. Corfe

Gibbs Hill, Nettlestead, Maidstone ME18 5HT. Tel: (01622) 812244; www.rockfarmhousebandb.co.uk

6m SW of Maidstone. From A26 turn S onto B2015, then turn right 1m S of Wateringbury

Open for NGS, and by appt

Entrance: £4

● WC B&B

ROGERS ROUGH

A gem of a garden – 1.5 acres created by a plantsman who is also a garden writer. The setting is idyllic, with views out to farmland and Bedgebury Pinetum (see entry), where the neutral pH of the soil allows a wide variety of plants to be grown. Hedges of beech and yew enclose individual rooms filled with cottage-garden plants, and the small, well-planted pond is fringed with interesting moisture-lovers. The scent within the rose garden is almost overwhelming. The meandering paths encourage the visitor to seek out surprises round every corner – *Azara lanceolata*, a white-berried sorbus, magnolias, mature shrubs with decorative foliage and a *Drimys winteri*.

Mr and Mrs Richard Bird

Chicks Lane, Kilndown, Cranbrook TN17 2RP. Tel: (01892) 890554

10m SE of Tonbridge off A21. 2m S of Lamberhurst turn left to Kilndown, and in village take 1st right into Chicks Lane; garden is on right

Open for NGS, and by appt May to July

Entrance: £3, children 50p

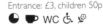

SCOTNEY CASTLE GARDEN AND ESTATE ★

(Historic Garden Grade I)

This is an unusual garden designed in the Picturesque style by the Hussey family, following the tradition established by William Kent and using the services of the artist and landscape gardener William Gilpin, who also advised on the

The National Trust

Lamberhurst, Tunbridge Wells TN3 8JN. Tel: (01892) 893868; www.nationaltrust.org.uk

8m SE of Tunbridge Wells, 1m S of Lamberhurst on E side of A21

Open 1st, 2nd, 8th and 9th March; 10th March to 2nd Nov, daily; all 11am – 5.30pm (last admission 1 hour before closing)

Entrance: £6.60, children £3.30, family £16.50

Other information: Possible for wheelchairs but hilly approach. Dogs in park only

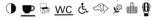

site of the new house, completed in 1843. The landscape garden includes smaller garden layouts in the overall area. A formal garden overlooks a quarry garden and the grounds of the Old Castle enclose a herbaceous border backed by roses and clematis; there is also a herb garden. The lakeside planting adds an air of informality. Evergreens and deciduous trees provide the mature planting, linking shrubs and plants to give something in flower at every season. Daffodils, magnolias, rhododendrons and azaleas are the most spectacular; also notable are the kalmias, hydrangeas and wisterias. In a good autumn, the colours are amazing. The planting is intentionally occasional and haphazard, 'Picturesque' in the true sense, but visit this 26-acre garden for its setting on a slope that gives fine views of open countryside, and for the romantic eighteenth- to nineteenth-century theme uniting it.

The National Trust
Sissinghurst, Cranbrook TN17 2AB.
Tel: (01580) 710700/ 710701 (Infoline);
www.nationaltrust.org.uk
13m S of Maidstone, 2m NE of Cranbrook, 1m E of Sissinghurst on A262
Open 15th March to 2nd Nov, Mon, Tues and Fri, 11am – 6.30pm, Sat, Sun and Bank Holiday Mons, 10am – 6.30pm (last admission 5.30pm or dusk if earlier). Parties of 11 or more by appt. Garden much quieter after 3.30pm
Entrance: £8.60, children £4, family £22
Other information: Coaches by appt. Wheelchairs restricted to 4 at one time because of narrow, uneven paths; pushchairs not admitted

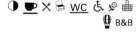 B&B

SISSINGHURST CASTLE GARDEN ★★
(Historic Garden Grade I)

The series of stylised outdoor rooms created among the ruins of a moated Tudor manor in the 1930s by poet and novelist Vita Sackville-West and her husband, writer and diplomat Harold Nicolson, still resonates with gardeners today. A little of the *genius loci* may have been subdued under the Trust's careful stewardship, but the famous and much-emulated colour palettes and the plantings of the highest subtlety and quality continue to inspire. Spring in the Lime Walk is spectacular, with drifts of bulbs creating a tapestry based on Nicolson's meticulous records. High summer in the incomparable White Garden and the heady delights of the old roses are followed by fiery and exuberant planting schemes in the cottage garden, lush ferns and foliage carpeting the nuttery, aromatic scents wafting across the herb garden, tall meadow grasses in the orchard and rustling poplars beside the moat. For many, this is the definitive English garden, evoking the poetic sensibility of its creators, their deep feeling for history and rural tradition and the influence of their aristocratic travels. On a more prosaic note, 2007 saw the replanting of a section of the Long Yew Walk which had succumbed to *Phytophthora cinnamoii*. The infected yews and surrounding soil were removed, new drains installed and the roots of the new plants treated with mycorrhizal fungus paste which fixes nitrogen and helps protect from harmful fungus attack. The replacement yews are expected to grow to their full height by about 2015; meanwhile a unexpected view into the orchard reinforces the importance of enclosure in this iconic garden. *Knole*, home to the Sackville family since 1603, will also be of interest to Vita's admirers, since she was born and brought up there. The house and its park (listed Grade I by English Heritage) were in her bones: 'It has the tone of England'. (Park open daily, Lord Sackville's garden on the first Wednesday of each month, May to September.)

Sissinghurst Castle Garden

SOUTHOVER

The typical fifteenth-century timber-framed Kentish house lies in the centre of a gently south-sloping site and is surrounded by a 1.5-acre garden full of plants and diversity which has been awarded several medals for its wildlife-friendly gardening. Work started in 1980, when the foundations of a much larger house were uncovered and planted with hedges to enclose a true garden room. A pond, filled in over the centuries, has been redeveloped as a wildlife feature. Elsewhere wildlife is encouraged through the planting of internal hedges, the creation of a spinney, a wildflower meadow and a long boundary 'eco-hedge', made from woody garden waste contained between two parallel rows of stakes. The upper spring bulb garden is now heavily naturalised by cowslips and fritillaries, and the lower spring garden has been enlarged to accommodate an ever-expanding collection of snowdrops. An autumn border features many colchicums. Nearer the house are two 'secret' garden rooms, one a large central paved area surrounded by borders containing a wide range of perennials blended with biennials and annuals; the other a more formal design with cool greens and soft yellows. A third enclosure has been developed as a kitchen garden. Impressive herbaceous borders to the south of the house contain many unusual plants. Other features are a sunken walk in green and white, a fern bank and a brown border featuring sedges and grasses.

Mr and Mrs David Way

Grove Lane, Hunton, Maidstone ME15 0SE. Tel: (01622) 820876

6m S of Maidstone between A229 and B2010. From Yalding take Vicarage Road to Hunton. Almost opposite school turn left into Grove Lane; house is about 180 metres on right. From Coxheath turn down Hunton Hill to Hunton; Grove Lane is immediately past school

Open for NGS, and by appt

Entrance: £3, accompanied children free

Other information: Wheelchair users must be accompanied. Teas by arrangement

 WC &

STONEACRE

The National Trust

Otham, Maidstone ME15 8RS.
Tel: (01622) 862871;
www.nationaltrust.org.uk

3m SE of Maidstone, 1m S of A20 from
Bearsted, at N end of Otham

House open as garden

Garden open mid-March to mid-Oct,
Sat and Bank Holiday Mons,
11am – 6pm (last admission 5pm), and
at other times by appt

Entrance: house and garden £3.50,
children £1.50

Other information: Disabled parking at
gate. Picnics in car park

The garden surrounding the fifteenth-century Kentish hall house, restored in the 1920s by Aylmer Vallance, Oxford aesthete, writer and biographer of William Morris, are set in a hidden valley of grazing sheep and distant views. Since 2000 the present tenants have considerably reworked the charming garden within the framework of yew hedges and ragstone walls, reshaping the borders and lawns to reflect the surrounding landscape. Their style combines boldness and subtlety, creating plantings that demonstrate a masterly use of foliage colour and texture; grasses are a particular feature. A tranquil white-and-green garden has been developed, and behind the house a sheltered courtyard, furnished with a collection of pots planted for all-year interest, leads along paths mown through meadow grasses billowing with cow parsley to an apple orchard and a wild area with three ponds. Other secret paths at tree-canopy height offer unexpected views of the garden below, with splendid flowering shrubs and shady banks filled with bulbs and ferns.

WYCKHURST

Chris and Judy Older

Mill Road, Aldington TN25 7AJ.
Tel: (01233) 720395

5m SE of Ashford off A20, leaving M20 at
junction 10. In village, turn right at village
hall and immediately left by Walnut Tree
pub onto Forge Hill, signed to
Dymchurch; after 0.5m turn right into Mill
Road

Open for NGS, and June, July and Sept by
appt

Entrance: £3, children free

NEW ● WC ♀

High above Romney Marsh, Judy Older has created a charming, inventive and continually evolving one-acre garden around the seventeenth-century farmhouse. Flowing spaces, defined by beds curving around mature trees, are divided and screened by hedges and linked by rose- and ivy-covered arches. A tiny thatched summerhouse beside a sunken bog garden, a diminutive potager and parterre, a miniature walnut orchard and a secret golden garden are punctuated by witty topiary. Those interested in learning how to achieve the same effects should enquire about the occasional topiary courses held here. Everywhere views look into the surrounding countryside and the wider landscape beyond.

OTHER RECOMMENDED GARDENS

BROADVIEW GARDENS

Hadlow, Tonbridge TN11 0AL (01732 850211;
www.hadlow.ac.uk). Open all year, daily, 10am – 5pm
(closes 4pm Sun)

The 10-acre gardens in the grounds of Hadlow College offer an inspiring range of old and new designs in a series of well-planted areas. Gardens sub-tropical, oriental, Heaven and Hell, sensory, gravel, Italian etc, plus National Collections of Japanese anemones and hellebores.

CHARTWELL

Mapleton Road, Westerham TN16 1PS (01732
866368; www.nationaltrust.org.uk). Open 15th March
to June, 3rd Sept to Dec, Wed – Sun; July and Aug,
Tues – Sun; all 11am – 5pm (or dusk if earlier) (last
admission 4.15pm). NT

The garden bought by Sir Winston Churchill for 'that view' is a place of mellow charm, with well-established trees and flowering shrubs, clouds of roses, terraces, fish ponds and vantage points from which to take in the vast panorama over the Weald of Kent. (Listed Grade II*)

COPTON ASH

Drs Tim and Gillian Ingram, 105 Ashford Road, Faversham ME13 8XW (01795 535919). Open for NGS, and by appt

In this 1.5-acre plantsman's garden many new plantings have been made recently with a particular emphasis on species adapted to warm and dry conditions. Over 3000 cluster in herbaceous borders and island beds; novelties and rarities may be spotted at any time. A large collection of snowdrops, early bulbs and woodland plants make spring a prime time to visit.

COTTAGE FARM

Phil and Karen Baxter, Cacketts Lane, Cudham TN14 7QG (01959 532506). Open June, Sun, 1.30 – 5.30pm, and for parties by appt

Tucked away in the byways of the North Downs, a delightful and original series of intimate garden spaces – among them an immaculate and luxuriant kitchen garden, a sheltered terrace blooming with exotics, a wildlife pond and a stumpery – has been created around a row of 18th-century brick and flint cottages. 1 acre.

DOWN HOUSE

Luxted Road, Downe BR6 7JT (01689 859119; www.english-heritage.org.uk). Open 4th Feb to 28th Sept, Wed – Sun and Bank Holiday Mons, 10am – 6pm

The 4-acre garden, with a flower garden, kitchen garden, meadows and woodland, was used by Charles Darwin as his open-air laboratory while he formulated his theories on evolution. It is being restored using plants described by the great scientist in his notes and letters, including the greenhouse where he studied plant growth and pollination and which now houses orchids, carnivorous and climbing plants. (Listed Grade II)

GARDEN ORGANIC YALDING

Benover Road, Yalding, Maidstone ME18 6EX (01622 814650; www.gardenorganic.org.uk). Open April to Oct, Wed – Sun and Bank Holiday Mons, 10am – 5pm

A whistle-stop tour through horticultural history: small gardens typical of each century, ranging from a 13th-century apothecary's

garden to a utilitarian 1950s allotment, finishing with an organic vision of the future. Impressive, well-maintained and an experience for the whole family. 5 acres.

115 HADLOW ROAD

Mr and Mrs Richard Esdale, Tonbridge TN9 1QE (01732 353738). Open for NGS, and by appt

The 0.4-acre suburban garden skilfully transcends the limitations of its space, for it is packed with the whole gamut of plants, from interesting specimen trees right down to summer bedding. There is even room for an attractively laid-out and well-stocked fruit and vegetable garden.

IGHTHAM MOTE

Mote Road, Ivy Hatch, Sevenoaks TN15 0NT (01732 810378; www.nationaltrust.org.uk). Open 15th March to 2nd Nov, Thurs – Mon, 11am – 5pm. NT

Set in a wooded cleft among 560 acres of farmland, the moated medieval and Tudor manor house has an extensive garden with a stream, a cascade and two ponds. The remains of a 19th-century garden sit on top of a medieval layout, including features from the 20th century. A restoration project is underway to open more areas to the public.

LAURENDEN FORSTAL

Mrs M. Cottrell, Blind Lane, Challock TN25 4AU (01233 740310). Open for NGS, and by appt

The 2-acre garden surrounding the 14th-century house is an enviable combination of informality, elegance and the owner's personal touches. The result is charming: sunny terraces, a white-flowered courtyard, velvety lawns, burgeoning herbaceous borders, a wildlife pond overlooked by a living willow tunnel, and a tiny vegetable garden with raised beds.

LONGACRE

Dr and Mrs G. Thomas, Perry wood, Selling, Faversham ME13 9SE (01227 752254). Open for NGS, and by appt

A 1-acre jewel in a tranquil country setting next to Perry Woods, into which the borders of the garden melt. Although at its best in spring and early summer, it offers all-year interest of colour and form, replicatin in miniature woodland, damp and dry areas.

LULLINGSTONE CASTLE

The Hart Dyke family, Eynsford DA4 0JA.
(01322 862114; www.lullingstonecastle.co.uk).
Open April to Sept, Fri and Sat, 12 noon – 5pm,
Sun and Bank Holiday Mons, 2 – 6pm

The World Garden of Plants is the dream of
plant hunter Tom Hart Dyke. In the 2-acre
walled garden of the ancient castle he has
created a map of the world and filled the beds
representing countries and continents with
indigenous plants. This is very much a work-in-
progress and the product of the vision and
boundless enthusiasm of one individual. The
garden is also worth a visit for its beautiful
location in an almost secret Kentish valley.

OWL HOUSE

Lamberhurst TN3 8LY (01892 891290;
www.owlhouse.com). Open all year, daily except
25th Dec and 1st Jan, 11am - 6pm

The atmospheric garden of 16.5 acres was
created and adored by the late Marchioness of
Dufferin and Ava. Flowers abound at every
season: bluebells, philadelphus, clematis, masses
of old roses, and walks of iris, apple blossom,
laburnum and blue hydrangea. Three water
gardens provide a peaceful setting for
contemplation.

THE PINES GARDEN

Beach Road, St Margaret's Bay CT15 6DZ
(01304 851737; www.baytrust.org.uk). Open all year,
daily, 10am - 5pm

Sheltered amongst trees, down a winding road
leading to the famous white cliffs, these
tranquil coastal gardens are immaculately
maintained and run on organic principles; the
Pines Calyx Centre, constructed from
excavated chalk, promotes sustainable living.
Undulating lawns, well-planted beds, a lush bog
garden, a grass labyrinth, a paved garden made
from the facade of a 17th-century town house
and a pathway that uses recycled materials
including seashells from Whitstable's oyster
beds combine to create a most unusual
atmosphere.

PRIORY GARDENS

Orpington (020 8464 3333; www.bromley.gov.uk).
Open all year, daily, 7.30am – dusk (opens 9.30am
Sat, Sun and Bank Holiday Mons)

Adjacent to an attractive medieval priory
building (now Bromley Museum), this is one of
the most tastefully gardened public spaces in
outer London. Pre-1939 the gardens were
extended in the formal Arts and Crafts style,
with patterned annual bedding, a rich rose
garden, a rock garden, fine mature trees and
shrubs and two lakes. (Listed Grade II)

RIVERHILL HOUSE

The Rogers family, Sevenoaks TN15 0RR
(01732 458802/452557). Open Easter to 22nd June,
Sun and Bank Holiday weekends, 11am – 5pm

This was originally one of the great smaller
country-house gardens, housing a plantsman's
collection of trees and species shrubs introduced
by John Rogers in the mid-1800s. His
descendants are custodians of the majestic
plantings that have survived, and there are also
good collections of bluebells, primroses,
rhododendrons and azaleas. 8 acres. (Listed
Grade II)

SQUERRYES COURT

Mr and Mrs John Warde, Westerham TN16 1SJ
(01959 562345; www.squerryes.co.uk). Open April to
Sept, Wed, Thurs, Sun and Bank Holiday Mons, 11.30am
– 5pm, and for parties by appt

The 15 acres of gardens, laid out around 1700 in
the formal Anglo-Dutch style, were landscaped
again later in the 18th century with a large lake,
a gazebo, a formal area framed by yew hedges,
and a woodland garden. Restoration has
breathed new life into this historic place. (Listed
Grade II)

WALMER CASTLE

Kingsdown Road, Walmer, Deal CT14 7LJ
(01304 364288; www.english-heritage.org.uk). Open
10th to 20th March and Oct, Wed – Sun, 10am – 4pm;
April to Sept, daily, 10am – 6pm (closes 4pm Sat).
Closed Nov to Feb and when Lord Warden in
residence

Historically the seat of the Warden of the Cinque
Ports, the Tudor walls of the castle conceal 10
acres of gardens. At its core is a double
herbaceous border backed by crinkle-crankle yew
hedges, a vegetable garden and the late Queen
Mother's garden in the former walled garden. This
was redesigned by Penelope Hobhouse complete
with a 30-metre-long formal pond, topiary and a
mount. (Listed Grade II)

LANCASHIRE

For further information about how to use the *Guide*
and for an explanation of the symbols, see pages vi–viii.
Specific dates and times are those given to us by garden owners for 2008.
For 2009 dates, check with the individual properties.
For opening dates under the National Gardens Scheme,
readers should consult *The Yellow Book* or www.ngs.org.uk.
Maps are to be found at the end of the *Guide*.

CLEARBECK HOUSE ★

This highly individual five-acre creation works on many levels.
On the bigger plan Rousham (see entry in Oxfordshire) has
been of influence, with vistas presenting views across
stretches of water and swathes of grass to the impressive
moorland beyond, punctuated by sculptures, ornaments and
follies. In some areas space is more enclosed, and here the
influence is Sissinghurst (see entry in Kent). An allegorical
theme inspires some parts – the Garden of Life and Death
with its unique pyramid, a maze and a folly named Rapunzel's
Tower all have a story behind them. A most successful recent
addition is a temple sitting at the base of a group of noble
poplar trees and overlooking a pool. Behind is a mount where
some visual trickery is intended – indeed a sense of fun
pervades the garden. The sculpture is varied and often
thought-rovoking, but whether classical or modern it is placed
to play an integral role in the structure of the garden. There is
strong planting too, with beds of mixed perennials
surrounding the stone cottage, marsh-lovers fringing the pools
and streams, and a large collection of shrub roses with many
scented varieties. Water is present throughout, and the largest
pool attracts a lot of wildlife – more than 80 bird species
noted in a single year. Perhaps the greatest achievement here
is the way the garden sits so perfectly within the landscape.

Peter and Bronwen Osborne

Higher Tatham, Lancaster LA2 8PJ.
Tel: (01524) 261029

10m E of Lancaster. From M6 junction
34 take A683 towards Kirkby Lonsdale,
turn right on B6480 and follow
signposts from Wray village

Open for NGS, and for parties by appt

Entrance: £2.50, children free

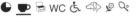

Clearbeck House

Gresgarth Hall

Sir Mark and Lady Lennox-Boyd

Caton LA2 9NB.
Tel: (01524) 771838;
www.arabellalennoxboyd.com

4m NE of Lancaster. From M6 junction
34 take A683 towards Kirkby Lonsdale,
then turn right in Caton village, signed
to Quernmore

Open 13th April, 11th May, 8th June,
13th July, 10th Aug, 14th Sept and 12th
Oct, 11am – 5pm

Entrance: £5

  WC & ☕

GRESGARTH HALL ★★

You expect something special from the garden of such a renowned designer as Arabella Lennox-Boyd, and you will not be disappointed. Within the 25-acre estate, she has experimented with different styles of gardening and produced some superb results – all the more surprising since the weather in this part of northern Lancashire can be harsh. At the front of the house are formal areas: herbaceous borders protected by yew hedges, and to the south a pool and bog garden with a large selection of ferns and other moisture-lovers. An arboretum contains a large sequoiadendron, acers, lilacs and many other fine specimens, while the walled garden has a happy mix of vegetables, fruit and flowering plants. To the east an attractive terrace and belvedere overlook a rocky beck that rushes through this part of the garden. A Chinese bridge leads to a woodland garden where azaleas, cornus, magnolias and many unusual plants flourish in the light shade. Sculpture, classical and modern, is used creatively throughout. There are woodland walks, a huge variety of plants and so much else that this description can only serve as the briefest of introductions to a fine garden. Evolution continues.

Mr and Mrs Richard Hodson

Marsh Road, Hesketh Bank, nr Preston
PR4 6XT. Tel: (01772) 812379;
www.hawthornes-nursery.co.uk

10m SW of Preston. Take A59 towards
Liverpool, turn right at traffic lights
signed to Tarleton, then on to
Hesketh Bank

HAWTHORNES NURSERY GARDEN

Complementing the family-run nursery, which stocks an interesting range of perennials and climbers, is a one-acre garden laid out informally as beds and sweeping grass paths. A tremendous number and variety of plants that thrive in a rich silt marshland with a high pH grow happily together. There are over 150 shrub roses, including many species and old-fashioned varieties – damasks, hybrid musks, centifolias and a few Bourbons, old and new varieties of *rugosa* hybrids.

Clematis are Mr Hodson's other love, and he has managed to assemble 200 of them, including a National Collection of *viticella* hybrids and some rare herbaceous varieties. Borders are well stocked with many varieties of phlox, thalictrum, lythrum, monarda and other eye-catching perennials with heleniums, dahlias and lobelias in a separate hot area. Close to the entrance is a large wildlife pond.

Open for NGS, and by appt

Entrance: £2.50, children free

Other information: Telephone for nursery opening times

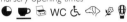

HOGHTON TOWER
(Historic Garden Grade II)

The tower, a sixteenth-century fortified manor built of local stone, occupies a hilltop position with good views to all sides and outwards to the surrounding countryside. The house and its outbuildings are constructed around two courtyards which, although not qualifying as gardens, are fine spaces. Surrounding the house are three walled gardens. The first, the Wilderness, contains a large lawn and herbaceous borders. The second, the rose garden, has a rectangular lawn flanked on two sides by clipped yews; in the centre is a raised square pond with an elaborate stone fountain. The third is mainly lawn with access to the tops of two crenellated towers. Around the walled gardens runs the Long Walk, which passes under large beech and holly trees (especially weeping hollies) and is planted with shrubs, mainly rhododendrons and azaleas. Legend has it that Shakespeare lived here during a formative period, and James I knighted a piece of beef 'Sir Loin' on 17th August 1617.

Hoghton Tower Preservation Trust

Hoghton, Preston PR5 0SH.
Tel: (01254) 852986;
www.hoghtontower.co.uk

5m SE of Preston mid-way between Preston and Blackburn, on old A675

House open for guided tours

Garden open July to Sept, Mon – Thurs, 11am – 4pm, Sun, 1 – 5pm; also Bank Holiday Suns and Mons (except Good Fri, Christmas and New Year)

Entrance: £3 (house and garden £6, concessions £5) (2007 prices)

LEIGHTON HALL

Very striking when first seen from the entrance gates, the white stone facade (c.1822) shines out in its parkland setting with the hills of the Lake District visible beyond. The Victorian conservatory by the house has been returned to its original elegance. The most interesting area of the 2.5-acre gardens, which lie to the west of the house, is the walled garden with its unusual labyrinth in the form of a gravel path running under an old cherry orchard; opposite is a vegetable garden made in a geometric design with grass paths. There are also herbaceous borders and an aromatic herb garden containing a wide variety of perennials, with climbing roses on the wall behind. High summer is a good time to visit, but there is something of interest during the whole of the visiting season.

Mr R. G. Reynolds

Carnforth LA5 9ST.
Tel: (01524) 734474/825604;
www.leightonhall.co.uk

8m N of Lancaster, 1m W of Yealand Conyers, signed from M6 junction 35

House and garden open May to Sept, Tues – Fri, 2 – 5pm (opens 12.30pm in Aug); in winter for parties by appt

Entrance: house and garden £6, OAPs £5, children (5-12) £4

MILL BARN ★

On the site of an old mill by the River Darwen, this garden has been designed to make the most of its superb setting. A path leading along a high stone embankment above the fast-flowing river passes through a series of features: a unique temple to alchemy created from an old sluice gate, a rose-clad pergola, a picturesque ruin constructed to hide a septic tank. Near here a fine 'Paul's Himalayan Musk' rose climbs high up into a

Dr C. J. Mortimer

Goose Foot Close, Samlesbury Bottoms, Preston PR5 0SS.
Tel: (01254) 853300

6m E of Preston on A677 Blackburn road, turn S into Nabs Head Lane, then Goose Foot Lane

Open 14th and 15th June, 11am –
4.30pm, for 'Art and Garden' exhibition;
for NGS; and mid-June to mid-July for
parties by appt

Entrance: £3, children free

Other information: Refreshments and
plants for sale on open days

 WC ♿ ♻ B&B

Gerald and Linda Hitman

Brockhall Village BB6 8DX.
Tel: (01254) 244811

5m N of Blackburn, turn N off A59, W
of junction with A666. Take minor road
signed to Old Langho and Brockhall
Village

Open March to Nov by guided tours
for parties of 15 or more staying or
eating at Avenue Hotel nearby
(suggested times 11am tour and 1pm
lunch, or 6pm and tour 8pm dinner)

Entrance: £16 for tour and meal

 ✖ WC   B&B

tree. Then comes a rectangular pool set into the wall containing a good variety of water plants and marginals, with a stretch of lawn and a heptagonal summerhouse beyond. A long herbaceous border containing plants chosen for their contrasting foliage and architectural effects runs back to the house, and a bridge over the river gives access to a belvedere looking back over the whole garden. The quarry is becoming a secret garden in a modern style.

THE OLD ZOO GARDEN ★

Although these sensational gardens are thoroughly modern in concept and design, there is an underlying feeling of the medieval pleasure grounds about them. The asymmetric and slightly austere house designed by Homa and Sima Farjardi sits perfectly within the 15-acre gardens and surrounding landscape. The use of water is spectacular. At the front a clear pool and canal are surrounded by a dramatic planting of phormiums, bamboos, rhus and pines, and from these a stream passes through a series of rocky pools under the house to emerge at a large area of decking that converts to a swimming pool. A long rill projects outwards across the terrace towards a stunning panorama of the Ribble Valley. To the north, looking for all the world like a medieval mount inverted, is an excavated spiral with a cascade flowing to a pool at its base. Below the terrace a unique step maze and an elongated hedge maze set out to puzzle the visitor. Fine

The Old Zoo Garden

sculptures appear throughout the garden, together with some notable green oak shelters designed by Derek Goffin. A small wooded valley is well planted with drifts of primulas, gunneras, hostas, hemerocallis and ligularias and backed by golden elder. There are more sculptures here and a bridge that incorporates a large curved tree trunk. A hot tub has a lid that has to be seen to be believed, and a *boules* rink is set within a glade of alders. Further up is a croquet lawn surrounded by banks of thickly planted *Rosa* 'Meifloplan', with gravel paths and rough-hewn stone steps winding up through swathes of hostas and grasses. Cloud trees in tubs also add a distinctive note. At the bottom of the valley is a wildlife lake surrounded by lush green foliage with a plantation of Lancashire apple trees on one bank.

RUFFORD OLD HALL

The 15 acres of gardens complement the exceptional sixteenth-century timber-framed house, laid out in the style of the Victorian/Edwardian period. On the south are lawns and gravel paths designed in a formal manner. The many island beds are formal in layout, too, but the shrubs, small trees and herbaceous plants they contain are planted in a more relaxed way. In the centre, a path leads from two large topiary squirrels to a beech avenue that extends beyond the garden towards Rufford. There are many mature trees and rhododendrons in this area dating back to the 1820s. To the east of the house by the stables is an attractive cobbled space with climbing plants on the surrounding walls. Look out for the cottage garden to the north side of the house, in which grow many old-fashioned plants enclosed by a rustic wooden fence. Spring and summer are good times to visit.

The National Trust

Rufford, Ormskirk L40 1SG.
Tel: (01704) 821254;
www.nationaltrust.org.uk

7m NE of Ormskirk, N of Rufford,
E of A59

House open as garden but 1 – 5pm

Garden open 15th March to 2nd Nov,
Sat – Wed, 11am – 5.30pm. Telephone
for winter opening times

Entrance: £4, children £2 (house and
garden £5.70, children £2.90)

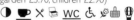

OTHER RECOMMENDED GARDENS

ASHTON MEMORIAL

Williamson Park, Quernmore Road, Lancaster LA1
1UX (01524 33318; www.williamsonpark.com). Open
all year, daily except 25th and 26th Dec and 1st Jan,
10am – 5pm (closes 4 pm Oct to March)

The superbly landscaped 54-acre park is dominated by John Belcher's 1906 Baroque Revival memorial, described by Pevsner as 'the grandest monument in England'. The restoration of the grounds, largely woodland, is nearing completion. (Listed Grade II)

GAWTHORPE HALL

Padiham, Nr Burnley BB12 8UA (01282 771004;
www.lancsmuseums.gov.uk). Open all year, daily,
10am – 6pm

Woodlands surround formal gardens including a parterre designed by Sir Charles Barry in swashbuckling Jacobean style, complementing the early-17th-century-house restored by him in the 1850s. 9 acres in all. (Listed Grade II)

PENDLE HERITAGE CENTRE

Park Hill, Barrowford, Nelson BB9 6JQ (01282) 661701; www.htnw.co.uk). Open all year, daily except 25th Dec, 10am – 5pm

The 0.25-acre walled garden set among a group of fine old stone buildings dates from the 1780s has been restored and replanted with known 18th-century culinary and medicinal herbs, fruit and vegetables under the watchful eye of the NCCPG. A small museum about the history of the garden opened in 2006.

THE RIDGES

Mr and Mrs J. M. Barlow, Cowling Road, Limbrick, Chorley PR6 9EB (01257 279981; www.bedbreakfast-gardenvisits.com). Open June and July, Wed, plus Bank Holiday Suns and Mons, May and Aug; all 11am – 5pm, and at other times by appt

The eighteenth-century house, with part of the old walled garden still extant, has been given a serene and gracious setting: a midsummer herbaceous border, seating arches planted for fragrance, a stream fringed with moisture-lovers, and a richly planted enclosure backed by woodland. A woodland walk and beds planted with wild flowers and grasses are recent developments. 2.5 acres.

TOWNELEY PARK

Todmorden Road, Burnley BB11 3RQ (01282 424213; www.towneleyhall.org.uk). Open all year, daily, during daylight hours

From the house front, late-18th-centry parkland stretches out, fringed by extensive woodlands, while formal beds and revitalised herbaceous and shrub plantings give colour around the hall (1500, reworked after 1816). 400 acres in all. (Listed Grade II)

WORDEN PARK

Leyland PR25 2DJ (01772 422316; www.southribble.gov.uk). Open all year, daily, 8am – dusk

The 63 acres here include formal plantings, open parkland and an arboretum; children will enjoy the circular hornbeam maze, activities and adventure playground. The stable block of the old house (a fire casualty) now contains craft and theatre workshops. A family day out. (Listed Grade II)

LEICESTERSHIRE

For further information about how to use the *Guide*
and for an explanation of the symbols, see pages vi–viii.
Specific dates and times are those given to us by garden owners for 2008.
For 2009 dates, check with the individual properties.
For opening dates under the National Gardens Scheme,
readers should consult *The Yellow Book* or www.ngs.org.uk.
Maps are to be found at the end of the *Guide*.

BEEBY MANOR ★

This atmospheric four-acre garden runs uphill from the house to a series of 'rooms' which feel lived-in and welcoming. The terrace near the house is laden with planters, and in late April the purple tulips in tubs are sensational, with *Rosa banksiae* going mad on the wall behind. Different species of narcissus also abound. To the west of the front lawn a doorway beckons the visitor into a great hall of old clipped yew hedges, left quite plain with a formal lily pond in the centre. The exit on the other side leads to an impressive modern sculpture in a bay of its own with a swimming-pool garden on one side and a wild garden on the other; beyond is an arboretum. A long and wide herbaceous border returns to the house, where an old, cloud-pruned Portuguese laurel looks positively Japanese. A lot of variety here.

Mr and Mrs Philip Bland

Beeby LE7 3BL.
Tel: (01162) 595238

5m E of Leicester. Turn off A47 in Thurnby and follow signs through Scraptoft

Open by appt

Entrance: £2

BELVOIR CASTLE
(Historic Garden Grade II)

The mock-Gothic castle, straddling an isolated hill at the edge of the Vale of Belvoir, is the fourth to occupy this dramatic natural belvedere. It was built by James Wyatt for the 5th Duke of Rutland; on her return from the Grand Tour in 1819 the Duchess redesigned the garden in the Renaissance manner. By the mid-nineteenth century terraced gardens had been created, divided into smaller enclosures by the discreet use of topiary and hedging. During the 1870s spring bedding was introduced; now various areas are devoted to roses and peonies, and elsewhere snowdrops and daylilies are naturalised. In the early twentieth century yew hedges were planted around two sides of the garden and the rose garden was laid out (it has now been replanted). To the north-east runs a curving terrace path, probably the broadwalk depicted in Badeslade's view of 1731; some of the Caius Cibber statues which lined it are now in the Statue Garden. The private woodland garden, known as the Spring Garden, was laid out in 1810; it is set in a natural amphitheatre and contains

The Duke of Rutland

Belvoir, Grantham, Lincolnshire NG32 1PD. Tel: (01476) 871002

10m NE of Melton Mowbray off A607 by Belvoir. Signposted

Castle open

Garden open 20th March to 6th April, daily; 12th, 13th, 19th, 20th, 26th and 27th April; May and June, daily except Mon and Fri; July and Aug, daily except Fri; Sept, Sat and Sun; all 11am – 5pm (closes 4pm Sat and Sun) (last admission 1 hour before closing). Spring Garden open all year for pre-booked parties

Entrance: £6, concessions £5, children (5–16) £2, family £15 (castle and gardens £12, concessions £10, children £6, family £32)

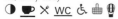

statuary and a recently restored hexagonal root house dating from 1841. Belvoir no longer relies on its history. The present Duchess is re-creating the brilliant colours of Victorian bedding with a tapestry of carefully chosen camellias, rhododenrons and azaleas, and the Duke has planted an avenue of *Quercus ruber* to reinforce the autumn colour.

GOADBY HALL ★

Mr and The Hon. Mrs Westropp

Goadby Marwood, Melton Mowbray LE14 4LN.
Tel: (01664) 464202

4m NE of Melton Mowbray between A606 and A607

Open by appt

Entrance: £3

Other information: Teas by arrangement

● 🪑 WC ♿ ⟁ ℺

The approach to this exciting and romantic six-acre garden is at the head of a string of five ornamental lakes extending to over a mile. These have been dredged and restored to the beauty the Duke of Buckingham must have imagined when he created them in the eighteenth century. Surrounding the handsome manor house remodelled in the 1760s is a variety of separate gardens planted substantially in creams and greens and variegated plants to offset the dominance of the ironstone buildings and walls, with many varieties of daffodils and tulips for spring colour. A children's garden leads to the croquet lawn, then past the church to the secret rose and walled gardens. There is also a potager and a recently restored stable garden, and a small orchard. All have been brought back to life over the past three years by the love, imagination and hard work of the knowledgeable owner.

Goadby Hall

LONG CLOSE ★

This is a true plantsman's garden, sometimes described as a Cornish garden in Leicestershire owing to the many quite tender trees and plants rarely to be found elsewhere so far north. When Mr and Mrs George Johnson bought the property in 1949, they began to restore the 5.5-acre garden, based on the framework and potential left by their predecessor, Colonel Gerald Heygate. Taking advantage of the lime-free loam, they nurtured a large collection of rhododendrons, azaleas and magnolias, which are now in magnificent maturity, adding many camellias and other shrubs and trees. Formal terraces lead to more informal gardens, with winding paths between specimen trees, and finally to a natural dappled pool. In spring there are drifts of snowdrops, daffodils and bluebells and in summer prolifically planted herbaceous borders. The present owners have extended the plantings, created a potager and penstemon collection in the old walled kitchen garden, and laid out a new cottage garden. A courtyard plays its sheltered part with magnificent wall-covering plants. For contrast, take a stroll within the 20 acres of ancient pasture, freckled with orchids in June.

John and Pene Oakland

Main Street, Woodhouse Eaves, Loughborough LE12 8RZ.
Tel: (01509) 890376;
www.longclose.org.uk

5m S of Loughborough between A6 and M1 junctions 22 and 23

Open March to July, Sept and Oct, Tues – Sat and Bank Holiday Mons, 9.30am – 1pm, 2 – 5.30pm, and for NGS. Parties by appt

Entrance: £4, accompanied children 50p

Other information: Tickets for daily visits to be purchased from gift shop opposite. Park in adjacent public car park. Teas on NGS open days, and for parties by appt

◑ WC 🏵

ORCHARDS ★

An unusual garden of 1.25 acres, very much the personal creation of Mr Cousins. Vistas have been created throughout, and at one point the garden peers out over the surrounding countryside to remind one that there is a world outside this enchanting enclosure. There are a number of distinct areas, bounded by hornbeam hedges or upright shrubs such as hazel, some cool and green, others bright with flowers chosen to emphasise the passage of the seasons. Trees, shrubs and climbers are shaped to underline their natural form and this gives the garden a sculptural quality. Distinctively, all the leaves are green – no variegated, gold or purple foliage here. Though not primarily a plantsman's garden, there are many interesting and unusual plants. Other features include an old orchard, an impressive wisteria draped over a large pergola, a circular reflective pool and a number of carvings and slate paving patterns by the owner's brother, Patrick Cousins.

Mr and Mrs Graham Cousins

Hall Lane, Walton, Lutterworth LE17 5RP.
Tel: (01455) 556958

4m E of M1 junction 20. In Lutterworth turn right at police station and follow signs to Kimcote and Walton. From Leicester take A5199 to Shearsby, then turn right signed to Bruntingthorpe and follow signs for Walton

Open for NGS, and by appt.

Entrance: £3, children free

 ● ☕ WC ♿ 🏵

PINE HOUSE ★

The facade of the house is clothed in clipped pyracantha and the terrace looks out across a grass tennis court to open countryside. On either side are mature trees including a Wellingtonia, yews, oaks, pines and a fine copper beech, with a woodland walk and water garden. Behind the herbaceous border a hidden winding path leads to a rockery on one side with interesting plants everywhere. Behind the house is a small yellow and green topiary garden and a wisteria walk unusually planted for summer interest with gourds which hang down attractively to resemble Chinese lanterns. The tunnel

Mr and Mrs Timothy Milward

Gaddesby, Leicester LE7 4XE.
Tel: (01664) 840213

9m SW of Melton Mowbray off A607. Turn E to Gaddesby on Rearsby bypass

Open by appt

Entrance: £3, children free

 ● ☕ WC ♿ 🏵

Pine House

goes to a Victorian vinery and a pot garden growing a wide variety of plants. A large gravel garden is a recent venture – much is packed into the two acres here.

STOKE ALBANY HOUSE

Mr and Mrs Alfred Vinton

Stoke Albany, Market Harborough
LE16 8PT. Tel: (01858) 535227

4m E of Market Harborough. Turn S off
A427 onto B669. Garden is 0.5m on left

Open 30th March (Daffodil Sun), 2 –
4.30pm; for NGS; and for parties by appt.

Entrance: £3, children free

Other information: Teas on Daffodil Sun only

A country-house garden set in four acres with picturesque landscape sweeping beyond. There are fine trees and wide herbaceous borders, striped lawns, good displays of bulbs in spring and roses in June. The walled garden contains a *potager* with topiary, a grey garden, an avenue of *Nepeta* 'Six Hills Giant' arched with 'Mme Alfred Carrière' roses and clematis, a garden centred around a water feature, and a beautifully maintained greenhouse. There is also a Mediterranean garden, a rose-filled parterre and an autumn garden – tradition brought up to date in a perfect English setting.

OTHER RECOMMENDED GARDENS

THORPE LUBENHAM HALL

Sir Bruce and Lady MacPhail, Lubenham, nr Market Harborough LE16 9TR (01858 433960). Open for NGS, and by appt

The Georgian mansion standing handsomely in its spacious park is well served by its 15-acre garden. Impressive herbaceous borders stretch along a walk, and the enormous swimming pool is concealed by climbers and surrounded by fragrant and colourful perennials. There is also a wildflower meadow, and a conservation garden being developed on the moated site of a ruined house.

ULVERSCROFT CLOSE

Mr and Mrs Michael Maddock, Ashby Road, Gilmorton LE17 5LY (01455 553226; www.maddockgarden.co.uk). Open for NGS, and by appt

An atmospheric and clearly loved garden of 0.5 acres. A fine conservatory, a short avenue of mop-head robinias and a diminutive box parterre occupy the top level, a pond and bog garden the lower. Roses, a plethora of clematis and a vegetable garden laid out in formal style add to the charm.

LINCOLNSHIRE

For further information about how to use the *Guide*
and for an explanation of the symbols, see pages vi–viii.
Specific dates and times are those given to us by garden owners for 2008.
For 2009 dates, check with the individual properties.
For opening dates under the National Gardens Scheme,
readers should consult *The Yellow Book* or www.ngs.org.uk.
Maps are to be found at the end of the *Guide*.

AUBOURN HALL ★

First impressions of the 10 acres of gardens surrounding the fine red-brick hall (*c.* 1600) are of spacious simplicity. Undulating lawns and borders sweep through rose arches or along grassy swathes to further lawns and gardens beyond. The enviably deep and diverse borders are carefully planted to give maximum effects of colour, shape and texture. There are also secluded areas in which to linger: the formal rose garden with its central tiered copper planter, the Golden Triangle edged with yew and planted with ornamental crab apple trees and spring bulbs, the ponds, the woodland dell and walks, and the swimming pool surrounded by a rose- and clematis-covered pergola. The grass maze is a new attraction. The nearby church, one of the smallest in Lincolnshire, is also open to visitors.

Mr and Mrs Christopher Nevile

Aubourn, Lincoln LN5 9DZ.
Tel: (01522) 788224

7m SW of Lincoln between A46 and A607

Open for NGS, and for parties by appt (telephone 07816 202 353)

Entrance: £3

● WC &

BELTON HOUSE ★

(Historic Garden Grade I)

The 33 acres of gardens set within 1000 acres of parkland are, like the house, composed with perfect harmony and proportion. The extensive woodland has two lakes, a

The National Trust

Belton, Grantham NG32 2LS.
Tel: (01476) 566116;
www.nationaltrust.org.uk

3m N of Grantham off A607

Belton House

House open

Gardens open Jan and Feb, 8th Nov to Dec, Fri – Sun, 12 noon – 4pm; March to June, 8th Sept to 2nd Nov, Wed – Sun and Bank Holiday Mons, 11am – 5.30pm; July to 7th Sept, daily, 10.30am – 5.30pm. Free access to park only on foot from Lion Lodge gates all year (closed for special events)

Entrance: gardens and grounds £7.50, children £4.50, family £20

small canal and noble cedars, and a maze re-created from the 1890 original. The radiating avenues are an impressive reminder of the late-seventeenth- and early-eighteenth-century predilection for introducing drama into the landscape. However, it is the formal area to the north of the house, beyond which the east avenue rises imperiously to the distant Bellmount Tower, that makes a visit memorable. The 1870s Dutch garden is a satisfying composition with pillars of green yew and cushions of golden yew, pale gravel, formal beds cleverly planted and edged with lavender, and generously filled urns. The earlier sunken Italian garden is more reliant on Wyatville's architectural features: a large central pond with a fountain, a lion-headed exedra and, the high point, the restored and replanted orangery. Behind the orangery a little church is glimpsed; it is filled with memorials to generations of Custs, who built the house, and Brownlows, who created the gardens.

Burghley House Preservation Trust

Stamford PE9 3JY.
Tel: (01780) 752451;
www.burghley.co.uk

0.5m E of Stamford on Barnack road, close to A1. Signposted

House open 21st March to 26th Oct, daily except Fri, 11am - 5pm

Sculpture garden and parkland open all year, daily, 10am – 5pm (closes 4pm in winter). Garden of Surprises open 21st March to 26th Oct, daily, 11am – 5pm; South Garden open April only for spring bulbs

Entrance: house and Garden of Surprises £10.90, concessions £9.50, children (5 – 15) £5.40, family £28 (2007 prices)

Other information: Limited access for wheelchairs. Dogs in park only, on lead

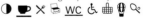

BURGHLEY HOUSE

The stupendous Elizabethan prodigy house built for William Cecil (later Lord Burghley), with its immense collection of art treasures, has survived the centuries miraculously intact. The park and gardens, however, were reinvented by each generation according to the horticultural fashion of the moment, including a Baroque garden designed by George London and a 'Capability' Brown landscape with a superb bridge and serpentine lake. Several acres of garden were reclaimed from Brown's lost lower gardens in 1994, and turned into a sculpture garden that includes a permanent collection of over twenty works, each positioned to draw attention to the surrounding spaces and plantings; neither sculpture nor horticulture is allowed to dominate. Now it has fallen to George Carter to create a distinctive contemporary statement. The one-acre Garden of Surprises nearby was inspired in part by another famous Cecil garden, Theobalds in Hertfordshire, constructed in the second half of the sixteenth century, of which no trace remains. In a succession of enclosed garden rooms, buildings and vistas, he has drawn on watery jokes beloved of the sixteenth- and seventeenth-century European designers and given them a very modern twist, including an artificial rain-tree, jets, water 'furniture', a long black-lined rill and curtain-like fountains of water. Topiary and sculpture, other Elizabethan hallmarks, are represented here by a maze, a parterre and bosquets and clipped hedges of box yew, phillyrea and hornbeam, together with busts of Roman emperors, mirrors and obelisks.

Mr and Mrs C. Curtis

Hacconby, Bourne PE10 0UL.
Tel: (01778) 570314

21 CHAPEL STREET

The gay and cottagey impression of this 0.5-acre village garden has been achieved by minimising lawn area and replacing it with planting space. The circuitous path passes rockeries and scree beds, small trees and shrub roses, rustic arches, troughs and a pond, all exuberantly planted and underplanted to ensure year-round colour, with splendid displays of snowdrops and hellebores in February, followed by a colourful herbaceous display that concentrates in late summer on red, yellow and gold; asters extend the season into October. There are hundreds of varieties of bulbs, alpines and herbaceous plants here to satisfy both the casual gardener and the seeker of the rare.

3m N of Bourne off A15, turn E at crossroads to Hacconby

Open for NGS, and by appt

Entrance: £2, children (under 16) free

DODDINGTON HALL ★
(Historic Garden Grade II*)

The large gardens of large houses (Elizabethan in this case) do not often impart an air of intimacy, but here grandeur and formality sit happily alongside the casual, comfortable style of the present owner. Formality is represented by a gravel, box and lawn courtyard, complete with topiary unicorns from the family crest, as well as beds of flag irises and a yew *allée* giving views along an extensive avenue of limes. The wild gardens beyond offer a choice of meandering walks through ancient trees, past a stream edged with flourishing *Lysichiton americanus*. From the Temple of the Winds, designed by the present owner, the natural landscape opens up. Snowdrops are followed by equally naturalistic plantings of narcissi and erythroniums, and then by rhododendrons. In May and June there is a tapestry of colour in the walled garden where box-edged parterres are filled with flag irises and herbaceous borders are massed with towering echiums, syringas, peonies, alliums and phlox. A turf maze designed by the owner's father is popular with children and adults alike. The old walled kitchen garden, with its original dipping pond and potting shed, has been restored with the aid of a grant from English Heritage and is bursting with vegetables and fruit, including many rare and heritage varieties.

Mr and Mrs J. Birch

Doddington, Lincoln LN6 4RU.
Tel: (01522) 694308;
www.doddingtonhall.com

5m W of Lincoln on B1190

House open as garden, but May to Sept only (opens 1pm)

Garden open 16th Feb to April, Sun and Bank Holiday Mon, 1 – 5pm; May to Sept, Wed, Sun and Bank Holiday Mons, 12 noon – 5pm; and for parties by appt at other times

Entrance: £4, children £2, family £11 (house and garden £6, children £3, family £16

Other information: Farmshop and cafe open all year, daily, 9 am – 6pm (opens 10am Sun and Bank Holiday Mons). Advisable to book for Sun lunch – telephone 01522 688581.

EASTON WALLED GARDENS

The 12 acres of garden date back to at least 1592. 'Improved' by the Victorians, photographs from *Country Life* in 1903 show an impressive array of glasshouses, lawns with statues, fountains and bedding schemes, ha-has, great terraces, fine trees and tremendous views. The manor house, however, was pulled down in 1951 and the garden lay untouched for fifty years. In 2002 Lady Cholmeley, aided by a dedicated team of helpers and volunteers, began to uncover the skeleton of the Victorian gardens in a massive undertaking to reclaim, restore and develop them. Already avenues have been cleared, glasshouses and stonework restored and planting schemes devised. Hand-in-hand with the ancient yew tunnel are new features such as the Pickery, in which a changing display of flowers for cutting is grown. New, too, are areas dedicated to herbaceous plantings, wild flowers and woodland plants, and collections of snowdrops, narcissi, auriculas, sweet peas and

Sir Fred and Lady Cholmeley

Easton, Grantham NG33 5AP.
Tel: (01476) 530063;
www.eastonwalledgardens.co.uk

7m S of Grantham, 1m E of A1 off B6403 N of Colsterworth roundabout. Follow signposts to village

Open 16th to 24th Feb for snowdrops; March to Aug, daily except Sat; Sept to 14th Dec, Sun; all 11am - 4pm

Entrance: £4.50, children 50p

Other information: Spring plant fair 4th and 5th May, 10am – 4pm, sweet pea week 22nd to 27th June

roses are expanding. A garden to revisit year by year as the restoration unfolds.

ELSHAM HALL

Mr and Mrs G. Elwes

Elsham, Brigg, DN20 0QZ.
Tel (01652) 688698;
www.elshamhall.co.uk

2m from M180 junction 5/A180 interchange at Barnetby Top

Open 22nd March to Sept, Sat, Sun and Bank Holiday Mons (daily during school holidays), 11am – 5pm, and by appt

Entrance: £5.00, concessions £4.50, children £4.00 (under 3 free)

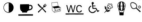

Although the 20-acre park and garden have been open to the public since 1970, the four-acre walled garden has been refurbished by the present custodians (artists both) in partnership with local landscape architect Ian Stubbs, so that it is now an intriguing, exciting and stimulating space. From the medieval-influenced viewing mound, the visitor takes in a panorama which includes the One-World Garden, whose planting reflects the different continents taken as its theme; a sensory garden where salvias, lavenders and santolinas reflect the combination of geometrical angles and gyrations with which it is landscaped; and the imaginative Nursery Garden offering a combination of plants and animals to delight the young. Modern aviaries reminiscent of Dutch glasshouses, enclosed areas of grass and wild flowers, and avenues of apple trees and hornbeams combine with boxed beech plantings to create an overall structure which places the design in a firm contemporary context. Add to this the existing lake flanked by developing herbaceous borders, a carp pond, an arboretum and woodland walks, and you are guaranteed a full, varied and interesting day's visit.

THE GARDEN HOUSE

Chris Neave and Jonathan Cartwright

Saxby, Market Rasen LN8 2DQ.
Tel: (01673) 878820;
mobile (07831) 263177;
www.thegardenhousesaxby.com

10m N of Lincoln, 4m S of Caenby Corner, 2.5m E of A15

Open 15th to 28th Feb for snowdrops; 30th April to Sept, Fri – Sun and Bank Holiday Mons, 10am – 5pm; and by appt

Entrance: £3, children free

One of the most striking aspects of this six-acre garden is the clarity of its design, so it comes as no surprise to learn that one of the owners is a landscape designer. Many different areas are fitted harmoniously into the overall design: three ponds; a long and formal lower terrace with symmetrical mixed planting; a Dutch Garden where rows of planted pots alternate with agapanthus; an upper lawn; a Mediterranean garden that tests the winter hardiness of sun-loving plants; a trio of walks (rose, thyme and hosta); and a pleached lime avenue. The owners have planted 100 specimen trees, and have a further half-dozen acres in their sights for reclamation, including two large ponds, copses of native trees and two wildflower meadows. Already maturing, this is a garden worth revisiting on a regular basis.

GOLTHO HOUSE

Mr and Mrs S. Hollingworth

Lincoln Road, Goltho LN8 5NF.
Tel: (01673) 857768;
www.golthogardens.com

10m E of Lincoln on A158, 1m on left before reaching Wragby

Open 16th to 24th Feb, 10am – 3pm; 2nd April to Sept, Wed and Sun, 10am – 4pm; and by appt

The 4.5-acre garden was only started in 1998, but already looks established and holds out much promise for the future. It is laid out with a strong feeling for colour, form and texture in flowers and foliage, and reflects the owners' interest in a wide range of plants, many of them rare. A long grass walk flanked by abundantly planted mixed borders forms a focal point; paths and walkways span out to other features – a nut walk, planted mostly for spring interest, an experimental prairie border, a small woodland area and a stunning wildflower meadow. Nearer the house and its range of interesting old farm buildings lies a large pond area, a peony and iris garden and a delightful rose garden. In contrast to the large-scale effect of the garden as a whole, the potager, with its brick and stone paths and geometric planting, offers an intimate experience of a wide variety of herbs and vegetables. A winter walk gives colour and structure in the colder months, and gravel gardens have been planted next to the nursery.

Entrance: £3

Other information: Teas on open days and by arrangement

GRIMSTHORPE CASTLE
(Historic Garden Grade I)

The impressive house, part-medieval, part-Tudor and part-eighteenth-century, with a dramatic forecourt and north front by Vanbrugh, is surrounded on three sides by good pleasure gardens in which 'Capability' Brown had a hand. The Victorian knot garden to the east of the house has beds of lavender, roses and catmint edged by clipped box. To the south are two yew-hedged gardens with topiary, a yew broad walk and a retreat. Leading to the west terrace is a double yew walk with classic herbaceous borders, and beyond is a shrub rose border. The yew hedging throughout the garden is superbly maintained and differs in design from one area to another. Beyond the pleasure gardens is an arboretum, a wild garden, an unusual geometrically designed kitchen garden with clipped box and bean pergola, and extensive parkland. Views of the old oak and chestnut avenues and of the parkland with its lake and Vanbrugh summerhouse are provided by cleverly positioned vistas and terraces. In all, 27 acres of gardens within 3000 acres of park.

Grimsthorpe and Drummond Castle Trust Ltd

Grimsthorpe, Nr Bourne PE10 0LY. Tel: (01778) 591205; www.grimsthorpe.co.uk

4m NW of Bourne on A151 Colsterworth – Bourne road

House open

Park and garden open April and May, Sun and Thurs; June to Sept, Sun – Thurs; all 12 noon – 6pm

Entrance: £3.50, OAPs £3, children £2 (house, park and garden £8, OAPs £7, children £3.50) (2007 prices)

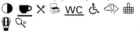

GUNBY HALL ★
(Historic Park and Garden Grade II)

The charming William and Mary house, its walls smothered in fine plants, sits in 1500 acres of parkland with avenues of lime and horse chestnut. The shrub borders, wild garden, lawns with old cedars and restrained formal front garden of nepeta and lavender beds backed by clipped yew provide a startling contrast to the main attraction of Gunby – its 8.5 acres of walled gardens. The dazzling pergola garden with an apple tree walkway has a maze of paths leading to beds of old roses, a herb garden and brimming herbaceous and annual borders. The second walled enclosure houses an impressive kitchen garden reached after passing more borders of perfectly arranged herbaceous plants and hybrid musk roses. Backing onto its wall is another wonderfully classic herbaceous border and, beyond that an early-nineteenth-century long fish pond flanked by the Ghost Walk, made eerie during autumn mists by the looming Irish junipers punctuating its length. Other seasons bring their own pleasures: a wildflower walk and

The National Trust

Gunby, Spilsby PE23 5SS. Tel: (01909) 486411; www.gunbyhall.ic24.net

7m NW of Skegness, 2.5m NW of Burgh-le-Marsh on S of A158

House open 4th June to 27th Aug, Wed, 2 – 5pm

Garden open 2nd April to 28th May, Wed; 3rd June to 28th Aug, Tues – Thurs; 3rd to 25th Sept, Wed and Thurs; all 2 – 5pm. Also open by written appt April and May, Tues and Thurs

Entrance: £4, children £2, family £9 (house and garden £6, children £3, family £14)

Other information: Possible for wheelchairs but some gravel paths; no wheelchair access to hall

Gunby Hall

spring bulbs in April and May, roses in June, and herbaceous borders at their glorious best from July to September.. This is a gorgeous garden. It is fitting that it was the subject of Tennyson's *Haunt of Ancient Peace*.

HALL FARM AND NURSERY ★

Mr and Mrs Mark Tatam

Harpswell, Gainsborough DN21 5UU.
Tel: (01427) 668412;
www.hall-farm.co.uk

7m E of Gainsborough on A631

Open all year, daily, 8am – 5.30pm
(nursery closed Sat and Sun); and
by appt

Entrance: donation to charity

Other information: Coaches by appt.

Teas on charity open day only

○ WC ⑂ ⬡ ⫰ ⬤

This 1.5-acre garden combines the formal and the informal in a most imaginative way. The owners' delight in plants, satisfied by their adjoining nursery, is evident everywhere; there are hundreds of varieties of unusual herbaceous plants, roses and shrubs. A rose pergola leads from a decorative paved terrace to the main area behind the farmhouse. Subdivided into six separate areas, each with at least two entry points, the whole becomes an intriguing maze of garden rooms linked by border-edged paths and pergolas; they include a walled top terrace, a formal double border walk, a sunken garden with seasonal planting, an orchard with a giant chessboard and a set of chessmen and a newly restored wildlife pond and walkway. Here the borders have been planted with moisture-lovers, grasses and bamboos, providing a peaceful contrast to the other, floriferous areas.

Hall Farm and Nursery

HARRINGTON HALL ★
(Historic Garden Grade II)

Given an idyllic setting in the wolds, the mellow red-brick of the Tudor and seventeenth-century hall walled gardens and raised terraces provide the perfect backdrop for a variety of superb wall shrubs, climbers and deep colour-themed mixed and herbaceous borders set off by good lawns. Referred to in Tennyson's *Maud*, it is hard to imagine that these romantic gardens and walks have ever changed, although they were in fact replanted during the 1950s after a spell of wartime vegetable cultivation. Ironically, the one-acre kitchen garden immediately east of the house is a much more recent restoration. Formal in design and subdivided by a variety of hedges and paths, it is a happy combination of the functional and the purely decorative, with trained fruit trees, borders and a raised sitting area with a pond. Two hedge-enclosed areas and their surrounding slopes are still in the early stages of development, but the inclusion of ornamental native trees serves to screen a swimming-pool pavilion and link the formal pleasure gardens to the parkland beyond. Six acres in all.

Mr and Mrs D.W. J. Price

Harrington, Spilsby PE23 4NH.
Tel: (01790) 754570 (Gardener);
harringtonhallgardens.co.uk

5m E of Horncastle, 2m N of A158

Open 8th and 29th June, 20th July, 10th Aug, 2 – 5pm, and by appt

Entrance: £2.50, children free

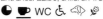

HOLMDALE HOUSE

Cleverly arranged around the Victorian farmhouse and spacious courtyard (used as the owners' plant nursery), several intimate gardens have evolved here, each with a different aspect and conditions. In the first a natural pond is edged by a gravel path and walled border. This leads to a grass walk flanked by deep rambling borders. The third area is a bordered lawn divided by a well-planted central bed. Existing trees and shrubs have been underplanted and supplemented, resulting in an eclectic mix of colour and texture. A fourth, recently acquired, 0.5-acre plot is in the process of development, already featuring a white garden (giving lovely views over the Lincolnshire fens), a prairie border and a snowdrop walk. Although there are flowers here, this garden, with its hosta bed, grasses and choice variegated plants, will appeal particularly to foliage lovers. Combining unusual plants, imaginative planting and quirkily placed seats and containers, a traditional 1.5-acre garden has been transformed into one with a highly individual feel.

Ian Warden and Stewart MacKenzie

55 High Street, Martin, Lincoln LN4 3QY.
Tel: (01526) 378838;
www.holmdalehouse.co.uk

15m SE of Lincoln, 4m SW of Woodhall Spa on B1191

Open all year, Tues – Sun and Bank Holiday Mons, 10am – 5pm

Entrance: free

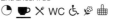

KEXBY HOUSE ★

The five-acre garden, begun at least as far back as 1881 when the impressive Victorian country house was built, is a visual feast. Impressive herbaceous borders betray the owners' passion for sumptuous colour combinations. Swathes of geraniums, irises, lupins, aquilegias, peonies, poppies, nepetas, euphorbias and a multitude of other well-grown plants spill over from the wide herbaceous vistas, enhancing the garden's defined Victorian structure. Cottage garden stalwarts jostle with less well-known hardy plants, the whole herbaceous

Herbert and Jenny Whitton

Kexby Lane, Kexby, Gainsborough DN21 5NE.
Tel: (01427) 788759;
www.kexbyhousegardens.co.uk

12m NW of Lincoln, 6m E of Gainsborough on B1241, on outskirts of Kexby village

Open 27th April, 18th May, 8th June, 6th July, 7th Sept, and by appt.

Kexby House

Entrance: £3, children free

● ● ✕ 🗑 WC ♿ ⬧ ▨

effect supported by judicious planting of shrubs, hundreds of roses and some fabulously ancient trees. It is obvious that an artist's eye has guided the design and planting, as one perspective after another invites the visitor into a series of intimate spaces, each with its own character and interest. To list the features – wildlife pond, bog garden, mixed and colour-coordinated borders, scree – doesn't begin to capture the spirit of a garden with a long history, tempered by the personal and modern approach of its present owners.

English Heritage
Medieval Bishops' Palace, Minster Yard,
Lincoln LN2 1PU.
Tel: (01522) 527468;
www.english-heritage.org.uk

LINCOLN CONTEMPORARY HERITAGE GARDEN

Mark Anthony Walker's small heritage garden is a landscaper's answer to the New York loft conversion – an antique terrace, first recorded as a garden site in 1320, has been given a pure,

Lincoln Contemporary
Heritage Garden

uncluttered design which must surely convert the anti-modernist. Deceptively simple, it makes clever allusion to the garden's history, linking it perfectly to the surrounding ruins and nearby cathedral. Brick paths create a lattice pattern across a lawn, and fastigiate hornbeams have been planted within steel discs at the intersections. Like the ribs and bosses of the cathedral's vaulted ceilings which inspired the design, the lattice succeeds in resolving the problem of asymmetry created by the irregular quadrilateral site. Clipped lavender – a splendid sight in flower in summers – and the red 'Guinée' rose give localised colour. The garden may be enjoyed from two seats set in yew niches, but the best views are from the East Hall terrace, where the full impact of what is in effect a contemporary knot garden can be appreciated. The entry charge includes access to the palace ruins and the flourishing vineyard on a lower terrace.

On S side of Lincoln Cathedral

Open April to Oct, daily, 10am – 5pm (closes 6pm in July and Aug); Nov to March, daily except Tues and Wed, 10am – 4pm. Closed 24th to 26th Dec, 1st Jan

Entrance: £3.90, OAPs £2.90, children £2, family £9.80 (2007 prices)

NORMANBY HALL ★

The Regency house designed by Sir Robert Smirke is set in 300 acres of parkland boasting some fine mature trees, including a grand old holm oak looking like a surreal climbing frame and good avenues of copper beech and Wellingtonia. There are also stream walks, a bog garden, a Christmas garden, a newly planted woodland garden and an accessible deer park. A Victorian woodland garden, still under development, has been planted with Japanese maples, camellias and azaleas, and acid-loving woodland perennials like the Himalayan blue poppy. Great strides have been made to restore the pleasure gardens to their former beauty. The formal area south of the hall includes a 'boar's head' parterre and a sunken garden with a rectangular pond surrounded by herbaceous borders. Further away are two gardens enclosed by tall old walls and holly and conifer hedges. The first has good wall shrubs and climbers and double herbaceous borders planted Jekyll-fashion to move along its length from hot to cool colours. The second is a lavish reconstruction of the original Victorian kitchen garden, complete with a potting shed, bothy, a vinery with a bed of subtropical plants, a fern house and a display house. Fruit trees are trained against the walls and over arches; those in the south-facing peach cases are under glass. There are decorative borders and four box-edged plots filled with organically grown fruit and vegetable varieties true to the period.

North Lincolnshire Council

Normanby Hall Country Park, Normanby, Scunthorpe DN15 9HU.
Tel: (01724) 720588;
www.northlinc.gov.uk/normanby

4m N of Scunthorpe on B1430

House and farm museum open 30th March to 28th Sept, daily, 1 – 5pm

Park open all year, daily, 9am – dusk (closes 9pm in summer); Victorian walled garden open daily except 25th and 26th Dec and 1st Jan, 10.30am – 5pm (4pm in winter)

Entrance: hall, gardens and farm museum £4.60, concessions £4.20, family £18. Season tickets available (2007 prices)

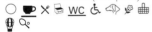

THE OLD RECTORY, EAST KEAL

With its orchard, vegetable garden and joyous planting, this is probably most people's dream of an English country garden. There are approximately 1500 different species and varieties in the 0.75 acre, tumbling, jostling for space and showing off in and on the lovely old walls, beds, borders, rockeries and ponds. To the casual observer it might seem that they had arrived by chance, but apart from the occasional happy

Mrs R. F. Ward

Church Lane, East Keal, Spilsby PE23 4AT.
Tel: (01790) 752477

12m W of Skegness, 2m SW of Spilsby on A16

Open for NGS, and 30th March and
17th Aug, 2 – 5pm, for other charities.
Also open by appt

Entrance: £2.50, children free

Other information: Refreshments by
arrangement

● ● WC ᕐ ֍

accident each part is carefully planned to provide different habitats, ensure year-round interest and avoid repeat-planting. Nestled on a hillside, the garden is criss-crossed by a myriad of steps and paths passing through the different areas to seats positioned for peaceful contemplation or for enjoying views of the rolling landscape of the Wolds. Converting a swimming pool into a pond and bog garden with a rose-laden pergola on one side has created an exotic new enclosure.

Denise and Derrick Targett

Somerby, Nr Brigg DN38 6EX.
Tel: (01652) 628268;
www.hostas.co.uk

4m E of Brigg off A1084

Open May to Sept, daily, 10am – 5pm,
and for parties by appt

Entrance: £2.50

◑ WC ᕐ ◁ ֍

THE OLD RECTORY, SOMERBY

Although little remains of the original nineteenth-century garden there is still a feeling of Victorian opulence in the 2.5 acres here, due to a preference for shrubs and herbaceous plants with form and stature. Specimens are permitted space to develop to their full potential in the generous borders (up to 10 metres deep in places) that edge the sweeping lawns. No froth or clutter; no island beds or secret walks, but anything that may have been forfeited in mystery has been gained in unobstructed views and plant beauty, epitomised by the exotic hot border with excellent rheums and *Lobelia tupa*. There is also a well-planted pergola, raised display beds and a formal fishpond. Hostas are a particular passion, displayed in a hosta walk, a large collection of unusual American hybrids (including National Collections of 'Mildred Seaver' and 'Lachman' hybrids), and the adjoining specialist nursery. It is worth visiting the Norman church sheltering on the wooded hillside opposite the house, and Normanby Hall (see entry) is only 14 miles away.

The Old Rectory, Somerby

OTHER RECOMMENDED GARDENS

AYSCOUGHFEE HALL

Churchgate, Spalding PE11 2RA (01775 761161; www.sholland.gov.uk). Open all year, daily except 25th Dec and 1st Jan, 8am – dusk

The 5-acre gardens of the late-medieval wool merchant's house are in a beautiful setting next to the River Welland. Mellow brick walls, bizarrely shaped clipped yews, an ice-house and an old fish pond with fountains create a feeling of antiquity, set off by modern plantings. (Listed Grade II)

THE LAWN

Sir Joseph Banks Conservatory, Union Road, Lincoln LN1 3BL (01522 560306). Open all year, daily: 10am – 4.30pm (closes 4pm Fri and Sun)

A 5-acre garden established after 1985 as a botanic collection representing plants appropriate to the parts of the world visited by Joseph Banks during his journey with Captain Cook. Exotic, interesting and well-arranged.

MANOR FARM

Mr and Mrs C. A. Richardson, Keisby, Bourne PE10 0RZ (01476 585607). Open by appt

Artistically planned and harmoniously planted, the pretty, informal 1-acre garden has narrow paths meandering through different areas, allowing a close inspection of the many choice plants. A streamside walk then leads to an entirely different experience: a south-facing continental garden, filled with grasses and sun-loving plants. February, summer and autumn are all good times to visit.

MARIGOLD COTTAGE

Stephanie Lee, Hotchin Road, Sutton-on-Sea LN12 2JA (01507 442151). Open 11th May, 1st June, 6th July and 3rd Aug for charities, and by appt

Essentially, this is a sparkling 0.5-acre cottage garden, with secret paths and tiny lawns, plant-laden pergolas, and rare and tender plants growing alongside old favourites in brimming mixed borders. However, artefacts and ideas gathered from long sojourns in Asia have helped to transform it into a place of great originality.

Marigold Cottage

LIVERPOOL & WIRRAL

For further information about how to use the *Guide*
and for an explanation of the symbols, see pages vi–viii.
Specific dates and times are those given to us by garden owners for 2008.
For 2009 dates, check with the individual properties.
For opening dates under the National Gardens Scheme,
readers should consult *The Yellow Book* or www.ngs.org.uk.
Maps are to be found at the end of the *Guide*.

BIRKENHEAD PARK ★
(Historic Park Grade I)

Metropolitan Borough of Wirral
Birkenhead, Wirral CH41 4HY.
Tel: (0151) 652 5197;
www.wirral.gov.uk
1m from centre of Birkenhead, S of
A553
Open all year, daily, during daylight hours
Entrance: free

A milestone in garden history, this – the world's first civic park – was designed by Joseph Paxton and opened in 1847. When Frederick Law Olmsted visited just three years later he wondered at 'the manner in which art had been employed to obtain from nature so much beauty'; he went on to incorporate much of what he had observed into New York's Central Park. Paxton's original vision is now re-emerging with an impressive restoration scheme. The sinuous shapes of the lakes have been re-established, gates, iron railings and stonework refurnished or replaced, the Swiss bridge and the Roman boathouse on the lower lake superbly restored, and an attractive new restaurant and gallery built. New plantings have been made too; although these are still immature, the many fine mature trees dominate the views as before. The bodies concerned with the restoration are to be congratulated on returning the park to much of its original elegance – let us hope that funds are available to keep it in this condition.

LIVERPOOL BOTANIC GARDENS ★

Liverpool City Council,
Environmental Services
Calderstones Park, Liverpool L18 3JD.
Tel: (0151) 225 4877;
www.liverpool.gov.uk
4m SE of city centre, S of A562
Park open all year, daily, during daylight hours. Old English garden and Japanese garden open all year, daily except 25th Dec, 8am – 5pm (closes 4pm Oct to March)
Entrance: free

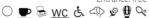

Essentially this is a well-landscaped park of 126 acres with mature trees, a lake and a rhododendron walk. At its heart, close to the house, a series of gardens is set around the old walled garden. To the front a long herbaceous border, 6 metres deep, has a range of strong-growing perennials; beyond, the flower garden features large clumps of grasses and daylilies and beds of annuals. Overlooking it is a greenhouse containing a sample of National Collections of codiaeums, dracaenas and aechmeas, many fine orchids in season, an impressive collection of cacti, and much else besides. To the rear of the greenhouse the Old English flower garden has beds of perennials, bulbs and shrubs set within a formal layout of paths, with a circular lily pool and pergolas bearing clematis, vines, golden hops and honeysuckle at its centre. In the Japanese garden a chain of rocky streams and pools is fringed by acers, pines and clumps of bamboo. On

Liverpool Botanic Gardens

the outer edges of the park is a recently restored rock garden, a large lake, a bog garden and a rose garden. Children will enjoy the 'text garden' maze and the £100,000 millennium playground. Altogether one of the best 'free' gardens in the country.

OTHER RECOMMENDED GARDENS

CROXTETH HALL

Croxteth Hall Lane, Liverpool L12 0HB
(0151 233 6910; www.croxteth.co.uk). Open mid-April to mid-Sept, daily, 10.30am – 4.30pm (winter times on request)

Hall, farm and gardens are integral parts of an historic estate comprising 540 acres of parkland and woodland. The centrepiece is a working and highly productive Victorian kitchen garden, complete with greenhouses and a mushroom house, and embellished by a broad herbaceous border. (Listed Grade II)

NATIONAL WILDFLOWER CENTRE

Court Hey Park, Roby Road, Liverpool L16 3NA
(0151 738 1913; www.nwc.org.uk). Open March to Sept, daily, 10am – 5pm (last admission 4pm)

A stimulating visitor centre, bringing Britain's native wild flowers and their habitats to the forefront of the popular imagination. Geometrical beds in the entrance courtyard, demonstration areas and a working nursery with a rooftop walkway running along the top of the award-winning modern building, all situated within a 35-acre Victorian park.

National Wildflower Centre

REYNOLDS PARK WALLED GARDEN

Church Road, Woolton, Liverpool L24 0TR
(0151 724 2371). Open all year, daily except 25th Dec,
10am – 6pm (closes 4pm in winter)

The diamond-shaped walled garden, perched
on a high hill, has traditional beds of dahlias and
seasonal bedding, in contrast to the broad and
luxuriant herbaceous borders along the south-
facing walls. In the park outside is an unusual
clipped yew hedge laid out in the 1920s in Art
Deco style.

SEFTON PARK

Liverpool (0151 225 4877; www.liverpool.gov.uk).
Open all year, daily, during daylight hours

One of the country's most impressive Victorian
parks, endowed and conceived on a grand
scale, and close in size to London's Hyde Park.

Cleverly landscaped and dotted with fine
buildings (including the magnificent 1896 palm
house), it is now being restored with lottery
funds. In all, 269 acres. (Listed Grade II*)

SPEKE HALL

The Walk, Liverpool L24 1XD (0151 427 7231;
0845 585702; www.nationaltrust.org.uk). Open all year,
daily except 24th to 26th Dec, 31st Dec and 1st Jan,
11am – 5.30pm (closes 4.30pm in winter). NT

These remarkable gardens, largely created in
Victorian times to frame the Elizabethan hall,
are located in a heavily industrial area yet seem
utterly rural, with vistas looking over to fields
and woodland. Restoration and development
continue to reveal them in all their impressive
variety. 45 acres in all.

LONDON AREA

For further information about how to use the *Guide*
and for an explanation of the symbols, see pages vi–viii.
Specific dates and times are those given to us by garden owners for 2008.
For 2009 dates, check with the individual properties.
For opening dates under the National Gardens Scheme,
readers should consult *The Yellow Book* or www.ngs.org.uk.
Maps are to be found at the end of the *Guide*.
Like other major cities, London's green spaces take two main forms: historic gardens
and public parks (the latter are usually free and open during daylight hours), and
private gardens that are often small and open rarely or by appointment only. For the
convenience both of visitors wishing to explore the capital's known attractions, and
residents interested in seeking out more hidden territories, they are grouped here
under those two categories.

PUBLIC PARKS AND GARDENS

BATTERSEA PARK
(Historic Park Grade II*)

There is something for everyone in this 200-acre Victorian
park. Much of the nineteenth-century landscape and the 1951
Festival of Britain pleasure gardens, designed by Russell Page,
have been restored. There is also an Old English Garden, a
herb garden, a sub-tropical garden and a 13-acre lake with a
Pulhamite cascade, where boats can be hired. The Buddhist
Peace Pagoda on the Riverside Promenade was built in 1985,
and dotted throughout the park are sculptures by Henry
Moore and Barbara Hepworth.

Wandsworth Borough Council

Battersea, London SW11 4NJ.
Tel: (020) 8871 7530/8800;
www.wandsworth.gov.uk

On S side of River Thames, from
Chelsea Bridge to Albert Bridge

Open all year, daily, 7am – dusk

Entrance: free, but parking charge

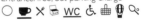

CAPEL MANOR COLLEGE

There are many hours of enjoyment in the 30-acre grounds
of this well-known land-based college, first established in
1968. The historic landscape around the Georgian manor
house includes a walled garden, an Italianate maze, a magnolia
border and seventeenth-century gardens. There are
sponsored demonstration gardens in a variety of styles,
including a delightful Japanese garden, and trial grounds of
plants and products run by *Gardening Which?* magazine. The
area of themed gardens includes a potager and topiary. In the
National Gardening Centre, design is explored in seven small
gardens which make up Sunflower Street, created in 2005 by
former students of the college. Over and above the
educational aspects of the college gardens, they are a fertile
source of inspiration for anyone seeking to reinvent their own
garden, or to start a new one from scratch.

Capel Manor Charitable Corporation

Bullsmoor Lane, Enfield EN1 4RQ.
Tel: (08456) 122122;
www.capelmanorgardens.co.uk

From M25 junction 25, via Turkey
Street/Bullsmoor Lane (signposted), or
walk from railway station

Open March to Oct, daily; Nov to Feb,
Mon – Fri; all 10am – 6pm (last admission
4.30pm). Closed 25th Dec to 1st Jan

Entrance: £6, concessions £5, children £2,
family £14. Special rates for winter and
show weekends

Other information: Full programme of
shows, events and concerts – telephone or
consult website for details

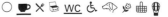

Chelsea Physic Garden Company
66 Royal Hospital Road, Chelsea, London SW3 4HS.
Tel: (020) 7352 5646;
www.chelseaphysicgarden.co.uk

Entrance in Swan Walk, off Chelsea Embankment and, for wheelchair users only, in Royal Hospital Road

Open 2nd, 3rd, 9th and 10th Feb, 11am – 4pm; 19th March to Oct, Wed – Fri, Sun and Bank Holiday Mons, 12 noon – 5pm. Also open 19th and 20th May, 12 noon – 5pm; July and Aug, Wed, late opening (last admission 8.30pm)

Entrance: £7, students and children £4, under 5 free

Other information: Winter Fair 7th Dec

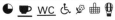

CHELSEA PHYSIC GARDEN ★
(Historic Garden Grade I)

A wrought-iron gate in Swan Walk opens on to England's second oldest botanic garden and one of London's most fascinating secret gardens. Founded in 1673 as a place to train apothecaries' apprentices in plant identification, the 3.5-acre garden now offers a stroll down the ages of plant taxa and discoveries and, through the Garden of World Medicine and the Pharmaceutical Garden, their uses worldwide. Its walled microclimate enables tender plants to flourish, including the largest outdoor fruiting olive tree in Britain, towering echiums and a National Collection of cistus. The beds radiate from an imposing statue of Sir Hans Sloane, who leased the land in perpetuity to the Society of Apothecaries in 1722. In one glasshouse is the rare *Musschia aurea* with starry cream flowers pollinated in the wild by lizards living on the volcanic slopes of Madeira; another houses an exceptional collection of species pelargoniums.

London Borough of Hounslow and English Heritage

Burlington Lane, Chiswick, London W4 2RP. Tel: (020) 8995 0508; www.english-heritage.org.uk

5m W of central London; entrance on A4

House open 21st March to Oct, Wed – Sun, 10am – 5pm (closes 2pm Sat). Private tours by arrangement Nov to March (telephone for details)

Gardens open all year, daily, 8am – dusk

CHISWICK HOUSE ★★
(Historic Park and Garden Grade I)

The celebrated eighteenth-century gardens, now stretching over 66 acres, with a lake, statues, temples, bridges, an orangery and magnificent trees, were created from 1715 and extended by William Kent to complement the Palladian villa built by Lord Burlington in 1729. Kent opened up views, added an exedra lined with statuary, and gave the lake a more serpentine shape. He also created a cascade at one end of the lake designed to mimic an underground river flowing from a rocky hill; it never worked in Kent's day but has recently been activated by English Heritage. An Italian garden with parterres

Chiswick House

and a conservatory (built to house the famous camellia collection) were added in the nineteenth century. In 2006 the Chiswick House and Gardens Trust was set up to oversee the restoration of both house and garden, and already the sphinxes on the gate piers in front of the villa have been reinstated and a new outdoor camellia garden is planned for the area south of the Italian garden.

Entrance: garden free (house £4, concessions £3.20, children £2.10) (2007 prices)

Other information: Dogs outside Italian garden only

ELTHAM PALACE GARDENS
(Historic Garden Grade II*)

The 19-acre grounds surrounding the moat of the original manor house are largely the creation of Stephen and Virginia Courtauld, who bought the site and built their adjoining Art Deco house in the 1930s. The garden is divided into a series of rooms and includes a sunken rose garden which has recently been replanted with the early hybrid tea and hybrid musk roses popular at the period. The Westmorland stone rock garden, now housing shrubs and alpine plants, originally featured a series of pools and cascades descending to the moat – these are also due to be restored. There are also areas of contemporary planting in the 120-yard-long South Moat border and White Wood by designer Isabelle Van Groeningen. A walk up to the wildlife lawn for wide views of London brings home the timeless allure of this remarkable historic enclave.

English Heritage

Court Road, Eltham, London SE9 9QE.
Tel: (020) 8294 2548;
www.elthampalace.org.uk

Near Eltham High Street, 0.5m from Eltham railway station (then Bus 161) or 0.75m from Mottingham railway station (then Bus 126 or 131)

Palace open as garden

Garden open 4th Feb to 20th Dec, 10am – 5pm (closes 4pm Nov to March)

Entrance: £4.80, OAPs £3.60, children £2.40 (house and garden £7.60, OAPs £5.70, children £3.80, family £19)

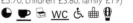

FENTON HOUSE

The 1.5-acre garden located behind the seventeenth-century house, approached along a cool avenue of *Robinia pseudoacacia*, is interesting as much for its structure as its planting, and for the features that make it a country-house garden in miniature. The immaculate lawn is separated from the rear of the house by a double row of lollipop hollies. A raised terrace runs along the east and north sides of the lawn, with climbers and espaliered fruit trees set against the walls and box-edged plants of summer-flowering perennials punctuated by tubs of dark blue agapanthus, while the west border is planted with shrubs and spring bulbs. Tall and immaculate yew hedges enclose a sunken rose garden and an informally planted gravelled area. Steps lead down into the old orchard with its 30 varieties of apple trees; filled in spring with narcissi, fritillaries and bluebells, in summer mown paths wind through the long grass. There is also a herb, vegetable and cutting garden, a restored greenhouse and even a beehive.

The National Trust

Hampstead Grove, London NW3 6RT.
Tel: (020) 7435 3471;
www.nationaltrust.org.uk

In centre of Hampstead in Hampstead Grove behind Heath Street

House open

Garden open 1st to 16th March, Sat and Sun, 2 – 5pm; 19th March to 2nd Nov, Wed – Sun and Bank Holiday Mons, 11am – 5pm (opens 2pm Wed – Fri); and for parties by appt at other times

Entrance: £1, children free (house and garden £5.40, children £2.70, family £13)

Other information: Toilet facilities if house visited

HALL PLACE
(Historic Garden Grade II*)

On the banks of the River Cray stands this fine example of a Tudor mansion house in its award-winning grounds. A raised walk overlooks the topiary lawn where the Queen's beasts,

Bexley Heritage Trust

Bourne Road, Bexley, Kent DA5 1PQ.
Tel: (01322) 526574;
www.hallplace.com

Just N of A2 near A2/A223 junction

House open April to Oct, daily, 10am – 5pm (opens 11am Sun); Nov to March, Tues – Sat, 10am – 4.15pm

Garden open all year, daily, 9am – dusk. Model allotment, parts of nursery and glasshouses open all year except 25th Dec, Mon – Fri, 9am – 5pm (closes 4pm in winter)

Entrance: free

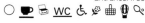

The National Trust

Ham Street, Richmond, Surrey TW10 7RS. Tel: (020) 8940 1950; www.nationaltrust.org.uk

On S bank of Thames, W of A307 at Petersham

House open 15th March to 2nd Nov, Sat – Wed, 12 noon – 4pm

Garden open all year, Sat – Wed, 11am – 6pm (or dusk if earlier). Closed 25th, 26th Dec and 1st Jan

Entrance: £3.30, children £2.20, family £8.80 (house and garden £9.90, children £5.50, family £25.30)

Other information: Parking 400 metres by river, disabled on terrace

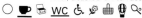

Historic Royal Palaces Trust

East Molesey, Surrey KT8 9AU. Tel: (0870) 950 4499; www.hrp.org.uk

On A308 at junction of A309 on N side of Hampton Court Bridge over Thames

Palace open

Gardens and park open all year, daily except 25th Dec, 10am – 6pm (closes 4.30pm Nov to March)

Entrance: Rose, Wilderness and Tiltyard Gardens free; Maze £3.50, children £2; Great Fountain, Twentieth-Century, Privy, and Sunken Gardens and Great Vine £4.50, concessions £3, children £2.50, family £13.50 (free to palace ticket-holders)

modelled on the originals at Hampton Court, stand proud against the backdrop of a mature *Solanum* 'Glasnevin' on the red brick wall. Further on, rose beds give way to a hedge-enclosed secret garden with wide herbaceous borders, and a wisteria-covered bridge leads to Italianate and herb gardens. A wildlife meadow, a time-garden which explores the history of plants through the ages, and a dipping pond are good places for budding young environmentalists. The horticultural area houses sub-tropical plant houses, a nursery, display gardens and a plant sales area. 50 acres in all.

HAM HOUSE ★

(Historic Garden Grade II*)

The approach to the impressive house is along an avenue running through meadows bordering the River Thames, giving no hint of the architectural framework of the gardens beyond, furnished in the seventeenth century with the 'Parterres, Flower Gardens, Orangeries, groves, Avenues, Courts, Statues, Perspectives, Fountains, Aviaries' remarked on by John Evelyn. Today, clipped balls of santolina and lavender are set amongst parterres of box and hedged with yew lead to the raised south terrace, where historic pots and planting are backed by healthy pomegranate trees. Beyond lie the grass plats. Replicas of seventeenth-century lead statues mark the entrance to the wilderness, and hornbeam hedges provide a setting for spring bulbs and summer wild flowers. The walled kitchen garden, planted with period herbs, fruit and vegetables, is the perfect adjunct to the earliest surviving orangery in the country. 18 acres.

HAMPTON COURT PALACE ★★

(Historic Park and Garden Grade I)

The gardens, which provide the setting for the palace, are an exciting and eclectic mixture of styles and tastes. They are traditionally famous for the Great Vine planted in 1768 – officially the largest vine in the world, probably the oldest and still producing hundreds of 'Black Hamburg' grapes each year (for sale to the public when harvested in late August) – and the maze, the oldest hedge-planted maze in Britain. The sunken Pond Gardens offer a magnificent display of bedding plants, and there is a 1924 knot garden with interlocking bands of dwarf box, thyme, lavender and cotton lavender infilled with bedding plants. On a truly grand scale, the Great Fountain Garden, an immense semi-circle of grass and flower beds with a central fountain, is probably the most impressive element, but the Wilderness Garden in spring, with its mass of daffodils and spring-flowering trees, has the most charm. The restored Privy Garden of William III is a spectacular and unique example of the Baroque, with parterres, cutwork, clipped yews and spring and summer displays of seventeenth-century plants. A yet more recent restoration is William III's unique Orangery Garden containing hundreds of exotics planted in ornate pots. A double row of 544 lime trees has been planted to flank the Longwater in Home Park, bringing Charles II's Long Walk Avenue back to its 1661 glory. An area of the gardens sometimes missed by visitors is the secluded Twentieth- Century Garden, located next to the Fountain Garden. Too much to see in one day – plan at least two trips; one in spring and one in summer to walk in only part of the 60 acres of gardens. *The Garden and Park at Hampton Court Palace* by Todd Longstaffe-Gowan, with photographs by Vivian Russell, is published by Frances Lincoln.

THE HILL GARDEN AND PERGOLA
(Historic Garden Grade II*)

From the entrance a spiral staircase climbs up to reveal one of the most dramatic garden structures in London: a 250-metre-long classical pergola with oak beams and stone columns planted with a wide variety of climbers. Designed by Thomas Mawson to link the garden to that of Inverforth House (built by Lord Leverhulme at the beginning of the twentieth century), it is at ground level on one side but supported by a red-brick colonnaded structure five metres above ground on the other. Views look out across the tree tops and down onto the old kitchen garden of the house, laid out now in sweeping beds containing cherries, magnolias, shrub roses, geraniums and bergenias, with a beautiful stand of birch in one corner. At the lower end, which is paved with brick and yet to be restored, the many mature climbers include what may be a wisteria from the original planting; a belvedere at the end looks out across to distant Harrow on the Hill. Steps descend past an ancient sweet chestnut into the Hill Garden proper – a peaceful retreat with lawns unfurling down the hill, mature trees, a long formal lily pond and well-maintained shrub and perennial borders. From the exit opposite the pergola, Golders Hill Park (see entry) is a short stroll away across the heath.

Corporation of London

Inverforth Close, North End Way, London NW3 7EX.
Tel: (020) 8455 5183

From Hampstead pass Jack Straw's Castle on left-hand side on road to Golders Green. Inverforth Close is off North End Way (A502)

Open all year, daily, 9am – dusk

Entrance: free

HOLLAND PARK
(Historic Park Grade II)

This much-loved public space has always been dominated by local families, who use it for walks around the well-maintained, box-edged gardens strutted by peacocks, or for informal picnics on the lawns. Sited around the remnants of Holland House where in 1812 Lord Holland created the formal gardens, the 55-acre park, which contains rare trees such as the Himalayan birch, Pyrenean oak and the May-flowering snowdrop tree, now provides admirably for the demands of a different society and includes summertime opera performances and a smart new garden shop. The tranquil,

Royal Borough of Kensington and Chelsea

Kensington, London W8/W11.
Tel: (020) 7471 9813

Between Kensington High Street and Holland Park Avenue, with several entrances.
Buses 9, 10, 27, 28, 49, C5; nearest underground stations Kensington High Street and Holland Park.

Parking (pay and display) from Abbotsbury Road entrance

Open all year, daily, 7.30am – dusk

Entrance: free

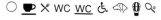

reflective Kyoto Garden is impeccably maintained, as is the bedding area with its changing displays of colourful planting. From the spring blossoming of camellias around the orangery to the autumn conker collecting, this welcoming public space gives horticultural pleasure for a very long season.

THE HOLME

Crown Estate Commissioners

Inner Circle, Regent's Park, London NW1 4NT

In Regent's Park, just W of Inner Circle

Open for NGS, and by appt

Entrance: £3, children £1, family £7 (2007 prices)

Other information: Refreshments and toilet facilities in cafe opposite

The four-acre garden attached to one of the best-positioned houses in Regent's Park is essentially in two parts: a south-facing formal garden, with a sunken lawn and circular pool ringed by generous beds of statuesque herbaceous perennials, and an expanse of lawn punctuated by fine specimen tree, including several mature willows and a *Taxodium distichum*, and beds planted with shrubs, grasses and swathes of herbaceous flowers. Four gardeners keep the whole place in immaculate order, cutting the lawn in summer several times a week in stripes that run the full width of the garden. By contrast the rock garden is a secret dell of lush growth and dripping water where ferns, bamboos, reeds, ivies and other water-loving plants are allowed to grow in profusion. The two parts of the garden are linked by a strip of woodland, heady with scent in spring from *Syringa microphylla* and viburnums. Throughout bedding plants are used generously to add elegant pools of colour. The garden richly deserves its 2005 award from BALI (British Association of Landscape Industries) for best-maintained domestic garden.

HYDE PARK

Royal Parks

Rangers Lodge, London W2 2UH. Tel: (020) 7298 2100; www.royalparks.org.uk

Open all year, daily, 5am – midnight

Entrance: free

(Historic Park Grade I)

It is tempting to nibble away at Hyde Park round the edges, enjoying the pockets of rich planting to be found around its entrances. You get a much better feel for the place, however, by walking from edge to edge, or better still making an entire circuit. That way you cannot fail to appreciate its majestic trees, and stately avenues with cool shade. Step away from the main paths and you will find patches of meadow grasses, full of insect life in summer. The south side of the park near Hyde Park Corner has most to offer gardeners, particularly the newish and very English rose garden, which is maturing well. Summer brings a profusion of roses in beds and on arches, with pinks and creamy yellows predominating, and tall foxgloves and eremurus adding an unexpected note. A short walk away, the Dell has waterfowl enjoying the waterfall and iris-lined stream. On the opposite side of the path is a quiet grove of silver birch underplanted with epimediums, cotoneasters and junipers, where a sombre holocaust memorial stone is set in gravel. The Diana Princess of Wales memorial fountain, whose agitated waters rather too closely mirror her troubled life, is the best-known and most recent of the monuments that mark the history of the place. The good maps placed at strategic points give as much information as the average visitor could need. 350 acres in all.

ISABELLA PLANTATION ★

Hidden away behind a wrought-iron gate within the sweeping tracts of Richmond Park, and commanding distant views of some of the capital's tower blocks, is a remarkably rich wooded plantation of 40 acres. Fine native trees – oaks, beeches and birches – shelter spring-flowering bulbs, colourful magnolias, camellias, rhododendrons and azaleas (a National Collection of Kurume azaleas is held here), coloured autumn leaves, and scented winter-flowering shrubs. Ponds, streams and a bog garden are planted with irises, daylilies and candelabra primulas. The garden is also a notable bird sanctuary – nuthatches, tree-creepers, kingfishers, woodpeckers and owls have all been spotted – and an atmosphere of secrecy and seclusion makes it a sanctuary for human visitors too.

Royal Parks

Richmond Park, Richmond, Surrey TW10 5HS. Tel: (020) 8948 3209; www.royalparks.gov.uk

Open all year, daily, dawn – dusk

Entrance: free

Other information: Parking in Broomfield Hill car park, Pembroke Lodge, Roehampton Gate, disabled at north entrance by way of Ham Gate. Refreshments at Pembroke Lodge. Motorised wheelchair available weekdays, telephone to book by 12 noon previous day

○ 🖼 **WC** க்

THE ISMAILI CENTRE

In this serene courtyard garden on the top floor of the Ismaili Centre, the sound of water running along rills masks the roar of traffic three storeys below. Designed by a Japanese firm, Sasaki Associates, in the early 1980s, its geometrical design and sense of enclosure recall the ancient Islamic *chahar bagh* or four-fold garden, common in Persian and Indian Muslim architecture. The garden, 60m square, symbolizes the celestial paradise found in the Koran, divided into quarters by rivers flowing with water, milk, honey and drink. The central fountain, an octagon of dark blue marble, feeds narrow channels set in the granite floor, and these lead to more fountains, one at a slightly raised level and all four in the shape of circular pools within a square. The late Lanning Roper advised on the planting, which is in shades of green with white, silver and blues in keeping with the traditional Muslim idiom. Structural plants include a fig tree, two silvery-grey weeping pears and cylinders of *Ilex aquifolium* 'J.C. van Tol' in beds 800mm deep.

Aga Khan Foundation

1 Cromwell Gardens London SW7 2SL. Tel: (020) 7581 2071

Opposite Victoria and Albert Museum. Entrance on corner of Thurloe Place and Exhibition Road. Nearest underground station South Kensington. Buses 14, 345, 49, 70, 74 and C1

Conducted tours hourly on London Gardens Day in June and London Open House in Sept. Also open at other times by appt

Entrance: free

● **WC** க்

The Ismaili Centre

Roses and jasmine provide scent and white oleanders in pots frame the main doorways. Look up to get your bearings from within the garden and on a clear day you can see the three domes of the V&A, the Natural History Museum and the Brompton Oratory.

KENSINGTON GARDENS
(Historic Park and Garden Grade I)

Royal Parks

London W2 2UH. Tel: (020) 7298 2100; www.royalparks.gov.uk

Entrances off Bayswater Road, Kensington Gore and West Carriage Drive, Hyde Park

Palace state apartments open all year, daily, 10am – 5pm (closes 6pm Sun, 4pm Nov to Feb). Orangery open daily; for information telephone 0870 751 5176

Gardens open all year, daily, from 6am (closing time displayed at gate)

Entrance: free (state apartments £12, concessions £10, children £6, family £33) (2007 prices)

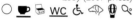

Water, statues and memorials dominate this elegant royal park, originally carved out by William III for its salubrious air. It was George II's wife, Caroline, who created the famous Serpentine and the Long Water, now edged with naturalistic planting. In the north-eastern corner are the fountains and pools of the Italian Water Gardens and, to the north of the palace, the Sunken Water Garden, surrounded by beds of bright seasonal flowers, can be viewed from 'windows' in a lime walk. The most recent of the memorials is the Peter Pan themed playground made in memory of Diana, Princess of Wales. The glittering Albert Memorial stands at the head of the Flower Walk, bordered by fine herbaceous beds. There is an elegant Baroque orangery by Hawksmoor and Vanbrugh with decoration by Grinling Gibbons, and a much photographed bronze of Peter Pan. The Serpentine Gallery, host to some of London's most exciting modern exhibitions, is distinguished by a crescent of slate benches and a stone circle by Ian Hamilton Finlay inscribed with the Latin names of all the trees in the park.

KENWOOD
(Historic Park Grade II*)

English Heritage

Hampstead Lane, London NW3 7JR. Tel: (020) 8348 1286; www.english-heritage.org.uk

On N side of Hampstead Heath, on Highgate – Hampstead road

House open April to Oct, daily, 11am – 5pm (closes 4pm Nov to March)

Park open all year, daily, 8am – 8.30pm (closes 4.30pm in winter)

Entrance: free

Other information: Parking at West Lodge car park, Hampstead Lane (charge)

The 112-acre picturesque landscape, currently being restored, was laid out by Humphry Repton at the end of the eighteenth century. Vistas, sweeping lawns from the terrace of Kenwood House and views over Hampstead Heath and London predominate. Large-scale shrubberies are dominated by rhododendrons. The pasture ground slopes down towards two large lakes, and woods to the south of the lakes fringe the heath, accessible through a number of gates. It is a good place to walk at any season, but particularly when the trees are turning in autumn. Look out for the ivy arch which opens out on to the lakes (one of Repton's famous 'surprises'), the sham bridge on the Thousand Pound Pond and sculpture by Barbara Hepworth and Henry Moore. Arabella Lennox-Boyd has designed the walled and terraced garden behind the cafe with some attractive shrub and perennial plantings.

LONDON WETLANDS CENTRE

The Wildfowl and Wetlands Trust

Queen Elizabeth's Walk, Barnes, London SW13 9WT. Tel: (020) 8409 4400; www.wwt.org.uk

Within this remarkable 105-acre wetland site you can spot nesting sand martins, admire colonies of snakes'-head fritillaries and southern marsh orchids, and explore three contemporary gardens designed to be sustainable and wildlife-friendly. The first of these gardens, by Land Art, has a loosely laid spiralling path of slate, with block planting of perennials rich in pollen and scent chosen to give interest for the partially sighted and to attract insects. Arne Maynard's garden consists of meadow-like planting with turf-topped walls formed from split oak logs, radiating across the site in undulating curves. The third design, by Cleve West and Johnny Woodford, employs strong vertical accent from a series of cobalt-blue spikes. The eye is led to the central pond with a 'bouncing bomb' sculpture skimming the surface; reed beds surround the pond and planting is simplified to increase the sculptural impact.

From M4 junction I take A4 to Hammersmith, then follow signs to Barnes (A306). Travel 0.75m along Castelnau to traffic lights; at Red Lion pub turn left into Queen Elizabeth's Walk. Nearest underground station Hammersmith. Buses 33, 72, 209, 283

Open all year, daily, except 25th Dec, 9.30am – 6pm (closes 5pm in winter) (last admission I hour before closing)

Entrance: £7.95, OAPs £6, children £4.50, family £19.95

REGENT'S PARK ★
(Historic Park and Garden Grade I)

This 410-acre royal park offers a series of delightful gardens, an open-air theatre, a large ornamental lake with a heronry, reedbeds, wildflower grassland, secluded woodland and expanses of lawn. In the Inner Circle the manicured and old-fashioned Queen Mary's Rose Garden, a collection of more than 60,000 roses – predominantly hybrid teas and floribundas – provides scent and colour in high summer while the surrounding herbaceous borders peak in late July and August. The Avenue Garden at the southern end of the Broad Walk is another exquisitely maintained Victorian-style area of planting; its side walks are lined with urns and fountains following Nesfield's originals and Italian cypresses line the paths. Adjacent to this is the charming English Garden added by Nesfield's son Marham. Do not miss the little St John's Lodge garden, with rose arbours, colourful borders and scalloped yew hedges.

Royal Parks

Inner Circle, Regent's Park, London NW1. Tel: (020) 7486 7905; www.royalparks.gov.uk

Off Marylebone Road. Many other entrances to park

Open all year, daily, dawn – dusk

Entrance: free

ROYAL BOTANIC GARDENS ★★
(Historic Park Grade I)

Stretching over 300 acres, the delightful gardens and grounds – a World Heritage Site since 2003 – have something for everyone: in spring, the flowering cherries, crocuses, daffodils and alpines; in May and June, the bluebell wood, the lilacs (made famous by the song) and the water-lily house; in summer the Duke's Garden, the rose garden; in autumn bulbs and trees; in winter, the winter-flowering cherries. The 14,000 trees include oaks, conifers and the famous ginkgo and pagoda trees. Year-round pleasures are Decimus Burton's Palm and Temperate Houses and the elegant modern Princess of Wales Conservatory with its computer-controlled microclimates. The huge glasshouses have their unique collections of exotic and unusual plants, ranging from banana trees to giant water lilies. The latest addition is the elegant Davies Alpine House, which opened in 2006. The somewhat formal rose garden, the

Trustees

Kew, Richmond, Surrey TW9 3AB. Tel: (020) 8332 5655; www.kew.org.

Kew Green, S of Kew Bridge

Palace open April to Oct, daily, 10am – 5.30pm

Gardens open all year, daily except 24th and 25th Dec, from 9.30am (closing times vary seasonally; glasshouses close earlier). Guided tours daily from Victoria Gate visitor centre, 11am and 2pm

Entrance: £12.25, concessions £10.25, children (under 17), blind, partially sighted and essential carers free (late-entry charge variable).

Royal Botanic
Gardens

rock garden and the grass and bamboo gardens should also be visited. The Japanese gateway has been completely restored and the surrounding area landscaped, and the Mediterranean gardens were being revitalised in 2007. All these buildings and gardens are elements in 'working' Kew, which is primarily a botanic research institution, collecting, conserving and exchanging plants from all over the world. There is another Kew – historic and royal. The recently restored palace became in 1729 home to Frederick, Prince of Wales and it was his wife Princess Augusta who commissioned the gardens, and the 3rd Earl of Bute who created them. Sir William Chambers designed the buildings which today give Kew its historical hinterland: the three temples dedicated to Aeolus, Arethusa and Bellona, the 1761 orangery, the ruined arch and the pagoda. A relic of an earlier age, the seventeenth-century Queen's Garden beside the palace, has been re-created in period style. The disabled will find most parts of Kew accessible. Children will enjoy the imaginative mangrove swamps, the marine display showing seaweeds and fish from around the world, and Climbers and Creepers, the UK's first botanical play zone.

THE ROYAL COLLEGE OF PHYSICIANS MEDICINAL GARDEN

Royal College of Physicians (contact: Dr Henry Oakeley, The Garden Fellow)

11 St Andrews Place, Regent's Park, NW1 4LE. Tel: (020) 7224 1539; www.rcplondon.ac.uk/garden

On SE corner of Regent's Park, at junction of Outer Circle and Park Square East. Nearest underground station Regent's Park and Great Portland St. Buses 18, 30, 205

When Mark Griffiths was asked to design and plant a physic garden for the twenty-first century, his brief was to make it a place of visual appeal as well as a living library and research resource. Retaining the best of earlier plantings, including a magnificent pomegranate, he replanted the small garden during 2005 and 2006, using thousands of plants from some 800 species. The result is an inspiring design based on a

The Royal College of Physicians
Medicinal Garden

fascinating range of plants, including some that are the source of current remedies such as *Illicium anisatum* (used to make Tamiflu), some, like *Veratrum nigrum,* long used in medicines, and more that have been taken by different peoples through the ages. The planting follows geographical regions and is split between the borders at the front (most colourful in spring and late summer) and those that encircle the undulating lawn to the rear. Here you will find plants associated with famous doctors from Dioscorides to Mead, and a range of dramatic exotics in a gravel bed. In 2007 head gardener Jane Knowles planted eight new beds with plants from the *Pharmacopoeia Londinensis* of 1618 that were used in medicine at that time.

Open all year, daily, 9am – 5pm, by appt (telephone Paula Crosier on (020) 7034 4901)

Other information: Garden behind college occasionally closed for private functions

Entrance: free

ST JAMES'S PARK ★
(Historic Park Grade I)

One of the smaller royal parks but one of the prettiest. Henry VIII turned a swampy field into a pleasure ground and nursery for deer and Charles II sought advice from Louis XIV's garden designer André Le Nôtre to refashion the park into a garden. He recommended a formal canal and included a pitch for the king to play the old French game of *paille maille* (hence nearby Pall Mall), a crude form of croquet. Between 1827 and 1829 Nash remodelled the gardens and the lake, whose islands are still home to a wide variety of birds. Don't miss the skyline view looking east from the bridge across the lake. Bands play on summer weekend afternoons near Marlborough Gate, and there is a small playground for younger children at the western end of the park.

Royal Parks

London SW1A 2BJ.
Tel: (020) 7298 2000;
www.royalparks.gov.uk

Extends from Buckingham Palace on W to Horse Guards Parade on E, The Mall on N and Birdcage Walk on S

Open all year, daily, 5am – midnight

Entrance: free

Thames Barrier Park

THAMES BARRIER PARK ★

London Borough of Newham

Barrier Point Road, off North Woolwich Road, London E16 2HP.
Tel: (0207) 511 4111;
www.thamesbarrierpark.org.uk

On N bank of River Thames, between North Woolwich Road and Thames Barrier in Silvertown. Nearest underground station Canning Town; Docklands Light Railway (DLR), Pontoon Dock; mainline station North London Line, Silverlink service between Richmond and North Woolwich Silvertown. Buses 69, 474

Open all year, daily, 7am – dusk

Entrance: free

Other information: No direct access between Thames Barrier Park on north bank and Thames Barrier Information and Learning Centre on south bank. No public access to Thames Barrier structure itself from either location

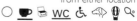

The finest modern park in Britain, opened in 2000, is simultaneously a brave act of regeneration and a landscape *tour de force*. The distinguished French designers Alain Provost and Alain Cousseran of Groupe Signes teamed up with English architects Patel Taylor and engineers Ove Arup to transform a contaminated brownfield site into a 22-acre park on the north bank adjacent to the river's most significant modern work of engineering, the giant stainless-steel 'cockleshells' of the Thames Flood Prevention Barrier. The river promenade gives a setting to the Barrier, and a raised walkway opens up views along and over the river. The flatness of the high-level plateau emphasises its spaciousness – think ten or more football pitches of lawns and wildflower meadows framed by bands of shrubs and interspersed with broad mown paths. The greatest surprise and pleasure is, however, the Green Dock, the largest sunken garden in London. Stretching the length of the park, this simulation of a marine dock is a glorious, accessible garden dug deep and crossed by two viewing bridges. Look down and the planting is a tidal flow of wave-cut hedges alternating with beds of perennials. However, the park has been bedevilled by problems with the fountain plaza and the theft of its stainless steel fencing – it would be a tragedy if its lustre were dimmed through neglect.

VICTORIA AND ALBERT MUSEUM
(The John Madejski Garden)

Cromwell Road, London SW7 2RL;
www.vam.ac.uk

On Cromwell Road, close to South Kensington underground station

Open all year, daily except 24th to 26th Dec, 10am – 5.45pm (closes 10pm Weds)

The V&A's new garden has been designed by Kim Wilkie. Within the 2800 square metres he has opted for a simple, elegant, flexible design, replacing the current row of trees by just two liquidambars to make the facade of the museum

Victoria and Albert Museum

more clearly visible. At the centre is an elliptical sunken stone area rather like a Roman bath, which can be flooded or drained at will. There are stone steps around the edge for people to sit on and water jets at the end. Specially designed planters containing lemon trees (replaced in winter by hollies) stand at the margins of grass; others around the perimeter hold colourful herbaceous perennials. A tranquil daytime garden can be transformed at the blink of an eye into a sparkling evening party space.

Entrance: free

Other information: Refreshments during summer only. Music, wine, food and lectures, etc. available on Fri evening openings (seasonal) – telephone (020) 7942 2000 for details

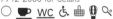

OTHER RECOMMENDED PUBLIC PARKS AND GARDENS

BARBICAN CONSERVATORY

The Barbican Centre, Silk Street, London EC2Y 8DS (020 7638 4141/8891; www.barbican.org.uk). Open all year, Sun and Bank Holiday Mons, 10am – 5.30pm

The conservatory houses a lush jungle of some 2000 species of temperate and semi-tropical plants, many of them recognisable as common house plants grown gigantic, and ponds swimming with large carp. Outside, there are trees and flowers, pools and fountains on every level of the walkways, and in summer most of the balconies on the lower rise buildings are a riot of colour, giving the lie to the idea of this listed 1960s development as a bleak and charmless place.

BONNINGTON SQUARE PLEASURE GARDEN

Off Langley Lane, Vauxhall, London SW8 1TE (www.bonningtonsquare.org.uk). Open all year, daily, dawn to dusk

A good example of a public space where residents working with the local authority have been able to put their stamp on the environment with lush planting. Containers of all shapes and sizes, window boxes and tiny spaces (once paving stones) now abound with trees and flowers. The small pleasure garden, with its large industrial water wheel, sub-tropical foliage

Bonnington Square Pleasure Garden

and secluded seating areas, was designed and is maintained by residents. Behind 37 Bonnington Square is the wonderful and secret *Harleyford Road Community Garden*, with a network of mosaic paths winding among trees and flowers.

CAMLEY STREET NATURAL PARK

12 Camley Street, London NW1 0PW
(020 7833 2311; www.wildlondon.org.uk). Open all year, Thurs – Sun, 10am – 5pm

A tranquil landscaped nature reserve filled with birds, insects and wildlife. Follow the winding path through 2 acres of meadow, ponds and woodland glade where more than 460 species of mainly native plants are kept in delicate balance.

CANNIZARO PARK

West Side Common, Wimbledon, London SW19 4UE
(020 8946 7349; www.merton.gov.uk). Open all year, daily, 8am – sunset (opens 9am Sat, Sun and Bank Holidays)

Year-round interest in this 39-acre park, planted with a wide variety of trees including cork oaks, mulberries, sassafras, mature beeches and red Japanese maples. The azalea dell is ablaze in late spring, while the pretty walled rose garden and sunken garden look their best in summer. (Listed Grade II*)

COLLEGE GARDEN

Westminster Abbey, London SW1P 3PA
(020) 7222 5152; www.westminster-abbey.org).
Open all year, Tues – Thurs, 10am – 6pm (closes 4pm Oct to March)

The one-acre garden, thought to be the oldest in England and under continuous cultivation for more than 900 years, was a busy place in the 15th century, with two ponds, fruit trees, a kitchen garden, meadow and an all-important herb garden where the monks tended their medicinal plants. Now it is mainly laid to lawn, with a few fruit trees and herbs around the edge as reminders of its roots, and some fine London planes and a fig tree planted in the 19th century.

FULHAM PALACE

Bishop's Avenue, London SW6 6EA (020 7736 3233).
Open all year, daily except 25th Dec and 1st Jan, 8am – dusk

A place of faded grandeur, steeped in history, with sweeping lawn and venerable trees, including a holm oak, estimated to be over 500 years old. The box-edged herb garden, dating from 1828, is enclosed by a pergola supporting a magnificent 100-year-old wisteria. (Listed Grade II*)

GOLDERS HILL PARK

North End Way, London NW11 7QP (020 8455 5183). Open all year, daily, 7.30am – dusk

The 36-acre park, with its mature trees, small zoo and water garden, is a pleasant place to wander, but the highlight is the walled garden behind the cafe. The walls are covered with climbers, and most of the space is taken up by an inspiring gravel garden where paths wind among Mediterranean shrubs and perennials. One edge is given over to seasonal bedding, designed with wit and often a startling combination of plants.

HORNIMAN MUSEUM AND GARDENS

100 London Road, Forest Hill, London SE23 3PQ
(020 8699 1872; www.horniman.ac.uk). Open all year, daily except 25th Dec, 7.15am – sunset (opens 8am Sun and Bank Holiday Mons)

16.5 acres of grounds with impressive planting, high standard of maintenance and stunning views across London. The sunken garden is planted in strong colours with an imaginative mix of tropical and traditional bedding schemes and the new African garden features planting from three different climate zones: temperate, tropical and desert.. There is also a nature trail along a stretch of disused railway line. (Listed Grade II)

LONDON WILDLIFE TRUST GARDEN

28 Marsden Road, Peckham, London SE15 4EE
(020 7252 9186; www.wildlondon.org.uk). Open all year, Tues – Sun, 10.30am – 4.30pm

This small haven is the place to head for if you are looking for ideas to make your personal space more attractive to local wildlife. Walk through Heather Burrell's intriguing metal gates down paths to small areas of enclosure where magnets for insects, butterflies and birds – evening primroses, buddleias, red valerian, hebes, globe thistles – simply romp away.

MILE END PARK

Mile End Road, London E3 (020 7364 5000). Open all year, daily

One of London's few new parks, extending for a mile southwards from Victoria Park alongside the Grand Union Canal, of interest for its contemporary approach to planting. Wildlife-friendly areas of trees and paths mown through long grass are combined with beds planted with swathes of lavenders, euphorbias, grasses and long-flowering perennials. Beyond the bridge a more formal terrace garden of shrubs and perennials descends to a water cascade and fountain.

MUSEUM OF GARDEN HISTORY

Lambeth Palace Road, London SE1 7LB (020) 7401 8865; www.museumgardenhistory.org.uk). Open all year, Tues – Sun, 10.30am – 5pm (closed 22nd Dec to 1st Jan)

The small garden, part of the old churchyard, houses the exotic tomb of the Tradescants, gardeners to Charles I and II. Combining historical authenticity and informality, it creates an impression of contained profusion. The centrepiece, designed by the Dowager Marchioness of Salisbury, is a knot garden filled with plants of the 17th century and surrounded by borders with clipped edging where standard topiary mixes with a choice selection of small trees, species roses, perennials, herbs and bulbs.

MYDDELTON HOUSE GARDENS

Bulls Cross, Enfield EN2 9HG (01992 717711; www.leevalleypark.org.uk). Open 23rd March to Sept, daily except Sat, 10am – 4.30pm (Suns and Bank Holiday Mons, 12 noon – 4pm); Oct to March, Mon – Fri, 10am – 3pm. Closed Christmas week

E.A. Bowles built up his diverse plant collection in this 4-acre garden, which includes an alpine meadow, a rock garden, a rose garden, a terraced lake and an award-winning collection of irises. Municipal planting around the house entrance soon gives way to a more informal Robinsonian style. (Listed Grade II)

THE NATURAL HISTORY MUSEUM WILDLIFE GARDEN

Cromwell Road, London SW7 5BD (0207 942 5011/942 5555 (school workshops); www.nhm.ac.uk). Open April to Oct, daily except in bad weather, 12 noon – 5pm

Brambles, nettles, wild garlic, bluebells, cowslips, marsh marigolds, newts, chalk blue butterflies and pipistrelle bats make up some of the 2000 or so species of plants and animals in this 1-acre network of British lowland habitats in a corner of the museum's grounds. Due to shading by the huge plane trees, the heathland plants are being overrun by ivy and ferns, but the other mini-habitats are thriving and include woodland, downland, meadow, reed-bed, hedgerow and pond. A retreat for the weary city visitor and a fascinating educational experience.

OSTERLEY PARK

Jersey Road, Isleworth TW7 4RB (020 8232 5050/01494 755566; www.nationaltrust.org.uk). Garden open 12th March to 2nd Nov, Wed – Sun and Bank Holiday Mons, 11am – 5pm. Park open all year, daily, 8am – 7.30pm (closes 6pm in winter). NT

Surrounding the neo-classical villa by Robert Adam, the 357 acres of grounds include a farm, ornamental lakes and classical buildings. A lengthy restoration programme has been initiated with the replanting of the flower beds around the garden house, using plants listed by Mrs Child in recently discovered documents; she it was who designed the formal flower gardens in the 18th century. (Listed Grade II*)

THE ROOF GARDENS

99 Kensington High Street, London W8 5SA (020 7937 7994; www.virgin.com/roofgardens). Telephone to check before visiting

A fantasy 1.5-acre garden 30 metres above the ground on the 6th floor of what was Derry and Toms 1938 department store, designed by Ralph Hancock to give three distinct illusions – a formal Spanish garden with a fountain, an English woodland garden and a Tudor courtyard. Over 500 varieties of trees and shrubs, including palms, figs and vines, survive up here, with ducks and flamingos swimming about in their high-rise ponds. (Listed Grade II*)

THE ROOKERY

Streatham Common South, London SW16. Open all year, daily except 25th Dec, 9am – dusk

Once part of a private garden, this green space includes an abundantly planted English garden with quiet seating areas, a rock garden and stream, a yew-hedged pond area, and a white

garden which is at its peak in midsummer.
(Listed Grade II)

ROOTS AND SHOOTS

Walnut Tree Walk, London SE11 6DN (020 7587
1131; www.rootsandshoots.org.uk). Open all year, Mon
– Fri (but closed Bank Holiday Mons), 9am – 4pm.
Telephone or consult website for other openings and
fairs

Lambeth's hidden green lung – a 0.75 acre
wildlife garden built on the rubble of a
demolition site, with a wildflower meadow,
ponds, beehives, arbours, and winding stony
paths through relaxed flowerbeds. Visit in
summer or during National Apple Week in
October, when you can buy the centre's single-
variety apple juice, pressed on site; there is also
a small plant sales area.

ROYAL HOSPITAL

Chelsea (Ranelagh Gardens), Royal Hospital Road,
London SW3 4SR (020 7881 5200;
www.chelseapensioners. org.uk). Open Jan to late
April, mid-June to Dec, 10am – sunset (opens 2pm
Sun). Closed 25th and 26th Dec, 1st Jan

The elegant and attractive gardens, 66 acres in
all, are sited to one side of the Royal Hospital,
with over a mile of wide walkways through
park-like grass and handsome tree and shrub
plantings. Formerly the pleasure grounds of
Ranelagh, they were redesigned by Gibson in
the 19th century, turned into allotments for
pensioners between the two world wars, and
later reconstructed according to Gibson's plan.
(Listed Grade II)

THE WATER GARDENS

Sussex Gardens, London W2. Edgware Road tube.
Open all year, daily, during daylight hours

The residents of the blocks of flats off the
major artery that is the Edgware Road look
down over a network of bridges, walkways and
grilles straight off a set of *West Side Story* to a
series of gardens where water in all its moods
is the pervasive theme. Visitors can walk among
pools and fountains surrounded by aquatic or
architectural plantings, a profusion of grasses,
weeping willows and other mature trees – the
overall effect is tranquil, lush and Japanese.

PRIVATE GARDENS

Lady Barbirolli

London NW3 5DH.

Tel: (020) 7586 2464

Open for NGS, and by appt.

Entrance £2.50, children free

15A BUCKLAND CRESCENT ★

The strong sense of space and line that musicians often
possess is expressed in this dignified 0.35-acre town garden,
designed by the present owner, in which the ground plan
combines flowing lines and ingenious geometry. A small knot
garden has a sundial mounted on a carved stone slab at its
centre. Planting is everywhere discriminating, ranging from a
functional but decorative vegetable patch to well-stocked
borders, bamboo groves and arches festooned with clematis.
A generous terrace is enhanced by boldly planted containers.

Crawford and Rosemary Lindsay

Herne Hill, London SE24 9HJ.

Tel: (020) 7274 5610

Close to Half Moon Lane. Nearest
station: Herne Hill

Open for NGS, and by appt

Entrance: £2.50

5 BURBAGE ROAD

An attractive garden (50m x 15m) in a tranquil and sheltered
setting, with well-kept lawns, a quietly splashing fountain and
herb beds. There is year-round interest and a continual
introduction of unusual plants; borders are filled with choice
arrangements of herbaceous perennials and shrubs, and good
use is made of a variety of pots holding climbers, ferns and
tender plants. Newly planted gravel areas are stocked with
species that are drought-tolerant.

66A EAST DULWICH ROAD

The 30-metre-long garden, which won ITV's 'Britain's Best Back Garden' in 2004, is distinguished by lush planting, ponds, a willow tree and climbing plants. The owner is an artist and a garden designer, and his unique method of festooning maypoles with climbers and his use of head-height seating areas and plant-filled antique hip baths defy all the rules. A viewing platform made from decking, a seating area and a plunge pool beside the owner's studio entice you to the end of the plot where another Robinson Crusoe-esque verandah, sundeck and summerhouse are concealed.

Kevin Wilson

East Dulwich, London SE22 9AT.
Tel: (020) 8693 3458

Behind Goose Green, opposite Dulwich swimming baths. Underground station East Dulwich (20 mins); Buses 37, 175, 176

Open for NGS, and by appt for parties of 10 or more

Entrance: £2.50, children £1 (evening opening £3.50 including glass of wine)

ELM TREE COTTAGE

If you need inspiration or persuasion to plant a Mediterranean garden, visit this well-designed garden with its wide variety of grasses and strong agaves in pots anchored in a surface of interesting pebbles and stones. The royal purple Lutyens-style seats and garden shed are vibrant statements, supported by golden daylilies, *Muehlenbeckia complexa*, varieties of blue clematis, alliums of all sizes and a pond edged with white lavender. There is a small grove of olive trees, figs and pots of ornamental vines, while the clipped yews and box balls and glowing copper beech hedge stand the test of winter time.

Michael Wilkinson and Wendy Witherick

85 Croham Road, South Croydon CR2 7HJ. Tel: (020) 8681 8622

2m S of Croydon. Take B275 from Croydon or A2022 from Selsdon. Bus 64; nearest mainline station South Croydon

Open for NGS, and by appt for parties at other times

Entrance: £2.50

NEW ● WC

70 GLOUCESTER CRESCENT

This jewel of a garden, just 350 metres square, is wrapped in a wedge shape around three sides of an elegant 1840s end-of-terrace house, once the home of Mrs Charles Dickens. It is the creation of Lucy Gent, erstwhile garden designer and writer, and Malcolm Turner. The strong geometry takes you through the awkwardly shaped plot, creating vistas and surprises within the secluded space. The planting is luscious, clearly that of a plantswoman. Skilful pruning restrains mature small trees and large shrubs – among them an Indian bean tree, a sophora, a cercidiphyllum, a ceanothus and a myrtle – leaving space for layers of smaller shrubs and perennials. A *Magnolia grandiflora* stands against the house wall, and the high garden walls are covered with climbers including clematis, decorative vines and roses. Interest continues throughout the year in both shady and sunny areas, with a climax of colour in late summer. The sheltered aspect nurtures tender shrubs such as a pomegranate, and the central paving is provided with a changing display in pots, including tender salvias, francoas and eucomis.

Lucy Gent and Malcolm Turner

London NW1 7EG.
Tel: (020) 7485 6906

Near junction of Gloucester Crescent and Oval Road 350 yards SW of Camden Town underground station

Open by appt

Entrance: £2

116 HAMILTON TERRACE

Spot the house duck on the small front-garden pool in this prize-winning garden. The considerable visual appeal of the neighbouring church and surrounding trees gives a peaceful quality to the large and interesting back garden. Prize hostas flourish at different levels and the walls are covered with a

Mr and Mrs I. B. Kathuria

116 Hamilton Terrace, St John's Wood, London NW8 9UT.
Tel: (020) 7625 6909

116 Hamilton Terrace

Nearest underground station Maida Vale (5 mins), St John's Wood (10 mins). Buses 16, 98 from Marble Arch to Cricklewood.

Open for NGS, and by appt

Entrance: £2.50

◐ 🍵 WC

variety of clematis, roses and other climbers. Exuberance is balanced by restraint in many effective planting combinations, as the changes are rung in open areas, damp and shady sites, and containers which provide glorious mid- and late-summer colour from fuchsias, daturas and cannas.

239A HOOK ROAD

This established suburban garden of 45m x 14m reflects the artistic skill of the garden-photographer owner and his wife. An attractive patio leads out onto a gravel garden and dining area planted with grasses and drought-tolerant plants. Around the circular lawn are standard hollies, and box balls act as edging to the wide and effective borders. A circular pond and an L-shaped rose tunnel lead into the potager, where vegetables scramble up handsome willow supports and fruit trees are underplanted with herbs, vegetables and low hedges. Look out for the picturesque garden shed with its cobwebby windows, which has appeared in many magazines and books.

Derek and Dawn St Romaine

Chessington, Kingston-upon-Thames, Surrey KT9 1EQ. Tel: (020) 8397 3761; www.gardenphotolibrary.com

On Hook road (A243) close to Hook underpass and A3. Opposite recreation ground (parking available)

Open for NGS, and by appt

Entrance: £2.50, children £1, evening opening £3.50 (2007 prices)

◐ ♿ B&B

38 KILLIESER AVENUE

This much-visited South London garden, 34m x 10m, is full of carefully chosen plants and shrubs evoking a romantic atmosphere. From a York-stone terrace, adorned with huge pots of agapanthus, the garden divides into three distinct areas: a grassed part, a gravel garden planted with small grasses and black-leaved species, and a final raised level reached via a rose-clad arch, where a parterre filled with white roses and a wall fountain create an element of formality. An obelisk, a Gothick arbour and a water cascade provide additional architectural interest.

Mrs Winkle Haworth

Streatham Hill, London SW2 4NT. Tel: (020) 8671 4196

Off Streatham Hill, near Streatham Hill station. From Sternhold Avenue take second turning right

Open for NGS, and by appt for parties of 5 or more

Entrance: £3.50

◐ 🍵 B&B

LITTLE HOUSE A

These front and back gardens are superb modern interpretations of Arts and Crafts design and plantsmanship. Created in 2002 to respond to the 1920s house built by Danish artist Arild Rosenkrantz, both gardens are made with the kind of symmetry and attention to detail that Edwin Lutyens bestowed on Hestercombe (see entry in Somerset). The elegant front garden is centred on an octagonal bed set in stone paving punctuated by squares of brick and sinuous roof tiles laid on their sides that echo motifs on the house

Linda and Stephen Williams

16a Maresfield Gardens, Hampstead, London NW3 5SU

Off Fitzjohn's Avenue, near Freud Museum. Nearest underground Swiss Cottage or Finchley Road (5 mins)

Open for NGS, plus 9th and 10th June, all 2 – 6pm

Entrance: £2.50

◐

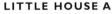

itself. There is a similar attention to detail in the back garden, where beautiful curving steps flanked by pots lead from a flagstone terrace to a lawn at a higher level. Here, a dark yew hedge set with niches for sculptural pots makes a dramatic backdrop to the garden's crowning glory – a stainless steel water feature that feeds a narrow stone rill running across the garden. In the centre it widens into a rectangular basin and then flows into a little stream that disappears beneath a *Dicksonia fibrosa* before trickling through colourful damp plantings down one side of the garden; on the other side a pergola is smothered with glorious roses, wisteria, clematis and vines. A garden fascinating for plant lovers and of immense interest to architects.

PEMBRIDGE COTTAGE

This small and carefully maintained artist's garden, interesting at all seasons, has been an excellent example of a green garden without the ubiquitous lawn. The narrow plot is designed by an artist and photographer with recessed areas framed by structural herbs, elaeagnus, fig, olive, pittosporum, viburnum, box and photinia. Gravel paths are outlined by groups of river stones. Bamboos, ferns and grasses have stylishly planted terracotta pots placed among them, while Italian cypresses add height. The journey ends at the artist's studio – ask to see the scrapbook showing the garden's creation and development.

Ian and Lydia Sidaway

10 Strawberry Hill Road, Twickenham TW1 4PT. Tel: (020) 8287 8993

1m from Twickenham town centre, approached from Cross Deep or Waldegrave Road. Strawberry Hill station. Buses 33, 110, 267, 281, 290, 490, R68, R70

Open for NGS, and by appt

Entrance: £2

 WC

PETERSHAM HOUSE

The best way to approach this stylish two-acre garden is to walk along the river from Richmond Bridge, past the tranquil water meadows of Petersham. The wide lush lawns that lead out from the house give time for the eye to take in the many features, including the exemplary borders designed by Mary Keen, and the glorious semi-rural setting. An Anthony Gormley statue stands proudly under an old yew tree with young clipped yews arranged sentinel-fashion in the lawn. The massed double borders, running down from the lawns,

Francesco and Gael Baglione

Church Lane, Petersham Road, Petersham, Surrey TW10 7AG. Tel: (020) 8940 5230; www.petershamnurseries.com

Entrance in Church Lane, off Petersham Road. Nearest station Richmond. Bus 65. Or take Hammerton Ferry from Marble Hill Park to Ham House

Petersham House

Open for NGS

Entrance: £3

provide colour, texture and creativity. There is a well-designed vegetable and small cutting garden with a stylish abode alongside for bantams. Allow time to visit the nursery with its well-maintained plants, restored propagation house filled with conservatory plants and original pieces of garden furniture and equipment, and cafe serving delicious lunches (booking advised).

Karen Grosch

London SW19 8HR.
Tel: (020) 8893 3660;
www.whettonandgrosch.co.uk

Off Dunsford Road. Nearest underground Wimbledon Park (10-min. walk) Bus 156.

Open for NGS, and by appt in June

Entrance: £2

101 PITT CRESCENT

The owner of this 30m × 7.5m garden is a set designer who has created a theatrical solution to the problem of a plot that slopes upwards away from the house. A series of terraces of different sizes makes the journey from an intimate cobbled patio to the wooden dacha. Along the way a rose- and clematis-covered pergola with a seating area looks onto a raised wooden-edged vegetable and herb garden containing fruit trees and a glasshouse. Ornamental trees make focal points for several varied and highly textured beds, while tall tapering planters, designed by the owner, give elements of height in shady areas.

Mr and Mrs A. Pizzoferro

West Dulwich, London SE21 8LW.
Tel: (020) 8766 7846

Off South Circular Road at junction of Rosendale and Lovelace Roads. Nearest train stations Tulse Hill or West Dulwich

Open for NGS, and by appt

Entrance: £2

167 ROSENDALE ROAD

The warm colour theme of the front garden gives no hint of the charm to be found in the small woodland area, the natural winter stream and wildlife pond behind the house. This is a place to visit for ideas: bamboo canes topped with holed flints; massed perennials and winding bark paths, one of which leads to an old wooden ladder leaning against a fruit tree. Grasses massed in pots, houseleeks at home in bricks, hostas planted at eye level for inspection, agapanthus and bulbs in pots are just a few of the visual delights.

Mr and Mrs Christopher Whittington

33 Kingsley Place, Highgate, London N6 5EA. Tel: (020) 8348 2785

Off Southwood Lane, Highgate

Open for NGS, and April to July by appt

Entrance: £2.50, children free

Other information: Plants for sale on NGS Sun only

SOUTHWOOD LODGE

An imaginatively designed garden created in 1963 from a much larger, older one. Set at the highest part of London with magnificent views to the east, the sloping 0.35-acre site offers much variety of mood and planting. By the house, dense planting and container displays surround a paved area enclosed on two sides by tall hedges. Through an arch in the beech hedge, steps lead down to a grassy walk edged with mixed borders. A wooded area in the lowest part of the garden is planted with many shade-lovers and here, in late June, a far-reaching 'Kiftsgate' rose scents the air.

Mr and Mrs R. Raworth

St Margaret's, Twickenham TW1 1QS.
Tel: (020) 8892 3713;
www.raworthgarden.com

Off A316 between Twickenham Bridge and St Margaret's roundabout

7 ST GEORGE'S ROAD ★

If you are a new owner of a London garden or seek inspiration to revamp your own garden, make an appointment to visit this stimulating place, where a wide variety of planting ideas is firmly held together by formal clipped hedges. Among the striking features is a large north-facing conservatory, a rose- and clematis-covered pergola and wide borders that

7 St George's Road

give shape and colour for nine months of the year. You enter through a sunken Mediterranean garden and an area filled with interesting containerised plants. A tiered variegated cornus leads the eye to the bog garden with its decked walkway, on the far side of the lawn, and then to the newest part of the garden, a charming knot garden designed by the artist daughter of the house. 0.5 acre.

Open for NGS, and for parties of 10 or more by appt

Entrance: £3, children 50p

Other information: Home-made teas and plants for sale on open days only

 WC ♿ 🌿

SYON PARK

(Historic Park Grade I)

This historic park, like its northern counterpart Alnwick, was shaped by 'Capability' Brown and still offers visitors to this suburban part of London views of watermeadows and hayfields, complete with grazing cattle. The entrance to the 40-acre garden to the rear of the neo-classical villa opens onto the magnificent Great Conservatory with its curved wings, designed by Charles Fowler in the 1820s. Beyond is one of Brown's two lakes, fed by the Thames; a lakeside path

The Duke of Northumberland

Brentford TW8 8JF.
Tel: (020) 8560 0882;
www.syonpark.co.uk

2m W of Kew Bridge, marked from A315/310 at Bush Corner

House open – telephone for dates, times and entrance charges

Syon Park

Garden open all year, daily except 25th and 26th Dec, 10am – 5.30pm (or dusk if earlier)

Entrance: £4, concessions and children £2.50, family £9 (house and garden £8, concessions £7, children £4, family £18)

winds through a collection of specimen trees, including a champion koelreuteria. Much of the garden was given over to the Festival of Gardens in the 1960s, which resulted in the view back to the conservatory being spoiled by garden buildings and a line of *leylandii*. Plans are in place to restore this view and extend the lake. For the past few years, midsummer visitors who arrive by car have been rewarded by the delightful spectacle of a band of vibrant cornfield flowers stretching the length of the drive. This helps to draw the eye away from the extensive car park and commercial outlets on the site of the former riding stables, just beyond the house.

Paul Minter and Michael Weldon

London E10 5LL.
Tel: (020) 8558 5895

Off Oliver Road, near Leyton Orient football ground. Nearest underground Leyton (10-min. walk). Buses 69, 58, 158

Open for NGS, and by appt

Entrance: £3

● ☕ WC

64 THORNHILL ROAD

In the unusually elongated garden stretching behind the 1888 house, the owners have gone for geometry and drama. The space is divided into four distinct areas, linked by a central brick path and focusing on a weeping lime which casts its huge shadow at the far end; a handsome wooden gate into this last enclosure is cleverly positioned to give the impression that infinite woodland stretches beyond. Plants are skilfully combined throughout, with a quincunx of birches, fruit trees, a metasequoia and 'Paul's Himalayan Musk' and 'Rambling Rector' roses adding exuberant height. Near the house a Gorgon fountain is surrounded by succulents, and mature box spirals stand alongside blue-and-gold Korean incense burners. An intriguing and enjoyable piece of theatre.

Sue Roscoe Watts

London SW18 1RB.
Tel: (020) 8874 2590

On A3 close to Wandsworth High Street Nearest underground station Putney East. Buses 37, 337 to West Hill Library

Open 21st and 22nd May, 9th and 10th July, 11am – 4pm, and by appt at other times

Entrance: £2 (for charity)

NEW ◑

29 WEST HILL

This 100ft × 35ft walled garden, at the back of the handsome Georgian house fronting a busy main road, is a leafy box of delights that exudes the owner's artisitic flair and originality. Divided into a series of small areas by ivy-clad brick walls and clipped hedges, it opens onto a lawned stage framed by borders raked with bold planting from clipped pittosporum, box, yew, and clumps of acanthus, *Melianthus major* and *Echium pininana*. The backdrop is an ivy-clad wall, topped by huge clay pots, with an off-centre painted filigree door – a wardrobe door from Rajasthan – that leads into the second half of the garden screened by giant sycamores. Here gravelled paths wind through a small herb parterre and past seating areas under birches and eucalyptus, returning along a charming painted garden room shaded by roses, clematis and a vine. Adding impact throughout the year are containers planted with twigs, stems and colourful foliage, like so many giant outdoor flower arrangements.

Nigel and Linda Fisher

London SE23 3ED.
Tel: 07789 865156;
www.woodvalegarden.blogspot.com

82 WOOD VALE ★

The sizeable back garden sloping gently uphill to the disused Crystal Palace railway line is confirmation (if any were needed) that Christopher Bradley-Hole's medal-winning

82 Wood Vale

show plots at Chelsea translate triumphantly into a real garden setting. Design as a relaxed space for the Fisher family, it is given structure by a matrix of hornbeam hedges. Now running with the grain of the garden, now at right angles to it, they rein in but do not fully enclose a jigsaw of perennial and grass bays. These low barriers almost give the impression that they could be moved around at will to change the flow and articulation of the garden. A canal is set in paving at the base of the slope; halfway up is a decking area, while the lawn at the top, a play area for the children, is planted simply with amelanchiers. A clever, intricate design. It is the army of perennials and grasses, however, that pack the real punch. *Calamagrostis* × *acutiflora* 'Karl Foerster', *Achillea* 'Feuerland', *Euphorbia amygdaloides* var. *robbiae* and *Verbena bonariensis* are just some of the stalwarts in the simple, restrained palette of oranges, browns, clarets and purples.

Near Dulwich Park, off South Circular where it joins Lordship Lane, but before Horniman Museum. House is between Langton Rise and Melford Avenue.

Nearest station Forest Hill. Bus 63 passes house, or 176,185, 312 nearby

Open for NGS, and for parties of 10 or more June and July, Sat and Sun by appt

Entrance: £2.50

OTHER RECOMMENDED PRIVATE GARDENS

BUCKINGHAM PALACE

Westminster, London SW1A 1AA (020 7766 7300; www.royalcollection.org.uk). Open Aug and Sept (but opening and closing dates may vary), daily, 9.45am – 6pm (last admission 3.45) by timed ticket

The 39-acre garden, enclosed by high walls, is part parade ground, part wildlife habitat. It may be glimpsed from a 450-metre guided route along the naturalistic lake, which is host to more than 30 types of bird. Many of the fine trees were established by William Aiton, head of Kew, in the 19th century, and succeeding generations of the Royal Family have been planting new ones in acts of commemoration. (Listed Grade II*)

156 DALLING ROAD

Kim Whatmore, Hammersmith, London W6 0EU (020 8741 2994). Open by appt

In this tranquil 4m × 10m garden every inch of space is made to count. Key plants – large tree ferns, camellias and box – are repeated throughout to give cohesion. Trellises covered with honeysuckles make secret partitions, and Yorkstone paving liberally interspersed with pebbles and planting leads to an enchanting retreat.

62 RATTRAY ROAD

Elspeth Thompson, London SW2 1BD (020 7733 2752). Open by appt

Tiny front and back gardens of artistry and imagination at a writer's terraced house. A drought-tolerant display of silver-leaved and scented plants greets the visitor; behind is a secluded oasis dominated by bold, shade-tolerant evergreens, with *Clematis montana* and other climbers romping up the back wall. Decking and a metal grille on several levels, large zinc troughs and a reflecting mirror on the back wall are stylish personal touches.

MANCHESTER

For further information about how to use the *Guide*
and for an explanation of the symbols, see pages vi–viii.
Specific dates and times are those given to us by garden owners for 2008.
For 2009 dates, check with the individual properties.
For opening dates under the National Gardens Scheme,
readers should consult *The Yellow Book* or www.ngs.org.uk.
Maps are to be found at the end of the *Guide*.
We have included some gardens with Manchester postal addresses in Cheshire and
Lancashire for convenience, so it is also worthwhile consulting pages 32–43 and
pages 189–194.

DUNHAM MASSEY ★

(Historic Garden Grade II*)

The National Trust

Altrincham, Cheshire WA14 4SJ.
Tel: (0161) 941 1025;
www.nationaltrust.org.uk

3m SW of Altrincham off A56

House open as garden but
Sat – Wed only, 12 noon – 5pm

Garden open 8th March to 2nd Nov, daily,
11am – 5.30pm.
Park open all year, daily

Entrance: car park £4, garden £6
(house and garden £8.50)

Other information:
Manual wheelchairs and batricars available.
Dogs in park only, on lead

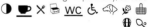

Between the conurbations of Liverpool and Manchester sits
the 3000-acre estate of Dunham Massey, where fallow deer
still roam freely in their 300-acre park. The house is an
eighteenth-century replacement of the Elizabethan mansion,
but the broad stretch of water curling around its north and
west sides is the original Elizabeth moat, while the semicircular
promontory jutting out into the moat was the site of an
Elizabethan mount and possibly even of the Norman motte
which preceded it. The other miraculous survivals are the five
avenues, which predate the English Landscape School of the
eighteenth century. Enough of the formal, seventeenth-
century Baroque lay-out of the park to the west and the
south remained for the Trust to replant the long avenues
radiating out from a *patte d'oie* in front of a triple row of lime
trees each side of the southern forecourt. The 29 acres of
gardens seem to improve every year, with some excellent
new planting. Close to the entrance, bordering a small stream,
are huge drifts of moisture-loving perennials, including hostas,
rodgersias and a striking clump of *Rheum palmatum rubrum*.
Further along, beside a rustic bridge, are *Meconopsis* ×
sheldonii, damp-loving ferns and a collection of acers. Fine
specimen trees, including a *Quercus suber*, are to be found on
the expansive lawn, which is overlooked by an eighteenth-
century orangery containing abutilons and surrounded by
banks of shrubs. In the Garden Wood is a large collection of
azaleas and hydrangeas. Don't miss the formal courtyard
garden at the centre of the house. A winter garden walk will
open in autumn 2008.

FLETCHER MOSS BOTANICAL GARDENS ★

Here, close to a busy part of south Manchester, is a tranquil green oasis of 21 acres, with a large range of plants, an historic rockery, and a water garden. What's more, it's free. It was in 1889 that Robert and Emily Williamson began to create this garden, focusing on its most important feature, the large rockery (in effect a mountainside in miniature) on which to grow their collection of alpines. It is still impressive. Large stones embedded in the steep south-facing slope form a series of terraces with pockets of soil for the plants and paths for the visitor, and in them are massed alpines, bulbs and small shrubs, plus many conifers and the odd well-placed small tree. Japanese maples cast their light shade in places; there is a large tulip tree, and sheltered at one end of the garden a collection of Chusan palms. A small stream cascades down the rocky terraces to the rich foliage of the water garden. A restful walled terrace gives views across the garden to the meadows and trees of the Mersey Valley. Emily Wiliamson had another interest beside plants: she founded the RSPB here in 1889. Close by are the public *Parsonage Gardens,* entered through an old stone arch in Didsbury's busy High Street. Rhododendrons, camellias, magnolias, hellebores and ferns flourish beneath the canopy of trees, and a deep L-shaped herbaceous border is backed by a wisteria-covered wall.

Manchester City Council Leisure Department

Mill Gate Lane, Didsbury M20 2SW. Tel: (0161) 445 4241

5m S of city centre on Mill Gate Lane, S of A5145, close to centre of Didsbury

Open all year, daily, 9am – dusk

Entrance: free

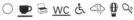

LYME PARK ★

(Historic Garden Grade II*)

The Palladian-style mansion is set in spectacular parkland in the foothills of the Pennines with panoramic views of the Cheshire Plains. The 17-acre gardens are of great historic importance, retaining many original features from Tudor and Jacobean times. It is regarded as one of the foremost National Trust gardens for its high-Victorian-style bedding in

The National Trust

Disley, Stockport, Cheshire SK12 2NX. Tel: (01663) 762023/766492; www.nationaltrust.org.uk

6m SE of Stockport just W of Disley on A6

House open

Lyme Park

237

Garden open 1st to 9th March, Sat and Sun; 15th March to 2nd Nov, daily; all 11am – 5pm; 8th Nov to 21st Dec, Sat and Sun, 12 noon – 3pm. Guided tours by arrangement

Entrance: garden £4.80, children £2.40; park: pedestrians free, car and occupants £4.60 (house and garden £7.60, children £3.80, family £19)

magnificent formal beds, using many rare and old-fashioned plants such as *Penstemon* 'Rubicundus' (bred at Lyme in 1906). Important features include Lewis Wyatt's orangery of 1814, which contains two venerable 150-year-old camellias; a spectacular Dutch garden with a rare example of a *parterre de broderie* using Irish ivy; a fine Jekyll-style herbaceous border designed by Graham Stuart Thomas; a wooded ravine garden with a stream and fine collections of rhododendrons, azaleas, ferns and other shade-loving plants; a collection of rare trees and plants associated with the eminent plantsman, the Hon. Vicary Gibbs; a large lake; a 300-year-old lime avenue; extensive lawns and an Edwardian rose garden. A garden designed by Lewis Wyatt in 1817 has been re-created and the Sundial Terrace restored.

Gordon Cooke
Sale M33 3AX.
Tel: (0161) 969 9816;
www.gordoncooke.co.uk

SW of city centre off M60 junction 6. From A6144 at Brooklands Station turn into Hope Road; Poplar Grove is 3rd turning on right

Open June by appt

Entrance: £3, children free

Other information: Exhibition late June – consult website for details

17 POPLAR GROVE ★

That the owner is a landscape gardener and potter is soon evident, for in a small space and suburban setting he has created a most distinctive garden. A masterstroke was to set the paths at diagonals to the main axis and this, together with the changes in level and varied use of building materials, creates interest throughout. Many of the plants are chosen for their foliage shape and colour: phormiums, thistles, alliums,

17 Poplar Grove

euphorbias, cordylines, grasses and ferns all contribute to the variety. A 'living roof ' has been added to a porch, and an unusual grotto sunk into the ground with plants growing over the top, overlooking a long rectangular pool surrounded by pieces of modern sculpture. Other water features and fine ceramics are spread around the garden, and within a new exhibition space.

RIVINGTON TERRACED GARDENS
(Historic Garden Grade II)

These are not gardens as such but the remains of gardens built by Lord Leverhulme and designed by Thomas Mawson in the early part of the twentieth century. Set mainly in woodland on a steep west-facing hillside, they have fine views across Rivington reservoirs. Particularly impressive is a rocky ravine, the remains of a Japanese garden and the restored pigeon tower. The number and variety of mature trees indicate that this must once have been a very grand estate. Take care on the steep, sometimes slippery paths. 45 acres.

United Utilities

Rivington Lane, Horwich, Bolton, Lancashire BL6 7SB. Tel: (01204) 691549; www.unitedutilities.com

Im NW of Horwich. Follow signs to Rivington from A673 in Horwich or Grimeford. Gardens are 10-min. walk from Rivington Hall and Hall Barn

Open all year, daily, during daylight hours

Entrance: free

OTHER RECOMMENDED GARDENS

HAIGH HALL GARDENS

Haigh Country Park, Haigh, Wigan WN2 IPE (01942 832895). Open all year, daily, during daylight hours

The house stands in mature parkland, with an array of formal gardens and three walled gardens a short span away. Another area is left wild, and an arboretum featuring acers set in woodland is developing well. 250 acres.

HEATON PARK

Manchester M25 2SW (0161 773 1085; www.heatonpark.org.uk). Open all year, daily, during daylight hours

The planting in the pleasure grounds here is appropriate to the magnificent house designed by James Wyatt in 1722. The 650-acre park, landscaped between 1770 and 1830, contains many neo-classical garden buildings which, together with the historic core of the park, have been restored with lottery funding. (Listed Grade II)

WOODSIDE

Princes Park, Shevington, Wigan WN6 8HY (01257) 255255; www.woodsidegarden.net. Open by appt

This exceptionally well-kept 0.6-acre garden is on an attractively undulating site surrounded by mature trees. It is landscaped around beds and borders filled with an enviable number of mainly acid-loving plants, together with gravel beds and water features.

WYTHENSHAWE HORTICULTURAL CENTRE

Wythenshawe Park, Wythenshawe Road M23 0AB (0161 998 2117). Open all year, daily except 25th Dec, 10am – 4pm

Within the Grade-II-listed park is a series of diverse demonstration gardens. Moisture-lovers grown along a chain of pools, collections of greenhouse plants, a well-labelled herbaceous border, a heather garden and a rockery are just a few of those on offer within the 5 acres.

NORFOLK

For further information about how to use the *Guide*
and for an explanation of the symbols, see pages vi–viii.
Specific dates and times are those given to us by garden owners for 2008.
For 2009 dates, check with the individual properties.
For opening dates under the National Gardens Scheme,
readers should consult *The Yellow Book* or www.ngs.org.uk.
Maps are to be found at the end of the *Guide*.

BESTHORPE HALL ★

Mr J. A. Alston

Besthorpe, Attleborough N17 2LJ.
Tel: (01953) 450300

14m SW of Norwich, 1m E of
Attleborough on Bunwell Road.

Open by appt only

Entrance on right, past church

● WC ♿

The present owner inherited these expansive formal gardens with their raised, box-edged pools and fountains from his grandparents, and clearly also inherited their plantsmanship. Since 1978, he has redesigned the space to enable the five acres to be run by a smaller number of gardeners – hence wall-to-wall cut flowers and vegetables in the kitchen garden have been replaced with equally colourful but less demanding herbaceous borders and a nuttery. The enclosures and much of the brickwork are Tudor in date and include a former tilt yard, now laid out with rows of yew topiary; what appears to be a ha-ha was in fact the ditch to keep ordinary spectators away from the jousters. Climbers are a special passion, and from late spring the walls are clothed with magnificent wisterias and every type of rose and clematis. A new collection of magnolias has joined the mature ones planted 30 years ago, and in May and June a fascinating collection of bearded irises saved from the garden of the artist Cedric Morris at Benton End is in full flower. Although most groups visit in spring and summer, the seasons is prolonged by buddlejas, a collection of colchicums from Felbrigg Hall and trees planted for their interesting winter bark.

BLICKLING HALL ★
(Historic Garden Grade II*)

The National Trust

Aylsham, Norwich NR11 6NF.
Tel: (01263) 738030;
www.nationaltrust.org.uk

15m N of Norwich, 1.5m NW of
Aylsham on N side of B1354

House open

Garden open all year: 15th March to
2nd Nov, Wed – Sun and Bank Holiday
Mons, plus Mons in Aug, 10.15am –
5.15pm; Nov to March, Thurs – Sun,
11am – 4pm

Although the gardens appear to be the perfect setting for the handsome Jacobean house, they represent a panorama of garden history from the seventeenth to the twentieth centuries. The massive yew hedges flanking the entrance to the gardens date from the earliest period. To the east is the parterre with a central pool, where four large corner beds planted by Norah Lindsay in the 1930s are surrounded by borders of roses edged with nepeta. Flights of steps mount to the highest terrace, from which a vista cut through blocks of woodland leads to the 1730 Doric temple raised above parkland beyond. The two blocks are intersected by *allées* replanted in the seventeenth-century style with Turkey oak, lime and beech. To the south, the 1782 orangery houses half-hardy plants and a 1640s statue of Hercules by Nicholas Stone. On the corner of the northern block is the Secret Garden, originally eighteenth-century, which now consists of a lawn with a central sundial surrounded by high beech hedges. The shrub border through which it is approached is by Norah Lindsay, who was also responsible for the dry moat surrounding the house. North of the parterre is a raised grassy area, possibly a remnant of the Jacobean mount; here grows an enormous, sprawling Oriental plane. Landscaped parkland to the north-west descends to the curving lake, formed before 1729 and later extended. West of the house stands a cedar of Lebanon and a collection of magnolias. In the park too is the 1773 Gothic tower and Bonomi's 1796 pyramidal mausoleum. The Trust has now restored the park to its 1840 extent and replanted the Great Wood. Truly a garden which is a palimpsest of gardening history, but also one filled with colour and interest right through from the spring flowering of over 100,000 narcissi to the spectacular display of autumn leaves. 55 acres in all.

Entrance: £6, children £3, family £16 (house and garden £9.10, children £4.50, family £24)

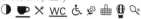

BRADENHAM HALL ★

The birthplace of the boys'-own adventure novelist Rider Haggard, the imposing eighteenth-century house surrounded by extensive and finely kept lawns has been the home of the Allhusen family since 1951. The gardens are probably best known for the arboretum – a collection of some 800 varieties of trees and shrubs started by the current owner's late father – and for its extensive narcissus collection. It is, however, the walled gardens and barns that give the garden its character, around which a series of clearly defined 'rooms' has been divided by yew hedges to defeat the windy site. In spring, the pleached lime walk looks particularly fine; later bearded irises flower against the courtyard walls and the kitchen garden with its quirky 'dog's breakfast' borders (a bit of everything, according to Mrs Allhusen Sr) flushes with colour. The small rose garden is a delight, with not an inch of bare space and masses of old-fashioned varieties packed in. Although lacking the history of some longer established gardens, the appealing atmosphere in the 23 acres here is of intimate spaces, well-cared-for and well-labelled plants and a sense of fun and experimentation.

Mr and Mrs Christian Allhusen

Bradenham, Thetford IP25 7QP.
Tel: (01362) 687243/687279;
www.bradenhamhall.co.uk

8m E of Swaffham, 5m W of East Dereham S off A47

Open April to Sept, 2nd and 4th Suns in month, 2 – 5.30pm, and for NGS. Coach parties on open days or at other times by written appt

Entrance: £4, children (under 12) free

Other information: Plant sale 24th Aug

BRESSINGHAM GARDENS ★

The 16 acres of beautiful gardens are still being developed by the Bloom family with over 8000 species and varieties of plants on display in five gardens. Alan Bloom created the six acre Dell Garden with its famous island beds set in park-like meadow between 1955 and 1962. Planted with perennials to give colour and interest from spring to autumn, the wide and varied collection includes many Bressingham-raised varieties.

Blooms Nurseries Ltd and Mr and Mrs Adrian Bloom

Bressingham, Diss IP22 2AB.
Tel: (01379) 686900;
www.bressinghamgardens.com

2.5m W of Diss on A1066

Open 20th March to 2nd Nov, daily, 10.30am – 5pm

Bressingham
Gardens

Winter Garden open all year, daily except 25th, 26th Dec and 1st Jan, 11am – 4pm

Entrance (inc. entry to Bressingham Steam Experience): £7, OAPs £6, children £4 (£3.50 out-of-season charge for Winter Garden only)

Other information: Special guided tours available outside normal open season

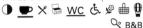 B&B

The Summer Garden at the entrance includes a National Collection of miscanthus. Foggy Bottom, designed and created by Adrian Bloom since 1966, sparkles with colour, not only from the excellent collection of blue and gold conifers, shrubs and ornamental trees, but also from seasonal plantings of perennials, grasses and bulbs. The 'River of Blood', a snaking broad drift of massed planting of the Japanese blood grass *Imperata cylindrica* 'Rubra', is a stunning sight from midsummer onwards. Linking the Dell Garden and Foggy Bottom, a pathway goes through the Fragrant Garden and Adrian's Wood, now being developed and planted with a collection of North American native plants. A winter garden opened in 2006. The famous nursery specialises in hardy perennials. Then visit the national Dad's Army Collection and the steam museum where engines and trains chug away and whistle – these nostalgic sounds do not detract from the overall peace.

CORPUSTY MILL GARDEN ★

Roger Last

Corpusty, Norwich NR11 6QB
Tel: (01263) 587223;
www.corpustymillgarden.co.uk

6m S of Holt. Turn off B1149 at Corpusty; mill is in centre of village

Open for parties by appt

Entrance: £6

Other information: Teas by arrangement

The 4.5-acre garden is as unexpected as it is intriguing, gradually revealing itself as a complex series of interlinked spaces. The planting is varied and lush with a rich collection of trees, shrubs, herbaceous and water-loving plants. Water is everywhere, in fountains, ponds, a stream, a small lake and a river. Buildings and follies are discovered as the garden unfolds: a long high flint wall inset with heads of Roman emperors, a Gothic arch with knapped flints, and a pitch-dark and mysterious four-chambered grotto built of moss-covered ginger sandstone. Elsewhere, a Gothick ruin with a spiral staircase, a flint humpback bridge and a classical pavilion in the highly formal kitchen garden, with ornamental compost containers. A separate area, rich in trees, has been developed

Corpusty Mill Garden

as a landscaped meadow. Here a small lake with a raised bank and walkway on one side is dominated by a gunnera and a tall, slender stainless steel cone and a water-filled cave reveals a figure drowning or rising up from the mud. To the north, the River Bure forms a tranquil natural boundary. By the house a contemporary formal garden, with a stainless steel water column and a central rill and pool, completes a highly eclectic but well-judged sequence of different styles and moods.

COURTYARD FARM ★

The primeval gardener was a stone-age farmer who enjoyed the wild flowers that spattered his little fields of ripening grain, and Courtyard Farm harks back to those prehistoric days of marigolds and corncockles. The best time to visit is in July. Take a circular walk through fields of ripening grain and acres of wild flowers – 150 plant species have been identified to date. This is not gardening on a small scale, but it is a most praiseworthy effort to retain our natural heritage of wild and cultivated plants. As the whole 800 acres are managed organically, wildlife abounds and hares and skylarks are spotted regularly. Most heartening.

Lord Melchett

Ringstead, Kings Lynn PE36 5LQ.

16m NE of King's Lynn, 3.5m E of Hunstanton, 2m E of Ringstead, on road crossing Ringstead Common to Chosely and Burnham Market

Open all year, daily, during daylight hours

Entrance: free

EAST RUSTON OLD VICARAGE ★★

The twin strengths of this much-publicised garden are the architectural framework of walls and hedges and an astonishing profusion of plants. Two Norfolk churches and a lighthouse play a fundamental role as focal points at the end of skilfully crafted vistas, and within the garden the value of theatre is not forgotten. Tall dark hedges with openings beckon the visitor on to yet more discoveries: a box parterre and sunken garden, superb herbaceous borders, a Mediterranean garden and, one of the most striking elements, a sizeable exotic garden. Rare plants are everywhere, set in gravel or in borders; because of the garden's coastal setting, many are semi-hardy and shrubs from the southern hemisphere are well represented. A three-acre woodland

Graham Robeson and Alan Gray

East Ruston, Norwich NR12 9HN.
Tel: (01692) 650432 (daytime);
www.eastrustonoldvicarage.co.uk

15m NE of Norwich, 4m E of North Walsham. Turn off A149 onto B1159 signed to Walcot and Bacton, then left at T junction. House is next to church after 2m

Open 21st March to 25th Oct, Wed, Fri – Sun and Bank Holiday Mons, 2 – 5.30pm, and by appt for coach parties

Entrance: £5, children £1, season ticket £15

East Ruston Old Vicarage

garden has been planted to give colour and interest from snowdrops and aconites in spring and a brilliant show of hydrngeas in summer through to trees and shrubs chosen for their autumn foliage. On the perimeter, a cornfield achieves an astonishing density and brilliance of summer colour, and a Desert Wash has mature palms, agaves, dasylirions, colourful lampranthus, delospermas, cacti and self-sown annuals, all left out for winter. In all, 32 vibrant acres.

THE EXOTIC GARDEN

Will Giles

6 Cotman Road, Thorpe, Norwich NR1 4AF. Tel: (01603) 623167; www.exoticgarden.com

In E Norwich off A47 Thorpe road, 0.25m from Norwich station. From Yarmouth follow one-way system towards city centre, turn right at traffic lights opposite DEFRA building. New entrance and car park via side entrance of Alan Boswell Insurance, 126 Thorpe Road, next to DEFRA building

Open 14th June to 26th Oct, Sun, 1 – 5.30pm, and for parties of 10 or more by appt

Entrance: £4, children free

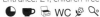

An exciting 0.5-acre garden set on a south-facing hillside, with tall trees and hedges creating a sheltered microclimate. The unusual collection of plants includes gingers, bananas, aroids and succulents. The garden reaches its peak in high to late summer, when such exotics as cannas and brugmansias are in full bloom. It is renowned for its use of house plants as bedding plants – tillandsias may be spotted in the branches of trees which are underplanted with codiaeums, guzmanias and tradescantias, and philodendrons and *Monstera deliciosa* are also used in this way, flourishing in the summer months. There are many flint walls and two raised pools. A feeling of fantasy pervades the whole place, especially in the evening when the various scents are at their headiest. A new 0.5-acre garden has been added for hardy exotics that need far less maintenance and tolerate winter cold.

FAIRHAVEN WOODLAND AND WATER GARDEN ★

The Fairhaven Garden Trust

School Road, South Walsham, Norwich NR13 6DZ. Tel: (01603) 270449; www.fairhavengarden.co.uk

9m NE of Norwich. Signposted from A47 at junction with B1140

Open all year, daily except 25th Dec, 10am – 5pm (closes 9pm Wed and Thurs, May to Aug). Guided walks for parties

Three miles of wide, level pathways wind past ancient oaks and rhododendron groves, across bridges and man-made waterways to a small private inland broad with a picture postcard thatched boathouse. The 13 acres here are the perfect place to escape into, particularly in spring when the foliage of the oaks, willows and alders creates a light green canopy above honey-scented *Rhododendron luteum*, dramatic

Fairhaven Woodland and
Water Garden

skunk cabbages and carpets of bluebells. In a county well-known for its dry climate, it is a treat to find a substantial collection of candelabra primulas growing in the organic, leafmould-rich soil built up over the years by the garden's creator, the second Lord Fairhaven, brother of the creator of the gardens at Anglesey Abbey (see entry in Cambridgeshire). Regular signposting encourages older children to stop and listen for woodpeckers and watch for tree creepers, and having reached the broad, there are regular 20- and 50-minute boat trips.

Entrance: £4.75, OAPs £4.25, children £2.25, under 5 free

Other information: Boat trips available April to Oct

FELBRIGG HALL ★
(Historic Garden Grade II*)

The Jacobean house faces south across the park, which is notable for its fine woods and lakeside walk. A ha-ha separates the park from the lawns of the house, where there is an orangery planted with camellias. To the north the ground rises and there are specimen trees and shrubs, including many of North American origin. At some distance to the east, across a paddock, is the richly productive 3.5-acre walled kitchen garden, set on a south-facing slope. It is now richly planted with a combination of fruit, vegetables, herbs and flowers in a formal design behind clipped hedges, and contains a vine house and a great octagonal brick dovecot with a flock of doves. In early autumn there is a display of many varieties of colchicums: a National Collection is kept here. The 7.5 acres are kept in immaculate order, and restoration, renewal and replacement continue at a brisk pace.

The National Trust

Felbrigg, Norwich NR11 8PR.
Tel: (01263) 837444;
www.nationaltrust.org.uk

2m SW of Cromer off A148. Entrance on B1436

Hall open 3rd March to 2nd Nov, Sat – Wed, 1 – 5pm

Garden and walled garden open 3rd March to 26th Oct, Sat – Wed; plus 26th May to 1st June, 21st July to Aug, 27th to 31st Dec daily; all 11am – 5pm. Park and woodland walks open all year, daily, dawn – dusk

Entrance: £3.70, children £1.60 (house and gardens £7.90, children £3.70, family £19.50)

Garden: ⬤ ☕ ✕ WC ♿ 🌿 🏛 💡
Park: ○ ♿

HALES HALL

A moat surrounds the remaining wing of a vast late-fifteenth-century house and a central lawn with well-planted borders and box and yew topiary backed by high brick walls. Work is continuing on the restoration of the two-acre garden after centuries of neglect. A fruit garden has been planted and

Mr and Mrs Terence Read

Hales, Loddon NR14 6QW.
Tel: (01508) 548507; www.haleshall.com

12m SE of Norwich, off A146. Signposted

Open all year, Wed – Sat, 10am – 4pm;
plus 25th March to 29th Oct, Sun and
Bank Holiday Mons, 11am – 4pm.
Guided parties by arrangement

Entrance: £2 (Great Barn and gardens)

○ WC &

there is a pot-grown orchard and a rose garden. The owners
specialise in rare and unusual perennial plants, and look after
National Collections of citrus, figs and greenhouse grapes. The
associated century-old nurseries offer an extensive range of
conservatory plants, vines, figs, mulberries, and many peach,
apricot, nectarine and greengage varieties. The fifteenth-
century thatched Great Barn is well worth a visit.

HINDRINGHAM HALL

Linda Tucker

Blacksmiths Lane, Hindringham,
NR21 0QA.
Tel: (01328) 878226

7 miles NE of Fakenham off A148 at
Thursford. Passing village hall, turn left
into Holme Lane after church

Open for NGS, and for parties of 30–40
by appt

Entrance: £3, children free

Other information: Refreshments by
arrangement

NEW ● WC ⬇ ☺ ℺

When the present owners arrived at Hindringham in 1993,
the lovely hall (not open) had almost lost its garden under a
layer of grass and nettles. Now it is has evolved into a
delightful place, with a sloping walled vegetable garden and
stream and wild meadow areas. Water is the heart of the
garden: the stream is planted with primulas and yellow tree
peonies, and the house is surrounded by a moat. It is fun to
see potatoes and asparagus growing near the water's edge.
The garden looks good at many different times. In May and
early June the view across to the west front of house, where
the moat is edged with bearded irises, is spectacular, and
visitors approach the house along paths mown through cow
parsley. Traditional roses mingle with pink-leafed actinidia on
the old flint walls and the eclectic borders progress through
the seasons to a hot crescendo in late summer. The Tudor
flint house and medieval moat are a most atmospheric
backdrop to a garden that manages to integrate tradition
with modern twists.

HOLKHAM HALL ★
(Historic Garden Grade I)

The Earl of Leicester

Wells-next-the-Sea NR23 1AB.
Tel: (01328) 710227; www.holkham.co.uk

23m W of Cromer, on A149

Hall open June to Sept, Sun – Thurs; Bank
Hols. Sat – Mon; all 12 noon – 5pm

Park open all year, daily except 25th Dec

Terrace gardens open 29th May to Sept,
Sun – Thurs (except Bank Holiday Mons),
12 noon – 5pm

Entrance: Terrace gardens free (hall £7,
children £3.50; museum £5, children £2.50)

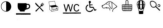

The vast park, famous for its holm oaks and its herd of 800
fallow deer, was laid out originally by William Kent then
altered by 'Coke of Norfolk' and the 2nd Earl. On the west
side of the house, lawns sweep down to the great lake. There
is now a nature trail around the lake and three designated
walks within the park. The terrace which fronts the south
facade was added in 1854, but the scale of the house and
park is so great that, from a distance at least, this does not
seriously disrupt the vision of the two. The formal beds
designed by W.A. Nesfield flank a great fountain representing
St George and the Dragon.

HOUGHTON HALL ★★
(Historic Garden Grade I)

The Marquess of Cholmondeley

King's Lynn PE31 6UE.
Tel: (01485) 528569;
www.houghtonhall.com

13m NE of King's Lynn off A148

Hall open as garden, but 11 am – 5pm

One of the most magnificent houses in Britain curiously never
seems to have had a formal garden in the eighteenth century:
it was not until the 1890s that it acquired a garden on the
west front. Recent tree-planting on an impressive scale will
settle the house into its landscape, but it is the five-acre walled
kitchen garden that has undergone the most radical change.

Houghton Hall

The centrepiece is a double herbaceous border; the remainder of the space is divided by yew hedges into 20 different garden rooms, each with an individual character and all immaculately maintained. One is a box-edged rose parterre, and a wide outer border has some of the older rose varieties and a mixture of foxgloves, pinks and delphiniums. In the kitchen garden proper are trained fruit trees, an outsize rustic fruit cage and vegetable beds filled with unusual varieties; elsewhere, pleached limes surround a grassy area planted with plum trees and 200 spring and summer bulbs. The cherry walk is underplanted with irises, and a wisteria pergola runs along the western edge of the garden. Behind, a border is given over to peonies and lilies, while an autumn border of asters, Japanese anemones and sunflowers provides a blaze of colour from August onwards. The rebuilt glasshouses contain an expanding orchid collection and an unusual water feature by Julian Bannerman. A rustic temple, a Kent seat, Italian statues, a sunken pool and a modern obelisk add architectural flourishes.

Park and gardens open
23rd March to 28th Sept, Wed, Thurs, Sun and Bank Holiday Mons, 11am – 5.30pm

Entrance: £5, children £2, family £12 (house, park and gardens £8, children £3, family £20)

Other information: Battery-powered buggies available for disabled visitors

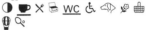

HOVETON HALL GARDENS ★

It is impossible to separate this 15-acre garden from the wetlands of Wroxham Broad, which it abuts. Walkways winding between primulas and other bog plants lead eventually to a long lake (dug out by hand in the eighteenth century); in late spring and early summer this area is a ablaze with mature azaleas and rhododendrons, and entymologists old and young can look out for the rare Norfolk Hawker, hairy dragonflies and White Admiral butterflies. The garden itself splits neatly into three: a water garden, woodland planted with spring-flowering narcissi and featuring a kidney-shaped lake, and two formal walled gardens. One is the original nineteenth-century kitchen garden, where nicely labelled vegetables are still set out in the time-honoured way. In the other, enclosed in the 1930s, two features stand out – a spider's web gate commissioned from wrought-iron artist Eric Stevenson in 1936, and a much-photographed

Mr and Mrs Andrew Buxton

Wroxham, Norwich NR12 8RJ.
Tel: (01603) 782798;
www.hovetonhallgardens.co.uk

9m NE of Norwich, 1m N of Wroxham on A1151

Open 23rd, 24th and 30th March; then April to 14th Sept, Wed – Fri, Sun and Bank Holiday Mons; all 10.30am – 5pm, and for parties of 25 or more by appt

Entrance: £5, children (5–14) £2, wheelchair users and carers £2.50

247

gardener's cottage covered with roses – and the borders encompass a wide range of traditional herbaceous and dry plantings. The whole atmosphere is of a living, evolving place, well maintained and well loved. A new arboretum was planted in 2004.

HOW HILL FARM ★

Mr P. D. S. Boardman

Ludham, Gt. Yarmouth NR29 5PG.
Tel: (01692) 678558

15m NE of Norwich, 1m W of Ludham off A1062. Follow signs to How Hill. Farm; garden is S of How Hill

Open for NGS. and for parties by appt at other times

Entrance: £3, children free

 WC

The garden around the farm is comparatively conventional, with a new garden and pond in the old bullock yard and a large Chusan palm planted in a dog cage from which it threatens to escape. Here, too, is a collection of over 100 varieties of *Ilex aquifolium* as well as many other rare holly species. Over the road in the river valley a rich combination of exotics mingles with native vegetation, and a wide variety of trees and shrubs. Around a series of pools, banks of azaleas merge into reed beds, rhododendron species rise over thickets of fern, wild grasses skirt groves of the giant *Arundo donax*, with birches, conifers and a collection of 40 different bamboos set against a background of a three-acre broad, thick with water lilies. In all, nine acres.

KETTLE HILL ★

Richard and Frances Winch

Blakeney NR25 7PN.
Tel: (01263) 741147

11m W of Cromer, just outside Blakeney on B1156 Langham road

Open for parties by appt

Entrance: £5 (incl. coffee), children free

With the help of Mark Rumary, the owners have transformed this garden into a luxurious and elegant delight. A box-edged rectangular parterre with heart-shaped beds, heightened by topiary spirals and mop heads, reflects their interest in the *Romantic Garden Nursery* at Swannington. A cleverly sited brick wall shelters a long mixed border packed with colour and unusual plants and leads to a circular secret garden. A large lawn, featuring a delightful Gothick summerhouse by George Carter, extends from the house to mature woodland, where many ornamental trees have been added and bluebells

Kettle Hill

and naturalised lilies carpet the ground in spring. A new rose garden has been planted adjoining the house, and the old one deep in the wood has been rejuvenated.

LAWN FARM

The 6.5-acre garden was designed and laid out by the owners in 1987. There are five natural ponds with three water gardens, and a damp wooded area with hydrangeas and azaleas. A completely different atmosphere is to be found in the two medieval flint-walled courtyards; here roses and many interesting and unusual shrubs and climbers flourish in the hot and sheltered microclimate. Mrs Deterding has a magpie's eye for the rare and difficult to find, including a good collection of unusual trees. April and June are good times to visit.

Mr and Mrs G.W. Deterding

Lawn Farm, Cley Road, Holt NR25 7DY.
Tel: (01263) 713484

From Holt take Cley Road opposite King's Head pub. After 1m, turning is signposted on right after school

Open March to Aug by appt

Entrance: £3.50, children free

WC &

LEXHAM HALL

(Historic Garden Grade II)

The seventeenth- and eighteenth-century hall sits well amid beautiful parkland filled with interesting trees and grazing sheep. The ground falls away to the river forming a lake and canals crossed by elegant bridges; the nine-acre garden was the inspiration of the present owner's mother who, with the help of the late Dame Sylvia Crowe, laid out its bones. Massive yew hedges reveal intimate views of the park, taking the eye to the distance beyond. Wide terracing to the south of the house is well planted and colourful, and a long grass walk edged with herbaceous plants and shrubs progresses to woodland full of rhododendrons, azaleas, camellias, rare trees and spring bulbs. (In early spring, the parkland and adjoining churchyard are also awash with snowdrops.) There is a colourful rose garden, and the kitchen garden has an early eighteenth-century crinkle-crankle wall covered with fruit, a cutting border, greenhouses sheltering plants for the house and tender vegetables, the whole a picture of health. A wood to the south, known as the American Gardens, is reputedly planted from seeds collected in America.

Mr and Mrs Neil Foster

East Lexham, King's Lynn PE32 2QJ.
Tel: (01328) 701288/701341

6m N of Swaffham, 2m W of Litcham off B1145

Open 10th, 11th and 24th Feb for snowdrops (provisional and weather permitting), 11am – 4pm; for NGS; and May to July mid-week for parties of 20 or more by appt

Entrance: £4

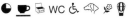 WC &

MANNINGTON HALL ★

(Historic Garden Grade II)

This is a 20-acre garden of romance and charm, where lawns run down to a moat crossed by a drawbridge, to herbaceous borders backed by high walls of brick and flint. The moat also encloses a secret, scented garden in a design derived from one of the ceilings of the fifteenth-century house. Outside the moat are borders of flowering shrubs flanking a Doric temple, and woodlands beyond contain the ruins of a Saxon church and nineteenth-century follies. Within the walls of the former kitchen garden, a series of rose gardens has been planted following the design of gardens from medieval to modern times and featuring roses popular at each period. A twentieth-

Lord and Lady Walpole

Saxthorpe, Norwich NR11 7BB.
Tel: (01263) 584175;
www.manningtongardens.co.uk

5m SE of Holt off B1149. Signposted

Open May and Sept, Sun, 12 noon – 5pm; June to Aug, Wed – Fri and Sun, 11am – 5pm

Entrance: £5, concessions £4, children free

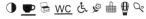 WC &

century rose garden incorporates a planthouse, a vegetable plot and a children's garden. There are now more than 1500 varieties of roses here. In 2003 a sensory garden was created on the south lawn with a narrow channel of water and four large beds with plants chosen for scent, touch, sight, taste and hearing. A lake, woods and meadowland with extensive walks are other features.

The National Trust

Oxborough, King's Lynn PE33 9PS.
Tel: (01366) 328258;
www.nationaltrust.org.uk

7m SW of Swaffham off A134

House open

Garden open 2nd Feb to 9th March,
8th Nov to 21st Dec, Sat and Sun;
15th March to July, Sept to 2nd Nov,
Sat – Wed; Aug, daily; all 11am – 5pm
(closes 4pm in winter)

Entrance: £3.70, children £2.10 (hall and
garden £7.10, children £3.70, family
£17.85)

OXBURGH HALL

(Historic Garden Grade II)

The gatehouse is the glory of Oxburgh, and the mellow redbrick early-Tudor manor house seems to float in its rectangular moat. Both house and garden are concealed from view until you have walked past the orchard of pears, quince, plum and greengage trees. Then you look down over the formal parterre, a Victorian copy of a Le Nôtre design consisting of a moderately restrained pattern of beds edged with clipped box hedges, punctuated by clipped clumps of yew. Yellow, red, violet and silver are the colours of the annual bedding – a vibrant carpet. Behind a long yew hedge is a narrow border edged with wispy catmint, with repeat-clumps of colourful perennials. There are some fine trees, and circular walks lead into the park and woodland, full of snowdrops and winter aconites in early spring. In all, 76 acres.

Mr and Mrs W. Jordan

Pensthorpe, Fakenham NR21 0LN.
Tel: (01328) 851465;
www.pensthorpe.com

1m E of Fakenham on A1067 Norwich
– Fakenham road. Signposted

PENSTHORPE ★

Although Pensthorpe's *raison d'être* is as a nature reserve for water birds and wildlife, it also includes two important gardens within its 200 acres of lakes and riverside walks. These are only a tiny part of the whole park and the approach to them – through a covered aviary – is rather disorientating.

Pensthorpe

However, the determined visitor will be rewarded for their efforts. The Millennium Garden designed by Piet Oudolf in 1999 is a masterpiece of perennial planting (at its height from July to October) and possibly the best place in Britain to see his style of planting using sedums, grasses, astrantias, eupatoriums and even bronze fennel to form huge bold 'colonies' beside the water and winding gravel paths. The smaller Wave Garden, designed by Julie Toll in 2005, combines wild and cultivated plants to great effect, peaking earlier, in late spring and summer. Striking and colourful, both gardens somehow manage to merge gently into the natural landscape.

Open all year, daily, 10am – 5pm (closes 4pm Jan to March)

Entrance: £7, OAPs £5.50, children £3.50

SANDRINGHAM HOUSE ★
(Historic Garden Grade II*)

The huge Victorian house stands among broad lawns with an outer belt of woodland through which a path runs past plantings of camellias, hydrangeas, cornus, magnolias and rhododendrons, with some fine specimen trees. The path passes the magnificent cast- and wrought-iron Norwich Gates of 1862. In the open lawn are specimen oaks planted by Queen Victoria and other members of the royal family. To the south-west of the house the eastern side of the upper lake is built up into a massive rock garden using blocks of the local carrstone, and now largely planted with dwarf conifers. Below the rock garden, opening onto the lake, a cavernous grotto was intended as a boathouse; above is a small summerhouse built for Queen Alexandra. There are thick plantings of hostas, agapanthus and various moisture-loving plants around the margin of the lake. The path passes between the upper and lower lakes set in wooded surroundings. To the north of the house is a garden designed by Jellicoe for King George VI: a long series of box-hedged beds, divided by gravel and grass paths and flanked by avenues of pleached lime, one of which is centred on a gold-plated statue of a Buddhist divinity. As one would expect, maintenance is immaculate throughout the 60 acres of garden, set within the 600-acre park.

H.M. The Queen

Sandringham, King's Lynn PE35 6EN. Tel: (01553) 772675; www.sandringhamestate.co.uk

9m NE of King's Lynn on B1440 near Sandringham Church

House open as garden, but from 11am

Garden and park open 22nd March to late July, early Aug to 26th Oct, daily, 10.30am – 4.30pm

Entrance: museum and grounds £6, concessions £5, children £3.50, family £15.50 (house, museum and grounds £9, concessions £7, children £5, family £23)

SHERINGHAM PARK ★
(Historic Garden Grade II*)

The house and 1000-acre park, both designed by Humphry Repton, are located in a secluded valley at the edge of the Cromer/Holt ridge, close to the sea but protected from its winds by steep wooded hills. The park is remarkable not only for its beauty and spectacular views but also for an extensive collection of rhododendrons which thrive in the acid soil. Crowning an eminence is a modern classical temple based on a Repton design and erected to mark the 70th birthday of Mr Thomas Upcher, the last descendant of the original owner to live at Sheringham. As Repton's most-admired and best-preserved work, it is well worth a visit.

The National Trust

Wood Farm, Upper Sheringham NR26 8TL. Tel: (01263) 820550; www.nationaltrust.org.uk

4m NE of Holt off A148

Open all year, daily, dawn – dusk

Entrance: £4 per car inc. parking and all occupants; coaches £10

Other information: Coaches must prebook during rhododendron season. Refreshments available April to Sept only

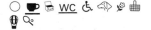

Stow Hall

Lady Rose Hare

Stow Bardolph, King's Lynn PE34 3HU.
Tel: (01366) 383194

2m N of Downham Market, E of A10

Open March to Oct, Wed, 10am – 4pm;
and for parties by appt

Entrance: £3.50, children free

STOW HALL ★

Set in a lawned park surrounded by majestic plane trees, cedars of Lebanon and an ancient fern-leaf beech is a series of imaginative gardens, all linked by a central path. The high, warm walls of the courtyard gardens are swathed in old roses and wisteria, and shrubs more usually seen in milder gardens also have congenial homes in the shelter of these walls. Off the main path are small and elegant formal gardens: a mixed perennial garden including irises; a sunken Dutch garden; cloisters with scented climbers; a lavender-edged pond and a croquet lawn. In the kitchen garden a rose border stretching either side of the main gate complements box-edged beds of fruit and vegetables, an arched tunnel with gnarled apple and pear trees, a venerable mulberry and many local apple varieties. The 20 acres of gardens also include a cottage garden around the greenhouse which is an exuberant mixture of scented plants and herbs.

Mr Gordon Alexander

Wretham Lodge, East Wretham,
Thetford IP24 1RL.
Tel: (01953) 498997

6m NE of Thetford off A1075.
Turn left by village sign, right at
crossroads, then bear left

Open for NGS, and for parties by appt

Entrance: £3, children free

WRETHAM LODGE

Extensive lawns and wide mixed borders surround the handsome flint-built former rectory set in its own walled park. There are substantial mixed borders within the walled kitchen garden too, together with roses massed in informal beds and covering the high flint walls. Plants worthy of note here include espalier and fan-trained fruit trees, a large indoor fig and unusual vegetables. A wide grass walk runs around the park and through mature and recently established trees where daffodils are naturalised; a long walk among narcissi and bluebells leads to a grove of ornamental trees. Spring sees the flowering of many bulbs, and in summer the double herbaceous borders and the wildflower meadows are a haze of colour. In all, 10 acres.

OTHER RECOMMENDED GARDENS

CONGHAM HALL HOTEL

Lynn Road, Grimston, King's Lynn PE32 1AH
(01485 600250; www.conghamhallhotel.co.uk).
Open all year, daily, 9am – 6pm

Set in 30 acres of parkland, the garden surrounding the hotel is noted for its extensive collection of culinary and medicinal herbs, many of which are for sale. Over 700 varieties are planted formally in a walled garden amid herbaceous borders and rose-covered pergolas, others grouped in a 'woodery' constructed from fallen estate trees.

FRITTON LAKE COUNTRYWORLD

Lord and Lady Somerleyton, Fritton, Great Yarmouth NR31 9HA (01493 488208; www.somerleyton.co.uk).
Open April to Sept, daily, 10am – 5.30pm

Separate from the other attractions of the country park are formal lakeside plantings, a Victorian garden laid out in the gardenesque style, and woodland walks winding among rhododendrons and azaleas – a reminder of those surrounding a mansion destroyed by fire in 1957.

THE GARDEN IN AN ORCHARD

Mr and Mrs R.W. Boardman, Mill Road, Bergh Apton, Norwich NR15 1BQ (01508 480322). Open Bank Holiday weekends and several others May to Sept, 11am – 6pm (check before visiting)

The garden has evolved little by little from a commercial orchard, and now covers 3.5 delightful and densely planted acres, filled by the owner (a professional plantsman) with a wide variety of rare and unusual plants and trees.

LAKE HOUSE WATER GARDENS

Mr and Mrs Garry Muter, Roman Drive, Postwick Lane, Brundall, Norwich NR13 5LU (01603 712933).
Open for parties by appt

An informal water garden of 2 acres in a deep cleft in the river escarpment, falling away from the top of the hillside to a waterlily-covered lake. The formal plantings of rare species are interesting at every season; there are drifts of spring-flowering bulbs under great forest trees, and an abundance of wild flowers.

NORFOLK LAVENDER

Caley Mill, Heacham, King's Lynn PE31 7JE
(01485 570384; www.norfolk-lavender.co.uk).
Open all year, daily except 25th and 26th Dec and 1st Jan, 9am – 5pm (closes 4pm Nov to March)

Fields of lavender stretching into the distance are the amazing backdrop in July and August to 6 acres of intimate gardens near the Victorian water mill that houses the visitor centre. These include a display designed as a National Collection, a herb garden and a fragrant meadow. 45 acres in all.

THE PLANTATION GARDEN

4 Earlham Road, Norwich NR2 3DB (01603 621868; www.plantationgarden.co.uk). Open all year, daily, 9am – 6pm (or dusk if earlier). Closed some Sats – check website for details

The extraordinary high-Victorian suburban garden of 3 acres created in the 1850s in a disused chalk quarry is both typical of its period and the personal vision of its strong-minded creator. The exuberant and eccentric architectural features he scattered among trees, shrubs and floral beds give the place a unique atmosphere. (Listed Grade II)

RAVENINGHAM HALL

Sir Nicholas Bacon, Raveningham, Norwich NR14 6NS (01508 548152; www.raveningham.com). Telephone for dates and times of opening

The peaceful, richly planted garden within a fine landscape park has gracious echoes of its 18th-century and Victorian past. The present is not forgotten: sculpture is sited sensitively throughout, and an arboretum of unusual trees is extending steadily towards the lake. 27 acres. (Listed Grade II)

THRIGBY HALL WILDLIFE GARDENS

Mr K.J. Sims, Filby, Great Yarmouth NR29 3DR
(01493 369477; www.thrigbyhall.co.uk). Open all year, daily, 10am – 5pm (or dusk if earlier)

The chief attraction in this unusual 10-acre garden, originally laid out in the style of William III, is a collection of Chinese plants arranged to form the landscape of the willow-pattern plate, complete with pagoda and bridges crossing a small lake.

NORTHAMPTONSHIRE

For further information about how to use the *Guide*
and for an explanation of the symbols, see pages vi–viii.
Specific dates and times are those given to us by garden owners for 2008.
For 2009 dates, check with the individual properties.
For opening dates under the National Gardens Scheme,
readers should consult *The Yellow Book* or www.ngs.org.uk.
Maps are to be found at the end of the *Guide*.

CASTLE ASHBY GARDENS
(Historic Garden Grade I)

Earl Compton

Castle Ashby, Northampton NN7 1LQ.
Tel: (01604) 696187;
www.castleashby.co.uk

5m E of Northampton, between A45 and
A428 Northampton – Bedford road

Open all year, daily, 10am – 5.30pm (closes
4.30pm Oct to March)

Entrance: (tickets from machine when
entrance unattended) £2.80, OAPs and
children £1.90, family £8 (2007 prices)

Other information: Teas available for
groups if pre-booked. Possible for
wheelchairs but uneven paths

The first impression as you walk past the Elizabethan house is of a vast space. 'Capability' Brown worked on the park, but the gardens open to the public are more intimate, laid out by Matthew Digby Wyatt in the 1860s with sunken lawns and immaculate yew cones surrounded by well-planted borders. The fine orangery has a central circular fish pool seven feet deep and is filled with borderline-hardy shrubs. More garden buildings, also glazed to their rear, close this view and, beyond, tall box hedges enclose the Butterfly Garden, the Summerhouse Garden and the Rainbow Border. Rare breeds of sheipp, pygmy goats, pigs, rabbits and guinea pigs run and hop in the child-friendly farmyard. A spring walk leads to an informal arboretum, where dogs are invited to roam free and paths meander to the terracotta bridge spanning a series of ponds; the wider water of the lake is in view, but inaccessible.

CEDAR FARM

Mr and Mrs R. Tuffen

Desborough NN14 2QD.
Tel: (01536) 763992;

6m N of Kettering, 5m S of Market
Harborough – telephone for directions.

Open for NGS, and by appt

An unpretentious drive on the outskirts of Desborough (a town made prosperous by the manufacture of shoes and corsets), opens out to a radiant 10-acre garden (originally a pig farm) which has been developed over the last decade. Now the main thrust is a wide lawn to the north of the house with formal yews marching up it and enclosed by lavish mixed borders. Roses and clematis love the clay soil, and almost anything that can act as a support has a mantle thrown over it – the circular pergola near the house drips colour in June and July. Mrs Tuffen has a flower-arranger's eye for form and colour, and foliage is especially important to her. East of the formal garden an arboretum slopes down to springs excavated to make three linking natural ponds; another large reflecting pool was dug near the house in 2004.

COTON MANOR GARDEN ★★

Mr and Mrs Ian Pasley-Tyler

Guilsborough, Northampton
NN6 8RQ. Tel: (01604) 740219;
www.cotonmanor.co.uk

Blessed with a south-facing slope, an abundance of springs and streams and a predominantly neutral soil, the present owners – the third generation of keen and knowledgeable gardeners

Coton Manor

to live here – have made this the finest garden in the East Midlands. Most visitors enter beside the pergola clothed with clematis and *Rosa* 'Madame Alfred Carrière'. Nestled below is the herb garden, on the site of a large shed formerly used to house the waterfowl which now greet and entertain you throughout the lower garden along with hens and surreal Alice-in-Wonderland flamingoes. The view across the Goose Park has been opened up and leads to a three-acre meadow, filled with a wide range of species giving colour from late spring to August. Beside this is the quintessential bluebell wood whose perfume permeates the air in May. The more formal area near the house contains a new rose garden, each of its quadrant beds containing the same plants but making no attempt at mirrored symmetry. The terrace pots are always innovative and abundant, softened by valerian billowing from every cranny and pavement crack. Massed hellebores and snowdrops start the year in the woodland walk, and this theme of areas for seasons continues down to the autumnal meadow border. The restraint of the formal rill is in restful contrast to the exuberantly planted Mediterranean bank and the luxuriant stream garden leading down to a new bog garden. The whole canvas is divided into precincts, each with its own mood and atmosphere but flowing from one into the next. Although the planting is thoughtfully composed, nowhere is there a slavish adherence to themed colours and everywhere the standard of maintenance and attention to detail are impeccable.

10m NW of Northampton, 11m SE of Rugby near Ravensthorpe Reservoir, signed from A428 and A5199

Open 21st March to 27th Sept, Tues – Sat and Bank Holiday Suns and Mons, plus Suns in April and May, all 12 noon – 5.30pm

Entrance: £5, OAPs £4.50, children £2.50

COTTESBROOKE HALL ★★
(Historic Garden Grade II)

When the imposing house was built in 1702, the landscape would have come up to its walls, but of that period only the magnificent cedars to the west of the house remain. The garden we see today was created between 1910 and 1930 and resounds with the names of famous landscapers down the years. Geoffrey Jellicoe designed the entrance court with great restraint, enhancing the distant view of Brixworth's Saxon church. Edward Schultz was called in, as was Sylvia Crowe in the 1970s (her neat summerhouse in the pool garden provides a spot for restful contemplation), and latterly James Alexander-Sinclair advised on the replanting of the double herbaceous borders. The Macdonald-Buchanans have

Mr and Mrs A. Macdonald-Buchanan

Cottesbrooke, Northampton NN6 8PF.
Tel: (01604) 505808;
www.cottesbrookehall.co.uk

10m N of Northampton between A5199 and A508

House and garden open May to Sept, Thurs and Bank Holiday Mons, plus Weds in May and June; all 2 – 5.30pm. Also open by appt

Entrance: £5.50, concessions, £4.50, children £2.50 (house and gardens £8, concessions £6.50, children £5.30)

lived and gardened here since 1930. The formal area is divided into a series of individual gardens. Brick Court is restrained, surrounding a huge pine cloaked in a climbing hydrangea, and opposite is the Dutch garden of boxed beds richly planted for autumn display. A new venture is the knot garden, where the box patterns show clearly against the pebble floor; beyond, more box surrounds massed *Rosa* 'Penelope' in the Philosopher's Walk. Throughout, sumptuous pots add summer luxuriance. Then walk across the drive to the relaxed and informal wild garden on the banks of a tributary of the River Nene. Detailing and maintenance are everywhere superb.

DEENE PARK

(Historic Garden Grade II)

Mr Edmund Brudenell

Corby NN17 3EW.
Tel: (01780) 450278/450223;
www.deenepark.com

6m N of Corby off A43 Kettering – Stamford road

House open as garden from March

Garden open 17th and 24th Feb, 11am – 4pm, for snowdrops; 23rd and 24th March, 4th, 5th, 25th and 26th May; then June to Aug, Sun and Bank Holiday Mons; all 2 – 5pm

Parties by appt

Entrance: £4, children (10–14) £1.50, accompanied children under 10 free (house and gardens £6.50, concessions £5.50, children (10–14) £2.50, accompanied children under 10 free) (2007 prices)

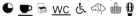

The 17-acre gardens enhance the noble house, which captures the imagination as the home of the Earl of Cardigan who led the Charge of the Light Brigade in 1854. Running the whole length of the building is a box-edged parterre designed by David Hicks, now mature and redolent of summer scents. The main thrust to the west of the house is a long grass terrace beginning and ending with an octagonal folly. The upper side is clothed with a mixed border planted against a high and mellow brick wall; the *enfilade* effect of this great stretch is broken by hornbeam hedges and a central round garden enclosing a large and richly planted font. To the other side the land slopes down to a canal-shaped lake. Water and trees dominate here: beyond the formal garden the arboretum leads down to a large lake that feeds two other lower-lying stretches of water, the lowest spanned by an elegant stone carriage bridge. Something of interest here from the snowdrop days of February to the tail end of summer.

EVENLEY WOOD GARDEN

Mr and Mrs R. T. Whiteley

Mill Lane, Evenley NN13 5SH.
Tel: (01280) 703329;
www.evenleywoodgarden.co.uk

0.75m S of Brackley on A43. Go through village towards Mixbury, then turn left down unmade road for 0.25m

Open for NGS, and for parties by appt

Entrance: £3.50, children free

Few plantsmen are as fortunate as Tim Whiteley in possessing 60 acres of private woodland in which to indulge his passion for planting and propagating (and helpfully labelling) a huge variety of species. Not only that, but 60 acres that combine the usual alkaline soil of the area with a band of acid soil. Thus, flowering alongside notable collections of quercus, malus, pyrus, euonymus and magnolias, roses and many climbers are rhododendrons, camellias and magnolias. Beneath this rich and rare mix of trees and shrubs drifts and groups of flowers appear season by season, ranging from the earliest snowdrops to narcissi, scillas and other spring bulbs, followed by many lilies, all set against the natural setting of woodland and water. The autumn colour is, needless to say, very fine.

HILL GROUNDS

Bob and Janet Cropley

Hill Grounds, Evenley NN13 5RZ.
Tel: (01280) 703224

Tucked away behind a large village green where cricket is still played on summer weekends, the garden – all four acres of it – is managed single-handedly by its plant-mad owners. Janet

Cropley cut her horticultural teeth at Waterperry and Cambridge University Botanic Garden and shares her knowledge generously with visitors. New areas are constantly being annexed and new beds colonised, so that the garden as a whole has an appealing fluidity about it. Some magnificent trees, yew hedges which if rolled up would cover a quarter-acre and several pergolas all add height, while the different enclosures contribute structure. The plants, however, rule the roost. They are massed in every conceivable situation: on the terrace in front of the house, around a small pond, in a seating area, in island beds, in a round garden and in an arboretum that doubles as a wildflower meadow. The house is smothered with *Campsis radicans* and *Magnolia grandiflora*, an aged apple tree is dressed in a weighty 'Rambling Rector' rose. This is a garden to visit for anyone seeking inspiration to refresh an existing garden or to start a new one.

1m S of Brackley on A43. From village green in Evenley, turn into Church Lane, then right up drive to automatic gate beneath copper beech

Open all year by appt

Entrance: £4, children free

KELMARSH HALL ★

James Gibbs's 1730s Palladian house was set in a contemporary landscape with obligatory lake and vistas in its 54 acres; in the twentieth century, Nancy Lancaster lived here and created a more intimate garden of 14 acres with advice from Norah Lindsay and Geoffrey Jellicoe. Huge, bulgy box hedges entice you on to a strategic seat with quintessentially English views across an old-fashioned rose garden and meadows grazed by British White cattle. The old drying-ground is enclosed by ancient yews, rather like a screens passage in a Tudor house, and planted with rich herbaceous borders. Another long border in brighter hues for later summer is now maturing after restoration work. The triangular walled garden, planted anew with vegetables, fruit and cut flowers, includes ornamental elements like a simple

The Kelmarsh Trust

Kelmarsh, Northampton NN6 9LY.
Tel: (01604) 686543;
www.kelmarsh.com

11m N of Northampton on A508 near A14 junction 2

House open as garden, but Thurs and Bank Holiday Suns and Mons only

Garden open 23rd March to 28th Sept, Tues – Thurs, Sun and Bank Holiday Mons, 2 – 5pm

Entrance: £4, OAPs £3.50, children £2.50 (house and garden £5, OAPs £4.50, children £3)

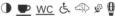

Kelmarsh Hall

257

turf maze and beautifully restored central glasshouse. Dazzling pots of tulips on steps and by doorways are replaced later in the season by dahlias and glowing annuals. For the sophisticate there is a shaded white garden, for the naturalist a rural lakeside ramble.

KIRBY HALL
(Historic Garden Grade II*)

English Heritage
Deene, Corby NN17 3EN.
Tel: (01536) 203230;
www.english-heritage.co.uk

4m NE of Corby off A43 on road W of Deene

Open Jan to June, Sept to Dec, Thurs – Mon; July and Aug, daily; all 10am – 5pm (closes 6pm July and Aug, 4pm Nov to March). Closed 24th to 26th Dec, 1st Jan. Please telephone before travelling

Entrance: £4.70, concessions £3.50, children £2.40, family £11.80

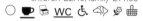

At the close of the seventeenth century, under the ownership of the 4th Sir Christopher Hatton, this was acclaimed as 'ye finest garden in England'. In 1994, after much archaeological excavation and research, English Heritage embarked on the creation of a garden of the 1690s on the west side of this noble ruin; it was completed in 2007. The character of the restored grass and gravel cutwork, impressive topiary grown in wooden planters, statues and other garden ornaments are strongly architectural. The surrounding terrace walks, with views over the garden from above, are a good place to take in the original design. Period plants are used throughout: old varieties of fruit trees are trained against the walls, and the north border has been replanted with species referred to in Hatton's papers. An exhibition about the gardens is located in the hall.

THE MENAGERIE
(Historic Park Grade II)

Mr A. Myers
Horton, Northampton NN7 2BX.
Tel: (01604) 870957 (leave message for Administrator);
www.menageriehorton.co.uk

6m SE of Northampton, on B526 turn left 1m S of Horton into field. Watch out for tiny notice on gate

Open May to Sept, Mon, Wed and Thurs, 2 – 6pm, also last Sun of these months, 2 – 6pm

Entrance: £5, concessions £4, children £1.50

When Horton House was demolished in the 1930s, a few of the landscape follies remained; this fine late-1750s building was the 2nd Earl of Halifax's private zoo and is one of the most important surviving works of Thomas Wright of Durham. In a ruinous state, it was rescued by Gervase Jackson-Stops and Ian Kirby, who set about creating the garden anew in the 1980s, planting 'the bones and the formal structure of a lime avenue, adding an acaena-covered mount and radiating hornbeam *allées*, each with a dramatic pond and fountain. Following the untimely deaths of its creators, years of neglect left the flesh of their garden sadly puffy and misshapen, but since 2000 much has been done to restore it. Although this is an uphill task on a wetland site and heavy clay, moisture-loving plants are in their element: the camassias stand four feet tall and trilliums burgeon in the rich planting of the Vernal Garden. One of the pair of thatched follies is now a chapel, and there is a newly built walled garden.

THE OLD RECTORY, MIXBURY

Mr and Mrs Ben Collins
Mixbury, Brackley NN13 5RR.
Tel: (01280) 848336

5m SE of Brackley, 6m W of Buckingham off A421. Turn left off A421 to Mixbury, house is on right just before church

This is a country garden of traditional bones and sophisticated planting – the two in perfect harmony. On the left-hand side a broad, delicately coloured herbaceous border swirls past characterful garden buildings before giving way on both sides to meadows spangled with alliums and oxeye daisies; to one side a mown path winds to a secluded little garden with a circular bed and a laburnum tunnel. Facing the house at the end of the lawn is a bold contemporary statement – a large oval bed planted with grasses and perennials, plus three rectangular beds defined by box edging and topiary and filled with stronger-coloured flowers and foliage. The surround to the tennis court, with its tumbledown Hansel and Gretel cottage, and the swimming pool hidden behind a waterfall of roses triumphantly resolve the problems of these twin evils.

Open for charity June to mid-Oct, for individuals and parties by appt

Entrance: £3.50 (£4.50 for parties, including refreshments)

Other information: Garden design courses by Angela Collins all year; email: ac.gardendesign@talk21.com for details

THE OLD RECTORY, SUDBOROUGH ★

'Garden open by appointment. However, as you're here, please come and enjoy it.' So reads the notice on the gate at the unassuming entrance dignified by clipped panels of osmanthus and jasmine against the churchyard wall. Once you reach the intimate courtyard leading to the back door, with its huge pots of *Polygala* x *dalmaisiana* and aromatic geraniums, the high standard becomes apparent. The garden proper lies to the south of the house and opens onto a broad lawn leading to an informal and fecund pond, with Harpers Brook marking the boundary. The lawn is embraced by generous mixed borders planted with a painterly eye for colour; to the west is a rose garden and peony border; to the east a spring garden and hellebore collection. Here too is the potager, with brick paths separating productive beds and apples appearing in many guises – hanging from step cordons and arches, trained into globes. Every possible attention is paid to detail (even the wall-trained peaches have glass 'hats' to prevent leaf curl). The neighbouring stable courtyard is richly planted in shades of peach and lemon. Near the house there is a hot, dry 'salviary' for late colour with daphnes thriving in the cool shade beyond. Everywhere in the two acres the planting is held together by clipped box and holly, hebes and other formal elements. Masterly.

Mr and Mrs Anthony Huntington

Sudborough, Kettering NN14 3BX.
Tel: (01832) 733247;
www.oldrectorygardens.co.uk

7m SE of Corby off A6116 Corby – Thrapston road, A14 junction 12

Open April to Sept, Tues, 10am – 4pm, and by appt

Entrance: £4 (£5.50 with tea and biscuits), children under 16 free

Other information: Evening parties by arrangement

The Old Rectory, Sudboough

James and Elizabeth Saunders Watson

Market Harborough LE16 8TH.
Tel: (01536) 770240;
www.rockinghamcastle.com

2m N of Corby on A6003. Signposted

Castle open as garden, but from 1pm

Garden open 23rd March to June, Sun and Bank Holiday Mon; July to Sept, Tues, Sun and Bank Holiday Mons; all 12 noon – 5pm

Entrance: £5 (castle and gardens £8.50, OAPs £7.50, children £5, family £22)

ROCKINGHAM CASTLE GARDENS
(Historic Garden Grade II*)

The castle commands a magnificent position on a scarp with vast views northwards and a good arboretum tumbling down the slope below. The most memorable feature in the garden is the Elephant Wall, huge recumbent yew pachyderms that are a happy result of neglect two centuries ago. The Cross Garden is planted with roses and lavender, and more roses are massed in the central roundel of the New Garden, which is surrounded by castellated yew. Extensions to this area, site of the original motte and bailey, were designed by Robert Myers, and the yew hedges will be clothed in time with shrubs and herbaceous plants densely planted in mixed borders.

Sir Michael and Lady Connell

Brackley NN13 6DP.
Tel: (01280) 705899

On A422 between Brackley and Banbury, 1m E of Farthinghoe, signed Steane Park only

Open for NGS, and March to Oct for parties of 10 or more by appt

Entrance: £4.50, children under 5 free

Other information: Refreshments by arrangement

STEANE PARK

Set within 60 acres of landscaped parkland, the seven-acre gardens surround the seventeenth-century house (not open) and its enchanting matching private chapel. Today its stone walls are enhanced by old varieties of climbing roses in pastel colours and beds of traditional cottage-garden flowers. The gardens have been kept appropriately restrained to an elegant formality but with soft curving lines which blend with the landscape beyond the ha-ha. Spacious lawns are punctuated by handsome trees and features like the rose- and clematis-festooned gazebo and the sundial fringed by two tones of lavender. Borders shaded by the house and a magnificent copper beech are arranged in subtle blends of foliage provided by shrubs and herbaceous plants. There are beds of culinary and medicinal herbs, white borders, and a pavilion reached by a lavender walk. The wild area of the garden is dominated by seventeenth-century fishponds and a stream which winds from a bog garden under the blue Monet bridge to a landing stage and seating area. This part of the garden is full of surprises: a leafy tunnel, a grass walk edged by cow parsley spanned by a drystone moon gate, a bower of terracotta pots, a folly and a tiny willow 'hermitage'.

Richard Bashford and Valerie Bexley

Juniper Hill, Nr Brackley NN13 5RH.
Tel: (01869) 810170

2.5m S of Brackley off A43. 200 yds after junction with B4031 (southbound exit only), turn left signed to Juniper Hill, and continue for 0.3m. Park on grass verge at 30mph sign and walk down unmade road on right; house is last on left

Open 20th Feb to 26th March, Wed, 2 – 5pm; for NGS; and by appt

Entrance: £3

WOODCHIPPINGS

Juniper Hill – Lark Rise in Flora Thompson's 1945 account of a dying rural tradition – is a hamlet of cottages hidden among hedges. Furthest from the road lies a horticultural gem. The owners are enamellers by profession, and it shows in their enchanting 0.3-acre garden, where clumps of rare and unusual flowers and foliage are studded among thick layers of bark, all grown to perfection despite the difficulties of deep chestnut shade and greedy hedges. They have divided the small space between them, and each has a distinctive style and palette of favoured plants. Visit in January or February for the snowdrops and hellebores, in June for the old roses and alstroemerias, in July the grasses and bright-coloured perennials. And so on into autumn. The small nursery attached to this plantsman's paradise offers some of the rarities on show.

OTHER RECOMMENDED GARDENS

ALTHORP HOUSE

Earl Spencer, Althorpe, Northampton NN7 4HQ;
(01604) 770107; www.althorp.com). Open July to
Aug, 11am – 5pm (telephone for exact dates).
Closed 31st Aug

The gardens were made in the 1860s by the
architect W. M. Teulon. Dan Pearson has planted
subtle and attractive borders near the house
and devised a memorial 2-mile walk through
the grounds (which include a fine arboretum)
to the island where Diana, Princess of Wales is
buried. 22 acres. (Listed Grade II*)

BOUGHTON HOUSE

The Duke and Duchess of Buccleuch and
Queensberry, Kettering NN14 1BJ (01536 515731;
www.boughtonhouse.org.uk). Garden open Aug, daily,
2 – 5pm. Park and plant centre open May to July, daily
except Sat, 1 – 5pm

The historic park was laid out before 1700 and
developed on a monumental scale during the
18th century. The landscape consists of
extensive lime avenues and a network of formal
canals. Within the house gardens are long
herbaceous borders, a lily pond and a walled
garden. 350 acres in all. (Listed Grade I)

CHURCH FARMHOUSE

Alexander and Gillian Foster, Blakesley, Towcester
NN12 8RA (01327 860364). Open April to July and
Sept by appt

A traditional garden of 1.5 acres, combining flair
and plantsmanship. Clever engineering means
that the different areas – a broad terrace, sunny
and shady borders, a stream-fed pond – flow
naturally into one other, full of interest, surprise
and ideas to take home.

HOLDENBY HOUSE GARDENS AND FALCONRY CENTRE

Mr and Mrs James Lowther, Holdenby NN6 8DJ
(01604 770074; www.holdenby.com). Open April to
Sept, Sun, 1 – 5pm. Falconry Centre open as garden,
but May to Aug

The 20-acre gardens are best known for
Rosemary Verey's miniature replica of the
original centrepiece of the extensive formal
gardens which once surrounded the vast
Elizabethan mansion – of which only one-eighth

remains – using plants available in the 1580s. An
abundant fragrant border and formal planting
fringing a pond were designed by Rupert Golby.
The falconry centre is a rival attraction. (Listed
Grade I)

LAMPORT HALL

Lamport, Northampton NN6 9HD (01604 686272;
www.lamporthall.co.uk). Open for guided tours 23rd
March to 12th Oct, Sun and Bank Holiday Mons,
2.30pm and 3.15pm; Aug, Mon – Fri, 2.30pm. Also
open for non-guided tours 23rd and 24th March,
25th and 26th May, 24th and 25th Aug, 11th and 12th
Oct, 2.15 – 4.15pm

The original 5-acre grounds were laid out in
1655 and now consist of a mellow and
attractive combination of lawns and fine mixed
and herbaceous borders. A line of huge and
shapely Irish yews marches in front of the
mounded ha-ha, and an impressive ironstone
rockery was home to the first garden gnome.
(Listed Grade II)

LYVEDEN NEW BIELD

Oundle PE8 5AT (01832 205358;
www.nationaltrust.org.uk). Open April to Oct,
Wed – Sun; Aug, daily; all 10.30am – 5pm; Nov,
Feb and March, Sat, Sun, 10.30am – 4pm. NT

Set in front of the roofless ruin of an
Elizabethan banqueting house are the fascinating
remnants of an elaborate water garden with
truncated pyramids and circular mounds,
surrounded by moats and terraces. A formal
orchard has been replanted with over 300 trees
of the period, and wildflower meadows are a
riot of summer colour. 15 acres. (Listed
Grade II*)

THE PREBENDAL MANOR HOUSE

Mrs Jane Baile, Nassington, Peterborough PE8 6QG
(01780 782575; www.prebendal-manor.co.uk). Open
24th March to Sept, Wed, Sun and Bank Holiday
Mons, 1 – 5pm

Reconstructions of different kinds of medieval
garden – a scented, grass-seated herber, a
vegetable patch protected by ancient walls, a
vineyard, a nut walk and two fishponds – are a
perfect accompaniment to the early-13th-
century house and its old tithe barn.

NORTHUMBERLAND

For further information about how to use the *Guide*
and for an explanation of the symbols, see pages vi–viii.
Specific dates and times are those given to us by garden owners for 2008.
For 2009 dates, check with the individual properties.
For opening dates under the National Gardens Scheme,
readers should consult *The Yellow Book* or www.ngs.org.uk.
Maps are to be found at the end of the *Guide*.

The Alnwick Garden

Denwick Lane, Alnwick NE66 1YU.
Tel: (01665) 511350
www.alnwickgarden.com

35m N of Newcastle upon Tyne. Take A1
and turn W at Alnwick.

The Alnwick Garden open all year, daily
except 25th Dec, 10am – 7pm (or dusk if
earlier)

Entrance: £8, OAPs and students £7.50,
accompanied children (under 16) free
(2007 prices)

THE ALNWICK GARDEN ★

(Historic Park and Garden Grade I)

In 2001 the first stage of an ambitious new garden was completed within a walled garden which had been derelict since the 1950s. The new contemporary garden is the vision of the present Duchess of Northumberland. A grand cascade designed by the Wirtz father and sons team from Belgium is the spine of the garden. Enclosed by an arched hornbeam tunnel with clipped openings along its length, it sends water tumbling down a series of 27 weirs; the pattern of the fountains changes every half hour. The path then leads up through trees to a formal ornamental garden, reached through three interlinked stone arches. This walled enclosure contains 16,500 European plants, the largest collection in Britain. Pergolas and arbours are covered in ramblers and vines, and rills lead to secret enclosed gardens with yew hedges. To the right of the entrance is a pretty rose garden.

The Alnwick Garden

Four equally grandiose projects have also been completed: one of the largest treehouses in the world – the size of two Olympic swimming pools – containing a restaurant, rope bridges and walkways in the sky; a poison garden featuring some of the world's deadliest plants; a bamboo labyrinth by Adrian Fisher; and the Serpent Garden, where masterly William Pye water sculptures rise above a sinuous holly hedge. A new pavilion and a visitor centre are the latest additions. The pavilion terrace looks south over the Grand Cascade and is linked to the rest of the garden by east and west terraces planted with specimen trees and topiary.

BELSAY HALL CASTLE AND GARDENS ★★
(Historic Garden Grade I)

The 30-acre gardens are the creation of two men who owned Belsay in succession from 1795 to 1933. Sir Charles Monck built the severe neo-classical hall with formal terraces leading through woods to a 'garden' inside the quarry which provided the building with its stone. Sir Arthur, his grandson, took over in 1867, adding Victorian features. Both were discerning plantsmen. The result is an exceptionally well-cared-for collection of rare, mature and exotic specimens in a fascinating sequence; the lily and snowdrop collections are also important. The terrace looks across to massed June rhododendrons. Other areas (flower garden, magnolia terrace, winter garden) lead to woods, a wild meadow and the quarry garden itself. This was carefully contrived, dominated by massive hewn slabs silvered by lichen and stocked to achieve a wild romantic effect. The sheltered microclimate has resulted in the luxuriant growth of some remarkable and exotic trees and shrubs, dramatically beautiful in the light and shade of the sandstone gorge. The path from the eighteenth-century hall leads through formal gardens to the quarry garden and thence to the fourteenth-century castle, a distance of about half a mile, all on fairly level ground. The winter garden, with its heathers, also has rhododendrons and a 28-metre-high Douglas fir planted in 1839. An unexpected pleasure is the croquet lawn, which is in regular use. The one-and-a-half-mile Crag Wood walk is a stepped, serpentine path which passes by the lake and through the hanging woods opposite the hall to the south.

English Heritage

Belsay, Newcastle-upon-Tyne NE20 0DX. Tel: (01661) 881636; www.english-heritage.org.uk

14m NW of Newcastle on A696

Hall and castle open

Gardens open 21st March to Oct, daily, 10am – 5pm (closes 4pm Oct); Nov to March 2009, Thurs – Mon, 10am – 4pm. Closed 24th to 26th Dec, 1st Jan

Entrance: £6.50, OAPs £4.90, children £3.90, family £16.30

Other information: Refreshments Easter to Oct only. Wheelchairs available for loan

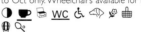

BIDE-A-WEE COTTAGE ★
One of the most enchanting and richly planted gardens in the North-East. Combining formal, informal and wild features, it occupies a long-abandoned stone quarry and some of the higher surrounding land – 2.5 acres in all. The varied topography, soil and climate allow for a diversity of plants to be grown, from marsh-loving to drought-tolerant species. The beauty of the natural rock faces has been

Mark Robson

Stanton, Netherwitton, Morpeth NE65 8PR. Tel: (01670) 772238; www.bide-a-wee.co.uk

7m NW of Morpeth, 3m SW of Longhorsley, off A697 Morpeth – Coldstream road towards Stanton

Bide-a-wee Cottage

Open 19th April to 30th Aug, Wed and Sat, 1.30 – 5pm. Parties of 20 or more by appt at other times

Entrance: £2.50

exploited to the maximum and enriched by truly sympathetic planting. More quarry wall has been exposed with new planting and another seat from which to view the garden. As well as being a highly refined plantsman, the owner is also a splendid mason whose stonework has done much to embellish the garden, and a shady corner has a timber summerhouse with an adjacent planting of arisaemas. A National Collection of centaureas is held here. Many of the plants are well labelled, and there is an excellent plant sales area with unusual species (catalogue available).

Sir Humphry Wakefield, Bt

Chillingham NE66 5NJ.
Tel: (01668) 215359/215390;
www.chillingham-castle.com

12m NW of Alnwick between A1 (signposted), A697, B6346 and B6348

Castle open as garden, but from 1pm

Gardens open May to Sept, Sun – Fri, 12 noon – 5pm, and by appt

Entrance: £6.75, OAPs £5.50, children (5–16) £3, under 5 £1

Other information: Self-catering accommodation available

CHILLINGHAM CASTLE
(Historic Park and Garden Grade II)

Since the 1200s this has been and continues to be the family home of the Earls Grey and their kin. The present owner has restored the ancient castle and garden along with the grounds, landscaped in 1828 by Wyatville (of Windsor Castle and Royal Lodge fame). The Elizabethan-style walled garden has been virtually excavated to rediscover its intricate pattern of clipped box and yew (enlivened by scarlet tropaeolum), with rose beds, fountains, a central avenue and a spectacular herbaceous border running the whole length. Outside are lawns and a rock garden, delightful woodland and lakeside walks through drifts of snowdrops, spring displays of daffodils, bluebells and, later, rhododendrons. The medieval castle provides a spectacular backdrop.

CRAGSIDE HOUSE
(Historic Garden Grade I)

Lord Armstrong, one of the greatest of Victorian engineers, clothed this hillside above the Coquet Valley with millions of trees and shrubs as the setting for a house designed by R. Norman Shaw that was then the wonder of the world. The rock gardens below the house are planted with an impressive display of heathers, shrubs, alpines and dwarf rhododendrons, spectacular in spring. The path descends sharply into the Debdon valley, crosses the river by a rustic bridge (magnificent views of the elegant iron bridge soaring above) and climbs through majestic conifers to the 1864 clock tower overlooking the high-Victorian formal garden set on three terraces with a quatrefoil pool as its centrepiece. The middle terrace contains the imposing orchard house with rotating fruit pots of sixteen types of fruit, to one side of which is a bed planted with small foliage plants in formal patterns typical of the 1870s. Carpet bedding is taken literally at Cragside: the two beds are planted with a different design each year, often inspired by designs in the house. In the formal beds some 6000 tulips are planted in autumn for spring colour. Between the middle and lower terraces is the dahlia walk, filled annually with 650–700 mixed cultivars and at its best in September and October. On the lower Italian terrace a loggia made of bold, pierced cast-iron is a remnant of the extensive range of glass structures once found here. The walk back through the valley impresses on the visitor the contrasting forces of wild romanticism and industrial technology which influenced this estate in equal measure. Rare North American coniferous species, given to the Trust by the Royal Botanic Gardens in Edinburgh, have been planted on the estate. In all, 1000 acres.

The National Trust

Rothbury, Morpeth NE65 7PX.
Tel: (01669) 620333;
www.nationaltrust.org.uk

13m SW of Alnwick off A697 between B6341 and B6344

House open as garden, but 1 – 5pm (closes 4.30pm Oct)

Gardens and estate open 15th March to 2nd Nov, Tues – Sun and Bank Holiday Mons, 10.30am – 7pm or dusk if earlier (last admission 5pm)

Entrance: £7.70, children (5– 17) £7.30, family £8.80 (reduced rates in winter) (house, gardens and estate £12.10, children £6.10, family £29.20)

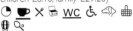

THE GARDEN COTTAGE

Protected by a long south-facing wall, the present owners have created a 1.5-acre garden of great artistry and imagination. The centrepiece is a large bed modelled on a dry gravelled river course and surrounded by a terrace with beds built up to suggest river banks, creating the impression of a sunken garden. A recent addition is the Contemplation Garden with low maintenance, naturalistic plantings. Everywhere there is an exuberance of colours, both warm and cool, and an inspiring range of planting variations, with new and unusual plants regularly introduced. Structural planting is well conceived – a beech arch, buttressed by a pair of cone-shaped yews, finds an echo in a single beech near the southern boundary – and winter interest is sustained by the coloured stems of cornus and willow. Abstract and animal sculptures enliven the main garden, where there are also secluded areas with seats for relaxation. North of the protective wall a large meadow garden is maturing.

Heather and John Russell

Bolam Hall, Bolam, Morpeth NE61 3UA.
Tel: (01661) 881660

15m NW of Newcastle. Turn off A696 after turn to Belsay Hall, follow sign to Bolam – telephone in advance for directions

Open for NGS and charity, and by appt

Entrance: £3

Other information: Possible for wheelchairs but gravel paths.

Refreshments for parties by arrangement

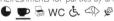

Herterton
House

HERTERTON HOUSE ★

The present owners took over the land and near-derelict Elizabethan building, with commanding views over picturesque upland Northumberland, in 1976. With vision and skill they have divided their one-acre plot into four distinct areas. In front is a formal winter garden; alongside, a cloistered 'monastic' knot garden of mainly medicinal, occult and dye-producing herbs; and to the rear, their most impressive achievement, a flower garden with perceptively mingled hardy flowers chosen with an artist's eye. This part of the garden contains some impressive topiary (spirals, columns and balls), which is altogether appropriate to this formal setting in front of a period house. Many unusual varieties of traditional plants (including species from the wild) flourish within the newly built sheltering walls. The fourth area, the Fancy Garden, has a parterre and a gazebo raised on a terrace. The views from the gazebo contrast well: to the north over a large field of cattle and to the south over this new garden and beyond to the formal garden with its flowers and topiary. A visit to the nursery will not go amiss.

HOWICK HALL ★
(Historic Garden Grade II)

There have been Greys at Howick since 1319, and the church and graveyard within the 75 acres of park and gardens are filled with their tombs and memorials, including that of the 2nd Earl, the great reforming Prime Minister. Surrounding the imposing Georgian house reconfigured by George Wyatt in 1809 and Sir Herbert Baker in 1928 are gardens created largely between 1920 and 2001. The present generation has continued the tradition – essentially that of plantsmanship and dendrology on a grand scale executed with appealing informality (the excellent guide book is likewise written with scholarship lightly worn). It is worth visiting at every season. Drifts of snowdrops are followed by a spectacular display of old daffodil varieties, with fritillaries to follow and tulips mingling with wild flowers in a 'Botticelli' meadow. The borders around the hall then burst into life, and the woodland garden (Silverwood) flowers with a rich variety of rhododendrons, camellias and magnolias, including two magnificent *M. campbellii*, all underplanted with drifts of shade-lovers. The bog garden surrounding a pond has an interesting range of late-summer-flowering plants grown from seed collected from the wild. Woodland walks to the west and east take in an arboretum planted with over 10,500 trees and shrubs.

Open Mid-Feb to March, Wed, Sat and Sun, 12 noon – 4pm; April to Oct, daily, 12 noon – 5pm

Entrance: £5, concessions £4, children under 16 free (reduced rates in winter)

LOUGHBROW HOUSE

The nine-acre garden here is expansive and a source of inspiration for both plant lovers and those who enjoy original design ideas. The lawns are generous, the planting of shrubs and roses bountiful. On the terrace is an interesting canal. The two deep herbaceous borders show the owner's colour concepts to great advantage, and beyond is a woodland garden. There is also a kitchen garden. The small lake from which the house derives its name ('lake on the brow of the hill') has been re-created, the bog garden extended, and an arboretum developed around the lake.

Mrs Kenneth Clark

Hexham NE46 1RS.
Tel: (01434) 603351

20m E of Newcastle, 1m S of Hexham. Take B6306 off Whitley Chapel road; at fork is brick lodge and long drive to house

Open May to July, Wed, 12 noon – 3pm; 5th Aug, 2 – 5pm, and by appt

Entrance: £3, children free

 WC B&B

NUNWICK ★
(Historic Garden Grade II)

This is one of the most interesting gardens in a county full of remarkable ones. The beautiful 1760 house (not open) looks out over lawns and parkland filled with fine and well-cared-for trees. Walking down to the gardens, it is clear that the design combines a clever sense of colour and shape with an interest in unusual plants. The herbaceous borders are cut back from their sheltering wall to ease maintenance, while beech hedges and shrub roses provide shelter on the orchard side. In the large and excellently maintained Victorian walled kitchen garden, Mrs Allgood experiments with varieties of vegetables, and there are good flowers, too, along the walks. Behind one wall is a small and elegant orangery containing a camellia over 100 years old. The other fascinating feature is the woodland path to the bog garden (en route note the stone wellhead), where the visitor first becomes aware of a profusion of hostas. The latter become evident again after crossing the recently built stone bridge over the burn and reaching the eighteenth-century Gothick kennels. Its four rooms, now open to the sky, house a spectacular collection of hostas, and the walls are planted with purple erinus, ivies of many kinds, toadflax and ferns. Trees and plants are well labelled. Back

Mrs L.G. Allgood

Simonburn, Hexham NE48 3AF.

8m NW of Hexham on B6320

Open 15th June, and for parties by appt in writing

Entrance: £3

Other information:
Teas on open day only

beside the house is a large collection of stone farm troughs with alpines, and an attractive large fountain. It is difficult to do justice in words to the charm of this garden.

WALLINGTON ★
(Historic Garden Grade II*)

The National Trust

Cambo, Morpeth NE61 4AR. Tel: (01670) 773600; www.nationaltrust.org.uk

20m NW of Newcastle off A696 (signed on B6342)

House open 15th March – 2nd Nov, 1 – 5.30pm (closes 4.30pm Oct and Nov)

Walled garden open April to Oct, daily, 10am – 7pm or dusk if earlier; Nov to March, daily, 10am – 4pm. Grounds open all year, daily, during daylight hours

Entrance: £5.80, children £2.90, family ticket £14.50 (house and garden £8.40, children £4.20, family £21)

Other information: Self-drive scooters and guided tours available

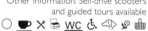

The handsome eighteenth-century house is set in a 65-acre landscape of lawns, terraces (fine views) and flower beds – serene and quintessentially English – but it is the walled garden, some distance away across the entry road via an attractive woodland walk, which has the most appeal. A rill runs from the pond to narrow lawns fringed with beds on two levels, and climbers cluster in prodigal numbers on the lovely old walls. (Alas, two of the elegant statues that graced the balustrade were stolen and the rest have been removed for safe-keeping.) The sloping site reveals the layout and invites exploration of the harmonious and generously filled herbaceous border. There is a garden house designed in Tuscan style by Daniel Garrett; the Victorian peach house is now restored, and the spectacular Edwardian conservatory is home to many treasures, with a rich tapestry of colour at every turn. Outside, the walks step down from a classical fountain past beds re-designed by Lady Trevelyan in the 1930s, including notable heathers and many herbaceous perennials. Trees planted by the Duke of Atholl in 1738 include a great larch, the survivor of three, by the China Pond.

Wallington

OTHER RECOMMENDED GARDENS

ASHFIELD

Barry and Rona McWilliam, Hebron, Morpeth NE61 3LA (01670 515616). Open for NGS, and by appt

This 5-acre garden, owned by a keen plantsman, is filled with unusual plants, many of them grown from seed collected abroad, all skilfully disposed within a variety of settings: scree beds planted with alpines, mature woodland trees sheltering bulbs, shade-lovers and small trees, colourful herbaceous borders, a small pinetum, and much more.

CHIPCHASE CASTLE

Mrs P. Torday, Wark NE48 3NT (01434 230203).
Open mid-April to July, Thurs – Sun and Bank Holiday
Mons, 10am – 5pm

The 18th-century walled garden with its
immaculate beds of vegetables and herbaceous
borders has been redesigned, together with the
fine borders in the formal terraced garden
beneath the castle walls. Colourful plantings in
the pond garden and beside the lake give a long
season of interest. 5 acres, plus a good 1.5-acre
nursery in the adjoining walled garden.

THE GARDEN STATION

Langley, Hexham NE47 5LA (01434 684391;
www.thegardenstation.co.uk). Open May to Aug,
Tues – Sun and Bank Holiday Mons, 10am – 5pm, and
for small parties Mon – Fri by appt

The unusual and attractive woodland garden,
approximately 250 metres long, is framed by
two Victorian railway bridges and overlooked by
a charming Victorian wooden station. There is
also a woodland walk. Many garden, art, and
craft courses are held here.

JESMOND DENE

Jesmond, Newcastle upon Tyne NE7 7BQ (0191 281
0973; www.newcastle.gov.uk). Open all year, daily,
during daylight hours

Presented to the city in 1883 by Lord
Armstrong, the famous engineer, and only a mile
from the city centre, this steep-sided, thickly
wooded dene provides walks in an entirely
natural setting, complete with a waterfall, a
ruined mill and some fine old buildings. 80
acres. (Listed Grade II)

LINDISFARNE

Holy Island, Berwick-upon-Tweed TD15 2SH
(01289 389244; www.nationaltrust.org.uk). Castle open
15th March to 2nd Nov, Tues to Sun and Bank Holiday
Mons. Garden open all year, daily (crossing times for
causeway vary according to tides – telephone for
details). NT

An essential visit for admirers of Gertrude Jekyll
– the re-creation of the walled garden just 30
metres square that she designed for the
founder and owner of *Country Life* in 1911 on a
lonely hillside north of the castle, making a
selection of her favourite plants and setting
them out in gradations of colour within paving
designed by Lutyens. (Listed Grade II)

MINDRUM

The Hon. P. J. Fairfax, Cornhill-on-Tweed TD12 4QN
(01890 850246). Open for NGS, and by appt

The steeply sloping 3-acre garden, 90 metres
above sea level, has wonderful views as far as
the Scottish Borders. Bowmont Water plays an
leading and dramatic role, its rocky banks richly
planted with perennials and flowering shrubs; a
walled garden and rose garden add their
colourful blooms in season.

NORTHUMBERLAND COLLEGE AT KIRKLEY HALL

Ponteland NE20 0AQ (01670 841200). Open April to
Sept, daily, 10am – 3pm

The 10-acre grounds, with their long
herbaceous border, succession of beds, sunken
garden and 3-acre Victorian walled garden, have
long been a valued northern showcase, and it is
welcome news that they are being restored
and revitalised. A National Collection of
beeches is here.

SEATON DELAVAL HALL

Lord Hastings, Seaton Sluice, Whitley Bay NE26 4QR
(0191 237 1493/0786). Open May, Bank Holiday
Mons; then June to Sept, Wed, Sun and Bank Holiday
Mon; all 2 – 6pm

Although the original grounds of Vanbrugh's
architectural masterpiece have been swept
away, the box-hedged rose garden is a
venerable survival, and the garden at the back
of the west wing compensates with a
spectacular parterre by Jim Russell. An attractive
shrubbery, herbaceous borders and a laburnum
walk have been established on the south side.
(Listed Grade II*)

NOTTINGHAMSHIRE

For further information about how to use the *Guide*
and for an explanation of the symbols, see pages vi–viii.
Specific dates and times are those given to us by garden owners for 2008.
For 2009 dates, check with the individual properties.
For opening dates under the National Gardens Scheme,
readers should consult *The Yellow Book* or www.ngs.org.uk.
Maps are to be found at the end of the *Guide*.

The National Trust

Clumber Estate Office, Clumber Park,
Worksop S80 3AZ.
Tel: (01909) 476592;
www.nationaltrust.org.uk

4.5m SE of Worksop off A1 and A57,
11m from M1 junction 30

Open all year, daily during daylight hours,
except 16th Aug (concert day),
and 25th Dec. Walled kitchen garden
open 21st to 28th March, 11am – 4pm;
29th March to 28th Sept, daily,
10am – 5pm (closes 6pm Sat and Sun);
Oct, Sat and Sun, 11am – 4pm

Entrance to walled garden: £2.50, children
free. Vehicle charge to park £4.80

Other information: Wheelchairs available
for adults and children. Bicycles for hire.
Chapel open (telephone for details)

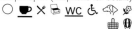

CLUMBER PARK

(Historic Park and Garden Grade I)

The 3800-acre park was enclosed from Sherwood Forest in the eighteenth century, and the garden was largely the creation of the 9th Earl of Lincoln (subsequently the 2nd Duke of Newcastle) in the second half of the eighteenth century. He landscaped the park, laid out the pleasure ground, serpentine walks and shrubberies, and commissioned two temples and a bridge for the lake, which remain today. The Atlantic cedars and sweet chestnut trees in the pleasure ground are of breath-taking size. In 1824 William Sawrey Gilpin created the Italianate terrace to the south of the house, island beds and picturesque walks in the pleasure ground. The two-mile-long lime avenue of 1838 and the Lincoln Terrace of 1845 were completed by other hands. From the nineteenth century also are Charles Barry's stable block and clock tower and G.F. Bodley's ornate Gothic chapel built in the pleasure garden. Since the demolition of the great house in 1938 (Barry's being the last in the line), the chapel has become the focus of the garden. The vinery and palm house have been restocked and the extensive glasshouses (138 metres) are the best and longest in the Trust's properties. The four-acre walled kitchen garden contains a 110-metre-long double herbaceous border, now replanted to an historic colour gradation, as well as cut-flower, fruit and vegetable and herb borders, a collection of old varieties of apple trees and a working Victorian apiary. The lower kitchen garden has now been taken in hand by the Trust, and is open as a 'work-in-progress'.

The Hon. Mrs Chaworth Musters

Underwood NG16 5FJ.
Tel: (01773) 810230;
www.snowdrops.co.uk

10m NW of Nottingham, 0.5m from M1
junction 27. Take A608 signed to Heanor
and Derby. Garden is on left

FELLEY PRIORY ★

The beautiful house blends into the slope as if it had become part of the land in the four centuries it has been there. The bland lawns and drive at the front do not prepare plant lovers for the sweetshop in the garden behind the house, which is full of rare delights, some old-fashioned and many reputedly tender but thriving here; helpfully, most are labelled. Plants for sale in the large nursery are mainly grown in the garden itself.

Felley
Priory

Grass banks step down to a large pond in the dip at the bottom; all around are fields, with woods on the other side of the valley. The site, on clay with a tendency to wet, is 600 feet above sea level and open in feel, despite the original walls and interior dividing hedges planted to protect the house from the winds. It is difficult to believe that the 2.5-acre garden was only established after 1976 by the present owner. She has laid out colourful double herbaceous borders, their shape and structure beautifully planned, undulating down from the house through stone-stepped terraces and between yew hedges. A deep border shelters a Jargonelle pear reputedly over 400 years old, while a perfectly sited mulberry, 30 years old but looking much older, is spectacular in fruit. There are pergolas, knot gardens and tasteful topiary (swans and peacocks, nothing overdone), a shrubbery that is almost a small and youthful arboretum, and a rose garden also planted with lavender and agapanthus. Spring brings an astonishing display of snowdrops, followed by hellebores and daffodils massed under orchard trees. Old-fashioned and unusual plants are for sale in the adjoining nursery.

Garden and nursery open all year, Tues, Wed, Fri, 9am – 12.30pm (March to Oct, 2nd and 4th Weds in month, 9am – 4pm, 3rd Sun in month, 11am – 4pm). Snowdrop Sun 10th Feb, 11am – 4pm. Also open for NGS, and for parties by appt at other times

Entrance: £3, OAPs £2.50, children free.

Other information: NCCPG plant fairs 1st June, 5th Oct, 12 noon – 4pm

HODSOCK PRIORY ★

Beyond the imposing red-brick Tudor gatehouse which is the entrance to Hodsock Priory (not open) stretches one of the most beautiful winter gardens in England. Snowdrops, magenta cyclamen and golden aconites are everywhere – spreading through the borders of the five-acre garden, in the grass and under the trees, and there is an additional walk in the snowdrop wood from which to enjoy the astonishing

Sir Andrew and Lady Buchanan

Blyth, Worksop S81 0TY.
Tel: (01909) 591204;
www.snowdrops.co.uk

5m NE of Worksop, 2m W of A1 at Blyth off B6045

Open 1st Feb to 2nd March, daily, 10am – 4pm

Entrance: £4.50, children (6–16) £1

Other information: Best displays depend on weather (telephone before travelling). Parties and coaches must prebook.

Mr and Mrs R. Brackenbury

Nottingham NG12 2LD.
Tel: (0115) 933 2371;
www.holmepierreponthall.com

5m SE of Nottingham off A52/A6011. Continue past National Water Sports Centre for 1.5m

House open as garden

Garden open 4th Feb to 19th March, Mon – Wed; 10th Feb, 9th March, 13th April; all, 2 – 5pm. Also open for NGS and for parties mid-week by appt

Entrance: £2 (house and garden £5, children £1.50)

Mr and Mrs R. J. Gregory

Elston Lane, East Stoke, Newark NG23 5QJ. Tel: (01636) 525460

5m SW of Newark. Take A46, turn left into Elston Lane (signed to Elston); house is first on right

Open for NGS, and April to Sept by appt

Entrance: £2, accompanied children free

Other information: Parking 100 metres past house on right

Nottingham City Council

Newstead Abbey Park, Nottingham NG15 8NA.
Tel: (01623) 455900;
www.newsteadabbey.org.uk

11m N of Nottingham on A60

display. Coloured stems of cornus and willow, and the brilliant white trunks of *Betula jacquemontii* reflect in the lake. There are two ferneries and banks of hellebores (almost 1000 plants in one), and the hedges of sarcococca and avenues of winter honeysuckle add fragrance to the whole. The working Victorian apiary is a great attraction, and the Victorian fan garden was re-created in 2002. Among the many old and interesting trees are *Cornus mas*, *Catalpa bignonioides*, swamp cypress, tulip trees, acers and a paulownia.

HOLME PIERREPONT HALL
(Historic Garden Grade II)

Described as 'Nottingham's best-kept secret', the garden surrounding the beautiful red-brick medieval manor house come indeed as a lovely surprise. Three outstanding features make a visit worthwhile. In the courtyard garden, surrounded by castellated walls, is a box parterre laid out in 1875 alongside modern herbaceous borders, and in spring an old *Viburnum carlesii* fills the air with scent and camellias flower in profusion. On Tulip Sunday – a special mid-April event – pass through the courtyard to the fields, where native *Tulipa sylvestris* flower wild *en masse* in a site deemed by Anna Pavord one of the best in the country. Finally, beyond the house lies the main garden, laid out by the present owners in 1973 with now-sizeable yews, stunning white-flowering cherries and continually developing winter borders. In this peaceful and welcoming place, the Jacob's sheep, with sprightly lambs in season, are friendly lawnmowers. 30 acres of garden and park.

MILL HILL HOUSE

A 0.5-acre cottage garden generously filled with a wide variety of plants provides year-round interest and tranquillity. The garden is well screened from the road and is a haven for birds, bees and butterflies. Trees now stand on the site of the former nursery, with mown paths winding among them, and in the sheltered corner once occupied by the polytunnel a path circles around a cobbled area, with a seat from which to enjoy the collection of herbaceous and climbing plants not usually found in this cold county: euryops, melianthus, berberidopsis, and a stunning *Euphorbia characias* 'Silver Swan'. The garden also holds a National Collection of berberis.

NEWSTEAD ABBEY ★
(Historic Garden Grade II*)

Water predominates in the estate which the poet Byron inherited and where he lived from 1808 to 1814. In most of the extensive and immaculate 33-acre gardens there is much of interest. The Japanese gardens are justly famous and the rock and fern gardens worth visiting. The tropical garden and the monks' stewpond are visually uninteresting but they are of laudable age. It is a pity that the large walled kitchen garden is now a rose garden – rose gardens, however pretty, are commonplace, but large kitchen gardens to the great houses are now rare. The old rose and carnation garden, until recently the iris garden, has been replanted as a herb garden. The waterfalls, wildfowl, passageways, grottoes and bridges provide plenty of fun for children, and there is also an imaginatively equipped play area with bark mulch for safety.

House with Byron memorabilia open April to Sept, 12 noon – 5pm

Open all year, daily except 30th Nov and 25th Dec, 9am – 6pm (closes at dusk in winter)

Entrance: £3, children £1.50 (house and grounds £6, children £2.50) (2007 prices)

OTHER RECOMMENDED GARDENS

'Pure Land' Japanese Garden

set among shrubs and cloud-pruned trees, waterfalls and streams; a 'landscape' created with gems and semi-precious stones glitters in the sunlight. May is a good time to visit.

RUFFORD ABBEY COUNTRY PARK

Ollerton, Newark NG22 9DF (01623 822944; www.nottinghamshire.gov.uk/ruffordcp). Open all year, daily except 25th Dec, 9am – 5pm

Everything that might be expected of an important country park: a ruined abbey, a lake and majestic trees, formal gardens, a rose garden and a maturing arboretum. Different areas are set aside for wildlife and ball games. 150 acres. (Listed Grade II)

WOLLATON PARK

Nottingham NG8 2AE (0115 915 3900); www.wollatonhall.org.uk. Open all year, daily, 11am – 5pm (closes 4pm Oct to March)

The grandiose 500-acre setting for Robert Smythson's astonishing centrepiece serves now as a great green oasis in the heart of the city. Bedding schemes provide vibrant spring and summer colour, and from the formal gardens at the top of the hill views stretch out, of huge cedars, holm oaks, lime avenues and the deer in the park. (Listed Grade I)

'PURE LAND' JAPANESE GARDEN

Buddha Maitreya, North Clifton, Nr Newark NG23 7AT (01777 228567). Open end-March to end-Oct, daily except Mon (but open Bank Holiday Mons), 10.30am – 5.30pm

The 1.5-acre garden laid out in traditional Japanese style is a place of calm and contemplation. Paths, steps and stepping stones lead among ornamental features and sculpture

OXFORDSHIRE

For further information about how to use the *Guide*
and for an explanation of the symbols, see pages vi–viii.
Specific dates and times are those given to us by garden owners for 2008.
For 2009 dates, check with the individual properties.
For opening dates under the National Gardens Scheme,
readers should consult *The Yellow Book* or www.ngs.org.uk.
Maps are to be found at the end of the *Guide*.

APPLETON MANOR

Appleton OX13 5PP.
Tel: (01865) 861614

In Appleton, 6m W of Oxford on A420;
drive is on right past The Plough pub
next to church

Open for parties by appt

Entrance: donation to charity

 &

Traces of antiquity linger here both in the characterful and irregular house and in the three-sided remains of a moat and some magnificent trees. In 2000 the present owners called Arne Maynard to the rescue of the then-dilapidated 10 acres. He placed a gravel and box enclosure beneath the front facade, shielded by a screen of pleached crab apples and furnished now with lavenders, *Verbena bonariensis* and self-seeded verbascums. To the rear he made a courtyard with more lavender and a large flat box table; a weeping willow presides over this sunny, butterfly-haunted spot. He joined the two with a luxuriant summer wall border, and down the slope towards the moat placed a tactile group of caterpillar-like box topiary shapes. Now Maynard's imprint on this sophisticated but informal family garden is being supplemented by those of

Appleton Manor

the design-minded owners and the talented head gardener, Thomas Unterdorfer. The wall separating the garden from the Norman church has been planted with a cloud hedge of yew, the beds in the wonderful vegetable garden are filled to bursting with many old varieties of fruit and vegetables, and plans are afoot for a woodland walk, a new orchard and more spiral hedging. It is worth many visits to see the future unfold.

ASTHALL MANOR ★
(Historic Garden Grade II)

The six-acre garden, set in the unspoilt Windrush valley with an early-seventeenth-century Cotswold stone manor house at its heart and a Norman church peering over the wall, is a beguiling mix of traditional and contemporary. The plants in the generous herbaceous borders around the house are country-garden favourites, while the paving stones in the broad courtyard are all but obliterated by tussocks of alchemilla and dianthus. On the steeply sloping bank facing the courtyard, however, you become aware of a gently subversive element at work. Two yew-edged squares flanked by twin box parterres filled with vibrant perennials slope downwards from way above head height; higher still are solid and substantial wedges of yew set in short mown rides. This inspired modern core is the creation of Julian and Isabel Bannerman. A large and long flat lawn is punctured at both ends by sextets of *Prunus* 'Taihaku', with mighty trees – a silver birch, a cut-leaved black walnut and two copper beeches – compelling the eye to the countryside beyond and leading to a delightfully unkempt area of wild woodland with two tree houses and a naturalistic pond. The biennial exhibition, 'on form 08 sculpture in stone', takes place from 8th June to 6th July – don't miss it.

Rosanna Taylor

Asthall, Nr Burford OX18 4HW.
Tel: (01993) 824319;
www.onformssculpture.co.uk

3m E of Burford off A40. At roundabout take turning to Minster Lovell; turn immediately left signed to Asthall and at bottom of hill, follow avenue of trees and look for car parking sign

Open 8th June to 6th July for sculpture exhibition, 12 noon – 6pm, and for NGS
◗

BLENHEIM PALACE ★★
(Historic Park and Garden Grade I)

Walking through Hawksmoor's triumphal arch, the visitor is greeted by one of the greatest contrived landscapes in Britain, entrusted by the 1st Duke of Marlborough to Vanbrugh, who enlisted the help of Bridgeman and Henry Wise, Queen Anne's master gardener and the last of the British formalists. Wise constructed a bastion-walled 'military' garden, laid out kitchen gardens, planted immense elm avenues and linked Vanbrugh's bridge to the sides of the valley. The gardens were ready when the Duke moved into the palace in 1719. Major alterations were made by the 4th, 5th and 9th Dukes, one of the earliest of which was the removal of Wise's formal and military gardens by 'Capability' Brown. After 1764; he also landscaped the park, installing the lake and cascade. Today the gardens include formal areas designed by Achille Duchêne in the early nineteenth century to replace those destroyed by Brown. He made formal gardens to the east and west, the

Blenheim Palace

Woodstock, Oxford OX20 1PP.
Tel: (01993) 811091;
www.blenheimpalace.com

8m NW of Oxford. At Woodstock on A44

House open as garden

Garden open 16th Feb to 14th Dec, daily (but closed Mons and Tues in Nov and Dec), 10.30am – 5.30pm (last admission 4.45pm). Park open all year, daily except 25th Dec, 9am – 6pm (closes at dusk in winter)

Entrance: Park and formal gardens only, £9.50, concession £7.50, child (5-16) £4.80, family £24.50 (peak prices)

Park: ○ 🍴 ♿ ⌂ 🏛 🍴 ♿

Gardens: ◑ ♿ ✕ <u>WC</u> ♿ 🏛 🍴 ♿

latter as two water terraces in the Versailles style. To the east of the palace is the elaborate Italian garden of patterned box and golden yew, interspersed with various seasonal plantings. To the south-west from the terraces lie the rose garden and arboretum. Beyond the vast south lawn is a grove of venerable cedars, laurel shrubberies and a box and yew exedra. A maze was planted in part of the kitchen garden in 1991, and the former garden centre has been redeveloped as a lavender and herb garden. The park extends over 2100 acres, and there are 100 acres of formal gardens.

Mrs D. Hodges

Well Lane, Alkerton, Banbury
OX15 6NL.
Tel: (01295) 670303/670590;
www.brookcottage.co.uk

6m NW of Banbury. From A422 turn W
signed to Alkerton. With small war
memorial on right, turn left into Well
Lane and right at fork

Open 24th March to Oct, Mon – Fri,
9am – 6pm, and by appt

Entrance: £5, OAPs £4, children free

Other information: Refreshments for
parties must be pre-booked.

BROOK COTTAGE ★

A four-acre garden of great originality and variety, created since 1964 in a west-facing valley as a series of interconnecting and intensively planted areas. It is the work of the plantswoman owner and her late husband and shows what can be achieved by those who 'Consult the Genius of the Place in all'. Once past the terrace below the house, slivers of paths force visitors into single file, making their emergence onto open lawn above the stream and lower pond all the more exciting. Here, the planting is bold and confident, grouped tellingly in individual clumps or in beds with skilful combinations of colour. In the bog garden a splendidly broad band of foliage plants contrasts with feathery or piercing flower spikes. The hanging garden of shrub roses is the most famous feature in its season, but for those who wish to see a

Brook Cottage

profusion of plants disposed in a masterly way, Brook Cottage is a living workshop of ideas at any time.

BROUGHTON CASTLE ★

(Historic Garden Grade II)

More of a house than a castle, with gardens that are unexpectedly domestic within the confines of the moat, Broughton sits in a beautiful flat-bottomed valley. In 1900 there were 14 gardeners, now just one maintains the overall splendour of its 60 acres. The most important changes were made after 1969 following a visit from Lanning Roper, who suggested opening up the views across the park. There are two magnificent borders, where great planting skill is evident in the serpentine flows of colour. The west-facing border, backed by the battlement wall, is based on blues and yellows, greys and whites, the other on reds, mauves and blues. On the south side is the walled 'ladies' garden' with box-edged, *fleurde-lys*-shaped beds holding floribunda roses. Another wonderful border rises up to the house wall. Everywhere is a profusion of old-fashioned roses and original planting. The castle is well worth visiting, not least for the views of the garden from the upper windows.

Lord Saye and Sele

Broughton, Banbury OX15 5EB.
Tel: (01295) 276070;
www.broughtoncastle.demon.co.uk

2.5m SW of Banbury on B4035

Castle open

Garden open 23rd and 24th March; May to 15th Sept, Wed, Sun and Bank Holiday Mons (plus Thurs in July and Aug); all 2 – 5pm. Also open by appt for parties

Entrance: £2.50 (house and garden £6.50, OAPs and students £5.50, children £2.50, family £15)

Other information: Teas on open days only. Refreshments for parties by arrangement

BROUGHTON GRANGE ESTATE ★★

This is a garden grand in both scale and vision. Parterres and topiary shapes anchor the front and rear facades of the Cotswold manor house into its immediate surroundings, while a generous double herbaceous border introduces a succession of gardens concealed further behind the house. First comes a shady woodland garden newly planted with ericaceous plants confined within black peat retaining walls; then a young grove of rare and rustling bamboos; most unexpected of all, a thumping great stumpery straddling the woodland path like a fortress gateway. After all these theatrical effects, the land opens out to light, space and height – a 50-acre arboretum set to double in size over the coming years. At its apex is a grass terrace with Mediterranean planting, from where the eye is led down two grand avenues of chestnut and lime to the river, where a wet garden is being established. Back within the garden proper, a spring walk passes a turreted tree house and ends in a series of high-hedged rooms sheltering tennis court, swimming pool and open-air jacuzzi, planted with perennials and grasses by Tom Stuart-Smith. He was also responsible for the exceptional walled garden created in 2001. It is screened on one side by Ptolemy Dean's striped, stepped and buttressed wall, and descends on its longest axis between a pleached lime *allée* and a beech tunnel. Stuart-Smith divided the vast sloping space into three broad terraces, with a greenhouse and viewing platform occupying the top level, a rill and water tank crossed by stepping stones the centre ground, and at the

Wykham Lane, Broughton OX15 5DS.

From Banbury take B4035 to Broughton. At Saye and Sele Arms turn left up Wykham Lane (one-way) and follow road for 0.5m out of village; entrance is on right

Open for NGS, and by appt (telephone 07701 098161)

Entrance: £6

Other information: Teas and plants on open days only

lowest point three *parterres de broderie* tracing in box the veins of a beech, an ash and an oak leaf. If the design is ingenious, the planting is masterly – a controlled explosion of colour, texture and height that wells down the slope in crests and troughs. It is worth visiting on both open days to see the garden in its very different spring and summer attire.

BUSCOT PARK ★
(Historic Park and Garden Grade II*)

Administered by Lord Faringdon on behalf of The National Trust

Faringdon SN7 8BU.
Tel: (01367) 240786;
www.buscotpark.com

On A417 between Lechlade and Faringdon

House open as garden (but closed Mon and Tues)

Garden open 21st March to Sept, Mon – Fri and Bank Holiday Mons; plus 22nd and 23rd March, 5th, 6th, 19th and 20th April, 3rd, 4th, 10th, 11th, 24th and 25th May, 14th, 15th, 28th, 29th June, 12th, 13th, 26th and 27th July, 9th, 10th, 23rd and 24th Aug, 13th, 14th, 27th and 28th Sept; all 2 – 6pm

Entrance: £5, children £2.50 (house and grounds £7.50, children £3.75)

Other information: Teas available when house open

The huge walled estate – 150 acres in total – is situated in the flatlands of the Thames, with a house built between 1780 and 1783 and a garden developed during the twentieth century. The water-garden-within-a-wood was created by Harold Peto in 1904; later, avenues linking lake to house were cut through, branching out from a goose-foot near the house, with fastigiate and weeping varieties of oak, beech and lime. The Egyptian avenue created by Lord Faringdon in 1969 is guarded by sphinxes and embellished with Coade-stone statues copied from an original from Hadrian's Villa. Two new gardens at *allée* intersections – the Swinging Garden and the Citrus Bowl – provide enclosed areas of great charm. The large walled kitchen garden was rearranged in the mid-1980s, and is now intersected by a pleached avenue of ostrya (hop hornbeam) and a Judas tree tunnel. Deep borders under the outside walls have unusual and skilled planting by Tim Rees, mixing old roses and climbing vegetables (gourds, marrows, beans, cucumbers) which lay themselves out over the rose bushes after their flowering is over. Walkways both outside and inside the kitchen garden lie between wide borders which use the exterior and interior walls and trellises as screens. In the latter the planting by the late Peter Coats and imaginative development by Lord Faringdon is exceptionally effective. The small garden at the elegant seventeenth-century *Buscot Old Parsonage*, also a Trust property, has different opening times.

CHASTLETON HOUSE
(Historic Garden Grade II*)

The National Trust

Chastleton GL56 0SU.
Tel: (01608) 674355;
www.nationaltrust.org.uk

6m NE of Stow-on-the-Wold off A436

Open 26th March to Nov, Wed – Sat, 1 – 5pm (closes 4pm Oct and Nov) (last admission 1 hour before closing). Ticket numbers restricted; visitors strongly advised to telephone in advance. Groups of 11 – 25 by prior appt only

Entrance: (house and garden) £7, children £3.50, family £17.50

The beguiling, somewhat gawky early seventeenth-century house was in a state of pleasing decay when it was in private hands, but the Trust has sensitively retained the atmosphere. The garden, which was at its peak in the early twentieth century and survived more or less intact until the 1960s, has been treated in the same spirit. The impressive topiary, probably a Victorian re-creation of a seventeenth-century design, still makes an emphatic statement; the rest provides a pleasant setting for the enchanted house. The rules of modern croquet are said to have been codified at Chastleton and one of the original croquet lawns has been restored. At *Chastleton Glebe* Prue Leith's garden is usually open one day a year for the NGS.

CLOCK HOUSE

Situated on a hillside with inspiring views over the Vale of the White Horse, this exuberant – and now somewhat overgrown – garden was created by Michael and Denny Wickham in the last forty years on the site of one of the most beautiful Caroline houses, Coleshill (tragically burned, then wilfully demolished in the 1950s). The ground-plan of the original house is planted out in box and lavender, to show the layout of walls and windows. The gravel 'rooms' are full of self-sown poppies in June and *Verbena bonariensis* in late July. The courtyard holds a collection of plants in pots, and roses and mixed plantings thrive in a sunny walled garden in the old laundry yard. The mixed herbaceous borders are filled with interesting and unusual plants. The lime avenue at the front of the house sweeps down to the views, and a pond and terrace are sheltered by tall shrubs. This is an original garden, designed by an artist, with a large collection of plants in imaginative settings.

Denny Wickham and Peter Fox

Coleshill, Swindon, Wiltshire SN6 7PT.
Tel: (01793) 762476

3.5m SW of Faringdon on B4019

Open by appt only

Entrance: £2, children free

COTSWOLD WILDLIFE PARK AND GARDEN ★

Varied and extensive grounds – 140 acres in all – surround the listed Victorian Gothic manor house. Head gardener Tim Miles and his team have achieved wonders here in the last few years. The tropical house, which has been completely refurbished and replanted, is outstandingly atmospheric with its spectacular plants and birds – the original Eden Project in miniature – and the exotic theme is carried through into the

John and Reggie Heyworth

Burford OX18 4JW.
Tel: (01993) 823006;
www.cotswoldwildlifepark.co.uk

Open all year, daily except 25th Dec; March to Sept, 10am – 6pm (last admission 4.30pm), Oct to Feb, 10am – 4.30pm (last admission 3.30pm)

Entrance: £10, OAPs and children (3–16) £7.50

Other information: Miniature train runs through part of park, April to Oct, usually 11.30pm – 4.30pm (£1 extra, OAPs and children 50p)

Cotswold Wildlife Park and Garden

exuberant walled garden. Here are hot colours and the largest collection of tender perennials in the country, together with immaculate traditional bedding in an effective combination of pink and silver shades, fruiting bananas and avocados, and a range of containers and hanging baskets with original and flamboyant displays. The planting schemes throughout complement and enhance the settings of the various animals and birds: don't miss the meerkats in their landscaped desert with its flowering cacti and succulents. The terrace beside the house, which has a formal pond and parterre, is in cool contrast, featuring blues and mauves and masses of white roses. Areas of prairie planting with grasses and bamboos continue to develop, and the parkland, home to many endangered animals, has fine specimen trees: Wellingtonias, giant redwoods, cedars and an immense oak six hundred years old. There are delights here for all ages, whether in buggies or wheelchairs.

GREYS COURT ★

(Historic Garden Grade II)

The National Trust

Rotherfield Greys, Henley-on-Thames RG9 4PG. Tel: (01491) 628529; www.nationaltrust.org.uk

W of Henley-on-Thames, E of B481. From town centre take A4130 towards Oxford, at Nettlebed mini-roundabout take B48. Signposted to left shortly after Highmoor

House closed in 2008

Gardens open 22nd March to 27th Sept, Tues – Sat and Bank Holiday Mons, 12 noon – 5pm

Entrance: £4.50, children £2.25, family £11.25

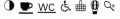

Six acres of beautiful and varied walled gardens are set against the ruins of a fourteenth-century fortified house. An ancient wisteria forms a canopy over one garden room, an ornamental kitchen garden is packed with unusual vegetables and a tamed wildflower meadow stretches out under the old apple orchard. Billowing herbaceous borders and fragrant shrub roses herald the summer season. The grass Archbishop's Maze, designed by Adrian Fisher, is interesting for its symbolism, and modern touches include decorative ironwork and statues. Seek out also the donkey wheel and the restored ice-house, and be sure to climb the thirteenth-century tower to view the whole garden from above.

THE HARCOURT ARBORETUM

(Historic Arboretum Grade I)

Oxford University Botanic Garden

Nuneham Courtenay, Oxford OX44 9PX. Tel: (01865) 343501; www.botanic-garden.ox.ac.uk

6m S of Oxford off A4074

Open Dec to March, Mon – Fri, 10am – 4.30pm (closed Christmas period); April to Nov, daily, 10am – 5pm (last admission 4.15pm)

Entrance: free, but £2 car parking charge

Other information: Guided tours available – telephone (01865) 286690 (Botanic Garden). No coaches

The village and church were demolished in the 1670s to make way for a classical landscape to be seen from the Georgian house (not open); Oliver Goldsmith's 1770 poem *The Deserted Village* is said to be based on that upheaval. Horace Walpole, in 1780, described the gardens designed by 'Capability' Brown and William Mason (the poet-gardener) as the most beautiful in the world. The garden was then full of flowers, not only along the walks, but also in carefully planted beds. The 85-acre site, one and a half miles from the house, is now owned by Oxford University Botanic Garden. It dates from 1835 when Lord Harcourt, who owned the Nuneham estate at the time, planted an eight-acre pinetum with the help of William Sawrey Gilpin. Many of those plantings – of such mighty trees as noble fir, Wellingtonia, Japanese and incense cedars – are now magnificent mature specimens underplanted with camellias, rhododendrons, bamboos, magnolias and a collection of acers. There is also a 10-acre bluebell wood and a 30-acre wildflower meadow. The pleasure of walking among these majestic and ancient trees almost cancels out the traffic noise and gigantic pylons that bedevil the site.

HOME FARM

With views over the village roof-tops of grazing sheep and nearby Claydon Wood, this peaceful garden has been cleverly designed to make the most of its 0.5 acre. It is a gem, with abundant flowering shrubs, herbaceous plants and bulbs, foliage and grasses achieving a natural effect full of interest and colour all year. In early summer deep purple abutilons beside the paler wisteria against the walls of the seventeenth-century house catch the eye, along with the rock garden and the brilliant cascade of helianthemums next to the terrace, where you can sit and enjoy it all. Potentillas creep between the steps, and pink perennial geraniums frame a stone seat in a shady far corner – a haven of refreshingly uncluttered informality.

Mr G. C. Royle
Balscote, Banbury OX15 6JP.
Tel: (01295) 738194
5m W of Banbury, 0.5m off A422
Open April to Sept by appt
Entrance: £3
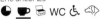

KINGSTON BAGPUIZE HOUSE

The beautiful mellow brick Baroque house, set in its compact park, was owned by Miss Marlie Raphael, an enthusiastic and much-travelled plant collector, from 1939 until her death in 1976. With the help of Sir Harold Hillier and other friends, she created a 10-acre garden planted with a mind-boggling variety of rare and unusual trees, shrubs and plants. The present owner, together with her late husband Francis, successfully uncovered and restored much of the original planting, complementing it with their own innovative ideas. Within the framework of mellow brick walls and hedges of yew, beech and laurel (and even of brachyglottis), there is an air of relaxed and luxuriant informality. An enormous mixed border 10 metres deep is packed with tall perennials covering a broad spectrum of harmonious colours. At every turn in the three-acre woodland garden are rare and interesting trees and shrubs, including several spectacular magnolias; beneath the jungle canopy are carpets of snowdrops and other bulbs, followed by drifts of geraniums, astrantias, campanulas, vincas, hellebores, lilies and other shade-loving perennials. In spring, Church Copse is a mass of naturalised snowdrops, native woodland bulbs and perennials. Along the edge of the Garden Park with its beech avenue, Wellingtonias and other specimen trees, the shrub border reveals yet more rarities. The terrace walk has a growing cistus collection and provides an excellent vantage point from which to enjoy a view of the house and different aspects of this informal and fascinating garden, where reminders of past glories survive alongside continued development.

Mrs Virginia Grant
Kingston Bagpuize, Abingdon OX13 5AX.
Tel: (01865) 820259;
www.kingstonbagpuizehouse.org.uk
5.5m W of Abingdon off A415. Follow signs to house along Rectory Lane
House and garden open 3rd, 10th, 17th and 24th Feb, 2nd, 16th, 23rd and 24th March, 6th and 20th April, 4th, 5th, 18th, 25th and 26th May, 1st, 2nd, 15th and 16th June, 6th, 7th, 20th and 21st July, 3rd, 4th, 17th, 18th, 24th and 25th Aug, 7th and 21st Sept. Telephone or consult website for further openings.
Also open for parties by appt all year. Guided tours available
Entrance: £3 (house and garden £5, OAPs £4.50, children (5–15) £2.50) (2007 prices)
Other information: Home-made teas. Meals available for parties by arrangement
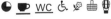

Lime Close

M. C. de Laubarede

35 Henleys Lane, Drayton OX14 4HU.

2m S of Abingdon off B4017; turn left into Henleys Lane, house is 200 yds on left

Open for NGS, and Feb to June and Oct for parties of 10 or more by written appt

Entrance: £3, children under 12 free

Other Information: Teas and plant sales on NGS open days only.

LIME CLOSE ★

The owner, a garden designer, has created an unexpected three-acre oasis here. Grassy walks and vistas, and mixed and shade borders distinguished by rare perennials (including *Clematis recta* 'Lime Close') and clever colour combinations, are all surrounded by mature trees and a wide variety of more recently planted rare trees and shrubs. Yew hedges and topiary are beautifully maintained, and privet hedges enclose the flower-filled potager with its Italian-Renaissance-style pergola and increasing iris collection, including 100 different bearded irises, spectacular in early summer. Beside the Elizabethan house formal areas include a parterre, a charming little herb garden designed by the late Rosemary Verey, a lawn and herbaceous borders. Peonies, roses, honeysuckles and clematis put in an appearance everywhere. The planting throughout is relaxed and informal, the colour effects enviably subtle and delicate. Masses of bulbs from late February onwards, and good autumn colour and berries. A beautifully planted cottage garden was made in 2004.

Dr and Mrs Dick Squires

2 Priory Road, Wantage OX12 9DD. Tel: (01235) 762785

Near Wantage Market Square opposite Vale and Downland Museum

Open April to Oct, Tues – Sat, 10.30am – 4.30pm, Sun, 2 – 5pm, and by appt

Entrance: By donation to charity (tickets available at museum)

OLD CHURCH HOUSE

An unusual and exciting one-acre town garden running down to Letcombe Brook. The present owner and his wife have transformed his childhood garden into a series of rooms leading away from the existing lawns and mature trees. There is a sunken water garden, a Mediterranean garden, a pergola garden and a wild garden, all filled with unusual plants and shrubs, with follies and highly imaginative building for architectural interest. Late May to June is the best season to visit, but it is an inspiration at any time to see what can be achieved in just a few years.

THE OLD RECTORY ★

At nearly 250 metres, and despite being prey to winds from the Downs, this outstanding four-acre garden has been created over thirty years, based on a good original structure of large trees and hedges, with magnificent views. The house is as pretty as any village old rectory could be, and sits at the heart of the garden looking out at the downs. Deep, parallel herbaceous borders are backed by yew hedges and within them are groupings of rare and interesting plants skilfully selected for colour and texture. Caroline Todhunter is both a talented garden maker and a marvellous plantswoman, with a masterly eye for unexpected combinations. The planting by the front of house is subtle and effective, and smaller areas have been laid out for sun- or shade-loving plants. Woodland contrasts with shrubs and lawns, and the fast-growing arboretum now contains over 150 trees. The swimming pool is surrounded by a large *Hydrangea sargentiana* and potted lilies, with mixed roses and clematis around the outside walls. There is a collection of old roses and small-flowered clematis, and wild flowers line the front lawn by the ha-ha. The tennis court has been turned into a shady and delightful *boule à drôme* garden, with four large beds, pretty wrought-iron gates and a gazebo; and the vegetable garden, presided over by an energetic scarecrow, is prodigiously neat and productive. Those who like John Betjeman's poetry will be interested to know that he lived here from 1945 to 1950 and can look for the ghost of Miss Joan Hunter Dunn in the shrubberies. A beautiful John Piper window in the church is in his memory.

Mr and Mrs Michael Todhunter

Farnborough, Wantage OX12 8NX.
Tel: (01488) 638298

4m SE of Wantage off B4494

Open for NGS, and by appt

Entrance: £3.50, children free

Other information: Teas nearby on charity open days and for parties

The Old Rectory

James and The Hon. Mrs Price

Lower Wardington, Banbury OX17 1RU.
Tel: (01295) 750232

5m NE of Banbury on A361 Daventry
Road (from M40 junction 11),
opposite church

Open by appt

Entrance: £6 for garden clubs (min. 20),
£10 for private visits

Other information: Workshop days with
photographer Clive Nichols – enquire for
dates and details

PETTIFERS ★★

The narrow, sophisticated garden in front of the seventeenth-century house does not prepare visitors for the beautifully planted garden and stunning landscape that lie behind. A rectangle of lawn is flanked by deep borders, resplendent in spring with tulips and alliums, followed later in the season by grasses and perennials. The lower terrace is quite different in character: a parterre with four yews and domes of *Phillyrea angustifolia* are the centrepiece of an area planted in summer with dahlias, agapanthus and roses. A flight of steps then descends to a 'Gustav Klimt' border, designed to peak in July; and at the bottom of the garden, and running its full width, is a richly colourful autumn border. Finally comes the tranquillity of a long green paddock with an avenue of *Malus transitoria* – a sea of camassias in early summer. Gina Price, whose travels in India have liberated her sense of colour, has a passion for plants – many of them rare or unusual – and an instinctive, unconventional ability to combine them. Discerning and knowledgeable plant lovers will find here a horticultural feast, with July, August and September perhaps the peak months to book a visit.

Charles Cottrell-Dormer

Nr Steeple Aston, Bicester OX25 4QX.
Tel: (01869) 347110;
www.rousham.org

11m N of Oxford, 2m S of Steeple Aston
off A4260 and B4030

House open for parties by appt

Garden open all year, daily,
10am – 4.30pm

Entrance: £4

Other information: Children under 15 not
admitted

ROUSHAM HOUSE ★★
(Historic Park and Garden Grade I)

Before William Kent's design of 1738 effectively froze the garden in time, it was already famous, described by Alexander Pope as 'the prettiest place for water-falls, jetts, ponds, inclosed with beautiful scenes of green and hanging wood, that ever I saw'. The enchantment of the setting and the use Kent made of it exercise a powerful impression on every visitor. Influenced perhaps by stage scenery, he set out to create a series of effects, choreographing splendid small buildings and follies, fine sculpture, water, seats and vantage points. The best way to view the garden is to follow these in the guidebook one by one in the order he intended. This was also one of the first places where the garden took in the whole estate, 'calling in' the surrounding countryside, to use Pope's phrase. Walled gardens next to the house, which pre-date Kent, are a major attraction in their own right, with a parterre, a rose garden, a fully tenanted dovecote and a productive vegetable garden; particularly attractive are the exuberant herbaceous borders spilling out over their box edging. 27 acres in all.

University of Oxford

Rose Lane, Oxford OX1 4AZ.
Tel: (01865) 286690;
www.botanic-garden.ox.ac.uk

In city centre opposite Magdalen
College near bridge

UNIVERSITY OF OXFORD
BOTANIC GARDEN ★★
(Historic Garden Grade I)

This is the oldest botanic garden in Britain, founded in 1621 for physicians' herbal requirements, surrounded by a Grade-I listed wall and entered through a splendid archway by Nicholas Stone. Nowhere else on earth, it is claimed, are so

University of Oxford
Botanic Garden

many different plants clustered in 4.5 acres: 6500 species in all, representing over 90 per cent of families of flowering plants. One yew survives from the 1650 plantings, and there is a series of family beds containing herbaceous and annual plants in labelled systematic groups. The old walls back beds with tender plants, including roses and clematis. To the left is a collection of glasshouses, modern ones replacing those built in 1670. A rock garden has been renovated, as has the water garden and late summer/autumn borders. A National Collection of euphorbias is held here. Recently, Nori and Sandra Pope were commissioned to plant autumn borders, and they have used dark and silver shrubs with spectacular autumn foliage at the back of the border.

Open all year, daily: 9am –6pm (closes 5pm March, April, Sept and Oct; closes 4.30pm Jan, Feb, Nov and Dec) Closed 25th Dec and 6th April

Entrance: £3, children in full-time education, accompanied by a family member free

Other information: Guided tours available. Plants for sale March to Oct. Professional photography by arrangement

WATERPERRY GARDENS ★

The eight acres of ornamental gardens date back to the 1930s when Miss Beatrix Havergal opened up a small horticultural school. The herbaceous nursery stock beds are in the fine and well-planted ornamental gardens extending over eight acres and form a living catalogue, with the plants grown in rows and labelled. Intermixed with this are major features of the old garden, lawns and a splendid herbaceous border – also beds containing collections of alpines, dwarf conifers and other shrubs, a rose garden, a formal knot garden, a water-lily canal and a clay bank planted with shade-lovers. A National Collection of saxifrages is held here. There is also a

Waterperry, Near Wheatley OX33 1JZ. Tel: (01844) 339254; www.waterperrygardens.co.uk

9m E of Oxford, 2.5m N of Wheatley off M40 junction 8 from London, or 8A from Birmingham. Signposted

Open all year, daily, 10am – 5.30pm (closes 5pm Nov to March) except Christmas period. 17th to 20th July open only to visitors to Art in Action (enquiries (020) 7381 3192)

Waterperry Gardens

Entrance: £4.95, concessions £3.95, children (10 – 16) £3.30 (under 10 free). Extra charge for Art in Action

Other information: Coach parties of 20 or more by appt only. Art and craft gallery. Teashop and museum closed 17th to 20th July

commercial garden centre occupying large areas of the walled garden. The greenhouses in the nursery are interesting; one in the old walled garden has an enormous citrus tree 100 years old. Five acres of commercial orchards yield thousands of bottles of Waterperry apple juice. A few miles east down the M40 is *Le Manoir aux Quat' Saisons*, in Church Road, Great Milton (off A329 Thame–Stadhampton road). The 12-acre garden surrounding Raymond Blanc's renowned hotel includes an impressive potager, a water garden, a Japanese garden, an orchard etc. It is open of course to patrons, and once a year for the NGS.

Mr and Mrs T.H. Gibson

Westwell, Burford OX18 4JT.

10m W of Witney, 2m SW of Burford off A40

Open for NGS, and by written appt for horticultural parties of 20 or more (£10 per person)

Entrance: £4

Other information: Teas available in village on open day

 WC

WESTWELL MANOR ★★

It is worth braving the inevitable crowds on the one day a year on which this seven-acre garden set within 30 acres of meadow, is open for the sheer variety and ingenuity which Mrs Gibson, a garden designer, has achieved here since 1979. Each of the 20 or so garden rooms behind the house and barn leads to another, some traditional, others – a charming water garden and a black-dyed *pièce d'eau* complete with boat – surprising and original. Notable too are twin rills lined by a pleached lime *allée*, an unusual lavender terrace, a sundial garden, a moonlight garden, an alder basket, a knot garden and splendid deep herbaceous borders in muted pastels contrasting with areas of meadow and long grass. There is also a vegetable garden, a nut walk and a Bunny Walk laid along a ley line. Mown paths lead to a mount constructed from surplus earth moved during the making of a ha-ha. The garden continues to develop with flair and unrestrained enthusiasm: a miniature paddy-field with rice from the Camargue, in all its varying shades of greeny-yellow, a grass amphitheatre in the old orchard, a late-summer border with umbelliferous plants, an orchard with carefully selected old fruit tree varieties, and a mown grass spiral. Mid-May to early July is the peak season of this exceptional garden.

WILCOTE HOUSE ★

Surrounding and complementing a fine sixteenth- to nineteenth-century Cotswold stone house, the large and peaceful garden is itself a period piece, with extensive beds of old-fashioned roses and mixed borders and a 40-metre laburnum walk with a vista to a stone gazebo. A leisurely stroll leads through the wild garden with its effective juxtaposition of over 200 species of unusual trees of different ages chosen for colour and interest at all seasons. Sweeps of lawn give glimpses of classic countryside beyond. An unusual feature is the large wild garden intersected by grass paths, planted since the early 1970s with nearly 200 varieties of trees chosen for both spring flowering and autumn colour.

The Hon. and Mrs Charles Cecil

Wilcote, Finstock, Chipping Norton OX7 3DY. Tel: (01993) 868606

4m N of Witney, 3m S of Charlbury E of B4022

Open Mon – Fri by appt; guided tours available

Entrance: £3, children free, parties negotiable

Other information: Conducted tours for private parties on weekdays by arrangement. Teas available by prior arrangement

 WC &

WOOLSTONE MILL HOUSE ★

When the present owners came here in 1976, the two-acre garden was little more than a field. Luckily both have gardening in their blood – Anthony Spink is the great-grandson of Thomas Mawson – and now within sheltering yew hedges delightful spaces are planted with a sure eye for colour, form and juxtaposition. Some of the plants used are traditional country garden favourites, others – tree ferns, swamp cypresses, the highly poisonous Indian pokeweed, *Davidia involucrata* and *Schizophragma hydrangeoides* – are more unusual. The main area behind the house is light and airy in feeling, with a wide terrace and box parterres opening out to a large circular lawn surrounded by generous curving herbaceous borders in a palette that changes colour season by season. These give way in their turn to open countryside; two amusing sheep with box bodies and carved stone heads stand boldly in the view. The clever and interesting parts of the design are the secret, densely planted pathways leading off this space, and the element of surprise that awaits in each enclosure in turn. There is a small white garden in gravel sandwiched between the stream and an old barn and dovecot; a mound planted with medlars and purple lace-cap hydrangeas; a barn walk leading to a vegetable garden designed by Justin Spink. Each one would make a charming small garden in its own right.

Anthony and Penny Spink

Woolstone, near Faringdon SN7 7QL. Tel: (01367) 820219

7m W of Wantage, 7m S of Faringdon off B4507 below Uffington White Horse Hill. 500 yards from White Horse Inn in Woolstone take road signed to Uffington

Open May to Sept, Wed, plus 6th July, all 2 – 5pm; and by appt at other times

Entrance: £3, children free

 WC &

OTHER RECOMMENDED GARDENS

BRIDEWELL ORGANIC GARDENS

Wilcote, Finstock, Chipping Norton OX7 3DY
(01993 868445; www.bridewellorganicgardens.co.uk).
Open one day in May, June and Sept (telephone or
consult website for details) and for parties by appt

Once the kitchen garden of Wilcote House,
supports people with mental health problems. It
includes a Celtic cross parterre, a herb wheel, a
working smithy, an imaginative tribute to
Giverny, and a 5-acre vineyard.

HILL COURT

Mr and Mrs Andrew C. Peake, Tackley (enquiries to
Court Farm, Tackley, Kidlington OX5 3AQ; 01869
331218). Open for NGS, and for parties by appt

The 2-acre, 16th-century walled garden, the
design of which was influenced by Russell Page,
unusually slopes uphill from the entrance.
Sensitive and original plantings in shades of
silver, pink and blue were created by Rupert
Golby to replace the old rose beds, and there
are many unusual plants.

OXFORD COLLEGE GARDENS

Most colleges are helpful about access, although
the Master's or Fellows' Gardens are often
private or rarely open. The best course is to ask
at the porter's lodge of each college, or to
telephone in advance. The following are among
those of particular interest: Christ Church,
Corpus Christi, Exeter, Green College, Holywell
Manor, Kellogg College, Lady Margaret Hall,
Magdalene, Nuffield, Queen's, St Catherine's, St
Hilda's, St Hugh's, St John's, Trinity, Wadham and
Worcester. The University Parks are open daily.

THE PRIORY

Dr D. El Kabir and others, Charlbury OX7 3PX
(01608 810417). Open for NGS, and occasionally
by appt

Formal terraces, topiary and Italianate features
combine in this 1-acre town garden with a
poetic and contemplative atmosphere created
by many unusual specimen trees and shrubs,
statuary and water features. Beyond is an
arboretum containing 200 different trees. In all,
6 acres.

STANSFIELD

Mr and Mrs D. Keeble, 49 High Street, Stanford-in-
the- Vale, Faringdon SN7 8NQ (01367 710340). Open
April to Sept, first Tues in each month, 10am – 4pm;
also for NGS and by appt

A 1-acre plantsman's garden packed with a
profusion of plants for both damp and dry
conditions. Year-long interest is ensured by the
widespread use of foliage and seasonal flowers.

STONOR PARK

Stonor, Henley-on-Thames RG9 6HF (01491 638587;
www.stonor.com). Open April to mid-Sept, Suns and
Bank Holiday Mons; July and Aug, Wed; all 1 – 5.30pm.
Also open for coach parties by appt.

Open parkland of 280 acres with majestic trees
and a wild herd of fallow deer give a timeless
quality to one of the most ancient estates in
the Chilterns. The complex E-shaped Tudor
house is set in a bowl on the south side of a
hill, with flower and vegetable gardens at a
higher level, and an attractive orchard planted
with cypresses and espaliered fruit trees.
(Listed Grade II*)

WROXTON ABBEY

Wroxton, Banbury OX15 6PX (01295 730551;
www.wroxtonabbey.org). Open all year, daily, dawn –
dusk, but closed last 2 weeks of Dec and early Jan.

The 56 acres of garden and parkland, furnished
with extensive lawns, specimen trees and
woodlands, natural-looking waters and 'eye-
catcher' buildings, were laid out in the mid-18th
century by Sanderson Miller. A fine example of
the early Picturesque style of gardening and of
considerable historical interest. (Listed Grade II*)

The Priory

RUTLAND

For further information about how to use the *Guide*
and for an explanation of the symbols, see pages vi–viii.
Specific dates and times are those given to us by garden owners for 2008.
For 2009 dates, check with the individual properties.
For opening dates under the National Gardens Scheme,
readers should consult *The Yellow Book* or www.ngs.org.uk.
Maps are to be found at the end of the *Guide*.
For gardens in Leicestershire see pages 195–198.

ACRE END

Developed since the mid-1970s from an old one-acre orchard, this is a sophisticated cottage garden created by a plantsman with style. Part of its charm lies in its secret nature and the surprises it springs within a series of very different garden rooms. In front of the house a knot of dwarf box is interplanted with salvias, heliotropes, verbenas, grasses and shrubs. An archway leads to the barnyard at the side of the house, where cacti, agaves, succulents and salvias in pots predominate. The Japanese-style courtyard garden at the rear contains the essential stepping stones, water basin and stone lanterns, together with maples, a cloud-pruned pine, shrubs pruned to reveal their lower limbs, foliage plants and a small collection of bonsai. Steps lead to a small garden where *Cortaderia richardii* makes the setting for a studio housing Mima Bolton's paintings. An arch in the yew hedge leads to substantial mixed borders, and a further arch, this time in an imposing beech hedge, reveals topiary shapes and an ancient pear tree. Then the mood changes again, to a more relaxed style with a circular lawn, island beds and a predominantly yellow herbaceous border; the purple Dawyck beech, blue Arizona cypress and fastigiate Scots pine contrast with a fine specimen of *Juniperus chinensis* 'Kaizuka'. A leafy tunnel introduces the croquet lawn, flanked by a herb and scented garden, with a kitchen garden with raised vegetable beds beyond. In the woodland garden unusual trees, especially birches grown for their bark, are underplanted with shrubs, woodland perennials and ferns, and Jim Bolton's wildlife woodcarvings. Returning to the house, the vista is of long double herbaceous borders, colour-themed in stages.

Jim and Mima Bolton

The Jetties, North Luffenham LE15 8JX. Tel: (01780) 720906

6m SW of Stamford, 5m NE of Uppingham off A6121

Open for NGS, and mid-June to mid-Aug by appt

Entrance: £3.50, children free

Other information: Teas on NGS open day only

NEW ● ᕕ ✏

ASHWELL HOUSE

Next to the fourteenth-century church of St Mary's Ashwell, the two-acre vicarage garden has been designed by the present owners to provide all-year colour in the shrubs and borders. Fine trees on all sides, some distant, give the impression of a park-like setting. Architectural features by

Mr and Mrs David Pettifer

Ashwell, Oakham LE15 7LW. Tel: (01572) 722833

3m N of Oakham via B668 towards Cottesmore, turn left to Ashwell

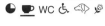

George Carter enliven shaded areas, and a classical summerhouse offers a peaceful retreat. The colour schemes achieve a successful balance of light and dark: in the front garden *Cedrus atlantica* 'Glauca', eucalyptus and white roses act as a cool foil to the copper beech and red-leaved berberis on the other side. A striking group of silver birches fans out in two arcs, surrounded by purple cut-leaf alders and 'Ispahan' and 'Blanche Double de Coubert' roses. The old walled vegetable garden, although still well stocked with fruit and vegetables, has in part been taken over by the pool and millennium gardens, planted with an abundance of roses: an avenue of standard 'Iceberg', a fan of 'Wedding Day', and columns draped with purple 'Raubritter'.

Brian and Judith Taylor

18 Teigh Road, Market Overton,
Oakham LE15 7PW.
Tel: (01572) 767337

6m N of Oakham off B668, beyond
Colttesmore

Open June to Sept for parties by appt

Entrance: £2

HILL HOUSE

The 0.5-acre garden is the work of plant enthusiasts who have a natural instinct for informal planting and design. Sinuous strips of lawn serve as pathways to a series of well-manicured borders that see-saw between dry shade and full sun. In each, architectural plants and shrubs often act as foils to a wide range of mainly hardy and half-hardy herbaceous perennials arranged in combinations designed to provide a continuous spectrum of colour and foliage effects during the whole of the open season.

Hill House

OTHER RECOMMENDED GARDENS

BARNSDALE GARDENS

Nick and Sue Hamilton, The Avenue, Exton, Oakham LE15 8AH (01572 813200; www.barnsdalegardens.co.uk). Open all year, daily: March to Oct, 9am – 5pm (closes 7pm June to Aug); Nov to Feb, 10am – 4pm (last admission 1 hour before closing). Closed 23rd and 25th Dec

Here are the show gardens immortalised by the late Geoff Hamilton on *Gardeners' World* and now run by his son and daughter-in-law. Impressive in their range and variety, they are excellent aids to planning or redesigning green spaces. Many of the plants on display may be bought from the adjoining nursery. 8.5 acres.

THE COURT HOUSE

Mr and Mrs Bas Clark, Geeston, Ketton, Stamford PE9 3RH (01780 720770). Open by appt

The terraced garden behind the attractive 17th century-style house was designed by Bunny Guinness to reinforce the Elizabethan impression; below, a wild meadow leads down through a well-planted copse sheltering cleverly placed follies to the river. 2.5 charming acres.

LYDDINGTON BEDE HOUSE

Blue Coat Lane, Lyddington LE15 9LZ (01572 822438; www.english-heritage.org.uk). Open April to Oct, Thurs – Mon, 10am – 5pm. EH

It is the setting and atmosphere that make a visit memorable. Originally a medieval palace of the Bishops of Lincoln and later converted into an almshouse, the beguiling house sits in a small garden of herbs and box-edged beds among picturesque golden stone cottages and beside the handsome parish church.

THE OLD RECTORY

Mrs D. B. Owen, Teigh, Oakham LE15 7RT (01572 787681). Open by appt April, June and July

A delightful, partially walled garden of 0.75 acres. The colour schemes and juxtaposition of plants, mostly traditional favourites with roses used to connect the shapes and contrasting foliage of their neighbours, are harmonious and masterly. The visiting period is timed for spring and midsummer, when the garden is at its peak.

SHROPSHIRE

For further information about how to use the *Guide*
and for an explanation of the symbols, see pages vi–viii.
Specific dates and times are those given to us by garden owners for 2008.
For 2009 dates, check with the individual properties.
For opening dates under the National Gardens Scheme,
readers should consult *The Yellow Book* or www.ngs.org.uk.
Maps are to be found at the end of the *Guide*.

BROWNHILL HOUSE

Roger and Yoland Brown

Ruyton XI Towns, Shrewsbury SY4 1LR.
Tel: (01939) 261121;
www.eleventowns.co.uk

10m NW of Shrewsbury on B4397

Open for NGS, and May to Aug by appt

Entrance: £3, children free

Other information: Parking at Bridge Inn
100 metres away

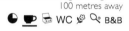 WC ♿ ℗ ⊘ B&B

Out of an impossible north-facing cliff a most unusual and distinctive two-acre garden of great variety has been created since 1972. The slope has been transformed from a scrap-covered wilderness into a series of terraces and small gardens connected by over 600 steps that wander up and down the hill through plantings of trees and shrubs, patches of wild flowers and open flower-filled spaces. At the bottom a riverside garden runs from an open lawn to a bog garden. A series of formal terraces includes a laburnum walk, and at the top there are paved areas with a pool, gazebo, parterre, a long walk with a herbaceous border, flower beds and a large kitchen garden with glasshouses. Also incorporated into the design are a folly, a Thai spirit house, a grotto, a summerhouse, a large Arabic arch, a cascade and a unique design of Menorah. Developments are continuing on the extensive terracing on which grow many of the collection of over 100 varieties of hedera, and a Japanese 'dry' garden has replaced the rockery. This is a garden that has to be seen to be believed, and fun for children, who can tax their brains with a challenging quiz.

CRUCKFIELD HOUSE

Mr and Mrs G. M. Cobley

Shoot Hill, Ford, Shrewsbury SY5 9NR.
Tel: (01743) 850222

5m W of Shrewsbury off A458. Turn left
signed to Shoot Hill

Open for NGS, and June and July for
parties of 25 or more by appt

Entrance: £4.50, children £1

● ▶ WC ♿ ℗

Sheltered and surrounded by mature trees, the romantic and tranquil four-acre garden, managed organically for many years, is designed in traditionally English formal style with an abundance of roses and peonies as part of the attraction. There are exuberant plantings of shrubs and herbaceous plants, many of them rare or unusual. Specimen trees set in wildflower grassland and a pretty bog area surround a large pond. The ornamental kitchen garden is set off by attractive outbuildings and an adjoining courtyard garden.

THE DOWER HOUSE

The National Trust

Morville Hall, Morville, Bridgnorth
WV16 5NB.
Tel: (01746) 714407;
www.stmem.com/dower-house-garden

Starting in 1989, the present tenant, well-known gardening writer Katherine Swift, has transformed a 1.5-acre site within the grounds of Morville Hall, with the aim of relating the history of English gardens in a sequence of separate features: a turf maze, a medieval cloister garden, a knot garden, a

seventeenth-century plat and flower beds, a William and Mary canal garden with formal water feature and box-edged *platesbandes*, an eighteenth-century flower garden, a Victorian rose border, a nineteenth-century wilderness and, finally, an ornamental fruit and vegetable garden. Particular attention is given to the use of authentic plants and construction techniques; old varieties of tulips and roses are a speciality.

3m NW of Bridgnorth at A458/B4368 junction, within Morville Hall grounds

Open 2nd April to 28th Sept, Wed. Sun and Bank Holiday Mons, 2 – 6pm; and at other times, inc. evenings, for parties by appt

Entrance: £4, children (under 16) £1

DUDMASTON
(Historic Park and Garden Grade II)

To garden historians, Dudmaston is a shrine. Its valley wilderness is the best surviving exemplar of William Shenstone's gardening philosophy of the Picturesque – 'pleasing the imagination by scenes of grandeur, beauty or variety'. The Dingle is a romantic creation of the late eighteenth century by one of Shenstone's former gardeners, working directly with the owners, the Whitmores of Dudmaston. The William and Mary house sits on the other side of the park, in a landscape of woods, hills and water. The terraces which connect the hall to the Big Pool – actually the largest of a series of lakes – were made in 1816; they anticipated the creation of more formal gardens here. Today eight acres of garden in proximity to the house include a large pool and bog garden, island beds filled with shrubs, azaleas, rhododendrons, viburnums and fine old roses. Large specimen trees, old fruit trees and mature shrubs lend an established feel. The rock garden has been restored and the Big Pool is now framed by attractive plantings. There are two estate walks.

The National Trust

Quatt, Bridgnorth WV15 6QN.
Tel: (01746) 780866;
www.nationaltrust.org.uk

4m SE of Bridgnorth on A442

House open as garden but, Tues, Wed and Sun, 2pm – 5pm

Garden open 23rd March to 23rd Sept, Mon – Wed and Sun, 12 noon – 6pm. Special Mon openings for pre-booked parties.

Estate open free of charge for pedestrian access all year

Entrance: £4.90, children £2.45, family £12.20, (house and garden £6.10, children £3.05, family £15.25

Other information: Batricar available. Dogs in Dingle only, on lead

GATE COTTAGE

The two-acre garden is changing and developing all the time to accommodate a vast range of plants. Roses and clematis scramble through old fruit trees, and there are many other fine roses along the exterior fence and in the herbaceous borders. Aquatic interest comes from pools and a bog garden with primulas. In the extended area shrubs have been planted

G.W. Nicholson and Kevin Gunnell

English Frankton, Ellesmere SY12 0JU.
Tel: (01939) 270606

10m N of Shrewsbury on A528. At Cockshutt take road to English Frankton; garden is 1m on right

Open for NGS, and for parties by appt

Entrance: £2.50, children 50p

Other information: Teas on charity open days only

The Redemptionists

Weston-under-Redcastle, Shrewsbury SY4 5UY. Tel: (01939) 200611; www.hawkstone.co.uk

13m NE of Shrewsbury via A49, 6m SW of Market Drayton on A442. Entrance on road from Hodnet to Weston-under-Redcastle. Signed from Hodnet

Open Jan to 10th Feb, 23rd Feb to 16th March, Sat and Sun; 11th to 17th Feb, 21st March to 7th April, 26th May to Aug, 27th Oct to 2nd Nov, daily; 9th April to 25th May, 3rd Sept to 26th Oct, Wed – Sun; all 10am – 3.30pm (closes earlier in winter). Closed Nov and Dec except for special pre-booked Christmas openings

Entrance: £6, concessions £5, children £4, family £17

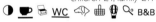

Mr A.E.H. and The Hon. Mrs Heber-Percy

Hodnet, Market Drayton TF9 3NN. Tel: (01630) 685786

12m NE of Shrewsbury, 5.5m SW of Market Drayton, at A53/A442 junction

Open 5th, 18th, 25th and 26th May, 8th, 15th and 22nd June, 13th July, 19th, 24th and 25th Aug, 14th Sept; all 12 noon – 5pm. Also open for parties by appt

Entrance: £4, OAPs £3.50, children £2

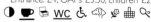

Lee and Pam Wheeler

Kenley, Shrewsbury SY5 6NS. Tel: (01694) 771279; www.stmem.com/jessamine-cottage

6m W of Much Wenlock. Signed from B4371 and from A458 Shrewsbury – Much Wenlock road at Harley

for colour effect. Large pebbles create attractive features, and there are unusual brown and black foliage plants and some interesting grasses. The rock and gravel plantings now include an area of hardy carnivorous plants. Other eye-catchers are a collection of zantedeschias and a large bed of meconopsis flowering under dogwoods with a backing of foxgloves.

HAWKSTONE PARK

(Historic Park Grade I)

In its day Hawkstone, owned by the Hill family of postage stamp fame, was as famous as Stowe and Stourhead, and the grounds have now been returned to their eighteenth-century grandeur and sublimity (the latter was supposed to induce awe if not fear). A series of monuments, now reconstructed, is linked by winding paths and tunnels. Ascending towards the White Tower, the visitor passes the thatched buildings, in one of which was a mechanical hermit famous for his artificial cough (now replaced by a hologram), then a grotto and the so-called Swiss bridge (a fallen tree across a gorge). Much remains to be done to the Red Castle, which is genuinely medieval. The whole thing is a triumph for all involved, including English Heritage. A walk through the park is approximately three and a half miles, but visitors should be warned that it involves climbing and descending many steps; allow time for a visit.

HODNET HALL ★★

(Historic Park Grade II)

The 60-acre parkland offers a constant succession of interest, although the greatest effect comes in autumn when the acers, sorbus and birches present their display. The grounds are grouped around a series of lakes and water gardens, home to black swans. This is essentially splendid large-scale parkland planting: magnolias, azaleas, rhododendrons in late spring are followed in summer by fuchsias, astilbes and gunneras, matched with water lilies on the lakes. For the herbaceous gardener there are shrub roses, tree peonies and the more traditional border plants. The working walled kitchen garden is well maintained, and there are also displays of flowers and pot plants, together with many varieties of fruit and vegetables.

JESSAMINE COTTAGE

This is Housman country, and Wenlock Edge raises its densely wooded hackles behind the house. Since they started designing their three-acre garden from a field in 2000, the owners have remained conscious of the wider landscape. There are two quite different gardens here. In front of the house and the adjacent wooden tea room is a bright splash of geraniums set in gravel, and to the left a substantial pair of colourful and boldly planted island beds draws the eye down to a lime avenue focusing on two towering ash trees perfectly positioned on the perimeter. In the rear garden the colours are more uniform, the design equally forceful. Nearest the house a wedge-shaped parterre in four sections is planted with lavenders, *Origanum laevigatum* and *Verbena bonariensis*. Lawns left partially unmown stretch down past a bed of scented red, pink and white roses, with others clambering up hefty wooden posts, to a large pond fringed with perennials, home to irises, water lilies and wildlife. Beyond is a young arboretum of specimen trees, and a wooden walkway crosses the pond and disappears into a cool and shady patch of woodland. There is also a well-stocked vegetable garden. The garden may not be subtle, but it is innovative, assured and full of ideas for aspiring gardeners.

Open May to Aug, Wed – Sun, 2 – 6pm

Entrance: £3, children £1

LOWER HALL ★

This modern 4.25-acre plantsman's garden has been developed by the present owners since 1964, helped originally by Lanning Roper. The courtyard and its fountain are featured in many design books. The walled garden has a magnificent display of roses, clematis and irises in season. Everywhere the use of colour combinations and plant associations is good – a red border, another of white and green giving a cool effect. Roses abound. The water garden is separated from the woodland garden by the River Worfe with two bridges and two weirs. A deck built over the pool exploits the view across to the colourful primula island. The woodland garden includes rare magnolias, a collection of birches with bark interest, acers, cornus, azaleas and amelanchiers – all-year variety and colour.

Mr and Mrs C. F. Dumbell

Worfield, Bridgnorth WV15 5LH. Tel: (01746) 716607

4m NE of Bridgnorth. Take A454 Wolverhampton-Bridgnorth road, turn right to Worfield and right again after village stores and pub

Open April to July for parties by appt

Entrance: £4, children under 12 free

Other information: Access for large coaches nearby. Garden room available for parties of 20–40 for pre-booked refreshments and meals

MILLICHOPE PARK

(Historic Park Grade II*)

The glory of Millichope is its magnificent landscaping, commissioned in the 1760s by a father seeking a fitting memorial to his four sons, all of whom had predeceased him. The main memorial was an elegant Ionic temple now dramatically sited away from the house across a lake. The present owners have commissioned a fine Chinese-style bridge across one of the gorges, and Mrs Bury has added a set of herbaceous borders disposed in elegant 'rooms' framed by yew hedges. Away from the Georgian classicism, romantic wilderness plantings of roses and philadelphus combine to make this a most beautiful park and garden; below the lake the grass has been managed as a flower-rich hay meadow. 13 acres.

Mr and Mrs L. Bury

Munslow, Craven Arms SY7 9HA. Tel: (01584) 841234

8m NE of Craven Arms, 11m N of Ludlow on B4368

Open 3 Suns in Feb for snowdrops(telephone for details); for NGS; and by appt

Entrance: £3, children 50p

Other information: Teas on snowdrop days and Bank Holidays only

THE PATCH

Although only 1.5 acres in extent, this garden has much to offer. Essentially the garden of a dedicated conservationist, holding National Collections of camassias, dictamnus,

Mrs Margaret Owen

Acton Pigot, Acton Burnell, Shrewsbury SY5 7PH. Tel: (01743) 362139

8m SE of Shrewsbury between A49 and A458. From Acton Burnell take Cressage Road; after 0.5m turn left signed to Acton Pigott

Open 26th Feb, 11am – 3pm for snowdrops and hellibores; 23rd and 24th March; in May by appt for camassias; 18th June, 13th July, 24th Sept; all 11am – 5pm; and for coach parties by appt

Entrance: £2.50, children free

 WC   ♿

veratrums and hardy nerines, together with other less commonly grown shrubs and herbaceous plants, it is filled with beauties, starting in spring with snowdrops, hellebores, erythroniums, dicentras, trilliums and violas. Easter sees the flowering of fine magnolias (and on the two open days visitors may take tea in the beautifully decorated Acton Burnell church). On into summer go *Paeonia mlokosewitschii* and *P. daurica*, roses and epimediums..The garden is bordered by a broad grassy path, and at its centre lies a white garden with several rare trees. The open days, geared to the garden's highpoints, indicate the impressive length of seasonal interest.

PREEN MANOR

Mrs A. Trevor-Jones

Church Preen, Church Stretton SY6 7LQ. Tel: (01694) 771207

5m W of Much Wenlock on B4371. After 3m turn right for Church Preen and Hughley; after 1.5m turn left for Church Preen, over crossroads. Drive is 0.5m on right

Open for NGS, and for parties of 15 or more in June and July by appt

Entrance: £3.50, children 50p

 WC

The 12-acre grounds are blessed with a beautiful south-east aspect facing Wenlock Edge. Despite the attractions of the more formal part of the gardens, it is the wooded landscaped walks beside the pools and natural stream that are the most outstanding feature. Rodgersias, *Primula japonica*, *Rhododendron ponticum* hybrids and magnificent yews and cedars create a noble setting on the banks which fall away from the former manor house. The formal gardens are actually akin to a pretty cottage garden, with roses, deutzias and violas planted to good effect. Other distinctive areas, including a chess garden, a pebble garden and a gazebo complete with parrot and cat, demonstrate an esoteric style of gardening which may appeal to some. 6m east of Preen are *Wenlock Abbey* (Historic Park Grade II) and the ruined *Wenlock Priory* with imaginative topiary.

RADNOR COTTAGE

Mr and Mrs David Pittwood

Clunton, Craven Arms SY7 OJA. Tel: (01588) 640451

12m W of Ludlow, 8m W of Craven Arms, 1m E of Clun on B4368 between Clun and Clunton

Open for NGS, and for parties by appt

Entrance: £2.50, children 50p

Overlooking the Clun valley in A.E. Housman's Marcher countryside, the 2.5-acre garden has been continually developing since it was taken on in the 1980s by its present enthusiastic owners. Set on a south-facing slope, it embraces the surrounding countryside by means of drystone walling, a wildflower meadow with snakes'-head fritillaries and the old cottage-garden pheasant's eye narcissi. The wide range of garden habitats includes sunny terracing and paving, alpine troughs, and damp shade lightened by golden foliage. There is a pond, a stream, and a small arboretum with native sorbus; roses are of the old-fashioned variety such as *Rosa mundi*.

SWALLOW HAYES ★

Mrs Michael Edwards

Rectory Road, Albrighton WV7 3EP. Tel: (01902) 372624

9m SE of Telford, 7m NW of Wolverhampton. Turn off M54 at junction 3, then off A41 into Rectory Road after garden centre

Open for NGS, and by appt

Entrance: £3 (on open days), children free

A modern garden of two acres, with many design features, colour and foliage contrasts, and an exuberant display of plants, shrubs and trees. Although easy maintenance is an object, it contains nearly 3000 different types of plants (most of them are labelled) and gives year-round interest. The Mediterranean wall has tender plants, and elsewhere small pools, ferns and a woodland area provide contrast. National Collections of witch hazels and lupins are here, plus an interesting area of small gardens to copy at home, vegetables and fruit trees, nursery stock beds and a hardy geranium trial of over 100 labelled hardy varieties.

WALCOT HALL
(Historic Park Grade II)

The handsome red-brick eighteenth-century house was remodelled by Sir William Chambers for the 1st Lord Clive of India (don't miss the courtyard stabling), and its beautiful landscape setting enhances the 30-acre arboretum planted by his son. Rhododendrons and azaleas sweep down to pools amid many fine specimen trees, and the lake and pools display the fine collection to advantage, enhanced by the lovely vision of Chambers' clock towers among the rolling borderland hills.

WESTON PARK ★
(Historic Park Grade II*)

The handsome seventeenth-century house has a 'Capability' Brown park as its distinctive setting; he also laid out pleasure grounds to the east and west of the house. There are almost 1000 acres of delightful woodland planted with spring bulbs, bluebells, rhododendrons and azaleas, together with beautiful pools; magnificent trees form a handsome backcloth to the many shrubs. A rose walk leads to the deer park, and the rose garden by the house and the Italian parterre garden have been restored. The architectural features in the park – Temple of Diana, Roman bridge and orangery – were all designed by James Paine. Children will enjoy the adventure playground, the railway and the maze in the walled garden.

WOLLERTON OLD HALL ★★

In design and layout this is a garden in the classic English mode. Within a little over four acres is a series of beautifully planted rooms, each distinct in character yet very much part of the whole. This effect is achieved through the careful positioning of a number of principal and secondary axes upon which the overall plan of the garden depends, with yew hedging creating an all-embracing, deeply green framework. Within the different garden rooms, contrasts are much in evidence. Fiery borders in the hot garden, stunning in August,

Other information: Teas on open days only

Mr C. R.W. Parish
Lydbury North SY7 8AZ.
Tel: (01588) 680570; www.walcothall.com

7m NW of Craven Arms, 3m S of Bishop's Castle, off B4385

House open for parties by appt

Garden open May to Oct, Fri – Mon, 12 noon – 4.30pm

Entrance: £3.50, children free

Weston Park Enterprises
Weston-under-Lizard, Shifnal TF11 8LE.
Tel: (01952) 852100; www.weston-park.com

6m E of Telford on A5, 7m W of M6 junction 12, 3m N of M54 junction 3

House open 1 – 5pm

Garden open 22nd to 30th March, daily; 5th to 27th April, 3rd to 18th May, 7th to 22nd June, Sat, Sun and Bank Holiday Mons; 24th May to 1st June, 28th June to Aug, daily except 26th July and 14th to 20th Aug; all 11am – 6.30pm (last admission 5pm)

Entrance: park and gardens £4, OAPs £3.50, children £2.50, family £12

John and Lesley Jenkins
Wollerton, Hodnet, Market Drayton TF9 3NA.
Tel: (01630) 685760 (Daytime); www.wollertonoldhallgarden.com

12m NE of Shrewsbury off A53. Brown signed off A53 between Hodnet and Tern Hill

Open 21st March to Sept, Fri, Sun and Bank Holiday Mons, 12 noon – 5pm

Entrance: £5, children £1

Wollerton Old Hall

are tempered with cool whites in a scented garden; openness, in the form of a broad expanse of lawn, contrasts with the intimacy of a pergola dripping with roses and clematis. But this garden is not just about plantsmanship and design. It is charged with atmosphere, enhanced by a number of most appealing structures; in recalling the Arts and Crafts Movement of the early years of the last century, it is redolent of many fashionable ones of the present.

OTHER RECOMMENDED GARDENS

ATTINGHAM PARK

Attingham, Shrewsbury SY4 4TP (01743 708162; www.nationaltrust.org.uk). House open as garden, but closed Wed. Garden open all year, daily, 9am – 6pm (closes 4pm Feb to 12th March, Nov to Jan). NT

A restored Reptonian landscape of large trees and shrubs, including a magnificent grove of Lebanon cedars, conceived as the setting for the grand neo-classical house. A mile-long ambulatory walk beside the River Tern is planted with daffodils, shrubs and trees, and longer walks may be enjoyed within the deer park. In all, 4000 acres. (Listed Grade II*)

BENTHALL HALL

Broseley TF12 5RX (01952 882159). Open 23rd March to Sept, Tues, Wed and Bank Holiday Suns and Mons, plus other Suns July to Sept, 1.30 – 5.30pm. NT

The intimate plantsman's garden of 3 acres, 19th-century in origin, encompasses a wilderness area, a rockery, a rose garden, a bowling green and a kitchen garden filled with fruit, vegetables and cut flowers. Combining formality with a relaxed and painterly style, it has been enhanced by a succession of gifted resident plantsmen, botanists, designers and generations of Benthalls. A tranquil, beautiful retreat and a monument to botanical history.

DAVID AUSTIN ROSES

Bowling Green Lane, Albrighton, Wolverhampton WV7 3HB (01902 376334). Open all year, daily except 25th Dec to 1st Jan, 9am – 5pm

An ideal place to inspect the roses grown by one of the country's leading breeders and growers – about 900 varieties in all, including shrub, climbing, species and old roses. The famous plant centre also sells an extensive range of herbaceous perennials, trees and shrubs. 2 acres.

LIMEBURNERS

Mrs Ann Derry, Lincoln Hill, Ironbridge, Telford TF8 7NX (01952 433715). Open April to Sept by appt

The 13-acre garden, with its pool, stream and waterfall, was started as a haven for wildlife in 1970 (years before fashion caught up), with an abundance of insect-attractants such as buddleias and shrub roses, nectar-rich flowers and native trees and shrubs. Now it is mature and delightful.

OTELEY

Mr and Mrs R. K. Mainwaring, Ellesmere SY12 0PB (01691 622514). Open for NGS and parties of 10 or more by appt

The gracious country garden of 10 acres, set in parkland and farmland with glimpses of the Mere beyond surrounding trees, is richly robed with plants set among extensive lawns, beneath handsome trees and in deep borders protected by high walls festooned with climbers. A folly and walled kitchen garden provide the finishing touches. Late spring is a fine time to visit.

RUTHALL MANOR

Mr and Mrs G.T. Clarke, Ruthall Road, Ditton Priors, Bridgnorth WV16 6Tn (01746 712608). Open for NGS and by appt

Set below the heights of Abdon Burf, the 1-acre garden has been designed for ease of maintenance in a variety of attractive and well-designed settings which include a delightful old pond, formal plantings, woodland and rare trees. A gravelled area is given over to an increasing collection of modern sculpture.

SOMERSET

For further information about how to use the *Guide*
and for an explanation of the symbols, see pages vi–viii.
Specific dates and times are those given to us by garden owners for 2008.
For 2009 dates, check with the individual properties.
For opening dates under the National Gardens Scheme,
readers should consult *The Yellow Book* or www.ngs.org.uk.
Maps are to be found at the end of the *Guide*.

AMMERDOWN HOUSE

(Historic Garden Grade II*)

The Bath-stone house was designed by James Wyatt, with panoramic views on one side and a garden on the other; the 15-acre garden was a brilliant conception by Lutyens, who wanted to link the house with the orangery. Walking through the Italianate 'rooms' of yew and sculpture and parterre, one is unaware of the tricks of space that are being played. Massive yew planting, now mature and nearly four metres high, creates enclosed formal areas which lead irresistibly one from another, and fountains and statues add architectural interest at all seasons. There has been much replanting in recent years, and beautiful meadows and ponds now link the formal gardens with the fine surrounding parkland.

The Hon. Andrew Jolliffe

Radstock, Bath BA3 5SH

10m S of Bath, 0.5m off A362 Radstock – Frome road on B3139

Open 24th March, 5th and 26th May, 28th Aug, 11am – 5pm, for charities, and for parties by appt at other times

Entrance: £4, concessions £3, children free

Other information: Pre-booked catering for parties at Ammerdown Centre – telephone 01761 433709

● ☕ ⟐ WC ♿ ⟨⟩ ✿

BARFORD PARK ★

The mellow brick eighteenth-century house is in perfect scale with its surrounding classic parkland and further distinguished by the acres of exceptional woodland gardens. Here spring-fed streams run through clearings framed by majestic oaks and sparkle through glades planted with well-placed ferns and thousands of candelabra primulas in harmonious colours. The two-acre formal garden around the house has an unusually placed walled garden – linked to the house and similar in proportion. Its great width allows deep double borders to flourish in each quarter. Developed since the 1960s by the present owners, this is a garden of rare charm and discernment. In all, 43 acres.

Mr and Mrs M. Stancomb

Spaxton, Bridgwater TA5 1AG.
Tel: (01278) 671269

5m W of Bridgwater. From Bridgwater – Spaxton road, turn to Enmore

Open for NGS

Entrance: £3, children free

● ⟐ WC ♿ ⟨⟩

BREWERY HOUSE

The 0.75-acre garden, tightly packed with interesting plants, is set on two levels and has magnificent views over rolling countryside to the south. The planting is dramatic, aimed at achieving strong contrasts in shape and size as well as colour, with perennials appearing next to huge specimens of phyllostachys or miscanthus. Bamboos, hydrangeas and hardy geraniums abound, and *Rosa* 'Kiftsgate' and *Magnolia*

John and Ursula Brooke

Southstoke, Bath BA2 7DL.
Tel: (01225) 833153)

2.5m S of Bath, off A367 Bath – Radstock road. At top of dual carriageway, turn left onto B3110 to double roundabout, then next right into Southstock; house on left behind high wall, by white railings

Open for NGS, and in July by appt

Entrance: £3, children 50p

Other information: Large plant sale in early June – telephone for details

NEW ● WC ⅙ ⏴⏵ 🐾

soulangeana are dominant presences. In the top garden, enclosed by a high stone wall, roses and clematis jostle for space with wall fruit and other climbers. There are many mature trees, including davidia, ptelia, medlar, apple and pear, and large specimens of walnut and mulberry. At the far end the swimming pool has been converted into a water garden with water lilies, gunneras and other aquatic plants. The garden has been run organically since 1983.

The American Museum

Claverton, Bath BA2 7BD.
Tel: (01225) 460503;
www.americanmuseum.org

2m SE of Bath off A36, signed to American Museum

House and garden open mid-March to Oct, Tues – Sun, 12 noon – 5pm. Pre-booked private garden tours by arrangement

Entrance: £5, concessions £4, children (5–16) £3 (house and garden £7.50, concessions £6.50, children £4)

◐ ♥ ✕ 🗊 WC ⏴⏵ 🐾 ⊞ 🎈 ♀

CLAVERTON MANOR

(Historic Garden Grade II)

The house, designed by Jeffry Wyatville, and garden are set on the side of the valley of the Avon in a stunning position with splendid views. The rather stark high walls of the house and the terrace support honeysuckle, clematis and old climbing roses, and fastigiate yews make strong buttress shapes up the south-facing wall. The Colonial Herb Garden is modest in size but the little herbarium is popular for seeds, herbs, tussie-mussies and so on. The Mount Vernon Garden, a colonial interpretation of George Washington's famous garden, with rampant old-fashioned roses, trained pear trees and box and beech hedges, is surrounded by white palings. There is a replica of the octagonal garden house used as a schoolroom for Washington's step-grandchildren. The seven-acre arboretum, which contains a fine collection of exclusively native American trees and shrubs, is believed to be the only one of its kind outside the USA. An orchard contains American apple varieties, and there is also a fernery, a cascade and a waterfall. The Lewis and Clark trail includes a selection of the flora encountered by the explorers as they made their way to the west coast of North America, and a short circular walk through the old parkland and a woodland walk above the manor house have also been opened up.

Mr and Mrs Alastair Robb

Greenham, Wellington TA21 0JR.
Tel: (01823) 672283
www.cothaymanor.co.uk

Cothay Manor

COTHAY MANOR ★★

Although these outstanding 12-acre gardens appear integral to the beautiful medieval manor house – each a natural extension of the other – they were in fact laid out only in the

1920s. They have been redesigned and replanted over the last few years, within the original yew-hedged compartments which were created to provide a seventeenth-century promenade complete with 'conversation arbours'. A 70-yard-long avenue of *Robinia pseudoacacia* 'Umbraculifera' underplanted with *Nepeta* 'Six Hills Giant' is a wonderful sight in May when a thousand white tulips are in bloom. Surrounding meadows, dotted with specimen trees, shrubs and spring bulbs, lead on to herbaceous borders, a cottage garden and a magical white garden. Masterly planting is everywhere evident, exuberance balanced by restraint; note for example the effective way in which complementary greys and mauves flow into the house walls. The pond beyond the main garden and the bog garden alongside the fast-flowing river are beginning to make an impact.

CROWE HALL ★
(Historic Garden Grade II)

These gardens, which extend to 11 acres on the hillside above Widcombe, are some of the most mysterious and beautiful in Bath. The owner describes the place as an island of classical simplicity surrounded by romantic wilderness. Around the Regency-style house are Italianate terraces, a pond, grottoes, tunnels, woods, glades, kitchen gardens and a long walkway with a stone statue facing a stunning view of Prior Park (see entry). Vistas and views are a feature of this steeply banked site, where down one walk you suddenly come upon the roof of the fifteenth-century church of St Thomas à Becket. Beyond the restored grotto is a meadow garden and an amusing garden dedicated to Hercules, with a theatrically ferocious hero who appears in a mosaic pool as well as on dry land. Magnificent trees include mulberries, beeches and limes. The charming little enclosed Sauce Garden, with its trelliswork and canal-like pool, was created in 1995, and the 1852 greenhouse has been restored. The Teazle Garden (in memory of a much-loved dog) has a cascade, a fountain, a pergola and many climbing plants. For its stunning setting and for the romantic ambience, Crowe Hall is an experience not to be missed.

DUNSTER CASTLE ★
(Historic Garden Grade II*)

The Luttrell family, who had lived here since the fourteenth century, gave the castle – a Jacobean mansion castellated by Salvin in 1868 – and the 17-acre gardens to the Trust in 1976. A fine border of rare shrubs surrounds a lawn by the keep, while sub-tropical plants, camellias and azaleas thrive on the formal terraces below. The profusion of plants on the wooded slopes and along the riverside walk is astonishing. Thousands of bulbs have been planted, and after the daffodils and snowdrops come fine displays of forsythias, camellias and early

5m W of Wellington. From W (M5 junction 27) take A38 signed to Wellington, then after 3.5m turn left to Greenham. From N (junction 26) take Wellington exit; at roundabout take A38 signed to Exeter. After 3.5m turn right to Greenham (1.5m) and right again on left-hand corner at bottom of hill. House is 1m further, always keeping left

House open for parties by appt

Garden open Easter to Sept, Wed, Thurs, Sun and Bank Holiday Mons, 2 – 6pm; parties welcome by appt

Entrance: £4.50, children (under 12) £2.50

Other information: Coaches by appt

Mr John Barratt

Widcombe Hill, Bath BA2 6AR.
Tel: (01225) 310322

Behind Bath Spa station off A36 within walking distance of station

Open for NGS, plus 1st June, all 2 – 6pm, and for parties by appt

Entrance: £4, children £1

The National Trust

Dunster, Minehead TA24 6SL.
Tel: (01643) 821314;
www.nationaltrust.org.uk/dunstercastle

3m SE of Minehead on A39

Castle open

Gardens open all year, daily: Jan to 14th March, 3rd Nov to Dec, 11am – 4pm; 15th March to 2nd Nov, 10am – 5pm

Entrance: £4.80, children under 16 £2.20, family £11.80 (castle and gardens £8.60, children £4.20, family £20.50)

Other information: Self-drive batricar and
volunteer-driven multi-seater available

Robert and Marianne Williams

South Petherton TA13 5HH.
Tel: (01460) 240328;
www.eastlambrook.com

2m NE of South Petherton off A303.
Follow brown flower signs

Open all year, daily, 10am – 5pm

Entrance: £3.95, OAPs, students £3.50,
children £1

Other information: Snowdrop study day
9th Feb (ticket only)

Alison and Brian Shingler

Bruton BA10 ODB.
Tel: (01749) 812393;
www.gantsmill.co.uk

0.5m SW of Bruton, signed off A359

Open June to Sept, Sun and Bank
Holiday Mons, 2 – 5pm, and for parties
by appt

Entrance: £3 (mill and garden £5)

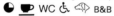 B&B

Greencombe Garden Trust
(Miss Joan Loraine)

Porlock TA24 8NU. Tel: (01643) 862363

7.5m W of Minehead, 0.5m W of Porlock
off B3225

Open 23rd March to July, Sat – Wed,
2 – 6pm

Entrance: £5, children £1

Other information: Coaches by appt only

rhododendrons, making it a good place for a walk in winter
and in spring. There is a National Collection of arbutus and a
huge *Magnolia campbellii*. Views stretch across to Exmoor, the
Quantocks and the Bristol Channel. 28 acres in all.

EAST LAMBROOK MANOR GARDENS
(Historic Garden Grade I)

In essence this is a cottage-style garden of two acres, with
mixed areas of planting, small lawns and narrow paths, but it
remains iconic as the creation of the great plantswoman
Margery Fish, who established the garden for endangered
species famous in its day for its controlled luxuriance of
growth, colour and scent. It still houses a remarkable
collection of rare plants, many of which she saved from
extinction. An extensive collection of geranium (cranesbill)
species and cultivars also remains here. The present owners
aim to improve all areas of the Grade-I-listed garden: the
terrace area and the hellebore woodland garden have been
restored, and Margery Fish's nursery has been relocated to its
original site.

GANTS MILL AND GARDEN

Approached down the greenest of lanes on the edge of
historic Bruton are the old buildings of Gants Mill. The mill
itself (still working) dates from 1290, but today's visitor can
also revel in the 0.5-acre English summer garden designed by
Philip Brown and realised by Alison Shingler since 1995. The
emphasis is on the masses of repeat-flowering climbing roses
and clematis on pergolas, surrounded by swathes of
perennials and summer bulbs in complementary shades. The
vibrant scent and colour from successive waves of irises and
Oriental poppies, roses and delphiniums, daylilies and dahlias
create an unforgettable effect from June until late September,
while the strong and intricate design holds all together. The
backdrop of river and trees provides a calm setting, and the
skilful use of water as a main feature contributes sound and
movement overall. An annually changing exhibition of
sculptures – some abstract, many figurative, and all for sale –
benefits the garden as well as the artists.

GREENCOMBE ★★

Created in 1946 by Horace Stroud, this 3.5-acre garden has
been extended by the present owner over the last three
decades. Set on a dark hillside overlooking the Bristol
Channel, it glows with colour, especially in spring and summer.
The formal lawns and beds round the house are immaculate.
Roses, lilies, hydrangeas, maples and camellias thrive. By
contrast the woodland area, traversed by a maze of narrow
paths, provides a walk of great interest; here a wide variety of
rhododendrons and azaleas flowers in the shelter of mature
trees, and ferns and woodland plants flourish. No sprays or

chemicals are used in the cultivation of this completely organic garden, which contains National Collections of erythroniums, gaultherias, polystichums and vacciniums. Woodborough (see entry) is nearby.

HESTERCOMBE GARDENS ★
(Historic Garden Grade I)

This is a superb product of the collaboration between Edwin Lutyens and Gertrude Jekyll, blending the formal art of architecture with the art of planting. The detailed design of steps, pools, walls, paving and seating is Lutyens at his most accomplished, and the rills, pergola and orangery are also fine examples of his work. A major reassessment and renewal of

Hestercombe Gardens Trust
Cheddon Fitzpaine, Taunton TA2 8LG.
Tel: (01823) 413923;
www.hestercombe.com

4m NE of Taunton off A361, just N of
Cheddon Fitzpaine. Signposted

Hestercombe Gardens

Open all year, daily except 25th Dec,
10am – 6pm (last admission 5pm).
Parties by written appt only

Entrance: £7.50, OAPs £6.95, children
under 5 free

Other information: Coaches by
arrangement

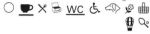

Jekyll's planting is underway and the formal garden has been replanted as closely as possible to her original plans. To the north of the house is the Combe, laid out two centuries earlier than the main gardens and a unique example of eighteenth-century pleasure grounds unchanged until the timber was felled in the 1960s. Visitors are now able to see the eighteenth-century parkland designed between 1750 and 1786 by Coplestone Warre Bampfylde, and his (restored) Great Cascade; he also designed the cascade from the lake at Stourhead (see entry in Wiltshire). This ambitious restoration of a Grade-I-listed landscape will eventually form a 35-acre landscape garden in its own right. The repair of the Victorian terrace is now complete, and a programme is well advanced to re-create the shrubbery in the style of William Robinson, c. 1880. Be sure to see the Doric temple, the mausoleum, the rebuilt witch's hut and the Gothic alcove, which commands views of Taunton Vale. In 2005 a new visitor and interpretation centre was opened in the restored Victorian stables. 50 acres in all.

HOLT FARM

Mr and Mrs Tim Mead

Bath Road, Blagdon, Bristol BS40 7SQ.
Tel: (01761) 462215

12m S of Bristol off A368 between
Blagdon and Ubley. Entrance to Holt
Farm, through Yeo Valley Farms, is 0.25m
outside Blagdon on left

Open for NGS, and by appt

Entrance: £2.50, children free

Other information: Teas and plants on
NGS open days only

 WC

A varied five-acre garden with a relaxed but very contemporary feel. The owner has worked with landscape architect Eileen O'Donnell since 1984 to create a place that is full of life and interest throughout the year. The woodland and meadow gardens are brilliant with fritillaries and camassias in spring, while in high summer the main gravel garden is filled with colour, shape and movement achieved by bold and imaginative repeat-planting on a generous scale, and autumn colour is maintained with many late perennials, dahlias and grasses. Grasses are also extensively used to link the newer parts of the garden to the fine rural landscape to the north of the house, while a simple sweep of lawn leading down to pastureland gives a view over Blagdon Lake to the south. There is also an attractive vegetable garden, with raised beds, brick paths and pool, all linked by wrought-iron gates and screens of great charm and originality.

LADY FARM ★★

Malcolm and Judy Pearce

Chelwood, Bristol BS39 4NN.
Tel: (01761) 490770;
www.ladyfarm.co.uk

9m S of Bristol on A368, 0.5m E of
Chelwood roundabout (A37/A368)

Open July to Sept, Wed, 2 – 6pm, and
for parties of 20 or more by appt

Entrance: £5, children free

The garden is blessed with a south-west-facing valley setting and with an abundance of natural water, but it is the vision and commitment of Judy Pearce that have since 1992 turned the 12 acres into an outstanding amalgam of contemporary styles. The formal plantings around the farmhouse include a modern interpretation of a cottage garden with a thatched summerhouse and a 'bobble garden' of standard topiary. The style becomes more natural as the garden extends down the valley and blends into the surrounding fields. A spring-fed water course, planted in shades of gold and russet, flows into the top lake, where an impressive rockwork by Anthony Archer-Wills is sited to command the view. A shady hosta walk, with birches and hydrangeas, leads to the bottom lake created from a stream, which is surrounded by natural planting and blends into a wildflower meadow. The stream cascades into a deep ravine before returning to its natural course. The innovative planting schemes elsewhere, initiated by Mary Payne, are the hallmark of the garden – none more so than the widely praised 'steppe' and 'prairie' areas. The first, peaking from May to July, has rhythmical clumps of foliage plants and splashes of colour from strong-hued summer flowers. The other, at its most colourful from July to December, is filled with substantial groups of heleniums, achilleas, rudbeckias, eupatoriums and the like, and many ornamental grasses. A 'formal prairie' has also been developed using different grasses and perennials, colour-themed from silver and cerise through to purple. Magnificent.

MILTON LODGE ★
(Historic Garden Grade II)

The terraced garden, planted c. 1914 in Arts and Crafts style and replanted by the present owner in the 1960s, is cultivated down the side of a hill overlooking the Vale of Avalon, affording a magnificent view of Wells Cathedral. A wide variety of plants, many of them tender and all suitable for the alkaline soil, provides a succession of colour and interest from March to October. Many fine trees can be seen in the four-acre garden and in the separate seven-acre arboretum with its good range of native and exotic specimens.

Mr D.C. Tudway Quilter

Wells BA5 3AQ. Tel: (01749) 672168
www.miltonlodgegardens.co.uk

0.5m N of Wells. From A39 turn N up Old Bristol Road; first gate on left

Open Easter to Oct, Tues, Wed, Sun and Bank Holiday Mons, 2 – 5pm, and for parties and coaches by appt

Entrance: £4, children under 14 free

MONTACUTE HOUSE ★
(Historic Garden Grade I)

This Elizabethan garden of grass lawns surrounded by clipped yews set in terraces is a triumph of formality. The surrealism of the topiary, which some claim was inspired by a dramatic snowfall, adds immensely to the effect. A large water feature has replaced the original Elizabethan high circular mount, and there is a charming raised walk, two original pavilions and an arcaded garden house probably devised by Lord Curzon while he was a tenant. Colour is provided by herbaceous borders and from midsummer by twin scented rose borders. An avenue of 72 limes is now established, and the gardens are surrounded by graceful parklands giving vistas and an impression of space.

The National Trust

Montacute TA15 6XP. Tel: (01935) 823289;
www.nationaltrust.org.uk

4m W of Yeovil. Signposted from A3088 and A303 near Ilchester

House open 9th March, 15th March to 2nd Nov, 11am – 5pm, Wed – Mon

Park open all year, daily, dawn – dusk.

Garden open 1st to 14th March, 5th Nov to 1st Jan 2009, Wed – Sun, 11am – 4pm; 15th March to 2nd Nov, Wed – Mon, 11am – 6pm

Entrance: £5.70. Children £2.80 (house, garden and park £9.50, children £4.50, family £23.50.

PRIOR PARK LANDSCAPE GARDEN ★
(Historic Garden Grade I)

The Palladian mansion, designed by the architect John Wood from 1735 for Bath's leading entrepreneur and philanthropist Ralph Allen, dominates the steeply sloping landscape and provides stunning views of the city. While the mansion is owned and used by Prior Park College and is not open to the public, the grounds below are well worth the circular walk

The National Trust

Ralph Allen Drive, Bath BA2 5AH.
Tel: (01225) 833422 (General Enquiries);
www.nationaltrust.org.uk

No parking at garden or nearby; catch bus from city centre or walk up A3062 from Widcombe

Open March to Oct, Wed – Mon, 11am
– 5.30pm; Nov to 22nd Feb 2009, Sat
and Sun, 11am – dusk (last admission
1 hour before closing). Closed 25th and
26th Dec, 1st Jan

Entrance: £5, children £2.80,
family £12.80

Other information: Small area for
pre-booked disabled parking, but
limited access for disabled

(allow 90 minutes) from the entrance gate off Ralph Allen
Drive. Allen landscaped and planted continuously from 1734
to 1764, helped by several gardeners, notably 'Capability'
Brown, who eliminated areas of formality, and Alexander
Pope, who inspired the Wilderness. The serpentine lake
stretching out from the Rococo sham bridge has been
restored, and much new planting of shrubs and herbaceous
perennials to achieve the theatrical effect beloved of
eighteenth-century landscapers is taking place in this area,
especially around the Cabinet – a gravel clearing at the base
of the main cascade and the grotto. The walk continues from
the mansion viewpoint down the east side of the valley (steep
in places) to the lakes and the Palladian bridge of 1755,
returning by the west side of the valley via the Rock Gate.
Undoubtedly two-star are the views of the Palladian bridge,
the mansion from the bridge and the city of Bath; the 'Priory
path' leading into the field next to the garden gives a
panoramic view over the whole city.

Mr and Mrs J. Southwell

Pear Tree House, Litton BA3 4PP.
Tel: (01761) 241220

15m S of Bristol, 7.5m N of Wells on
B3114, 0.25m beyond Litton and The
Kings Arms

Open mid-Feb for snowdrops and
hellebores; then 25th May to 28th Sept,
Mon; all 11am – 6pm.
Telephone for details of Feb and Oct
opening dates and times

Entrance: £3, children free

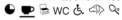

SHERBORNE GARDEN

This rather surreal garden displays a very personal choice of
specimen trees, grasses and water garden features in a 6.5-
acre site reclaimed from farmland. It is an excellent example
of how natural pasture land may be tamed and surface water
channelled into ponds. The owners are compulsive tree
people who since 1963 have planted hundreds of native and
exotic trees, expanding the original cottage garden and
paddock into a mini-arboretum. The garden now boasts a
one-acre grove of native species, a pinetum, nut hedges, a
collection of species roses, gravel beds with collections of
giant grasses and about 200 varieties of hemerocallis, a Prickly
Wood bristling with 100 varieties of holly, and a collection of
over 250 ferns. The demise of several Leyland cypresses has
prompted the making of a new shrubbery and a 'circus' of
dwarf conifers. In such experienced and creative hands this
garden never stands still, and the twin themes of trees and
water – a *wadi* was constructed as a millennium project – are
continually being celebrated and extended.

Von Essen Hotels

Ston Easton, near Bath BA3 4DF.
Tel: (01761) 241631;
www.stoneaston.co.uk

11m SW of Bath, 6m NE of Wells
on A39

Open all year, daily, during daylight hours

Entrance: free

Other information: Teas and toilet
facilities in hotel

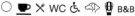

STON EASTON PARK ★

(Historic Garden Grade II)

The magnificent Palladian house is set in a 36-acre park
replanned and replanted by Humphry Repton in 1792,
reached by a suitably impressive drive winding past the old
stables. The glory is the view from inside the great Saloon, or
from the terrace immediately outside, over the River Norr
with a bridge and an elegant stepped cascade. Repton made
a Red Book with his proposals for improvement, and the
previous owners worked on the restoration of the park to his
plans. Beyond the terrace are wide lawns with fine specimen
trees and extensive woodland with many glades and paths. At

some distance from the house is a vast sheltered walled garden, partly ornamental and partly productive, divided by Penelope Hobhouse into beech-hedged enclosures. Many new projects and plans are now underway in this area.

WAYFORD MANOR ★
(Historic Garden Grade II)

Four acres of gardens surround a fine manor house dating from the thirteenth century with Elizabethan and Victorian additions. This is a good example of the work of Harold Peto, who redesigned the garden in 1902. The formal upper terrace with yew hedges and topiary fronting the house has panoramic views over west Dorset. Steps down to the second terrace lead to a new stone-pillared pergola complementing the loggia designed by Peto, which in turn complemented the Elizabethan porch to the house. Below the rockery and grass tennis court is an area of partly wild woodland gardens with plantings of mature trees and shrubs, including fine maples, cornus, magnolias, rhododendrons and spring bulbs. Colourful displays of candelabra primulas, arum lilies, gunneras and other moisture-lovers fringe the lower ponds. Natural spring water is used throughout this south-facing, multi-layered garden, where widespread planting continues apace.

Mr and Mrs R. L. Goffe
Crewkerne TA18 8QG.
Tel: (01460) 73253
3m SW of Crewkerne off B3165 at Clapton
Open for NGS, and for parties of 10 or more by appt at other times
Entrance: £3, children (6-15) £1
 WC

YARLINGTON HOUSE

The varied formal garden is blessed with an ideal mix of design and planting. The fine pleached lime square surrounding the rose garden and the romantic sunken Italian garden, complete with classical statuary and balustrades and awash with scent and soft colours, complement the scale and style of the distinguished 1780s house. Created by the present owners over forty years, the garden is at a satisfying stage of maturity within the setting of the fine surrounding parkland. Within 2.5 acres it achieves skilful mood changes, moving

Count and Countess Charles de Salis
Yarlington, Wincanton BA9 8DY.
Tel: (01963) 440344
In village of Yarlington S of Castle Cary, signposted off A371
Open for parties of 10 or more by appt
Entrance: £3.50, children free

Yarlington House

307

Other information: Lunch or tea by arrangement, can include visit to house.

 WC &♿ 🏠 B&B

gradually from the more formal areas to an unusual circle of crab apples trained in the shape of a bandstand (J.C. Loudon's 'apple house') and down towards a dell replete with ferns and shade-loving specimens. Vegetables and fruit trees are grown within a magnificent walled garden approached through impressive gates. Early in the year the daffodils make their point before the laburnum walk comes into flower over a Gothic-arched pergola. The Emperor Napoleon is commemorated in the Italian garden, surrounded by roses – 'Empress Josephine' and 'Souvenir de la Malmaison' of course. A dovecote is stationed within the small children's garden.

Louise and Fergus Dowding

East Street, Martock TA12 6NF.
Tel: (01935) 822202

6m NW of Yeovil off A303. Turn off main street through village at Market House onto East Street; garden is 150 yards on right after post office

Open June to Aug for parties of 15 or more by appt

Entrance: £3.50, children free

NEW ●

YEWS FARM

Located on the edge of the Somerset Levels in the lovely small town of Martock, the dramatic one-acre garden lies behind a thirteenth-century cruck-framed house. Surrounded by walls and buildings built of rich golden Hamstone and sheltered by its setting, it has a strong layout set off by a long season of wonderfully natural plantings, mainly of perennials. Inspired by shape, height and texture, Louise Dowding has used block planting in a restricted and imaginative palette to achieve skilful effects with colourful head-high plant associations accented by judicious self-seeding and formal clipped box shapes. The heavy accent on soil fertility comes courtesy of the farmyard pigs and chickens, with the healthy and intensive plantings and superb organic vegetable garden as living proof of its benefits. Visitors leave with memories of a contemporary garden of personal inspiration and discovery.

OTHER RECOMMENDED GARDENS

BARRINGTON COURT

Barrington, Ilminster TA19 0NQ (01460 241938; www.nationaltrust.org.uk). Open March to Oct, daily except Wed, 11am – 5pm (closes 4.30pm March and Oct. NT

Set in parkland, the 2 acres of formal garden are in the Hidcote style of garden rooms, with many of the planting schemes based on the plans Gertrude Jekyll drew up in 1917. The walled kitchen garden is vast and productive. (Listed Grade II*)

BECKFORD'S TOWER

Lansdown Road, Bath BA1 9BH (01225 460705). Open Easter to Oct, Sat, Sun and Bank Holiday Mons, 10.30am – 5pm

William Beckford's Graeco-Italian tower, standing high above Bath, was designed as a place for reading, writing and reflection, and it

was also to be his burial place. The site is now planted with shrubs known to have been used by the eccentric recluse in his extensive gardens. (Listed Grade II)

CITY OF BATH BOTANICAL GARDENS

Royal Victoria Park, Upper Bristol Road, Bath BA1 2NQ (01225 448433). Open all year, daily, 8.30am – dusk

The gardens created in 1887 to house a collection of plants assembled over a lifetime by an enthusiastic amateur botanist and plant collector, and extended and improved 100 years later, have become one of the finest collections, certainly in the West Country, of plants on limestone. 9.5 acres.

HERSCHEL MUSEUM OF ASTRONOMY

New King Street, Bath BA1 2BL (01225 446865; www.bath-preservation-trust.org.uk). Open Feb to 15th Dec, daily except Wed, 1 — 5pm (opens 11 am Sat, Sun and Bank Holiday Mons)

Historical research has enabled the re-creation of a charming Georgian town garden with a curious arbour, using plants that might have existed there in the astronomer s time.

JASMINE COTTAGE

Mr and Mrs Michael Redgrave, 26 Channel Road, Clevedon BS21 7BY (01275 871850; www.bologrew.pwp.blueyonder.co.uk). Open May to July, Thurs, 11am — 4pm; for NGS; and by appt May to Sept

Concealed behind a perfectly ordinary house front is a stylish and imaginative 0.35-acre garden, with herbaceous borders, island beds, a pergola walk and a decorative potager all crammed into a tiny patch. The exuberant plantings range from old-fashioned roses, climbers and mixed shrubs to a 50-strong collection of salvias.

LITTLE GARTH

Roger and Marion Pollard, Dowlish Wake TA19 0NX (01460 52594). Open for NGS, and June to Aug by appt

An immaculate 0.5-acre garden with a long season of superbly colourful plantings, achieved mainly by the skilful and artistic use of a wide range of perennials, grasses and bulbs. The different sections surrounding the house include a glorious rainbow border, a gentle species-based bed and colour-themed terraces with many unusual herbaceous plants.

LOWER SEVERALLS

Mary Pring, Crewkerne TA18 7NX (01460 73234; www.lowerseveralls.co.uk). Open March to July and Sept, Tues, Wed, Fri, Sat and most Bank Holiday Mons, 10am — 5pm

Several different garden rooms thrive in the sheltered valley setting of the 2.5-acre cottage garden, including water and bog gardens fed by a spring and a dry garden built up to form a windbreak. Quirky features and everything delightful. The attached nursery stocks a good range of herbs and garden plants.

LYTES CARY

Charlton Mackrell, Somerton TA11 7HU (01458 224471). Open 15th March to 2nd Nov, Sat and Wed (plus Good Fri), 11am — 5pm. NT

The 6-acre Arts and Crafts garden is a pleasing setting for the Elizabethan house, with a long, wide border replanted to Graham Stuart Thomas s original design, lawns with hedges in the Elizabethan style, topiary and a large orchard. (Listed Grade II)

TINTINHULL HOUSE

Farm Street, Tintinhull, Yeovil BA22 9PZ (01935 822545). Open 15th March to 2nd Nov, Wed — Sun and Bank Holiday Mons, 11am — 5pm. NT

A 2-acre garden developed from the 1930s by a great gardener, Phyllis Rees, in the Hidcote style, with a sequence of garden rooms divided by walls and hedges. (Listed Grade II)

WATCOMBE

Peter and Ann Owen. 92 Church Road, Winscombe BS25 1BP (01934 842666). Open for NGS, and for parties by appt

The 0.75-acre garden is traditional, with an unusual Edwardian feel, and this has inspired the present owners to refine and improve the generous and varied planting within a strong, somewhat Italianate framework. A handsome pergola dripping with selected wisterias and a pleached lime avenue underplanted with rare narcissi are special features. The more formal part is distinguished by stately trees and exceptional topiary.

WOODBOROUGH

Porlock Weir TA24 8NZ (01643 862406). Open April and May by appt

An interesting garden of 2 acres created on a steep hillside with magnificent views over Porlock Bay. The wide variety of shrubs includes unusual rhododendrons and azaleas.

STAFFORDSHIRE

For further information about how to use the *Guide*
and for an explanation of the symbols, see pages vi–viii.
Specific dates and times are those given to us by garden owners for 2008.
For 2009 dates, check with the individual properties.
For opening dates under the National Gardens Scheme,
readers should consult *The Yellow Book* or www.ngs.org.uk.
Maps are to be found at the end of the *Guide*.

Alton Towers

Alton ST10 4DB.
Tel: (08705) 204060;
www.altontowers.com

From N take M6 junction 16 or M1 junction 28, from S take M6 junction 15 or M1 junction 23A. Signposted.

Theme park, ruins and grounds open March to Oct daily, 9.30am – 5pm, 6pm or 7pm

Entrance: see website for current pricing. Tickets from £24 adults, £16 children

○ WC B&B

ALTON TOWERS ★

(Historic Park Grade I)

This fantastic Elysium of ornamental garden buildings was created between 1814 and 1827 by the 15th Earl of Shrewsbury. It contains many beautiful and unusual features, including the three-storey cast-iron Chinese pagoda fountain – a copy of the To Ho pagoda in Canton. W. A. Nesfield was active here (one of his parterres is still *in situ* though in need of restoration). The enormous rock garden is planted with a range of conifers, acers and sedums. The fine domed conservatory houses pelargoniums etc. according to the season, and the terraces have rose and herbaceous borders. There is a Dutch garden, Her Ladyship's Garden, featuring yew and rose beds, an Italian garden, a yew-arch walkway and woodland walks. Water adds further beauty and interest. All this plus the manifold attractions of the theme park. In all, 500 acres.

The National Trust

Grange Road, Biddulph, Staffordshire, Moorlands ST8 7SD.
Tel: (01782) 517999 (Garden Office);
www.nationaltrust.org.uk

BIDDULPH GRANGE GARDEN ★★

(Historic Garden Grade I)

This is one of the most remarkable and innovative gardens of the nineteenth century, 15 acres in extent. The Egyptian garden is marked by a pyramid and obelisks of clipped yew, the Chinese garden by a joss house, a golden water buffalo

Biddulph Grange Garden

overlooking a dragon parterre, a watch tower and a temple reflected in a calm pool. In front of the house terraces descend to a lily pond. The stumpery demonstrates an innovative Victorian way of displaying suitable plants. The verbena, araucaria and rose parterres and the Shelter House and dahlia walk (with over 600 dahlias) have now been restored just as they were in the middle of the nineteenth century, and the long Wellingtonia avenue, felled and replanted in 1995, is beginning to make its presence felt again. In all, one of the country's most unusual gardening rediscoveries and restorations, worth visiting at any time of year – it should not be missed.

3.5m SE of Congleton, 7m N of Stoke-on-Trent. Access from A527 Biddulph-Congleton road

Open 15th March to 2nd Nov, Wed – Sun and Bank Holiday Mons, 11.00am – 5.00pm

Entrance: £6.40, children £3.20, family £14.90

12 DARGES LANE

A 0.25-acre garden on two levels, attractively laid out, well stocked and of great interest to plantsmen. Fine trees and a large variety of shrubs and foliage plants are the background to a comprehensive collection of flowering plants and small shrubs, among them prunus, spiraea, azara and abutilon. Some are unusual, even rare, and there is room too for 93 varieties of clematis and a National Collection of lamiums. Borders are complemented by island beds, and a small water garden with a circular paved area and a water feature. Every inch is used to grow or set off the plants, and there is year-round appeal for flower arrangers. Spring is the owner's favourite time, when hellebores, erythroniums and trilliums are in flower, along with tulips and *Paeonia* 'Joseph Rock'. The overall effect is attractive as well as enticing to the plant lover. Plants for sale include some more unusual ones.

Mrs A. Hackett

Great Wyrley, Walsall WS6 6LE.
Tel: (01922) 415064

2m SE of Cannock. From A5 (Churchbridge junction) take A34 towards Walsall. First turning on right over brow of hill. House on right on corner of Cherrington Drive

Open for NGS, and by appt

Entrance: £2.50

Other information: Plants for sale on open days

THE DOROTHY CLIVE GARDEN ★

Created by the late Colonel Clive in memory of his wife, this 12-acre garden has wide appeal in terms both of design and inspired planting, including a quarry garden filled with rhododendrons and azaleas, and a pool with a scree garden rising on the hillside above it which will give gardeners many

Willoughbridge Garden Trust

Willoughbridge, Market Drayton, Shropshire TF9 4EU. Tel: (01630) 647237; www.dorothyclivegardens.co.uk

7m NE of Market Drayton, 1m E of Woore on A51 between Nantwich and Stone

The Dorothy Clive Garden

Open 15th March to Oct, daily,
10am – 5.30pm

Entrance: £5, concessions £4,
children (11–16) £1, under 11 free

Other information: Disabled parking

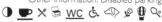

good ideas. The guidebook identifies the highlights season by season. In spring there are unusual bulbs and primulas, a daffodil and a tulip walk; in summer colourful shrubs combine with unusual perennials and conifers; many other trees provide autumn colour. The garden has been extended, and new features include a laburnum arch with roses and other climbers, and a gravel garden.

SHUGBOROUGH ★
(Historic Park Grade I)

Shugborough Estate

Milford, Stafford ST17 0XB.
Tel: (01889) 881388;
www.shugborough.org.uk

6m E of Stafford on A513

Estate open 14th March to 24th Oct,
daily 11am-5pm, and for parties by
appt all year

Entrance: £12, OAPs £9.50, children £7,
family £30

Other information: Guided tours and
demonstrations available. Batricars
available.

Shugborough is of interest to garden historians because Thomas Wright of Durham worked here. Many of the buildings and monuments in the 878-acre park are ascribed to James 'Athenian' Stuart and were built for Thomas Anson from the 1740s onwards. These are some of the earliest examples of English neo-classicism, and there is also an early example of Chinoiserie based on a sketch made by one of the officers on Admiral Anson's voyage round the world. In the 22-acre formal gardens, the Victorian layout with terraces by Nesfield was revitalised for the Trust in the mid-1960s by Graham Stuart Thomas, who also worked on the Edwardian-style rose garden. Due to an outbreak of phytophthora, all the roses except the ramblers have been replaced by herbaceous plantings specifically chosen to attract bees and butterflies, harmoniously grouped in small beds. Seasonal attractions include massed plantings of daffodils along the river bank, azaleas, rhododendrons, a fine long-flowering herbaceous border and good autumn colours. In the park the aim is to restore the landscape to its eighteenth-century appearance; over 1000 trees, predominantly oak and sweet chestnut, have already been planted, and wild flowers and grasses are also being re-established. Parkland walks include the re-created eighteenth- and nineteenth-century woodland walks with fine views and the impressive Hadrian's Arch monument.

Shugborough

15 ST JOHN'S ROAD

The small garden is skilfully landscaped so as to appear larger. It contains a wide range of delights, from a tropical area near the house, past a pool and a varied collection of trees, shrubs, climbers (33 different clematis) and flowers, to a Japanese feature at the far end, where a stream runs under a little bridge. The smaller trees include acers, and there are shrubs, grasses, ferns, hostas, perennials and clematis blooming through the season, with annuals adding splashes of colour. In 2004 a new garden was reclaimed from waste land, trees and shrubs planted in gravel, a wildlife pool dug, and a shaded woodland path made under a large willow tree.

Maureen and Sid Allen

Pleck, Walsall WS2 9TJ.
Tel: (01922) 442348

10m NW of Birmingham. From M6 junction 10, head towards Walsall on A454, and turn right into Pleck Road (A4148). St John's Road is fourth right

Open by appt

Entrance: £2, children free

TRENTHAM GARDENS ★
(Historic Park Grade II*)

Over several centuries, the progressive aggrandisement of Trentham Hall and the Leveson-Gower family went hand-in-hand. In 1759 'Capability' Brown was brought in to re-landscape the 750-acre park and in 1833 Charles Barry commissioned to lay out the Italian Flower Gardens – the two most important features remaining today. When in 1911 the 2nd Duke of Sutherland sold up, most of the hall was demolished and the grounds degenerated into a public amenity space, although some magnificent trees and decaying garden buildings remained as reminders of the glory days. Now Dominic Cole, Piet Oudolf, Tom Stuart-Smith and Michael Walker are masterminding its salvation. The upper part of the Italian Gardens has been restored and the lower part reinterpreted in the modern perennial style. Following this, trees will be planted in perimeter woodlands and in the western pleasure ground to connect the formal gardens to the park, while wildflower and perennials meadows will lead to a grass amphitheatre overlooking the lake. If the project fulfils its ambitions it will be a worthy chapter in a grandiose history.

Trentham Leisure Ltd

Stone Road, Trentham,
Stoke-on-Trent ST4 8AX.
Tel: (01782) 657341;
www.trenthamgardens.co.uk

2m S of Stoke-on-Trent on A34,
2m E of M6 junction 15

Open all year, daily, 10am – 6pm

Entrance: £6.50, concessions £6,
children £5.50, family £22 (2007 prices)

OTHER RECOMMENDED GARDENS

THE GARTH

Mr and Mrs David Wright, 2 Broc Hill Way, Milford, Stafford ST17 0UB (01785 661182). Open for NGS, and for parties by appt

The 0.5-acre garden laid out of a steep slope, with old caves to discover at the bottom, is divided into areas filled with an astonishing range of plants. Inspiration here to suit the taste of any gardener.

MOSELEY OLD HALL

Fordhouses, Wolverhampton WV10 7HY (01902 782808; www.nationaltrust.org.uk). Open March to 2nd Nov, Wed, Sat and Sun, plus Bank Holiday Mons and Tues following (except 6th May), 12 noon – 5pm; 9th Nov to 21st Dec, Sun, 12 noon – 4pm. NT

The 1-acre garden, surrounding the Elizabethan house where Charles II hid after the Battle of Worcester, is of particular appeal to those interested in 17th-century species, disposed in the fashion of the period in knot, walled and herb gardens, a nut walk and a small orchard. Fine spring blossom and autumn colour.

SUFFOLK

For further information about how to use the *Guide*
and for an explanation of the symbols, see pages vi–viii.
Specific dates and times are those given to us by garden owners for 2008.
For 2009 dates, check with the individual properties.
For opening dates under the National Gardens Scheme,
readers should consult *The Yellow Book* or www.ngs.org.uk.
Maps are to be found at the end of the *Guide*.

Mr and Mrs Timothy Easton

Bedfield, Woodbridge, IP13 7JJ
Tel: (01728) 628380

15m N of Ipswich off A140. Turn right
onto A1120, and in Earl Soham turn left
after church, signed to Bedfield. With
Bedfield primary school and red phone
box on left, take right turn into Church
Road; house is just past church. Parking
on green by church

Open June to Oct by appt for parties of
8 or more

Entrance: £3 for independent viewing or
£6 per person inc. tea/coffee and
introductory talk

● ▭ ఉ

BEDFIELD HALL ★

Timothy Easton is an artist and architectural historian,
Christine a painter. Their artistic bent is immediately obvious
in the two-acre garden surrounding the Gothicised house
dating from 1421 to *c*.1830. One acre – The Platform – is
girdled by a thirteenth-century moat, with a secondary
moated area of nuttery and wild woodland; there is also an
island. Central to the plan is a formal herb, vegetable and
picking garden hidden behind high yew hedges and arched
wooden gates. It is ringed by calmer areas of varied
greenery: yew and box topiary, grey-olive wooden arches,
and no fewer than five bridges, also painted grey-olive and
inspired by the Gothick finials on the house. The way
forward leads over these bridges and high walkways from
one area to another with elevated views over colourful and
exuberant plantings of irises, roses, lavender, clematis,
honeysuckles, grasses and much more. Without ever
retracing your steps, you then pass through a new orchard
with a hen-house and along a topiaried yew walk beside the
water, lengthened by false perspectives, with vistas
deliberately drawing in the surrounding arable fields. The

Bedfield Hall

whole two acres exhibit strong bones and instinctive, well-informed planting. Church, tower and house make an interesting architectural group with the garden.

BLAKENHAM WOODLAND GARDEN

The Tory cabinet minister who became Lord Blakenham planted five acres on a hill above the village between 1950 and 1982. It was his rural retreat from urban political life where he could hear the birdsong and relax in its peace. He succeeded admirably, and his passion for planting and the atmosphere he created have been intensified by the present generation. Though the woodland is clearly managed, the birds still sing in the trees above a carpet of native primroses and bluebells in due season. Other planting is more exotic: rhododendrons, azaleas and magnolias now flower blithely alongside bamboos and phormiums, interspersed with sculptures, belvederes and rustic huts from which to enjoy the serenity. At the heart of the wood is a surprise which never fails to enchant visiting children: a tilting, spiralling grass landform with a central chalk 'plughole', ringed by tall sycamores. At Blakenham even the badgers have their own reserved dell. A delight on a spring or early summer day.

Little Blakenham, Ipswich IP8 4LZ.
Tel: (07760) 342131

4m NW of Ipswich, 1m off B1113.
Signed from The Beeches in
Little Blakenham, 1m off old A1100
(now B1113)

Open March to June, daily, 10am – 5pm.

Parties welcome by appt

Entrance: £3

BUCKLESHAM HALL ★

The great interest of Bucklesham is how these 7.5 acres of interlocking gardens, terraces and lakes have been created from scratch since 1973 by the previous owners and added to and further improved by the present owners since 1994. A Monet-type bridge was built in 1999 with a waterfall falling between two lakes, and a 16-step water staircase has also been made so that the water flows from an island lake into the streams. Round the house are secret gardens packed with flowers; beds of old-fashioned roses overflow their borders, and a courtyard garden created with the use of every kind of container. Descending terraces of lawns, ponds and streams lead to the woodland and beyond; round each corner is a new vista and a fresh delight. Spring and summer are spectacular here, with displays of daffodils and tulips, rhododendrons, camellias and rare Japanese maples, followed by an abundance of roses.

Mr and Mrs D. R. Brightwell

Bucklesham, Ipswich IP10 0AY.
Tel: (01473) 659263

6m SE of Ipswich, 0.5m E of
Bucklesham. Entrance opposite and
N of primary school

Open for parties by appt

Entrance: £5

COLUMBINE HALL ★

A nine-acre garden of great subtlety, gentle order and picturesque charm, with planting interest assured from April through to July. The lime-washed manor house, a characterful example of medieval craftsmanship, stands proudly in its rhomboidal moat like a ship in dock. In the entrance courtyard, French in feeling, architectural plants – clipped standards and box mounds, cardoons, a fig and a vine – spring out of gravel or hug the house. The architectural embellishments are eye-catching too. What is clever about the

Hew Stevenson and
Leslie Geddes-Brown

Stowupland, Stowmarket IP14 4AT.
Tel: (01449) 612219;
www.columbinehall.co.uk

1.5m NE of Stowmarket. Turn N off
A1120 opposite Shell garage across
village green, then right at T-junction into
Gipping Road. Garden drive is on left
just beyond de-restriction sign

Open for NGS, and by appt

Entrance: £3, children free

Other information: Self-catering accommodation available.

 WC &

garden (much of it the work of George Carter) is that it has a series of uncluttered spaces defined by hornbeam hedges. These are not outdoor rooms, for they allow movement through generous openings, glimpses into other parts of the garden and views out to the countryside. Flowers cluster at the base of pleached limes or in strips running parallel to grass paths. Towards the perimeter, rides are mown through meadows beneath native trees. There is one surprise: a hidden, sinuous bog garden planted with great discrimination. In all, 29 acres.

David and Yvonne Leonard

Field Road, Mildenhall IP28 7AL. Tel: (01638) 712742

15m W of Bury St Edmunds off A11, 1m from Mildenhall centre. From Fiveways roundabout at Barton Mills follow signs to Mildenhall

Open by appt May and June only

Entrance: £3, children free

NEW 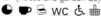 WC

CROSSBILLS

In their 0.3-acre garden on the sandy soil of Suffolk's Breckland, the present owners decided around 1995 to root up their lawns and create instead two quite different gravel gardens using drought-tolerant plants. They have travelled the world from Arizona to South Africa searching for the right wild species. His fiefdom, the front garden, is filled with cistus, grasses and Mediterranean herbs, giving the effect of a Provencal wilderness on the flat. Hers is the back garden, where the gravel is more hidden, the effect – due in part to lots of lavender and atmospheric Douglas firs – more cultivated and cottagey. Both are gloriously colourful, unusual and inspiring for designers and plantsmen alike.

Mr and Mrs Rupert Eley

East Bergholt CO7 6UP. Tel: (01206) 299224

8m SW of Ipswich, 2m E of A12 on B1070

Open March to Oct, daily, 10am – 5pm. Closed 23rd March

Entrance: £3, children free

EAST BERGHOLT PLACE

The bones of this charming, meandering woodland garden were laid out over the 20 acres by the current owner's great-grandfather, Charles Eley, between 1900 and 1914; some of the rare mature trees, azaleas and rhododendrons came from George Forrest, the great plant collector. Rupert Eley has built on this sure foundation, creating woodland walks, formal and informal ponds and streams while keeping the atmosphere of an English garden loosely inspired by the Himalayas – the whole is a mixture of the romantic and the disciplined. Many of the exotic trees and shrubs are labelled. The walled garden has been turned into an extensive and well-kept nursery.

The Duke and Duchess of Grafton

Thetford, Norfolk IP24 2QP. Tel: (01842) 766366; www.eustonhall.co.uk

11m NE of Bury St Edmunds, 3m S of Thetford on A1088

House open as garden

Garden open 19th June to 18th Sept, Thurs, plus 29th June, 13th July and 7th Sept; all 2.30 – 5pm

Entrance: £4 (house and garden £6)

EUSTON HALL ★
(Historic Park Grade II*)

This is the epitome of the English landscape park. The 74-acre pleasure grounds laid out in the seventeenth century by John Evelyn have grown into a forest of yew, but straight rides trace out the original formal layout. Also from this period are the stone gate piers which, together with the remnants of a great avenue, mark the original approach to the house. Fronted by terraces, the mellow red-brick hall stands among extensive lawns and parkland along a winding river, composed by William Kent in the 1740s, as is the splendid domed temple isolated on an eminence to the east and the pretty garden house in the formal garden by the house. The small lake was

Euston Hall

the work of 'Capability' Brown. Today, the planting is admirably restrained, with many fine specimen trees and a wealth of shrub roses, leaving the original designers' genius intact; further evidence of their brilliance is visible from the rooms of the house.

HAUGHLEY PARK ★

A curious mixture of eighteenth-century-style landscaped park and nineteenth-century evergreens, plus rhododendrons and azaleas, gives this huge garden a unique atmosphere. Unexpected secret gardens with clipped hedges or flint and brick walls hide immaculate flower beds, climbers and flowering shrubs; each garden has its own character. The main lawn is surrounded by herbaceous borders, with a splendid lime avenue at the end drawing the eye across open countryside. Rhododendrons, azaleas and camellias grow on soil which is, unexpectedly for Suffolk, lime-free. The trees include a 12-metre-wide magnolia and a flourishing oak reputed to be a thousand years old. Beyond are the walled kitchen garden, greenhouses and shrubbery. In spring the broad rides and walks through the ancient woodland reveal not only the newly planted trees, specimen rhododendrons and other ornamental shrubs, but also 10 acres of bluebells, two acres of lilies-of-the-valley and half a mile of mauve *ponticum* rhododendrons.

Mr R. J. Williams

Stowmarket IP14 3JY.
Tel: (01359) 240701;
www.haughleyparkbarn.co.uk

4m NW of Stowmarket, signed to Haughley Park (not to Haughley) on A14

House open by appt

Garden open 20th April and 5th May for bluebells, then May to Sept, Tues, 2 – 5.30pm

Entrance: £3, children under 16 free

Other information: Coaches by appt. Teas and plants for sale on bluebell Suns

 <u>WC</u>

HELMINGHAM HALL GARDENS ★★

(Historic Garden Grade I)
Nineteen generations of Tollemaches have lived here, and though there have been many changes over the past five centuries the property retains a strong Elizabethan atmosphere. The double-moated Tudor mansion house of great splendour and charm, built of warm red brick, stands in a 400-acre deer park. A nineteenth-century parterre, edged with a magnificent spring border, leads to the Elizabethan kitchen garden which is surrounded by the Saxon moat with banks covered in daffodils. Within the walls the kitchen garden has been transformed into an enchanting potager most subtly planted; the meticulously maintained herbaceous borders and old-fashioned roses surround beds of vegetables separated by

Lord Tollemache

Helmingham, Stowmarket IP14 6EF.
Tel: (01473) 890799 (Sarah Harris);
www.helmingham.com

9m N of Ipswich on B1077

Open 4th May to 14th Sept, Wed and Sun, 2 – 6pm, and for parties by appt

Entrance: £5, concessons £4.50, children £3

 <u>WC</u>

Helmingham Hall
Gardens

arched tunnels of sweet peas and dangling gourds. Large beds along the walls have been cleverly split up by iron dividers and planted with geometrically arranged herb and box beds. Outside is a lushly planted south-facing spring border which includes many irises and peonies. There are also wildflower areas, fruit trees, a shady yew walk, knot and herb gardens. Lady Tollemache is a gifted plantswoman and designer, and her own garden increasingly benefits from her skill.

Mark Rumary

High Street, Yoxford IP17 3EP.
Tel: (01728) 668321

4m N of Saxmundham on A12.
In main street, next to Griffin Inn

Open for NGS, and by appt

Entrance: £3

 WC

MAGNOLIA HOUSE ★

In this 1.4-acre garden laid out behind a village house and surrounded by high walls, the designer Mark Rumary has managed to create at least four different moods and a coherent plan – paths always lead somewhere. Near the house is a paved area. The largest part of the garden is laid to lawn surrounded by plants chosen for their leaf shapes, colours and textures: phormiums, berberis, cardoons. A beech arch leads to a more formal Italian section with a lily pond and fountain; the walls are planted with figs and daturas, and colours here are basically white, yellow and blue. Behind a yew hedge a shady garden, Victorian and inspiration combines order and informality with box heding and bedding plants, spotted laurels, ferns, bamboos and ivies. A dell at the far end has shady bamboos and ferns beside a water trough. A delight all summer.

Mr and Mrs B. Blower

North Cove, Beccles NR34 7PH.
Tel: (01502) 476631

3.5m E of Beccles, 50 metres off
A146 Lowestoft road

Open under Invitation to View
scheme – telephone for details

Entrance: £3, children free

 WC 🚻 ⬧

NORTH COVE HALL ★

Climbing roses adorn the sunny Georgian house set in lawns surrounded by a 25-acre park full of mature trees. The walled garden partly encloses the half-acre pond studded with water lilies and bordered by majestic *Gunnera manicata*, *Taxodium distichum* var. *imbricatum* 'Nutans', a group of *Betula jacquemontii* and *Alnus glutinosa* 'Imperialis'. A small stream with waterfalls is planted with marginals. Inside the walls are herbaceous and shrub borders, pergolas and a kitchen garden, This part occupies five acres. Outside are woodland walks among mature trees and various younger conifers; the autumn colours make this a good time to visit. It is worth walking across the park to see the church and its restored wall paintings.

PLAYFORD HALL

The Tudor red-brick house is the central feature of this 10-acre garden. Its surrounding moat runs between high brick walls and a bridge at one side and then, because of the lie of the land, the water is level with the ground at the other. Huge old roses like 'Paul's Himalyan Musk' cover the walls and drip down towards the water. Beyond the moat, the gardens vary from gently sloping lawns planted with splendid trees – a weeping lime, a swamp cypress and the poisonous Persian wing nut – to rose-hedged orchards, a formal vegetable and herb garden and wild woodland walks. The carefully thought-out borders of herbaceous plants and shrubs backed by evergreen hedges draw the eye irresistibly back to the impressive house.

Mr and Mrs Richard Innes

Playford, Ipswich IP6 9DX.
Tel: (01473) 622509

3m NE of Ipswich, 1m N of A1214 between Ipswich and Woodbridge, on edge of Playford

Open by appt

Entrance: £5

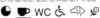 WC &

THE PRIORY ★

Set on several levels with sweeping views over Constable country, the nine-acre garden has been in the care of one family for several generations. Linked man-made and spring-fed lakes nurture waterside and aquatic plants, including masses of water lilies, and in spring the water reflects the colour of early rhododendrons and azaleas. The focal point of the largest lake is a bright red oriental-style bridge leading to a pavilion, with views back towards the house. The terrace running the full length of the house from a corner loggia, built by a local architect, shelters blue agapanthus and nerines. The walled garden created in 1929 with a wood-framed conservatory for tender and scented plants along most of one wall holds a wayward and colourful cottage-garden display of towering hollyhocks and other summer perennials. This follows on from the massed plantings of spring bulbs in neat box-edged compartments in the former formal garden. Running along the outside of the south-facing wall is a deep double border where hyacinths and tulips flower in spring, followed by perennial geraniums, lilies and delphiniums bulked out with tall plume poppies and other stately perennials. The kitchen garden has a raised bed, a rose cutting garden and a stylish pigsty. At every turn there are views across to interesting collections of plants, as well as vistas that take in two borrowed ornaments – the steeples of Stoke and Polstead churches.

Mr and Mrs Henry Engleheart

Stoke by Nayland CO6 4RL.
Tel: (01206) 262216

8m SE of Sudbury on B1068

Open for NGS, and by appt in writing

Entrance: £3, children free

 WC &

SOMERLEYTON HALL AND GARDENS ★★
(Historic Garden Grade II*)

The Jacobean house was extensively rebuilt in the mid-nineteenth century by Sir Morton Peto as an Italianate palace, and the gardens splendidly reflect this magnificence

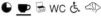

Hugh Crossley

Somerleyton, Lowestoft NR32 5QQ.
Tel: (0871) 222 4244;
www.somerleyton.co.uk

5m NW of Lowestoft, 8m SW of Great Yarmouth on B1074. Signposted

SUFFOLK

Somerleyton Hall
and Gardens

House open as garden (closed Nov),
but 11.30am – 4pm

Gardens open 16th March to June, Thurs,
Sun and Bank Holiday Mons; July and Aug,
Tues – Thurs, Sun and Bank Holiday Mon;
Sept and Oct, Thurs and Sun; Nov, Sun; all
10am – 5pm

Entrance: £5, OAPs £4, children (5–16) £3
(hall and gardens £8.25, OAPs £7.25,
children £4.25, family £23)

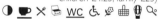

Michael Loftus

Blackheath, Wenhaston, Halesworth
IP19 9HD. Tel: (01502) 478258;
www.woottensplants.co.uk

14m SW of Lowestoft, 0.5m S of
Blythburgh off A12. Turn left in
Wenhaston by marked sign

Garden open April to Sept, Tues – Thurs;
iris field open 24th May to 10th June, daily;
hemerocallis field open 12th, 13th, 19th,
20th, 26th and 27th July; all 9.30am – 5pm

Entrance: donation box

Sir Kenneth and Lady Carlisle

Stanton, Bury St Edmunds IP31 2DW.
Tel: (01359) 250287;
www.wykenvineyards.co.uk

9m NE of Bury St Edmunds on A143.
Leave A143 between Ixworth and
Stanton. Signed to Wyken Vineyards

Open April to Oct, daily, except
Sat, 2 – 6pm

with 12 acres of formal gardens, a beautiful walled garden, an aviary, a loggia and a winter garden surrounding a sunken garden displaying statues from the original nineteenth-century winter garden. Of special note are the 1846 William Nesfield yew hedge maze, the 90-metre-long iron pergola covered in wisteria, vines and roses and the extraordinary peach cases and ridge-and-furrow greenhouses designed by Sir Joseph Paxton and now containing peaches, grapes and a rich variety of tender plants. The Victorian kitchen garden has been redeveloped, and there is also a museum of bygone gardening equipment.

WOOTTENS OF WENHASTON ★

Excavating a car park for the nursery's new iris field left the owner with enough topsoil to remove the lawn from his private garden and create a series of raised beds. These are now planted, with an excellent eye for a good plant and a good combination, in a glorious herbaceous abandon. Beds range from shaded greens and whites to exuberant mixes of poppies, alliums, columbines and irises. The two-acre iris field and one-acre hemerocallis field have special openings (see left) for their brief but fabulous flowering seasons. Since most of the plants are clearly labelled and many are for sale in the exceptional nursery adjoining, inspired visitors can take his ideas home and re-create the effects in their own gardens. An informative and well-designed handbook is also available.

WYKEN HALL ★

The combination of Sir Kenneth Carlistle, a RHS committee member, and his enterprising American wife Carla, has created an exuberant four-acre garden full of invention and surprise. It is divided into a series of rooms, starting with the wild garden and winter garden, which leads into the south and woodland garden, and so into the dell. Mown paths meander between shrubs and into the newly planted copper beech maze next to the nuttery and gazebo, then on to the rose garden, enclosed on three sides by a hornbeam hedge and on

320

the fourth by a rose-laden pergola. Beyond the wall are the knot and herb gardens, separated by yew hedges and designed by Arabella Lennox-Boyd. An 'edible garden' and a kitchen garden have been planted to the north of the house, and there is a pond just beyond the garden. The whole place is remarkable for its colours and scents, particularly in spring and early summer. Fields and orchards with wandering hens, peacocks, guinea fowl and llamas enhance the relaxed atmosphere, while the outbuildings painted in American pioneering colours are the personal touches of Lady Carlisle.

Entrance: £3.50, OAPs £3, children under 12 free

OTHER RECOMMENDED GARDENS

ABBEY GARDENS

Bury St Edmunds (01284 757067; www.stedmundsbury.gov.uk). Open all year, daily, 7.30am – dusk (opens 9am Sun)

A most surprising 14-acre municipal garden, set around the flinty stumps of the ruined Benedictine abbey. A multitude of brightly planted beds on a circular plan traces the site of the early-19th-century botanic garden, and there are scented and water gardens to stimulate other senses. (Listed Grade II)

ICKWORTH PARK

Ickworth House Park and Gardens, Horringer, Bury St Edmunds IP29 5QE (01284 735270; www.nationaltrust.org.uk). Open all year, daily except 24th to 26th Dec, 11am – 4pm; 15th March to 14th Nov, 10am – 5pm; 5th Nov to 14th March 2009, 11am – 4pm. NT

33 acres of varied gardens – Italian, spring, silver and gold – lie south of the house with its great domed rotunda. The vast park, girdled by woodland dominated by majestic trees and threaded by miles of way-marked paths, hides other pleasures, including an ornamental canal and summerhouse, walled gardens and a vineyard. (Listed Grade II*)

THE LUCY REDMAN SCHOOL OF GARDEN DESIGN

6 The Village, Rushbrooke IP30 0ER (01284 386250; www.lucyredman.co.uk). Open for NGS and Red Cross, and by appt

Sited around a charming thatched cottage, the 0.75 acre is a designer's working garden. It is therefore busy, interesting and full of ideas, both in its unusual planting – many

grasses, bamboos and herbaceous perennials – and in its design elements – a turf seat, large sculptures, decorative stone paths, a copper beech spiral. Colourful and children-friendly.

MELFORD HALL

Long Melford, Sudbury CO10 9AA (01787 379228; www.nationaltrust.org.uk). Open 22nd to 24th, 26th to 30th March, April and Oct, Sat and Sun, May to Sept, Wed – Sun (plus all Bank Holiday Mons), 1.30 – 5pm. NT

A classically English 9-acre garden of fine trees, formal gardens and a gracious lawn punctuated by great domes of yew is the harmonious setting for the mellow red-brick Elizabethan house and its rare and beautiful banqueting house.
(Listed Grade II*)

THE OLD RECTORY

Mr and Mrs Tim Fargher, Orford, Woodbridge IP12 2NN (01394 450063/450266). Open mid-April to early July, Tues – Sat, 10am – 4pm (please telephone in advance)

As might be expected in a garden designed largely by Lanning Roper with later additions by Mark Rumary, the design is classic 1960s, the planting exceptional. Woodland, wildflower meadows, a vegetable garden and fine modern sculptures. 4.5 acres.

THE THUMBIT

Mrs Ann James, Badwell Road, Walsham-le-Willows IP31 3BT (01359 259414). Open for charity by appt

A charming garden in scale with its tiny thatched cottage, skilfully designed to incorporate a fish pond and ornamental herb garden as well as curvaceous beds divided by immaculate grass paths and thickly planted with climbing roses and perennials.

SURREY

For further information about how to use the *Guide*
and for an explanation of the symbols, see pages vi–viii.
Specific dates and times are those given to us by garden owners for 2008.
For 2009 dates, check with the individual properties.
For opening dates under the National Gardens Scheme,
readers should consult *The Yellow Book* or www.ngs.org.uk.
Maps are to be found at the end of the *Guide*.
We have included some gardens with Surrey postal addresses in the London
section for convenience. So before planning a day out in Surrey it is
worth consulting pages 213–235.

BUSBRIDGE LAKES

(Historic Park Grade II*)

Mr and Mrs Douetil

Hambledon Road, Godalming GU8 4AY.
Tel: (01483) 421955;
www.busbridgelakes.co.uk

1.5m S of Godalming off B2130
Hambledon road

Open 21st to 30th March, 4th, 5th,
25th and 26th May, 17th to 25th Aug;
all 10.30am – 5.30pm; also for parties
April to Sept by appt

Entrance: £5, OAPs £4, and children
£3.50, under 5 free

Other information: Refreshments
weekends and Bank Holidays only

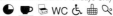 ● ● 🍵 🏠 WC & 🏛 ℺

Parkland was created here in the 1650s and the grounds were landscaped in 1750 by Philip Webb MP. Beside the largest of the three lakes stands an early-nineteenth-century Gothick boathouse, recently restored, with delicate blind windows, a room with a fireplace and two verandahs. At the end of the lake, what appears to be a bridge, multi-arched and built of rocks, proves to be an illusion. Huge plane trees dominate the lakeside; the 30-metre chestnuts, probably planted in 1660, may be the tallest in England. Tulip trees and a fine cedar of Lebanon stand near the orchard; a sequoia towers above the house. Across the canal lake is a hermit's cave, excavated in 1756 as a tomb for the then owner's wife and two of their children. Further up, a late-eighteenth-century Doric temple with two porticoes has recently been restored; below it a grotto contains the spring which feeds the lakes. There are peacocks on the lawns, and the site abounds with attractive, rare and endangered species of ducks, geese, swans and pheasants, all flourishing – as are the gardens, all 40 acres of them.

CHERKLEY COURT ★

The Beaverbrook Foundation

Reigate Road, Nr Leatherhead KT22 8QX.
Tel: (01372) 380980;
www.cherkleycourt.com

3m NE of Dorking off B2033. From M25
junction 9 take A24 towards Leatherhead,
then Dorking; passing signs to Headley
Court (Military Hospital) turn left at
roundabout onto B2033 signed to
Headley, then second right into driveway

Open April to Sept, Tues – Thurs, Sat
and Sun, 10.30am – 5pm

The grandiose 1894 mansion built in French *château* style is blessed with an astonishingly rural setting: its own parkland plus the borrowed wooded hillside of Norbury Park opposite and the National Trust lands of Box Hill and Polesden Lacey adjoining. The 400-acre estate was bought in 1911 by Max Aitken, later created Lord Beaverbrook, and from here the tentacles of his publishing empire reached out. Now the house is open for private parties, weddings and business conferences, and the 16 acres of garden have been redesigned by Simon Johnson as a reinterpretation of those glory days. His planting schemes are both robust and elegant, the hard landscaping is

Cherkley Court

beautifully done, and new sculptures and garden buildings blend in to a nicety. The main garden lies on two terraces behind the house. A broad path closed off by handsome gates and flanked by a row of tulip trees drops to an expanse of lawn with a rill, two pavilions and a grotto decorated in style by Belinda Eade. This lower terrace is backed by a long and boldly planted herbaceous border; beyond is a walnut grove planted by Lord Beaverbrook. Other areas are full of interest: a cool Italian garden contrived around an existing formal pool; an exotic planting of lilies, salvias, bananas, dahlias and cannas recreating in spirit the interior of a magnificent vanished conservatory; rising ground behind the house that is positively Mediterranean in planting and atmosphere.

Entrance: £6, concessions £4.70, children (5-16) £3.50, under 5 free.

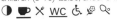

CLANDON PARK
(Historic Park Grade II)

The Palladian house was built by the Venetian architect Giacomo Leoni in the early 1730s for the 2nd Lord Onslow, whose family still owns the park even though the house and garden are now in the care of the National Trust. The wealth of successive generations of Onslows enabled them to adapt the seven acres of garden to suit changing design tastes, from formal through to Brownian and ornamental. Remnants of each survive or have been re-created – note the grotto, the parterre with its seasonal bedding schemes, the herbaceous border and the sunken Dutch garden. An oddity is the Maori meeting house, known as 'Hinemihi', brought from New Zealand over a century ago by the then Lord Onslow.

The National Trust

West Clandon, Guildford GU4 7RQ. Tel: (01483) 222482; www.nationaltrust.org.uk

3m E of Guildford on A247 at West Clandon; or take A3 to Ripley then join A247 via B2215

House open as garden

Garden open 16th March to 2nd Nov, Tues – Thurs, Sun and Bank Holiday Mons, 11am – 5pm, and for parties by appt

Entrance: house and garden £7.70, children £3.90, family £19.80

CLAREMONT LANDSCAPE GARDEN ★
(Historic Park Grade I)

This is one of the most important historic landscapes in England. Practically all the great landscape designers of the eighteenth century adapted it in turn for the new owner, the immensely wealthy man who became Duke of Newcastle. He bought the house from Sir John Vanbrugh and, for him

The National Trust

Portsmouth Road, Esher KT10 9JG. Tel: (01372) 467806; www.nationaltrust.org.uk/claremont

E of A307, just S of Esher

House (not NT) and Belvedere open – telephone for details

Garden open Jan to March, daily except Mon, 10am – 5pm; April to Oct, Mon – Fri, daily, 10am – 6pm (closes 6pm Sat, Sun and Bank Holiday Mons); Nov to Dec, daily except Mon, 10am – 5pm or sunset if earlier. Closed 25th Dec.

Entrance: £5.60, children £2.80, family £14

Other information: Coach parties must pre-book.

Vanbrugh designed the Belvedere (the views from the top are amazing). The Duke then employed Bridgeman in 1716, followed by Kent in the 1730s; the latter adapted the garden to create picturesque settings evoking various moods, and also enlarged the pond to make the lake, with a pavilion (recently restored). When the Duke died, the new owner, Clive of India, brought in 'Capability' Brown, who also redesigned the house and, in typical form, diverted the London–Portsmouth road to improve the viewpoints, the most striking of which is the grass amphitheatre. In the nineteenth century Claremont was a favourite retreat of Queen Victoria and her younger son. The 49 acres restored by the Trust are only a part of the original estate, which was broken up in 1922 when the house became a school. A useful leaflet describes the various contributions to the park, which will appeal to everyone interested in a sensitive reconstruction of the eighteenth-century English style, even if it has little to please a plant lover, except perhaps the camellia terrace. Late spring, early summer and autumn are good times to visit.

The Metson family

Peaslake Road, Ewhurst, Cranleigh GU6 7NT. Tel: (01306) 731101; www.coverwoodlakes.co.uk

7m SW of Dorking, 6m SE of Guildford, 0.5m S of Peaslake off A25

Open for NGS, and for parties by appt

Entrance: £4, children £2

COVERWOOD LAKES, GARDEN AND FARM

Immensely tall rhododendrons, planted in Edwardian times, tower over camellias and azaleas, with little paths bordered by hostas, candelabra primulas, trilliums and lilies-of-the-valley winding among them. In the bog garden, the tiny streams that moisten groups of lysichitum and *Gunnera manicata* flow on to feed the four lakes that lie at the heart of the woodland estate. The first and most formal of these has a pergola with stone pillars and seats running along one side; the furthest and largest lies beside a 3.5-acre arboretum planted in 1990 with specimens from all over the world. A marked farm trail gives wonderful views from the highest field. In all, 14 acres.

Mrs R D Millais and family

Millais Nurseries, Crosswater Lane, Churt, Farnham GU10 2JN. Tel: (01252) 792698; www.rhododendrons.co.uk

6m SE of Farnham, 6m NW of Haslemere, 0.5m N of Churt off A287. Signed 'Millais Nurseries'

Open 21st April to 6th June, daily, 10am – 5pm

Entrance: £3, children free

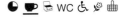

CROSSWATER FARM

These six acres of woodland gardens were begun in 1946 by Ted and Romy Millais, who specialised in azaleas and rhododendrons and assembled an exceptional international collection. Among the mature and some more recent plantings are rare species collected in the Himalayas and hybrids raised by them, including *Rhododendron* 'High Summer'. The plants are labelled and most are available from the adjoining four-acre nursery, which grows more than 750 different varieties. There is also an excellent collection of sorbus trees. The surrounding garden features a stream, ponds and attractive companion plantings, including magnolias, Japanese maples and woodland perennials.

Baron and Baroness Sweerts de Landas Wyborgh

DUNSBOROUGH PARK ★

The restoration of the 10-acre garden, together with its Victorian glasshouses and palm house, is now virtually complete and makes a fitting showcase for the extensive collection of statuary and ornaments displayed among the plants. Double herbaceous borders have been cleared of bindweed and replanted by Rubert Golby with perennials in a colour scheme of blue and white, and a former colour-themed border has been replaced with vibrant late-summer herbaceous perennials. There are two walled gardens. One has been divided by Penelope Hobhouse into separate rooms, each one different and each filled with unusual and interesting plants; the other shelters shrub roses and, behind a unique ginkgo hedge, a display of garden ornaments. The main part of the water garden, crossed by stepping stones, has been restored and replanted to Mykola Khrystenko's design, and can be viewed from the delightful belvedere on the bridge. The secluded white garden is dominated by an ancient, spreading mulberry.

Ripley, Woking GU23 6AL.
Tel: (01483) 225366;
www.sweertsdelandas.com

3m NE of Guildford. Take A247 or A3 to Ripley. Entrance across Ripley Green

Open 12th April, 14th June, 13th Sept, 12 noon – 5pm, for charity, and by appt

Entrance: £4, children free

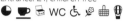

FEATHERCOMBE

The romantic 12-acre garden was designed and created from 1910 by Surrey author and journalist Eric Parker and his wife Ruth, daughter of Ludwig Messel of Nymans (see entry in West Sussex); now it is maintained by their grandchildren. High banks of rhododendrons, azaleas, tree heathers and shrubs, including a huge exochorda, are sheltered by mature trees – in spring spectacular tall *Embothrium coccineum* (Chilean firebush) blaze out their scarlet flowers. A mature yew topiary garden surrounds a formal goldfish pool, and *Wisteria floribunda* cascades from a pergola. There are amazing views to the Surrey and Sussex hills: Blackdown, Hindhead and the Hog's Back.

Campbell

Feathercombe Lane, Hambledon, Godalming GU8 4DP.
Tel: (01483) 860264

4m SW of Godalming between A283 and B2130. Feathercombe Lane is off Hambledon Road between Hydestile crossroads and Merry Harriers pub

Open May by appt

Entrance: £3.50

GATTON PARK ★
(Historic Park Grade II)

The Domesday Book records a manor and deer park here, and a diminutive town hall still stands as a reminder of Gatton's days as a rotten borough. In the eighteenth century 'Capability' Brown landscaped the grounds and created the 28-acre lake, and in the late-nineteenth and twentieth centuries Jeremiah Colman, the mustard magnate, built a dramatic rock and water garden, together with a Japanese garden with a thatched tea house, bridge and lanterns. An enthusiastic band of volunteers has been restoring the gardens since 1996, most recently the ponds, cascades and the serpentine river feeding the lake, which is home to a heronry on one of the islands. The rock garden has been planted anew with alpines and small shrubs, and the drystone arch restored too; next on the list is the walled garden. Set in a circle near North Downs Way are ten Caithness stones, three metres high, engraved for the millennium with texts from the past 1000 years. 250 acres in all.

The Royal Alexandra and Albert School.

Foundation Office, Gatton Park, Reigate RH2 0TW.
Tel: (01737) 649068 or (0794) 157 2434;
www.gattonpark.com

3m NE of Reigate. From A23 or Gatton Bottom, turn into Rocky Lane

Open for NGS for snowdrops, then Feb to Oct, 1st Sun of each month, 1 – 5 pm

Entrance: £3.50, children free. Snowdrop talk and walk 2nd Feb, £8 per person

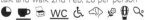

Great Fosters

Stroude Road, Egham TW20 9UR.
Tel: (01784) 433822
www.greatfosters.co.uk;

1m SW of Staines off M25 junction 13,
1m S of Egham. From railway station
follow Manorcroft Road into Stroude
Road and continue 1m. Hotel on left

Open all year, daily, during daylight hours

Entrance: free

Other information: Refreshments and
toilet facilities in hotel

GREAT FOSTERS ★
(Historic Garden Grade II*)

Although the house was built in the late-sixteenth century, the topiary parterres were created in 1918 within an original U-shaped moat and more recently restored. A Japanese bridge, festooned with wisteria, leads to a pergola and a circular, sunken rose garden with an octet of steps leading down to a lily pond and fountain. Nearby are two modern gardens and a vista garden with serpentine hedges. A lake surrounded by marginals and a woodland area are recent additions. But the most dramatic and innovative development is undoubtedly Kim Wilkie's vast amphitheatre at the end of the lime avenue, carved out against a *bund* made especially to block out the pervasive roar of the M25. In all, 50 acres.

Hannah Peschar

Black and White Cottage, Standon Lane,
Ockley RH5 5QR. Tel: (01306) 627269;
www.hannahpescharsculpture.com

6m S of Dorking, 1m SW of Ockley off
A29. Follow signs for 'Golf and Country
Club'. Entrance on right in Standon Lane
400 metres past low bridge over stream

Open May to Oct, Fri and Sat, 11am – 6pm;
Sun and Bank Holiday Mons, 2 – 5pm; other
days, except Mon, by appt only

Entrance: £9, OAPs £7,
children under 16 £6

Other information: Refreshments and meals
for parties by arrangement only.

Details of lecture tours, party and school
visits on request

HANNAH PESCHAR SCULPTURE GARDEN

In Victorian times the heart of the 10-acre valley garden was part of the Leith Vale Estate, and when Hannah Peschar and her husband, the landscape designer Anthony Paul, came here in 1977, the place had been neglected for many years. He kept the old trees, and under their canopy has encouraged some 400 native species to spread among his favourite, more restricted palette of architectural plants – dynamos such as gunneras, *Ligularia* 'The Rocket', vast groups of petasites, giant hogweed (be warned), a variety of grasses and stands of bamboo. It is an other-worldly experience to wind along the narrow paths looking down on streams, lakes and precarious wooden bridges; and the romantic buildings at the heart of the garden enhance the effect. But the garden is only half the story. It has primarily been designed as a showcase for Hannah Peschar's own business – the sale of high-quality contemporary sculpture, placed among vegetation or against water to bring out the character and quality of each piece.

HATCHLANDS PARK

The eighteenth-century house is surrounded by 430 acres of parkland, and Humphry Repton was employed as landscaper in 1800. There are four way-marked walks to enjoy, including a bluebell wood. In 1913 Gertrude Jekyll submitted plans for a south and a west parterre garden; the former alone was executed, and has now been reinstated. At its summer peak it is a pretty scheme, but it does sit somewhat awkwardly in its parkland setting. Beside the garden is a magnificent 200-year-old London plane tree, a temple and an ice-house. A wildflower meadow is left uncut until July. The Trust's task is now to reconcile the conflicting styles and contours, and more importantly to raise the overall standard following the decline between 1959 and 1980, when the property was let to a finishing school. Slowly but surely the garden is becoming again a fine accompaniment to the house.

The National Trust

East Clandon, Guildford GU4 7RT.
Tel: (01483) 222482;
www.nationaltrust.org.uk

5m NE of Guildford, E of East Clandon.

House and garden open 23rd March to Oct, Tues – Thurs, Sun and Bank Holiday Mons, plus Fri in Aug, 2 – 5.30pm

Park open 23rd March to Oct, daily, 11am – 6pm

Entrance: Park £3.50 (house, garden and walks £6.60, family £17

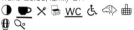

KNOWLE GRANGE ★

The house, which sits on a hilltop with a wide and verdant view to the north, was built in 1928, and the gardens were started in 1990 following a clear-up after the great storm of 1987, with the inspiration coming from Mrs Wood's visits to gardens in this country and abroad. Eighteenth-century stone steps from France lead down to a circular lawn with a long curve of French Gothic balustrading. Behind the house the ground has been levelled to make a wide lawn with flower borders; a Burgundian fountain and pool are at one end, a belvedere at the other. To the west the land slopes down to a series of outdoor rooms – an Italianate garden with columns and pencil cypresses, and woodland, Japanese and knot gardens. A charming stone gazebo is festooned with roses. To the south Mr Wood, clearly a philosopher, is creating a mile-long Universal Path of Life encompassing a hilltop with distant views, a bluebell valley and a holly labyrinth. An amazing garden of strong architectural lines softened by planting, recently created but traditional in its effect.

Mr and Mrs P. R. Wood

Hound House Road, Shere GU5 9JH.
Tel: (01483) 202108

8m SW of Guildford off A25. Go through Shere and after railway bridge, continue 1.5m past house on right (stone dogs on gatepost) to end of lane.

Open for NGS, and for parties of 15 or more by appt in May, June and Sept

Entrance: £5, children free

NEW

LITTLE LODGE

The house rests comfortably in its own lush 0.3-acre surround, and in the front garden a pond and wild planting with formal topiary beds give little hint of the cottage garden to the rear. Against the densely covered house walls is a paved suntrap with a wide variety of containers and unusual plants, and the main lawned area has herbaceous borders and island beds with secret spots defined by yew hedges. A vegetable garden with well-stocked raised beds edged in box adds to the charm of this much-visited garden.

Mr and Mrs Peter Hickman

Watts Road, Thames Ditton KT7 0BX.
Tel: (020) 8339 0931

1m N of Esher. From London take A3. In Thames Ditton village follow High Street down Watts Road

Open for NGS, and by appt

Entrance: £2.50, children free

LONGER END COTTAGE

The 1.5-acre garden surrounding the sixteenth-century yeoman's cottage (not open) is packed with interest and beautifully presented. Lawns are punctuated by rose beds, an

Ann and John McIlwham

Normandy Common Lane,
Normandy, Guildford GU3 2AP.
Tel: (01483) 811858

4m W of Guildford on A323. In village, turn right at crossroads into Hunts Hill Road, then first right again

Open for NGS, and by appt for parties of 15 or more

Entrance: £3, children free

NEW

atmospheric sunken pond, herbaceous plantings and an intricate knot garden designed by the late Rosemary Verey. Roses grow in profusion – on the house walls, woven through apple trees and draped over trellis. Beyond a bed of 'Iceberg' roses and a hidden stumpery, a rose arch beckons to a circular herb garden with a camomile seat. Another area is filled with herbaceous colour, and a sheltered corner with cannas, bananas and tree ferns leads to a laburnum walk. A small wildflower meadow provides naturalistic contrast, mature trees give shelter and structure, and a folly and a Wendy house are decorative additions to this attractive and interesting place.

Mr and Mrs M. G. More-Molyneux

Compton, Guildford GU3 1HS.
Tel: (01483) 304440;
www.loseley-park.com

3m SW of Guildford, W of A3, off B3000

House open as May to Aug, Tues – Thurs, Sun and Bank Holiday Mons, 1pm – 5pm

Garden open May to Sept, Tues – Sun and Bank Holiday Mons, 11am – 5pm

Entrance: £4, concessions £3.50, children £2 (house and garden £7, concessions £6.50, children £3.50)

LOSELEY PARK ★

The Elizabethan house is surrounded by parkland. Hidden away at the side of the house, the 2.5-acre walled garden has been transformed: five gardens have been created based on a Gertrude Jekyll design, each with their own theme and character, and an old mulberry survives, together with a medlar planted with a group of palms. An enchanting rose garden with low box hedges is filled with old-fashioned roses, carefully labelled; box balls and circles emphasise the design, while pillars of roses and hollies give height. Along one side is an arcade of vines and clematis. A herb garden displays culinary, medicinal and ornamental herbs in triangular beds and others used in cosmetics, lotions and dyes, all well labelled. Quartets of domed acacias stand at the intersections of the main paths, and golden crab apples form a square avenue in the fruit and flower garden, which is planted in bold fiery colours. In contrast, the fountain garden is laid out with white and silver flowers and foliage to create a romantic atmosphere. A wide range of produce is grown in the attractive organic vegetable garden. A new wildflower meadow opened in 2006. The moat walk shelters a long border of sun-loving plants, including yuccas. Near the entrance to the garden is an ancient wisteria and a good herbaceous border.

Penny and Maurice Snell

The Fairmile, Cobham KT11 1BG.
Tel: (01932) 864532

2m NE of Cobham on A307, adjacent to car park by A3 bridge

Open for NGS, and for parties of 10 or more by appt

Entrance: £3, children free

MOLESHILL HOUSE

The Victorian house was originally surrounded by a vast garden, much of which was sold off by previous owners for modern housing. The 0.75 which remains has been delightfully planted to complement the house and express the owners' ideas. The bold circular lawn wears a necklace of box balls, and plants and shrubs in soft colours are closely packed into the surrounding borders. An avenue of *Sorbus lutescens* opens out to a rose-covered gazebo and colour-themed beds; returning to the entrance you come upon a semi-circular pool with a fountain and a short, attractively planted woodland path leading to a dovecot and bee alcoves. The latest project is to grasp the nettle of climatic change and embark on a significant replanting programme that will also extend the garden's season.

MUNSTEAD WOOD

(Historic Garden Grade I)

Gertrude Jekyll began to make her own garden here in 1883, when she was forty; the house, designed by Edwin Lutyens, was built thirteen years later. The garden, carefully restored to Jekyll's original plans since the early 1980s, reveals the extent of her genius for both planting and design. A river of daffodils flows onto the front lawn from a birch copse. A wide grass path through mature rhododendrons creates a vista to and from woodland and the house, and there are walks among scented azaleas in soft and vibrant colours. The wide west lawn leads past a sunken rock garden and shrubbery to the main border, 60 metres long, backed by a high wall of local Bargate stone. Jekyll grew hot red and orange flowers in the centre, shading out through yellows, blues and mauves to white at either end. The spring and summer gardens are reached through an arched doorway. Returning towards the house, past the rose-covered pergola and summerhouse, visitors discover the nut walk, the aster garden and lavender-fringed paths; a primula garden is hidden away to one side. At the back of the house is a cool courtyard with festoons of *Clematis montana*, paving and a pool. Jekyll had eight gardeners tending 15 acres: now 10 acres are maintained by just two.

Sir Robert and Lady Clark

Munstead Wood, Heath Lane, Busbridge, Godalming GU7 1UN.
Tel: (01483) 417867

From Godalming take B2130 to Busbridge. Heath Lane is on left opposite church

Open for NGS, and by appt

Entrance: £3, OAPs £2, children free

Other information: Teas and plants for sale only on NGS open days

🌑 WC ♿ ⟨⟩

PAINSHILL PARK ★★

(Historic Garden Grade I)

The Hon. Charles Hamilton created the 158-acre landscaped park – contemporary with Stowe and Stourhead – between 1738 and 1773, when it was sold after he ran out of funds. The garden was well maintained until World War II, then in 1948 it was sold off in lots and all but lost. Between 1974 and 1980 Elmbridge Council bought up most of the land; the following year the Painshill Park Trust was formed and began the task of restoration. To the north is a crescent of parkland with clumps of trees, and the ornamental pleasure grounds

Painshill Park Trust

Portsmouth Road, Cobham KT11 1JE.
Tel: (01932) 868113;
www.painshill.co.uk

4m SW of Esher, W of Cobham. From M25 junction 10, take A3 and A245. Entrance 200 metres from A245/A307 roundabout

Painshill Park

Open all year, daily except 25th
and 26th Dec: March to Oct,
10.30am – 6pm (last admission
4.30pm); Nov to Feb, 11am – 4pm or
dusk if earlier (last admission 3pm).
Parties of 10 or more (incl. school
parties) by appt

Entrance: £6.60, concessions £5.80,
children (5–16) £3.85, family £22

Other information: Children under 16
must be accompanied. Wheelchairs and
pre-booked buggy tours for disabled
(max 3) available

to the south were designed around a serpentine 14-acre lake
and spectacular waterwheel fed from the River Mole. The
restored Chinese bridge, opened in 1988, leads to an island
and a magical grotto, the main chamber of which is 12 metres
across, hung with stalactites and lined with shards of glistening
felspar. The mausoleum, near the river, was depicted on one
of the plates of Catherine the Great's Wedgwood 'Frog
Service'; a further reach of the lake reflects an abbey ruin.
The focal point of the garden is the elegant Gothick temple
on higher ground. It is approached across a grassed
'amphitheatre' encircled by formal eighteenth-century-style
shrubberies. A dramatic blue and white Turkish tent with a
gold coronet stands on a plateau among informal plantings; in
the distance is the Gothick tower. The great cedar of
Lebanon, 36.5 metres high and with a girth of 10 metres, is
reputedly the largest in Europe. The vineyard has been
replanted on a southern slope and the hermitage rebuilt,
while the restoration of the grotto and rebuilding of the
'missing' Temple of Bacchus are ongoing. The acclaimed
'American Roots' exhibition continues within the old walled
garden, and in 2006 Painshill was awarded full National
Collection status for the John Bartram Heritage Plant
Collection – a well-researched round-up of the plants sent to
Hamilton from Philadelphia by the famous plant collector.

The National Trust

Dorking RH5 6BD.
Tel: (01372) 452048/ 458203 (Infoline);
www.nationaltrust.org.uk

5m NW of Dorking, 2m S of Great
Bookham off A246 Leatherhead –
Guildford road

House open

Gardens and grounds open all year, daily,
11am – 5pm, or dusk if earlier; telephone
for details of snowdrop openings

Entrance: £6.50, children £3.20, family
£16.20 (house and grounds £10.50,
children £5.20, family £26.20) (2007 prices)

Other information: Disabled parking area.
Batricar available on pre-booked basis.
Braille guide available

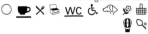

POLESDEN LACY ★
(Historic Garden Grade II*)

Richard Brinsley Sheridan, the dramatist, lived here for twenty
years until his death in 1816, and extended the Long Walk
with its fabulous views across the valley. A few years later the
present house was built by Cubitt in the Greek classical style
and over 20,000 trees were planted. The Edwardian society
hostess, The Hon. Mrs. Greville, replaced the Edwardian facade
and laid out the formal walled gardens, although the outbreak
of the First World War and the death of her husband
prevented the plans for an original elaborate Italianate terrace
from being carried out. In her day 36 gardeners tended the
30 acres; today a quarter of a million people visit the garden
annually. Now pergolas draped with ramblers enclose the
paths in the rose garden, peony, lavender and iris gardens lead
to the winter garden and the thatched bridge, and there is a
long herbaceous border designed by Graham Stuart Thomas
sheltered by a wall. A programme of restoration is under way:
a new oak bridge has been built and walks have been created,
including one suitable for wheelchairs. The rock garden will be
restored and the orchard replanted.

Mr and Mrs P. Gunn

Chiddingfold, Godalming GU8 4SN.
Tel: (01428) 654167;
www.ramsterweddings.co.uk

RAMSTER

A local nursery originally laid out the garden in 1890 in the
Japanese style fashionable at the time, and bamboos, stone
lanterns and a splendid double row of *Acer palmatum*

'Dissectum Atropurpureum' remain from that era. In 1922 the property was bought by Sir Henry and Lady Norman, Mrs Gunn's grandparents. Lady Norman grew up at Bodnant (see entry in Wales) and many of the plants at Ramster came from there. The 15 acres of natural woodland, stream and lakes provide an ideal setting for rhododendrons and azaleas, camellias, magnolias and unusual trees. A collection of over 200 old hardy hybrid rhododendrons is a more recent addition, and a bog garden was planted in 1998. The paved millennium garden has two ponds connected by a rill, and four raised beds of three tiers each, built of concrete blocks; the planting follows the colour wheel, with an appropriate tree in each, underplanted with bulbs, herbaceous perennials and shrubs.

NE of Haslemere, 1.5m S of Chiddingfold on A283

Open 4th April to 22nd June, daily, 10.30am – 5pm, and for parties by appt

Entrance: £5, OAPs £4.50, children under 16 free

Other information: Possible for wheelchairs in dry weather only

RHS GARDEN WISLEY ★★
(Historic Garden Grade II*)

The garden was presented to the RHS in 1903 by Sir Thomas Hanbury, who created the famous La Mortola garden in Italy. The first major development was the rock garden, a fashionable feature at the time, sections of which were reconstructed in the 1980s. The broadwalk leads between generous double mixed borders to a country garden designed by Penelope Hobhouse, then to rose gardens and onwards to Battleston Hill and East Battleston, with azaleas, rhododendrons, hydrangeas and lilies. Over the crest of the hill, on the southern slope, is a Mediterranean garden planted since the 1987 storms and, beyond it, the Trials Field, where the Society, as the leading international trials institution, holds annual trials of plants, flowers and vegetables. To the west the

Royal Horticultural Society

Wisley, Woking GU23 6QB. Tel: (01483) 224234; www.rhs.org.uk

7m NE of Guildford, on A3. Signed from M25 junction 10 south. Trains to West Byfleet or Woking; taxi service usually available at stations

Open all year, daily, 10am – 6pm (opens 9am Sat, Sun and Bank Holiday Mons, closes 4.30pm Nov to Feb) (last admission 1 hour before closing)

Entrance: £7.50, children (6–16) £2, under 6 free; companion for wheelchair-bound or blind visitors free (2007 prices)

RHS Garden Wisley

Other information: Disabled and shaded parking

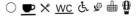

32-acre Jubilee Arboretum encircles the fruit field, where growing trees can be compared. The new bicentenary glasshouse, opened in 2007, is the latest magnificent achievement. Within the 12.5-metre high curves of glass and steel, the drama of a waterfall cascading down a rock structure is enhanced by the explosion of ferns, palms, creepers, exotic flowers and displays of species running the gamut from arid desert to tropical jungle; a separate root zone explores the secret life of plants beneath the soil. The building stands within a specially created landscaped garden that includes a lake intended as a reservoir for the glasshouse, and a striking new planting design by Tom Stuart-Smith linking the glasshouse to the Piet Oudolf borders. The popular model gardens include a collection of bonsai and prizewinning gardens transported from the Chelsea Flower Show; others display fruit and vegetables – 1000 varieties of top, bush and soft fruit are grown. Lucy Huntington has redesigned the herb garden. The peaceful pinetum, the riverside walk and the new heather garden in Howard's Field lie beyond the restaurant. The lakes nearby have been enlarged and made more naturalistic, with planting mainly for winter effect. Sir Geoffrey Jellicoe designed the canal and loggia in front of the laboratory. Martin Lane Fox and the garden staff have transformed the walled garden – a sun trap which now shelters Italian cypresses, Chusan palms, tree ferns and a host of tender plants. An avenue of *Cornus kousa* var. *chinensis* underplanted with shrubs backs herbaceous perennials and grasses laid out in diagonal drifts to give a ribbon effect. At the top is a fruit mount with a spectacular view of the Surrey countryside; step-over apples grow round the base and the spiral path is bordered by blackberries and vines. Excellent and innovative educational facilities add to those already provided by the laboratory (built in 1916 as the hub of the Society's advisory service to members), the library and the bookshop. The extensive plant centre is also well worth a visit.

SAVILL GARDEN (WINDSOR GREAT PARK) ★★

(Historic Park Grade I)

Administered by the Crown Estate Commissioners

Wick Lane, Englefield Green TW20 0UU. Tel: (01753) 847518; www.theroyallandscape.co.uk

4m W of Staines, 5m S of Windsor. From A30, turn into Wick Road and follow signs, or follow signs from Englefield Green

Open all year, daily except 25th and 26th Dec, 10am – 6pm (closes 4.30pm Nov to Feb).

Entrance: £6.50, concessions £6 , children (6– 6) under 6 free, family £17 (2007 prices)

This particularly fine woodland garden of some 35 acres is distinguished by its wide range of rhododendrons, camellias, magnolias, hydrangeas and its great variety of other trees and shrubs producing a wealth of colour throughout the seasons. Wonderful collections of hostas and ferns flourish in the shadier areas. Meconopsis and primulas are splendid in June, while lilies are the highlight of high summer and the tweedy autumn colours are almost as satisfying in their mellowness as the jauntier spring hues. A more formal area is devoted to modern roses, herbaceous borders, a range of alpines and an interesting and attractive dry garden. The Golden Jubilee Garden, planted in cool colours, has a central vista lined by

Savill Garden

pink and blue lavender; at its heart is a water sculpture designed by Barry Mason. An imposing temperate house was opened in 1995 where tender subjects – tree ferns, mimosas, eucryphias and delicate shrubs – are arranged in tiered beds and underplanted with exotics. Metal obelisks support non-hardy climbers; *Lapageria rosea* is on the main wall. The minimum temperature maintained in the 36m x 18m glasshouse is only 2°C (38°F), easily achieved in a conservatory. The Savill Building, an iconic new visitor centre, opened in 2006. Designed by architect Glen Howells, it features a unique grid-shelf roof constructed from timber grown on the Windsor estate.

Other information: Guided tours available. Wheelchairs available on loan

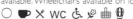

STUART COTTAGE

Originally this was a cowman's cottage. The present owners arrived in 1975 and, confronted with nothing but grass and two old trees, have made a delightful 0.5-acre garden on the alkaline clay soil, full of colour and interest from June through to September. It is partially walled, connected and divided by wisteria and rose pergolas. A formal, circular area has colour-themed borders curving round a central fountain, and a hot border of cannas and dahlias thrives in the shelter of a sunny wall. There is also a decorative organic kitchen garden and a small orchard. Secret places and a variety of nooks and crannies make the whole seem much larger than it is.

Mr and Mrs J. M. Leader

East Clandon, Guildford GU4 7SF.
Tel: (01483) 222689

4m E of Guildford. From A246, go through village, take road signed to Ripley and follow yellow signs

Open for NGS, and for parties of 20 or more by appt

Entrance: £3, children free

TITSEY PLACE

(Historic Garden Grade II)

The 18-acre gardens, nestling in a curve of the North Downs, have been in the same family for 400 years. In the walled garden unusual varieties of vegetables, fruit and flowers, grown from seed from all over the world, are most attractively displayed. The space is divided classically at crossing points by ironwork gazebos covered with roses and vines, and box-edged beds are filled with vegetables, salads, soft fruit and

Trustees of the Titsey Foundation

Titsey Hill, Oxted RH8 0SD.
Tel: (01273) 715362/715359 (Infoline);
www.titsey.org.

1m E of Oxted, 9m W of Sevenoaks. Leave M25 at junction 6. From A25 E of Oxted, turn left into Limpsfield (signed to Warlingham). At end of High Street fork left into Blue House Lane and first right into Water Lane

333

House open

Garden open 24th March; then 14th May to 24th Sept, Wed, Sun and Bank Holiday Mons; all 1 – 5pm

Entrance: £3.50, children £1 (house and garden £6, no concession for children)

Other information: Parking through park near walled garden, or by gate for woodland walks with long walk to garden

● ● ▣ WC 㐂 ⬥

flowers for cutting. The walls support espaliered fruit underplanted with borders of shrub roses and annuals; greenhouses against the south wall shelter nectarines and peaches, unusual tomatoes and collections of alstroemerias and pelargoniums; and the central glasshouse displays exotic and tender plants in pots. From here the central path, flanked by perennials, leads out into the main garden, where unusual sun-loving climbers and shrubs grow against the outside of the wall. Lawns sweeping down to a ha-ha give uninterrupted, spectacular views. A knot border stretches the length of the house; further down the slope, herbaceous beds curve round a fountain, and an ancient yew guards Saxon gravestones and modern dogs' graves. Below the two formal rose gardens, magnificent specimen trees dominate the lawns and lead down to a stream edged with marginals which feeds the lakes. The first, with its splendid fountain, water lilies and golden carp, is divided from the second – more informal, surrounding an island – by a deep cascade and a bridge. The whole is beautifully maintained.

VALE END

Mr and Mrs J. Foulsham

Chilworth Road, Albury, Guildford GU5 9BE.
Tel: (01483) 202296

4.5m SE of Guildford. From Albury take A248 W for 0.25m

Open for NGS, and by appt

Entrance: £3, evening openings £4 and £3.50

● ● WC ⬥ ✿

In an idyllic setting with views of a mill pond backed by woodland, the one-acre walled garden is arranged on different levels. In spring it has a mass of bulbs, especially tulips. The sloping lawn has a border filled with old roses and old favourites as well as less familiar perennials. The terrace in front of the house is a sun trap, the border and new gravel bed devoted to plants that thrive in hot, dry conditions. Beyond a yew hedge, a cool area is shaded by a spreading magnolia; above, edging a newly gravelled and planted walk, stand clipped yew boxes and a catenary of posts and rope swags, festooned with roses, wisteria and vines. An attractive courtyard is hidden behind the house. Steps by a new pantiled cascade lead up to a fruit, vegetable and herb garden level with the roof.

THE VALLEY GARDENS (WINDSOR GREAT PARK) ★★

Administered by the Crown Estate Commissioners

Wick Road, Englefield Green TW20 0VU.
Tel: (01753) 847518;
www.theroyallandscape.co.uk

4m W of Staines, 5m S of Windsor. From A30 turn into Wick Road and look for burgundy-coloured signs to car park entrance adjoining Valley Gardens, avoiding a 2m round walk

Open all year, daily, 8am – 7pm (or dusk if earlier); possible closure if weather inclement

Entrance: car and occupants £4 (April and May £6) (10p, 20p, 50p and £1 coins only) (2007 prices)

That discriminating and experienced garden visitor, the late Arthur Hellyer, suggested that the Valley Gardens are among the best examples of the 'natural' gardening style in England. With hardly any artefacts or attempts to introduce architectural features, they are merely a 200-acre tract of undulating woodland (on the north side of Virginia Water) divided by several shallow valleys, that has been enriched by the introduction of a fine collection of trees and shrubs. They were started by the royal gardener Sir Eric Savill when he ran out of room in the Savill Garden. One of the valleys is filled with deciduous azaleas. In another, the Punchbowl, evergreen azaleas rise in tiers below a canopy of maples. Notable too are collections of flowering cherries, a garden of heathers which amply demonstrates their ability to provide colour during all seasons, and one of the world's most extensive collections of hollies. Lovers of formal gardening might be forgiven for suggesting that the gardens have something of that rather too open, amorphous, scrupulously kept feel found in America. Off the A30 adjacent to the junction with the A329, *Virginia Water Lake* [Historic Park Grade I] was a grand eighteenth-century ornamental addition to Windsor Great Park created by the Duke of Cumberland, who became its Ranger in 1746. Alas, almost all his landscaping and architectural concepts have disappeared, but the woodland and the 1.5-mile lake, full of fish and wildfowl, survive, together with a pillared colonnade from the Roman site of Leptis Magna in Libya.

Other information: Refreshments and plants for sale at Savill Garden (see entry)

VANN ★

(Historic Garden Grade II*)

The Grade-II*-listed house (not open), standing in five acres of garden, dates from 1542 – the name is derived from the word 'fen'. The oldest part of the garden is at the front, enclosed by clipped yew hedges, divided by paths and planted in cottage-garden style. Behind the house a stone pergola (W.D. Caröe, 1907), underplanted with shade-lovers, strides out towards an old enlarged field pond. The woodland water garden was designed with Gertrude Jekyll, who supplied the plants in 1911. It has a winding stream, crossed and recrossed by Bargate-stone paths and swathed in lush planting; above the pond a narrow, stone-walled stream is enclosed by a yew walk planted in 1909. A serpentine crinkle-crankle wall supports fruit trees, and there are two mixed herbaceous borders in the vegetable garden and island beds in the orchard.

Mrs M. B. Caroe

Hambledon, Godalming GU8 4EF.
Tel: (01428) 683413;
www.vanngarden.co.uk

11m S of Guildford, 6m S of Godalming. On NGS open days, follow yellow signs. Otherwise, take A283 to 30mph sign at Chiddingfold; pass Winterton Alms pub on left, and after 50 metres turn left into Skinners Lane, then left again at T-junction signed to Hambledon. Garden is 1.2m on right

Open for NGS, and by appt (parties of 15 or more by written appt)

Entrance: £4.50, children 50p

WINKWORTH ARBORETUM ★

Dr Wilfrid Fox bought the curving, steeply sloping 110-acre hillside site from the actress Beatrice Lilley in 1937. Helped by his connections with Kew and Hilliers, he set about establishing extensive collections of trees – among them birch, holly, magnolia and a National Collection of sorbus. In 1952 he gave the arboretum to the National Trust. Eucryphias, glorious in August, stand sentinel on either side of his memorial looking down his beloved valley. Carpets of bluebells in spring are followed by cherries, rhododendrons and azaleas in bright splashes, and in autumn acers, liquidambars and nyssas provide rich colour. The hillside setting has glorious views over the lake to the hills beyond. After problems with the dams, the lower lake has been drained to form a wetland area, crossed by a handsome bridge with a viewing platform, built (somewhat improbably) of reconstituted plastic – it is the highpoint of a new woodland walk.

The National Trust

Hascombe Road, Godalming GU8 4AD.
Tel: (01483) 208477;
www.nationaltrust.org.uk

2m SE of Godalming, E of B2130

Open all year, daily, dawn – dusk (but may be closed in bad weather)

Entrance: £5, children (5–16) £2.50, family £12.50, cyclists and public transport users 50% discount, carers with the disabled free. Pre-booked guided tours available

Other information: Possible for wheelchairs but some steps and steep paths. Opening for shop and tearoom varies seasonally

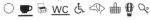

Mr and Mrs Peter Hutley

Bramley GU5 0LR.
Tel: (01483) 892167;
www.wintershall-estate.com

4m S of Guildford, 3m S of Bramley. On
A281 turn right, then next right; drive
next on left

Open for NGS, and by appt all year

Entrance: £3, disabled £1.50, children
free

NEW

WINTERSHALL MANOR

Cooing doves greet visitors to this peaceful two-acre garden, and a terrace with beds of roses and lavender gives spectacular views across a valley to the Surrey hills. Semi-circular steps lead down to a rectangular lily pond edged with irises, while pheasants strut across the lawn among beds of rhododendrons guarded by an immense sequoia. At the side of the house the garden is terraced, with delightful mixed borders at each level, an ancient mulberry planted by James II and lawns rolling down to garden railings erected to celebrate the Battle of Waterloo. Beyond is a lake and huge mature trees, including fine specimens of cherry and eucalyptus, and in the woodland, filled in spring with bluebells, a trail passes the Stations of the Cross. Two chapels and the Rosary Walk are other religious elements.

Hayley Conference Centres Ltd

Guildford Road, Dorking RH5 6HS.
Tel: (01306) 730000

3m W of Dorking on A25 Dorking –
Guildford road. Entrance signed next to
Wotton Hatch pub

Open for NGS, and for genuinely
interested visitors at other times

Entrance: £2.50, children free

 B&B

WOTTON HOUSE ★

John Evelyn, the diarist and gardening writer, was born here in 1620. Greatly influenced by his travels in Europe during the Civil War, he originally designed the garden for his elder brother George, but inherited the estate himself at the age of 79 on his brother's death. The dominant feature of the garden, set against a backdrop of mature trees, is the spectacular mound rising on three levels with a classical temple at its base; in front is a circular pool with a fountain, surrounded by a parterre of interlocking box triangles filled with a variety of plants. Near the house are two Pulhamite grottoes, one with a pool, and a fernery. Hidden away in a walled enclosure is a tortoise house in the style of an Italian temple, and rectangular pools, intended originally for terrapins. Waterers Landscape have restored the garden, and a drained lake is being transformed into a water meadow.

OTHER RECOMMENDED GARDENS

BUSHY PARK

Hampton (020 8979 1586; www.royalparks.gov.uk).
Open all year, daily, 9am – dusk

Once a royal hunting ground, the 1099-acre park – part country park, part formal landscape – adjoins Hampton Court to the north, and the spectacular mile-long avenue of horse chestnuts was part of the original grand approach to the palace. The famous 17th-century Arethusa Fountain will in time be restored to full working order, and areas of the landscaped Waterhouse Woodland Gardens refreshed. (Listed Grade I)

CHESTNUT LODGE

Mr and Mrs R. Sawyer, Old Common Road, Cobham
KT11 1BU (01932 862053). Open for NGS, and for
parties by appt

Rare trees, shrubs and exotic plants curve round the handsome Georgian house (not open). Formal pools are framed by a collection of bonsai, while flamingoes and water birds enjoy a naturalistic pond and tropical birds have spacious aviaries enclosing their own delightful gardens. 5 acres.

GODDARDS

Abinger Common, Dorking RH5 6JH (01306 730871
– office hours). Open 25 March to Oct, Wed only,
strictly by appt

In this unusual example of the famous
partnership, Lutyens designed the house around
a well-structured courtyard garden overlooked
by all the principal rooms, while Jekyll laid out
the flower borders and formal gardens,
providing vistas across lawns and a meadow to
a backdrop of woods. The house and gardens
are now in the care of the Landmark Trust. 7
acres.

GUILDFORD CASTLE GARDENS

Castle Street, Guildford GU1 3TU
(01483 505050).www.guildford.gov.uk. Open all year,
daily, dawn – dusk

The ruined keep erected by William the
Conqueror became part of a private town
garden in 1885. Shaped beds cut into the
sloping turfed sides of the moat are bedded-out
in vibrant Victorian fashion, and a tunnel leads
up to a bowling green with attractive borders
and clipped hedges. 6 acres.

LANGSHOTT MANOR HOTEL

Mr and Mrs Peter Hinchcliffe, Horley RH6 9LN
(01293 786680). Open all year, daily

The peaceful setting of the beautifully restored
Elizabethan manor house (now a hotel) is
enhanced by its mellow and attractive 3-acre
garden. It has a classic English layout: a sunken
rose garden, herbaceous borders, a croquet
lawn announced by pleached lime and
hornbeam avenues, and a lake with resident
swans.

LEITH HILL RHODODENDRON
WOOD

Tanhurst Lane, Coldharbour (01306 71271;
www.nationaltrust.org.uk). Open all year, daily, during
daylight hours. NT

Originally part of the estate owned by the
composer Ralph Vaughan Williams,
rhododendrons and azaleas blaze out in spring

and early summer. The views are spectacular,
with an immense tulip tree in the field beyond.
Further on, mature trees create a shady area
for soft-coloured rhododendrons. 12 acres.

41 SHELVERS WAY

Mr and Mrs K.G. Lewis, Tadworth KT20 5QJ
(01737 210707). Open for NGS, and by appt

A 0.5-acre back garden of dense and detailed
planting, interesting at all seasons, starting with a
mass of spring bulbs. In one part beds of choice
perennials are interlaced by paths and backed
by unusual shrubs and mature trees; in the
other cobbles and shingle support grasses and
special plants that prefer dry conditions.

THE WALLED GARDEN

Sunbury Park, Thames Street, Sunbury-on-Thames
TW16 6AB (01784 451499 – Community Services).
Open all year, daily except 25th Dec, 8am – dusk

A 2-acre walled garden originally attached to
an Elizabethan house has been developed as
an attractive public garden containing rose
beds, knot gardens, parterres and island beds
of plants from around the world. The award-
winning Sunbury Embroidery Gallery, home
to a locally crafted embroidery celebrating
the town, occupies one corner of this
ancient garden.

WESTWAYS FARM

Paul and Nicky Biddle, Gracious Pond Road,
Chobham GU24 8HH (01276 856163). Open for
NGS, and by appt

The Queen Anne house, clothed with *Magnolia
grandiflora*, has as its setting a formal terrace and
sunken pond garden which leads to a vast lawn
shaded by an immense red oak. Woodland
beyond was planted in the 1930s with a
colourful array of rhododendrons, azaleas,
camellias and magnolias underplanted with
dogwoods, erythroniums, lilies-of-the-valley and
bluebells. 8 acres.

SUSSEX, EAST

For further information about how to use the *Guide*
and for an explanation of the symbols, see pages vi–viii.
Specific dates and times are those given to us by garden owners for 2008.
For 2009 dates, check with the individual properties.
For opening dates under the National Gardens Scheme,
readers should consult *The Yellow Book* or www.ngs.org.uk.
Maps are to be found at the end of the *Guide*.

The National Trust

Burwash, Etchingham TN19 7DS.
Tel: (01435) 882302;
www.nationaltrust.org.uk

14m E of Uckfield, 10m SE of Tunbridge
Wells, 0.5m S of Burwash off A265

House and mill (which grinds flour most
Sats in open season) open as garden

Garden open 15th March to 2nd Nov,
Sat – Wed, 11am – 5pm

Entrance: £7.20, children £3.60, family
£18 (house, mill and garden)

Other information: Dog creche available

BATEMAN'S

(Historic Garden Grade II)

The spirit of Edwardian England pervades the tranquil gardens surrounding the Wealden ironmaster's house bought by Rudyard Kipling in 1902. All the elements of his original plan – formal lawns surrounding a reflecting pool emphasised by pleached limes, the pear *allée* he planted in the walled kitchen garden now bounded by a fine herb border, the sheltered Mulberry Garden in the former farmyard and the wild fringes of the little River Dudwell running to the working mill – combine to evoke the atmosphere of privacy and stability that he created here over three decades until his death in 1936. The house and garden are rich in associations with his stories and poems, especially *Puck of Pook's Hill* and *Rewards and Fairies*, which were both set here; the mill that featured in these stories is only a short walk away.

Mrs Carolyn McCutchan

Tye Hill Road, Arlington, Polegate
BN26 6SH.
Tel: (01323) 485152

7m NW of Eastbourne, 2.5m SW of
A22, 2m S of Michelham Priory (see
entry) at Upper Dicker. Approach
Arlington passing Old Oak Inn on right,
continue for 350 metres, turn right
along Tye Hill Road. Signposted

Open for NGS, and by appt

Entrance: £4

Other information: Monthly cookery
courses, inc. guided tour of garden

BATES GREEN ★

The present owner, a noted plantswoman, has transformed two acres of farmland around her Sussex farmhouse into a superb series of garden spaces embraced within the shelter of the Downs. Agricultural knowledge combined with artistic imagination has resulted in plantings that demonstrate an instinctive use of colour, light and shade. The huge borders of the Sundial Garden confidently combine washes of harmonious and contrasting colour with bold verticals and foliage texture. In the Oak Tree Garden, spring drifts of narcissi, fritillaries and later wild flowers thrive in the dappled shade. The garden is in the constant process of change and refinement, with the original cattle pond being transformed into a bog garden and a new monocot border filled with kniphofias, eremurus and grasses forming a visual link with meadows crossed by mown paths leading to woodland. The potager supplies fresh produce for the 'Garden to Kitchen' cookery courses run by daughter Philippa Vine.

CHARLESTON

The Bohemian circle of artists and writers around Vanessa Bell and Duncan Grant, known as the Bloomsbury group, spent many creative years at Charleston. The house and garden sheltering beneath the Downs have been painstakingly restored, and the idiosyncratic menage is skilfully evoked in thoughtful tours and exhibitions. The walled garden, replanted with quintessential cottage-garden flowers and filled with original sculptures and casts, was a place for painting and playing, and has been faithfully re-created from the correspondence, paintings and memories of weekenders of the period like Peggy Ashcroft and Dadie Rylands.

The Charleston Trust

Firle, Lewes BN8 6LL. Tel: (01323) 811265;
www.charleston.org.uk

6m E of Lewes on A27 between Firle and Selmeston

House and garden open April to Oct, Wed – Sun and Bank Holiday Mons, 2 – 6pm (opens 11.30am Wed and Sat in July and Aug)

Entrance: £2.50, children £1 (house and garden £7.50, children £4.50)

CLINTON LODGE ★

The house was enlarged by the Earl of Sheffield for his daughter, who married Sir Henry Clinton, one of the three generals of Waterloo. The eighteenth-century facade is set in a tree-lined lawn, flanked by a newly created canal and overlooking parkland. The 1987 storm removed the old oaks but these have been replanted in a Repton-style landscape leading to a tall stone pillar on the hill. The garden itself lies in six acres of clay soil divided into areas by period. The Elizabethan herb garden has camomile paths and turf seats, and four knot gardens. The Victorian era is represented by a tall white, yellow and blue herbaceous border; the Pre-Raphaelites by an *allée* of white roses, clematis, purple vines and lilies; the twentieth century by an unusual swimming pool garden encircled by an arcade of apples. A wildflower meadow is reached through an avenue lined with fastigiate hornbeams, and a pleached lime avenue leads to the medieval herb garden and a potager. An enclosed garden of old roses is trained at nose height to enjoy the scent. New gardens continue to be made: a small, shady glade, a small knot garden, a canal garden and an orchard planted with crinums.

Lady Collum

Fletching, Uckfield TN22 3ST.
Tel: (01825) 722952

4m W of Uckfield off A272. Turn N at Piltdown and continue 1.5m to Fletching. House is in main street surrounded by yew hedge

Open for NGS, and for parties by appt

Entrance: £4, parties £6 per person

GREAT DIXTER ★★
(Historic Garden Grade I)

Enfolded by its glorious gardens, the medieval house at Great Dixter appears historically authentic. It was in fact reinvented after 1910 by Christopher Lloyd's parents by the architect Edwin Lutyens, who enlarged it in the local vernacular, and designed the gardens. Christo, as his friends called him, lived and gardened here with his inimitable passion and flair for planting, assisted by Fergus Garrett, until his death in 2006. He left behind a garden that is inspirational at every turn. Meadow gardening is a striking feature, with the entrance flanked by long grass filled with *Camassia quamash*, and colonies of bulbs and early purple orchids in the orchard. The Long Border is a spectacular mixture of shrubs, climbers, perennials and annuals, reflecting Lloyd's determination to combine colours unconventionally to exuberant effect, while

Olivia Eller and the Great Dixter Charitable Trust

Dixter Road, Northiam, Rye TN31 6PH.
Tel: (01797) 252878;
www.greatdixter.co.uk

10m N of Hastings, 0.5m N of Northiam. Turn off A28 at Northiam post office

House open as garden, but 2 – 5pm

Garden open 21st March to 26th Oct, daily except Mon (but open Bank Holiday Mons), 2 – 5pm

Entrance: £6.50, children £3 (house and garden £8, children £3.50)

the sheltered Exotic Garden is a riot of tropical colours and unfamiliar shapes. In the High Garden, approached through superb topiary, stock plants and vegetables grow together in an intriguing and aesthetic melange. Many of the plants are propagated *in situ* and for sale in the attractive nursery.

HAILSHAM GRANGE ★

Noel Thompson

Hailsham BN27 1BL.
Tel: (01323) 844248

8m N of Eastbourne off A22. Turn off Hailsham High Street into Vicarage Road and park in public car park

Open for NGS, and for parties by appt

Entrance: £3.50, children free

● ● WC ※ B&B

The present owner has devised a horticultural stage set with the handsome early-eighteenth-century former vicarage centre-stage. Masterly use of stilted hornbeam and box hedging divides the one-acre garden into a series of formal rooms where the restraint of clipped foliage, gravel and brick contrasts with romantic, colour-themed planting. A central turf path leading to a rose-swagged gazebo reveals a *coup de théâtre* of hidden double borders filled with cream, yellow and apricot perennials, skilfully planted for texture and form and set against the backdrop of church and sheltering trees. Box parterres, a tiny white garden, a shady wilderness and a bulb-filled spinney combine with topiary and statuary to create a classical estate in miniature.

Hailsham Grange

MARCHANTS HARDY PLANTS

Graham Gough and Lucy Goffin

2 Marchants Cottages, Mill Lane, Laughton BN8 6AJ. Tel: (01323) 811737

6m E of Lewes. From Laughton crossroads on B2124 (at Roebuck Inn), travel E for 0.5m. At next crossroads turn S, signed to Ripe, down Mill Lane; entrance is on right

Garden open 5th March to 16th Oct, Wed – Sat, 9.30am – 5.30pm

Graham Gough, esteemed as a nurseryman and gardener, bought the derelict cottage sitting on two acres of neglected land on the spur of the moment. What he did not anticipate was the intractable clay that lay beneath. Building up the soil and improving its structure was a long haul and a terrible labour, but he was rewarded with a panoramic view of the South Downs. Now it is filled with grasses, trees and shrubs in harmony with the lush countryside. Personal herbaceous favourites – agapanthus, kniphofias and sedums – are guaranteed a place, together with other enthusiasms like sanguisorba, thalictrum and persicaria, and grasses such as *Miscanthus sinensis* 'Silberspinne', *M.s.* 'Malepartus' and the elegant *Stipa gigantea*. Most of the plants for sale are propagated on site. This is not just a nursery – it is also a fabulous garden with a view.

Nursery open as garden, but from 19th March

Entrance: £2.50, children free

MERRIMENTS GARDENS ★

In this fine four-acre garden, pools and pergolas surrounded by boldly curving beds of impressive colour-themed planting create a rich source of inspiration particularly relevant to modern gardens. Well-designed and labelled schemes show plant associations for every situation, from a shady bog garden filled with lush marginals to the sun-baked gravelled garden. Between these extremes are imaginatively stocked borders in every colour combination, filled with herbaceous plants and shrubs underplanted with tulips, alliums and hostas. Fine specimen trees like *Gleditsia triacanthos* 'Sunburst' and *Catalpa bignonioides* 'Aurea' have been chosen for their decorative foliage. Benches, arbours and summerhouses afford good vantage points, and handsome containers and sculpture make effective focal points. The health and vigour of the plants, which include many excellent varieties of clematis, is remarkable. A welcoming tea room and a shady terrace combine with a superbly stocked nursery.

David and Peggy Weeks

Hawkhurst Road, Hurst Green
TN19 7RA.
Tel: (01580) 860666;
www.merriments.co.uk

7m N of Battle, on A229 (formerly A265) between Hawkhurst and Hurst Green

Open 21st March to Sept, daily,
10am – 5.30pm (opens 10.30am Sun)

Entrance: £4.50, children £2

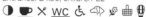

Merriments Gardens

MICHELHAM PRIORY ★

Sussex Past

Upper Dicker, Hailsham BN27 3QS.
Tel: (01323) 844224;
www.sussexpast.co.uk

10m N of Eastbourne off A22 and A27

House, museum and gardens open
March to 2nd Nov, Tues – Sun and Bank
Holiday Mons, 10.30am – 5pm (closes
4pm March and Oct) ; Aug, daily,
10.30am – 5.30pm

Entrance: £6, concessions £5,
disabled and carers, children (5–15) £3,
family £15.20 (2007 prices)

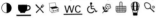

Initially, the main horticultural interest of this historic monastic site – more a Tudor manor than a monastery – was the physic garden, but every visit reveals new areas of interest within the moated site of the old priory. The stewponds have been re-excavated and fringed with exotic waterside plants, particularly those with dramatic foliage. The widely sweeping herbaceous border is planted in swathes of bold colour and form and leads into areas of mixed planting alongside the moat and adjoining the buildings. A fine ornamental potager with vegetables, flowers and a central pergola lies behind the walls of a yew hedge, and there is also an orchard. Young liquidambars and catalpas are gaining strength and enliven the foreground to the more natural moatside planting. A cloister garden in the well courtyard, inspired by illustrations of medieval Marian gardens, includes an arbour, turf seat and raised beds for medicinal plants. Sculptures are dotted throughout.

MONK'S HOUSE

The National Trust

Rodmell, Lewes BN7 3HF.
Tel: (01323) 870001;
www.nationaltrust.org.uk

4m S of Lewes off old A275 (now C7).
In Rodmell follow signs to church and
continue 400 metres to house

House and garden open 2nd April to
29th Oct, Wed and Sat, 2 – 5pm, and
for parties by appt (must book 4 weeks
in advance)

Entrance: £3.50, children £1.80,
family £8.70

The delightful cottage gardens surrounding the country retreat of Virginia and Leonard Woolf from 1919 are being restored by the present tenant. Scrambling roses and unpretentious plants tumble over paths leading to the orchard where Virginia created her famous writing room with views of the South Downs and the Sussex flint church. The tranquil spaces around the house are protected by mature trees and divided by rustic walls and cordon fruit into sunny or shady courtyards. The atmosphere of seclusion and privacy echoes a diary entry of 1932, when she wrote of 'all the garden green tunnels, mounds of green, never a person to be seen, never an interruption, the place to ourselves, the long hours'. The potager where Leonard worked is flourishing, there are three tiny pools, and the whole garden is filled with scent and birdsong. Several rooms in the house have also been evocatively re-created.

PASHLEY MANOR GARDENS ★

Mr and Mrs James A. Sellick

Ticehurst TN5 7HE.
Tel: (01580) 200888;
www.pashleymanorgardens.com

16m N of Hastings, 10m SE of Tunbridge
Wells on B2099 between Ticehurst and
A21. Signposted

Open 3rd April to Sept, Tues – Thurs, Sat
and Bank Holiday Mons,
11am – 5pm; Oct, Mon – Fri,
10am – 4pm. Coach parties by appt only

Entrance: £7

The Grade-I-listed house is a beautiful and atmospheric amalgam – a 1550 timber-framed front facade and a 1720 rear elevation – and is pivotal to the 11 acres of handsome gardens that surround it. The entrance drive leads through elegant parkland, and there are fine views of the surrounding countryside from all sides, but the garden proper lies mainly to the rear. Near the house, festooned with a mighty wisteria, is a progression of large curving borders and, stretching eastwards, a series of enclosed formal gardens, each one different and all immaculately maintained. In one golden flowers and foliage dominate; another is given over to roses; in a third an avenue of pleached pears is underplanted with box arranged to give a view through to a magnificent

Pashley Manor

hydrangea hedge. Major collections of tulips, lilies from Bloms Bulbs and Peter Beales roses ensure a spectacular progression of colour and scent from May through to early August, when the hot-coloured herbaceous borders facing outwards to the grazing fields take centre-stage. Sweeping lawns and water are the other key elements, enticing visitors down towards the perimeter of the garden, to the medieval moat and its island and to a string of ponds falling away into the distance, the top one furnished with a magnificent fountain. Gravel paths lead through camellia and rhododendron shrubberies in an intriguing circuit, and in every part of the garden there are sculptures to discover. A visit here is enjoyable for many other reasons: the restaurant is excellent, the plants for sale well-grown, the staff welcoming, and if the owners are in residence the whole place bubbles with infectious enthusiasm.

PENNS IN THE ROCKS

William Penn, celebrated Quaker and founder of Pennsylvania, owned Penns in the Rocks in the seventeenth century. The handsome house contrasts dramatically with surrounding sandstone outcrops, and in spring the wooded vale leading to a classical gazebo blazes with azaleas. In the 1930s, the poet Dorothy Wellesley and her friend Vita

Lady Gibson

Groombridge, Kent TN3 9PA.
Tel: (01892) 864244

7m SW of Tunbridge Wells on Groombridge – Crowborough road just S of Plumeyfeather Corner

Penns in the Rocks

343

Open for NGS, and for parties by appt

Entrance £4, children 50p

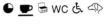

Sackville-West established the bold formal axis of garden spaces centred on the walled garden, where now topiary box globes and squares filled with lavender contrast with lush perennials. (Vita later wished she and Harold Nicholson had seen Penns the year they bought Long Barn, with intriguing implications for British gardening.) An avenue of white mulberries and an Ionic temple reflected in the lake link the garden to the wider landscape. 12 acres.

Mr and Mrs John Whitmore

Hartfield TN7 4JP.
Tel: (01892) 770266

7m E of East Grinstead, 1m N of Hartfield on B2026. Turn into unmade lane adjacent to Perryhill Nurseries, left fork, over bridge and up hill

Open for NGS, and by appt
May to Sept

Admission £4, children free

PERRYHILL FARMHOUSE

With far-reaching views to the Ashdown Forest, the medieval hall house forms a handsome backdrop to the quintessentially English country garden, its 1.5 acres now divided into contrasting areas surrounding a central lawn. Roses are a particular feature, smothering pergolas, clothing ancient barn walls, and planted in formal beds and burgeoning herbaceous borders. A sheltered parterre and sunken pool garden provide tranquil places to sit, and the fine Victorian greenhouse and kitchen garden produce vegetables, soft fruit and in late summer a stunning display of dahlias.

Brighton & Hove City Council

Brighton BN1 1EE.
Tel: (01273) 290900:
www.royalpavilion.org.uk

In central Brighton

House open April to Sept, daily, 9.30am – 5:45pm; Oct to March, daily except 25th, 26th Dec, 10am – 5.15pm

Garden open all year, daily

Entrance: free (house £7.70, concessions £5.90, children under 16 £5.10, family £20.50)

Other information: entrance to Brighton Museum and Art Gallery (open Tues – Sun)

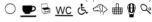

ROYAL PAVILION GARDENS

(Historic Garden Grade II)

The seven-acre gardens surrounding the Royal Pavilion have been restored to their original splendour, closely following John Nash's plans of the 1820s. Nash conceived the building and grounds as a unity, and his fascinating vision will be fully realised as the plants and shrubs continue to flourish and mature. The beds are of mixed shrubs and herbaceous plants, a combination first applied at that time, and species and varieties have been selected to conform as closely as possible to the original lists of plants supplied to the Prince Regent (later King George IV). In summer orange tiger lilies with their spotted purple markings, brought from China in 1804, provide an exotic foreground to more familiar and native plants, while a profusion of roses – such as R. 'Petite Lisette', a damask first introduced in 1817 – contribute their colour and scent to the ornamental shrubberies. The gardens and grounds reflect the great revolution in landscape gardening that began in the 1730s, when straight lines and symmetrical shapes were banished, and in their place appeared curving paths and 'natural' groups of trees and shrubs undulating gracefully over the lawn. As visitors pass through the grounds, the magical building is disclosed by a succession of varying views through the shrubs and thickets.

Sarah Raven and Adam Nicolson

Perch Hill Farm, Willingford Lane, Brightling, Robertsbridge TN32 5HP.
Tel: (0845) 050 4849;
www.sarahraven.com

SARAH RAVEN'S CUTTING GARDEN ★

Set high on a windy hill, with stunning views across valleys to the distant Brightling Beacon, the Sussex farmhouse is surrounded by a series of characterful garden spaces – two acres in all, packed with flowers for picking and produce of every imaginable kind. The Oast Garden, sheltered by a loggia and handsome walls, is planted with bold architectural plants and washes of brilliant colour from salvias, cardoons, artichokes, dahlias, zinnias, gladioli, cannas, jungly corn and banana foliage. The former vegetable garden is now given over to fruit, and in the new vegetable garden tepees of sweet peas look down on an ornamental display of artichokes, flowers and vegetables. The large cutting garden has four central beds filled with hardy and half-hardy annuals and biennials. Inspirational.

SHEFFIELD PARK GARDEN ★
(Historic Park Grade I)

Laid out in 1776 for the Earl of Sheffield by 'Capability' Brown and further developed in the early twentieth century, the park is a fine example of the landscape movement. What impresses most is the sheer scale. Two lakes, originally created in a valley below the neo-Gothic house, were later extended to four, linked by cascades. Now grown to magnificent maturity, towering specimen trees provide superb autumn colour, but the beauty and diversity of foliage, the continuing programme of tree and shrub planting, and the drifts of daffodils and bluebells followed by dramatic displays of rhododendrons and azaleas, make a visit here rewarding at any time. Bold waterside planting shelters swans, moorhens and mallards, and the lakes are planted with elegant water lilies.

5m E of Heathfield on A265. In Burwash village turn S at war memorial; after 3m turn R at crossroads into Willingford Lane (signed Burwash Weald). Garden is 0.5m on right (only suitable for small vehicles)

Open for NGS, and for parties by appt

Entrance: £4, children free

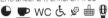

The National Trust

Sheffield Park TN22 3QX.
Tel: (01825) 790231;
www.nationaltrust.org.uk

5m NW of Uckfield, midway between East Grinstead and Lewes E of A275

Open 5th Jan to 2nd March, Sat and Sun; 4th March to 4th May, 3rd June to 5th Oct, 4th Nov to Dec, Tues – Sun; 5th May to 1st June, 6th Oct to 2nd Nov, daily; all 10.30am – 5.30pm (closes 4pm in winter) (last admission 1 hour before closing). Open Bank Holiday Mons, April to Aug

Entrance: £7.30, children £3.65, family £18.25

Other information: Wheelchairs and self-drive powered vehicles available – telephone (01825) 790302

Sheffield Park Garden

WARREN HOUSE

Mr and Mrs M. J. Hands

Warren Road, Crowborough TN6 1TX.
Tel: (01892) 663502

7m NE of Uckfield off A26. From
Crowborough Cross turn towards Uckfield,
take 4th turning on right; garden is 1m
down Warren Road. From south, take 2nd
turning on left after Blue Anchor pub

Open for NGS, and by appt

Entrance: £3 on NGS open days

 WC &

Situated in a commanding position overlooking Ashdown Forest, this is a splendid example of a garden made and tended by the owner alone – all nine acres of it. Extensive plantings of trees, shrubs, grasses and flowers skirt the sweeping lawns, and a series of different vistas displays a wealth of rhododendrons and azaleas. There are wisteria and laburnum walks, and the woodland, with its ponds and tree-lined avenues, is a peaceful place in which to stroll. The original infrastructure of walls, paths and terraces has been sensitively restored, blending the garden harmoniously into the surrounding forest.

OTHER RECOMMENDED GARDENS

HERSTMONCEUX CASTLE

Hailsham BN27 1RN (01323 833816;
www.herstmonceux-castle.com). Open 12th April
to 26th Oct, daily, 10am – 6pm (closes 5pm Oct).

The impressive moated 15th-century castle stands in 550 acres of magnificent wooded parkland, with formal gardens sheltered by high walls and hedges, roses and herbaceous borders, a herb garden and parterre inspired by Shakespearean quotations. (Listed Grade II)

KING JOHN'S LODGE

Mr and Mrs R. A. Cunningham, Sheepstreet Lane,
Etchingham TN19 7AZ (01580 819232);
www.kingjohnslodge.co.uk. Open all year, daily,
10am – 5.30pm, and for parties by appt

The romantic appeal of the fine, mostly Jacobean house has been enhanced by the restoration of its 8-acre gardens. Flowing borders and tranquil lawns bounded by a formal lily pond with fine parkland views contrast with a wildflower-filled orchard, shady woodland and a natural pool. A propagation nursery is now open.

LAMB HOUSE

West Street, Rye TN31 7ES (01580 762334;
www.nationaltrust.org.uk). Open 20th March to 25th
Oct, Thurs and Sat, 2 – 6pm. NT

Although the author Henry James professed to have no horticultural knowledge, with the help of Alfred Parsons he left a 1-acre town garden of charm and interest, with unusual trees and shrubs, vegetable and herb gardens and attractive herbaceous plantings.

STONE HOUSE HOTEL

Peter and Jane Dunn, Rushlake Green, Heathfield
TN21 9QJ (01435 830553;
www.stonehousesussex.co.uk). Open March to Oct by
appt

A succulent potager has been planted in the walled kitchen garden by master chef Jane Dunn to supply fresh produce for her hotel and culinary courses. Beyond is a traditional country-house garden of avenues, an impressive semi-circular lime walk, roses, pools and a huge herbaceous border. Across the lake lie the wooded valleys of deepest Sussex. 6.5 acres.

WELLINGHAM HERB GARDEN

Grant Bricknell, Wellingham Lane, Nr Lewes
BN75 8SW (01435 883187). Open Easter to Sept,
Sat and Sun, 10.30am – 5.30pm

Within sight of the South Downs, a fragrant garden and nursery have been laid out inside an old walled kitchen garden. Herbs shaded by fruit trees are planted in natural drifts within a formal pattern of beds and paths, with scented shrubs and trained fruit on the walls. Old roses, yew hedges, statuary and a summerhouse complete the elegant picture.

SUSSEX, WEST

For further information about how to use the *Guide*
and for an explanation of the symbols, see pages vi–viii.
Specific dates and times are those given to us by garden owners for 2008.
For 2009 dates, check with the individual properties.
For opening dates under the National Gardens Scheme,
readers should consult *The Yellow Book* or www.ngs.org.uk.
Maps are to be found at the end of the *Guide*.

ARUNDEL CASTLE GARDENS

(Historic Garden Grade II*)

Since 1996 the neglected 10-acre gardens surrounding the impossibly dramatic and romantic castle have been returned to their Victorian splendour by the Duchess of Norfolk and head gardener Gerry Kelsey. Within the grounds are a number of small gardens that have been faithfully restored but also bear the imprint of the Duchess's own personality. The delightful walled vegetable garden is based around a formal Victorian design of small paths and square beds; the central point is a lead fountain viewed through arches of apple trees, an enchanting sight in the spring, and flowers grow among the vegetables, adding to the tapestry of colour. A rare Clarke and Hope 1850 lean-to iron peach house once again has peaches flourishing on its wall along with citrus and other exotic fruits. The remaining third of the walled garden is being reclaimed from tarmac and transformed into a series of enclosures terraced on two levels that pays homage to the long-lost Renaissance garden created at Arundel House in London by the 14th Earl. The design, by Julian and Isabel Bannerman, is at once formal and contemporary, drawing on topiary, water

The Duke and Duchess of Norfolk

Arundel BN18 9AB.
Tel: (01903) 882173/884581;
www.arundelcastle.org

10m E of Chichester on A27

Castle and garden open 21st March to 2nd Nov, daily except Mon (but open Bank Holiday Mons and Mons in Aug), 10am – 5pm.

Garden tours available

Entrance: Gardens and castle keep £6.50 (full castle, gardens and grounds £12, OAPs £9.50, Children £7.50, family £32)

Arundel Castle

devices and sculpture of all kinds. In the small garden of the Fitzalan Chapel, planted in white and containing a small pool, an atmosphere of stillness and reflection prevails. The rose garden, a separate enclosure further from the castle, is well worth visiting. Planted with roses including 'Madame Isaac Pereire' and 'Winchester Cathedral', its seclusion gives it a feeling of timelessness.

BANKTON COTTAGE

Robin and Rosie Lloyd

Turners Hill Road, Crawley Down RH10 4EY.

Tel: (01342) 718907

2.5m E of M23 junction 10, 4m W of East Grinstead, B2028 1m N of Turners Hill crossroads

Open for NGS, and May to early Aug for parties by appt

Entrance: £3.50, evening opening £4.50 inc. wine

NEW

Redesigned in 2001 by the present owners, there is plenty to delight both the eye and the senses in the three acres here. The main, walled garden was originally the kitchen garden to Bankton House, built in 1864, but it has now been artistically divided into different sections. Entered through a small paved area with an eye-catching statue by Michael Speller, an abundance of delphiniums, hollyhocks, poppies and other cottage-garden favourites adds a romantic feel to this section. From there the route is either towards the conservatory overlooking a lavender parterre or on to the main lawn, cleverly divided by serpentine yew hedges and flanked on one side by a wonderful hot border planted with *Crocosmia* 'Lucifer', *Lysimachia* 'Firecracker', *Dahlia* 'Bishop of Llandaff' and *Phlox* 'Starfire' and the like. Opposite is a pergola covered in wisteria and 'Wedding Day' and other roses; beyond, a small vegetable garden is laid out in raised beds. Near the house is a fish pond and bog garden resplendent with hostas, irises and ferns, and the garden continues outside the main walled enclosure with a lake, woodland, a small gravel garden and a newly planted shrubbery. The charm of this tranquil and atmospheric garden lies not only in its planting but also in its fine and well-placed statuary and terracotta pots, including a huge planter containing an olive tree grown from a cutting taken from Crete in the early 1980s.

BORDE HILL GARDEN ★
(Historic Garden Grade II*)

Borde Hill Gardens Ltd

Balcombe Road, Haywards Heath RH16 1XP. Tel: (01444) 450326; www.bordehill.co.uk

1.5m N of Haywards Heath on Balcombe – Haywards Heath road

Garden open – telephone or consult website for details

Entrance: March to Oct £6.50, concessions £5.50, children £3.50 (reduced rates Oct to Dec) (2007 prices)

This is one of Sussex's fine plant-hunter gardens, created from 1893 with trees and shrubs collected from Asia, Tasmania, the Andes and Europe. It has award-winning collections of azaleas, rhododendrons, magnolias and camellias surrounded by 220 acres of parkland and bluebell woods. The classic rose and Italian gardens were designed by Robin Williams, and Heritage Lottery funds have been used to restore the glasshouse area and refashion the surroundings of the old potting sheds as a series of small rooms filled with rare southern-hemisphere shrubs. In the Long Dell Sino-Himalayan species surround Chusan palms, while the Round Dell is a lush hidden area with more Chusan palms, bamboos and huge gunneras. A white garden was created in 2002. Additional attractions include a pirates' adventure playground, coarse and children's fishing, extensive woodland walks and lakes.

BURPHAM PLACE

A small garden of great originality in its colour schemes and plant associations, largely redesigned in 2006 by the owner, a garden designer. New colour-themed herbaceous borders were introduced around two circles of grass with a succession of unusual and native plants. Special emphasis is on 'sad' colours – black, brown, peach, silver and grey plants and grasses flow through several beds. New varieties of verbascum, foxglove, hemerocallis, heuchera and iris are star players, and other beds feature mauve and lime and green and white plantings, with the emphasis on texture. A Gothic arch leads to a path in the small wild garden full of cow parsley and mullein which meanders around silver birch trees down to a stream and folly. The whole is designed to blend with the Downs beyond.

Elizabeth Woodhouse

Burpham, Arundel BN18 9RH.
Tel: (01903) 884833

0.5m S of Arundel, turn off A27 Arundel – Worthing road and continue for 2m through Wepham to Burpham

Open by appt

Entrance: charge

 WC B&B

CASS SCULPTURE FOUNDATION ★

Twenty-six acres of woodland have been shaped to give a finer setting for twenty-first-century British sculpture than any indoor gallery. The quality of the work is outstanding; the trees act as screens, giving each piece its own stage, and sometimes opening to give a backdrop of the Sussex countryside. Beautiful gates by Wendy Ramshaw herald the entrance to the park, while at the end of one walk the spire of Chichester cathedral is borrowed sculpture of the most majestic kind. Over 72 large, ever-changing outdoor works are on show at any one time, ranging from Steven Gregory's 'Fish on a Bicycle', Anthony Caro's 'Eastern' to Bill Woodrow's 'Regardless of History' and a DNA helix made from shopping trollies by Abigail Fallis. The largest exhibition of Tony Cragg's outdoor work in Britain to date can be seen in a newly landscaped chalk pit within the grounds.

Vicky Goodes

Goodwood, Chichester PO18 0QP.
Tel: (01243) 538449;
www.sculpture.org.uk

7m N of Chichester, 3m S of East Dean, between A286 and A285 (telephone (01243) 771114 for directions or consult website)

Open March to 4th Nov, Tues – Sun and Bank Holiday Mons, 10.30am – 5pm (last entrance 4pm)

Entrance: £10

Cass Sculpture Foundation

CHIDMERE HOUSE

Jackie and David Russell

Chidham Lane, Chidham, Chichester
PO18 8TD.

Tel: (01243) 572287;
www.chidmeregardens.com

6m W of Chichester, 4m E of Emsworth,
S of A259. Turn right at S end of Chidham

Open for NGS, and by appt

Entrance: £3.50, children free

  WC

The Tudor house (not open) is excitingly situated next to Chidmere Pond, so much so that the well-filled greenhouse which borders the mere feels almost like a houseboat. The garden was laid out in the 1930s, divided into separate compartments by tall hedges of hornbeam and yew. Flowering cherries, sheets of daffodils and bluebells ensure that it is spectacular in the spring. There are other fine flowering trees, while the house supports a Banksia rose and two wisterias. Later, the roses, a well-stocked herbaceous border, a tulip tree and a fine *Taxodium distichum* command attention. The garden has been expanded by 12 acres and now includes an alpine greenhouse, a wildflower meadow and orchards of fruit trees producing Chidmere Farm apple juice. In all, 32 acres.

COATES MANOR

Mrs G.H. Thorp

Fittleworth, Pulborough RH20 1ES.
Tel: (01798) 865356

3m W of Pulborough, 0.5m
S of Fittleworth off B2138

Open by appt

Entrance: £3, children free

This one-acre garden has an abundance of trees and shrubs carefully chosen to give long-term pleasure. There are ferns, grasses such as *Stipa gigantea* like frozen waterfalls, *Phlomis italica* and *P. chrysophylla*, blue and white agapanthus, and many specimen trees chosen for their foliage, berries or autumn colour. A small paved walled garden has *Clerodendrum trichotomum*, clematis, phlox and other scented flowers. The owner is particularly interested in colour contrasts and light and shade, and goes to considerable lengths to find the best species available. Look out for a variegated ivy contrasting well with *Cotinus coggygria* 'Notcutt's Variety' on a wall by the house; a mature copper beech tree stands nearby. The delightful Elizabethan house is partly covered in variegated ivy and euonymus, linking it to the surrounding countryside.

Coates Manor

DENMANS GARDEN ★

John Brookes, one of Britain's most influential designers, moved here in 1980. The whole of the four-acre site relies for its drama on foliage plants – even in spring, visitors come away with minds full of euphorbias, yuccas, phormiums and mounds of clipped box. The centre of the garden is a river of pebbles and gravel against which the leaves of thistles and bamboo show up dramatically. There are some choice tulips and other spring bulbs, interesting primulas and spring-flowering shrubs. In late summer a large border of *Romneya coulteri*, the Californian tree poppy, is at its best, while autumn and winter interest are given by the stems of willow and cornus, and by the leaves of staphylea and *Parrotia persica*. The walled garden contains many old roses as well as a herb garden and perennials. Outside the house is the south garden; very tender species are planted in another gravel area near a circular pond.

John Brookes and Michael Neve

Denmans Lane, Fontwell BN18 0SU.
Tel: (01243) 542808;
www.denmans-garden.co.uk

5m E of Chichester. Turn S off A27, W of Fontwell racecourse

Open all year, daily, except 24th to 26th Dec and 1st Jan, 9am – 5pm, and for parties of 15 or more by appt

Entrance: £4.25, OAPs £3.80, children over 4 £2.50, family £12.50

HIGH BEECHES GARDENS ★
(Historic Garden Grade II*)

The delightful woodland and water garden of over 25 acres encourages its visitors to explore the different walks that meander, like the streams, through the collection of rare trees and unusual shrubs. Alongside a National Collection of

High Beeches Gardens Conservation Trust

Handcross RH17 6HQ.
Tel: (01444) 400589;
www.highbeeches.com

High Beeches Gardens

5m S of Crawley, 1m E of Handcross,
S of B2110

Open mid-March to Oct, Thurs – Tues,
1 – 5pm

Entrance: £5.50, accompanied children
under 14 free

stewartias are glades of rhododendrons, azaleas and magnolias. Originally designed by Colonel Loder in 1906, the garden is always extending its well-labelled collection. There are many benches and a summerhouse from which to enjoy the scents and colours. Starting with bluebells in spring, stunning cornus, a wildflower meadow, a glade of *Gentiana asclepiadea* (the only naturalised site of willow gentian in Britain) and *Eucryphia glutinosa* in late August, and a carpet of *Cyclamen hederifolium* at the base of the oak tree at Centre Pond adding to the wonderful autumn colours, this is a garden of many seasons.

Worthing Borough Council

Littlehampton Road, Goring-by-Sea
BN12 6PF. Tel: (01903) 501054

3m W of Worthing, N of A259

Open April to Sept, daily, 10am – 6pm;
Oct to March, Mon – Fri,
10am – 4.30pm (closes 4pm
Dec and Jan)

Entrance: free – donation box

Other information: Refreshments at
adjacent Highdown Towers. Toilet
facilities available to wheelchair users
only with key

HIGHDOWN

(Historic Garden Grade II*)

Sir Frederick Stern created a succession of gardens and woodland glades overlooking the beautiful downland country side and with views to the sea, during the early part of the twentieth century. Among the abundance of fine and rare plants and trees he planted were many from China and the Himalayan regions. The atmosphere is magical, with paths leading from one enclosed space to another, or through a woodland glade awash in the spring with primroses, bluebells and daffodils. Covering ten acres, there are higher, middle and lower gardens. The first, begun in 1909 in the old chalk pit, is a pond and rock garden with a magnificent backdrop of deciduous trees clinging to the white cliff face. The second, reached through a beech wood, has a succession of colour through spring and early summer as irises, philadelphus and agapanthus follow on from the spring bulbs. In the third, entered through a pittosporum hedge, are many of the old cultivars of roses originally grown here, together with tree peonies and a wealth of herbaceous plants. These gardens are a secret crying out to be better known.

Laurence and Rebeka Hardy

Freshfield Lane, Danehill, Haywards
Heath RH17 7HQ.
Tel: (01825) 790237

7m S of East Grinstead on A275. In
Danehill, turn at war memorial into
Freshfield Lane. Latchetts is 1 mile
further (not Latchetts Farmhouse)

Open for NGS; and by appt

Entrance: £5, £4 on NGS open days

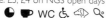

LATCHETTS ★

An eight-acre garden remarkable in its diversity, filled by its creative owners with assured planting for every situation, plus three acres of woodland with wooden sculptures and a fern stumpery. Five acres of flowing spaces surround the house high above its Wealden valley. Velvety lawns surrounded by mature trees and huge shrub borders slope to raised beds massed with sun-loving perennials; a rill trickles from a water garden fringed with giant gunneras into a cool wild wood sheltering tree ferns and bamboo. Bold swathes of prairie planting provide late colour sheltered by a high bank of shrub roses. At every turn there is something new: a mysterious pool with mist rising from the water and sculptures creating sound, a rose-laden tunnel leading to a vegetable garden, an intimate millennium garden filled with Christian symbolism and the soothing sound of water, a desert garden laid out around a giant sundial with a mound for the energetic to climb, looking over a wildflower meadow with a mini-labyrinth cut into it. In 2006 a sunken garden was created with a mural and a waterlily pond. Everywhere there are benches, summerhouses and vantage points from which to enjoy the varying views.

LEONARDSLEE – LAKES AND GARDENS ★★
(Historic Garden Grade I)

The gardens were originally started in 1801 and opened to the public in 1907; remnants of the original planting can still be found in the dell garden, including some of the oldest and largest specimens of rhododendrons and magnolias in the country. In 1889 Sir Edmund Loder, famously remembered for his *Rhododendron loderi* hybrids, moved to Leonardslee. These are a breathtaking sight on the top walk in May, as is the rock garden with its brilliantly coloured Kurume azaleas and rare Chusan palms. With 240 acres, seven lakes, sweeps of bluebells and important collections of camellias, acers and magnolias, this is not a place to rush round in a hurry. The immense scale and the mature trees give the garden a special quality and later in the season the autumn colours and their reflections in the water are incredibly beautiful. After the devastation of the 1987 storm new vistas were opened up, the whole area east of the lakes cleared and replanted with oaks and maples; plans are afoot to plant more cornus to extend the high points of the season. Other attractions are the temperate greenhouse and alpine house, the wallabies (assistant lawnmowers), the Loder family collection of Victorian motor cars, and a dolls' house exhibition incorporating all the components of a Victorian market town and country mansion. Selehurst (see entry) is opposite.

The Loder family

Lower Beeding, Horsham RH13 6PP.
Tel: (01403) 891212;
www.leonardslee.com

4m SW of Handcross and M23 on B2110/A281

Open April to Oct, daily, 9.30am – 6pm

Entrance: £9, children £4 (peak rates)

Other information: Victorian motor car collection

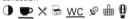

NYMANS ★★
(Historic Garden Grade II*)

An historic collection of fine trees, shrubs and plants in a beautifully structured setting, full of outstanding and almost theatrical effects: sheets of white narcissi under sorbus trees, a circle of camellias around a lawn with an urn in the centre, a vista down a lime avenue with a 'prospect' at the end and several borders of great splendour. It was started in 1890, by Ludwig Messel, who sponsored some of the great Himalayan plant-hunters, and given to the Trust in 1954. The garden still acquires rare wild-collected plants, with a particular focus on Chile. The library and drawing room are open to the public and lead out to the forecourt and a knot garden. The picturesque ruins of the original building (built c. 1928 to resemble a medieval manor house and largely destroyed by fire in 1947) are planted with clipped yew and other topiary. The original Messel creations include a pinetum, a heather

The National Trust

Handcross, Haywards Heath RH17 6EB.
Tel: (01444) 405250;
www.nationaltrust.org.uk

4m S of Crawley, off A23/M23 and A279, at southern end of Handcross

House open 19th March to 2nd Nov, Wed – Sun, 11am – 4pm

Garden open all year, Wed – Sun and Bank Holiday Mons, 10am – 5pm (closes 4pm in winter). Closed 25th and 26th Dec and 1st Jan

Entrance: £4, children £2, family £10 (house and garden £8, children £4, family £20) (reduced rates in winter)

Other information: Entrance may be restricted at peak times, and parts restricted in winter. Coaches must prebook. Batricar, wheelchairs and braille/audio guide available on free loan

garden, a rose garden, a wisteria-clad pergola and a walled garden, Some of these areas can be viewed from on high from the mound. Bedding is always beautifully done and the whole is exceptionally well maintained. *Magnolia* x *loebneri* 'Leonard Messel' and *Eucryphia* x *nymansensis* were both raised here. An exhibition of garden history situated within the garden is a recent welcome addition. On the opposite side of the road is the wild garden, and there are also 250 acres of free-access woodlands.

Nr Pulborough RH20 4HS.
Tel: (01903) 742021/744888;
www.parhaminsussex.co.uk

4m SE of Pulborough on A283, equidistant from A24 and A29

House open as gardens, but closed Tues and Fri, except in Aug, 2 – 5pm

Gardens open 23rd March to July and Sept, Tues to Fri, Sun and Bank Holiday Mons; Aug, Tues and Fri (but advisable to check before travelling); all 12 noon – 6pm (last admission 5pm). Also open by appt for private parties and guided tours

Entrance: £5, OAPs £4, children (5–15) £2.50, family £13 (house and garden £7, OAPs £6, children £3.50, family £19)

Other information: Advance notice required for wheelchairs. Garden study and flower arranging courses

PARHAM HOUSE AND GARDENS ★
(Historic Garden Grade II*)

Set in the heart of a medieval deer park on the slopes of the South Downs, the award-winning gardens surrounding the Elizabethan house are approached through Fountain Court. A broad gravelled path leads down a gentle slope through a wrought-iron gate guarded by a pair of Istrian stone lions to a walled garden of about four acres, which retains the original quadrant layout divided by broad walks and includes an orchard and teak walk-through greenhouse. The scope and character of this garden have been progressively replanted with huge herbaceous borders of Edwardian opulence to ensure a long season of interest. There are also cut-flower borders, a potager, a rose garden and a green border, planted along the outer west wall, and a lavender garden. In one corner is an enchanting miniature house with its own garden, a delight for both children and adults. The seven-acre pleasure grounds provide lawns and walks under stately trees to the lake, with views over the cricket ground to the South Downs. A brick and turf maze is a feature here. This is a garden for all seasons, and in spring it is dominated by carpets of bulbs and the splendid 'sacred' grove of white-flowering 'Mount Fuji' cherries, over fifty years old.

The National Trust

Petworth GU28 0AE.
Tel: (01798) 342207;
www.nationaltrust.org.uk

6.5m E of Midhurst on A272 in Petworth

House open as garden, but 11am – 5pm

Pleasure ground open March to Oct, Sat – Wed, 11am – 4pm; Nov, Wed – Sat, 10am – 3.30pm, Dec, Thurs – Sun, 10am – 3.30pm

Deer park open all year, daily, 8am – dusk

Entrance: pleasure ground £3.80, children £1.90; deer park free (house and pleasure ground £9.50, children £4.80, family £23.80)

PETWORTH HOUSE ★
(Historic Park Grade I)

The stately palace, with one of the finest late-seventeenth-century interiors in England, sits in a magnificent park developed over centuries from a small enclosure for fruit and vegetables in the sixteenth century to its present size of 705 acres; it is enclosed by an impressive five-mile-long stone wall. George London worked here at the end of the seventeenth century, and from 1751 to 1763 'Capability' Brown was employed by the 2nd Earl of Egremont to modify the contours of the ground, plant cedars and many other trees, and construct the serpentine lake in front of the house; it was one of his earliest designs. Turner painted fine views of the park (as well as the interior of the house) and it is interesting to see these and have them in one's mind. It is not a place for the botanist, but it is a splendid experience all year round, with a fine show of daffodils and bluebells and glorious autumn colour. The individual trees and shrubs, including Japanese maples and rhododendrons, deserve close study, and majestic veteran trees now tower over wildflower meadows and ornamental shrubs, providing interest throughout the year. It is worth noting that at the turn of the century Petworth had over two dozen gardeners (they were always counted in dozens). Far fewer staff have, since the storms of 1987 and 1990, planted in the region of 40,000 trees and continued to replant the pleasure grounds in Brownian style.

Other information: Parking 0.5m N of Petworth on A283. Disabled visitors by arrangement, special parking available. Refreshments only on days house open

Pleasure Ground: ◐ 🍵 ✕ 🖼 <u>WC</u> ♿ 🐾 ⊞ 🔍

Deer park: ○

RYMANS

Surrounding a fifteenth-century house with a mellow Ventnorstone exterior, the 20-acre garden is being developed by the present owner. Two new box parterres flank *Rosa odorata* 'Mutabilis' in front of the house. A walled garden filled with wisterias, flowering shrubs and roses and furnished with a new pergola leads to a long avenue of black poplars. The paddock opposite the old stables is now planted with a selection of trees and two wildflower glades. Seen from within the walled garden another avenue of black poplars, *Populus nigra*, stretches beyond a magnificent wrought-iron gate to nearby twelfth-century Apuldram church. Planted with massed daffodils, the avenue is a splendid sight in springtime. A spiral potager is maturing, and there is a new dahlia walk which, together with the collection of salvias, steals the show in August and September.

Mrs Suzanna Gayford

Apuldram, Dell Quay, Chichester PO20 7EG. Tel: (01243) 783147

1m SW of Chichester. Turn off A259 (old A27) at sign to Dell Quay, Apuldram, garden on left

Open for NGS, and by appt

Other information: Teas on open days

Entrance: £3.50

○ 🍵 🖼 ⬦ 🌹

Rymans

Mr and Mrs M. Prideaux

Lower Beeding, Horsham
RH13 6PR.
Tel: (01403) 891501

4.5m SE of Horsham on A281,
opposite Leonardslee

Open for parties by appt

Entrance: £5

Other information: Teas by
arrangement

● WC &

SELEHURST

Originally part of the Leonardslee estate (see entry) there are still original 'Loderi' rhododendrons to be found here, and the tallest *Eucalyptus gunnii* in the country, dating from the 1890s. The rest of this romantic landscape garden has been created since 1976 by garden designer and novelist Sue Prideaux. It is a place of glorious views, large-scale planting and a highly individual vision. Near the house the picture is classic and traditional: walled garden, Italian borders, laburnum and rose-tunnel, herb knot, herbaceous borders and topiary. Crossing the meadow down to bluebell woods and a stand of copper beeches is a different and enchanting world. Here is a crinkle-crankle hornbeam hedge, a 'magnolia axis' underplanted with bluebells, a calm green amphitheatre; nearby a 5000-year-old petrified Irish yew root is set on a mound within a copper beech circle. In the larch wood a walk is lined with columnar cypresses and *Cornus* 'Eddie's White Wonder'. There are no fewer than six ponds, each different in outline and atmosphere. In one is reflected a Gothick folly tower, and from here the path meanders through magnolias, azaleas, cornus and tree ferns to a hornbeam *allée*. Alternatively, you can take the original 1890s woodland walk back to the topmost pond and Chinese pavilion. On the other side of the house are plantings of eucryphia, stewartia and camellia, and a lime walk leading to a wildflower meadow.

Laura Ponsonby and Ian and
Kate Russell

Linchmere, Haslemere, Surrey
GU27 3NQ.
Tel: (01428) 653049

2m SW of Haslemere off B2131

Open 25th and 26th May, 24th and
25th Aug, 2 – 6pm, and by appt

Entrance: house and garden £3,
children £1

● ● ● WC & ●

SHULBREDE PRIORY

Originally an Augustinian priory, twelfth-century Shulbrede became the home of Lord Ponsonby, a writer and former pacifist MP early in the twentieth century. He and his wife Dorothea created a garden here which delighted Dorothea's father, Sir Hubert Parry, the composer and Director of the Royal College of Music, who often visited Shulbrede and composed the *Shulbrede Tunes* for piano. Their grand-daughter, Laura Ponsonby, continues to improve the 2.5-acre garden. Cottage-style borders are seen and smelt from the house, a sunken garden gives an Italianate air, a waterside walk in the wild garden inspires a sense of mystery, and vast yew hedges enclose a series of individual gardens planted to great effect.

Peter Thorogood

Bramber BN44 3WE.
Tel: (01903) 816205;
www.stmarysbramber.co.uk

8m NE of Worthing off A283 in
Bramber, 1m E of Steyning

Open May to Sept, Thurs, Sun and
Bank Holiday Mons, 2 – 6pm
(last entry 5pm). Parties by appt
April to Sept, except during public
open times

ST MARY'S HOUSE AND GARDENS

From the small gravel garden with clipped box and yew, the path leads over a pretty stone balustraded bridge to the topiary garden in front of the charming fifteenth-century timber-framed house, girdled by five mellow acres. The yew tunnel beyond the gate leads to the ivy-clad Monk's Walk. The upper lawn is enclosed by herbaceous borders, while the lower lawn has clipped yew hedges and roses; there is an exceptional example of the prehistoric *Ginkgo biloba*. The Victorian Secret Garden includes a rose garden and a border planted in memory of the late Queen Mother. The formerly circular orchard has been re-landscaped and includes a semi-circular pergola. A rural museum has been created in the Boulton and Paul potting shed, while the unusual 40-metre fruit wall has been cleared and replanted, and the pineapple pits proclaim their purpose once again. Two herbaceous borders and new yew hedges give structure to the herb and rose gardens. The woodland walk has been underplanted with bluebells and primroses but is mostly left to the native wildlife, with a huge fallen willow starting into growth again as an amazing living structure.

Entrance: house and gardens £6, concessions £5.50, children £3

TOWN PLACE ★

A wonderful three-acre garden created since 1990 by an ultrakeen husband-and-wife team – each year it gets a bit bigger. Wrought-iron gates open onto a lawn enclosed by low walls and old brick paths; the one to the left leads up steps to an apple tunnel and herb garden with wide downland views, then down past a big hollow oak to the dell with its attractive freeform raised pond and fountain. From here you look back across the main lawn to the 1650s house (not open) and a 46-metre-long herbaceous border backed by a magnificent flame tapestry hedge. A rose pergola shields a sunken rose garden, replanted in 2005 with over 140 English roses, and this in turn leads into the orchard and an area by the pool with gravel paths and beds block-planted with box, screened by a line of *Rosa* 'Excelsa'. Amble through the orchard, carpeted in spring with daffodils, to the 'circus', where beds of grasses and shrubs are surrounded by the astonishing circular, clipped, striped conifer hedge; beyond is the English rose garden, box-edged and planted with over 400 roses of 36 different cultivars. Tucked away in a corner

Mr and Mrs Anthony McGrath

Ketches Lane, Freshfield,
Nr Scaynes Hill RH17 7NR.

Tel: (01825) 790221;
www.townplacegarden.org.uk

3m E of Haywards Heath. From A275 turn W at Sheffield Green into Ketches Lane (signed to Lindfield); garden is 1.75m on left

Open for NGS, and June and July for parties of 20 or more by appt

Entrance: £4, children free

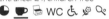

Town Place

are a spring garden and a hidden garden – follow the sound of water. There is more: copper beech hedges, a hornbeam walk, a potager and cutting garden and the New Territories, where a hornbeam *allée* and a cloister outline a 'ruined priory'. From here you can return to the main lawn to soak up a bit more of that sumptuous border.

TROTTON OLD RECTORY

Captain and Mrs John Pilley

Trotton, Petersfield GU31 5EN.
Tel: (01730) 813612

3m W of Midhurst on A272

Open for parties by appt

Entrance: £3

Set in the pretty Rother valley, the 3.5-acre garden consists of several different areas of varying shapes and sizes, each with its own character. Many are lavishly planted, and they are separated from each other by hedges of yew, holly and beech as well as a trellis screen and walls. To the north of the house are newly planted pleached limes and box, to the south a terrace leads out into a formal rose garden. This is planted with attractive pink and white roses, contrasting with the old roses in the circular rosarium in the garden beyond, which is surrounded by mixed borders where lavender, delphiniums, campanulas and many other plants provide a riot of colour. A restful enclosure dominated by a venerable oak has gunneras, clipped yew and a lawn speckled with bulbs in spring to give variations of texture and shades of green; against the hedge are the graves of family pets. Another garden surrounds the croquet lawn. To the east of the house at a lower level is a large pond surrounded by clumps of handsome *Iris ensata*. Walks lined with shrubs and hostas, hemerocallis and lilies link the different areas.

WAKEHURST PLACE GARDEN AND MILLENNIUM SEED BANK ★★

(Historic Garden Grade II*)

The Royal Botanic Gardens, Kew

Ardingly, Haywards Heath RH17 6TN.
Tel: (01444) 894066 (Infoline);
www.kew.org

5m N of Haywards Heath on B2028.
From London take A(M)23, A272,
B2028 or A22, B2110

Part of house open

Garden open all year, daily, except 24th and 25th Dec, 10am – 6pm (closes 4.30pm autumn and winter). Guided walks available 11.30am and 2.30pm on Sat, Sun and Bank Holiday Mons

Entrance: £9, children (under 17) free,
(2007 prices)

Other information: Many events throughout the year – telephone for details

Wakehurst is a place for the botanist, plantsman and garden lover, offering features of year-round interest, particularly the winter garden which bursts into colour about late November. Dating from Norman times, the estate was bought by Gerald W.E. Loder (Lord Wakehurst) in 1903. He spent thirty-three years developing the gardens, a work carried on by Sir Henry Price. The 500 acres have been managed by the Royal Botanic Gardens, Kew since 1965. They have a fine collection of hardy plants, which are arranged geographically and display four National Collections – betulas, hypericums, nothofagus and skimmias. A glade planted with species growing at over 3000 metres in the Himalayas is the only one of its kind in the country. A plantation of Japanese irises is part of the extensive and fascinating water gardens. There are two walled gardens, one given over to colourful bedding schemes, the other to herbaceous borders, delightfully planted in subtle shades. The Wellcome Trust Millennium Building, home to an international seed bank and interactive public exhibition, opened in 2000 – futuristic in appearance, the design and presentation are masterly.

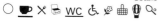

WEALD AND DOWNLAND OPEN AIR MUSEUM

Set in the heart of the South Downs, the main exhibits of this museum (founded in 1967) are 45 traditional buildings, ranging from medieval to Victorian, rescued from certain destruction, restored and rebuilt on the museum's countryside site. Complementing the buildings, six historic gardens have been researched and planted to demonstrate the changes and continuities in domestic gardens from the early 1400s to 1900. A complete medieval farmstead has been re-created around Bayleaf Farmhouse, and the replica fifteenth-century garden is planted to fulfil the gastronomic and medical needs of six adults, their children and servants from beds over four metres long and a metre wide. By the Victorian era, represented by a typical cottage garden of the period, the gardens were not only practical but showed the introduction of flowers for their beauty alone. In all, 45 acres.

Weald and Downland Open Air Museum

Singleton, Chichester PO18 0EU.
Tel: (01243) 811348;
www.wealddown.co.uk

6m N of Chichester on A286

Open 2nd Jan to 27th Feb, Wed, Sat and Sun; 18th to 22nd Feb, March to 23rd Dec, daily; all 10.30am – 6pm (closes 4pm in winter). Also open 26th Dec to 1st Jan for 'A Sussex Christmas'

Entrance: £8.25, OAPs £7.25, children £4.40, under 5 free, family £22.65 (2007 prices)

○ ☕ 🍽 <u>WC</u> ♿ ⟨🔊⟩ 🌿 🏛
🔦 ⚲

WEST DEAN GARDENS ★
(Historic Garden Grade II*)

There have been gardens here since 1622. In 1836 several rare trees were mentioned by J.C. Loudon, and in 1891 William James bought the property and Harold Peto

Edward James Foundation

West Dean, Chichester PO18 0QZ.
Tel: (01243) 818210;
www.westdean.org.uk

6m N of Chichester on A286

West Dean Gardens

Open March to Oct, daily,
10.30am – 5pm; Nov to Feb,
Wed – Sun, 10.30am – 4pm; and for
parties by appt. Closed over Christmas
and New Year period.

Entrance: £6, OAPs £5.50, children £3
(half price Nov to Feb)

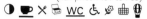

designed the magnificent 100-metre-long pergola. If you want to see fruit and vegetables growing in profusion, this is the garden to visit. The restored Victorian glasshouses are immaculate and the regimented rows of fruit and vegetables excellently labelled. In the orchard, backed by an old crinkle-crankle wall, are fruit trees trained in a variety of shapes and an unusual circular thatched apple store. The potting sheds now house garden-themed exhibitions. Outside the 3.5-acre walled garden you can explore the 35 acres of ornamental grounds – designed around the house (now an Arts and Crafts College). Stroll the length of the pergola with its lush planting designed to flower from spring through to early autumn, then relax in the sunken garden, a mass of tulips in spring, before taking the woodland walk. The west end of the garden has been restored and replanted. The spring garden, with its enchanting summerhouse, laburnum tunnel and flintwork bridges over the River Lavant, is given an exotic jungle atmosphere by a planting of Chusan palms and bamboos; beyond is the wild garden, which has some unusual trees and is planted in more naturalistic style to blend into the surrounding parkland. From here there is an enjoyable walk through the park, with panoramic views of the house, grounds and the surrounding downland landscape, to the 49-acre *St Roche's Arboretum*, carpeted in spring with wild daffodils, where Edward James is buried beneath the trees he loved so much.

OTHER RECOMMENDED GARDENS

CHAMPS HILL

Mr and Mrs D. Bowerman, Coldwaltham, Pulborough RH20 1LY (01798 831868). Open for parties by appt

A fine and unusual heathland garden, with over 300 varieties of heather grown alongside dwarf conifers and other interesting plants, complemented by spectacular views of the Arun Valley and South Downs. Visit in March and August for the heathers, in May for a walk in the rhododendron woods. Sculptures are an added feature. 27 acres in all.

GRAVETYE MANOR

Vowels Lane, East Grinstead RH19 4LJ (01342 810567; www.gravetyemanor.co.uk). Open all year to hotel and restaurant guests, perimeter footpath to public, Tues and Fri only

The historically important 35-acre garden, where several large shrubs and trees remain from the original planting, has been carefully restored in the style pioneered here by William Robinson. The path down a magnolia walk leads around a lake, and the public footpath to the north and south passes through wildflower meadows. (Listed Grade II*)

HAMMERWOOD HOUSE

Mr and Mrs M. Lakin, Iping, Midhurst GU29 0PF (01730 815627). Open for NGS

A peaceful country garden of 1.5 acres, planted with care and a fine eye for good plants, including some splendid specimen trees. The 2 May open days are geared towards the spectacular flowering of rhododendrons and azaleas, and the wild flowers abounding in the streamside woodland walk.

LITTLE WANTLEY

Hilary Barnes, Fryern Road, Storrington RH20 4BJ (01903 740747). Open for NGS, and parties by appt

The exuberant 4.5-acre garden has been landscaped and extensively planted by the present enthusiastic owners since 1997; the main lake alone covers 1.5 acres. Trees and roses are a passion, and round every corner there is a fresh surprise: nut and rose walks, a stumpery, and a new catenary. An inspiring visit.

STANDEN

East Grinstead RH19 4NE (01342 323029; www.nationaltrust.org.uk). Open 1st to 9th March, 8th Nov to 21st Dec, Sat and Sun; 15th March to 20th July, 3rd Sept to 2nd Nov, Wed – Sun and Bank Holiday Mons; 21st July to Aug, Mon, Wed – Sun and Bank Holiday Mons; all 11am – 5.30pm (closes 3pm Nov and Dec). NT

Like the Philip Webb house with its Morris and Co interiors, the 12-acre hillside garden is a reflection of the Arts and Crafts Movement. It is divided into small compartments, notably a quarry garden, a kitchen garden and a bamboo garden with a swimming pool, cascades and steps. Woodland walks and stunning views.

Little Wantley

WARWICKSHIRE

For further information about how to use the *Guide*
and for an explanation of the symbols, see pages vi–viii.
Specific dates and times are those given to us by garden owners for 2008.
For 2009 dates, check with the individual properties.
For opening dates under the National Gardens Scheme,
readers should consult *The Yellow Book* or www.ngs.org.uk.
Maps are to be found at the end of the *Guide*.

The Viscount and Viscountess Daventry

Arbury, Nuneaton CV10 7PT.
Tel: (024) 7638 2804

10m N of Coventry, 3.5m SW of
Nuneaton off B4102

House open as garden, but closes 5pm

Garden open Bank Holiday Suns and
Mons only, 1.30 – 6pm

Entrance: £5, children £3.50 (hall and
gardens £6.50, children £4.50, family £18)

ARBURY HALL ★

(Historic Garden Grade I)

An army of factories may be encamped at the very gate of the vast park, but within is a charmed survival – a picturesque landscape surrounding a seminal Gothic Revival house, with earlier stables by Wren, three rush-fringed lakes, a network of canals and magnificent trees. Daffodils, bluebells and rhododendrons, roses and irises, turning leaves of trees and shrubs provide a constant procession of colour from spring to autumn. The formal rose garden is memorable for its tilting terrain enclosed by a venerable yew hedge and a mellow brick orangery. 50 acres in all.

Arbury Hall

BARTON HOUSE ★

Borders of rhododendrons greet the visitor to the 6.5-acre garden, set around a manor house by Inigo Jones (not open), and throughout the garden an excellent collection of American, species and hybrid rhododendrons provides a long flowering period, with autumn colour filling many trees. A secret garden has magnolias and maples underplanted with a range of shrubs and perennials. Viewing points have been made to enjoy the surrounding countryside, and there are some fine mature trees, many rare plants plus National Collections of nothofagus, stewartias and arbutus, and masses of spring bulbs. Among the varied features and surprises are a catalpa walk, a collection of moutan tree peonies (*Paeonia suffruticosa*), *Paulownia fargesii and P. tomentosum*, a rose garden with beds of individual colours surrounding an oblong lily pool, a Himalayan garden, a Japanese garden, herbaceous and shrub beds, statues, archways and a copy of the portico of St Paul's, Covent Garden. A paved roundel in the centre of the walled kitchen garden is being developed as a Mediterranean garden with palm trees, olives and cypresses. The ornate cast-iron atrium from the Royal Exchange in Threadneedle Street forms the roof of the orangery. The ha-ha has been lined with clay, filled with water and furnished with an ornate iron bridge, a Neptune platform and a garden house. A vineyard was planted in 2000.

Mr and Mrs I. H. B. Cathie

Barton-on-the-Heath,
Moreton-in- Marsh, Gloucestershire
GL56 0PJ.
Tel: (01608) 674303

6m S of Shipston-on-Stour off A3400,
4m E of Moreton-in-Marsh off A44

Open for NGS, and for parties of 25
or more by appt

Entrance: £5, children £2

Other information: Refreshments and
plant sales in coach house on NGS
open day

 WC ♿ ♨

COUGHTON COURT ★

The 25-acre grounds complement the mid-sixteenth-century house and include a variety of gardens both formal and informal. The main garden, courtyard and walled garden were created by Christina Williams, the owner's daughter and a

Mrs C. Throckmorton

Alcester B49 5JA.
Tel: (01789) 400777;
www.coughtoncourt.co.uk

Coughton
Court

8m NW of Stratford-upon-Avon,
2m N of Alcester on A435

House and garden open April to June
and Sept, Wed – Sun; July and Aug,
Tues – Sun; Oct, Sat and Sun; all
11am – 5.30pm. Closed Good Fri,
open Bank Holiday Mons and Tues. Also
open for parties by appt

Entrance: £6.20, children £3.10, family
£15.80 (house and garden £9, children
£4.50, family £22.60)

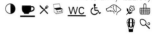

garden designer. The redesigned orchard contains many old local varieties and there is also a chef's herb garden. The large lawn is bordered by cloistered lime walks, while a peaceful stroll beside the River Arrow reveals willows, wild garlic, ferns, hellebores and native trees and shrubs. In spring there is a bluebell wood and many bulbs to enjoy. A second lake has been drained to form a bog garden. One of the finest features is the large walled garden with 'hot' and 'cold' herbaceous borders containing a superb display of plants to give colour and interest through the seasons. The red and white gardens are surrounded by hornbeam hedges being trained to provide windows. In the rose labyrinth masses of roses and clematis grow over arches and pedestals, with herbaceous underplanting. In the early-summer garden wisteria is trained over raised hoops with peonies beneath, and pale colours change to deeper shades of blue and red. The architectural features are also good. A pond and fountain is surrounded by benches and planted in green and white as a peaceful place for contemplation. Many of the plants seen here are stocked in the plant centre adjoining.

Mr and Mrs E.W. Dyer

Binton Road, Welford-on-Avon
CV37 8PT. Tel: (01789) 750793

5m SW of Stratford-upon-Avon on
B439. Turn left after 4.5m to Welford

Open for NGS, and for parties by appt

Entrance: £3, children free

ELM CLOSE

A 0.6-acre garden filled with fresh ideas and a wide range of plants. Clematis (over 300) are trained over pergolas and climb through trees and shrubs, and there are dwarf conifers, a rock garden, hellebores, a pool, alpine troughs, raised beds and an excellent range of bulbs. Herbaceous plants and shrubs, including a wealth of peonies, cornus, hostas, daphnes and magnolias, provide interest and colour throughout the year.

The National Trust/Mr Holbech

Farnborough, Banbury, Oxfordshire
OX17 1DU. Tel: (01295) 690002;
www.nationaltrust.org.uk

6m N of Banbury, 0.5m W of A423
or 1.5m E off B4100

House and grounds open 2nd April to
27th Sept, Wed and Sat, plus 3rd and
5th May, all 2 – 5.30pm

Entrance: Garden and terrace walk £2,
(house and grounds £4.50, children
£2.25) family £11.75 (2007 prices)

FARNBOROUGH HALL
(Historic Garden Grade I)

The house has been in the same family since 1684. It was reconstructed in the eighteenth century with fine Rococo plasterwork and the grounds were improved in the 1740s with the aid of Sanderson Miller, the architect, landscape gardener and dilettante, who lived at nearby Radway. Climbing gently along the ridge looking towards Edgehill is the fine S-shaped terrace walk built by William Holbech in order to greet his brother on the adjoining property. It has been described as a majestic concept marking the movement towards the great landscaped parks at the end of the eighteenth century. Two temples and a game larder lie along the walk and an obelisk at the end. The trees are beech, sycamore and lime. Beyond a giant cedar is part of the site of the former orangery, a rose garden, and a yew walk with steps at the end, where there is a seat with a fine view over the river, the cascade and the countryside towards Edgehill. The cascade fountain suppresses the otherwise-invasive hum of the M40. A uniquely interesting 18-acre site.

Garden Organic Ryton

GARDEN ORGANIC RYTON

Ryton was set up in 1985 to be a centre of excellence for organic horticulture. Since then the 10 acres have been steadily developed, in a beautifully landscaped setting, to provide a wide range of inspirational and educational displays of herbs, roses, unusual vegetables, fruit, wildlife gardening and plants for bees and the world's first bio-dynamic garden. At the heart of the garden is a vibrant display of herbaceous perennials in an informal drift of form and colour. The individual gardens include demonstrations of organic techniques, including composting and pest and disease control. There are also gardens for the visually impaired and those with other special needs, a bee garden, one for the enthusiastic cook, a Paradise Garden created by Isabelle Van Groeningen, and the Vegetable Kingdom, an interactive visitor centre which houses the Heritage Seed Library. Events and courses are held throughout the year, and there is plenty to amuse and interest children of all ages.

Garden Organic

Wolston Lane, Coventry CV8 3LG.
Tel: (024) 7630 3517;
www.hdra.org.uk

7m NE of Leamington Spa, 5m SE of Coventry. Turn off A45 onto Wolston Lane

Open all year, daily except Christmas period, 9am – 5pm

Entrance: £5, OAPs £4.50, children £2.50

Other information: Pre-booked guided tours available. Guide dogs only

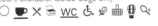

THE HILLER GARDEN

An established two-acre garden with year-round interest. Large beds of herbaceous perennials with frequent new introductions enable visitors to the garden centre to see mature, well-labelled plants in good colour combinations and so judge their suitability for their own gardens. The garden also embraces an extensive rose garden, which includes more than 200 varieties and has a Victorian rose area as its centrepiece. A miniature railway chugs around the perimeter – telephone to find out when it is in operation.

Hillers Farm Shop

Dunnington Heath Farm, Alcester B49 5PD.
Tel: (01789) 491342; www.hillers.co.uk

9m W of Stratford-upon-Avon, 3m SW of Alcester between A46 and A422, S of Weethley village

Garden open all year, daily, 9am – 5pm; Plant Centre closed Nov to Feb

Entrance: free

THE MASTER'S GARDEN

(Historic Garden Grade II)

The restoration work undertaken here is remarkable. Old cobbles from the summerhouse have been relaid in a new circular house with a thatched roof of Norfolk reeds, and

Board of Governors of
Lord Leycester Hospital

Lord Leycester Hospital, Warwick
CV34 4BH. Tel: (01926) 491422
(Contact: The Master);
www.lordleycester.com

In High Street

Open Easter to Sept, daily except
Mon (but open Bank Holiday Mons),
10am – 4.30pm

Entrance: £2

archways dating from the 1850s have been copied to support roses, clematis and other climbers. A brick pathway through the centre of the garden repeats the feathered pattern. The 150-year old pleached lime boundary remains. An eighteenth-century dovecot has been converted into a gazebo, and a pineapple frame has been restored. The kitchen garden has a sundial at its centre, and the vegetable and fruit area is bursting in season with gooseberries and redcurrants. A Norman arch frames a Nileometer – a finial from a stone column installed by the Romans on the Nile to record the rise and fall of the river – and leads into the other half of the garden, which includes a Victorian rock garden, shrubs, roses and perennials. Also in Warwick, at Hill Close, the *Victorian Pleasure Gardens*, an interesting example of nineteenth-century plots grown by local craftsmen and tradesmen, are being restored to their old pattern of high hedges, summerhouses and old fruit trees.

PACKWOOD HOUSE ★

(Historic Garden Grade II*)

The National Trust

Lapworth, Solihull, Birmingham
B94 6AT. Tel: (01564) 782024;
www.nationaltrust.org.uk

11m SE of central Birmingham, 2m E of
Hockley Heath on A3400

House and garden open 9th Feb to
2nd Nov, Wed – Sun and Bank Hol Mons,
11am – 5pm. Parties by written appt

Park open all year, daily

Entrance: £4.20, children £2.10
(house and garden £7.30, children £3.65,
family £18.25)

Other information: Picnic site opposite
main gates

Hidden away in a rather suburban part of Warwickshire, this seven-acre garden is notable for its intact layout, dating from the sixteenth and seventeenth centuries when the original house was built. There are courtyards, terraces and brick gazebos. Even more remarkable is the almost surreal yew garden, unique in design. Tradition claims that it represents the Sermon on the Mount, but in fact the 'Apostles' were planted in the 1850s as a four-square pattern round an orchard. Never mind, the result is now homogeneous. A spiral mount of yew and box is a delightful illusion; note also the clever use of brick. G. Baron Ash, who gave the property to the Trust, made a sunken garden in the 1930s and restored earlier design features. In spring drifts of daffodils follow the snowdrops and bluebells carpet the copse, while shrubs flower on red-brick walls. Herbaceous borders, a sunken garden, terrace beds and climbing roses and honeysuckles are a riot of summer colour, and autumn brings changes in foliage. The walled kitchen garden has been greatly improved after many years of neglect; it promises to be splendid. Don't miss the attractive lakeside walk and wildflower meadows.

UPTON HOUSE ★

(Historic Garden Grade II*)

The National Trust

Banbury, Oxfordshire OX15 6HT.
Tel: (01295) 670266;
www.nationaltrust.org.uk

12m SE of Stratford-upon-Avon,
7m NW of Banbury on A422

House open

Garden open March to Nov, Sat – Wed,
11am – 5pm. Telephone for winter opening
times. Parties of 15 or more by appt

The house, which dates from 1695, stands on ironstone, over 210 metres above sea level on Edgehill, near the site of the famous battle. Below a great lawn, the garden descends in a series of long terraces, along one end of which an impressive flight of stone steps leads down to the large lake. In the centre of the terraced area is a huge sloping kitchen garden, well labelled to indicate varieties, and below this a mirror pool has been restored to its eighteenth-century grandeur. The grand

Upton House

Entrance: £5 (house and garden £8.50, children £4.20)

Other information: Possible for wheelchairs in parts but steep in places. Motorised buggy with driver available. Banqueting house available as holiday cottage

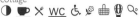

scale of the plan creates an immediate impression, but it is worth taking a closer look at the plantings, for there are many unusual species, particularly perennials and bog plants, and a National Collection of asters spp. *amellus*, *cordifolius* and *ericoides* is here. A rewarding day out, 37 acres in all.

WARWICK CASTLE ★

(Historic Park Grade I)

The magnificent castle stands on the banks of the River Avon, surrounded by 60 acres of beautiful grounds landscaped by 'Capability' Brown. His work at Warwick Castle for Francis Greville is thought to have been his first independent commission, for which he received much praise, encouragement and publicity. He removed the old formal garden outside the wall and shaped the grounds to frame a view using an array of magnificent trees, notably cedars of Lebanon. In 1753 he began to landscape the courtyard, removing steps, filling in parts of the yard and making a coachway to surround the large level lawn. He then worked on the creation of a park on the other side of the eleventh-century mound. In 1779, when Brown's remodelling was barely twenty years old, George Greville embarked on a grandiose scheme of expansion which involved demolishing several streets in the town. In 1786 he constructed the conservatory at the top of Pageant Field, which today houses a replica of the famous Warwick Vase. From here visitors can view the panorama before them – the Peacock Garden and the tree-lined lawn of Pageant Field which meanders down to the gently sloping banks of the River Avon. On the other side of the castle entrance is the Victorian rose garden re-created in 1986 from Robert Marnock's designs of 1868. Also in the town is The Master's Garden (see entry) at Lord Leycester Hospital.

Merlin Entertainments

Warwick CV34 4QU.
Tel: (0870) 442 2000;
www.warwick-castle.com

In Warwick

Castle open

Grounds open all year, daily except 25th Dec, 10am – 6pm (closes 5pm Oct to March)

Entrance: £14.50, OAPs £10.50, students £10.75, children £8.75, family £39 (peak rates)

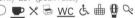

WOODPECKERS ★

This two-acre garden, planned for year-round interest, contains a wide range of design and planting ideas, and blends well with the surrounding countryside. A small arboretum with a wide selection of choice trees provide contrast in form and colour. Moving around the garden, there are many

Drs Andrew and Lallie Cox

The Bank, Marlcliff, Bidford-on-Avon B50 4NT. Tel: (01789) 773416

7m SW of Stratford-upon-Avon off B4085 between Bidford and Cleeve Prior

Open by appt

Entrance: £4, children free

Other information: Wheelchair users must be accompanied

surprises – a wooden figure of St Fiacre surrounded by old roses with clematis climbing through, an attractive small potager, colourful and unusual herbs and vegetables. A knot garden has been created in box, and room has been found for topiary, an ivy arbour with statue, a fern border, several island beds with splendid ranges of colour and plants, a Mediterranean garden, a cactus and succulent greenhouse and a round greenhouse for tender plants. The terrace has a range of troughs and alpine plants, and there is a delightful pool and bog garden. A belvedere of framed English oak affords fine views of the garden, including a wildflower area in spring. A two-storey oak building with a balcony overlooks the arboretum and rose garden. It is also worth visiting in winter to see the trees and a border designed to look interesting at this neglected time of year, and in February for the snowdrops in mass and variety.

OTHER RECOMMENDED GARDENS

BADDESLEY CLINTON

Rising Lane, Baddesley Clinton, Knowle, Solihull B93 0DQ (01564 783294; www.nationaltrust.org.uk). Open 9th Feb to 21st Dec, Wed – Sun and Bank Holiday Mons, 11am – 5pm (closes 4pm Nov and Dec). NT

The gardens evoke the atmosphere rather than the period of the moated medieval manor house with a colourful walled garden and a courtyard planted with red and golden annuals in the shape of the heraldic shield of the Ferrers, who lived here until 1633. A new kitchen garden provides fruit and vegetables for the acclaimed restaurant. (Listed Grade II)

CHARLECOTE PARK

Charlecote, Wellesbourne, Warwick CV35 9ER (01789 470277; www.nationaltrust.org.uk). Park and grounds open 2nd to 24th Feb, March to 28th Oct, 31st Oct to 31st Jan 2009, Fri – Tues, 10.30 – 4pm (closes 6pm March to 28th Oct). NT

The much-altered home of the Lucy family since the thirteenth century is girdled with a variety of gardens – courtyard, wild and sensory – and furnished with herbaceous borders planted for a long season of interest. 'Capability' Brown laid out the park. A well-stocked nursery is next door. (Listed Grade II*)

COMPTON SCORPION FARM

Mrs T. M. Karlsen, Ilmington, Shipston-on-Stour CV36 4PJ (01608 682552). Open 1st to 15th June, daily, 2 – 5pm, and by appt

The stunning view that unfolds as you drive along the ridge from Ilmington is an extra incentive to visit the garden created from a steeply sloping meadow since 1989. The farmhouse is now surrounded by spaces infused with mellow plantings: a Jekyll-inspired walled garden, a rose-encrusted slope, a vegetable garden, an orchard and a wildflower meadow.

COOMBE COUNTRY PARK

Brinklow Road, Binley, Coventry CV32AB (024 7645 3720). www.coventry.gov.uk/coombe) Open all year, daily, 7.30am – dusk

Parkland, lakeside and woodland walks, wildflower meadows, a vast 'Capability' Brown lake set within a SSSI, an arboretum and gardens by W.A. Nesfield and William Miller – 450 acres of natural and historical interest.

JEPHSON GARDENS

Leamington Spa CV32 4UJ (01926 450000). Open all year, daily, 8am – dusk

The principal formal public garden in a string of parks and gardens running right across the town has vibrant bedding displays and a remarkable collection of trees. A fine glasshouse contains a collection of sub-tropical plants, and the restored Victorian tea pavilion fulfils its intended function once more. (Listed Grade II)

RAGLEY HALL

The Marquess and Marchioness of Hertford, Alcester B49 5NJ (01789 762090; www.ragleyhall.com). Open 15th March to 28th Sept, Thurs – Sun and Bank Holiday Mons , 10am – 6pm

Within the 18th-century parkland and its lake enlarged by 'Capability' Brown are 27 acres of formal and informal gardens, including parterres, rose beds, a secret garden and a 'fumpery'. (Listed Grade II*)

THE SHAKESPEARE HOUSES AND GARDENS

Stratford-upon-Avon (01789 204016; www.shakespeare.org.uk). Open all year, daily, except 23rd to 26th Dec – times vary. NT

Seek out the Birthplace Garden and those at Mary's Arden's House, Anne Hathaway's Cottage, New Place and Hall's Croft for an interesting insight into the Bard's private life and works, created by the Trust using period plants and Elizabethan designs.

STONELEIGH ABBEY

Kenilworth CV8 2LF. Tel: (01926 858535; www.stoneleighabbey.org) Open 6th April to Oct, Tues – Thurs, Sun, 10am – 5pm

The park and gardens owe much to Humphrey Repton, who regarded the commission as one of his most prestigious – 'I look upon Stoneleigh Abbey as a place not to be compared to any other' – and who created for it one of his finest and largest Red Books. Over the last few years, much of the abbey (not open) and many of the estate and garden building have been restored. (Listed Grade II*)

UNIVERSITY OF WARWICK

Gibbet Hill Road, Coventry CV4 7AL (02476 524189). Open all year, daily, during daylight hours

An intelligent and sensitive landscaping of crowded campus grounds. Good use is made of tree plantings and bedding schemes, and for the more athletic there are lakes, wetlands and a nature reserve, varied walks and a sculpture trail. 700 acres in all.

WHICHFORD POTTERY GARDEN

Whichford, Shipston on Stour CV36 5PG (01608 684416; www.whichfordpottery.com). Open for NGS; telephone for details of special events

The rambling and romantic cottage garden is set between the house and the well-known pottery. Hedges, old walls and topiary hide one room from another, following the lines of vanished buildings or the contour of an old pond. Italian frescoed arches look onto antique pollarded willows, and mud walls hide a Paradise garden.

Stoneleigh Abbey

WILTSHIRE

For further information about how to use the *Guide*
and for an explanation of the symbols, see pages vi–viii.
Specific dates and times are those given to us by garden owners for 2008.
For 2009 dates, check with the individual properties.
For opening dates under the National Gardens Scheme,
readers should consult *The Yellow Book* or www.ngs.org.uk.
Maps are to be found at the end of the *Guide*.

ABBEY HOUSE GARDENS ★

Barbara and Ian Pollard

Malmesbury SN16 9AS.
Tel: (01666) 822212;
www.abbeyhousegardens.co.uk

In town centre next to Abbey

Open 21st March to 21st Oct, daily,
11am – 5.30pm (last admission
4.45pm), and for parties by appt

Entrance: £6.50, concessions £5.50,
children (5–15) £2

Other information: Car park close
to garden

A remarkable five-acre garden, created since 1996. The owners' passion and enthusiasm are reflected in the exuberant planting schemes. The setting around a late Tudor house beside the abbey is unique, the effect overwhelming, with an enormous arcade-encircled herb garden, a generously proportioned laburnum tunnel, a knot garden in the form of a Celtic cross echoing its historic surroundings, huge herbaceous borders in riotous colours, water features including a waterfall, a river and woodland walk (with kingfishers and water voles if you are lucky), foliage and maple walks and a scree garden. In all there are over 10,000 different species and varieties of plants here. The season starts with a dazzling display of 100,000 tulips and meconopsis followed by roses (the largest private collection in the country), clematis and rhododendrons, and continues right through to the autumn. There is also a large and interesting collection of cordon fruit trees around an arcade, with sweet peas for added colour. The owners are indefatigable, adding to the collections and planting new areas year on year.

BOLEHYDE MANOR ★

Earl and Countess Cairns

Allington, Chippenham SN14 6LW.
Tel: (01249) 652105

1.5m W of Chippenham on A420
Bristol road. Turn N at Allington
crossroads; garden is 0.5m on right

Open for NGS, and for parties by appt

Entrance: £3.50

Other information: Teas and plant sales
on NGS open day only

A four-acre garden at once steeped in tradition and bursting with innovative ideas. The characterful manor house dates from the fifteenth century. Owned by the Abbot of Glastonbury until after the dissolution of the monasteries, Bolehyde was sold in 1635 to the Case family, who lived there for the next 400 years. The house, outbuildings and gatehouses developed into a charming huddle of beautifully weathered Cotswold stone buildings, and this is reflected in the series of linked garden rooms disposed around the house. Within a semi-formal framework are splendid contrasts, gracefully achieved: a pear walk, some lovely wildflower meadow planting, an exciting potager. Sheltered and sunny formal areas are edged with colourful narrow beds, and satisfyingly chunky topiary abounds. Planted for

Bolehyde Manor

year-round interest, the garden is nevertheless at its stunning best in midsummer, when masses of roses bloom on the old walls, and the half-hardy planting of the courtyard – much of it in darkly glowing jewel colours – is nearing the peak of a brilliant display.

BOWOOD HOUSE ★

(Historic Park and Garden Grade I)

The house and its pleasure grounds extend over 100 acres and lie in the centre of 'Capability' Brown's 200-acre park. Other splendours include a tranquil lake, arboretum and pinetum, Doric temple, cascade waterfall and hermit's cave. Thousands of bulbs bloom in spring. The Robert Adam orangery (converted into a gallery) is particularly fine, and in front are formal Italianate terraces with rose beds, standard roses, fastigiate yews and flourishing *Fremontodendron californicum*. The upper terrace was laid out in 1817 and the present fountains were added in 1839. In the twentieth century, when elaborate bedding schemes became too time-consuming, the parterre was planted with hybrid tea roses, thus blurring the edges. Mary Keen advised replacing the grass paths with gravel and compensating for the loss of green by putting box hedges around the beds. New planting has ensured that the flowering season starts almost three months earlier than it used to. In the nineteenth century it was the aim of every garden to be 'as clean as a drawing room', and Bowood is now in this class once again. The rhododendron walks are situated in a separate 60-acre area, which is only open when the rhododendrons are flowering from late April to mid-June. Robert Adam's mausoleum (a little gem well worth a visit) is in this area.

The Marquis and Marchioness of Lansdowne

Bowood House, Derry Hill, Calne SN11 0LZ. Tel: (01249) 812102; www.bowood.org

3m SE of Chippenham, 2.5m W of Calne off A4, 8m S of M4 junction 17. Separate rhododendron walks off A342 Chippenham – Devizes road midway between Derry Hill and Sandy Lane

House open

Garden and pleasure grounds open 19th March to 4th Nov, daily, 11am – 6pm or dusk if earlier (last admission 1 hour before closing). Rhododendron walks open daily end-April to early June (depending on flowering season)

Entrance: house and gardens £8, OAPs £7, children (5–15) £6.50, (2–4) £4.50; rhododendron walks extra (£5.25, OAPs £4.75, children free) (reduced rates in winter)

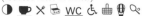

BROADLEAS GARDEN

This 9.5-acre garden, set in a combe below Devizes, was bought just after World War II by Lady Anne Cowdray. Mature and semi-mature magnolias grow on each side of a steep dell. As good as any Cornish garden, it is stuffed with fine things

Lady Anne Cowdray/ Broadleas Garden Charitable Trust

Broadleas, Devizes SN10 5JQ. Tel: (01380) 722035

1m S of Devizes on A360.
Signed from Devizes town centre

Open April to Oct, Sun, Wed and
Thurs, 2 – 6pm

Entrance: £5.50, children (under 10) £2

Other information: Coaches must use
Devizes town centre approach. Teas for
parties by arrangement

◑ <u>WC</u> ᴕ ⬠ ▨

that one would think too tender for these parts – large specimens of everything (much of it now over forty years old), including *Paulownia fargesii*, *Parrotia persica* and all manner of rare and notable magnolias, azaleas, hydrangeas, hostas, lilies and trilliums. There has also been much planting in recent years, including many rhododendrons and camellias. It is a garden of tireless perfectionism, at its most stunning in spring when sheets of bulbs stretch out beneath the flowering trees. Rarely seen in such quantities are the erythroniums or dogtooth violets. There is also a woodland walk, a sunken rose garden and a silver border. This is serious plantsmanship and dendrology. Some of the more unusual plants, both shrubs and perennials, are grown for sale.

CHISENBURY PRIORY ★

Mr and Mrs John Manser

East Chisenbury, Nr Pewsey SN9 6AQ.
Tel: (07810) 483984

3m SW of Pewsey. Turn E off A345 at
Enford, then N to East Chisenbury;
main gates 1m on right

Open for NGS, and by appt

Entrance: £3

Other information: Teas on NGS
open day

◑ WC ᴕ

In this traditional English garden, a broad vision and close attention to detail have combined to produce an atmosphere of romantic, controlled exuberance within an ancient and peaceful framework. A fine avenue of mature chestnuts and sycamores leads to the handsome eighteenth-century house front, with richly planted herbaceous borders on each side of the lawn. The rest of the priory is much older than that, however, and 400 years of history have been enriched by skilful and imaginative planting in its surrounding four acres of garden. A great curving pergola by Paul Elliot in galvanised steel, dripping with roses and late-flowering *Clematis viticella*, forms a dramatic and unique feature. Also his work is the fine bridge over the leat in the wild garden, an offspring of the River Avon. Water was an important element in the redesign of the garden in the 1960s, when many of the mature shrubs and trees were planted. Now mown paths wander past iris-fringed pools, down a nut walk and through flowery orchards offering glimpses of striking modern sculptures. Sheltered enclosures nearer the house are ablaze with colour from early spring to the end of July – successive waves of alliums and aquilegias followed by superb delphiniums, lilies, campanulas and masses of roses.

CONOCK MANOR

(Historic Garden Grade II)

Mrs Bonar Sykes

Conock, Devizes SN10 3QQ.

5m SE of Devizes, off A342
near Chirton

Open for NGS, and by appt

Entrance: £3, children under 16 free

◑ ▬ ᴕ ▨

Set between distant views of Marlborough Downs and Salisbury Plain, the Georgian house looks out over lawns with specimen trees, ha-has and a recently planted arboretum, which includes unusual trees such as *Aesculus* × *mutabilis* 'Induta' and *Catalpa fargesii* f. *duclouxii*. From a Reptonesque thatched dairy near the house, a long brick wall and a mixed shrub border lead to the stable block, designed in early Gothic Revival style with a copper-domed cupola. Between the house and the stable block is an unusual and elaborate water feature. Beyond, yew and beech hedges and brick walls frame unusual trees and shrubs and a 1930s shrub walk. Beech forms attractive bays and box makes clipped balls. Notable are the pleached limes and a magnolia garden also planted with malus, sorbus, prunus and eucalyptus. Five acres in all.

THE COURTS GARDEN
(Historic Garden Grade II)

The distinguished eighteenth-century house is surrounded by a seven-acre garden with a well-defined framework of lawns, topiary and hedging, laid out originally in the 1920s, overlaid by modern plantings. Passing through huge stands of cotinus and other red-leaved shrubs, the visitor reaches water gardens which include a rectangular lily pond bordered by hundreds of pale *Iris sibirica*; the luxuriantly planted dye pond beyond dates from its old history as a mill. Borders are contained within traditional enclosures of yew, beech and holly, and the arboretum beyond has some rare and splendid trees carpeted in spring by scillas and daffodils.

The National Trust

Holt, Trowbridge BA14 6RR.
Tel: (01225) 782340/782875;
www.nationaltrust.org.uk

3m SW of Melksham, 3m N of Trowbridge, 2.5m E of Bradford-on-Avon on B3107

Open 15th March to 2nd Nov, daily except Wed, 11am – 5.30pm, and by appt at other times

Entrance: £4.80, children £2.40, family £12.20

Other information: Parking at village hall

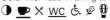

THE GARDEN LODGE ★

In 1990 the present owner bought the house and its abandoned two-acre Victorian walled garden, and since then, taking advantage of a sheltered, sloping site, she has created within the mellow surrounding walls a formal garden of immaculate design. The upper level consists of a long curving sweep of lawn, backed by a deep raised border which leads to a fine mature oak tree. A large pond on a lower level is lavishly furnished with marginal and water plants, and a stone rill drops to an amphitheatre and a central area planted with 'Sander's White' rambler roses. Clematis and roses abound on walls, pillars and pergolas. Original features include a grass and brick maze and a brick sundial let into the grass, and a serpentine yew-edged path leads to an elegant pavilion complete with an ingenious snakes-and-ladders game. The seclusion in this appealing garden is accentuated by the borrowed landscape of mature trees on the encircling skyline. Late spring, summer and late autumn are fine times to visit.

Mrs Juliet Wilmot

Chittoe, Chippenham SN15 2EW.
Tel: (01380) 850314

Off A342 Chippenham – Devizes road, signed to Chittoe; garden marked on right after 1m

Open by appt

Entrance: £3

GOULTERS MILL

The idyllic 0.75-acre garden lies deep in seclusion and silence. Ancient tracks radiate from the mill, mentioned in the Domesday Book, and the present seventeenth-century house preserves an atmosphere of timelessness and peace. Looking out from the house a sea of colour and movement is achieved with well-chosen hardy perennials and self-sown annuals, framed by attractive paths and accented by topiary figures. The dense planting leads to a small lawn surrounded by ancient apple trees entwined with roses and overlooking a lily-fringed stream and pool, then on to a happily planted gravel area. Irises and sisyrinchiums abound here, and poppies and eremurus are also a speciality. The river, tree house and vine planting may be glimpsed beyond a wild area currently

Mr and Mrs Michael Harvey

Nettleton, Nr. Castle Combe, Chippenham SN14 7LL.
Tel: (01249) 782555

6m W of Chippenham on B4039 between Burton and The Gibb

Open for NGS, and April to Sept by appt

Entrance: £3.50

 B&B

under review. The spring invites walks to bluebell woods beyond, and in the summer there is a wash of wild flowers and rare butterflies in the meadow paths.

HAZELBURY MANOR
(Historic Garden Grade II)

Box, Corsham SN13 8HX.
Tel: (01225) 865322

5m SW of Chippenham. From Box take A365 towards Melksham, turn left onto B3109, next left, and right immediately into private drive

Open for NGS, and by appt

Entrance: £2.80, OAPs £2, children £1, under 6 free

Other information: Teas and plants on NGS open days

● WC &

Richly architectural in character, the gardens are entirely in keeping with the history and scale of the fifteenth-century fortified manor house they surround. Following an Edwardian renaissance, they were largely rescued in the 1970s by Ian Pollard, who reconfigured them on a lavish scale with eight acres of formal gardens around the house and 10 more of landscaped grounds. Since 1997 the present owner has restored and improved them, and added a profusion of organically grown medicinal herbs and plants. The glory of the garden is the main lawn, dramatic in its proportions and framed by magnificent yew hedges and compartmented colour-themed borders backed by grassy banks leading to mature beech *allées*. A topiary chess set, and an imaginatively and richly underplanted laburnum tunnel and lime walk, add extra dimensions. The front of the house is seen across lawns and borders ablaze with spring bulbs, while behind is an historic archery walk – exactly 40 paces long. To the west of the house the mood becomes more relaxed and intimate, with informal plantings of shrubs and perennials opening onto the surrounding landscape. There is a fine organic vegetable garden and a flowery mead sprinkled with crocuses, fritillaries and martagon lilies. Beyond the garden lies a mound and a circle of seven megaliths placed in a great saucer in homage to the famous prehistoric monuments of this ancient part of Wiltshire.

HEALE GARDEN ★
(Historic Garden Grade II*)

Mr and Mrs Guy Rasch

Middle Woodford, Salisbury SP4 6NT.
Tel: (01722) 782504;
www.healegarden.co.uk

4m N of Salisbury between A360 and A345

Open Feb to Sept, Wed – Sun and Bank Holiday Mons, 10am – 5pm

Entrance: £4, children (5–15) £2, under 5 free

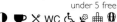

This is an idyllic garden of eight acres with mature yew hedges, much of it designed by Harold Peto. A tributary of the Avon meanders through, providing the perfect boundary and obvious site for the sealing-wax red bridge and thatched tea-house straddling the water. This was brought over from Japan and assembled in 1910 with the help of four Japanese gardeners; it extends under the shade of *Magnolia* × *soulangeana* along the boggy banks planted attractively with moisture-lovers. There are two terraces to the west of the house linked by a Yorkstone path rampant with alchemilla. The topmost has beds containing two aged wisterias among tall herbaceous plants, backed by clipped yew, the other two stone lily ponds and two small borders given height by tall wooden pyramids bearing roses, clematis and honeysuckles. The Long Border contains many dark-leaved plants, including *Sambucus* 'Black Beauty', *Physocarpus* 'Diabolo' and interesting

Heale Garden

herbaceous perennials; behind is a border of musk roses. It is tempting to linger in the tranquil walled kitchen garden that manages to achieve a satisfying marriage between practicality and pleasure. The wonderful flint-and-brick wall provides protection for many plants, including *Cytisus battandieri* and an ancient fig tree. Look out for the ancient mulberry, the very old *Cercidiphyllum japonicum* (the second tallest known in Europe), and the *Magnolia grandiflora*. The plant centre is comprehensive and the shop appeals to the discerning. Unique wrought-iron plant supports can be bought here.

HOME COVERT GARDENS AND ARBORETUM ★

The 33-acre garden, developed in the 1960s, has been created out of amenity woodlands of the now-demolished Roundway House by the present owners, charming plant fanatics who are always ready to share their knowledge with their visitors. In front of the house a splendid wide view opens up from a large lawn on a plateau edged with grasses, herbaceous plants and alpines producing colour throughout the year. Beyond this, grass pathways meander through a collection of trees and rare shrubs. A steep path drops from the plateau to a water garden, lake, waterfall and bog garden, rich with colour from bog primulas and other moisture-loving plants, and shaded by fine specimen trees. Excellent collections of magnolias, camellias, erythroniums and hydrangeas are scattered informally throughout, and roses and clematis scramble over walks and through trees. Described as 'a botanical madhouse' by Mr Phillips, this is a garden of wonderful contrasts, worth visiting at any time, but especially from mid-April through to the end of July.

Mr and Mrs John Phillips
Roundway, Devizes SN10 2JA.
Tel: (01380) 723407

1m N of Devizes. Turn off A361 on edge of built-up area NE of town, signed to Roundway. In Roundway turn left towards Rowde. House is 0.75m on left. Signposted

Open by appt; guided parties (12–40 persons) welcome

Entrance: £4, children free

IFORD MANOR ★★

(Historic Garden Grade I)

Harold Peto found himself a near-ideal house in the steep valley through which the River Frome slides languorously towards Bath. The topography lends itself to the strong

Mrs Cartwright-Hignett
Bradford-on-Avon BA15 2BA.
Tel: (01225) 863146;
www.ifordmanor.co.uk

2m S of Bradford-on-Avon off B3109, 7m SE of Bath via A36. Signposted

Open 23rd and 24th March; April and Oct, Sun; May to Sept, Tues – Thurs, Sat, Sun and Bank Holiday Mons; all 2 – 5pm. Also open at other times and for parties by appt

Entrance: £4.50, OAPs, students and children over 10 £4, children under 10 free, Tues – Thurs only (2007 prices)

Other information: Full teas May to Aug, Sat, Sun and Bank Holiday Mons only

architectural framework he favoured and to the creation of areas of entirely differing moods. The overriding intention in the 2.5 acres is Italianate with a preponderance of cypresses, junipers, box and yew, punctuated at every turn by sarcophagi, urns, terracotta, marble seats and statues, columns, fountains and loggias. In a different vein is a meadow of naturalised bulbs, most spectacularly martagon lilies. A path leads from here to the cloisters – an Italian-Romanesque building of Peto's confection made with fragments collected from Italy. From here one can admire the whole, and the breathtaking valley and the walled kitchen garden on the other side. Peto's hand is also evident in the artefacts and planting of the Japanese garden; the central pond and rockwork are of a later date. Westwood Manor (see entry) is nearby.

The Marquess of Bath

Warminster BA12 7NW.
Tel: (01985) 844400;
www.longleat.co.uk

3m SW of Warminster, 4.5m SE of Frome on A362

House open

Garden open all year, daily: Easter to Sept, 10am – 5.30pm; Oct to March, 11am – 3pm, except 25th Dec

Entrance: £3, OAPs and children £2, coaches free (house extra)

Other information: Helicopter landing pad available by prior request

LONGLEAT

(Historic Park and Garden Grade I)

This garden has been rearranged and developed by most of the great names in English landscape history. 'Capability' Brown ironed out the formality of the previous Elizabethan and London and Wise garden, and landscaped a chain of lakes set among clumps of trees and hanging woods, best admired today from Heaven's Gate. The 9000-acre park was slightly altered by Repton in 1804 and added to in the 1870s when it became fashionable to collect exotic trees and to make groves of rhododendrons and azaleas. It remains both beautiful and rewarding for all who delight in trees. In the twentieth century the fortunes of the garden came under the guiding hand of Russell Page. The nineteenth-century formal garden in front of the orangery to the north of the house was simplified and improved upon by him to great effect, although, alas, most of his work has since been swept away. The orangery itself is a dream of wisteria. A quarter of a mile to the south there is a pleasure walk in a developing arboretum, with many spring bulbs and wild flowers. The 6th Marquess planted one of the world's longest hedge maze at Longleat in 1975, and others planted by the present Marquess are at various stages of growth; future examples of the genre will encompass a variety of styles and materials. Elsewhere, the safari park and other attractions.

Simon and Amanda Relph

Lower Westwood, Bradford-on-Avon BA15 2AG. Tel: (01225) 864905

1.5m NW of Trowbridge, 1.5m SW of Bradford-on-Avon on B3109

Open for NGS, and April to Sept by appt

Entrance: £2.50, children free

THE OLD MALTHOUSE

In this one-acre garden created by a film producer and his ex-actress wife, it is appropriate that drama and wit should be at the forefront of the design. A work in progress since 1995, its level has been raised to create vistas of Westwood Manor (see entry) and the church of this medieval village. Within the garden the scene changes constantly: from the Arts and Crafts mood at the front of the house, with its drystone walls, water rills and spouts, lavenders and lavateras, via a large rustic barn to a stretch of lawn overlooking fields and a long herbaceous

The Old Malthouse

border in shades of green and white. An old orchard with long grass and daisies elides into a potager where fruit and vegetables are presented with panache. The main garden has a stream and a view into the cloister garden, where espaliered fruit trees and roses roam over pergolas. On the paved terrace above, silver, white and blue planting makes a soft background for sculpted furniture; the enclosing walls support wisterias and ramblers in drifts, and self-seeding plants are encouraged to rampage. Above all, and everywhere, there is sculpture – carvings, seats, fountains, cages and surreal details – setting and stealing the scene in every part of this original and inspiring garden.

Other information: Teas on NGS open days only

 🖶 WC ⚙ ⟨♿⟩ ✏

THE OLD MILL

It would be hard to imagine a more idyllic setting for a garden than the grounds of this ancient rambling mill house. The River Kennet runs through and therefore divides the garden, so that from the formal areas near the house on one side of the river there are lovely views of a wilder and more natural landscape across the flow of water. The pool, mill stream, mill race and numerous channels, all once part of the original working mill, dominate and shape the five acres of cultivated land, giving the garden its special allure and character. The design never intrudes on the natural beauty of the site – this is due to Annabel Dallas's light touch with colour and choice of plants, many of them grown from seed, which veers away from anything that looks too contrived. The whole place is full of experiment, and new features and buildings seem to spring up all the time. There are many spring bulbs and good autumn colour, but summer is the high point here. Close to the house are ebullient borders of salvias, other colour-themed borders and an attractive area combining an informal arrangement of pots with planting in gravel. Wooden bridges cross streams to extend the garden in different directions: an enclosure of lawn and herbaceous borders leads into a green garden backed by an old brick wall.

James and Annabel Dallas

Ramsbury SN8 2PN.
Tel: (01672) 520266

5m NE of Marlborough. Go down High Street, turn right at The Bell pub (signed to Hungerford); garden is 90 metres on right behind yew hedge

Open for NGS, and by appt

Entrance: £3.50, children free

 ⚙ 🐾

THE OLD VICARAGE ★

Every year new discoveries mark the travels of a peripatetic gardener who has created a varied, scented garden on a three-acre escarpment set high on the north side of Salisbury Plain. Swags of clematis, cistus and mahonias enliven the plain

J. N. d'Arcy

Edington, Westbury BA13 4QF.
Tel: (01380) 830512

4m NE of Westbury on B3098 to West Lavington. Signposted

Open once for charity in mid-June,
and by appt

Entrance: £4, children free (includes
other neighbouring gardens)

Other information: Parking in church
car park

 WC &. ⟨⟩

façade of the former vicarage; a wide lawn – croquet of course – leads to a meadow artful with wild flowers beneath rare varieties of chestnut, sorbus and maple. A National Collection of evening primroses gives pleasure after dusk. Stunning views towards Edington Church lift the visitor's eyes through well-planted vistas. Dividing the garden is a yew hedge, an *allée* of fastigiate hornbeams points the view towards Devizes, and brick walls create rooms and shelter exotic plants and trees. Waves of phlomis species mark the hot garden, while a sunken garden to the rear of the house is romantically planted in cool shades round a 15-metre well. Nepetas, a particular passion, run riot. Towards the end of the tour a gravel bed is a sea of agapanthus and eryngiums, and everywhere seedlings push through the gravel.

Mme Anita Pereire

Kington St Michael, Chippenham
SN14 6JG. Tel: (01249) 750360

3m N of Chippenham off A350
between Chippenham and M4 junction
17. Drive through village, then turn left
down lane opposite stud farm on right
at bottom of hill

Open by appt only

Entrance: £3

 WC &. ⟨⟩

THE PRIORY ★

Since 1994 the owner, a respected writer and garden designer, has created a magical two-acre garden around the buildings of an ancient priory. A firm overall structure and lavish planting have combined to make this a most satisfying and elegant garden. Radiating from a central patchwork stone path lined with an avenue of weeping silver pears (Mme Pereire's signature tree) are well-defined and separate areas. These include a breathtaking 'French' garden of topiary and standard roses (the long-lasting 'The Fairy' and 'Ballerina'), an exquisite water garden, a ha-ha ablaze with rock plants, perennials and flowering shrubs, and a classic rose garden filled with colour and scent from masses of old-fashioned varieties. Beyond the hedge-enclosed part of the garden lies a meadow with mown paths forming a maze among the long grasses. In the wild garden further mown grass paths, edged with wild roses, lead down to a gravel garden which blends seamlessly into the surrounding meadowland. The latest additions are a white and silver sun garden full of artemisias and cistus, and another rose garden built into a stone walk.

Mr and Mrs Antony Young

Mountain Bower, Chippenham
SN14 7AJ.
Tel: (01225) 891204

8m W of Chippenham off A420.
Turn N at The Shoe, take second left,
then first right

Open for NGS, and for parties by appt

Entrance: £3.50, children under 14 free,
parties of 10 or more £4.50 per person

Other information: Picnics in meadow
only, from 1pm

 B&B

RIDLEYS CHEER ★

This stylish garden, filled with treasures, has been created since the early 1980s by a garden designer and his wife. It covers some 14 acres, two of which hold a most attractive and interesting arboretum, and there is also a three-acre wildflower meadow, a splendid sight in July and August. The garden is on two levels, connected by a broad flight of steps with a wrought-iron rose arbour at the top and a grass walk, and contains many fine examples of rarer shrubs and trees. Spring is ushered in with bulbs and magnolias. The shrub roses, including some 125 species and hybrids seldom encountered, are a major summer feature; notable too are the displays of white martagon lilies and *Meconopsis betonicifolia*. There is a small potager, and a gravel garden planted with box and yew outside the conservatory. Autumn colour is given by a growing number of maples, beeches, tulip trees, oaks and

Ridleys Cheer

zelkovas. In the main, this in an informal garden, full of appeal for plantsmen, who can derive much information from the knowledgeable owners. A small nursery sells trees, shrubs and perennials, many of them unusual.

STOURHEAD ★★
(Historic Garden Grade I)

An outstanding example of an English landscape garden, designed by Henry Hoare II between 1741 and 1780, a paragon in its day and almost the greatest surviving garden of its kind. The sequence of arcadian images is revealed gradually if one follows a route anti-clockwise around the lake, having come from the house along the top route, so seeing the lake from above. Each experience is doubly inspiring: visitors glimpse classical temples across the water, almost unattainable and mirage-like, and when they reach their goal some other architectural vision always attracts the eye. To gain a better idea of how these buildings would have looked had the surrounding planting remained as it was originally, take a walk by Turner's Paddock Lake below the cascade. Between 1791 and 1838 Hoare's grandson Richard Colt Hoare planted many new species, particularly from America, including tulip trees, swamp cypresses and Indian bean trees. He also introduced *Rhododendron ponticum*. From 1894 the 6th Baronet added to these with the latest kinds of hybrid rhododendrons and scented azaleas, and a large number of copper beeches and conifers, of which many are record-sized specimens. In the early nineteenth century Stourhead boasted one of the best collections of pelargoniums in the world, over 600 varieties, and the latest effort to emulate Richard Colt Hoare's passion consists of over 100 varieties in a 1910 lean-to greenhouse. The garden is especially atmospheric in the quiet of winter when more views are afforded through the bare trees.

The National Trust

Stourton, Warminster BA12 6QF.
Tel: (01747) 841152;
www.nationaltrust.org.uk

3m NW of Mere via A303 at Stourton off B3092

House open 15th March to 2nd Nov, Fri – Tues, 11.30am – 4.30pm (or dusk if earlier)

Garden open all year, daily, 9am – 7pm (or dusk if earlier)

Entrance: house or garden £7, children (5–16) £3.80, family £16.60 (house and garden £11.60, children £5.80, family £27.60)

Other information: Refreshments in restaurant or at Spread Eagle Inn at garden entrance. Wheelchairs available. Buggy service from car park in peak season. Dogs Nov to Feb only

○ 🛏 WC ⚹ 🕸 🐾 🏛 🍴 ⚲

Stourhead

Adjacent to Stourhead, and sharing the same car park but with separate entry charges, is *Stourton House Flower Garden*, a colourful five-acre garden of interest at all times of year, where a wide range of wild and cultivated plants grow happily together. Telephone Mrs Bullivant on (01747) 840417 for details. [Open April to Nov, Wed, Thurs, Sun and Bank Holiday Mons, 11am – 6pm.]

Mr and Mrs Neil Campbell-Sharp

Manton Drove, Manton, Marlborough
SN8 4HL. Tel: (01672) 515380

1m W of Marlborough off A4. In
Manton bear right past Odd Fellows
Arms, then after 180 metres left into
Manton Drove. House is up hill on right

Open by appt

Entrance: £5

WEST WIND

An outstanding and very personal one-acre garden created since 1987 by the present owners in a wonderful downland setting. Their expertise as garden photographers is allied to wide horticultural experience to achieve a visual feast and fine perspectives, and the garden is alive with colour, form and scent from May right through to November. Viewpoints highlight the strong outlines and lush planting radiating from the house. A restful enclosed garden leads to a skilfully planted double border awash with old-fashioned roses, then descends to a woodland walk planted for spring flowering. The garden fits happily into the surrounding landscape, viewed through slender silver *Betula jacquemontii* and home to a rich assortment of wildlife. The superbly grown and placed grasses are an outstanding feature.

The National Trust

Bradford-on-Avon BA15 2AF.
Tel: (01225) 863374;
www.nationaltrust.org.uk

WESTWOOD MANOR

Turning from the Italianate glories of Iford Manor (see entry), topiarists and lovers of geometric design will enjoy the dense green of the garden here. There are no flowers, other than the lilies in the pond set into the lawn and the swathes of wisteria on the wall leading to the entrance. A small garden links the ancient barns to the medieval manor house which the yew hedges enfold and enclose. This simple design looks centuries-old but dates from the early part of the twentieth century, when Edgar Lister bought and restored the house and created and designed the garden, both of which he later left to the Trust. The garden should be visited as an adjunct and a complement to the house.

WILTON HOUSE ★
(Historic Garden Grade I)

Currently the home of the 18th Earl of Pembroke, the house built by Inigo Jones in 1647 is surrounded by quintessentially English parkland dotted with statues and eye-catchers – the Whispering Seat, with its interesting accoustic properties, is a good vantage point looking down towards the Tudor entrance of the house. Formal gardens were created by Isaac de Caus in 1633, sweeping 1000 feet to the south. When this style fell from favour, one of the earliest examples of English landscaping took its place. The River Nadder runs right through the park beneath the 1736 Palladian bridge; taking the riverside walk today, visitors come across a loggia and an avenue of liquidambars. The woodland walk leads along a tributary of the River Wylye, overlooking the arboretum; cedars of Lebanon, some introduced in the 1630s, others newly planted, appear throughout the park. After he succeeded to the title in 1969, the 17th Earl commissioned four gardens. The one in the north courtyard, designed by David Vickery in 1971, incorporates formal pleached limes within formal box hedges; before the foliage becomes a feature, colour comes from white and pink tulips, followed by

1.5m NW of Trowbridge, 1.5m SW of Bradford-on Avon off B3109. In Westwood beside church

Open April to Sept, Tues, Wed and Sun, 2 – 5pm, and at other times for parties of up to 20 by written appt with s.a.e.

The Earl of Pembroke
Wilton, Salisbury SP2 0BJ.
Tel: (01722) 746720;
www.wiltonhouse.com

3m W of Salisbury on A30

House open – please see website for details

Garden open 21st to 24th March, 5th April to 28th Sept, daily, 11am – 5.30pm (last admission 4.30pm)

Entrance: £5, children £3.50 (house and garden £12, concessions £9.75, children £6.50)

Other information: Plants for sale in garden centre

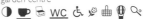

Wilton House

standard honeysuckles and lavenders. Xa Tollemache created a box-hedged parterre bordered by cotton lavender, echoing designs from the central ninth-century wellhead. The Oriental water garden and a hedged garden of old roses complete the quartet, and a Miz-maze of crushed white stone and turf is a work-in-progress. For children there is fun and excitement in a large adventure playground.

OTHER RECOMMENDED GARDENS

AVEBURY MANOR

Avebury, Marlborough SN8 1RF (01672 539250; www.nationaltrust.org.uk). Open April to Oct, Fri – Tues, 11am – 5pm. NT

Surrounding the atmospheric house, monastic in origin, is a neat, secretive garden that suits it perfectly, furnished with a rose garden flowering under the shadow of the church tower, herbaceous borders set behind low box hedges, a splendid lavender walk and a topiary garden with distinctive box hedges. 6 acres.

CORSHAM COURT

James Methuen-Campbell, Corsham SN13 0BZ (01249 701610; www.corsham-court.co.uk). Open 20th March to Sept, Tues – Thurs, Sat, Sun and Bank Holiday Mons, 2 – 5.30pm; Oct to 19th March, Sat and Sun, 2 – 4.30pm. Closed Dec. Also for parties by appt

In a landscaped park devised by 'Capability' Brown some superlative trees (notably a mighty *Platanus orientalis*) survive, together with a delightful bath house, while Humphry Repton added a lake and a boat house. 17 acres of formal gardens near the house are graced by some fine shrubs and trees. 350 acres. (Listed Grade II*)

GREAT CHALFIELD

Melksham SN12 8NH (01225 782239). Open April to Oct, Tues – Thurs, 11.30am – 5pm, Sun, 2 – 5pm. NT

The 7-acre garden designed by Alfred Parsons provides a serene and spacious setting for this most romantic of moated 15th-century houses. Spacious lawns are broken up by vast topiary yews and surrounded by substantial borders, at their best in June and early July, with a semi-natural shrubbery and a woodland walk stretching beyond. (Listed Grade II)

LACOCK ABBEY

Lacock, Chippenham SN15 2LG (01249 730227; www.nationaltrust.org.uk). Open March to Oct, daily except 21st March, 11am – 5.30pm. NT

The medieval abbey buildings dominate the meadowland beside the River Avon. A woodland garden is massed with spring bulbs, a rose garden has been re-created from an 1841 photograph, and for dendrologists and plantsmen there are many unusual trees and a walled 'botanic garden'. 9 acres. (Listed Grade II)

SHARCOTT MANOR

Captain and Mrs David Armytage, Pewsey SN9 5PA (01672 563485). Open April to Sept for NGS, first Wed in month, 11am – 5pm, plus two Suns, 2 – 6pm, and for parties by appt

In this fine 6-acre garden, filled with a rich choice of plants grouped with a sure eye for colour and effect, the widely varied plantings ensure interest at every season.

Great Chalfield

WORCESTERSHIRE

For further information about how to use the *Guide*
and for an explanation of the symbols, see pages vi–viii.
Specific dates and times are those given to us by garden owners for 2008.
For 2009 dates, check with the individual properties.
For opening dates under the National Gardens Scheme,
readers should consult *The Yellow Book* or www.ngs.org.uk.
Maps are to be found at the end of the *Guide*.

ARLEY ARBORETUM

The arboretum forms part of what remains of an important Picturesque landscape, laid out and planted over the late-eighteenth and nineteenth centuries by two families with distinguished botanical connections. Embellishing the already renowned grounds of Arley House, George Annesley, Earl of Mountnorris, a Fellow of the Royal and Linnean Societies, began planting trees in the 1790s; and through the nineteenth century the Woodward family, related by marriage to Joseph Hooker, the famous plant collector who was also Director of Kew, continued his work. Situated above the River Severn, with exquisite views over the surrounding countryside, the remaining walled garden and arboretum retain a romantic atmosphere. The mature trees include Crimean pines and an ancient layered beech, and walks wind beneath them through daffodils in spring, followed by bluebells, magnolias and rhododendrons. The arboretum has recently been extended and planting continues, while the walled garden, with its intact castellated gatehouse, is also being restored and replanted. Fourteen acres in all.

R. D. Turner Charitable Trust

Upper Arley DY12 1XG.
Tel: (01299) 861368/861868;
www.arley-arboretum.org.uk

6m NW of Kidderminster 9m SE of Bridgnorth, between A442 and B4194

Open April to mid-Nov, Wed – Sun, 11am – 5pm

Entrance: £5, children £1

◑ ⬤ 🖺 <u>WC</u> ⟟ ⟨🖐 🌢 ⬚ ℺

BURFORD HOUSE AND GARDENS ★

The late John Treasure's seven-acre gardens, planned and planted over a period of forty years from 1954, are now mature and a classic of their time. A huge variety of species is grown here in the broad sinuous mixed borders which cross the smooth lawns, with much of the herbaceous planting devised for late summer colour; elsewhere, streamside gardens are attractive in spring and early summer, while *Erigeron mucronatus* clothes the more formal terraces against the house, which is draped with a magnificent *Wisteria macrobotrys* 'Burford'. The gardens remain a showcase for clematis, in which the garden centre specialises; National Collections of *C. texensis*, *viticella* and herbaceous varieties are held here. Across the brook which skirts the main garden is the meadow garden, the work of the designer Charles Chesshire: mown grass paths curve through the meadows into circular enclosures of amelanchier or cherry, or dive into

Burford Garden Company

Tenbury Wells WR15 8HQ.
Tel: (01584) 810777;
www.burford.co.uk

19m SW of Kidderminster, 1m W of Tenbury Wells on A456; 8m S of Ludlow via A49 and A456

Open all year, daily, except 25th and 26th Dec, 9am – 6pm (or dusk if earlier). Parties of 20 or more by appt

Entrance: £3.95, children £1 (2007 prices)

Other information: Plants for sale, especially clematis

◯ ⬤ ✕ 🖺 <u>WC</u> ⟟ 🌢 ⬚ ℺

a maze of beech hedging, and a tiny track leads down through the wild flowers to the banks of the River Teme. The whole forms a perfect counterbalance to the more contrived informality of the original gardens.

The National Trust

Builders Yard, High Green, Severn Stoke WR8 9JS. Tel: (01905) 371006; www.nationaltrust.org.uk/croomepark

8m SW of Worcester off A38 and 6m W of Pershore off B4084

Open 1st to 30th March, 3rd Sept to 26th Oct, Wed – Sun; 31st March to Aug, 26th Dec to 1st Jan, daily; Nov to 21st Dec, Sat and Sun; all 10am – 5.30pm (closes 4pm in winter). Guided tours by appt in writing

Entrance: £4.80, children £2.40, family £12

CROOME PARK
(Historic Park Grade I)

Capability' Brown's career as an independent landscape designer and architect was effectively launched at Croome Court, of which today's 670-acre park was once an integral part. The house (not open) was sold by the family who commissioned it and remains in private hands. Brown created a serpentine lake, complete with grotto, and a mile-long artificial river. Paths wind through shrubberies and past charming and ornate garden buildings, and the wider parkland contains stunning follies by Robert Adam, James Wyatt and others. The Trust's ambitious ten-year restoration, completed in 2006, has involved dredging the lake and river and restoring the bridges across the lake, the classical temples and grotto, and the listed park buildings. More than 45,000 trees and shrubs have been planted to replace those lost from the original scheme.

Croome Park

EASTGROVE COTTAGE GARDEN NURSERY ★

An intimate, deceptively simple five-acre garden which is both superbly planted and impeccably maintained, with the added value of a nursery full of choice plants. The masterly planting, with a careful but also relaxed and instinctive approach to colour and wonderful use of foliage, divides the small plot into smaller sections of distinct character. A garden of cottage favourites – aquilegias, geraniums, irises and violas – invites quiet sitting, while the Great Wall of China displays alpines and other small plants deserving of close study in an admirably natural manner. A stroll leads through shady walks and open lawns, with luscious planting on all sides, and even wilder areas further from the cottage are carefully presented. A young two-acre arboretum has an oval concave 'labyrinth' for children to enjoy.

Malcolm and Carol Skinner

Sankyns Green, Shrawley, Little Witley WR6 6LQ. Tel: (01299) 896389; www.eastgrove.co.uk

8m NW of Worcester on road between Shrawley (B4196) and Great Witley (A443)

Open 24th April to 19th July, 11th Sept to 11th Oct, Thurs to Sat; plus 4th, 5th, 25th and 26th May; all 2 – 5pm

Entrance: £4, children free

Other information: Home-made ice cream available

HANBURY HALL ★

(Historic Garden Grade I)

The hall, remodelled in 1701, is a jewel of a house, and the setting provided by the surrounding gardens and parkland is magnificent. The restoration of the early-eighteenth-century gardens on the west side is proving a triumph as they acquire maturity. The sunken parterre, surrounded by yew hedges, and the adjoining fruit garden with its trellis pavilions, have been authentically planted. The pattern of clipped box is filled with individual specimens of choice small plants of the period – auriculas, tulips and marigolds – laid out in colourful regular patterns; citrus and clipped bay trees in pots are displayed on the surrounding gravel walks. Beyond, in the wilderness and especially the grove, fastigiate junipers and low box in a calm green space backed by sprightly young trees give a fine and unaccustomed sense of how such formal woodland gardens would have appeared to their creators. Shrubberies rejuvenated with box, laurel, phillyrea and philadelphus stand neatly on vast expanses of smooth lawn, contrasting with fine trees extending into the parkland. The orangery has been brought back into use, with pots of tender plants lining its terrace in the summer, as has the curious mushroom house attached. An orchard of old apple varieties occupies part of the vast walled gardens, and a walk across the park leads past a well-preserved ice-house and offers spectacular views of the ancient parkland. 20 acres in all.

The National Trust

School Road, Hanbury, Droitwich WR9 7EA. Tel: (01527) 821214; www.nationaltrust.org.uk

4.5m E of Droitwich, off B4090 or B4091

House open

Garden open 1st to 16th March, Nov to Feb, Sat and Sun; 17th March to 29th Oct, Sat – Wed (but open Good Fri); plus July, Aug and all school holidays, daily; all 11am – 5.30pm (closes 4pm in winter)

Entrance: £4.80, children £2.40, family £12 (house and garden £7.20, children £3.60, family £18)

Other information: Batricar available

LITTLE MALVERN COURT ★

Tucked into the side of the Malvern Hills and spread out beside an ancient gabled manor house and priory church, this 10-acre garden has great romantic charm. The medieval fish ponds, bulging yew hedges clipped into fantastic shapes and a venerable lime tree remain from earlier gardens, but much dates from 1982 onwards, originally laid out by Arabella

Mrs T. M. Berington

Little Malvern, Nr Malvern WR14 4JN. Tel: (01684) 892988

4m S of Great Malvern on A4104 S of junction with A449

Little Malvern Court

Open 16th April to 17th July, Wed and
Thurs, 2.15 – 5pm, and Mon – Fri
by appt

Entrance: £4.50, children £1 (house and
garden £5.50, children £2)

Lennox-Boyd and continued by Michael Balston. Close to the house, a classic English combination of clipped hedges and pergolas defining formal areas filled with soft planting creates satisfying contrasts. Moving from area to area, themes develop and vistas are opened up. Pale colours and soft textures are used to great effect, and the garden gains a modern edge by the elegant simplicity of some of the planting, such as a clipped box hedge set against a clipped yew hedge and a billowing choisya in the entrance forecourt, and elsewhere a simple horseshoe of pleached limes around a small lawn. Below the house a series of small lakes connected by weirs is embraced by mown grass paths, flanked by wild flowers and maturing trees. At the top of the first lake is a new rock garden and a watery gravel bed where primulas and irises are naturalising. This evolving, imaginative and immaculately presented garden repays several visits, especially in spring for the blossom and early summer for the array of old-fashioned roses.

LUGGERS HALL

Mr and Mrs R. Haslam

Springfield Lane, Broadway WR12 7BT.
Tel: (01386) 852040;
www.luggershall.com

In Broadway turn off High Street by
Swan Hotel, bear left into Springfield
Lane, garden is 270 metres on left

Open for NGS, and May to July for
parties of 20 or more by appt

Entrance: £3, children free

Alfred Parsons, the Victorian painter of gardens and landscapes, built the house for himself in 1911 and designed the 2.5-acre garden in the style typical of the Arts and Crafts Movement centred around Broadway at that time. The present owners have been gradually restoring the garden since 1995, retaining its overall character and adding ideas of their own. The main lawn, with hedged compartments opening off it, has a splendid battlemented yew hedge to one side, and the rose garden remains unchanged with criss-cross paths of broken Cotswold stone. The parterre, reconstructed with the aid of an original black-and-white aerial photograph, has been replanted with white roses and blue perennials. The colour effects are superb, especially in summer: themed borders in the walled garden and elsewhere range from palest yellows through blues to intense shades of pink, with many unusual plants including a wide variety of salvias. A white garden is tucked away, and there is also a potager and a tranquil leafy corner where the former swimming pool has been transformed into a home for the koi carp. Gravel paths with strategically placed seats connect the different areas, and Broadway Tower can be glimpsed between the trees.

OVERBURY COURT ★
(Historic Garden Grade II*)

The superb six-acre garden, largely laid out in the late nineteenth and early twentieth centuries, provides the setting for a fine early-eighteenth-century house; an interesting church adjoins. It is bordered by lush parkland giving unspoiled views in all directions. Everywhere there is water. Behind the house, a brook issues into a tufa grotto. Rough steps wind between cascades and through naturalistic plantings of hostas, filipendulas, wild garlic and ferns, backed by mature box bushes. The brook, emerging along a broad rill bordered on one side by meadow and on the other by lawn, descends through gentle cascades and winds around a series of pools beyond a great lawn. Huge plane and lime trees contrast with the smoothness of grass and water; the simplicity is magical. Massive yew hedges separate this part of the garden from the more formal area to the south, where the centrepiece is an avenue of Irish yews flanked by a sunken bowling lawn and a formal pool. Again, the planting is simple yet stunning – to the east a crinkle-crankle border of gold and silver foliage by Peter Coates, and to the west a sunken double mixed border displaying old-fashioned and species roses, underplanted with geraniums and *Alchemilla mollis*. Near the house is a terrace with silver and white borders, and well-trained shrubs and climbers clothe the house walls.

Mr and Mrs Bruce Bossom

Overbury, Tewkesbury, Gloucestershire GL20 7NP.
Tel: (01386) 725111 (office hours); www.overbury.org

9m SW of Evesham, 5m NE of Tewkesbury, 2.5m N of Teddington (A46/A435) roundabout

Open by appt only

Entrance: minimum charge £20

● WC &

THE PICTON GARDEN

Ernest Ballard began selling asters, many of his own breeding, at Old Court Nurseries in 1906. The present owner's father, Percy Picton, took over in 1952, and the impressive plantsman's 1.5-acre garden has developed alongside the continuing breeding programme and National Collection as a setting for a splendid late-summer display of asters (nearly 400 varieties) and other late-summer perennials. It owes much to the naturalistic prairie planting style, with rudbeckias and echinaceas, heleniums and helianthus mingling with great swathes of Michaelmas daisies, together with seedheads of spent flowers and towering stands of bamboos. Trees and shrubs for autumn interest – cornus, acers, hydrangeas and liquidambars – have been added, and a new shrub bed was planted in 2006.

Mr and Mrs P. Picton

Old Court Nurseries, Colwall, Great Malvern WR13 6QE.
Tel: (01684) 540416;
www.autumnasters.co.uk

3m SW of Great Malvern on B4218

Open Aug, Wed – Sun, 2.30 – 5pm; Sept to 11th Oct, daily, 1 – 5pm

Old Court Nurseries open as garden, plus May to July, Fri – Sun, 2.30 – 5pm

Entrance: £3, children under 15 free

◐

SHUTTIFIELD COTTAGE

This unusual three-acre plantsmans garden has lawns leading down to a woodland rose garden through a succession of beds and borders containing shrubs and flowering plants designed to give pleasure and interest throughout the year.

Angela and David Judge

Birchwood, Storridge, Malvern WR13 5HA. Tel: (01886) 884243

Shuttifield Cottage

8m SW of Worcester off A4103. Turn right opposite Storridge church to Birchwood. After 1.25m turn left down tarmac drive. Park on road and walk down this drive (limited parking at house for disabled)

Open for NGS, and by appt

Entrance: £3.50, children free

● ☕ WC ♿

The rose garden has space for a large collection of old varieties to spread, sprawl, climb and bloom abundantly. Beyond is a 20-acre wood carpeted with wood anemones and bluebells, azaleas and rhododendrons, traversed by winding paths. In other parts are colour-themed beds, including stump and primula beds, splendid trees and a vegetable garden. The seven-acre valley to the south is home to a small herd of sika deer, and contains two ponds set among wild flowers and orchids. There is also a thatched tea house. The planning is skilful, the effect natural and unstudied.

Trustees of Spetchley Gardens Charitable Trust

Spetchley, Worcester WR5 1RS.
Tel: (01453) 810303;
www.spetchleygardens.co.uk

3m E of Worcester on A44

Open 21st March to 30th Sept, Wed – Sun and Bank Holiday Mons, 11am – 6pm (last admission 5pm); Oct, Sat and Sun, 11am – 4pm (last admission 3pm)

Entrance: £6, OAPs £5.50, children free

◑ ☕ ✕ WC ♿ ♨ ⚑

SPETCHLEY PARK ★
(Historic Park Grade II*)

The grand Victorian garden of 30 acres, surrounded by seventeenth-century parkland, were laid out and extended by successive generations of the Berkeley family. Ellen Willmott, a relative, was a frequent visitor and helped to fashion the planting, evidenced by *Eryngium* 'Miss Willmott's Ghost' still self-seeding in the vast herbaceous borders. The current owner, a plant collector, is expanding the area under cultivation, with a view to allowing the plants to do their own thing, even in more formal parts within and around the old walled garden. Everywhere gravel or daisy-strewn grass walks lead you on between yew hedges or old shrubberies to discover further areas punctuated by statue and fountain, and a visit in June is rewarded by spectacular expanses of naturalised martagon lilies, together with *Campanula lactiflora*. In the woodland garden, the collection includes dogwoods, acers, and hydrangeas, and recent planting has introduced an array of rare trees and shrubs beneath the mature canopy. Park Lake is fringed with water lilies and bulrushes, with views to the deer park beyond.

Mr and Mrs James Arbuthnott

Stone, Kidderminster DY10 4BG.
Tel: (01562) 69902;
www.shcn.co.uk

STONE HOUSE COTTAGE GARDENS ★

The 0.75-acre plantsmans garden has been created since 1975, and looking round it now, it is difficult to believe that the whole area was once flat and bare. The owners have skilfully built towers and follies to create small intimate areas

Stone House Cottage Garden

and at the same time provide homes for many unusual climbers and shrubs. Yew hedges break up the area to give a vista with a tower at the end, covered with wisteria, roses and clematis. Hardly anywhere does a shrub grow in isolation – something will be scrambling up it, often a small late-flowering clematis. Raised beds are full to overflowing, shrubs and unusual herbaceous plants mingle happily and in a grassed area shrubs are making good specimens. Mrs Arbuthnott acknowledges herself to be a compulsive buyer of plants – her money has not been wasted. Visitors may ascend the towers to view the garden as a whole for the price of a donation to the Mother Theresa charity. The highly regarded adjacent nursery specialises in wall shrubs, climbers and unusual herbaceous plants.

2m SE of Kidderminster via A448

Open mid-March to mid-Sept, Wed – Sat, 10am – 5pm, by appt

Entrance: £3, children free

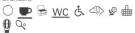

WITLEY COURT

(Historic Garden Grade II*)

The spectacular ruin of Witley Court looks out now over the gardens to ploughed farmland where once would have stretched acres of parkland. However, the gardens have been brought to life by the restoration of the truly magnificent Italianate fountain which formed the centrepiece of a vast and elaborate Nesfield parterre. The planting is partly replicated, to give an impression of the setting for the fountains and other remaining stonework: twin pavilions flanking the semi-circular bowl of the parterre, with an elaborate and decaying ha-ha dividing this from the land beyond. The imagination provides the rest, and to see the fountains playing again with all the guests departed cannot fail to be a moving experience. Elsewhere in the grounds are the nineteenth-century woodland and wilderness walks, also restored, and a picturesque lake with a cascade. The ruined mansion and the superb Baroque church adjoining can also be visited. 46 acres in all.

English Heritage

Worcester Road, Great Witley, Worcester WR6 6JT. Tel: (01299) 896636; www.english-heritgage.org.uk

10m NW of Worcester on A443

Open March to Oct, daily, 10am – 5pm (closes 6pm June to Aug); Nov to Feb, Wed – Sun, 10am – 4pm

Entrance: £5.40, concessions £4.10, children £2.70, family £13.50 (2007 prices)

Other information: Disabled parking available

OTHER RECOMMENDED GARDENS

24 ALEXANDER AVENUE

David and Malley Terry, Droitwich WR9 8NH
(01905 774907). Open for NGS, and by appt

High hedges threaded with clematis protect and
conceal a small town garden of immaculate
artistry, filled with a dazzling array of plants,
many of them rare. April is a good time to visit
to enjoy the bulbs and early-flowering
perennials, July for the clematis.

PERSHORE COLLEGE

'Avonbank', Pershore WR10 3JP (01386 552443;
www.pershore.ac.uk). Open Mon – Fri by appt for
large parties

As might be expected, the 10-acre grounds of
the horticultural college display a flourishing
range of specialist gardens, including 'model
gardens' created by students, an arboretum,
orchards, automated glasshouses and a hardy
plant production nursery and plant centre.
National Collections of penstemons and
philadelphus are here.

RIVERSIDE GARDENS

Wychbold, Droitwich Spa WR9 0DG (01527 860000;
www.webbsdirect.co.uk). Open all year, daily except
23rd March, 25th and 26th Dec, 9am – 8pm (closes
6pm Jan and Feb, plus Sat and Bank Holiday Mons);
1st Jan and all Suns, 10.30am – 4.30pm

Below the huge garden centre a number of
imaginative themed gardens, among them The
New Wave designed by Noel Kingsbury, have
been planted in over 2 acres on the banks of
the River Salwarpe. Great thought has been
given to show plants for every situation;
gardeners will gain insight and inspiration here.

YORKSHIRE (N. & E. RIDING)

For further information about how to use the *Guide*
and for an explanation of the symbols, see pages vi–viii.
Specific dates and times are those given to us by garden owners for 2008.
For 2009 dates, check with the individual properties.
For opening dates under the National Gardens Scheme,
readers should consult *The Yellow Book* or www.ngs.org.uk.
Maps are to be found at the end of the *Guide*.

BURTON AGNES HALL

The beautiful Elizabethan house is the work of Robert Smythson, who also designed Longleat, Wollaton and Hardwick (see entries in Wiltshire, Shropshire and Derbyshire), but of the Elizabethan garden mentioned by Celia Fiennes in 1697 nothing remains. The yew topiary leading from the gatehouse towards the house was planted in the nineteenth century, while the charming Gothic summer house, the work of Bridlington architect Francis Johnson, was built in 1972; his also the canal garden to the east created in the 1950s. The walled garden probably forms part of the original Elizabethan layout and since 1990 has been imaginatively redeveloped, with a large potager of herbs and vegetables filling the western corner and a central herbaceous border running towards the greenhouses. Contrasting with the structured confusion of a maze created using 700 yews is the Jungle Garden, full of exotic-looking plants encroaching over gravel paths, which leads to a pool where Agnes the Elephant acts as the fountain. Beyond the glasshouses is a series of colour-themed gardens, each one focused on a different game. Opening off a central sunken garden laid out with a giant chess set and surrounded by a pergola festooned with roses and honeysuckles is a dark red and purple garden, where snakes and ladders is the name of the game, while in the white garden draughts is the thing. Young and old are kept amused for hours, and it is by no means uncommon to see ladies of mature years showing off their skills at hopscotch.

Mrs Susan Cunliffe-Lister/Burton Agnes Preservation Trust Ltd

Burton Agnes, Driffield, East Riding YO25 4NB. Tel: (01262) 490324; www.burton-agnes.co.uk

5m S of Bridlington, 5m NE of Great Driffield on A166

House open

Garden open mid-Feb for snowdrops, then April to Oct, daily, 11am – 5pm

Entrance: £3 (hall and garden £6, OAPs £5.50)

Other information: Gardeners' Fair 8th and 9th June

WC

CASTLE HOWARD ★★

(Historic Park Grade I)

Built by the 3rd Earl of Carlisle between 1699 and 1712 to a design by Sir John Vanbrugh and Nicholas Hawksmoor, Castle Howard is one of Yorkshire's finest houses. The extensive grounds, running to about a 1000 acres, are populated by several buildings, the most famous being the mausoleum in the park and the Temple of the Four Winds at the extremity of the garden. The formal gardens around the house were redesigned by William Nesfield, who added the famous Atlas

Castle Howard Estates Ltd

York YO60 7DA. Tel: (01653) 648333; www.castlehoward.co.uk

15m NE of York, 5m SW of Malton off A64

House open

Garden open all year, daily except 25th Dec, 10am – 4.30pm. Special tours of woodland garden and rose gardens available for pre-booked parties

Castle Howard

Entrance: £8, concessions £7.50, children (4-16) £5.50, family £21 (house and garden £10.50, concessions £9.50, children £7, family £27)

Other information: Separate entrance arrangements for 'Kew at Castle Howard' arboretum

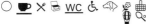

Fountain in 1853 as a centrepiece of an elaborate south parterre which was swept away barely fifty years later. The eighteenth-century walled garden has been comprehensively redeveloped since 1975, when a rose garden filled with Albas, Gallicas and Damasks was created in memory of Lady Cecilia Howard. Further plantings of old roses, notably Chinas, Bourbons and older hybrid teas and floribundas, enrich the air and delight the eye, forming one of the most extensive collections of old-fashioned and species roses in the country. Delphinium borders add further interest and the old sundial garden has been transformed into an elegant and interesting potager. The large woodland garden, known as Ray Wood, contains a fine collection of species and hybrid rhododendrons, together with good collections of magnolias, acers and vacciniums. A separate 127-acre arboretum known as 'Kew at Castle Howard' has been developed since 1975. Originally the brainchild of Lord Howard and the nurseryman James Russell, with a nucleus formed by the Sunningdale Nursery Collection, it has been further enriched and enhanced to form an important collection of specimen trees. In 1997 an agreement between Castle Howard and the Royal Botanic Gardens, Kew resulted in the setting-up of The Castle Howard Arboretum Trust.

Mr Charles Wyvill

Leyburn, North Yorkshire DL8 5LJ.
Tel: (01677) 450428;
www.constableburtongardens.co.uk

16m NW of Ripon, 3m E of Leyburn on A684

CONSTABLE BURTON HALL
(Historic Park Grade II)

In a walled and wooded parkland setting is a perfect Palladian mansion designed by John Carr of York in 1768. Built of beautiful honey-coloured sandstone, it rises from the lawns shaded by fine mature cedars. A delightful terraced woodland garden of lilies, ferns, hardy shrubs, roses and wild flowers drops down to a lake enhanced by an eighteenth-century bridge (no access). Near to the entrance drive are a stream and rock garden, and a new lily pond has been added. This eight-acre garden is a particular pleasure to visit because, after placing their entry coins in the honesty box, visitors can follow the numbered directional arrows using the concise notes to pass from one area of the garden to another – a technique that many other gardens could use with advantage. Surprises abound, such as the yellow Turk's cap lily in profusion and many mad climbers and shade-loving ground-cover plants. A herbaceous garden and several grand borders (over 6000 tulips planted each year to spectacular effect in May) have replaced the old formal rose garden.

Open 17th March to 28th Sept, daily, 9am – 6pm. Tulip Festival 3rd to 5th May

Entrance: £3, OAPs £2.50, children 50p (honesty box)

DUNCOMBE PARK

(Historic Park Grade I)

Built in 1713, possibly with advice from Vanbrugh, it is the grass terrace, similar to that at nearby Rievaulx (see entry), for which the garden is justly famous. As Christopher Hussey observed, these two are 'unique, and perhaps the most spectacularly beautiful among English landscape conceptions of the eighteenth century'. From the Ionic rotunda a broad sweeping grass terrace stretches half a mile in extent, resembling a wonderful green crescent moon. It leads to another, grander temple in the Doric order, where the river in the valley below turns 300 degrees, giving the impression that the temple is set upon a promontory. Further back towards the house, partly hidden in woodland, is a conservatory built by Barry in 1851, of which only the central orangery remains intact. On either side of the house are sunken parterres (one white and grey, another red and purple) originally laid out in 1846 and recently restored. They contrast well with the huge yews partially encircling the perimeter, which in spring are bedecked with *Clematis montana*. The house dominates the great square lawn with its large figure of Father Time (attributed to van Nost and dating from 1715) sitting at the junction of grass and terrace. As a landscape it is a wonderfully simple composition – an essay in tones of green broken only by the extravagant display of a roaming peacock. In all, 35 acres.

Lord Feversham

Helmsley, North Yorkshire YO62 5EB. Tel: (01439) 772625/771115 (during open hours); www.duncombepark.com

12m E of Thirsk, 1m SW of Helmsley off A170

House open as garden, by guided tour (12.30pm, 1.30pm, 2.30pm and 3.30pm)

Garden open 23rd March to 26th Oct, Sun – Thurs, 11am – 5.30pm (last admission 4.30pm). Closed 11th, 12th and 16th June

Parkland Centre and part of National Nature Reserve also open

Entrance: park £2, children (10–16) £1; gardens and park £4, concessions £3.50, children £2; (house, garden and park £7.25, concessions £5.50, children £3.25, family £15)

Other information: Parking at Parkland Centre. Alternative entrance for wheelchair users

HUNMANBY GRANGE

Situated three miles from the sea high on the chalk wolds, this atmospheric and carefully thought-out garden has been carved slowly but steadily since 1984 from pasture land, with nearly two thirds of the three acres intensively gardened. Now generous shelter belts cut out the winds, and the garden has been further subdivided by hedges to create a series of characterful rooms. The orchard, underplanted with daffodils and camassias, with irises on the sunnier face, greets the visitor. To the north lies a pond and gravel garden complete

Mr and Mrs T. Mellor

Wold Newton, Driffield YO25 3HS. Tel: (01723) 891636; www.hunmanbygrange.co.uk

Midway between Bridlington and Scarborough, off A165 or B1249, 4m SW of Filey. House is between Wold Newton and Hunmanby on Burton Fleming – Fordon road.

Hunmanby Grange

Open for NGS, plus July to Sept,
Wed, 1 – 5pm

Entrance: £2.50, children free

with two ponds; beyond lies the croquet lawn, its eastern edge defined by a laburnum tunnel. The tone changes yet again with the more intense planting of an enclosure created as an outdoor dining room and filled with plants for scent and autumn colour, a particular feature of the garden as a whole. On the windier east side of the house is a border of shrub roses underplanted with bulbs and hardy geraniums, all in grass, giving onto a bold circular lawn forming a hub, with 'hot' borders making a good contrast to the cool grasses and shrubs which went before. The woodland garden runs down to the tennis court, flanked by a border planted on a spoil mound with bold groups of shrubs; backing onto this a small copse is centred on a fine view of the open countryside. The large elliptical house lawn, with an almost 270-degree view, is even more exposed. Shrubs and some good island-bed planting abounds, revealing the same flare for originality: an old greenhouse base has been turned into an annual and biennial garden with an outdoor chess set.

Kelberdale

KELBERDALE

In this one-acre plantsman's garden created since 1970, the eye is immediately caught by a broad and sweeping herbaceous border imaginatively and skilfully planted, set against a backdrop of neighbouring trees. Across the lawn, laid out beneath a *Robinia pseudoacacia* 'Frisia', is a bed planted in tones of yellow and orange, and as an experiment a conifer bed, essential for winter structure, has been given an underplanting of grasses. The lawn leads on to a small woodland glade filled with shrubs and bulbs, the huge trees clinging to the rock face high above the river and its weir. At the other side of the house a recently acquired piece of land is gradually being transformed into a wildlife haven, with a meadow and a pond and many native trees, plus a few ornamentals for the human occupants. Two ponds, a vegetable garden, an alpine house and a collection of troughs complete the picture.

Mr and Mrs S. Abbott

Wetherby Road, Knaresborough HG5 8LN. Tel: (01423) 862140

1m SW of Knaresborough on B6164 Wertherby road. Turn left immediately after roundabout at intersection with A658

Open for NGS, and April to mid-July by appt for parties of 10 or more

Entrance: £3

 ● ● ● WC ᕕ ᵚ

MILLGATE HOUSE ★

From the Market Square a green-painted door opens onto a corridor leading to a narrow stepped lane ('snicket' in the Yorkshire vernacular) set between house and boundary wall. Pots filled with bold foliage line the path, while a golden hop and a *Clematis montana* festoon the walls. The three-acre garden, especially delightful in June and July, opens off to the right, laid out before the charming Regency-fronted house, and is composed of two small rectangles set on two different levels linked by broad rustic steps. The top area has a small naturalistic shaped lawn, but the space is dominated by a large *Rosa helenae* trained over an iron support in the shape of a medieval tent – an appropriate nod at Richmond's long military history. This is balanced near the house by a fine *Magnolia × kewensis* casting its shade over a small tank with a

Austin Lynch and Tim Culkin

Richmond, North Yorkshire DL10 4JN. Tel: (01748) 823571; www.millgatehouse.com

In Richmond, in corner of Market Square opposite Barclays Bank

Open for NGS, and special snowdrop days Feb and March (weather permitting), by appt; then mid-March to mid-Oct, daily, 10am – 5pm; and at other times by appt

Entrance: £2

◗ B&B

Millgate House

lion mask; the sound of water echoes that of the waterfalls on the River Swale in the valley below. The garden is rich in old roses and there are well over forty different varieties scattered throughout the garden. These are allied with evergreen shrubs to give winter interest, including many specimens of variegated holly, yew and box. The skilful underplanting never feels contrived, just natural and generous. This delightful garden, like York Gate at Adel near Leeds (see entry in S. & W. Yorkshire), is a wonderful education in the art of handling a small restricted space.

NAWTON TOWER ★

Mrs Sylvia Ward

Highfield Lane, Nawton, York YO62 7TU. Tel: (01439) 771218

14.5m E of Thirsk, 2.5m NE of Helmsley, off A170. In Nawton and Beadlam, turn left up Highfield Lane for 2m

Open 26th April to 26th May, Sat, Sun and Bank Holiday Mons, 2 – 6pm; and in spring by appt

Entrance: £1.50, children 75p

This remarkable, atmospheric 12-acre garden on the edge of the North York Moors was created during the 1930s by the Earl of Feversham. It consists of a series of formal grassy walks between living tapestries woven from a masterly selection of trees, rhododendrons, azaleas and old shrub roses, underplanted by drifts of bluebells and other spring bulbs. Every junction from the central walk leads to a fresh surprise: a statue on a pedimented gazebo as the focal point of another pathway; a yew-hedged topiary garden; a quiet contemplative clearing with a silent stone fountain at its centre.

NESS HALL

Mr and Mrs D. Murray Wells

East Ness, Nunnington, Helmsley YO62 5XD. Tel: (01439) 748223

22m N of York, 6m E of Helmsley

Open for NGS, and by appt

Entrance: £3

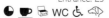

Since 1290 only three families have owned Ness Hall, which in its present guise is an early-nineteenth-century house bedecked with climbing roses. An undulating yew hedge separates the house lawn from the surrounding countryside. Within the three acres here, sweeping borders lead through a sequence of gates to the walled garden, and around the forecourt to the orchard, where a cherry tree is festooned with a wonderful 'Bobby James' rose. Set on a slight slope, the walled garden is quartered in the usual manner – one is a tennis court, another has more natural planting. The sundial lawn is flanked by scree beds planted with shrubs and alpines, its simplicity in marked contrast to the summerhouse garden, which is a riot of colour and texture with drifts of *Nepeta* 'Six Hills Giant' leading the visitor on to a welcoming seat. The main axial walk has skilfully designed double borders with a yellow and blue colour scheme, while beyond the central pool, encircled by yew hedges, is a pergola planted with climbing roses strewn with lavender at their feet. Unusually, the garden has been planned so there is much to see late in the season.

NEWBY HALL AND GARDENS ★★
(Historic Garden Grade II*)

In 1697 Celia Fiennes described Newby as 'the finest house I saw in Yorkshire'. Some three centuries later she would have no cause to change her opinion – greatly enriched after 1766 by Robert Adam and Thomas Chippendale, it is indeed exceptional. The 25-acre garden we see today is mostly the work of Major Edward Compton, who inherited the property in 1921. He swept away most of the Victorian features and seems to have had a fine eye for proportion and perspective; he was also a patient man, planting hedges and shelter belts. Grassing over some Victorian parterres on the south front, he created a pair of grand herbaceous borders more than 200 metres long, backed by yew hedges and leading down towards the River Ure. They remain Newby's most famous feature and are a magnificent sight at the height of the season. On either side of a broad cross-axis known as the Statue Walk is a series of enclosed gardens, each with a different theme and planting style. A formal rose garden, filled with old-fashioned roses and herbaceous plantings, is flanked by an autumn garden that brings the gardening year to a rich and fiery finale. Nearer to the house the large enclosed garden known as Sylvia's Garden was formerly brought to a peak in time for the York races in May, but it has a longer season now. Elsewhere a curving pergola festooned with laburnum leads down to an enormous rock garden built by the Backhouses of York and resplendent with an aqueduct and waterfall. In the more naturalistic areas off the two axis walks are extensive plantings of trees and shrubs. The garden also contains a National Collection of cornus and is rich in rhododendrons and magnolias. There is also a well-stocked plant centre.

PARCEVALL HALL GARDENS ★
(Historic Garden Grade II)

Purchased in 1926 by Sir William Milner Bt., a godson of Queen Mary, the 0.25-acre garden is set on a steep hillside with a glorious view to a craggy distant peak known as 'Simon's Seat'. Broad graceful terraces follow the slope, and the whole composition is strongly in the Arts and Crafts tradition, respecting local vernacular style. The planting has been sympathetically renovated and includes a border of

Richard Compton

Ripon, North Yorkshire HG4 5AE.
Tel: (0845) 450 4068;
www.newbyhall.com

4m SE of Ripon on B6265, 3m W of A1

Open 31st March to June, Sept,
Tues – Sun and Bank Holiday Mons;
July and Aug, daily; all 11am – 5.30pm

Entrance: £7, OAPs £6, children £5.50
(house and gardens £9.50, OAPs £8.50,
children £6.60) (2007 prices)

Other information: Wheelchairs
available

Walsingham College
(Yorkshire Properties) Ltd

Skyreholme, Skipton, North Yorkshire
BD23 6DE.
Tel: (01756) 720311;
www.parcevallhallgardens.co.uk

10m NE of Skipton, 1m NE of
Appletreewick off B6265
Pateley Bridge – Skipton road

Open 21st March to Oct, daily, 10am – 6pm; and in winter by appt

Entrance: £5.75, concessions £4.75, children £2.75

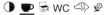

hardy fuchsias, a white border and two fine *Prunus* x *yedoensis*. A newly planted orchard containing old late-flowering apple varieties flanks the red borders which form the finale. The garden and its environs lie on the South Craven Fault, so above the house a magnificent rock garden was created by stripping away the thin soil to expose the bedrock. The result, set within light woodland and bisected by small streams, is spectacular. Masses of Himalayan poppies enjoy the dappled shade, while in summer the air is rich with the scent of the *Primula florindae* naturalised among the rocks and little rills. Below, a rose garden said to be based on a traditional Mogul design has been replanted with modern English varieties. A camellia walk leads back down the hill towards the beck, where the acid soil is ideal for rhododendrons, many unique to the garden. Set within the Dales National Park, with only the call of the curlew to be heard, such an utterly peaceful place with so glorious a view deserves to be much better known.

Royal Horticultural Society

Crag Lane, Harrogate, North Yorkshire HG3 1QB. Tel: (01423) 565418; www.rhs.org.uk/harlowcarr

1.5m W of Harrogate on B6162 Otley road

Open all year, daily except 25th Dec, 9.30am – 6pm (closes 4pm Nov to March) (last entry 1 hour before closing)

Entrance: £6.50, accompanied children (6–16) £2.20, under 6 free

Other information: Wheelchairs for loan. Guide dogs only

RHS GARDEN HARLOW CARR ★

Acquired by the RHS in 2001, Harlow Carr had been the home of the Northern Horticultural Society since 1949. The beautifully planted streamside, criss-crossed by numerous

RHS Garden Harlow Carr

picturesque 'packhorse' bridges, is still an object lesson in such planting and justly famous for its wonderful strain of candelabra primulas. From the lake a magnificent avenue rolls through the woodland and into the arboretum, passing a broad wildflower meadow and bird hide. Elsewhere are display gardens, including a large herb garden, a shrub rose walk, a scented garden and a border of ornamental grasses. A kitchen garden has been created using the raised-bed system, separated from the neighbouring winter walk by modern herbaceous borders, and during the summer of 2005 the old long walk, leading from the former entrance gates to the streamside, was replanted with perennials in the fashionable prairie style. To celebrate the RHS bicentenary in 2004, the BBC commissioned a landmark gardening series, 'Gardens through Time'. Seven gardens were created exploring fashions and tastes from the Regency period through to the present day. With 58 acres, Harlow Carr may not be as extensive as its southern sister Wisley, but in its position and diversity it more than holds its own. It also has the benefit of a plant centre stocking a wide range of plants that reflects those to be seen in the garden – alpines, roses, herbaceous perennials, shrubs for particular situations, and shade-lovers in a new shade house.

RIEVAULX TERRACE ★
(Historic Park Grade I)

This is a unique example of the eighteenth-century passion for the romantic and the picturesque – that is, making landscape look like a picture. The work was done at the behest of the third Thomas Duncombe around 1754 and consists of a half-mile-long serpentine grass terrace high above Ryedale with views of the great ruins of one of the finest of all of Britain's Cistercian abbeys. At one end is a Palladian Ionic temple-cum-banqueting-house with furniture by William Kent and elaborate ceilings, at the other a Tuscan temple with a raised platform and splendid views to the Rye Valley. The concept is wonderfully achieved, its beauty breathtaking. Those who want to see flowers must concentrate their attention on the grass bank below the terrace, which is managed for wildflower content – fine displays of cowslips, primroses, orchids, violets, bird's foot trefoil, ladies' bedstraw, etc. Blossom throughout the spring season comes from cherries, blackthorns, rowans, whitebeams, elders and lilacs.

The National Trust

Rievaulx, Helmsley, North Yorkshire YO6 5LJ. Tel: (01439) 798340; www.nationaltrust.org.uk

10m E of Thirsk, 2.5m NW of Helmsley on B1257

Open 15th March to 2nd Nov, daily, 10am – 6pm (closes 5pm Oct) (last admission 1 hour before closing). Ionic temple closed 1 – 2pm

Entrance: £4.80, children £2.60, family £12

Other information: Possible for wheelchairs but steps to temples. Electric runaround and manual wheelchair available for pre-booking. Exhibition of landscape design in basement of Ionic temple

SCAMPSTON HALL ★★
(Historic Park and Garden Grade II*)

The 70 acres of gardens and park were originally laid out by Charles Bridgeman, although they were much altered later in the eighteenth century by 'Capability' Brown, who built the unusual Ionic 'bridge building' in 1772 to terminate a vista at

Sir Charles and Lady Legard

Malton YO17 8NG.
Tel: (01944) 759111;
www.scampston.co.uk

5m E of Malton off A64

Scampston Hall

House and surrounding gardens open 23rd May to 22nd June, daily except Mon (but open Bank Holiday Mon), 1.30 – 5pm (last entry 4pm)

Walled Garden open 22nd March to 2nd Nov, daily except Mon (but open Bank Holiday Mons), 10am – 5pm. Also open for parties of 20 or more, and for garden tours by appt

Entrance: £5, concessions £4.50, children (12–16) £3

the end of the lake. The large rock garden, built in 1890 by W. H. St Quintin and recently restored, looks at its best in May and June. In 1998 the Dutch landscape designer Piet Oudolf, a leading figure in the 'new wave planting' movement, was commissioned to produce a scheme for the almost-derelict 4.5-acre walled garden. He came up with an imaginative modern design, creating a series of rooms each with a distinct character. Running the length of the perimeter wall is a border planted with spring-flowering shrubs and perennials underplanted by bulbs and autumn-flowering hydrangeas. The first space encountered is called Drifts of Grasses, with swathes of molinia – over 6000 plants – alternating with mown turf to create waves of purple spikelets in August. To the north lies a cut-flower garden laid out as a series of circular beds, while to the south is the Silent Garden, where an army of yew pillars three metres tall guards a large square reflecting pool. Around the old dipping pool and conservatory, a perennial meadow demonstrates Oudolf's skill at naturalised planting, using colour, texture and form to give a long season of interest. A grove of katsuras (*Cercidiphyllum japonicum*) underplanted with woodlanders acts as a backdrop and foil to the meadow plantings, the dappled shade being in marked contrast to the bright sunlight elsewhere. Beyond the Summer Box Garden – huge three-metre cubes of box – lies the Serpentine Garden, echoing the waves of Drifts of Grasses but using undulating two-metre-high walls of yew, backed by broad shrub borders. Across a beech *allée* set in a cherry orchard and surrounded by wild flowers is the Mount. Resembling an Aztec pyramid, it provides a superb vantage point from which to survey the whole garden and affords long views into the park. Outstanding.

Dr and Mrs O. James

Fadmoor, Kirbymoorside, North Yorkshire YO62 7JG. Tel: (01751) 431942; www.shdcottages.co.uk

SLEIGHTHOLME DALE LODGE

The three-acre garden occupies a unique position on the side of a wooded valley opening onto the moors. In the spring it is a blaze of blossom, wild daffodils and azaleas, and through the summer the walled garden, which runs steeply up the hill to the north, is breathtaking in the colour and exuberance of its parallel borders. It has been described as 'a gardeners' garden' and there are many rare plants to be seen, notably meconopsis. Descending terraces, built at the beginning of the century to the south of the house, have deep shrubberies, and a grass platform at the bottom separated from the meadow beyond by a ha-ha. A fine series of steps runs down through the terraces.

20m NE of Thirsk, 3m N of Kirbymoorside off A170

Open for NGS and NHS, and by appt in writing

Entrance: £3, children free

Other information: Self-catering accommodation available

STILLINGFLEET LODGE ★

This charming and imaginative two-acre garden has developed gradually since 1974 on a windswept plot sloping down to the River Fleet. The modest house is surrounded by small, intimate spaces planted with great skill and knowledge, each based upon a colour theme but with an emphasis on foliage and form. It is also a garden full of surprises. Beyond a simple country hedge the scale is larger and bolder with an avenue of rowans flanked on either side by long double borders – one part in shade, the other in full sun. A few carefully selected shrubs provide structure, but it is the herbaceous perennials, grouped tellingly together, that make the most impact. Beyond again is a meadow, recently doubled in size, planted with a collection of specimen trees and species roses chosen both for their flowers and hips. Enveloped by naturalistic plantings, the pond sits comfortably with the meadow and leads into a play area complete with swings and climbing frame and a chicken run occupied by an interesting collection of rare breeds. More recently a modern interpretation of a rill garden has been created, its simplicity in marked contrast to the luxuriant planting all around. The whole garden is rich in unusual herbaceous plants and has a particularly fine collection of hardy geraniums and pulmonarias, while the small nursery is stocked with a collection of interesting plants.

Mr and Mrs J. Cook

Stillingfleet, York YO19 6HP.
Tel: (01904) 728506;
www.stillingfleetlodgenurseries.co.uk

6m S of York. From A19 York – Selby road take B1222 signed to Sherburn in Elmet. In Stillingfleet turn opposite church; garden is at end of lane

Open 16th April to Sept, Wed, Fri and 1st and 3rd Sats each month (closed Sats in Aug), 1 – 5pm

Entrance: £4, children (5–16) 50p

Other information: Plant sales only available when garden open

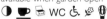

STUDLEY ROYAL AND FOUNTAINS ABBEY ★★

(Historic Park Grade I)

The gardens of Studley Royal were created by John Aislabie, who had been Chancellor of the Exchequer but whose career was ended by his involvement with the South Sea Bubble in 1720; he retreated to his estate in 1722 and worked until his death in 1742 to make the finest water garden in the country. The lakes, formal canals and water features, with buildings such as the Temple of Piety, turned what is essentially a landscape with large trees and sweeping lawns into one of the most beautiful green gardens in the world. The views from Colen Campbell's Banqueting House are remarkable. Then there is its intimate and dramatic relationship with Fountains Abbey – probably the noblest monastic ruin in Christendom

The National Trust

Ripon, North Yorkshire HG4 3DY.
Tel: (01765) 608888;
www.fountainsabbey.org.uk

4m SW of Ripon, 9m N of Harrogate. Follow Fountains Abbey sign off B6265 Ripon – Pateley Bridge road

Abbey and garden open all year, daily, 10am – 5pm (closes 4pm Nov to Feb). Closed Nov, Dec and Jan, Fri, plus 24th and 25th Dec. Deer park open all year, during daylight hours

Entrance: Park free. Abbey and garden £7.90, children £4.20, family £20.90

Studley Royal

Other information: Parking free at main visitor centre car park but £3 at Studley Park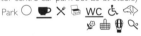

– visible at first only distantly from the Surprise View, a door in a small building. Studley Royal Park is deservedly a World Heritage Site. Restoration of Anne Boleyn's seat, a timber gazebo with a fine view, is now complete, and a further £10 million is being sought to continue a major programme of restoration. 880 acres.

Sir Reginald and Lady Sheffield

SUTTON PARK ★

Sutton-in-the-Forest, York YO61 1DP.
Tel: (01347) 810249/811239;
www.statelyhome.co.uk.

8m N of York on B1363

House open as garden but Sun, Wed, and Bank Holiday Mons only, and for parties by appt at other times

Gardens open Easter to Sept, daily, 11am – 5pm

Entrance: £3.50, concessions £3, children £1.50 (house and gardens £6.50, concessions £5.50, children £4)

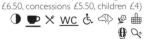

Moving reluctantly from Normanby Hall (see entry in Lincolnshire) in 1962, Nancie Sheffield, herself a keen and knowledgeable gardener, engaged Percy Cane to help redesign her new garden. They set about enclosing part of the 72-acre park laid out in the 1750s by Adam Meikle, a follower of 'Capability' Brown, and planted three terraces, each with a distinct and different character. Large panels of lawn and crisp paving characterise the topmost one, flanked by borders filled with shrubs, old roses and herbaceous perennials, with a wisteria tumbling out of a large old conifer. Broad steps lead on down past a fine Judas tree to a narrower terrace with a double parterre punctuated by eight weeping pears clipped to resemble silvery green umbrellas. On the lowest terrace a beech hedge marks the boundary while a magnificent cedar of Lebanon gives an air of instant maturity. This terrace became a water garden with a stone-edged canal pool characteristic of Cane's work; a pair of white painted wirework gazebos festooned with roses act as full stops at either end. To the west the garden becomes more natural. An old Edwardian rock garden is being developed as a fernery, and beyond some fine old trees stretches a long low laburnum walk. Since 1997 the garden has been developed further by the present generation, and the old walled kitchen garden is now a wildflower maze, with a smaller organic kitchen garden created in its stead.

THORP PERROW ARBORETUM AND WOODLAND GARDEN ★
(Historic Arboretum Grade II)

The arboretum was established many years ago and has one of the finest collections of trees in England, containing over 2000 species. Within the 85 acres is a Victorian pinetum, sixteenth-century woodland and National Collections of ash, limes, laburnums and walnuts. You can follow the tree trail, the nature trail or simply amble at your own leisure. Thousands of naturalised daffodils and bluebells in spring, glorious wild flowers in summer and stunning autumn colour. There are new plantings, a new one-acre bog garden with raised walkway, and continual improvements in the arboretum. Falconry demonstrations and children's play area.

Sir John Ropner, Bt
Bedale, North Yorkshire DL8 2PR.
Tel: (01677) 425323;
www.thorpperrow.com
10m N of Ripon, 2m S of Bedale, signed off B6268 Masham road
Open all year, daily, dawn – dusk
Entrance: £6.10, concessions £4.80, children (4–16) £3.30, family £18
Other information: Electric wheelchair available. Tea room open mid-Feb to mid-Nov, thereafter weekends only

VALLEY GARDENS ★
(Historic Public Park Grade II)

One of the best-known public gardens in the north of England, laid out earlier this century at the time Harrogate was fashionable as a spa. The Sun Pavilion has been restored, the standard of formal bedding remains high, and the dahlia border gives a fine display in late summer. Children will enjoy the range of activities on offer – paddling and boating pools, a play area, tennis courts, a pitch-and-putt course and crazy golf.

Harrogate Borough Council
Valley Drive, Harrogate, North Yorkshire.
Tel: (01423) 500600; www.harrogate.gov.uk
In centre of Harrogate; main entrance near Pump Room Museum and Mercer Art Gallery
Open all year, daily during daylight hours
Entrance: free
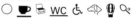

WYTHERSTONE GARDENS

An expanding and enchanting plantsman's garden of eight acres created from a greenfield site since 1970, with a wide range of rare shrubs, trees and perennials not normally considered hardy in the north of England, such as *Melianthus major*, thriving and flowering year after year. It consists of a series of garden rooms, interlinked so that the whole is revealed little by little. The spring garden is a riot of colour with azaleas, rhododendrons, meconopsis, trilliums and other ericaceous plants. This leads into a Mediterranean garden and a small rock garden, home to some rather rare alpines. The front of the house is covered in pineapple brooms and carpenterias. Behind the tall beech hedges are smaller spaces, each with its own individual feel. A pathway meanders along a large terrace made of railway sleepers up to a secret doorway; beyond lie a young arboretum that includes a newly planted *Wollemia nobilis*, a unique species of pine discovered in the Wollemy Park north of Sydney in 1994, and a wildlife pond. Steps flanked by peony borders lead to the colour-themed and highly scented conservatory garden where roses threaten to smother the trees. Two Chinese peony borders and a small fernery were laid out in 2006.

Lady Clarissa Collin
Pockley, Nr Helmsley, York YO62 7TE.
Tel: (01439) 770012;
www.wytherstonegardens.co.uk
15m E of Thirsk, 2.5m NE of Helmsley off A170. In Pockley, past church
Open for NGS, and for parties by appt
Entrance: £3.50, children (6-16) £1

OTHER RECOMMENDED GARDENS

ARDEN HALL

The Earl and Countess of Mexborough, Hawnby,
York YO62 5LS (01439 798396). Open two or three
times a year for charity, and for suitably interested
parties by appt – telephone for details

Tulips, foxgloves and sweet rocket are informally
planted in the formal terraced gardens
dominated by an ancient and massive yew
hedge, with water features fed by a natural
spring. A fabulous 80-foot-long laburnum tunnel,
splendid herbaceous borders and a wildflower-
rich valley make May and June a fine time to
visit. 2 acres.

BURNBY HALL GARDENS AND MUSEUM

33 The Balk, Pocklington, East Riding YO42 2QF
(01759 307125; www.burnbyhallgardens.com).
Open April to Sept, daily, 10am – 6pm

When it was first established in 1904, the
8-acre garden included 2 acres of fishing lakes,
which were converted in 1935 to water-lily
cultivation on a considerable scale. At their peak
in July and August they are a spectacular sight,
covered in blooms from 80 different varieties
including a National Collection of hardy
water lilies.

HACKFALL WOOD

Grewelthorpe (01476 581135). Open all year, daily,
during daylight hours

Set in a spectacular gorge cut out by the River
Ure, the 117-acre romantic woodland garden
was laid out by William Aislabie in the mid-18th
century. Paths wind beneath tall native trees
through undergrowth massed with wild garlic,
bluebells and ferns to a pool, a grotto and a
number of Arcadian ruins. (Listed Grade I)

HELMSLEY WALLED GARDEN

Cleveland Way, Helmsley YO62 5AH (01439 771427;
www.helmsleywalledgarden.org.uk). Open April to
Oct, daily, 10.30am – 5pm

The 5-acre walled garden lying beneath the
walls of Helmsley Castle is an appealing and
edifying mixture of demonstration, show and
ornamental gardens, and dedicated to
horticultural therapy. The walls are thickly
clothed with clematis, for it is the national
display garden of the British Clematis Society.

MOUNT GRACE PRIORY

Staddle Bridge, Northallerton DL6 3JG
(01609 883494). Open April to Sept, Thurs – Mon,
10am – 6pm; Oct to March, Thurs – Sun, 10am – 4pm.
Closed 25th and 26th Dec and 1st Jan

The gardens here reflect the time-span –
medieval, 17th-century, Arts and Crafts – of the
priory buildings. Thus a cell-garden has a design
of paths and herb-filled raised beds, there are
shrubberies, borders and specimen trees, and
an Edwardian garden has been laid out in
stepped terraces spilling with rock plants.

NORTON CONYERS

Sir James and Lady Graham, Wath, Nr Ripon HG4 5EQ
(01765 640333). Open 3rd June to 11th Aug, Sun and
Mon; 2nd to 5th July, daily; all 2 – 5pm. Also open Bank
Holiday Suns and Mons except Easter

Charlotte Brontë modelled Thornfield Hall in
Jane Eyre on the ancient house and Charles I
played bowls on the green. The sense of
historical continuity is palpable in all its
elements: a sweeping ha-ha dividing the broad
terrace from the park, an 18th-century walled
garden with an orangery and deep herbaceous
borders filled with traditional plants. 4 acres.
(Listed Grade II)

ORMESBY HALL

Ormesby, Middlesborough TS7 9AS (01642 324188).
Open 15th March to Oct, Sat, Sun and Bank Holiday
Mons, 1.30 – 5pm

An unostentatious 5-acre garden of lawns,
broad gravel paths and specimen trees,
accompany traditional, colourful planting in beds
and on terraces. Yews, Portugal laurels and a
holly walk add shelter and gravitas, and the walls
of the sober Palladian-style house are thickly
draped in climbers.

PLUMPTON ROCKS

Edward de Plumpton Hunter, Plumpton,
Knaresborough HG5 8NA (01289 386360;
www.plumptonrocks.co.uk). Open March to Oct,
Sat, Sun and Bank Holiday Mons, 11am – 6pm

A dramatic natural feature – a massive outcrop
of reddish-purple rocks – enhanced by man.
Or rather one man, Daniel Lascelles, who in
the mid-18th century laid out his wonderful
pleasure grounds with 2000 mixed trees,

flowering shrubs and evergreens. Painted by Turner, they survive to this day. 30 acres, including woodland. (Listed Grade II*)

RICHMOND CASTLE (THE COCKPIT GARDEN)

Richmond DL10 4QW (01748 822493). Open all year, Thurs to Mon (daily in Aug), 10am – 5pm (closes 4pm Oct to March). Closed 24th to 26th Dec and 1st Jan

A masterly contemporary garden created within an historic space by Neil Swanson. Laid out on grass terraces sloping down towards the river is an unusual topiary garden of yew circles set in gravel, with a thoroughly modern herbaceous border below. Hedges divide and shelter, and the outer bailey wall is thickly planted with shrubs.

RIPLEY CASTLE

Sir Thomas Ingilby Bt, Ripley, Harrogate HG3 3AY (01423 770152; www.ripleycastle.co.uk). Open all year, daily, 9am – 5pm

This is the restoration success story of a 100 acre 'Capability Brown' landscape, its 4-acre formal garden and its 8-acre pleasure grounds. To the enjoyment of lakeside and woodland walks among ancient trees and spring bulbs (including a National Collection of hyacinths) must be added spectacular long herbaceous borders, rare vegetables, and tropical plants in the listed greenhouses. (Listed Grade II)

SHANDY HALL

Coxwold, York YO61 4AD (01347 868465). Open May to Sept, daily except Sat, 11am – 4.30pm

A 2-acre garden full of year-round interest surrounds the pretty 15th-century cottage in which Laurence Sterne wrote *Tristram Shandy*. It is tripartite: an enclosed room with a view towards Byland Abbey and the moors; raised beds of old-fashioned roses and herbaceous plants; a tree-fringed quarry garden, filled with wild flowers and wildlife. Delightful.

SLEDMERE

Sir Tatton Sykes, Bt, Sledmere, Great Driffield, East Riding YO25 3XG (01377 236637). Open 27th April to Sept, Tues – Thurs and Sun (plus June to Aug, Fri), all 10.30am – 5pm. Also open Easter period and Bank Holiday weekends

Dating from the 1770s, this is one of 'Capability' Brown's best-preserved landscape schemes, revealing his characteristic belting and clumping of trees and diagonal vistas to distant eye-catchers, with extensive tree-planted lawns sweeping across a ha-ha up to the house walls. A well-stocked border, a parterre and an 18th-century walled garden filled with roses and herbaceous plants broaden the appeal. (Listed Grade I)

SWINTON PARK

Masham, Ripon HG4 4JH (01765 680900; www.swintonpark.com). Open all year to hotel guests.

Most of the 200-acre park and landscape created in the middle of the 18th century in the Picturesque style, and set in fine country, lies some distance from the house. Nearer to hand is a spring garden planted with a good collection of rhododendrons and azaleas, an old walled garden and a Gothic orangery, now a romantic ruin. Colour and interest here from May through to September. (Listed Grade II)

YORKSHIRE LAVENDER AND HOWARDIAN HERBS

Terrington, York YO60 6PB (01653 648008; www.yorkshirelavender.co.uk). Open 15th March to 2nd Oct, daily, 10am – 5pm

A colourful display of various lavenders, grown on an exposed hillside with glorious views over the Vale of York; many are for sale in the nursery. A Mediterranean dry garden leads to a lavender maze. 60 acres.

YORKSHIRE (S. & W. AREA)

For further information about how to use the *Guide*
and for an explanation of the symbols, see pages vi–viii.
Specific dates and times are those given to us by garden owners for 2008.
For 2009 dates, check with the individual properties.
For opening dates under the National Gardens Scheme,
readers should consult *The Yellow Book* or www.ngs.org.uk.
Maps are to be found at the end of the *Guide*.

BRAMHAM PARK ★

G. Lane Fox

Wetherby LS23 6ND.
Tel: (01937) 846000;
www.bramhampark.co.uk

10m NE of Leeds, 15m SW of York,
5m S of Wetherby, just off
northbound A1

House open for parties of 10 or more
by written appt

Garden open April to Sept, daily,
10.30am – 4.30pm (closed for horse
trials and Leeds festival; please
telephone for dates)

Entrance: £4, OAPs and children £2,
under 5 free (2007 prices)

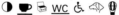

(Historic Park Grade I)

Together with St. Paul's Walden Bury in Hertfordshire (see entry), Bramham is an almost unique survival of an early formal landscape garden. Created by Robert Benson (later Lord Bingley) both house and garden seem to have been completed by 1710. Near the house is a formal parterre and rose garden, with a broad herbaceous border flanking one of the avenues leading down to the obelisk ponds and cascades. These water features and broad avenues are what make Bramham so unique. The formal grounds run to over 70 acres, bounded by a ha-ha with view points into the surrounding park (a further 900 acres) at the culmination of avenues cut through the woodland or hedge-lined *allées*, very much in the French formal manner after André Le Nôtre. Many of the buildings which adorn this remarkable landscape are the work of James Paine and date from the 1740s and '50s, commissioned by Harriet Benson, Lord Bingley's daughter. To compare a plan of the garden made in 1728 by John Wood the Elder of Bath with a plan of today makes the visitor realize just how little has changed. A unique landscape.

EAST RIDDLESDEN HALL

The National Trust

Bradford Road, Riddlesden, Bradford
BD20 5EL. Tel: (01535) 607075;
www.nationaltrust.org.uk

1m NE of Keighley off B6265, 3m
NW of Bingley

House open

Garden open 15th March to 2nd Nov,
Mon – Wed, Sat and Sun, 12 noon – 5pm.
Also open Good Fri and Bank Holiday
Mons

Entrance: £4.50, accompanied children
£2.25, family £10

Other information: Parties must pre-book

Set on a promontory overlooking the River Aire, there has been a dwelling on the site since at least AD680. The oldest parts of the present house date from the thirteenth century, although it was 'modernised' in 1640 and a later eighteenth-century west wing was partially demolished in 1905. Seen across the small lake, the house with its large rose window presents a particularly romantic prospect. The garden on the south face was laid out in the 1970s by the late Graham Stuart Thomas, with a simple holly hedge partly enclosing the site and pyramidal fruit trees lining a central path. A sunken rose garden wraps around the surviving west facade, and the ghostly outline of the whole wing has been traced by a chequered pattern of standard acacias planted on a strip of lawn. Further west still an old orchard containing a number of old varieties of apple traditional to Yorkshire gardens is being

406

developed as a wild garden in homage to William Robinson and Gertrude Jekyll. A fragrant medicinal herb border based on Culpeper's *Herbal* lies at the foot of the east front of the house, overlooking a grass maze and picnic area in the meadow beside the riverbank. 50 acres in all.

FIRVALE ALLOTMENT

What have the Oxford Botanical Gardens and a 230-square-metre allotment on the edge of Rotherham in common? Well, between them they hold the National Collection of euphorbias. As is the way with allotment holders, Don Witton used to grow vegetables before an obsession with herbaceous perennials took hold; now most of his growing space is devoted to them. The plants are grown in informal beds divided by slate paths, mingled with a great range of other perennials: ajugas, astrantias, hostas, phlox, sedums, pulmonarias and lychnis. Where Oxford concentrates more on the species euphorbias, Don has over half his collection in hybrid forms – over 140 of them, ranging from the giant *E. x pasteurii*, over 2 metres high, to *E. capitulata* from the Balkan Mountains, just 10cm. He favours *E. polychroma* 'Midas' for the brightness of its flowers, and also has some lovely variegated forms such as *E. characias* 'Silver Swan'. Indeed it is the variety offered by this genus in colour, shape and habit that make so many of them ideal garden plants.

Don Witton

26 Casson Drive, Harthill, Sheffield S26 7WA. Tel: (01909) 771366; www.euphorbias.co.uk

Between A57 and A619. 3 miles NE of M1 junction 30. Allotment is at S end of Harthill village

Open 4th May, 1 – 4pm, and March to July by appt

Entrance: Donation to NCCPG

Other information: No unaccompanied visitors permitted on the allotment

 WC

Firvale Allotment

Leeds City Council

Otley Road, Leeds.
Tel: (0113) 2610374

NW of Leeds off A660 Leeds – Otley
road at approach to Bramhope

Open all year, daily, during daylight hours

Entrance: free

GOLDEN ACRE PARK ★

A privately owned pleasure park until 1945, this has been developed as one of the city's finest public parks, transformed with a wide range of different gardens – limestone, sandstone, courtyard, heather, water and bog – and borders for both spring and late-season interest. The pleasantly undulating site, well provided with trees, leads down to a lake, and at the heart of the park are demonstration gardens that follow horticultural trends and provide visitors with inspiration and ideas for their own gardens. Each one is devoted to a different theme, ranging from wildflower, tropical and prairie plantings to formal, pottage, container and basket plots. The Chrysanthemum and Dahlia Societies exhibit, and several National Collections, including syringa, hemerocallis and large-leaved hostas, are held here. 137 acres.

Harewood House Trust

Harewood, Leeds LS17 9LG
Tel: (0113) 218 1010
www.harewood.org

7m N of Leeds on A61

House open

Grounds open March to Oct, daily;
Nov to mid-Dec, Sat and Sun;
all 10am – 4pm

Entrance: Grounds and bird garden
£8.80, OAPs £7.95, children £5.90 (rates
increase during peak period)

Other information: Regular garden tours
and talks programme

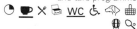

HAREWOOD HOUSE ★

(Historic Park and Garden Grade I)

In 1772 'Capability' Brown was commissioned to 'improve' the park surrounding a new mansion built by Carr of York. The natural terrain was much in his favour, and his refashioned landscape, described as 'most delectable' by Dorothy Stroud, was painted by Turner. He would still recognise the park, but the house was Italianised in 1843 by Sir Charles Barry, who also laid out a broad terrace. His elaborate box parterre with its mile of hedging has been restored and planted with blue hyacinths in spring and heliotropes in summer – the effect against the yellow-tinged stone of the house and walls is quite stunning. A broad herbaceous border, mixing perennial and tender plants as in Victorian days, continues the soft pastel colour scheme. On the upper west terrace a simple and sophisticated modern garden was laid out by David Hicks in 1993, with hornbeam hedging reflecting the massive bulk of the house centred around a terracotta dolphin fountain. Beneath the bastion wall, as a contrast to the cool subtle

Harewood
House

colours directly round the house, lies another border planted with hot colours, using many tender subjects not readily associated with Yorkshire gardens. Behind Carr's stable block lies the famous Bird Garden, where the geographical zones are defined by plants; this leads on to a woodland garden densely planted in the nineteenth century with a fine collection of rhododendrons. At the head of the lake is the Himalayan garden, a sunken glade originally laid out in the 1770s and now graced by a *stupa*, a Buddhist memorial shrine built of local stone under the supervision of a Bhutanese lama. With the installation in 1999 of a spiral labyrinth in the old walled garden, the family's interest in developing the grounds clearly continues unabated.

THE HOLLIES PARK ★

The original layout is Victorian, and the gardens were given to Leeds Corporation in 1921 by the Brown family in memory of a son killed during World War I. The fine informal, largely woodland garden features woody plants, especially rhododendrons. Ferns flourish throughout the gardens and a varied collection of hydrangeas provides late summer colour. Many slightly tender subjects thrive in the pleasant microclimate. Several National Collections are held here, including those of hemerocallis, hostas and deutzias, and probably the most comprehensive philadelphus collection in Europe.

Leeds City Council

Weetwood Lane, Leeds LS16 5NZ. Tel: (0113) 247 8361 (Parks and Countryside)

In NW Leeds, off A660 Leeds – Otley road

Open all year, daily, during daylight hours

Entrance: free

○ 🅱 WC ◁◊

LAND FARM ★

The four-acre garden created by the owners on a north-facing site high in the Pennines combines good design, excellent planting and interesting sculpture. Planted for ease of maintenance, the emphasis is on shrubs, herbaceous perennials and alpines. In the woodland garden, acers, cornus and rhododendrons have an understorey of herbaceous plants. Large banks are massed with *Cardiocrinum giganteum*, making a fantastic display in July and August with their tall and scented spires, and *Tropaeolum speciosum* runs in glorious riot through other parts of the garden. The impact of sculpture in a garden depends so much on its positioning – here it is done to perfection and at times achieves a real drama. The former barn is now an art gallery.

Mr and Mrs J. Williams

Colden, Hebden Bridge, Calderdale HA7 7PJ. Tel: (01422) 842260

3.5m NE of Todmorden, off A646 between Sowerby Bridge and Todmorden. Call at visitor centre in Hebden Bridge for map

Open May to Aug, Sat, Sun and Bank Holiday Mons, 10am – 5pm, and for parties by appt

Entrance: £4

◑ 🅱 WC ♿ ◁◊ 🌱 ▥ ⚲

SHEFFIELD BOTANICAL GARDENS

(Historic Public Park Grade II)

These historic gardens, designed by Robert Marnock in the Gardenesque style with several interesting garden buildings, opened in 1836. Today they provide residents and visitors to Sheffield with an invaluable 19-acre green lung; more importantly, they are the only botanical gardens in the UK to have undergone a major (£6.69m) facelift. The jewels in the

Sheffield Council

Sheffield S10 2LN. Tel: (0114) 267 6496; www.sbg.org.uk

0.5m from A625, 1.5m SW of city centre

Open all year, daily except 25th and 26th Dec and 1st Jan, 10am – dusk

Entrance: free

○ ☕ ✕ WC ♿ ▥ ⚱

crown – the three impressive glass pavilions with their linking glass corridors (one of the earliest curvilinear glass house complexes in the country) – have been beautifully restored and display plant collections from around the warm temperate world. An evolutionary garden shows the development of plants, the rosarium the history of the rose. National Collections of weigelas and diervillas are displayed on the main lawn, and an archive of botanical illustrations depicting plants growing in the gardens is being built up.

TROPICAL WORLD ★

(within Roundhay Park – Historic Park Grade II)

Leeds City Council

Roundhay Park, Roundhay, Leeds LS8 2ER. Tel: (0113) 266 1850; www.leeds.gov.uk

S of A6120 northern ring, off A58 Roundhay Road from city centre

Open all year, daily, except Bank Holidays, 10am – 6pm

Entrance: £3, children (8–15) £2, under-8s and Leeds card holders free (2007 prices)

Other information: Children under 16 must be accompanied

The 700-acre parkland with its fine trees and wildflower meadows is a wonderful setting for the pure horticultural extravaganza of the canal gardens with their formal bedding and generous collections. Nearby are the Monet and the Alhambra gardens. These were once the kitchen and ornamental gardens of the estate purchased in 1803 by Thomas Nicholson, who developed a ravine, landscape gardens, woodland, a lake, waterfalls and a sham castle – all the trappings of the time – before selling up to the Leeds Corporation in 1871. The exotic houses, aflutter with butterflies and birds, have the largest collection outside Kew. Waterfalls and pools are surrounded by tropical plants, and the arid house holds a large number of cacti and succulents. There is an underwater world of plants and fish, a re-created rainforest environment and a nocturnal house where bush babies, monkeys and other animals can be spotted.

WENTWORTH CASTLE GARDENS ★

(Historic Park Grade I)

Wentworth Castle and Stainborough Park Heritage Trust

Lowe Lane, Stainborough, Barnsley S75 3ET. Tel: (01226) 776040; www.wentworthcastle.org

3m SW of Barnsley off M1 junction 37, 2m along minor roads between Stainborough and Hood Green. Follow signs for Northern College

Open daily, 10am – 5pm (last admission 4pm); and for parties by appt

Entrance: Park free. Garden £3.95, concessions £3.25, children (5-16) £2. Guided tour £2 extra.

Less than an hour from Leeds and Sheffield is one of the most exciting gardens in Yorkshire – 500 acres of parkland, 60 acres of pleasure gardens, a walled garden and a three-quarter-mile-long serpentine lake, laid out mainly under the direction of Thomas Wentworth and his son William between 1708 and 1791. A £15m project, which includes a £10.3m Heritage Lottery Fund grant, is nearing completion, and visitors are encouraged to tour the garden and parkland to see this ambitious work in progress. The first phase includes the restoration of the gardens, including the Union Jack Garden, the Victorian secret garden, Stainborough Castle, and the park and woodland. The derelict home farm has been transformed into a visitor centre and cafe.

YORK GATE ★

Perennial (formerly The Gardeners' Royal Benevolent Society)

Back Church Lane, Adel, Leeds LS16 8DW. Tel: (0113) 267 8240; www.perennial.org.uk

A one-acre garden created by the Spencer family and bequeathed by the late Sybil Spencer to the Gardeners' Royal Benevolent Society. Bought by the Spencers in 1951, this was a bleak farmhouse and unpromising area of land. When her

York Gate

York Gate

husband died, her son took over the design and in a tragically short life achieved a garden of rare delight, using local stone, cobblestones and gravel to create a structure of impeccable taste and style and great horticultural interest. The late Arthur Hellyer remarked on its debt to Hidcote and commented on the clever use of architectural features and topiary. It is also a plantsman's garden, with rare and unusual plants to be discovered in a sequence of individual settings. These include an extraordinary miniature pinetum, a dell with a stream, a canal garden, fern and peony borders, a herb garden with a summerhouse, a kitchen garden and white borders. Sybil's Garden has recently been redesigned by Alistair Baldwin in a more contemporary style but using materials sympathetic to the rest of the garden.

2.25m SE of Bramhope, off A660

Open 23rd March to Sept, Thurs, Sun and Bank Holiday Mons, 2 – 5pm, and for parties by appt. Telephone for details of special evening openings in midsummer

Entrance: £3.50, children free

 WC

OTHER RECOMMENDED GARDENS

BRODSWORTH HALL

Brodsworth, Doncaster DN5 7XJ (01302 722598).
Open April to Sept, Tues – Sun and Bank Holiday
Mons, 10am – 5.30pm; Oct to March, Sat and Sun,
11am – 4pm

Neglected for 50 years, the 15-acre garden has
now been triumphantly returned to its full-
blooded Victorian persona by English Heritage,
with Italianate terraces, statues and follies, fine
rockwork bridges in the old quarry and a fern
dell with an elegant cascade, plus evergreen
shrubberies, herbaceous borders, colourful
bedding schemes and a mass of roses. (Listed
Grade II*)

HILLSBOROUGH WALLED GARDEN

Middlewood Road, Sheffield S6 4HD (0114 281 2167;
www.hcd.4t.com). Open March to Oct, daily,
9am – 4.30pm; Nov to Feb, Mon – Fri, 9am – 3pm

A wildlife area, a lawn with herbaceous borders,
a woodland glade and a formal garden with
raised beds – 2 peaceful acres, managed by
Sheffield City Council working in partnership
with the local community.

Yorkshire Sculpture Park

NOSTELL PRIORY

Doncaster Road, Nostell, Wakefield WF4 1QE
(01924 863892; www.nationaltrust.org.uk). Park open
all year, daily, 9am – 6pm (or dusk if earlier). Garden
open 9th, 10th, 16th and 17th Feb; 1st, 2nd, 9th and
10th March; 15th March to 2nd Nov, Wed to Sun and
Bank Holiday Mons; 8th to 30th Nov, Sat and Sun; all
11am – 5.30pm. Also open 5th to 14th Dec,
11am – 4.30pm. NT

The saturnine 18th-century house built by
James Paine with additions by Robert Adam sits
in open parkland with an attractive lake, a
wealth of well-established trees and several
Adam buildings. A fine rose garden and
extensive lakeside plantings of magnolias and
rhododendrons are the main garden features.
350 acres of park, 45 acres of garden. (Listed
Grade II*)

TEMPLE NEWSAM

Leeds LS15 0AD (0113 264 5535;
www.leeds.gov.uk/templenewsam). Estate open all year,
daily, dawn – dusk

Traces of 'Capability' Brown's landscape remain
in the 1500-acre parkland surrounding the
prodigy house full of treasures, and a wide
diversity of gardens, including a large walled
garden with magnificent traditional borders.
Several National Collections of favourite garden
flowers are held here. (Listed Grade II)

YORKSHIRE SCULPTURE PARK ★

West Bretton, Wakefield WF4 4LG (01924 832631;
www.ysp.co.uk). Open all year, daily except 23rd to
25th Dec, 10am – 6pm (closes 5pm in winter)

The first permanent open-air sculpture gallery
in Britain was established here in 1977, within
500 acres of formal gardens, woods, lakes and
parkland. This is sculpture in the round –
temporary and permanent, international and
own-collection.

THE REPUBLIC OF IRELAND & NORTHERN IRELAND

For further information about how to use the *Guide*
and for an explanation of the symbols, see pages vi–viii.
Specific dates and times are those given to us by garden owners for 2008.
For 2009, check with the individual properties.
Maps are to be found at the end of the *Guide*.

NORTHERN IRELAND

ANNESLEY GARDEN AND NATIONAL ARBORETUM ★

(Historic Demesne)

The walled garden contains an outstanding collection of mature trees and shrubs, planted after 1849 by the Earl Annesley. Original specimens of some of Castlewellan's cultivars thrive here, in fine condition. In the spring and summer there are many rhododendrons in bloom and scarlet Chilean fire bushes (*Embothrium coccineum*). In midsummer, a snow-carpet consists of the fallen petals of an unequalled collection of eucryphias. In all, there are 34 champion specimen trees in one area of just nine acres, including 15 southern-hemisphere broad-leaved champions; half of these specimens are also thought to be the oldest examples in cultivation. Apart from the trees there are bulbs, herbaceous borders, two restored fountain pools, topiary of Irish yew and, in summer, an impressive show of tropaeolum. Beyond the walls the arboretum extends for a further 85 acres in the Forest Park; signposted walks lead round a magnificent lake, and the Cypress Pond, where the dramatic view to the Mourne Mountains has been restored. A major piece of landscaping, the largest and longest yew-hedge maze in the world, represents the path to peace in Northern Ireland. In all, 112 acres.

Forest Service, Dept of Agriculture (Northern Ireland)

Castlewellan, Co. Down BT31 9BU.
Tel: (028) 4377 8664;
www.forestserviceni.gov.uk

25m S of Belfast, 4m NW of Newcastle, in Castlewellan

Open all year, daily, 10am – dusk

Entrance: cars £4, minibuses £10, coaches £25 (2007 prices)

Other information: Disabled parking. Refreshments in summer only. Caravan and camping ground in park

BALLYWALTER PARK

(Historic Garden)

The fine mid-nineteenth-century Italianate house by the architect Lanyon, with an elegant conservatory wing, was praised by John Betjeman. The surrounding 30-acre grounds are an amalgam of two earlier 'landscaped' demesnes, which were embellished for the present house by the creation of a rock garden around a stream crossed by bridges; Lanyon was also responsible for this scheme. The notable rhododendron

Dunleath Estates

Ballywalter, Nr Newtownards, Co. Down BT22 2PP. Tel: (028) 4275 8264;
www.ballywalterpark.com

10m SE of Newtownards off B5 between Greyabbey and Ballywalter. Turn right at T-junction facing gates and follow wall to entrance on left

Open by appt (telephone Mon – Fri, 9am – 1pm)

Entrance: house or garden £6 (house and garden £10) (2007 prices)

Belfast City Council Parks Department

Stranmillis Road, Belfast City BT7 ILP.
Tel: (028) 9032 4902;
www.belfastcity.gov.uk/parks

Between Queen's University and Ulster Museum, Stranmillis. Buses 8A, 8B and 85

Open all year, daily, 7.30am – dusk. Palm House and Tropical Ravine, summer, weekdays, 10am – 5pm, weekends and public holidays, 1 – 5pm (closes 4pm in winter). Guided tours and parties at any time by arrangement

Entrance: free. Guided tours £10

Mr and Mrs Hugh Montgomery

Ballybogey, Ballymoney, Co. Antrim BT53 6NN. Tel: (028) 2074 1331; www.benvarden.com

4m E of Coleraine off B67. Signposted

Open June to Aug, Tues – Sun and Bank Holiday Mons, 12 noon – 5pm, and by appt at other times

Entrance: £3.50, children free

The National Trust

Portaferry Road, Newtownards, Co. Down BT22 2AD. Tel: (028) 4278 8387; www.nationaltrust.org.uk

15m E of Belfast, 5m SE of Newtownards on A20 Portaferry road

House open

Lakeside gardens and walk open all year, daily, 10am – dusk. Formal garden open 8th to 30th March, Sat and Sun 10am – 4pm; April to Oct, daily, 10am – 8pm (closes 6pm April and Oct)

collection is sheltered by mature trees throughout the park. A rose pergola and seven restored glasshouses decorate the walled garden.

BELFAST BOTANIC GARDENS PARK
(Historic Park)

Established in 1828, this became a public park in 1895. As well as two magnificent double herbaceous borders and a rose garden with 8000 roses, there is another reason to visit the 14 acres here – the exceptional curvilinear iron and glass palm house (1839–52). Richard Turner built only the wings; the dome is by Young of Edinburgh, restored in the 1970s. It contains a finely displayed collection of tropical plants, while massed pot plants are changed throughout the seasons in a cooler wing. The Tropical Ravine House is an even greater delight, a perfect piece of High Victoriana with ferns, bananas, lush tropical vines and tree ferns, goldfish in the Amazon lily pond, and a waterfall worked with a chain-pull. Marvellous, evocative of crinoline days.

BENVARDEN HOUSE
(Historic Garden)

The eighteenth-century house is set in lawns where the visitor can wander along the banks of the Bush River, which is spanned at this point by an elegant Victorian iron bridge, 36 metres long. A large pond is surrounded by Irish yews and many rhododendrons, camellias and azaleas. The walled garden has a curved and brick-faced three-metre-high wall, lined with old espalier-trained apple and pear trees and focused on a round goldfish pond and fountain. Climbers scramble over the former glasshouse frames, beneath which seats are provided. The adjoining one-acre traditional kitchen garden is in full production and contains fruit trees and box hedges, melon and tomato houses, potting sheds and a gardener's bothy. In all, five acres.

MOUNT STEWART ★★
(Historic Garden)

Of all Ireland's gardens this is the one not to miss. Any adjective that evokes beauty can be applied to it, and it's fun too. In the gardens fronting the eighteenth- and nineteenth-century house is a collection of statues depicting British political and public figures as animals. The planting here is formal, with rectangular beds of hot and cool colours. Beyond in the informal gardens are mature trees and shrubs – a botanical collection with few equals, planted with great panache and maintained with outstanding attention to detail. Spires of cardiocrinums, aspiring eucalyptus, banks of rhododendrons, ferns and blue poppies, rivers of candelabra

Mount Stewart

primulas, and much more. Walk along the lakeside path to the hill that affords a view over the lake to the house. Rare tender shrubs such as *Metrosideros umbellata* from Australasia flourish here outside the walled family cemetery; leading from it is the Jubilee Avenue with its statue of a white stag. The Temple of the Winds, James 'Athenian' Stuart's banqueting hall of 1782–5, is also memorable. The garden should be seen several times during the year truly to savour its rich tapestry of plants and water, buildings and trees. 94 acres in all.

Entrance: £5.35, children £2.70, family £13.40 (house and garden £7, children £3.50, family £17.50)

Other information: Parking 300 metres away. 4 pre-bookable battery wheelchairs available

ROWALLANE GARDEN ★★
(Historic Garden)

While famous as a 52-acre rhododendron garden and certainly excellent in this regard, Rowallane has much more to interest keen gardeners. In summer, the walled garden

The National Trust

Saintfield, Ballynahinch, Co. Down BT24 7LH. Tel: (028) 9751 0131; www.nationaltrust.org.uk

0.5m S of Saintfield on A7 Belfast – Downpatrick road

Open all year, daily except 25th, 26th Dec and 1st Jan, 10am – 4pm (closes 8pm 12th April to 13th Sept)

Entrance: £4.80, children £2.40, family £12

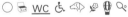

Rowallane Garden

blossoms in lemon and blue, while hoherias scatter their white petals in the wind and in secluded places a pocket-handkerchief tree blows. There is a restored Victorian bandstand (music-filled on some summer weekends) and a rock garden with primulas, meconopsis, heathers, etc. Any season will be interesting, and for the real enthusiast there are rhododendron species and cultivars in bloom from October to August. A National Collection of large-flowered penstemons is here. A feature is made of *Hypericum* 'Rowallane' at the entrance to the walled garden; within is the original plant of *Viburnum plicatum* 'Rowallane' and the original *Chaenomeles* × *superba* 'Rowallane'. The wildflower meadows are famed for such comparative rarities as wild orchids, and wildlife abounds.

Mr Patrick and Lady Anthea Forde

Downpatrick, Co. Down BT30 8PG.
Tel: (028) 4481 1225;
www.seafordegardens.com

22m S of Belfast on A24
Belfast – Newcastle road

Open March to Oct, Mon – Sat,
10am – 5pm, Sun 1 – 6pm; Nov to Feb,
Mon – Fri, 10am – 5pm.
Closed 25th Dec to 1st Jan

Entrance: £3.50, children £2.30

SEAFORDE HOUSE
(Historic Garden)

The fine landscaped park can be glimpsed on the way to the vast walled garden. Half of this is a commercial nursery with the attraction of a butterfly house which also displays a collection of tropical plants, the other half an ornamental garden bedecked in late summer with blooms of eucryphia that make up a National Collection. The hornbeam maze has a rose-clad arbour at the centre, the vantage point for which is a 1992 Mogul tower. Beyond the walled garden is the Pheasantry, a verdant valley enclosed by mature trees, full of noteworthy plants collected over many years and still expanding. 7.5 acres.

Belfast City Council

237 Upper Malone Road, Dunmurry,
Belfast BT17 9LA
Tel: (028) 906 03359/903 20202;
www.parks.belfastcity.gov.uk

S of Belfast city centre

Open all year, daily, 8am – sunset

Entrance: free

SIR THOMAS AND LADY DIXON PARK
(Historic Park)

This 128-acre park, presented to the City of Belfast in 1959, is part of a demesne established in the eighteenth century. The main feature today is the International Rose Trial area, where some 40,000 rose bushes can been seen in carefully labelled beds following the contours of the park. One display has old varieties demonstrating the history of the rose. Elsewhere there are riverside meadows by the River Lagan, a walled garden, international camellia trials and a Japanese garden. A secluded children's playground and band performances during the summer make it enjoyable for all the family.

OTHER RECOMMENDED GARDENS

ANTRIM CASTLE

Randalstown Road, Antrim, Co. Antrim BT41 4LH (028 9448 1338; www.antrim.gov.uk). Open all year, daily, 9.30am – dusk

The ornamental gardens were created in the early 18th century by the magnificently named Clotworthy Skeffington, 3rd Viscount Massereene, to complement his now-demolished castle. Canals, connected by a cascade, are lined with tall clipped hedges, paths criss-cross through a wooded wilderness, and a large parterre has been replanted with period varieties. A spiral path leads up an ancient motte to give splendid views of garden and countryside. 37 acres. (Historic Garden)

THE ARGORY

Moy, Dungannon, Co. Tyrone BT71 6NA (028 8778 4753; www.nationaltust.org.uk). Open all year, daily, 10am – 6pm (closes 4pm Oct to April). NT

From the house with its colourful summer border and enclosed rose garden, the lawns slope down past yew arbours to two pavilions, with a tranquil landscape of riverside and woodland walks opening up beyond. 5 acres. (Historic Demesne)

BROCKLAMONT HOUSE

Mrs Margaret Glynn, 2 Old Galgorm Road, Ballymena, Co. Antrim BT42 1AL (028 2564 1459). Open by appt

Mature trees and shrubs grace the lawns of this well-laid-out and well-maintained 2.5-acre town garden, and the fine collection of plants is beautifully presented throughout the year. A new woodland garden with a planted understorey combine with waterside plantings, scented and colourful mixed borders, troughs and scree beds to give ever-changing pleasure. Alpines and snowdrops are specialities.

CASTLE WARD

Strangford, Downpatrick, Co. Down BT30 7LS (028 4488 1204; www.nationaltrust.org.uk). Open all year, daily, 10am – 8pm (closes 4pm Oct to April). NT

The well-wooded 820-acre landscape park stretches out beside Strangford Lough. Impressive canal and yew walks are remnants of the early-18th-century formal garden. The sunken Windsor Garden has new colourful sub-tropical borders guarded by a sentinel row of cordylines and Florence Court yews. 40 acres. (Historic Demesne)

FLORENCE COURT

Florencecourt, Enniskillen, Co. Fermanagh BT92 1DB (028 6634 8249; www.nationaltrust.org.uk). Open all year, daily, 10am – 7pm (closes 4pm Nov to March). NT

It is worth the taking the woodland paths for the walk up from the splendid mansion to pay respects to the original, the mother of all Irish yews (*Taxus baccata* 'Fastigiata'), surviving since 1760. The 12-acre Victorian pleasure grounds have exotic trees and shrubs and a restored heather house. (Historic Demesne)

FOX LODGE

Brian Mooney, 20 Leckpatrick Road, Ballymagorry, Artigavan, Strabane, Co. Tyrone BT82 0AL (028 7188 2442). Open April to July by appt

This informal 2-acre country garden, developed and expanded since the late 1960s, can be enjoyed from daffodil time to summer. Water is everywhere present, flowing through a succession of rock-sided ponds to a bog garden lavishly filled with water-loving plants, while informal planted woodland contrasts with the ordered scree and raised peat beds for the collection of alpines, all adding to the variety of the merging but contrasting areas.

28 KILLYFADDY ROAD

Ann Buchanan, Magherafelt, Co. Londonderry BT45 6EX (028 7963 2180). Open April to Sept, Wed – Sat, 2 – 5pm, and by appt

This informal country garden of 1.2 acres is packed with every choice thing one could wish for – perennials, alpines, trees, fruit, vegetables, a small orchard and a wildlife pond and meadow. The long season of interest is reflected in its opening dates

THE REPUBLIC OF IRELAND

The GGIRP refers to The Great Gardens of Ireland Restoration Programme, initiated in 1994, which has seen the renaissance of 26 historic parks and gardens. The National Inventory of Historic Gardens and Designed Landscapes, now well underway, aims to identify sites using the first edition Ordnance Survey maps of 1833-46 and comparing these with current aerial photography to assess the level of survival and change. Visit the website on www.buildingsofireland.ie/surveys/gardens.

ALTAMONT

Office of Public Works

Tullow, Co. Carlow.
Tel: (00353) 59 91 59444;
www.heritageireland.ie

19km SE of Carlow, 8km S of Tullow,
off Tullow-Bunclody road
(N80/81) near Ballon

Open all year, daily, telephone for times

Entrance: Free; Pre-booked guided tours
€2.75, OAPs €2, students/children
€1.25, family €7

◐ 🚻 WC ⚹ 🌿 🍴

The lily-filled lake, surrounded by fine, mature trees, forms a backdrop for a gently sloping lawn; a central walkway formally planted with Irish yews and roses leads from the house to the lake. There is a beautiful fern-leaved beech, and other ancient beeches form the Nun's Walk. The passion of the late owner, Mrs Corona North, for trees, old-fashioned roses and unusual plants is evident, and the garden is kept in the spirit she intended. The walled garden has a fine double herbaceous border planted in 2000 and a nursery, *Altamont Plant Sales*, separately run by Robert Mille (Tel: (00353) 87 982 2135). A long walk through the demesne leads to the River Slaney through an Ice-Age glen of ancient oaks undercarpeted with bluebells. 40 acres.

ANNES GROVE

Mr and Mrs F. P. Grove Annesley

Castletownroche, near Mallow, Co. Cork.
Tel: (00353) 22 26145;
www.annesgrovegardens.com

2.5km N of Castletownroche, between
Fermoy and Mallow

Open 17th March to Sept, Mon – Sat,
10am – 5pm, Sun, 1 – 6pm, and at
other times by appt

Entrance: €6, concessions €4,
children €2

Other information: Self-catering
accommodation available

◐ 🚻 <u>WC</u> ⚹ ◁▷ 🌿

This is an archetypically Robinsonian wild garden. Rhododendron species and cultivars arch over and spill towards the pathways, carpeting them with fallen blossoms.

Annes Grove

Steep, sometimes slippery paths descend at various places into the valley of the Awbeg river (which inspired Edmund Spenser). Seek out the eighteenth-century pen pond at the bottom of the valley – a pond with a narrow extension once used for trapping wild duck. The statuesque conifers planted in the valley make a colourful tapestry behind the river garden, with mimulus, daylilies and candelabra primulas in profusion. The glory of the garden is, however, the collection of rhododendron species, many of them introduced through subscription to Kingdon Ward expeditions. Visitors may spot hidden surprises – a superb *Juniperus recurva* 'Castlewellan', a mature pocket-handkerchief tree (*Davidia involucrata*) and other exotic flowering trees. The small nursery specialises in woodland plants. 28 acres in all.

ARDCARRAIG ★

The oldest part of the five-acre garden is a collage of heathers and conifers, with spring and autumn-flowering bulbs; ordinary but attractive. This leads on to a formal, sunken garden, with a clematis-draped pergola and a terracotta *pithoi* as the focal point; handsome, but not unusual. The path then enters a wild hazel wood carpeted with bluebells, ramsons and ferns; nature's garden. A clearing ablaze with scented azaleas in spring and roses and geraniums in summer is the first surprise. The path winds on to a pool surrounded by blue Himalayan poppies, hostas and candelabra primulas. And on – to a bubbling peat-stained stream that chatters over granite rocks to a bog garden with heathers and skunk cabbages, to a tranquil Japanese hill and pool garden, while the boulder beyond suggests Mount Fuji. And on – to Harry's Garden, planted in memory of Lorna's late husband. The latest venture is a moss garden.

Mrs Lorna MacMahon

Oranswell, Bushypark, Co. Galway.
Tel: (00353) 91 524336

4km W of Galway city centre off N59. Oranswell turn 2km past Glenlo Abbey Hotel; house 230 metres up hill on left

Open 11th, 18th and 25th May, 2 – 6pm, and by appt

Entrance: €5

 WC

ARDGILLAN CASTLE AND GARDEN

The approach to the castle is one of the most spectacular in Ireland, with views northwards along the coast to Carlingford and the Mourne mountains, and the castle itself nestled in a hollow. Built in 1738 by the Rev. Robert Taylor, it now houses an eclectic assortment of eighteenth- and nineteenth-century furniture, and an important collection of seventeenth-century 'Down Survey' maps of Ireland. The demesne today covers about 194 acres. A fine Victorian conservatory rescued from another house forms the centrepiece of the formal rose garden. The walled garden is divided into sections, including box-edged herb and vegetable gardens, a fruit garden and ornamental gardens displaying shrubs, perennials and rock plants. Many of the beds were created recently and are not part of the original layout, but they contain some choice plants. A unique, free-standing brick wall with 20 alcoves is now planted with fruit. The gardens and demesne have been grant-aided under the GGIRP for the woodland paths, the rose garden (which

Fingal County Council Parks

Balbriggan, Co. Dublin.
Tel: (1) 849 2212 (Castle),
(1) 849 2324 (Garden)

24km N of Dublin, between Balbriggan and Skerries. Signposted off M1 and N1

Castle open all year, daily except Mon (but open Bank Holiday Mons and Mons in July and Aug). Closed 23rd Dec to 1st Jan

Garden open all year, daily, 10am – 6pm (closes winter 4.30pm). Park open all year, daily, 10am – 6pm (closes up to 9pm depending on season). Conducted tours June to Aug, Thurs, 3.30pm

Entrance: €6, groups €5 guided tours €6 (castle tours €6, concessions €3.50, family €12)

includes Edwardian and Victorian cultivars) and a small garden museum, and to provide some new plant stock to extend its collections. A National Collection of potentillas is held here. Don't miss the icehouse, a short way along the woodland walk. July is a fine time to visit.

BALLINDOOLIN HOUSE AND GARDEN

The Molony family

Carbury, via Edenderry, Co. Kildare. Tel: (00353) 46 973 1430; www.ballindoolin.com

5km N of Edenderry on R401

House open; guided tours only (extra charge)

Garden open May to July, Wed – Sun, 12 noon – 6pm, and at other times by appt

Entrance: €6, children over 5 €4

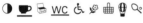

A seven-acre demesne surrounds the 1821 Georgian house, which still retains its original interior and furnishings. Some of the farmyard buildings and outhouses await repair, but the gate lodge and the two-acre walled garden have been faithfully restored under the GGIRP. Espaliered apple trees in various stages of decrepitude, which have been carefully kept and are charming, set the atmosphere, and a ruined melon-pit has also been conserved. The old borders have been replanted with a wide range of herbaceous perennials, roses and herbs, and a good range of vegetables and fruit thrives once again in the microclimate. The wonderfully preserved walls include a high, brick-lined south-facing fruit wall, which has also been replanted. Outside the walled garden a path runs past a quirky little rockery towards the unique trefoil-shaped dovecote, on to the lime kiln, the 'Iron Age' mound and the woodland walk, where a long beech avenue leads into the woods and back towards the house. A delightful place for a detour with a real flavour of the local countryside.

BALLYMALOE COOKERY SCHOOL GARDENS

Tim and Darina Allen

Kinoith, Shanagarry, Co. Cork. Tel: (00353) 21 464 6785; www.cookingisfun.ie

36km E of Cork, between Cloyne and Ballycotton

Open April to Sept, Mon – Fri, 10am – 6pm

Entrance: €5 (2006 price)

Other information: Pre-booked tours for parties available

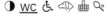

Take the bones of an old seven-acre Quaker garden and begin afresh – that is what has been done at Kinoith. The antique beech hedges are clipped again, and within their shelter are compartments, each one different and refreshing. The first is the flower garden with short herbaceous borders, and beside a small pool is a summerhouse, its floor patterned with shards of Delft. Beyond is the herb garden, where dwarf box hedges delineate a formal pattern of beds planted mainly with culinary herbs. These compartments can be enjoyed from a viewing platform. The pool garden lies outside the old hedges, and has a folly. A double herbaceous border leads to a Gothic-windowed garden house decorated with myriad shells. The organic vegetable garden appeals directly to the eye with its tapestry of vegetables and edible flowers.

BANTRY HOUSE AND GARDENS ★

Mr and Mrs E. Shelswell-White

Bantry, Co. Cork. Tel: (00353) 27 50047; www.bantryhouse.com

On outskirts of Bantry on Cork road

House and gardens open 17th March to Oct, daily, 10am – 6pm

It is worth paying a visit just to see the house in its setting, quite apart from its magnificent garden, created from 1844 to 1867 while in the ownership of the 2nd Earl of Bantry, Richard White. His artistic ambitions, influenced by his Grand Tour experiences, inspired him to lay out formal parterres, terraces and beds around the house; behind is his amazing staircase of a hundred steps stretching up the steep hillside. Those who

Bantry House and Gardens

reach the top are rewarded with a stunning view of the house and gardens below and Bantry Bay sweeping out to the broad Atlantic beyond. Statues, urns and balustrading encircle and embellish the gardens. There is a definite Italian air about the place, and its warm humid climate has inevitably influenced the plants that will grow there towards wisterias, magnolias, myrtles, *Trachelospermum asiaticum* – the lakeside gardens of Como and Maggiore spring to mind here. The results achieved under the GGIRP are impressive: the extensive drainage system has been recovered, the parterre surrounding the nineteenth-century wisteria circle and fountain completed, the round bed at the entrance to the house replanted, the woodland walk along the stream to the walled garden reclaimed, the 14 round beds to the north overlooking the bay re-created, and the old rose garden laid out afresh with a mixture of roses and herbaceous plants. In all, 45 acres

Entrance: €5, children under 14 free, (house and garden €10, concessions €8, children free)

Other information: Annual music festival early July (house closed) – telephone (27) 50047 for details

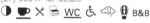

BELVEDERE

Surrounding the Neo-Palladian villa perched on a beautiful site overlooking Lough Ennell is a jewel of woodland and landscape park dotted with beguiling Gothick follies, restored thanks to a major GGIRP grant. There are fine views of the lough and islands from the terraces. The Jealous Wall, a Gothick folly, is the largest in these islands. There are also three kilometres of trails and three children's play areas. An exhibition in the stables relates the story of the Wicked Earl and the Mary Molesworth scandal, the history of the estate and its restoration. Its real glory is the eighteenth-century parkland, follies – including Thomas Wright's Gothick arch – and woods. 160 acres in all.

Westmeath County Council

Mullingar, Co. Westmeath.
Tel: (00353) 44 934060;
www.belvedere-house.ie

5km S of Mullingar on N52 Tullamore road

House open as garden but last entry 5pm

Garden open all year, daily, 10.30am – 7pm (closes 9pm May to Aug, 4.30pm Nov to Feb)

Entrance: €8.75, concessions €6.25, children €4.75, family €24

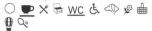

BIRR CASTLE DEMESNE ★

The Gothick front of the castle (not open) dominates vistas which strike through the park and at whose centre is the restored 'Leviathan', the Great Telescope which made Birr the world's astronomical Mecca in the mid-nineteenth century

The Earl and Countess of Rosse

Birr, Co. Offaly.
Tel: (00353) 57 912036;
www.birrcastle.com

130km SW of Dublin, 38km S of
Athlone, on N52 in Birr

Open all year, daily, March to Oct,
9am – 6pm; Nov to Feb, 10am – 4pm.
Guided tours by arrangement

Entrance: €9, OAPs and students €7.50,
children €5, family €24

Other information: Parking outside
castle gates

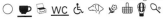

and of which regular demonstrations are given. All around are rare trees and shrubs, many raised from seed received from central China from the 1930s. Crossing one of the rivers is a fine suspension bridge, while a hidden glen boasts a Victorian fernery. Conifers, golden willows, carpets of daffodils, and world-record box hedges, magnolias galore, a cherry avenue and the original *Paeonia* 'Anne Rosse' are just some of the many attractions. The old formal parterres have recently been restored to complement the hornbeam cloisters, and a winter garden with a thatched bower has also been restored, all under the GGIRP. The demesne contains over 50 of the champion trees, as well as geographic collections from Mexico, Pakistan and Yunnan. 120 acres in all.

Alfred Cochrane

Woodbrook, Bray Co. Wicklow.
Tel: (00353) 1 282 2821/
(00353) 0 872 447006
www.corkelodge.com

On old Dublin road between
Shankill and Bray, on Woodbrook
Golf Club Avenue

Open by appt for parties of 10 or more

Entrance: €5 (house and garden €8)

CORKE LODGE

The elegant two-acre gardens of this classical 1815 house have been re-created since 1980 by the present owner, architect Alfred Cochrane, to reflect the spirit of the original design. The atmosphere is of a secluded Mediterranean garden, both dramatic and romantic. A champion cork tree stands at the centre of an entirely green space planted with evergreen foliage plants and white flowers. Beyond, paths wind through woodland skilfully thinned to give the effect of slender columns reaching to the sky. The fine architectural remains provide a strong focus, while avenues of cordylines and palms contrast with a distant view of surrounding cornfields.

Charles Bigham

Lauragh, Killarney, Co. Kerry.
Tel: (00353) 64 83588

DERREEN

The broad sweep of plush lawn and the bald outcroppings of rock by the house do not prepare visitors for the lushness of the walks which weave through native woodlands and palisades of jade-stemmed bamboo. The evocatively named

Derreen

King's Oozy – a path that has a hankering to be a river – leads to a grove of tall, archaic tree ferns (*Dicksonia antarctica*) underplanted with species of filmy hymenophyllum ferns. Wellies and anti-midge cream are the plantsman's only requirement to enjoy the large collection of rhododendrons and rare and tender shrubs that shelter among clipped entanglements of *Gaultheria shallon*. This is probably one of the wettest places in these islands, a fact you're reminded of by the lushness of planting throughout.

24km SW of Kenmare on R571 road along S side of Kenmare Bay, towards Healy Pass

Open all year, daily, 10am – 6pm or dusk if earlier

Entrance: €8, children €4, family €25

Other information: Picnic area near car park only

 WC

THE DILLON GARDEN ★★

This superlative 0.5-acre town garden is the creation of the renowned plantswoman Helen Dillon. The front garden is a plain square of pink granite surrounded by *Betula* 'Fascination', and the rectangular walled garden at the rear, typical of Dublin's Georgian town houses, lost its lawn to a canal a while back. In the mixed borders of shrubs and herbaceous perennials planted against the walls, each season brings unusual plants and exciting colour combinations. Exploration reveals a necklace of secret rooms with raised beds for rarities, such as lady's slipper orchids or double-flowered *Trillium grandiflorum*. On the sunken terrace, terracotta pots sprout more rare plants. Clumps of *Dierama pulcherrimum* arch over the sphinxes, and a small alpine house and conservatory shelter the choicest species, including ferns, alpines and bulbs. A new area of dramatic foliage plants is being developed.

Helen and Val Dillon

45 Sandford Road, Ranelagh, Dublin 6; www.dillongarden.com

10-min. drive or 30-min walk from city centre in cul-de-sac off Sandford Road just after Merton Road and church

Open March, July and Aug, daily; April to June and Sept, Sun; all 2 – 6pm Parties of 15 or more by written appt

Entrance: €5

Other information: Refreshments for pre-booked parties. Possible for wheelchairs but limited access

 WC

Dillon Garden

FERNHILL GARDENS

Mrs Ann Burnett

Sandyford, Dublin 18.
Tel: (00353) 8 726 46053;
www.gardensireland.com

13km S of city centre on R117
Dublin — Enniskerry road

Open all year, Tues — Sat and Bank
Holiday Mons, 11am — 5pm, Sun, 2 — 6pm

Entrance: €5, concessions €4, children €4
(under 5 free)

 WC ♿

The 40-acre garden is situated on the eastern slope of the Dublin Mountains and has a laurel lawn, some fine nineteenth-century plantings and an excellent flowering specimen of *Michelia doltsopa*. The plantings of rhododendron species and cultivars provide spectacles of colour from early spring into midsummer; many of the more tender rhododendrons flourish here. The walkways through the wooded areas wind steeply past many other shrubs — pieris and camellias are also outstanding. Nearer the house are water and rock gardens. Daffodils appear in sheets in spring, and summer sees the flowering of roses and a good collection of herbaceous plants, many used as underplanting through the woodland.

FOTA ARBORETUM AND GARDENS

Office of Public Works

Fota Estate, Carrigtwohill, Co. Cork.
Tel: (00353) 21 481 2728;
www.heritage.ireland.ie

15.5km E of Cork, on Cobh road

Arboretum open all year, daily,
9am — 6pm (closes 5pm Nov to March). Closed 25th Dec. Walled garden open April to Oct, daily except Sat, 9am — 3.30pm (2 — 5pm Sun), plus Sat in June, July and Aug, 12 noon — 5pm

Entrance: free. Automatic pay barrier to car park

Other information: Refreshments and shop in Fota House

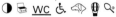

Perhaps the wonders of Fota are best appreciated in summer when the obvious distractions like camellias, embothriums, drimys, pieris and most of the rhododendrons have finished flowering. There is no lack of colour: the walls sparkle with abutilons and cestrums, and the myrtles take on a pinkish hue. *Davidia involucrata* may be bereft of handkerchiefs, but admire instead the elaborate flowers of *Magnolia* x *wieseneri* or the frothy white blooms of *Eucalyptus delegatensis*. Now is the time to appreciate the complicated growth of the Chilean hazel, the immense canopy of the fern-leaved beech, a perfect *Pinus montezumae* and the marvellous bark of the stone pine. Note the wickedly spiny species of colletia and the elegance of *Restio subverticillatus*, then spend a few minutes in the cool fernery and the Victorian orangery, which contains a fine collection of contemporary plants. This, and a section of the Pleasure Gardens known as the Italian Garden, have both been restored.

GLENVEAGH CASTLE GARDENS ★

Department of Environment

Glenveagh National Park, Churchill,
Co. Donegal.
Tel: (00353) 74 37090;
www.heritageireland.ie

24km NW of Letterkenny

Castle open

Grounds open all year, daily, during daylight hours. Garden open all year, daily, 10am — 6pm

Entrance: Grounds free, (castle €3, shuttle bus €2)

Other information: Parking at visitor centre. Access to garden and castle by shuttle bus only. Garden tours by appt (telephone 00353 749 137391)

The centrepiece of the Glenveagh National Park is the castle and surrounding gardens, set above Lough Veagh and encircled by high peat-blanketed mountains in the middle of the Donegal highlands — there can be few places where the contrast between the wild and rugged landscape and the gardens is so marked outside of Scotland. In the garden the surprises are countless, with each compartment given a different treatment. The two-acre lawn in the pleasure grounds is fringed by rhododendron shrubberies, tree ferns, eucryphias and mass plantings of hostas, rodgersias and astilbes. Beyond, pathways wind through oak woods in which grow scented rhododendrons and tender trees and shrubs. Here classical elements are added, including terraced enclosures furnished with Italian statuary and massive terracotta pots. The potager, bounded by herbaceous borders, is planted with heritage vegetable varieties, Irish apple cultivars and rank upon rank of flowering herbs. This is a paradise for plantsmen and gardeners. Linger, tour the castle, and walk the mountain sides, then take the last bus back to the remarkable heather-roofed visitor centre.

HEYWOOD GARDEN

Edwin Lutyens' garden with its pergola and lawns is acknowledged as his masterpiece work in Ireland; it has much in common with Hestercombe (see entry in Somerset). This gem has now been recognised as a heritage garden of historic and architectural importance and is undergoing restoration close to its original state as far as the walls and ornaments are concerned. A four-year programme will see some of the follies restored and plantings redone. These have a long way to go, however, and although it is intended that the borders should be replanted in Gertrude Jekyll style, it remains to be seen whether this will be successfully accomplished. On the driveway leading towards the school buildings is an eighteenth-century folly within an eighteenth-century designed landscape, the vestiges of which can still be enjoyed. Sadly the original seventeenth-century house, set in 45 acres of parkland, burnt down in the 1950s.

Department of Environment

Ballinakill, Co. Laois.
Tel: (00353) 502 33563;
www.heritageireland.ie

5km SE of Abbeyleix. Turn E in Abbeyleix signed to Ballinakill. Outside Ballinakill

Open all year, daily, during daylight hours

Entrance: free

HUNTING BROOK

Take a panoramic view of the Wicklow Mountains, an ancient woodland glen, a trickling stream, a sloping tract of open fertile ground, a sturdy Polish log cabin, and a plantsman with the greenest of fingers, and you get one of Ireland's most compelling contemporary gardens all five acres of it. The

Jimi Blake

Lamb Hill, Blessington, Co. Wicklow.
Tel: (00353) 8 728 56601;
www.huntingbrook.com

Hunting Brook

On N81 9.3 m from Tallaght exit
towards Blessington. Take road opposite
sign to Sally Gap and Kilbride, then
follow signs to house

Open 17th and 18th May, 14th and
15th June, 19th and 20th July, 16th and
17th Aug, 13th and 14th Sept,
12 noon – 5.30pm, and by appt
at other times

Entrance: €6, children €2

Other information: Refreshments by
arrangement. Gardening courses and
demonstrations

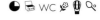

owner, former head gardener at the historic Airfield Gardens in Co. Dublin, has found a new voice here since 2003. In the generous herbaceous borders below the house he has painted an Impressionistic picture using a huge range of grasses and herbaceous perennials (many of them propagated from seed collected in far-flung continents) in shades of orange, purple and brown set off by a variety of foliage. The overall style is a seductive modern combination of tropical and prairie planting. Completely different in character and planting is the woodland walk winding down to the Hunting Brook, a shady haven of mature larches, interesting specimen trees, rhododendrons and bluebells. Different again is the woodland garden created within the remains of a seventh-century ring fort and planted with such treasures as *Trochodendron aralioides* from Korea, *Diphylleia cymosa* from the Appalachian Mountains and *Deinanthe bifida* from Japan. Jimi Blake's sister June owns the adjacent nursery, where many of the rare and unusual herbaceous perennials, ornamental grasses and shade-loving plants found in the garden are on sale.

Office of Public Works

Glengarriff, Co. Cork.
Tel: (00353) 027 63040;
www.heritageireland.ie

On island in Bantry Bay

Open March and Oct, Mon – Sat,
10am – 4.30pm, Sun, 1 – 5pm; May to
Sept, daily, 10am – 6.30pm (opens
9.30am July and Aug; 11am Suns)
(last landing 1 hour before closing).
Closed Nov to Feb

Entrance: €3.70, OAPs €2.60, students
and children €1.30, family €8.70
(2007 prices)

ILNACULLIN (Garinish Island)

The boat trip across the sheltered inlets of Bantry Bay past sun-bathing seals, with views of the Caha Mountains, is doubly rewarding; landing at the slipway you gain entrance to one of Ireland's gardening jewels, begun in the early 1900s. Most visitors cluster around the Casita – an Italianate garden – and reflecting pool, designed by Harold Peto, to enjoy (on clear days) spectacular scenery and nowadays some quite indifferent annual bedding. But walk beyond, to the Temple of the Winds, through shrubberies filled with plants usually confined indoors, tree ferns, southern-hemisphere conifers, rhododendron species and cultivars. A flight of stone steps leads to the Martello tower, and thence the path returns to the walled garden with its double-sided herbaceous border. Alas, these days the admirable attention paid to maintenance is not matched by investment in the tired and diminishing collection of rare and tender plants and the regeneration of its once-delightful borders. Late spring through to early summer sees the 37-acre gardens at their most colourful.

Office of Public Works

Clonmel Street, Dublin 2.
Tel: (1) 475 7816; www.heritageireland.ie

Open all year, daily, 8.30am – 6pm
(opens 10am Sun and Bank Holiday
Mons, closes earlier Oct to March).
Closed 25th Dec, 17th March

Entrance: free

IVEAGH GARDENS

Ranked among the finest and least known of Dublin's parks and gardens, they were designed by Ninian Niven in 1863 and include a rustic grotto, a cascade, fountains, a maze, a rosarium, archery grounds, a wilderness and woodlands. An ongoing programme of restoration is underway, and many of the highlights of the gardens – the fountains, the cascade and the rosarium – have already been tackled, but a lot remains to be done and good plantings are needed.

Killruddery House and Gardens

KILLRUDDERY HOUSE AND GARDENS ★

Killruddery is unique in having the most extensive early formal gardens surviving in Ireland in their original style. They date largely from the seventeenth century with nineteenth-century embellishments. The joy of the gardens is the formal hedging, known as 'The Angles', set beside the formal canals or 'long ponds' which lead to a ride into the distant hills. There is a collection of nineteenth-century French cast statuary, a sylvan theatre created in sweet bay, and a fountain pool enclosed in a beech hedge. The fine nineteenth-century orangery, inspired by Paxton's Crystal Palace, has been completely re-roofed, its original Turner dome put back and its unique collection of statues conserved and restored under the GGIRP. This 80-acre garden deserves to be better known.

KILMOKEA

The seven-acre gardens of the rectory, developed since 1940, have matured splendidly in the gentle microclimate of Waterford Harbour. The contrast between the formal and the informal is marvellously displayed here. It is impossible to decide which is the more inspired – a series of enclosed gardens featuring among others an herbaceous border, topiary and an Italian garden, or the woodland garden, which was started in 1968 on the site of an old mill and where the smaller and rarer rhododendrons, candelabra primulas and tender shrubs excel beneath a canopy of conifers and exotic trees, alongside a stream and its falls. The influence of Peto is discernible; the imaginative hand of the previous owners, the Prices, is paramount. Admire also the pergolas, gazebos and boardwalks. A yin and yang garden has been planted by the present owners, with white and yellows representing the cool element and reds and oranges the hot, and a large organic potager was added in 2003.

The Earl and Countess of Meath

Southern Cross Road, Bray, Co. Wicklow.
Tel: (00353) 128 63405;
www.killruddery.com

23km S of Dublin, just beyond Bray.

House open

Garden open April, Sat and Sun;
May to Sept, daily; all 1 – 5pm

Entrance: €6, concessions €5, children €2
(house and garden €10, concessions €8,
children €3).

Other information: All children must be
accompanied. Teas and meals for parties by
arrangement

◑ WC ⅗ ⛱

Mark and Emma Hewlett

Great Island, Campile, Co. Wexford.
Tel: (51) 388109;
www.kilmokea.com

13km S of New Ross, 0.5km off R733
New Ross – Great Island road towards
River Barrow

Open 17th March to 5th Nov, daily,
10am – 5pm

Entrance: €7, OAPs €6, accompanied
children under 15 €4

Other information: Guided tours
available

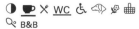

KYLEMORE ABBEY AND GARDEN

Order of Benedictine Nuns in Ireland

Kylemore, Connemara, Co. Galway.
Tel: (00353) 95 41146;
www.kylemoreabbey.com

On N59 9km NE of Letterfrack

Abbey, church and mausoleum open all year, daily except Christmas week and Good Fri, 9.30am – 5.30pm; Nov to March, 10am – 4.30pm

Garden open mid-March to Oct, daily, 10am – 4.30pm

Entrance: Abbey buildings and garden €12, concessions €7

Set in spectacular Connemara landscape, the 1860s Scottish Baronial house is reflected in a lake and backed by tree-covered mountains. The trees are some of the hundreds of thousands planted by the original owner, Mitchell Henry, who also established an elaborate six-acre walled garden in a clement spot a mile away from the castle. Kylemore Castle became Kylemore Abbey when it was bought by Benedictine nuns in the 1920s. A portion of the walled garden was maintained for many years, but it had become overgrown and the buildings dilapidated until the nuns, aided by a GGIRP grant, decided in 1995 to restore the walled garden to its late-nineteenth-century splendour and to conserve the buildings. Half the garden has become again an ornamental flower garden, containing typical annual beds in lawns, the other half, once a fruit and vegetable garden, is now fully replanted. The two areas are separated by a tree-lined stream. Two of the 21 glasshouses in a handsome range have been restored. The head gardener's house (sadly not lived in), bothy, toolshed and lime kiln (from which the heat for the glasshouses was piped) are on view, and traditional Victorian favourites and exotic plants can be enjoyed once more.

LAKEMOUNT ★

Brian Cross

Barnavara Hill, Glanmire, Co. Cork.
Tel: (00353) 86 811 0241;
www.lakemountgarden.com

8km E of Cork off R639, at top of Barnavara Hill above Glanmire

Open all year, by appt

Entrance: €7

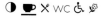

A skilfully designed and immaculately maintained two-acre hillside garden, with rhododendrons, azaleas and camellias in spring and a wealth of summer interest and colour, especially from hydrangeas. There are paved areas on different levels, a poolhouse and planthouse with exotics such as iochromas cassias and tibouchinas, while to the rear of the house a lawn slopes gently to a rock garden to beds with a mixed planting of trees, shrubs and herbaceous plants. This is an evolving garden with many unusual plantings, most recently in the old orchard and in meadows now filled with wild flowers fringed by rare trees and shrubs. A large pond and a cottage garden have also been added.

LARCHILL ARCADIAN GARDENS

Michael and Louisa de las Casas

Kilcock, Co. Kildare.
Tel: (00353) 1 628 7354;
www.larchill.ie

5km from Kilcock on Dunslaughlin Road

Open May to Sept, Sat, Sun and Bank Holiday Mons, 12 noon – 6pm, and appt at other times

Entrance: €7.50, children €5.50, family €27.50

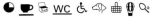

The modest mid-eighteenth-century house overlooks a tree-lined parkland landscape of 63 acres. A circulatory walk through the trees leads to several unique rustic follies, including the Fox's Earth and a sham fort on an island in the lake (no longer used for mock sea battles but by nesting wild fowl). The follies have been conserved and the lake and the entire site restored with the aid of a grant from the GGIRP. Larchill is that unusual survival, an intact *ferme ornée*, with a large collection of rare breeds of cattle and other domestic animals, living in fields and in the handsome eighteenth-century farmyard. Contemporary design and colourful planting in the walled garden contrast with the restful greens of the parkland.

LISMORE CASTLE GARDENS

The situation of the castle overlooking the River Blackwater is stunning; Edmund Spenser is said to have written *The Faerie Queene* here (Annes Grove, on the other hand, claims that he was inspired by the Awbeg river that runs through its own demesne). There are two beautiful gardens linked by the gatehouse entrance: the upper, reached by a stairway in the gatehouse, leads to a Jacobean-style terrace with vegetables and flowers, a reduced original Paxton glasshouse (with his typical ridge-and-furrow roof) and a fine view from the main axis to the church spire emphasised by a new herbaceous border. In the lower garden, several steps down from the gatehouse, are some fine plants, but the principal feature, an ancient yew walk, is wonderful. Remarkable too are the contemporary sculptures inserted into the landscape. The west wing of the castle has been converted into a contemporary art space to host exhibitions from all over the world. Seven acres in all.

The Duke and Duchess of Devonshi.
Lismore, Co.Waterford.
Tel: (00353) 58 54424;
www.lismorecastle.com

57.5km SW of Waterford in Lismore

Open 15th March to 5th Oct, daily,
1.45 – 4.45pm (opens 11am June
to Sept)

Entrance: €7, children under 16 €3.50

Other information: Toilet facilities, inc.
disabled, nearby

LODGE PARK WALLED GARDEN

The two-acre walled garden dates from the late eighteenth century and provided produce and flowers for the house. The present owners have been restoring it over a number of years, adding their own personal touches to the layout. It is filled with a great assortment of rare flowering plants, herbs, salad crops and fruit and is beautifully kept – the potting shed must be the most perfect example of its kind for cleanliness and order. Head gardener, take a bow. The lack of commerciality is refreshing, and despite being relatively unknown its high standards mark it out as a true gardener's garden.

Mr and Mrs Robert Guinness
Straffan, Co. Kildare. Tel: (00353) 1 628 8412;
www.steam-museum.ie

20km W of Dublin. Take N4 to Maynooth
or Lucan or N7 to Kill. Leave N7 at sign for
Straffan and follow signs for Steam Museum

Open June to Aug, Wed – Sun and Bank
Holiday Mons, 2 – 6pm; May and Sept by
appt

Entrance: €7.50, concessions €5, family €20

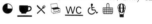

LOUGHCREW HISTORIC GARDENS

An extraordinary survival of a seventeenth-century demesne, retaining many of its features through the waxing and waning of the family fortunes. The remarkable yew walk dates from the mid-1660s and has few rivals for the beauty and girth of its individual trees. The lime avenue runs down in a straight and elegant sweep to an ancient burial ground. The tower house alone is worth a visit. A massive ancient motte is the focal point of the garden; behind it a huge cedar spews a water cascade from its base into a dark pool. This 'devil's cauldron' has been planted in fiery colours and terminates the main herbaceous border. A yew parterre delineates the site of the ruined seventeenth-century longhouse, and a carved wooden doorframe echoes the original. A slender canal flows parallel to the replanted herbaceous border, which itself skirts the outside of the old walled garden (not accessible). Many of the original features of the garden and pleasure ground have been repaired, restored or unashamedly reinvented, all achieved under the GGIRP. The atmosphere of the whole 11 acres is one of considerable antiquity.

Mr and Mrs Charles Naper
Oldcastle, Co. Meath.
Tel: (00353) 49 854 1922;
www.loughcrew.com

85km NW of Dublin off N3, 5km from
Oldcastle off Mullingar road

Open April to Sept, daily, 12.30 – 6pm;
Oct to March, Sun and Bank Holiday
Mons, 1 – 5pm. Closed 25th Dec. Also
open for parties by appt

Entrance: €7, concessions €5, children €4

B&B

aoghaire-Rathdown County Council

Grange Road, Rathfarnham, Dublin 18.
Tel: (00353) 1 493 4059;
www.irishtabletop.com

In Rathfarnham, signposted on
Brehon Road/Grange Road

House open by appt

Park open, all year, dawn – dusk. Walled
garden open May to Sept, Tues – Sun,
12 noon – 5pm

Entrance: park free, walled garden €3,
children €2

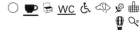

MARLAY PARK

The extensive 200-acre public park under the Dublin mountains, with the Little Dargle River running through, contains a lake, lawns and fine old trees. Once the demesne of the La Touche banking family, the late-eighteenth-century house has recently been sensitively restored for public use; the adjacent large walled garden has also been restored with the aid of a grant from the GGIRP. The garden was traditionally divided into three walled parts, two of which are on view. On entering through the head gardener's house, the central position is taken by an attractive Regency-style ornamental flower garden, containing colourful flowerbeds of mixed bedding fashionable in that era. Features of interest, such as a shrubbery, an orangery, a rustic summerhouse and a fountain embellish the site. Another section houses a large kitchen garden, set out in a traditional early-nineteenth-century manner and containing vegetables and fruit known to have been grown at that time, many now rare.

Mr Ambrose Congreve

Kilmeaden, Co. Waterford.
Tel: (00353) 51 384115 (Office)

8km W of Waterford by N5

Open March to Oct, Thurs, 9am – 5pm;
and strictly by appt for conducted tours
and coach parties

Entrance: free but €15 for pre-booked
guided tour

Other information: Adults only please

 WC

MOUNT CONGREVE ★★

Ambrose Congreve has amassed here an unequalled collection of rhododendron, camellia and magnolia species and cultivars, and many other fine specimen trees. It is a staggering collection which cannot be described adequately in a single entry: 70 acres of shrubs, mass upon mass, since every cultivar is planted in groups. In addition to the flowering shrubs, which include Mount Congreve hybrids, there are many other splendours, including a whole series of surprises, one of the most spectacular being a pagoda at the base of 25-metre cliffs. Highlights are memorable. In early March a forest of *Magnolia campbellii* offers pink to white goblets to the rooks. A languid walled garden has a fine eighteenth-century vinery and range of glasshouses. In the borders is an extensive collection of herbaceous plants arranged in order of monthly flowering – May to July, a large arrangement for August, plus a border for September and October – an unusual idea. There is far too much here to appreciate on a single visit.

Mount Congreve

Mount Usher

MOUNT USHER ★★

The Vartry River flows through this exquisite 22-acre garden over weirs and under bridges which allow visitors to meander through the collections. It is a plant-lovers' paradise. *Pinus montezumae* is always first port of call, a shimmering tree, magnificent when the bluebells are in flower. Throughout are drifts of rhododendrons, fine trees and shrubs, including many that are difficult to cultivate outdoors in other parts of Britain and Ireland. The grove of eucalyptus at the lower end of the valley is memorable; a kiwi-fruit vine (*Actinidia chinensis*) cloaks the piers of a bridge, and beside the tennis court is the gigantic original *Eucryphia* x *nymansensis* 'Mount Usher'. In spring, bulbs, magnolias, a procession of rhododendrons and camellias, in summer eucryphias and leptospermums, in autumn russet and crimson leaves falling from maples – a garden for all seasons, but at its finest in spring and autumn.

Mrs Madelaine Jay

Ashford, Co. Wicklow.
Tel: (00353) 404 40116/40205;
www.mount-usher-gardens.com

50km S of Dublin, 6.5km NW of Wicklow, off N11 at Ashford

Open mid-March to Oct, daily,
10.30am – 6pm

Entrance: €7, OAPs, students and children €5.50. Special rates for parties of 20 or more. Guided tours (€40) must pre-booked

MUCKROSS GARDENS AND ARBORETUM ★

The gardens are almost incidental to the spectacle of the lakes mountains of Killarney; indeed, are principally renowned as a viewing area for the wild grandeur of the mountains. The lawns sweep to clumps of old rhododendrons and Scots pines, and there is a huge natural rock garden. Quiet corners abound along the lough-shore walks, and anyone interested in trees and shrubs is strongly recommended to head for the recently developed arboretum area, easily reached by car (follow the signpost) and is a short walk from the house). There, good specimen trees surround a wooden pergola of

National Parks and Wildlife Service

Killarney National Park, Killarney,
Co. Kerry. Tel: (00353) 64 31947/31440;
www.killarneynationalpark.ie

6.5km S of Killarney on N71
Kenmare road

House open (admission charge)

Gardens open all year, daily

Entrance: free

imaginative design, and there are plantings of tender shrubs in the wild, shaded woods beyond, which, with their unique flora and ancient yews and the almost immortal strawberry trees (*Arbutus unedo*), are enticing.

NATIONAL BOTANIC GARDENS, GLASNEVIN ★

Office of Public Works
Glasnevin, Dublin 9.
Tel: (00353) 1 804 0300/ 857 0909
(Visitor Centre);
www.botanicgardens.ie

1.5km N of city centre on Botanic Road close to cemetery

Open all year, daily except 25th Dec:
9am – 6pm (closes 4.30pm in winter)

Entrance: free, parking €2

Other information: Pre-booked guided tours €2; free tour Sun, 12 noon and 2.30pm

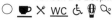

This historic 50-acre garden is changing yearly but retains some of its Victorian atmosphere. The plant collections and glasshouses are undergoing restoration and renewal, there are interesting new planting schemes near the entrance and around the Curvilinear Range, and the Great Palm House of 1884, with its tropical rainforest display. The Turner Conservatory (1843–69), the finest in Ireland, has been restored and planted with cycads and related plants, south-east Asian rhododendrons (sect. Vireya) and plants from the South African fynbos and dry temperate areas of Australia and South America. Recent developments include a greatly expanded display of Chinese plants and a new organic fruit and vegetable garden. Glasnevin is undoubtedly worth visiting and highlights are hard to enumerate, but a few outstanding plants should be mentioned: *Zelkova carpinifolia*, a marvellously architectural tree; the ancient wisteria on the Chain Tent (c. 1836); the weeping Atlas cedar (*Cedrus atlantica* 'Pendula'); a Chusan palm planted outdoors in 1870; a *Parrotia persica* near the entrance; and of course 'The Last Rose of Summer'.

THE PHOENIX PARK

Office of Public Works
Dublin 8. Tel: (1) 821 3021

N of River Liffey. From city centre follow signs to 'The West', or take No. 10 bus to Phoenix Park

Open all year, daily

Entrance: free

Other information: Guided tours of àras an Uachtarin (residence of President of Ireland) and Farmleigh Estate from visitor centre, Sat, from 9.45am

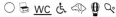

At 1760 acres, this is the largest enclosed park in any European city, replete with a herd of fallow deer, some splendid monuments and great houses, most of which are accessible to the public by request. The Phoenix Monument has been relocated to its original position on the main avenue. The planting is large-scale – the avenues of horse chestnuts, limes and beeches are spectacular in blossom and in autumn, and gas lights twinkle at night the whole way along the ceremonial avenue. The People's Garden, near the main city entrance, is the only part where there is intensive gardening, but the park is a place to be lost in among the hawthorns and wild flowers.

POWERSCOURT ★

Slazenger family
Enniskerry, Co. Wicklow.
Tel: (00353) 1 204 6000;
www.powerscourt.ie

19km S of Dublin, just outside Enniskerry

House open, with exhibition on history of estate and gardens

This is a 'grand garden', of 47 acres, a massive statement of the triumph of art over the natural landscape. Although its evolution took place over 250 years or more, it was the 7th Viscount Powerscourt, a lover both of trees and of European culture, who stamped his imprint most strongly on its layout and planting in the mid-nineteenth-century. The most arresting part of the design was largely the work of the inimitable Daniel Robertson. In some ways it is beyond compare – the amphitheatre of terraces guarded by winged

horses, and the great central axis formed by the ceremonial stairway leading down to the Triton Pond and jet and stretching beyond to the Great Sugarloaf Mountain, are justly famous. The Pepperpot tower has been restored and visitors can climb it to view 'the killing hollow' and the North American specimen trees in the tower valley. Wander on to the edge of the pond and look up along the staircase past the monumental terraces to the south facade of the house. That's the view of Powerscourt that is breathtaking. Statuary and the famous perspective gate, an avenue of monkey puzzles and a beech wood along the avenue add to its glory.

Powerscourt

Gardens open all year, daily except 25th and 26th Dec, 9.30am – 5.30pm (closes dusk Nov to Feb)

Entrance: charge

Other information: Self-catering apartments available

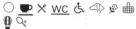

PRIMROSE HILL ★

The garden is approached up a beech avenue, flanked by a developing three-acre arboretum. The garden itself is not much bigger than one acre, yet it succeeds in housing a fine collection of snowdrops, including some of its own 'Primrose Hill' seedlings, glorious in flower. It is unusual for a garden to boast that February is its best month – but undoubtedly it is here, starting the visiting season; to return in late spring and summer when the borders are in full colour is an added joy. The herbaceous plants are lovingly cared for and planted in humus-rich compost in large clumps, giving a generous effect to the borders. Irises are high on the priority list, and so are lobelias (two named ones originated here), lilies, kniphofias and, of course, *Primula auricula* 'Old Irish Blue', plus many others.

Robin Hall

Lucan, Co. Dublin.
Tel: (00353) 1 628 0373

13km W of city centre off N4. Turn right signed to Lucan, drive through village and, after Garda (police) station, take steep, narrow Primrose Lane on left. Continue to top and through black gateway

House open

Garden open Feb, June and July, daily, 2 – 6pm (or dusk if earlier), and by appt at other times

Entrance: €5

STROKESTOWN PARK ★

The Neo-Palladian house in its parkland, entered from one of the broadest village streets in Ireland, was purchased in 1979 by a local company, who put in motion a restoration plan

The Westward Group

Strokestown, Co. Roscommon.
Tel: (00353) 071 96 33013;
www.strokestownpark.ie

23km W of Longford on N5

House open

Park open mid-March to Oct, daily, 10am – 5.30pm. Parties by arrangement

Entrance: park free; house, Famine Museum and garden €14, concessions €12.50, children €7, family €29.50

Other information: Restaurant, garden shop and toilet facilities at museum

involving the refurbishment of the house and the creation of new gardens within the old walls. In this six-acre walled garden is one of the largest double herbaceous borders in these islands, 146 metres long. Handsome gates (moved here from Rockingham near Boyle) have been rescued and re-erected, the pool and the pergola completed, a yew and beech hedge planted. The old summerhouse is close by the new maze and croquet lawn. A rose garden, a wildflower meadow and a fern walk are other achievements. Under the GGIRP the other two-acre Georgian walled fruit and vegetable garden, the 1780 vinery, the 1740 banqueting folly and the Regency gazebo tower have all been restored.

Fingal County Council

Malahide Castle, Malahide, Co. Dublin. Tel: (00353) 1 846 2456; 1 890 5629 (Parks Department, Dublin); www.fingalcoco.ie

16km N of Dublin in Malahide

Castle open

Gardens open May to Sept, daily, 2 – 5pm, and for parties by appt. Conducted tour of walled garden and glasshouses, May to Sept, Wed, 2pm, and by appt

Entrance: €4, OAPs free

TALBOT BOTANIC GARDENS ★

A 22-acre botanic garden lies within the 290-acre estate of Malahide with the castle centre stage. This was home to the Talbot family for 800 years until the death of Lord Milo Talbot in 1973; in 1976 the estate was acquired by Fingal County Council. The garden is in two sections – the 18-acre west lawn area of southern-hemisphere plants, and a four-acre walled garden of more tender species, including many Tasmanian and other southern-hemisphere species, making this a plantsman's delight. The seven glasshouses range from a large Victorian conservatory to a small pit house. A National Collection of olearias is here, and pittosporums, nothofagus, azaleas and hoherias are also well represented. Other features and entertainments include a model railway, a doll's museum and a children's playground.

Thomas Pakenham

Castlepollard, Co. Westmeath. Tel: (00353) 44 9661159; www.tullynallycastle.com

1.5km NW of Castlepollard on R395

Castle open to pre-booked parties only

Gardens open May and June, Sat, Sun and Bank Holiday Mons; July to 17th Aug, daily; all 2 – 6pm. Open at other times by appt

Entrance: €6, children €3

TULLYNALLY CASTLE

An elaborate early-eighteenth-century formal garden of canals and basins was succeeded by romantic parkland and pleasure grounds in the best Reptonian manner. They encompass two artificial lakes and a recently restored grotto, made of eroded limestone from nearby Lough Derravaragh and decorated within by carved wooden gargoyles. The present owners have added new features: Gothick summerhouses, a Chinese garden complete with pagoda and a Tibetan garden of waterfalls and streams. The walled gardens have extensive flower borders and an avenue of memorable 200-year-old Irish yews. The energetic can undertake a mile-long walk around the lower lake, which offers splendid views of the castle.

Kilkenny County Council

Inistioge, Co. Kilkenny. Tel: (00353) 87 8580502/8549785; www.woodstock.ie

Just outside Inistioge midway between Kilkenny and New Ross off R700

WOODSTOCK GARDENS AND ARBORETUM

The 50-acre gardens surrounding the now-ruinous mid-eighteenth-century house were redesigned in the latter half of the Victorian era in fashionable style and became renowned for the arboretum and intricately planted terraced gardens. Much has recently been conserved and restored with the aid of a GGIRP grant after seventy years of neglect. Beautifully situated on a sloping site, high above the attractive village of Inistioge and the River Nore, many fine mature exotic trees are well spaced in grass and paths lead through the towering monkey puzzle and noble fir walks. The walled garden now contains a double herbaceous border. The old rose garden beyond has been replanted and the rustic summerhouse rebuilt, and a newly installed fountain is enclosed by rhododendrons. A dovecot and a garden building (later tiled as an ornamental dairy) pre-date the Victorian lay-out. A vast granite and white quartz rockery and an original, once-tiled bath house are sympathetically planted. A circular conservatory is currently being constructed, a replica of an original Turner Conservatory which was removed from the gardens in the 1950s.

Open all year, daily, dawn – dusk

Entrance: €4 car parking. Bus charges on request

OTHER RECOMMENDED GARDENS

BALLINLÓUGH CASTLE GARDENS

Clonmellon, Co. Westmeath (00353 46 943 3234). Open May to Sept by appt

A long avenue leads to the impressive, largely 17th-century castle, which stands on a mound overlooking two lakes. The formality of the four walled enclosures, filled with choice plants, fruit, herbs and vegetables, gives way to free-style wild plantings along woodland paths leading to a rockery and a glade. 40 acres, all restored under the GGIRP.

THE BAY GARDEN

Frances and Iain MacDonald, Camolin, Ennicorthy, Co. Wexford (00353 53 938 3349; www.thebaygarden.com). Open May to Sept, Sun; June to Aug, Fri and Sun; all 2 – 5pm; and at other times by appt

The fertile, free-draining 2.5-acre garden is filled with diverse spaces, each flowing effortlessly into the next: a tiny cottage garden fronting the house, mixed borders and a serpentine lawn swooping around the side, a tiny rose parterre, 'hot' and 'funereal' borders. A formal pond garden leads to a modern planting of grasses and perennials, and there is room too for a woodland and bog garden and a small but interesting nursery.

BUNRATTY CASTLE

Bunratty, Co. Clare (00353 61 360788). Open all year, daily, 9.30am – 5.30pm

The castle grounds are now occupied by the vernacular buildings of the Folk Park, each complemented by an appropriate garden. Especially successful is the 0.5-acre walled flower garden charmingly planted in Regency style by Belinda Jupp as a horticultural match for the 1804 house.

COOLCARRIGAN GARDEN

Mr and Mrs Wilson-Wright, Naas, Co. Kildare (00353 45 863527/863524; www.coolcarrigan.ie). Open April to Sept, by appt

The large and much-admired collection of rare and unusual trees and shrubs dotted informally about the 20-acre garden was formed with the advice of Sir Harold Hillier. A large and attractive Victorian greenhouse backed by towering trees dominates the spacious lawn and its fine herbaceous border.

Coolcarigan Garden

DUCKETT'S GROVE

Rainestown, Co. Carlow (00353 59 913 1554/917 0776;
www.carlowtourism.com/gardens). Open all year, daily
except 25th and 26th Dec, 10am – 6pm

The massive, turreted Gothick ruin of Duckett's
Grove was gutted by fire in 1933, and the estate,
once one of the most important in the county,
was vastly reduced and near-derelict when it was
acquired by Carlow County Council in 2004. It is
early days in this major work of reclamation, but
two interconnecting walled gardens have been
restored and replanted – one filled with
ornamental plants, the other with good things to
eat, including historic Irish apple cultivars – and a
woodland walk has been reinstated. 11 acres.

DUNLOE CASTLE GARDENS

Hotel Dunloe Castle, Beaufort, Killarney, Co. Kerry
(00353 64 44111; www.killarneyhotels.ie). Open early
April to Sept, 9am – 7pm, and for parties by appt

A modern hotel opened on this superb site
facing the Gap of Dunloe and the imposing
ruined fort of Dunloe Castle. It is surrounded by
acres of parkland and gardens with magnificent
and unusual trees and shrubs, in which the
plantings of 1920 have been continually added to
and maintained.

ENNISCOE GARDENS

Mrs Susan Kellett, Castlehill, Ballina, Co. Mayo
(00353 96 31112; www.enniscoe.com). Open April to
Oct, daily, 10am – 6pm (opens 2pm Sat and Sun)

Set near the shores of Lough Conn and its
beautiful surrounding landscape, the 4-acre
pleasure grounds of the 200-acre estate were
developed in the 1870s. The ornamental walled
garden has been restored to its Edwardian
trimness and vibrancy with the aid of a GGIRP
grant. The picturesque 18th-century house is now
a country-house hotel.

AN FÉAR GORTA
(TEA AND GARDEN ROOMS)

Catherine and Brendan O'Donoghue, Ballyvaghan,
Co. Clare (00353 65 707 7157). Open, June to mid-Sept
Mon – Sat, 11am – 5.30pm

A garden bursting with luxuriance, its different
compartments filled with shrubs and perennials
that thrive by the edge of the sea, is set before
and behind the traditional cottages, with the
Burren, John Betjeman's 'Stony seaboard, far
and foreign' as the dramatic backdrop. An
oasis of hospitality for garden-lovers.

GASH GARDENS

The Keenan Family, Castletown, Portlaoise, Co. Laois
(00353 57 8732247). Open May to Sept, daily
except Sun, 10am – 5pm. Parties welcome by appt

A 4-acre plantsman's garden full of treasures
stretching down to the River Nore.
A laburnum arch introduces a riverside walk,
with fine and varied herbaceous borders to
admire on the way. Water is omnipresent – in
a circular pond, a stream garden, a cascade
and a bog garden – and a large rock garden is
bright with alpines and perennials.

GEORGIAN HOUSE AND GARDEN

2 Pery Square, Limerick, Co. Limerick
(00353 61 314130; www.limerickcivictrust.ie).
Open all year except Christmas period and Bank
Holidays, Mon – Fri, 9am – 4.30pm, Sat and Sun for
parties by appt

The handsome early-19th-century town
house and small rear garden, enclosed by high
brick walls and backed by its coach house,
have both been sensitively restored. A central
lawn is surrounded by neatly maintained wall
borders planted with favourites of the period
to sustain interest throughout the year.

GLEBE GARDENS

Jean and Peter Perry, Baltimore, Co Cork
(00353 28 20232; www.glebegardens.com)
Open 21st March to 2nd April, daily; May to Sept,
Wed – Sun; all 10am- 6pm; plus Bank Holiday Mons

This 5.5-acre organic plot is an imaginative
fusion of productivity and prettiness, with
cornucopian potager, well-stocked cutting
garden, goldfish-flecked lily pond, wildflower
meadow, woodland walk and turf
amphitheatre. Facing north-east, it fans out
behind the pleasingly square former rectory
and runs down to the seashore.

GLIN CASTLE GARDENS

Madam Fitzgerald and the Knight of Glin.
Glin, Co. Limerick (00353 68 34173/34112;
www.glincastle.com). Open March to Nov, daily,
10am – 4pm

The stylish and romantic castle looks over a formal setting of lawns and topiary to the south leading to a well-wooded demesne. An outstanding feature is the productive walled kitchen garden set on a steep slope, with its castellated henhouse and rustic temple. Behind a path ascends to a circle of 20th-century standing stones and Gothic hermitage. 12 acres in all.

GRAIGUECONNA

Mr and Mrs John Brown, Old Connaught, Bray, Co. Wicklow. Open by written appt only

A fascinating 4-acre garden created early last century by Lewis Meredith, author of one of the earliest textbooks on rock gardens. His own lies hidden at the end of a grassy path punctuated by Irish yews and lined with excellent mixed borders. Interesting plants abound, including 'old' roses and tender and unusual plants.

THE JAPANESE GARDEN

Irish National Stud, Tully, Kildare, Co. Kildare (00353 45 521617/522963; www.irish-national-stud.ie). Open 12th Feb to 15th Nov, daily, 9.30am – 6pm (last admission 5pm)

The 4-acre garden commissioned by Colonel William Hall Walker in 1910 is now part of the Irish National stud. Laid out by a Japanese father-and-son team to symbolise the 'Life of Man', it is a serene place of flowering cherries and mature topiary, with exquisite Scots pines shading pools, rocky outcrops and meandering paths. The curious, watery *St Fiachra's Garden* adjoining was created in 1999.

JOHN F. KENNEDY ARBORETUM

New Ross, Co. Wexford (00353 51 388171). Open all year, daily except 21st March and 25th Dec, from 10am (closes 6.30pm April and Sept, 8pm May to Aug, 5pm Oct to March)

A spacious modern arboretum of 623 acres laid out in botanical sequences with rides. From the summit of a nearby hill a superb panorama stretches out, not only of the arboretum but also of parts of six counties. Planting began in the 1960s, and now 4500 different trees and shrubs are established, including a fine rhododendron collection.

KILFANE GLEN AND WATERFALL

Thomastown, Co. Kilkenny (00353 56 772 7105; www.NicholasMosse.com) Open July and Aug, daily, 11am – 6pm, and for parties of 20 or more by appt

This romantic woodland garden dates from 1790, when the glen was designed to display nature in all her terrifying beauty, *à la* Wordsworth. It has the requisite romantic traits including a hermit's grotto, a delightful *cottage orné* and an impressive waterfall. Another area above the glen has sculptures and modern touches. Nine acres.

KNAPPOGUE CASTLE

Bunratty, Co. Clare (00353 61 360788). Open end-April to early Oct, daily, 9.30am – 5pm (last entry 4.15pm). Telephone for Easter opening details

The walled garden planted as a flower and herb garden in a tranquil setting close by the castle has been restored under the GGIRP. The wall borders are filled with an attractive mixture of shrubs and herbaceous plants, and the old paths divide spacious lawns amply supplied with seats.

KNOCKABBEY CASTLE

Cyril O'Brien, Louth, Co. Louth (00353 16 778816; www.knockabbeycastle.com). Open May and Sept, Sat and Sun; June to Aug, Tues – Sun and Bank Holiday Mons; all 10.30am – 5.30pm

The 30-acre grounds have been revived with the aid of a GGIRP grant. Terraces lead past herbaceous borders to parkland, where mown paths weave through woodland and around ponds to an 18th-century stone building encircled by majestic lime trees.

NATIONAL BOTANIC GARDENS

Kilmacurragh Arboretum, Kilbride, Co. Wicklow (00353 0 404 48844). Open all year, daily, 9am – 6pm (closes 4.30pm in winter)

The 50-acre arboretum created by Thomas Acton in the latter half of the nineteenth century is highly rated for its magnificent heritage collection of plants. Many specimens, including towering rhododendrons, are unequalled and rare conifers abound. A programme of replanting is underway.

SALTHILL GARDENS

Elizabeth Temple, Mountcharles, Co Donegal
(00353 74 9735387; www.donegalgardens.com)
Open May to 25th Sept, Mon – Thurs, plus Sats in
May and June; all 2 – 6pm

The 2-acre walled garden is enclosed by aged
and lichened brick and stone, yet its abundant
planting dates from the last two decades. Roses
ramble over arches and behind crowded
herbaceous borders, lilies and cannas pack the
greenhouse, and a collection of daylilies
explodes in July. Vegetables are grown in flat-
topped, traditional Donegal ridges, refashioned
each year.

ST ANNE'S PARK

Raheny, Dublin 3 (00353 1 833 8898/1859;
www.dublincorp.ie). Open all year, daily, during
daylight hours

Within the large public park (once the
demesne of a grand Victorian mansion
belonging to Lord Ardilaun of the Guinness
family) is a 14-acre rose garden with an
outstanding display of roses, flourishing in their
thousands in summer and peaking with the
Rose Festival held each July.

TURLOUGH PARK

Castlebar, Co. Mayo (00353 9490 2444). Open all year,
daily except Bank Holiday Mons, 10am – 5pm
(opens 2pm Suns)

The core of the fine 18th-century landscape
park survives; the gardens were created as the
setting for the Victorian mansion that houses
part of the National Museum collections. The
grounds and gardens, restored under the
GGIRP, are a pleasurable visit in their own right.
The Castlebar River flows through, servicing an
ornamental lake overlooked by grass terraces,
formal bedding and two glasshouses.

VANDELEUR WALLED GARDEN

Vandeleur Demesne, Killimer Road, Kilrush, Co. Clare
(00353 65 905 1760; www.vandeleurwalledgarden.ie).
Open all year, daily, 10am – 6pm (closes 5pm Oct
to April)

Set among 420 acres of native woodland, the
2.2-acre walled garden hidden from view
behind fine stone walls has been redesigned for
the 21st century around the old path system.
Unusual and tender plants thrive in the
sheltered microclimate, and a horizontal maze,
unusual water features and a free-standing
Victorian-style glasshouse add to the attractions
of the contemporary plantings.

SCOTLAND

For further information about how to use the *Guide*
and for an explanation of the symbols, see pages vi–viii.
Specific dates and times are those given to us by garden owners for 2008.
For 2009, check with the individual properties.
For opening dates under Scotland's Gardens Scheme,
readers should consult *Gardens of Scotland* or www.gardensofscotland.org.
Maps are to be found at the end of the *Guide*.

ABRIACHAN GARDEN AND NURSERY

Although this is officially a retail nursery selling many unusual plants, it is also a fascinating hillside garden of over four acres – a plantsman's joy with paved viewing areas and secluded seats from which to contemplate the ever-mysterious Loch Ness. The clever terracing of the beds ensures that plants are seen from every angle and level, and visitors will not be able to resist climbing onwards and upwards along the network of paths meandering into the woodland. The planting content is comprehensive and professional, ranging from bog plants to gravel lovers and alpines. Snowdrops start the flowering season, followed by auriculas, meconopsis and primulas. After the riches of summer come crocosmias, schizostylis, kniphofias and a wealth of autumn leaves. Several new beds have been planted with unusual woodland plants. Enticingly, most of the plants on view are also for sale.

Mr and Mrs Davidson

Loch Ness Side, Inverness, Highland
IV3 8LA. Tel: (01463) 861232;
www.lochnessgarden.com

On A82 Inverness – Fort William road.
Ignore side roads signed to Abriachan
(centre of village is in hills 2 miles above
garden and nursery)

Open Feb to Nov, daily, 9am – 7pm
(closes 5pm Oct, Nov and Feb)

Entrance: £2, OAPs £1 (collecting box)

○ ☕ ⬙ ✿

ACHAMORE GARDENS

(Historic Scotland Inventory)

An amazing idea to create such a superb garden on the Isle of Gigha. The journey there is through beautiful countryside finishing up with the ferry trip, surrounded by squawking sea birds. In 1944 Sir James Horlick purchased the whole island with the sole purpose of creating a garden in which to grow the rare and the unusual. This was accomplished with the advice of James Russell, and the overall effect is tropical. A delightful woodland landscape was planted with a vast collection from around the world. Few gardens outside the national botanic collections can claim such diversity and rarity. The rhododendrons are unsurpassed in variety, quality and sheer visual magnitude, with fine specimens of tender species, and there are many varieties of camellias, cordylines, primulas and Asiatic exotica. Many genera are represented by very good specimens, thriving in the mild climate. There is a *Pinus montezumae* in the walled garden; drifts of Asiatic primulas feature around the especially pretty woodland pond. Now that Gigha has been put in trust for the local community, its future seems secure. 40 acres in all.

Isle of Gigha Heritage Trust

Isle of Gigha, Argyll and Bute PA41 7AD.
Tel: (01583) 505390;
www.gardensatgigha.org.uk

Take A83 to Tayinloan then ferry to
Gigha (check www.calmac.co.uk for
details)

Open all year, daily, dawn – dusk

Entrance: £3.50, children £1.50
(under 10 free)

Other information: Home-made teas
available summer only; refreshments at
hotel all year

○ ☕ WC ♿ ⬙ ✿

AIKET CASTLE

Katrina Clow

Aiket Castle, Dunlop, Ayrshire KA3 4BW.
Tel: (01560) 483926

10m SW of Glasgow off A736
Barrhead – Irvine road. At Burnhouse turn
left onto B706; after 1.5m turn right

Open end-April to mid-Sept for parties
by appt

Entrance: £3

Other information: Meals available by
arrangement. Children must be supervised

NEW ● ◗ ▢ WC ♿ ◁▷ ◊

Hidden away in the rolling Ayrshire country, the fifteenth-century castle was bought as a burned, abandoned and roofless ruin by the present owners in 1976. It has been lovingly restored to its original medieval outline and stands proud above the River Glazert, providing the spectacular backdrop and focal point of the undulating seven-acre garden. The approach, along an avenue of handsome *Alnus rubra* underplanted with spring-flowering woodland plants, leads to the front of the castle, where azaleas, hybrid rhododendrons, sambucus, eucryphias, magnolias and hoherias, variegated cornus and hydrangeas thrive within a shelter belt of conifers. The summer garden to the east slopes gently down towards the burn with fine views across to Barr Hill. Two large oval ponds reflect the colours of the richly planted surrounding borders, which contain a good backbone of perennials with masses of tulips in spring followed by beautifully colour-co-ordinated cosmos, geraniums, nicotianas and dahlias. *Iris ensata* thrive in the moist conditions with a companion planting of phormiums, dieramas and many different grasses. Immediately behind the castle is a terraced area and a natural amphitheatre where plays are sometimes performed. The river divides the garden so that from the formal areas near the castle there are stunning views of the wilder and more natural landscape on the other side. Wooden bridges cross the river to extend the garden in different directions – one way leads to a wildflower meadow, another to a quarry garden with a natural pond and cliff planted with tender plants thriving in the sheltered microclimate.

AN CALA ★
(Historic Scotland Inventory)

Mrs Sheila Downie

Easdale, Isle of Seil, Argyll and Bute
PA34 4RF.
Tel: (01852) 300237;
www.gardens-of-argyll.co.uk

16m SW of Oban. Signed to Easdale on
B844 off A816 Oban – Campbelltown
road

Open April to Oct, daily, 10am – 6pm

Entrance: £3

◗ ▢ WC ♿ ◁▷ ◊

A jewel of under five acres designed in the 1930s in front of a row of old distillery cottages, nestling into the surrounding cliffs. The stream, with its ponds and little waterfall, is an essential element in a series of different spaces filled with sophisticated colour, at their peak in spring and summer. A small wooden temple lined with a mosaic of fir cones stands at the far end of one of the ponds. This is how azaleas and rhododendrons should be planted on the small scale – enhancing rather than dominating the picture. Local slate paths invite the visitor into each well-planned corner. Just over the gate, in a different world, are ocean and islands.

ARBUTHNOTT HOUSE
(Historic Scotland Inventory)

The Viscount of Arbuthnott

Laurencekirk, Kincardineshire AB30 1PA.
Tel: (01561) 361226;
www.arbuthnott.co.uk

22m S of Aberdeen, 3m W of Inverbervie
on B967 between A90 (A94) and A92

The enclosed garden dates from the late seventeenth century and together with its policies is contained within the valley of the Bervie Water. The entrance drive is flanked by rhododendrons, and in spring the verges are full of primroses and celandines. The drive crosses a fine bridge topped by imposing urns before reaching the house set high on a promontory, with most of the five-acre garden sloping steeply to the river. The sloping part has four grassed terraces, and this pattern is dissected by diagonal grassed walks radiating out in a manner reminiscent of the Union Jack. This fixed structure creates long garden rooms and vistas as the garden is explored. Although the framework is very old, much of today's mature planting was done by Lady Arbuthnott in the 1920s, and this is continued by the present chatelaine. Herbaceous borders, old roses, shrub roses and ramblers, shrubs underplanted with hostas, primulas, meconopsis and lilies, lilacs and viburnums provide colour throughout the summer. A metal stag for target practice stands at the bottom of the slope by the lade (millstream).

House open by appt

Garden open all year, daily, 9am – 5pm

Entrance: £2.50, children £1

Other information: Refreshments available at Grassic Gibbon Centre in village

○ WC

ARDMADDY CASTLE

The handsome but modest fifteenth-century castle, with steps up to its *piano nobile*, faces both ways: outwards with wide views to the islands and the sea, inwards on the garden side towards steep surrounding woods and a formal walled garden. In the eighteenth century Ardmaddy marked the western extent of the Earl of Breadalbane's estate, enabling him to ride from one side of Scotland to the other on his own land – until all was gambled away in the early twentieth century. The walled garden set below the castle has traditional box hedge compartments, large numbers of species and hybrid rhododendrons and an increasing collection of herbaceous plants and flowering shrubs and trees as well as immaculate vegetables. A water garden with two ponds, and a woodland garden with walks, add further interest. There is always a good selection of home-grown plants and vegetables (in season) on sale. 10 acres in all.

Mr and Mrs Charles Struthers

By Oban, Argyll PA34 4QY.
Tel: (01852) 300353;
www.gardens-of-argyll.co.uk

13m SW of Oban. Signed from B844 to Easdale along narrow road

Open all year, daily, 9am – dusk

Entrance: £3

○ 🐾 WC ♿ ⟨⟩ 🐾 ♀

ARDTORNISH

(Historic Scotland Inventory)

A plantsman's garden of 28 acres with a particularly fine and extensive collection of unusual shrubs, deciduous trees and rhododendrons set against a background of conifers, a loch and outstanding Highland scenery. The first house on the site was built by a London distiller in the 1860s, and the gardens have developed over the past hundred years or more. They are on a steep slope and rainfall is heavy. Mrs Raven's late husband wrote a book, *The Botanist's Garden* (now republished), about their other garden, Docwra's Manor (see entry in Cambridgeshire), and here too he assisted his wife to follow in her parents' footsteps in trying to establish a plantsman's paradise. Apart from the area around the house, there is a pleasing air of informality about the gardens, which include Bob's Glen with *Rhododendron thomsonii* and *R. prattii*, a larger glen with still more species and hybrid rhododendrons, and a kitchen garden under separate management nearby, where good-quality plants are for sale.

Ardtornish Estate Company

Lochaline, Morvern, Highland PA34 5UZ.
Tel: (01967) 421288 (Estate Office)

30m SW of Corran. From Corran ferry, 9m SW of Fort William, cross to Morvern and take route left on A861 towards Lochaline, then left on A884. Gardens are 2m before Lochaline on left

Open April to Nov, daily, 9am – 6pm

Entrance: £3, children free (collecting box)

Other information: 12 self-catering units available, 5 in house

◑ 🐾 WC ♿ ⟨⟩

Arduaine Garden

ARDUAINE GARDEN ★★
(Historic Scotland Inventory)

The National Trust for Scotland

Oban, Argyll and Bute PA34 4XQ.
Tel: (01852) 200366;
www.arduaine-garden.org.uk

On A816, 20m S of Oban, 18m N of
Lochgilphead. Joint entrance with Loch
Melfort Hotel

Open all year, daily, 9.30am – sunset

Entrance: £5, concessions and
children £4, family £14 (2007 prices)

Other information: Refreshments at
hotel adjacent – coach parties must
pre-book, telephone (01852) 200233

This outstanding 20-acre garden, located on a promontory
bounded by Loch Melfort and the Sound of Jura, climatically
favoured by the North Atlantic Drift, was conceived and
begun in 1898 by James Arthur Campbell. The Essex
nurserymen Edmund and Harry Wright acquired the garden
in 1971, restored it and gave it to the Trust in 1992. Make
the effort to climb to the high viewing point to enjoy the
panorama of ocean, coasts and islands. Although Arduaine's
fame rests largely on its outstanding rhododendrons, azaleas,
magnolias and other rare and tender trees and shrubs, the
garden has far more than botanical interest to offer. Trees
and shrubs, some over a hundred years old and thickly
underplanted, tower overhead as they, and visitors, climb the
glen, while at the lower level hostas, ferns, candelabra
primulas, meconopsis and numerous other flower and
foliage perennials cluster around lawns and along the sides
of the watercourses.

ARNOT TOWER GARDENS

Helen and Benjamin Gray

Leslie, Fife KY6 3TQ.
Tel: (01592) 840 115;
www.arnottower.co.uk

Just W of Glenrothes on A911, 1.5m
outside Scotlandwell; signed on left

Open 6th May to Sept, Tues,
10am – 5pm, and for parties by appt

Entrance: £3.50, children free

Overlooked by the magnificent ruins of Arnot Tower and the
Victorian mansion, the outstanding feature of this
contemporary garden is the impressive flight of stone-paved
steps, flanked by herbaceous planting, which leads down
through three small terraces to an elegantly long rill and stone
ponds enlivened by five dramatic water jets. This rectangular
arena is kept deliberately simple as it is often used as a
wedding venue, but on the other side of the hornbeam
hedges are generous and colourful herbaceous borders. The
treatment of the gradient is a particularly good example of
how to turn a challenging slope into a successful and
handsome feature. The owners have opened up the view
down to Loch Leven and are continuing to restore and
expand the garden.

ASCOG HALL FERNERY AND GARDEN

Although the main reason for your visit will be the magnificently restored fern house built c.1875, the rest of the flourishing three-acre garden with its abundance of choice plants comes as a delightful surprise. Paths meander through immaculate beds, and undulating banks create themed areas: an enclosed rose garden with a pergola, exotic plants, a white-themed garden and a most successful gravel garden. The present owners bought the house in 1986 and only then stumbled on hidden rustic steps leading down to a sunken, derelict interior with strangely fashioned walls and rotting vegetation, all submerged under bracken, ivy and brambles. Thanks to a description and inventory in *The Gardeners' Chronicle* of 1879, professional help from Historic Scotland and a collection of ferns donated by the Royal Botanic Garden, Edinburgh, the glasshouse has been exactly reconstructed. Artfully planted in a grotto setting and sympathetically enhanced by a waterfall and pools, it now houses one of the most impressive collections to be found outside a botanic garden. Its star (and the only original survivor) is a 1000-year-old *Todea barbara* fern, a true Sleeping Beauty now thankfully awake in this fairytale fernery.

Wallace and Katherine Fyfe

Isle of Bute PA20 9EU.
Tel: (01700) 504555;
www.ascoghallfernery.co.uk

Car ferry (35 mins) from Wemyss Bay to Rothesay (www.calmac.co.uk). 5-min drive on A844; bus from Rothesay to Ascog and Mount Stuart (Easter to Sept); or 10-min ferry from Colintraive to N end of Bute

Open 21st to 24th March, daily; 26th March to Oct, Wed – Sun; all 10am – 5pm

Entrance: £3, supervised children free

ATTADALE

Water and sculpture combine to give this 20-acre garden its considerable appeal. Inside the gate a stream and ponds all along one side of the drive are beautifully planted with candelabra primulas, irises, giant gunneras and bamboos. A bridge over a waterfall links the water garden with the upper rhododendron walk, commanding views of the sea and hills.

Mr and Mrs Ewen Macpherson

Strathcarron, Wester Ross, Ross-shire IV54 8YX. Tel: (01520) 722217; www.attadale.com

15m NE of Kyle of Lochalsh, on A890 between Strathcarron and Strome

Open April to Oct, daily except Sun, 10am – 5.30pm

Entrance: £4.50, OAPs £3, children £1, disabled free

Other information: Car park 50 yards from garden; disabled parking by Attadale. House. Meals available at Carron Restaurant 1.5m away. Self-catering cottages available

Attadale

Sculpture from Zimbabwe and bronzes by Bridget McCrum and Elizabeth Macdonald Buchanan are reflected in the ponds, and a bronze crested eagle created by Rosie Sturgis perches on a cliff. The formal kitchen garden has a slate urn by Joe Smith; beyond, a recently built geodesic dome houses a collection of exotic ferns and is surrounded by hardy ferns, including tree ferns, backed by dripping cliffs. (Visitors should linger here, for over 50 species are on offer in the plant sales area.) A path leads down to a dell of rhododendrons planted by the Schroder family nearly a century ago, then on along a woodland path to the new Japanese garden, where lichened rocks and gravel imitate the River of Life and the Mystic Isles of the West. The symmetrical sunken garden in front of the 1755 house (not open) provides a complete contrast. Visitors are advised to wear waterproof shoes.

BALLINDALLOCH CASTLE

Mrs Oliver MacPherson-Grant Russell

Grantown-on-Spey, Banffshire AB37 9AX.
Tel: (01807) 500205;
www.ballindallochcastle.co.uk

Halfway between Grantown-on-Spey and Keith on A95. Signposted

Castle and garden open 21st March to Sept, daily except Sat, 10.30am – 5pm, and by appt

Entrance: £3.50, OAPs £3, children (6-16) £2, family £9 (castle and gardens £7.50, OAPs £6, children £4, family £20)

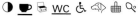

What a pleasure to find a garden of this scale and calibre set in the magnificent Spey valley. One of the most attractive feature is the 1937 rock garden, which comes tumbling down the hillside onto the most impressive lawn in the land. It takes three men two days to mow and edge it. The owners have completely renovated all the borders over the years and transformed the old walled garden into a rose and fountain parterre garden which has matured most attractively. The daffodil season and the river and woodland walks are particularly lovely. The grass labyrinth is an intriguing feature, and a small parterre at the side of the house shows how stunning humble nepeta and *Alchemilla mollis* can be when all else is eaten by the deer.

BALMORAL CASTLE
(Historic Scotland Inventory)

Balmoral Estate

Ballater, Aberdeenshire AB35 5TB.
Tel: (013397) 42534 (Estates Office);
www.balmoralcastle.com

6m W of Ballater on A93 at Crathie

Castle ballroom and carriage exhibitions open

Gardens and grounds open April to July, daily, 10am – 5pm

Entrance: £7, OAPs £6, children (5–16) £3, under 5 free, family (2 adults and 4 children) £15 (2007 prices)

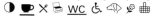

Balmoral, the personal home in Scotland of Her Majesty the Queen, is Gaelic for 'majestic dwelling'. There had been earlier castles on the same site before the estate was purchased in 1852 by Prince Albert, consort to Queen Victoria. She called the place 'this dear paradise', and the couple immediately began making a three-acre garden about the castle and planting the grounds with rare coniferous and broad-leaved forest trees. Queen Mary added the sunken rose garden in 1932, and since 1953 there have been improvements and extensions, including a water garden created in 1979 close to Victoria's garden cottage. There are herbaceous borders, but generally the gardens are natural in style. Throughout the grounds statues and cairns have been erected in memory of members of the House of Windsor, and specimen trees labelled with the names of the visiting dignitaries who planted them. The kitchen garden, developed by the Duke of Edinburgh, provides all the fruit and vegetables for the royal table.

BELL'S CHERRYBANK GARDENS AND SCOTTISH NATIONAL HEATHER COLLECTION

The garden was laid out originally in 1984 to display the whisky company's National Collection of heathers. Today there are over 900 varieties, all in superb condition and planted in sweeping swathes which flow in a surprising gamut of colour over mounded island beds. Water interest is provided by a trout stream, a bog garden and a modern fountain pool. The family-friendly activities include a good cafe, a putting green, an aviary, a playpark and a dedicated children's shop. It may not seem an obvious destination, but proves to be well worth a visit – not many gardens rely on a single genus to such good effect. Also of considerable interest is the detailed scale model of The Calyx, the proposed £30-million 'Scotland's Garden', the vision of Jim McColl, which is being developed on an adjacent 61-acre site and, pending lottery funding, will hopefully be opened in 2010. Described as a garden for the twenty-first century, it is intended to delight, inspire and educate, using the best in design and horticultural techniques and techology. Annual visitor numbers are expected to reach 250,000.

Bell's Cherrybank Centre, Cherrybank, Perth PH2 0PF. Tel: (01738) 472800

Off A93 S of Perth, approx 1m from Broxden roundabout; signposted. Regular bus services from city centre

Open Jan and Feb, Thurs to Sat; March to Dec, daily; all 10am – 5pm (opens 12 noon Sun, closes 4pm Nov to Feb)

Entrance: £3.75, concessions £3.40, children (12– 6) £2.50, under 12 free

Other information: Guide dogs only

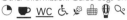

BENMORE BOTANIC GARDEN ★★

(Historic Scotland Inventory)

This regional garden of the Royal Botanic Garden Edinburgh is a magnificent mountainside garden of 120 acres, set in the dramatic location of the Cowal Peninsula. It is world-famous for its collections of flowering trees and shrubs. From Britain's finest avenue of giant redwoods (*Sequoiadendron giganteum*) planted in 1863, a variety of trails spreads out. More than 300 species of rhododendron and an extensive magnolia collection provide a positive array of colour on the hillside beside the River Eachaig. Other features include a

Dunoon, Argyll, Argyll and Bute PA23 8QU. Tel: (01369) 706261; www.rbge.org.uk

7m N of Dunoon, W of A815 at Benmore. Signposted

Open March to Oct, daily, 10am – 6pm (closes 5pm March and Oct), and at other times by appt

Entrance: £4, concessions £3.50, children £1, family £9

Benmore Botanic Garden

formal garden with stately conifers, an informal pond, the Glen Massan arboretum with some of the tallest trees in Scotland, a Chilean rainforest and a Bhutanese glade. A short climb leads to a stunning viewpoint looking out across the garden, Strath Eck and the Holy Loch to the Firth of Clyde and beyond.

BIGGAR PARK ★

Capt. and Mrs David Barnes

Biggar, South Lanarkshire ML12 6JS. Tel: (01899) 220185

30m SW of Edinburgh at S end of Biggar on A702

Open May to July by appt

Entrance: £4

A Japanese garden of tranquillity welcomes the visitor to this well-planned 10-acre plantsman's garden. The efficient labelling adds greatly to the enjoyment when walking through the woodland and the small arboretum and well-planted ornamental pond. The planting is carefully designed to give year-round interest, starting with a stunning display of daffodils, with a little field of snake's-head fritillaries blooming at the end of April, followed by masses of meconopsis, rhododendrons and azaleas in early summer before the huge herbaceous borders burst into colour. The high point, however, must be the outstanding walled garden, reached through a fine rockery bank beside the eighteenth-century house. The view through the wrought-iron gate stretches the length of a 45-metre double herbaceous border, attractively backed by swags of thick ornamental rope hanging from rose 'pillars', while the intensively planted sections either side are intersected by pleasing grass paths and plots of fruit and vegetables.

BLACKHILLS HOUSE

Mr and Mrs John Christie

Lhanbryde, Elgin, Moray IV30 8QU. Tel: (01343) 842223; www.blackhills.co.uk

4m E of Elgin off A96. Take B9103 southwards, then minor road

Open April to May by appt

Entrance: by donation

Other information: Teas and picnic lunches for parties by arrangement. Self-catering accommodation available

The east coast of Scotland is not, with a few exceptions, noted for its rhododendron gardens, but this 50-acre garden in the Laich of Moray should be visited for its collection of species rhododendrons in early May and hybrids in late May. Both sorts are spread under tree cover in a steep-sided valley with many fine specimen trees. These include a davidia, a Japanese red cedar (*Cryptomeria japonica*), Brewer's weeping spruce and *Chrysolepis chrysophylla*, a rare chestnut relative from North America. The finest rhododendrons are those in the subsections Falconera, Grandia and Taliensia, but the genus is well represented as a whole. The wooded valley opens to reveal two lakes with plantings of maples and other Asiatic plants. Thomas North Christie, who was responsible for the early planting in the 1920s, corresponded at length and exchanged the latest introductions with his neighbour the Brodie of Brodie.

BLAIR CASTLE ★

(Historic Scotland Inventory)

The Blair Charitable Trust

Blair Atholl, Pitlochry, Perthshire PH18 5TL. Tel: (01796) 481207; www.blair-castle.co.uk

35m N of Perth on A9 at Blair Atholl. Signposted

The blazing white castle remains one of Scotland's most important, most visited and best presented historic houses in private hands. The 2500-acre managed park and landscape were begun in 1730 by the 2nd Duke of Atholl in the French manner, with geometrically patterned avenues and walks radiating out from the castle. His most important legacy was the nine-acre walled Hercules Garden of 1758, named after the life-size lead statue by John Cheere which overlooks it. It is unique, not only for its scale, but also for the fact that it contains extensive water features. A series of delightful ponds, planted islands and peninsulas forms a central axis from which fruit tree orchards – faithfully reproduced, but without the original underplanting of fruit and vegetables – slope gently upwards to herbaceous borders, yew buttresses and elegant gravel walks backed by the original eighteenth-century walls. A charming apple-store museum, a nineteenth-century folly, statuary, an ogee-roofed pavilion and a Chinoiserie bridge all add to the beauty of this unusual garden in its splendid Highland setting.

House open as garden

Garden open 21st March to 24th Oct, daily, 9.30am – 5.30pm (last entry 4.30pm), Nov to March by appt

Entrance: £2.70, children £1.30, family £6 (house and grounds £7.90, OAPs £6.90, students £6.50, children £4.90, family £20.50)

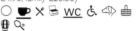

BOLFRACKS
(Historic Scotland Inventory)

There has been a garden on this site for over two centuries, but the present one was started by the owner's grandparents in the 1920s and reshaped by his uncle over the last thirty years. Three acres of plantsman's garden are well laid out within a walled enclosure and demonstrate the potential of an exposed hillside site with a northerly aspect. Astounding views over the Tay Valley are matched by the garden's own interesting features, including peat walls and a stream garden. There are masses of fine bulbs in spring and good autumn colour. An excellent collection of mainly dwarf rhododendrons has been established over the years and gives a wonderful display in May and June. Gentians, meconopsis, ericaceous plants and celmisias do well on this soil. The walled garden contains a collection of old and modern shrub roses and rambling roses and a great variety of herbaceous perennials.

Mr R. A. Price

Aberfeldy, Perth and Kinross PH15 2EX. Tel: (01887) 820344; www.bolfracks.com

2m W of Aberfeldy on A827 towards Loch Tay

Open April to Oct, daily, 10am – 6pm

Entrance: £4, children under 16 free (honesty box at gate)

BRANKLYN GARDEN ★
(Historic Scotland Inventory)

John and Dorothy Renton created this garden nearly within sight and certainly within sound of the centre of Perth. Work commenced in 1922, and in 1955 Dorothy was awarded the Veitch Memorial Medal by the Royal Horticultural Society. The National Trust for Scotland took over the garden in 1968. It extends to nearly two acres, the main interest being its Sino-Himalayan alpine and ericaceous plants and magnificent scree/rock gardens. There is also a splendid collection of dwarf rhododendrons and a National Collection of the Mylnefield lilies bred by Dr Chris North. Essential work continues to maintain Branklyn's rightful reputation as an outstanding plantsman's garden. It is impossible to describe all the fascinating things to be found here, from the fine trees to the

The National Trust for Scotland

116 Dundee Road, Perth, Perth and Kinross PH2 7BB. Tel: (01738) 625535; www.branklyngarden.org.uk

0.5m from Friarton Bridge on A90, then A859 to Perth

Open 21st March to Oct, daily, 10am – 5pm

Entrance: £5, concessions £4, family £14.

Other information: Steep lane to garden. Parking for disabled and coaches at entrance. Possible for wheelchairs but some paths too narrow

comprehensive collection of dwarf and smaller rhododendrons, the meconopsis to the notholirions. This is a garden that repays many visits.

Robert and Anna Dalrymple

Broadwoodside, Gifford, East Lothian EH41 4JQ Tel: (01620) 810351

On B6355 leaving Gifford towards golf course

Open for SGS, and for parties by appt

Entrance: £5, children under 16 free

NEW

BROADWOODSIDE

The East Lothian farmstead was rescued from dereliction in 2000 and with talented restoration has been turned into something much grander. The garden, shortlisted for the 2007 *Country Life* 'The Genius of the Place' award and still in its youth, will grow and grow – a magical and intimate place that literally clothes the buildings. An eye-catching door incorporating three garden forks forms the entrance to the kitchen garden and sets the atmosphere of this imaginative place. The centrepiece is a formal rectangular pond surrounded by willows that are cut back every winter. Vegetables in raised beds and flowers for cutting are arranged in symmetrical rectangular beds. From the kitchen garden a covered pond leads to the first of the two courtyards, where a simple formal layout is richly and informally planted with scented pink and white roses, white foxgloves, astrantias, bronze fennel, macleayas, geraniums and violas. The formality continues in the upper courtyard with an eye-catching chequerboard design, alternate squares being occupied by standard mop-top *Acer platanoides* 'Globosum', each with a different underplanting: one has clipped box balls, another two varieties of allium, and a third a solid block of clipped germander. Every detail executed with perfection. There is humour here too, with each tree boldly labelled with an erroneous name. The garden continues beyond the house and out into the beautiful East Lothian farmland with an iris canal, an *allée* of beech hedging, an orchard and a hornbeam avenue. Even the wider landscape has been treated in a style that is a cross between eighteenth-century Picturesque and Ian Hamilton Finlay and dotted with a temple and other follies. In all, 200 acres.

The National Trust for Scotland

Isle of Arran, North Ayrshire KA27 8HY. Tel: (01770) 302202; www.nts.org.uk

On Isle of Arran, 2m N of Brodick. Ferry from Ardrossan or Kintyre

Gardens and country park open all year, daily, 9.30am – dusk. Walled garden open 21st March to Oct, daily, 9.30am – 5pm

Entrance: £5, concessions £3, family £14 (castle and gardens £10, concessions £7, family £20)

Other information: Wheelchair available

BRODICK CASTLE
(Historic Scotland Inventory)

High above the shores of the Firth of Clyde and guarding the approaches to Western Scotland is a castle of locally quarried sandstone. The garden was an overgrown jungle of rhododendrons until it was restored by the Duchess of Montrose after World War I. She was much helped after 1930 when her daughter married John Boscawen of Tresco Abbey (see entry in Cornwall). Many trees and plants arrived at that time by boat from Tresco in the Scillies; others came from subscriptions to the second generation of great plant-hunters like Kingdon Ward and, in particular, George Forrest. Plants from the Himalayas, Burma, China and South America, normally considered tender, flourish in the mild climate. There is a good display of primulas in the bog garden. The walled

Brodick Castle

formal garden to the east of the castle is over 250 years old and has recently been restored as an Edwardian garden with herbaceous plants, annuals and roses. It is impossible to list all the treasures of the woodland garden, but perhaps the most surprising is the huge size of the specimens in the lower rhododendron walk. Opposite Brodick on the west side of the island, five miles north of Blackwaterfoot, is *Dougarie Lodge*, an impressive castellated terrace garden created in 1905 with a wide range of semi-hardy trees and plants, and lovely views towards the Mull of Kintyre. [Open one day in summer for SGS and by appt; telephone Mr and Mrs Gibbs on (01475) 337355.]

BROUGHTON HOUSE ★
(Historic Scotland Inventory)

Created by an artist, E.A. Hornel, who lived here from 1901 to 1933, this fascinating 1.5-acre garden reflects an interest in Oriental art following a visit to Japan, and incorporates both Japanese and Scottish features. After his death the house became a museum and its surroundings were gradually restored. The garden starts with a sunken courtyard, beyond which is a pleasant hybrid, a cross between 'fantasy Japan and fantasy old-world cottage garden'. Japanese cherries blossom over skilful low-level planting in the sunken courtyard, and further down are all the elements of a much larger garden: rose parterre, pergola, glasshouse, box hedges and herbaceous borders, all looking remarkably uncrowded. Charming lily pools have flat stepping stones and dramatic boulders. At the end of the long central walk, beyond a hedge, is the River Dee with its mudflats and saltings.

The National Trust for Scotland

12 High Street, Kirkcudbright, Dumfries and Galloway DG6 4JX.
Tel: (01557) 330437; www.nts.org.uk

28m SW of Dumfries. Take A75 from Dumfries past Castle Douglas, then 1m past Bridge of Dee take A711 to Kirkcudbright. Signposted

Garden open Feb and March, Mon – Fri, 11am – 4pm; April to June, Sept and Oct, Thurs – Mon, 12 noon – 5pm; July and Aug, daily, 12 noon – 5pm

Entrance: house and garden £8, OAPs £5, family £20

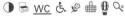

BUGHTRIG

Owned by just three families since the fourteenth century, the traditional Scottish garden of three acres, designed for amenity, but unusually is hedged rather than walled and sited close to the house. It contains an interesting combination of herbaceous, perennials, shrubs, annuals and fruit, surrounded by fine specimen trees which provide remarkable shelter.

Major General and
The Hon. Mrs Charles Ramsay

Coldstream, Berwickshire, Scottish Borders TD12 4JP.
Tel: (01890) 840678

5m N of Coldstream, 0.25m E of Leitholm on B6461

Open June to Sept, daily, 11am – 5pm

Entrance: £2.50, children £1

Bughtrig is a classic family home. Organised *bona fida* parties are welcome to make an appointment to visit the garden and occasionally also the Georgian house. Accommodation can sometimes be arranged for small groups of 6–8 people.

CALLY GARDENS AND NURSERY

(Historic Scotland Inventory)

Mr Michael Wickenden

Gatehouse of Fleet, Castle Douglas, Dumfries and Galloway DG7 2DJ. Tel: (01557) 815029 (Infoline); www.callygardens.co.uk

30m SW of Dumfries via A75. Take Gatehouse turning and turn left through Cally Palace Hotel gateway. Signposted

Open 22nd March to 28th Sept, daily except Mon, 2 – 5.30pm (opens 10am Sat and Sun)

Entrance: £2.50, children under 13 free

The house, built *c.* 1763-5 to designs by Robert Mylne, was once surrounded by an elegantly planned landscape with extensive woodland. In 1939, the 600-acre estate was sold to the Forestry Commission and 500 acres were promptly replanted. Three hundred Glasgow children 'dug for Victory' here in World War II. The gardens, however, have flourished since the arrival of the present owner. A specialist nursery in the large eighteenth-century walled garden has generous beds of herbaceous plants and many unusual varieties. There is a impressive collection of perennial geraniums, kniphofias, crocosmias and others – 3500 varieties in all. Almost all the plants in the sales area are propagated on the premises, some from seed collected abroad or sent in botanic garden exchanges, and a changing selection of several hundred is available pot-grown. A favourite with visitors is the spread of meconopsis (Himalayan blue poppies) when in season in early June. The Cally Oak Woods which surround the nursery have nature trails. The house is now run as a country house hotel, which has taken ownership of the remaining policies.

CAMBO GARDENS

Sir Peter and Lady Erskine

Kingsbarns, St Andrews, Fife KY16 8QD. Tel: (01333) 450313; www.camboestate.com

6m SE of St Andrews on A917 between Kingsbarns and Crail

Open all year, daily, 10am – 5pm

Entrance: £4, children free

Other information: Self-catering accommodation available

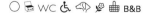

This romantic Victorian walled garden of 2.5 acres is designed around the Cambo burn with weeping willows, a waterfall and rose-clad wrought-iron bridges. Naturalistic plantings of rare and interesting herbaceous perennials add to the informal atmosphere of the garden. There are masses of spring bulbs, a lilac walk with 26 cultivars, over 250 old-fashioned and rambling roses, and glowing early autumn borders. Beyond the walled garden a woodland garden includes a September meadow of colchicums, and 70 acres of woodland walks leading to the sea are carpeted in early spring with snowflakes, aconites and a spectacular display of snowdrops (250 varieties, forming part of a National Collection).

CASTLE FRASER

(Historic Scotland Inventory)

The National Trust for Scotland

Sauchen, Inverurie, Aberdeenshire AB51 7LD. Tel: (01330) 833463; www.nts.org.uk

15m NW of Aberdeen, off B993 near Kemnay

Castle open

Garden open all year, daily, 9am – 6pm

The 328-acre grounds – the setting for one of the most spectacular of the castles of Mar – consist of a designed landscape of the late seventeenth and early eighteenth centuries with eighteenth-century agricultural developments. The deep, south-facing herbaceous border, designed in 1959 by James Russell, has been reworked to accommodate a greater selection of plants tolerant of the brisk climate. The historic walled garden has been completely replanted and the original cross- and perimeter paths have been reinstated. A woodland garden is being developed around the walled garden, together with a woodland play area with an amphitheatre. Extensive walks in the grounds include superb views of the castle in its parkland setting and outwards to the neighbouring hills.

Entrance: castle and garden £8, concessions £5, family £20 (2007 prices)

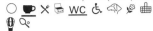

CASTLE KENNEDY ★★

(Historic Scotland Inventory)

One of Scotland's most famous gardens, set on a peninsula between two lochs and well worth a visit for its sheer 75-acre magnificence and spectacular spring colour. The gardens, originally laid out in the late seventeenth century, were later remodelled by Field Marshal the 2nd Earl of Stair. He used his unoccupied dragoons to effect a major remoulding of the landscape around the ruined castle, which had burnt down in 1716, combining large formal swathes of mown grassland with massive formal gardens, criss-crossed by avenues and *allées* of large specimen trees. The garden is internationally famous for its pinetum, its good variety of tender trees and its species rhododendrons, including many of Sir Joseph Hooker's original introductions from his Himalayan expeditions. The monkey puzzle avenue, now sadly a little tattered, was once the finest in the world; there is also an avenue of noble firs underplanted with embothriums and eucryphias. An impressive two-acre circular lily pond puts everyone else's in their proper place, and a good walk from this brings the visitor back to the ruined castle and its walled garden, well planted with themed borders. The adjacent garden centre sells some excellent plants.

The Earl of Stair

Stair Estates, Rephad, Stranraer, Wigtownshire, Dumfries and Galloway DG9 8BX.
Tel: (01776) 702024/(01581) 400225; www.castlekennedygardens.co.uk

5m E of Stranraer on A75

Open Feb and March, Sat and Sun; 21st March to Sept, daily; all 10am – 5pm; and by appt at other times

Entrance: £4, OAPs £3, children £1 (2007 prices)

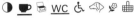

Castle Kennedy

The Queen Elizabeth Castle of Mey Trust

Thurso, Caithness, Highland KW14 8XH.
Tel: (01847) 851473; www.castleofmey.org.uk

1.5m from Mey on A836

Open May to 23rd July, 6th Aug to Sept, daily, 10am – 5pm

Entrance: £3, concessions £2.50, children free (castle and gardens £8, concessions £7, children £3, family £20)

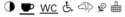

CASTLE OF MEY
(Historic Scotland Inventory)

The castle dates from the late sixteenth century and was renovated by H.M. The Queen Mother between 1952 and 1955. Gardening would not be possible in such an exposed position without the protection of the 'Great Wall of Mey'. Within the three-acre walled garden, she collected her favourite flowers; many were gifts and have special meaning. A personal feeling pervades the whole garden, which is well planted and well maintained. The colour schemes are good, blending the garden with the vast natural panorama within which it is situated.

The Dowager Countess Cawdor

Cawdor, Nairn, Highland IV12 5RD.
Tel: (01667) 404401;
www.cawdorcastle.com

Between Inverness and Nairn on B9090 off A96

Castle open

Garden open May to 14th Oct, daily, 10am – 5.30pm

Entrance: £4 (castle and garden £7.30, OAPs £6.30, children £4.50, family £23.50) (2007 prices)

Other information: Garden weekend 7th and 8th June

CAWDOR CASTLE ★
(Historic Scotland Inventory)

Frequently referred to as one of the Highland's most romantic castles and steeped in history, the castle consists of a fourteenth-century keep with seventeenth- and nineteenth-century additions. The surrounding parkland is handsome and well kept, though not in the grand tradition of classic landscapes. To the side of the castle is the formal garden, where wrought-iron arches frame extensive herbaceous borders, a peony border, a venerable hedge of mixed varieties of *Rosa pimpinellifolia* (the Scots or Burnet rose), a rose tunnel, old apple trees festooned with climbing roses, interesting shrubs and lilies. An abundance of lavender and pinks completes a rather Edwardian atmosphere. The castle wall shelters exochordas, *Abutilon vitifolium*, *Carpenteria californica* and *Rosa banksiae*. Pillar-box red seats create an unusual note in this splendidly flowery place, but the owner likes them. The walled garden below the castle has been restored with a holly maze, a thistle garden, a laburnum walk and a white garden. The latter is a 'Paradise garden', preceded by Earth represented as a knot garden, and between the two lies Purgatory. There are fine views everywhere of the castle, the park and the surrounding countryside, which one can enjoy more actively by walking one of the five nature trails, varying in length from half a mile to five miles. Further developments include the Auchindoune gardens, where Arabella Lennox-Boyd helped with the planting (open May to July, Tues and Thurs, 10am – 4pm; extra charge).

Mr J. and Mrs W. Mattingley

Aberfeldy, Perth and Kinross PH15 2JT.
Tel: (01887) 820795

32m NW of Perth. N of Aberfeldy, over Wade's Bridge, take A827 Weem – Strathtay road. House signed after 3m

Open March to Oct, daily, 10am – 6pm

CLUNY HOUSE ★
(Historic Scotland Inventory)

Unlike most other gardens, this is as truly wild as one can find – friendly weeds grow unchecked for fear of disturbing an extensive collection of Asiatic primulas. Sheltered slopes create a moist microclimate where all the plants flourish abundantly, including a *Sequoiadendron giganteum* with the British near-record girth of over 11 metres. In the superb woodland garden many of the plants were propagated from seed acquired by Mrs Mattingley's father on the Ludlow/Sherriff expedition to Bhutan in 1948. Special treats are the carpets of bulbs, trilliums and meconopsis, a fine selection of Japanese acers, *Prunus serrula*, hundreds of different rhododendrons, *Cardiocrinum giganteum*, massive lysichitons and many fine specimen trees. The six-acre garden is managed on strictly organic principles, and it is delightful to see native wild flowers and garden plants growing together in harmony and profusion, and red squirrels putting in a welcome appearance.

Entrance: £4, children free

COLZIUM LENNOX ESTATE

An outstanding collection of conifers, including dwarf cultivars, and rare trees, has been established in the beautifully designed 0.6-acre walled garden. Everything is well labelled and immaculately maintained; even the gravel paths are raked. There are also 100 varieties each of snowdrops and crocuses. An arboretum and a glen provide attractive walks, and a curling pond and clock theatre are unusual features. Of architectural interest are the fifteenth-century tower house and seventeenth-century ice-house. All in all, an unusual array of gardens and buildings, water features and outdoor activities are on offer. Maintenance is immaculate.

North Lanarkshire Council

Kilsyth, Glasgow G65 0PY.
Tel: (01236) 828150;
www.northian.gov.uk

14m NE of Glasgow on A803

Estate open all year, daily. Walled garden open April to Sept, daily, 12 noon – 7pm; Oct to March, Sat and Sun, 12 noon – 4pm

Entrance: free

CORSOCK HOUSE

A most attractive 25-acre woodland garden with exceptionally fine plantings both of trees (beech, Wellingtonia, oak, Douglas fir, cercidiphyllum, acer) and of rhododendrons (*R. thomsonii*, *lacteum*, *loderi*, *prattii*, *sutchuenense*). The knowledgeable owner has contributed most imaginatively to the layout of the gardens over the last forty years, creating glades, planting vistas of azaleas and personally building temples and a *trompe-l'oeil* bridge which give the gardens a classical atmosphere. An impressive highlight is the large water garden, again cleverly laid out and with water-edge plantings set off by a background of mature trees giving good autumn colour.

Mr and Mrs M. L. Ingall

Corsock, Castle Douglas, Dumfries and Galloway DG7 3DJ. Tel: (01644) 440250

10m N of Castle Douglas on A712. Signed from A75 onto B794

Open for SGS, and by appt

Entrance: £3, children free

Other information: Refreshments on open day

CRARAE GARDEN ★★
(Historic Scotland Inventory)

Thanks to a successful £1.5 million fund-raising campaign, a phased programme of restoration is underway in one of the most important of Scottish woodland gardens. The gardens were originally planned by Grace, Lady Campbell in the early part of last century, possibly inspired by her nephew Reginald Farrer, the famous traveller and plant collector. Subsequently her son, Sir George Campbell (1894–1967), spent many years creating this superb Himalayan ravine set in a Highland glen, the whole enlivened by splendid torrents and waterfalls. Using surplus seed from the great plant expeditions, numerous gifts

The National Trust for Scotland

Minard, Inveraray, Argyll and Bute PA32 8YA. Tel: (01546) 886614;
www.nts.org.uk

11m SW of Inveraray on A83

Open all year, daily, 9.30am – sunset

Entrance: £5, concessions and children £4, family £14 (2007 prices)

Other information: Visitor centre open April to Sept, daily, 10am – 5pm

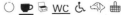

from knowledgeable friends and the shared expertise of a network of famous horticulturists, he planted a variety of rare trees (his first love), together with exotic shrubs and species rhododendrons, which now form great canopies above the winding paths. This must be a unique opportunity to see 440 different varieties of rhododendron, some exclusive to the garden, which, together with many other plants from the temperate world, make a magnificent spectacle of colour and differing perspectives. The autumn colouring of sorbus, acers, prunus, cotoneasters and berberis is one of the great features of the garden, which contains a National Collection of nothofagus. 126 acres in all.

The National Trust for Scotland

Banchory, Aberdeenshire AB31 5QJ.
Tel: (01330) 844525; www.nts.org.uk

3m E of Banchory, 15m SW of
Aberdeen on A93

Castle open

Garden and grounds open all year, daily,
9am – dusk

Entrance: £8, concessions and children
£5 (castle, garden and grounds £10,
concessions and children £7, family £25)

Other information: Parking 400 metres
from gardens (charge for non-Trust
members)

CRATHES CASTLE GARDEN ★★
(Historic Scotland Inventory)

The romantic castle, set in flowing lawns, dates from 1596, and looks much as it did in the mid-eighteenth century. There is no record of how the four-acre walled garden – one of the finest and most famous in Scotland – was laid out then, although the splendid yew topiary of 1702 survives. Sir James Burnett, who inherited the estate in the 1920s, was a keen collector, his wife an inspired herbaceous garden designer, and the garden today reflects their achievements. The terraces and sloping terrain increase the dramatic effect. Rare shrubs reflect Burnett's interest in the Far East, while the splendid wide herbaceous borders with clever plant associations were Lady Burnett's creation, the most famous being the white border. In all there are eight gardens, each with a different character and varied planting schemes, often compared to Hidcote but with evident inspiration from Jekyll. There are many specialist areas, such as the trough garden; the large greenhouses contain a National Collection of Malmaison carnations. The extensive wild gardens and 20 acres of parkland are furnished with

Crathes Castle Garden

picnic areas and marked trails, and there is a good plant centre stocking alpines, herbaceous perennials and some old varieties of plants to be seen in the garden.

CRUICKSHANK BOTANIC GARDEN

The garden was endowed in 1898 by Miss Anne H. Cruickshank, who stipulated that it should be used for the advancement of science at the university and for the enjoyment of the people of Aberdeen. Both hold good today. The original six acres were designed by George Nicholson of Kew, but that layout disappeared with World War I. The long wall, herbaceous border and sunken garden date from 1920, and in 1970 the garden was extended and a new rock garden made. The 1980s saw the creation of terrace and rose gardens and the restoration of the peat walls. There is also a sunken garden and beech, birch and azalea lawns. A small woodland area is rich in meconopsis, primulas, rhododendrons and hellebores. Proximity to the North Sea does not permit good growth of many large conifers, but there are fine species lilacs, witch hazels, and tender exotics protected by the long wall. The total area of the present garden is 11 acres, of which four are planted as an arboretum reached by a path from the summit of the rock garden.

The Cruickshank Trust and University of Aberdeen

St Machar Drive, Aberdeen AB24 3UU. Tel: (01224) 272704; www.abdn.ac.uk

1.5m N of city centre in Old Aberdeen. Entrance in Chanonry. Signposted

Open all year, Mon – Fri, 9am – 4.30pm; plus May to Sept, Sat and Sun, 2 – 5pm

Entrance: free

Other information: Children must be accompanied

CULROSS PALACE

(Historic Scotland Inventory)

This small historical showpiece, which runs on organic principles, is packed with fascinating plants and features, including the old poultry breed, the Scots Dumpy. The atmosphere of the seventeenth-century garden is evoked by such things as paths made from crushed shells, and great attention has been paid to the smallest details – clay watering cans, plants in baskets and hurdles, bee skeps in wall niches. On the walled terrace a kitchen and ornamental garden of the period is planted with an abundance of fruit, old-fashioned vegetables and herbs, all flourishing in a relatively frost-free environment.

The National Trust for Scotland

Culross, Dunfermline, Fife KY12 8JH. Tel: (01383) 880359; www.nts.org.uk

12m W of Forth Bridge off A985

Palace open March to Oct – dates and times vary

Garden open all year, daily, 9am – dusk (closes 4pm in winter)

Entrance: £2.50, children under 16 free (no charge when palace closed) (palace and garden £8, concessions and children £5, family £20)

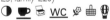

CULZEAN CASTLE ★★

(Historic Scotland Inventory)

Culzean is regarded by many as the Trust's flagship. The country-park landscape covers 563 acres with a network of woodland and cliff-top paths; the gardens themselves occupy a spacious 40 acres. The castle, originally a medieval fortified house atop the Ayrshire cliffs, was extensively restructured by Robert Adam from 1777 in what has become known as his 'Culzean style'. This is reflected in the many fine architectural features scattered throughout the grounds, and in particular the handsome home farm courtyard, now a visitor centre. Restoration work continues. A major undertaking was the

The National Trust for Scotland

Maybole, South Ayrshire KA19 8LE. Tel: (01655) 884400; www.culzeanexperience.org

12m S of Ayr on A719 coast road

Castle open 21st March to Oct (limited facilities Nov to March), 10.30am to 5pm (last admission 4pm)

Park open all year, daily, dawn – dusk

Gardens open, all year, daily, 9am – 5pm (closes 4pm Nov to March)

Culzean Castle

Entrance: £8, concessions and children £5, family £20 (castle, grounds and country park £12, concessions £8, family £30) (2007 prices)

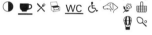

consolidation and partial rebuilding of Adam's unique viaduct. The camellia house, a picturesque 1818 glasshouse, has been restored to its original use as an orangery, the fountain in the garden below the castle repaired and replumbed, the southern walled garden completely redesigned and the vinery rebuilt on the original site based on its Victorian plan. The Swan Pond buildings have been conserved and repaired along with the beautiful bridge to the north. The restored pagoda is now spectacular, and the Dolphin House has been turned into an environmental education centre.

DAWYCK BOTANIC GARDEN ★
(Historic Scotland Inventory)

Royal Botanic Garden Edinburgh

Stobo, Peeblesshire, Scottish Borders EH45 9JU. Tel: (01721) 760254; www.rbge.org.uk

20m SW of Edinburgh, 8m SW of Peebles on B712

Open Feb to Nov, daily, 10am (closing times vary), and at other times by appt

Entrance: £4, concessions £3.50, children £1, family £9

Other information: Guide dogs only

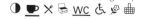

This is a specialist garden of the Royal Botanic Garden Edinburgh (see entry). With over 300 years of tree planting, it is one of the world's finest arboretums; its collections include

Dawyck Botanic Garden

rare Chinese conifers and the unique Dawyck beech. At the entrance is the formal azalea terrace which leads the visitor into Scrape Glen, and from here paths cross the slopes of Scrape Hill, with the burn tumbling down under the Swiss bridge in the middle of the glen. The mature specimen trees tower majestically above a variety of flowering trees and shrubs. From further up the hill there are magnificent views of the garden, including the beech walk with its tree-top outlook. In the Heron Wood is the first cryptogamic sanctuary and reserve for non-flowering plants; illustrated panels provide details of the essential role played by these plants. The fine stonework and terracing on bridges, balustrades and urns were produced by Italian craftsmen in the 1820s. Visit the 60 acres in February for the snowdrops, May and June for the meconopsis and azaleas, and September and October for autumn colour.

DOWHILL

This is an exceptional garden, perhaps best described as a 'proper' country garden. It carries the very personal signature of the present owners, who over two decades have transformed the six acres surrounding the early Georgian house designed by Robert Adam into a 'pleasure walk' based around nine linked ponds. Great respect has been paid to the borrowed landscape, and the garden itself has a natural feel and flow to it, enhanced by magnificent mature trees and many others planted more recently. Generous lawns swirl and eddy around traditionally planted borders, creating secluded areas which are a delightful alternative to more formal garden rooms. Visitors are led in a seemingly artless progression through well-planted woodland, over decorative iron bridges and down manicured mown paths circling an unexpectedly expansive and beautiful lakeland area, where informal shrub and waterside plantings provide shelter for wildfowl and tame hens. As if this were not enough, the owners are expanding further into a topiary walk and two quarry gardens.

Mr and Mrs C Maitland Dougal

Keltie, Perth and Kinross KY4 08Z.
Tel: (01577) 850 207

M90 Edinburgh to Perth, exit 5.
Turn left to Cleish; house is 0.75m on left

Open for SGS, and by appt

Entrance: £3

DRUIMAVUIC HOUSE GARDENS

The romantic five-acre site was begun after World War I but has now been replanted and cultivated by its dedicated owners. The humorous and descriptive guide states that the real architect of the gardens is Nature, but they have certainly embellished her work most successfully. The stream garden makes an immediate impact with colourful clumps of many varieties of primulas (*P. pulverulenta*, 'Inverewe' and *helodoxa*) and meconopsis mixed in with other varied spring plantings. The well-planted woodland garden has lovely open oil-painting views of cattle watering in the loch below. In the excellent working kitchen garden strawberries are grown at eye level.

Mr and Mrs Newman Burberry

Appin, Argyll and Bute PA38 4BQ.
Tel: (01631) 730242

4m S of Appin on A828
Oban – Fort William road, turn left at new road bridge. Signposted

Open April to June, daily, 10am – 6pm

Entrance: £2.50, children free

DRUM CASTLE
(Historic Scotland Inventory)

The National Trust for Scotland

Drumoak, by Banchory, Aberdeenshire
AB31 5EY.
Tel: (01330) 811204;
www.nts.org.uk

10m W of Aberdeen, 3m W of
Peterculter, off A93

Garden open 21st March to Oct, daily,
10am – 6pm. Grounds open all year

Entrance: £2.50, concessions £1.90 (castle,
garden and grounds £8, children and
concessions £5) (2007 prices)

Garden: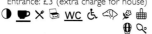
Grounds: ○ ⬠ ⚲

Within the old walled garden of the castle, the Trust has established a 'garden of historic roses' which was officially opened in June 1991 as part of its Diamond Jubilee celebrations. The four quadrants of the garden are designed and planted with roses and herbaceous or other plants appropriate to the seventeenth, eighteenth, nineteenth and twentieth centuries. The central feature is a copy of the gazebo at Tyninghame, East Lothian (see entry), and a small garden house in one corner, now restored, acts as an interpretative centre. The 40-acre grounds around the castle have other features of interest:: a pond garden, a collection of conifers, spacious lawns and walks in the Old Wood of Drum, designated a SSSI.

DRUMLANRIG CASTLE
(Historic Scotland Inventory)

The Duke of Buccleuch

Thornhill, Dumfries and Galloway
DG3 4AQ. Tel: (01848) 331555;
www.buccleuch.com

16m SW of M74 Junction 14, 18m NW
of Dumfries, 3m N of Thornhill on A76,
between A77 and A75. Signposted

Castle open

Gardens and country park open
25th March to Sept, daily, 11am-5pm

Entrance: £3 (extra charge for house)

◑ ⬤ ✕ ⬠ WC ♿ ⬠ ⚲ ⬚
🎈 ⚲

Built in the late seventeenth century by William Douglas, 1st Duke of Queensberry, Drumlanrig is one of Scotland's finest and most palatial residences. The formal terraces and parterres around and below the house reflect this contemporary 'grand manner', in a magnificent setting. The parterres were first restored to their former glory in the Victorian era by two of the foremost designers of their day, Charles M'Intosh and David Thomson, who, interestingly, used heathers instead of bedding plants as infill. They also introduced foreign plants and shrubs as well as many of the exotic conifers still thriving in the woodland walk today. These include one of the oldest Douglas firs in the UK, the tallest weeping beech (*Fagus sylvatica* 'Pendula') and an early fan-trained *Ginkgo biloba*. A charming heather-root pavilion in the woodland walk overlooks the tumbling Marr burn. The 40-acre gardens were simplified during the two world wars and are now being restored again to a very high standard. The four parterres, all with different plants and colour themes, are a stunning sight from the 200-metre-long terrace above; the Shawl Parterre in particular has a pretty design using circles, ovals and hearts. Annuals are used on an impressive scale.

DRUMMOND CASTLE GARDENS ★★
(Historic Scotland Inventory)

Grimsthorpe and Drummond Castle
Trust Ltd

Muthill, Crieff, Perth and Kinross PH7 4HZ
Tel: (01764) 681433;
www.drummondcastlegardens.co.uk

2m S of Crieff on A822

Open May to Oct, daily, 1 – 6pm
(last admission 5pm)

Entrance: £4, OAPs £3, children £1.50

These magnificent 17-acre parterre gardens were first laid out in 1630 by the 2nd Earl of Perth; at their centre was a multifaced obelisk sundial which still indicates the time all over the world. The gardens were greatly enhanced during the seventeenth century and reached their zenith during the 1830s when a descendant created one of the most significant revival gardens of the period, much admired by Queen Victoria. Parterres were traditionally designed as architectural

Drummond Castle Gardens

extensions of the mansion or castle. The one here takes the form of a long St Andrew's Cross and is one of the finest in Scotland, particularly when viewed from the 120-metre-long terrace 20 metres above. The whole garden is ornamented by 36 statues and numerous fountains and urns, all strategically placed as focal points or at the end of long vistas. Numerous box-edged compartments of intricate design are infilled, mostly with roses, antirrhinums, dahlias and lavenders, in the Drummond heraldic colours. The visual impact of the 207 clipped evergreens, intricate box compartments and stone masonry is unforgettable.

DUN ARD ★

An exceptionally well-planned organic garden incorporating many of the most stimulating elements of contemporary horticultural design, all carved out of a sloping three-acre field. Areas of exuberant planting are interspersed with minimalist, restful or wild areas, so that visitors are always ready for the next surprise as they climb ever onwards and upwards, culminating with a sandstone pyramid with a bird's-eye view over the whole garden, the valley and the mountains beyond. All the features sought after by today's gardeners are here – a potager, an early garden, a rose parterre, a bulb meadow, a still pool enclosed by a beech hedge, a bog garden, a formal pleached hornbeam avenue and, best of all, a late garden planted in hot colours in the increasingly popular continental matrix style, combining wild and herbaceous patchwork planting, viewed in all its deliciousness from a smart decking platform.

Alastair Morton and Niall Manning

Main Street, Fintry, Stirlingshire G63 0XE. Tel: (01360) 860369

17m SW of Stirling, 17m N of Glasgow on B822

Open by appt only

Entrance: £4

DUNBEATH CASTLE ★

The immaculately harled clifftop castle, dating from the fourteenth century, is dramatically outlined against the sea as one approaches down a tunnel of trees giving way to steep, deep-cut grass banks crowned on each side by two large

Mr and Mrs S.W. Murray Threipland

Dunbeath, Caithness KW6 6EY. Tel: (01593) 731308; www.dunbeath.co.uk

459

6m NE of Berriedale off A9. Turn right
to Dunbeath village post office, then
right again

Open for parties by appt

Entrance: £4, OAPs and children £2

walled gardens. The right-hand one has now been beautifully re-created with the help of the designer Xa Tollemache with a turret viewpoint over the garden as a whole and behind to the castle and the glinting sea. Although the layout of the two acres is traditional, with three mown grass axes and a central path creating eight compartments, these are broad and generously scaled, with the outer paths unusually wide and the whole threaded together by decorative metalwork. A water feature with cupola, a laburnum pergola across the width of the garden, a gazebo, plant supports and border backdrops are all designed using the same material, giving the garden structure, height and unity. Two well-clipped fuchsia hedges run the length of the garden, providing the outer shelter walls of the compartments and small parterres. These are paired so as to make a colourful and attractive pattern of vegetables, fruit and flowers. The outer walls themselves have herbaceous planting at their feet and are clad alternatively with an array of climbers chosen for flower or foliage effect. An exceptional visit, to be combined perhaps with Langwell and Dunrobin (see entries).

The Sutherland Trust

Golspie, Sutherland, Highland KW10 6SF.
Tel: (01408) 633177/633268;
www.great.houses-scotland.co.uk

1m NE of Golspie on A9

Castle open

Garden open 21st March to 15th Oct,
daily, 10am – 4.30pm (opens 12 noon
Suns, closes 5.30pm June to Aug)

Entrance: £7.50, concessions £6.50,
children £5, family £20

Other information: Falconry displays
11.30am and 2.30pm

DUNROBIN CASTLE GARDENS ★

(Historic Scotland Inventory)

The five-acre Victorian formal gardens were designed in the grand French style by Sir Charles Barry in 1850 to echo the architecture of the castle, which rises high above and looks out over the Moray Firth. Descending the stone terraces, one can see the round garden (evocative of the Scottish shield, perhaps), grove, parterre and herbaceous borders laid out beneath. The round ponds, all furnished with fountains, are a particular feature, together with the wrought-iron Westminster gates. Roses have been replaced with hardy geraniums, antirrhinums and *Potentilla fruticosa* 'Abbotswood'; the interest continues from tulips in spring through to hardy fuchsias, including *F*. 'Dunrobin Bedder' (raised *c*. 1860) and autumn-flowering dahlias. An eighteenth-century summerhouse, converted into a museum in the nineteenth century, is now also open to the public and well worth seeing. Other developments include the removal of the shrubbery and its replacement by 20 wooden pyramids covered in roses, clematis and sweet peas and interplanted with small ornamental trees to continue the French style visible elsewhere. In the policies there are many woodland walks.

MacLeod Estate

Isle of Skye IV55 8WF.
Tel: (01470) 521206;
www.dunvegancastle.com

14m NW of Portree, beyond
A850/A863 junction

DUNVEGAN CASTLE

(Historic Scotland Inventory)

A superb backcloth for the castle which stands on the shores of Loch Dunvegan, the gardens have three areas of interest. First, a round garden with a boxwood parterre of 16 triangular beds, three mixed borders for summer show and a fern house. Second, an expanding woodland waterfall dell, which carries the season on past rhododendron time. The meconopsis and giant cardiocrinums are breathtaking in this setting, but note also tiny maidenhair ferns, native wood sage and other treasures. Third, an exciting two-acre walled garden, created by head gardener Thomas Shephard on a long-derelict site and open to the public since 1998. Laid out on a formal plan, the four quarters each have a focus of interest: a lawn with a sorbus avenue; a raised pool with gravel surround pierced by plants; a triangle with an internal yew triangle; and an unusual stepped 'temple' evocative of Mayan architecture. The surrounding paths spill over with helianthemums, cistus and other Mediterranean plants. Non-gardeners can take an exciting boat trip to the nearby seal colony – on a calm day.

Castle open

Garden open all year, daily, mid-March to Oct, 10am – 5.30pm, Nov to mid- March, 11am – 4pm

Entrance: £5, OAPs £3.50, children £3 (castle and gardens £7.50, OAPs £6, children £4, family £20) (2007 prices)

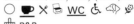 B&B

FINLAYSTONE
(Historic Scotland Inventory)

Designed in 1900 and enhanced and tended since the 1960s by the late Lady MacMillan, much respected doyenne of Scottish gardens, and her family, this spacious garden is imaginatively laid out over 10 acres, with a further 70 acres of mature woodland walks. There are large, elegant lawns framed by long herbaceous borders, interesting shrubberies and mature copper beeches looking down over the River Clyde. John Knox's tree, a Celtic paving 'maze', a paved fragrant garden and a bog garden are added attractions, and for children there are unusual woodland play areas. A walled garden is planted in the shape of a Celtic ring cross.

George Gordon MacMillan of MacMillan

Langbank, Renfrewshire PA14 6TJ.
Tel: (01475) 540505;
www.finlaystone.co.uk

8m W of Glasgow Airport, on A8 W of Langbank

Open all year, daily, 11am – 5pm

Entrance: £3.50, concessions and children (4– 6) £2.50

Other information: Doll museum and Celtic exhibition in visitor centre

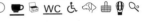

FLOORS CASTLE
(Historic Scotland Inventory)

Floors is, architecturally, one of Scotland's grandest country houses – a real swagger castle – magnificently situated with glorious views across a huge sweep of open parkland. The 1857 walled kitchen garden is of equally stately proportions and contains the classic mix of glasshouses, herbaceous borders, fruit, vegetables and annuals. The borders, long, broad and packed with colour, have a backing of chain swags covered with the bright pink rose 'American Pillar'. Groups of apple trees using the three historic Scottish cultivars – 'Bloody Ploughman' (thereby hangs a tale), 'Galloway Pippin' and 'Scottish Dumpling' – have been trained in the traditional French style as goblets and dwarf and full pyramids. The large children's playground is conveniently, but not aesthetically, sited within the walled garden. Recent additions are a woodland garden and a two-acre parterre, designed in the French style and featuring the intertwined initials of the present Duke and Duchess. Much use has been made of traditional box, with contrast and highlighting provided by *Euonymus fortunei* 'Emerald 'n' Gold'. 25 acres in all.

The Duke of Roxburghe

Roxburghe Estates Office, Kelso, Roxburghshire TD5 7SF.
Tel: (01573) 223333;
www.floorscastle.com

Well-signposted on outskirts of Kelso

Castle open as garden. but Easter and May to Oct only

Gardens and grounds open all year, daily, 11am – 5pm

Entrance: £3, OAPs £1.50 (house, grounds and garden £6.50, concessions £5.50, children £3.50, family £16)

The Garden of Cosmic
Speculation

Charles Jencks
Portrack House, Holywood, Dumfries
and Galloway DG2 0RW
5m N of Dumfries, 1.5m off A76
Open for SGS
Entrance: £5

THE GARDEN OF COSMIC
SPECULATION ★★

One of the most exciting and important contemporary gardens in Britain, 30 acres sculpted by the designer and architectural critic Charles Jencks and his wife Maggie Keswick, and expanded by him after her death in 1995. Using nature to speculate on the deeper ideas and laws underlying nature, it has several areas devoted to the fundamental discoveries of our time. Thus a water cascade tells the story of the universe, a terrace evokes the distortions caused by a black hole, a Quark Walk explores the smallest building blocks of matter, sinuous lakes and swirling landforms simulate fractal geometry. The Nonsense Building set in woodland was designed by James Stirling. The garden culminates in the Universe Cascade, the story of cosmogenesis at its heart. It is by no means a science lesson from the lab, rather a witty, intriguing and sensual apprehension of basic metaphors that run the universe. Jencks has written its story, *The Garden of Cosmic Speculation* (published by Frances Lincoln in 2005).

The Earl of Strathmore and Kinghorne
Glamis, Forfar, Angus DD8 1RJ
Tel: (01307) 840393 www.glamis-castle.co.uk
5m W of Forfar on A94
Castle open, (guided tours)
Garden open March to Dec, daily,
10am – 6pm (last admission 4.30pm)
Entrance: £3.70, concessions and children
(5–16) £2.70 (castle and grounds £7.50,
concessions £6.30, children 5–16) £4.30,
family £21.50) (2007 prices)

GLAMIS CASTLE
(Historic Scotland Inventory)

At the end of a mile-long, tree-lined avenue and against the backdrop of mountain and moorland, the turrets and spires of Glamis Castle beckon the visitor. Although much older, the park was landscaped in the 1790s by a garden designer working under the influence of 'Capability' Brown, and the avenue was replanted about 1820. On the lawn near the castle is an intriguing Baroque sundial, 6.5 metres tall and with a face for every week of the year. On the east side of the castle a two-acre Italian garden consists of high yew hedges, herbaceous borders, a fountain and seventeenth-century-style gazebos. The walled garden to the north, largely laid to lawn

with fruit trees, is being redeveloped. The pinetum, planted
c.1870, is now open to visitors. Glamis was the childhood
home of the late Queen Mother.

14 GLEBE CRESCENT

This delightful 0.5-acre plantsman's garden is designed to fill
every corner with a different plant setting and thus a different
'feel'. Clever terracing of the natural slope ensures that the
garden does not seem unduly overcrowded and yet, believe it
or not, there is a Japanese koi carp pool, a collection of bonsai,
a perfumed garden, a formal courtyard area, a conifer lawn,
over 40 ornamental grasses and a woodland area with a large
collection of rare ferns, arisaemas, hellebores and trilliums.
Notable are the unusual *Cercidiphyllum japonicum* 'Ruby' and
the variegated angelica tree (*Aralia elata* 'Aureovariegata'), and
many visitors covet the beautiful Japanese umbrella pine
(*Sciadopitys verticillata*). The owner says: 'There's a lot squashed
into this garden.' Indeed there is.

Mrs Joy McCorgray

Tillicoultry, Clackmananshire FK13 6PB.
Tel: (01259) 750484

8m W of Stirling on A91 at east end of
village; signed by yellow arrow at Glebe
Crescent

Open for SGS, and by appt

Entrance: £2, children free

GLENARN
(Historic Scotland Inventory)

Established in the 1920s by the Gibson family, the 10 acres of
woodland garden owe an incalculable debt to the Victorian
planthunters, and to twenthieth-century expeditions. Well-
kept paths eander round a sheltered bowl, sometimes
tunnelling under superb giant species rhododendrons
(including a *R. falconeri* grown from seed supplied by Hooker
in 1849), sometimes allowing a glorious vista across the
garden to the Clyde estuary, and sometimes stopping the
visitor short to gaze with unstinted admiration at huge
magnolias, pieris, olearias, eucryphias and hoherias. The
owners, both professional architects, acquired Glenarn in
1983. and with almost no help have successfully replanted and
restored where necessary, while retaining the special
atmosphere created by such magnificent growth. The rock
garden falls steeply down past the daffodil lawn to the house
with its tall, twisting chimney pots. Work has been completed
to expose the quarry face and is continuing on the
restoration of the scree bed.

Michael and Sue Thornley

Rhu, Helensburgh, Dunbartonshire
G84 8LL. Tel: (01436) 820493;
www.gardens-of-argyll.co.uk

On A814 between Helensburgh and
Garelochhead. Go up Pier Road to
Glenarn Road

Open 21st March to 21st Sept, daily,
dawn – dusk

Entrance: £3, OAPs and children £1.50

Other information: Refreshments on
certain open days only and by
arrangement. Plant sales March to June

GLENBERVIE HOUSE
(Historic Scotland Inventory)

Two very different gardens may be enjoyed here – a
traditional Scottish 1.25-acre walled garden on a slope, and a
woodland garden by a stream. Occupying one wall of an
enclosed garden is a fine example of a Victorian conservatory,
with a great diversity of pot plants and climbers on the walls.
Elsewhere in the walled area is a typical mix of herbaceous
plants, fruit, vegetables and summer bedding. There are many
shrub and old roses, and on walls and pillars a variety of

Mrs C.S. MacPhie

Drumlithie, Stonehaven, Kincardineshire
AB39 3YA. Tel: (01569) 740226

8m NE of Laurencekirk, 6m from
Stonehaven off A90 Laurencekirk –
Stonehaven road. On minor road 3m W
of Drumlithie

Open for SGS, and by appt

Entrance: £4, children £1

climbing and rambler roses. Spring brings good displays of bulbs, and the woodland garden with its drifts of primulas, ferns and interesting shrubs is beautiful in early summer. There are fine trees near the house.

GLENDOICK GARDENS
(Historic Scotland Inventory)

Mr and Mrs Peter Cox and Kenneth Cox

Glendoick, Glencarse, Perth and Kinross PH2 7NS. Tel: (01738) 860205 (Nursery); (01738) 860260 (Garden Centre); www.glendoick.com

8m E of Perth, 14m SW of Dundee on A90

Open 7th April to 6th June, Mon – Fri, 10am – 4pm, plus May, Sat and Sun, 2 – 5pm

Garden centre and display garden open all year, daily

Entrance: £3, children free

The gardens hold one of the most comprehensive collections of rhododendrons in the world, started by Euan H.M. Cox in the 1920s and considerably augmented since then by his son, daughter-in-law and grandson; many specimens were collected by them in the Himalayas and China. The rhododendrons are enhanced by an understorey of perennials, including meconopsis, primulas, trilliums, lilies and nomocharis, swelled by naturalised and native plants. Near the fine Georgian mansion are dwarf rhododendrons and azaleas; a small arboretum and a collection of conifers complement the many mature trees. Trial beds of new hybrid rhododendrons have been planted in the walled garden, and with azaleas are the main feature of the famous nursery and garden centre.

GLENWHAN GARDEN

Mr and Mrs Knott

Dunragit, Stranraer, Wigtownshire, Dumfries and Galloway DG9 8PH. Tel: (01581) 400222; www.glenwhangardens.co.uk

7m E of Stranraer, 1m off A75 at Dunragit

Open April to Sept, daily, 10am – 5pm, and by appt. Evening visits by arrangement

Entrance: £4, OAPs £3, children £1, family £8.50, season ticket £10, conducted tours for parties of 20 or more £15

Other information: Picnics permitted on request. Dogs strictly on leads (dog-walking area)

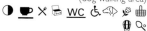

This magical 12-acre garden, started in 1981, has spectacular views over Luce Bay and the Mull of Galloway, and is set in an area of natural beauty with many rocky outcrops. Because of the Gulf Stream and consequent mild climate, exotic plants thrive amongst the huge collections of trees, shrubs and plants from all over the world. Seats and walkways abound in the maze of hilly plantings, mostly overlooking the central lakes and bog gardens, and sculptures are placed in carefully selected locations. Collections, whether of genera, reminders of friends or particular themes of interest, are to be seen everywhere. There are enchanting woodland walks where species rhododendrons flourish amongst many different kinds of primulas, and a 17-acre moorland walk sprinkled with native wild flowers. Most of the plants in the nursery are propagated on site.

GREENBANK GARDEN ★
(Historic Scotland Inventory)

The National Trust for Scotland

Flenders Road, Clarkston, Glasgow G76 8RB. Tel: (0141) 616 5125/5126; 0844 4932201 www.nts.org.uk

From Clarkston Toll in S Glasgow take Mearns Road for 1m. Signposted

Open all year, daily except 25th and 26th Dec, 1st and 2nd Jan, 9.30am – sunset

Entrance: £5, concessions and children £4, family £14

The 2.5-acre old walled garden of an eighteenth-century house has been divided into many sections, offering imaginative practical demonstrations to illustrate the design and planting of small gardens. The colour combinations are especially good. All the plants are in good condition and admirably labelled. An old hard tennis court in the corner has been converted into a spacious and pleasant area full of ideas for disabled and infirm gardeners, with raised beds and a waist-high running-water pond. Wheelchair access to the

Greenbank Garden

glasshouse and potting shed allows disabled people to attend classes and work here. Woodland walks are filled with spring bulbs and shrubs and there are usually Highland cattle grazing in the paddock. The garden holds a National Collection of bergenias.

Other information: Refreshments in summer only

GREYWALLS

Greywalls was designed in 1901 by Sir Edwin Lutyens as a golfing holiday house and enjoys refreshing views over Muirfield golf course and the Firth of Forth to distant hills known as the Paps of Fife. The whole property is surrounded by local honey-coloured stone walls topped with grey Dutch tiles – their relationship with the house is one of the most interesting features. The seven-acre formal garden is possibly the only one in Scotland attributed to Gertrude Jekyll. The main garden lying to the south, where a Yorkstone terrace opens onto the old rose garden, has recently been redesigned by Laura Mackenzie retaining the original design of 20 beds and using many of Jekyll's favourite plants. Honeysuckles, clematis and roses climb up ornamental metal pyramids. An *oeil-de-boeuf* in the stone wall provides a fine vista through to the Lammermuir Hills. Beyond this garden, box compartments contain whitebeams underplanted with vincas and white foxgloves, backed by holly-hedged chambers containing cherry trees and sculptures. Beyond this again are double herbaceous borders, a lavender border, and a charming parterre of box and santolina with green bean pyramids – all Jekyllian in design and content. The garden combines the 'prettiness' of that particular era of English gardening with wonderful Scottish views and the tang of the sea, while the house is an exceptionally comfortable hotel and open to visitors for lunch and dinner. Time your arrival carefully.

Mr and Mrs Giles Weaver

Gullane, East Lothian EH31 2EG.
Tel: (01620) 842144;
www.greywalls.co.uk

17m NE of Edinburgh on A198, 3m W of North Berwick. At east end of Gullane, signed to Greywalls Hotel; house is on right

Open March to Dec, daily, during daylight hours, and for parties by appt

Entrance: £3

 B&B

HOUSE OF TONGUE

(Historic Scotland Inventory)

Sheltered from wind and salt by tall trees, this four-acre walled garden is a haven in an otherwise-exposed environment, and especially colourful in high summer. Adjoining the

The Countess of Sutherland

Tongue, Lairg, Sutherland, Highland IV27 4XH. Tel: (01847) 611209

1m N of Tongue off A838

465

House of Tongue

Open for SGS, and at other times by appt

Entrance: £3, OAPs £2, children under 12 50p

● ♨ WC ☍ ⬀

seventeenth-century house, it is laid out after the traditional Scottish acre, with gravel and grass walks between herbaceous beds, hedged vegetable plots and orchard, and three beds filled with old-fashioned and new rose varieties. The glasshouse has been restored, and a wildflower meadow is in progress. A stepped beech-hedged walk leads up to a high terrace which commands a fine view over the Kyle of Tongue. The centrepiece of the garden is Lord Reay's 1714 sundial, a sculpted obelisk of unusual design.

INVEREWE GARDEN ★★
(Historic Scotland Inventory)

The National Trust for Scotland

Poolewe, Ross-shire, Highland IV22 2LG. Tel: (01445) 781200; www.nts.org.uk

6m NE of Gairloch on A832

Open all year, daily, 9.30am – 5pm (closes 4pm Nov to March)

This spectacular 54-acre garden on the shores of a sea loch, Loch Ewe, covers the Am Ploc Ard peninsula and has a long period of colour and interest. Planned as a wild garden around two dwarf willows on peat and sandstone, it has been developed since 1865 as a series of walks through herbaceous and rock gardens, a wet valley, pond gardens and woodland walks. A sloping traditional walled garden with glorious sea views and colourful terraces is filled with a mixture of

Inverewe Garden

herbaceous plants, roses and vegetables. It is a plantsman's garden (labelling is discreet), containing nearly 6000 different plants including many tender species from Australia, New Zealand, China and the Americas, sheltered by mature beech and pine trees. National Collections of olearias, brachyglottis and rhododendrons are held here. The garden is well tended and way-marked. Note: midge-repellent is advisable on still and muggy summerdays and is on sale at the main desk. In all, 62 acres.

INWOOD

A delightful plantsman's garden of just over an acre created since 1984. Full use is made of a small front garden designed for late summer colour containing an exciting variety of tender and lush-foliage plants. Through the garden gate boundary fences blaze with prolific rambling roses, and carefully chosen plants complement each other in colour-themed island beds, where roses and clematis scramble over shrubs to reach up into the central heights of *Viburnum plicatum* 'Pink Beauty', *Pyrus salicifolia* 'Pendula', and a beautiful *Cornus controversa* 'Variegata'. Neat mown lawn extends into the woodland area with appropriate shrubs and ornamental trees; rare plants are constantly being added to the shade beds and pond. The owner has also cleverly created a large polythene-lined 'bog-bed' that adds glamorous foliage to a dry shady area.

JURA HOUSE GARDENS ★

A circular walk around the estate reveals the rich natural history and geology of the island. Starting from the car park the visitor has a choice of walks to the walled garden. There is the direct route through native woodland, or a more

Entrance: £8, concessions £5.25, family £20

Other information: Restaurant and shop open April to Oct only

Irvine and Lindsay Morrison

Carberry, Musselburgh EH21 8PZ. Tel: (0131) 665 4550; www.inwoodgarden.com

6m E of Edinburgh. From A1 Edinburgh – Berwick Road take A6094 signed to Dalkeith. Turn left at roundabout and follow signs for Carberry; garden is signed on left

Open April to Sept, Tues, Thurs and Sat, 2 – 5pm, and by appt

Entrance: £3, children free

 B&B

Riley-Smith family

Ardfin, Isle of Jura, Argyll and Bute PA60 7XX. Tel: (01496) 820315; www.jurahouseandgardens.co.uk

Jura House Gardens

467

On Jura, 5m SE of ferry terminal off A846. Vehicle ferries from Kennacraig by Tarbert to Port Askaig, Islay, and from Islay to Feolin, Jura

Open all year, daily, 9am – 5pm

Entrance: £2.50, children (5-16) £1 (collecting box)

Other information: Teas available June to Aug, Mon – Fri only. Possible for wheelchairs but sloping gravel paths

○ ♨ WC ⬤ ⬦ ⬨ ⬩ ⬪

adventurous approach along the banks of a fuchsia-clad burn which plunges into a ravine filled with ferns and lichens. Spectacular views of the Islay coast accompany the steep path down to the shore, where dykes and rock formations are home to wild scree plants and scrubby trees. Entering the organic walled garden is like stepping into another world, a flourishing oasis within the rugged moorland of Jura. This is a haven for many half-hardy plants. *Geranium maderense* and *G. palmatum* grow in profusion in a parterre of clipped box; echiums tower over Australian bottle brushes, tree ferns, aeoniums and other non-hardy plants from Australasia, collected especially for this garden in 1999. Many unusual perennials are allowed to self-seed, creating a loose and natural look. Directly outside the garden wall, in the summer only, there is a tea tent sitting in a colourful wildflower meadow, and a plant nursery where it is possible to buy many of the plants seen growing in the garden.

KAILZIE GARDENS ★
(Historic Scotland Inventory)

Lady Angela Buchan-Hepburn

Peebles, Peeblesshire, Scottish Borders H45 9HT. Tel: (01721) 720007

2.5m SE of Peebles on B7062

Open all year, daily, 11am – 5.30pm (in winter, during daylight hours)

Entrance: 4.50, concessions £3.50, children £1 (peak rates)

Other information: Holiday cottage available

○ ♨ ✕ ⬚ WC ⬤ ⬦ ⬨  ⬩ ⬪

The gardens of 25 acres are situated in a particularly attractive area of the beautiful Tweed Valley and have breathtaking views. The old mansion was pulled down in 1962 and the vast walled garden, which still houses the magnificent greenhouse, has been transformed by the present owner into a garden of meandering lawns and island beds full of interesting shrubs and plants, notably fuchsias and geraniums. There are many surprises, including snowdrops in drifts in February and March, a choice flower area, secret gardens, loving seats invitingly placed under garlanded arbours and thoughtfully sited pieces of statuary. A fine fountain at the end of the herbaceous borders leads on to woods and stately trees, and from here you may stroll down the Major's Walk, lined with laburnum and underplanted with rhododendrons, azaleas, blue poppies and primulas. The less horticulturally minded might enjoy the 18-hole putting green and osprey-watch viewing centre.

KELLIE CASTLE
(Historic Scotland Inventory)

The National Trust for Scotland

Pittenweem, Fife KY10 2RF. Tel: (01333) 720271; www.nts.org.uk

3m NW of Pittenweem on B9171 towards Arncroach

Castle open April to Oct, daily, 1 – 5pm

Garden and grounds open all year, daily, 9.30am – 5.30pm

Entrance: £3, children £2 (castle extra charge)

Other information: Parking 100 metres, closer for disabled. Refreshments and shop only when castle open, 12 noon – 5pm

Entered by a door in a high wall, the 1.5-acre garden inspires dreams within every gardener's reach. It appears to be seventeenth-century in plan, embellished by Professor James Lorimer and his family in late Victorian times. Simple borders, such as one of nepeta, capture the imagination as hundreds of bees and butterflies work the flowers. Areas of lawn are contained within box hedges, and roses on arches and trellises abound. In one corner, behind a trellis, is a small romantic garden-within-a-garden. A large commemorative seat designed by the sculptor Hew Lorimer provides a focus at the end of one of the main walks. An orchard, wall-trained

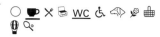

fruit, and a collection of old and unusual varieties of vegetables produced by organic gardening methods are other delights. Outside the walled garden, mown walks wind through the meadow and woodland, which is a haze of wild garlic in late spring.

KERRACHAR GARDENS ★

Horticulturally as far north-west as you can go, Kerrachar is one of the few inhabited homes in the UK accessible only by water. The half-hour boat trip down the loch is a scenic pleasure in itself, but this waterside garden would be well worth a visit wherever it was located. The areas either side of the house are not particularly large – under an acre each – but this is anyway a garden you want to wander around, so varied and abundant is the planting, with something seemingly continuously in flower, especially rewarding in mid- and late summer. Particular favourites are *Gladiolus cardinalis*, *Morina longifolia*, *Achillea grandiflora*. thalictrums, deep red Martagon lilies, verbascums, liatris, the little red 'thistle' *Cirsium rivulare* and the unfailingly hardy *Hebe elliptica*. As well as a host of roses and herbaceous perennials, there is a fine show of more tender shrubs, including crinodendrons, pittosporums, callistemons, olearias and the attractive *Ozothamnus rosmarinifolius* with its woolly white shoots. Finally, what a treat to be able to buy truly home-grown and reasonably priced plants from the well-stocked nursery area.

Peter and Trisha Kohn

Kylesku, Sutherland IV27 4HW.
Tel: (01571) 833288 (Garden);
(01971) 502345 (Boat);
www.kerrachar.co.uk

30m N of Ullapool, accessible by boat from Kylesku

Open mid-May to mid-Sept, Tues, Thurs and Sun. Additional visits arranged for parties of up to 40. Boat departs from Old Ferry Pier 1pm or by arrangement

Entrance: £3, children (12–16) £1.50, under 12 free (boat fare £12, children £6, under 12 free)

KILBRYDE CASTLE

The 20-acre garden was created by the present owner's parents, whose passions were rhododendrons, azaleas, clematis and bulbs. The garden is in two parts – a partly walled upper garden with island beds full of colour on a south-facing slope, and a lovely woodland garden on either bank of a stream well planted with rhododendrons and azaleas under a canopy of mature trees. The best time to visit is spring, particularly the end of May.

Sir James Campbell

Dunblane, Perthshire FK15 9NF.
Tel: (01786) 824897

9m NW of Stirling, off A820

Open for SGS, and by appt all year

Entrance: £3, OAPs and children £2

KILDRUMMY CASTLE GARDENS ★

(Historic Scotland Inventory)

The 20 acres of gardens are set in a deep ravine between the ruins of a thirteenth-century castle and a Tudor-style house, now a hotel. The rock garden, by Backhouse of York (1904), occupies the site of the quarry which provided the stone for the castle. The narrowest part of the ravine is crossed by a copy of the towering fourteenth-century Auld Brig O'Balgownie (Old Aberdeen Bridge) built by Colonel Ogston in 1900. This affords a spectacular bird's-eye view of both sides of the water garden commissioned from a firm of Japanese landscape gardeners in the same period; Backhouse continued the planting. In April the reflections in the still water of pools increase the impact of the luxuriant *Lysichiton americanus*, and

Kildrummy Castle Garden Trust

Alford, Aberdeenshire AB33 8RA.
Tel: (01975) 571203/563451;
www.kildrummy-castle-gardens.co.uk

2m SW of Mossat, 10m W of Alford, 17m SW of Huntly. Take A944 from Alford, following signs to Kildrummy, and turn left onto A97. From Huntly turn right onto A97

Open April to Oct, daily, 10am – 5pm (closing date may change depending on weather)

Entrance: £4, OAPs £3, children (5–16) free

Other information: Cars park inside hotel main entrance, coaches in delivery entrance. Woodland walks and children's play area

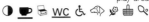

later come primulas, Nepalese poppies and a notable *Schizophragma hydrangeoides*. There are also fine maples, rhododendron species and hybrids, oaks and conifers. Although a severe frost pocket, the gardens can grow embothriums, dieramas and other choice plants. They are especially beautiful in autumn with colchicums in flower and acers in brilliant leaf.

KINROSS HOUSE GARDENS

Mr James Montgomery

Kinross, Kinross-shire KY13 8ET. Tel: (01577) 862900; www.kinrosshouse.com

Junction 6 of M90, into Kinross and follow signs

Open 21st March to Oct, daily, 10am – 7pm

Entrance: £3, concessions £2.50, accompanied children free

(Historic Scotland Inventory)

Ten acres of walled garden, all beautifully maintained, surround the seventeenth-century mansion. The gardens were designed in the 1680s and reconstructed early last century. The walls, surmounted by fine statuary, have decorative gates. Within, the scene is formal: a spacious lawn, clipped hedging, herbaceous borders, some with colour themes, and rose borders surrounding a fountain. There are yew hedges in interesting shapes, with well-placed seating for those in a contemplative mood or wishing to view *Loch Leven Castle* on the nearby island. It was here that Mary Queen of Scots was imprisoned in 1567, and visitors can make the short boat trip to its sombre walls from the adjoining Kirkgate Park.

LANDFORM UEDA AT THE GALLERY OF MODERN ART

National Galleries of Scotland

75 Belford Road, Edinburgh EH4 3DR. Tel: (0131) 624 6200; www.nationalgalleries.org

Between Scottish National Gallery of Modern Art and Dean Gallery

Open all year, daily, 10am – 5pm

Entrance: free

Designed in 2002 by American architectural historian Charles Jencks for the Scottish National Gallery of Modern Art, the Landform Ueda (named for a Japanese scientist) is a serpentine stepped mound of mown grass with three crescent-shaped pools from which rise gentle spiral paths. The design, which is both innovative and strangely pleasing to the eye, is based on the rhythmic patterns that occur in nature, such as weather systems. These create a series of curves which overlap but never repeat and are attracted to a point or basin. Jencks 'looked at the inherent principles of natural movement and designed the Ueda to reflect and heighten these natural forces'. Once you actually see it, this description becomes quite understandable. The Landform is seven metres high and occupies 300 square metres; from the paths there is also a good elevated view over the two galleries' grounds and their fine collection of sculptures, and towards the handsome Edinburgh skyline. Jencks' own sensational garden, The Garden of Cosmic Speculation (see entry) is open on one day for SGS.

LANGWELL

The Lady Anne Bentinck

Berriedale, Caithness, Highland KW7 6HE. Tel: (01593) 751237 or (01593) 751278 (Head Gardener)

2m W of Berriedale off A9

Open for SGS, and by appt

(Historic Scotland Inventory)

A lovely traditional two-acre walled garden. It has a sadly short season, due to the fact that it is almost as far to the north-east as it is possible to go, but inspires commensurate interest and admiration as a result. The cruciform layout lends itself to dramatic 64-metre-long herbaceous borders specialising in plants that are not only colourful but also manage to thrive in these conditions. They are framed by yew hedges, behind which lie vegetable and fruit sections — all immaculately maintained.

Entrance: £2

LAWHEAD CROFT

Nearly 300 metres up in the midst of the bleak Lanarkshire moors, the present owners have planted hedges and laboriously carved out a luxuriant garden, set out as an enchanting series of garden rooms, all with a different theme. Grass walks lead from one interesting border to another, full of unusual plants with carefully considered colour associations and leaf contrasts. Great ideas include an excellent bonsai collection. It is a place that never stands still: recently most of the vegetable garden has been swept away and replanted in a great sweep of curved, tiered and circular beds of spectacular and original design.

Sue and Hector Riddell

Tarbrax, West Calder, West Lothian EH55 8LW

12m SW of Balerno, 6m NE of Carnwath on A70 towards Tarbrax

Open for charity June to Sept, daily, at any reasonable time, and for parties by written appt only

Entrance: £2, children 20p

LEITH HALL AND GARDENS ★
(Historic Scotland Inventory)

It is the old garden, remote from the house, that offers the greatest pleasure to the enthusiast. Rising on a gentle slope from the west drive, a series of small spaces sheltered by walls and hedges contains long borders and a large, well-stocked rock garden with a stream and gravel paths. The simple, romantic design allows a tremendous display of flowers during the whole of summer and early autumn; especially fine are magenta *Geranium psilostemon* and an entire border of solid catmint. There are no courtyards and no dominating architecture, just massive plantings of perennials and the odd rarity amongst the rocks. The circular moon gate at the top of the garden leads to the old turnpike road. Woodland walks throughout the designed landscape take in ponds and views down the garden. Six acres in all.

The National Trust for Scotland

Huntly, Aberdeenshire AB54 4NQ. Tel: (01464) 831216; www.nts.org.uk

34m NW of Aberdeen, 1m W of Kennethmont on B9002

House open: telephone for details

Garden and grounds open all year, daily, 9.30am – dusk

Entrance: £2.50, OAPs and children £1.90 (house and gardens £8, OAPs and children £5) (2007 prices)

Other information: Dogs outside walled garden only

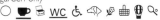

LINN BOTANIC GARDENS

The three-acre garden has been developed to its present form since 1971 by the current owner with thousands of unusual and exotic plants, including large collections of bamboos and temperate ferns. Colour is present at every season, from spring-flowering bulbs through rhododendrons to autumn leaves, set off by the dark foliage of conifers and evergreen trees. Water is a pervasive presence: in the extensive water garden, in formal ponds and fountains, in the glen with its tumbling waterfalls. There are also herbaceous borders, a rockery and a cliff garden; in 2004 a large oval lawn was dug up and replaced by a 'New Zealand heath'. A signed route takes visitors through all parts of the garden. Fine views look down to the Firth of Clyde and from the terrace across Loch Long to the hills of Argyll.

Mr J. H. K. Taggart

Cove, Helensburgh, Dunbartonshire G84 0NR. Tel: (01436) 842084

6m S of Garelochhead, 0.75m N of Cove on shore of Loch Long

Open all year, daily, dawn – dusk

Entrance: £3.50, concessions £2.50, children £1 (under 5 free)

Other information: Parking next to garden sign on shore side of road. Entirely unsuitable for wheelchairs and prams. Light refreshments for organised tours. Plants for sale in adjacent nursery, open daily, 11am – 5pm

Dunsyre, Lanark, South Lanarkshire
ML11 8NG. www.littlesparta.co.uk

Turn off A721 at Newbiggin for Dunsyre.
1m W of Dunsyre turn up unmarked farm
track signed to Stonypath and
Little Sparta; garden is 1m walk uphill.
Alternatively take A702 from Edinburgh,
turning off at Dolphinton; road signed
to Dunsyre

Open June to Oct, Fri and Sun,
2.30 – 5pm. Bus service from Edinburgh
available July and Aug, Wed – telephone
or consult website for details.

Entrance: £10

◑ WC

LITTLE SPARTA ★★
(Historic Scotland Inventory)

Described by Sir Roy Strong as the most original
contemporary garden in the country, the five-acre garden
remains open after the death of its mercurial, creative and
intellectual creator, Dr Ian Hamilton Finlay. On arrival at the
gate to the property a beautifully carved wooden sign greets
the visitor, giving a hint of the craftsmanship and artistry that
are combined in the work of this admired poet and sculptor.
He believed that a garden should appeal to all the senses and
provoke thought, both serious and light-hearted, and he
therefore revived the art of emblematic gardening which died
out in Britain in the seventeenth century, although his
personal philosophy was inspired more closely by the
eighteenth-century poet-gardeners Alexander Pope and
William Shenstone. He achieved an international reputation in
the process. It is impossible to describe Little Sparta briefly,
except to say that he transformed a sizeable hill farmstead
350 metres above sea level in the Pentland Hills (starting in
1966 with the idea of establishing a testing-ground for his
sculptures) into a unique garden full of classical inscriptions
and images, allusions and symbols. Not all are easily
understood or interpreted – *n'importe*, as this is a garden, not
a crossword puzzle. *Little Sparta* by Jessie Sheeler, with
photographs by Andrew Lawson, was published by Frances
Lincoln in 2003.

Royal Botanic Garden Edinburgh

Port Logan, Stranraer, Wigtownshire,
Dumfries and Galloway DG9 9ND.
Tel: (01776) 860231; www.rbge.org.uk

14m S of Stranraer off B7065. Signposted

Open March to Oct, daily, 10am – 6pm
(closes 5pm March and Oct), and by appt
at other times

LOGAN BOTANIC GARDEN ★★
(Historic Scotland Inventory)

This 24-acre garden deserves far more acclaim and repays
you tenfold for the extra effort required to journey to the
furthest north-west corner of the UK. Rightly described as

Logan Botanic Garden

the most exotic garden in Scotland, the balmy Gulf Stream climate is ideal not only for the tender sweet-scented rhododendrons which are a speciality, but also allows a remarkable collection of exotic half-hardy plants to flourish outside. Logan specialises in plants from the southern hemisphere (including 50 different species of eucalyptus), and about half of its holdings are fully documented wild-origin plants. In the walled garden paths flow between island beds always full of colour and interest. Scale and structure are well supplied by majestic tree ferns and *Cordyline australis*. Everywhere there are tender shrubs such as leptospermum, embothrium, olearia, pittosporum, eucryphia – an endless list. The woodland area has a similarly large collection of trees, including magnolias, shrubs such as carpodetus, metrosideros (related to callistemon), elegant bamboos and tree ferns like the lovely silver fern *Cyathea dealbata* and *Dicksonia fibrosa*. Wander through the Tasmanian Creek, gasp at the gunnera stand and admire the Chilean collection. Then, since the rainfall here is 40 inches a year, take shelter in the licensed salad bar which looks onto a good display of Scottish native plants before venturing out to check the rare and unusual plants in the nursery.

Entrance: £4, concessions £3.50, children £1, family ticket £9. Local membership scheme, inc. Dawyck and Benmore Botanic Gardens (see entries), available

Other information: Discovery Centre and Sound Alive guided tours. Guide dogs only

◑ ☕ ✕ 🖭 <u>WC</u> ♿ 🐾 ⛲
🔦 🎧

LOGAN HOUSE GARDENS

The elegant Queen Anne house was built in 1701, but the lands were documented as held by the McDouall family 'Ultra memoriam hominum' ('Before the memory of man'). The 20-acre gardens were planted by them in the 1870s with new shrubs from China, the Himalayas, Australasia and South America. In 1969 the main part of the garden became the Logan Botanic Garden (see entry), and the remaining mainly woodland section round the house was left relatively untended until 1995, when the present owners began an ongoing planting programme. Wide lawns and woodland glades set against the natural rock now enhance the mature trees and giant rhododendrons such as *R. maccabeanum*, *sinogrande* and *russelianum*. Two champion trees, *Eucryphia cordifolia* and *Leptospermum lanigerum*, are both the biggest of their kind in the UK, and there are also exceptional embothriums, nothofagus, auraucarias, clethras and Chilean hazels. If you can, time your visit for spring and early summer.

Mr and Mrs Andrew Roberts

Port Logan, by Stranraer DG9 9ND.
Tel: (01776) 860239
www.mull-of-galloway.co.uk/attractions

14m S of Stranraer on A716. 2.5m from Ardwell. Signposted

Open Feb to Aug, daily, 9am – 6pm (10am – 5pm, Feb and March)

Entrance: £3, children under 16 free

◑ 🖭 WC

MALLENY GARDEN
(Historic Scotland Inventory)

Aptly described as the Trust's secret garden, Malleny seems an old and valued friend soon after meeting and reflects the thoughtful planning by the head gardener and his talented wife. An impressive deodar cedar reigns over this three-acre walled garden, assisted by a square of early seventeenth-century clipped yews and by yew hedges. As well as holding a National Collection of nineteenth-century shrub roses,

The National Trust for Scotland

Balerno, Edinburgh EH14 7AF.
Tel: (0131) 449 2283
www.nts.org.uk

In Balerno, off A70 Edinburgh – Lanark road

Open all year, daily, 10am – 6pm (or dusk if earlier)

Entrance: £3, OAPs/children £2

○ 🏠 WC ⚬ 🏺

Malleny's four-metre-wide herbaceous borders are superb, as is the large glasshouse containing a summer display of flowering plants. Don't forget to admire the attractive herb and ornamental vegetable garden, laid out in traditional manner.

Lord Palmer

Duns, Scottish Borders TD11 3PP.
Tel: (01361) 883450;
www.manderston.co.uk

2m E of Duns on A6105

House open as gardens, but 1 – 5pm

Gardens open 8th May to 28th Sept,
Sun, Thurs and Bank Holiday Mons,
11.30 – dusk, and for parties at
any time of year by appt

Entrance: £4.50 (house and gardens £8),
children under 12 free

● 🍽 🏠 WC ⚬ 👁 ▦

MANDERSTON ★★

(Historic Scotland Inventory)

One of the last great classic houses to be built in Britain, designed by John Kinross and modelled on Robert Adam's Kedleston Hall, it was described in 1905 as a 'charming mansion inexhaustible in its attractions'. This might equally well apply to the gardens, which remain an impressive example of gardening on the grand scale. Four magnificent formal terraces planted in Edwardian style overlook a narrow serpentine lake, and a Chinoiserie bridging dam tempts visitors over to the woodland garden on the far side, elegantly effecting the transition from formal to informal. The woodland garden has an outstanding collection of azaleas and rhododendrons, and is at its best in May. The formal walled gardens to the north of the house are a lasting tribute to the very best of the Edwardian era, when 24 gardeners were employed to do what two now accomplish to the same immaculately high standard. Gilded gates open on to a panorama of colourful planting on different levels, with fountains, statuary and a charming rose pergola all complementing one other. Even the greenhouses were given lavish treatment, with the walls created from lumps of limestone to resemble an exotic planted grotto. In all, 56 acres of formal and informal beauty.

The Earl of Haddington

Gordon, Berwickshire TD3 6LG.
Tel: (01573) 410225; www.mellerstain.com

6m NW of Kelso off A6089

House open as garden

Garden open 17th and 24th Feb, 2nd and
9th March, 11am – 4pm; 21st to 24th March,
daily; 4th May to June and Sept, Wed, Sun
and Bank Holiday Mons; July and Aug, Mon,
Wed and Thurs; Oct, Sun; all 11.30am – 5pm.
Also open for parties by appt

Entrance: £3.50, children free
(house and garden £6)

● 🍽 ✕ 🏠 WC ⚬ 👁 🌱 🏺

MELLERSTAIN

(Historic Scotland Inventory)

The house is a rare example of the work of the Adam family; both William and his son Robert worked on the building. The formal garden created by Reginald Blomfield after 1909 to replace William Adam's original design is composed of a trio of dignified balustraded terraces with lawns, clipped yews and rose-filled parterres. The glory of the garden is the landscape, complete with lake and woodlands in the style of 'Capability' Brown and Humphry Repton, but redesigned by Blomfield – the view of the Cheviot Hills from the terraces is one of the finest to be found in this attractive stretch of the Scottish Borders. Fifty acres in all.

The Duke of Sutherland

St Boswells, Melrose, Roxburghshire
TD6 0EA. Tel: (01835) 823236

8m SE of Galashiels, 2m NE of
St Boswells on B6404

MERTOUN

(Historic Scotland Inventory)

Overlooking the Tweed and with the house in the background, this is a lovely garden in which to wander and admire the mature specimen trees, azaleas and daffodils, and the most attractive ornamental pond flanked by a good herbaceous border. The focal point is the immaculate three-acre walled garden, which is everything a proper kitchen garden should be. Walking up from a 1567 dovecot, thought to be the oldest in the county, through a healthy orchard, the visitor reaches the box hedges, raised beds and glasshouses of the main area. Vegetables, herbs and flowers for the house vie for attention with figs and peaches in the well-stocked glasshouses.

Open April to Sept, Fri – Mon, 2 – 6pm

Entrance: £2.50, OAPs £1.50, children under 14 50p

 WC &

MONTEVIOT
(Historic Scotland Inventory)

The river garden running down to the River Teviot has been extensively replanted with herbaceous perennials and shrubs to a more informal design. Beside it, the semi-enclosed terraced rose gardens overlooking the river have a large collection of hybrid teas, floribundas and shrub roses. The pinetum is full of unusual trees, and nearby a water garden has been created, planted with hybrid rhododendrons and azaleas. A new feature will incorporate cascading water flowing under bridges into a pool. A circular route has been laid out around the gardens, and there are fine views.

Jedburgh, Scottish Borders TD8 6HQ. Tel: (01835) 830380 (mornings); www.monteviot.com

5m NE of Jedburgh. Turn off A68 onto B6400 to Nisbet. Entrance second turn on right

House open

Garden open April to Oct, daily, 12 noon – 5pm, and for parties by appt

Entrance: charge, children under 16 free

MOUNT STUART ★★
(Historic Scotland Inventory)

Incorporated in the 300 acres of designed landscape and waymarked woodland walks, there is a wealth of horticultural interest here, and one of the most elegant drives in the country. The gardens contain a considerable mature pinetum of 1860 and a magnificent old lime tree avenue leading to the shore, but they have been restored and augmented over the last decade by the 6th Marquess and his wife. In conjunction with the Royal Botanic Garden Edinburgh, 100 acres have also been set aside to grow endangered conifer species from all

Mount Stuart Trust

Rothesay, Isle of Bute. Argyll and Bute PA20 9LR. Tel: (01700) 503877; www.mountstuart.com

Take ferry from Wemyss Bay. Garden is 5.5m S of Rothesay ferry terminal on A844

House open as garden but 11am – 5pm (10am – 2.30pm Sat)

Mount Stuart

Garden open May to Sept, daily,
10am – 6pm

Entrance: £3.50, OAPs £3, children £2
(house and garden £7.50, OAPs £6,
children £3)

over the world. Rock gardens provide decorative features near the house, but the two most important elements are the kitchen garden and the 'Wee' garden. The latter is actually eight acres of mixed and exotic plantings with emphasis on species from the southern hemisphere. It is set in the mildest part of the grounds and grows some of the most tender plants to be found outside the glasshouse, often flourishing to unusual size. The kitchen garden, originally designed as an ornamental potager by the late Rosemary Verey, has been partially redesigned for the 7th Marquess by James Alexander-Sinclair in the form of six large beds planted with bold imagination in a scheme based on the colour wheel. Set in the middle is the Pavilion Glasshouse sheltering rare flora from SE Asia. One of Scotland's finest gardens. The magnificent Victorian fern house at Ascog Hall (see entry), is nearby.

NOVAR

Mr and Mrs Ronald Munro Ferguson

Evanton, Ross-shire IV16 9XL.
Tel: (01349) 831062; www.novarestate.co.uk

7m NE of Dingwall off A9 and B817
between Evanton and junction with A836

Open for SGS, and for parties of 8 or more
by appt

Entrance: £5

Other information: Teas and plants
for sale on SGS open day

◐ WC &

A charming series of mature planted natural ponds forms part of the mansion house gardens, fed by streams gushing over stone steps and monumental waterfalls. A formal semi-circular parterre was built to celebrate the millennium, the back edge of which drops down as a 2.75-metre wall to form a handsome ha-ha overlooking the park. There is also a five-acre traditional walled garden with charming arched entrances. Peaceful lawns and mature trees offset a large eighteenth-century oval pond embellished with a contemporary bronze figure. Nine acres in all.

PITMEDDEN GARDEN

The National Trust for Scotland

Pitmedden Village, Ellon, Aberdeenshire
AB41 7PD.
Tel: (01651) 842352;
www.nts.org.uk

14m N of Aberdeen, 1m W of
Pitmedden, 1m N of Udny on A920

Open May to Sept, daily, 10am – 5.30pm

Entrance: £5, concessions £4, family £14

Other information: Coaches please book
if tea required. Wheelchairs supplied.
Museum of farming life

(Historic Scotland Inventory)

The Great Garden at Pitmedden, originally laid out in 1675 by Sir Alexander Seton, 1st Baron of Pitmedden, as the centrepiece of his estate, exhibits the taste of seventeenth-century garden-makers and their love of patterns made to be viewed from above. This rectangular parterre garden is enclosed by high terraces on three sides and by a wall on the fourth. Simple topiary and box hedging abound. The south- and west-facing walls, lined by fine herbaceous borders, are covered by a great variety of old apple trees in both fan and espalier styles, producing almost two tons of fruit at the end of the season. Ornamental patterns are cut in box on a grand scale, infilled with 40,000 annuals. The overall impact is striking when viewed from the original ogivally roofed stone pavilion at the north of the garden or when walking along the terraces. The old house was destroyed by fire in 1807, and when the Trust acquired the property in 1952, little was left in the garden of the original design, so contemporary seventeenth-century plans for the garden at the Palace of Holyrood in Edinburgh were used in re-creating what is seen today. Seven acres.

Pitmuies Gardens

PITMUIES GARDENS ★★

(Historic Scotland Inventory)

In the 20-acre grounds of an attractive eighteenth-century house and courtyard, these beautiful walled gardens lead down towards a small river with an informal riverside walk and two unusual buildings – a turreted dovecot and a Gothick wash-house. There are rhododendron glades with unusual trees and shrubs, but pride of place must go to the spectacular semi-formal gardens behind the house. Here exquisite old-fashioned roses and a series of long borders containing a dramatic and superbly composed palette of massed delphiniums and other herbaceous perennials in June and July constitute one of the most memorable displays of its type to be found in Scotland. Latterly the gardens have evolved with new plantings, vistas and focal points, and the conversion of a former tennis court has allowed for new habitats and a greater diversity of plants. The supremely knowledgeable owner has lived in the house since 1966 and known the place for half a century.

Mrs Farquhar Ogilvie

House of Pitmuies, Guthrie, By Forfar, Angus DD8 2SN. Tel: (01241) 828245; www.pitmuies.com

1.5m W of Friockheim, on A932

House open for parties by appt

Garden open Feb to mid-March as part of Scottish Snowdrop Festival; then mid-March to Sept, daily, 10am – 5pm, and at other times by appt

Entrance: £3.50 by collection box

Other information: Teas by arrangement for parties visiting house

 WC

PORTMORE ★

It is a joy to see an old neglected estate brought lovingly back to life. The long drive winds up through woods, fields and little lochs to the Edwardian mansion proudly surveying the rolling acres. A parterre has been planted at the far side of the house, and woodland walks are being developed with rhododendrons, azaleas and shrub roses. The wonder of the place is the large walled garden designed and replanted by Chrissie Reid with great taste and flair – she cares particularly about colours and the effect at the entrance is magical. The soft mixture of greys, blues, mauves, pinks and dark red delight the eye in the herbaceous borders and lead the gaze to the greenhouses stuffed full of geraniums, pelargoniums, streptocarpus, fuchsias. Leading off these is an enchanting Victorian Italianate grotto, cool, dripping and fern-filled. The remainder of the 10-acre garden is divided into squares of potagers, herb gardens, hawthorn walks, rose gardens, all surmounted by wonderful wrought-iron arches. Even the luxurious-looking fruit is protected by wire held up by three elegant cages. A recently developed water garden has been planted with shrubs and meconopsis.

Mr and Mrs D. Reid

Eddleston, Peebleshire, Scottish Borders EH45 8QU Tel: (01721) 730383

0.5m N of Eddleston, on A703 Peebles – Edinburgh road

Open for SGS, and for parties by appt

Entrance: £4, children under 12 free

 WC

Royal Botanic Garden
Edinburgh

Inverleith Row, Edinburgh EH3 5LR.
Tel: (0131) 552 7171;
www.rbge.org.uk

1m N of city centre at Inverleith.
Signposted

Open all year, daily except 25th Dec
and 1st Jan, from 10am (closes
4pm – 7pm depending on season).
Garden tours operate April to Sept,
daily, 11am and 2pm

Entrance: free. Glasshouses £3.50, OAPs
£3, children £1, family £8

Other information: Exhibition hall and
Inverleith House gallery open. Guide
dogs only

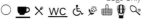

ROYAL BOTANIC GARDEN EDINBURGH ★★

Set on a hillside with magnificent panoramic views of the city, this is one of the finest botanic gardens in the world; arguably the finest garden of its type in Britain. Established in the seventeenth century on an area the size of a tennis court, it now extends to 75 acres. Rhododendrons and azaleas abound, and in spring their flowers provide a blaze of colour and intriguing scents. The world-renowned rock garden is spanned by a long bridge over the stream. In summer, marsh orchids, lilies, saxifrages and bell-shaped campanulas give brilliant colour. There are also peat and woodland gardens and a stunning herbaceous border. The arboretum sweeps along the garden's southern boundary. A relatively recent addition is the Chinese hillside on a south-facing slope, which includes a spectacular wild-water ravine crossed by bridges, tumbling down into a tranquil pond at the bottom of the hillside. A T'ing (pavilion) provides an ideal place to relax. The glasshouses, featuring Britain's tallest palm house, leads the visitor on a trail of discovery through the temperate and tropical regions of the world, including passion flowers, cycads (some over 200 years old) and species that provide everyday necessities such as food, clothes and medicine. A garden in memory of the late Queen Mother opened in 2006. Galanthophiles may wish to make the seven-mile trip west of Edinburgh city centre off the A90 to *Mons Hill*, within the Dalmeny Estate. It is open for charity one Sunday in late February or early March, when acres of wild snowdrops naturalised in woodland must be seen to be believed. Telephone (0131) 331 1888 for details.

Scone Palace

Perth, Perth and Kinross PH2 6BD.
Tel: (01738) 552300;
www.scone-palace.co.uk

Just outside Perth on A93
Perth – Braemar road

SCONE PALACE GARDENS

(Historic Scotland Inventory)

The 100 acres of gardens surrounding the site of Macbeth's ancient city of Scone include the famous nineteenth-century pinetum with magnificent towering trees, including *Sequoia giganteum* over 48 metres tall; a second pinetum with over 60 specimens was planted in 1977. There is also a 30-metre-long laburnum pergola and a beech maze designed by Adrian Fisher in the shape of the Murray Star. Taking their turn in season are spectacularly massed daffodils, a primrose drive, many honeysuckles, clematis and roses, and fine rhododendrons and azaleas. Butterflies abound in their designated garden, and red squirrels delight visitors for whom they are a rarity. The renowned explorer and plant collector, David Douglas, born at Scone, supplied the garden with many of his discoveries, and one of his firs survives. His life is marked by an exhibition in the palace. The owners have the largest orchid collection in the country and orchids are always in flower in the State Rooms. It is also worth travelling 7m further north to marvel at the *Meikleour Beech Hedge*, now 30 metres high and a quarter of a mile long, beside the A93. Legend has it that men who planted it in 1745 were called away to fight and not one returned alive from the battle of Culloden.

Palace and gardens open 21st March to Oct, daily, 9.30am – 5.30pm (closes 4pm Sat)

Entrance: £4.50, concessions £4, children £3 (palace and gardens £8, concessions £7, children £5, family £24)

SHEPHERD HOUSE ★

Shepherd House and its one-acre garden create a walled triangle in the middle of the eighteenth-century village of Inveresk. The present owners have lived here since 1957, and the garden has evolved slowly, from what was for many years a children's playground, into one of the best small gardens in Scotland. Symmetrical parterres of clipped box frame the front of the house, but the main garden is to the rear. There is a hint of formality here too, with a herb parterre and two symmetrical potagers, but this is balanced by the lack of formal divisions within the garden; the overriding impression is of romantic planting and joyful abundance. The two ponds are connected by a rill, flowing gently beneath a series of rose- and clematis-clad arches which are underplanted with nepeta. There are roses everywhere, up trees and on obelisks, through arbours and over arches, but the garden is best in April, May and June, when it is filled with hellebores, tulips and irises – all plants that provide inspiration for Lady Fraser's paintings.

Sir Charles and Lady Fraser

Inveresk, East Lothian EH21 7TH. Tel: (0131) 665 2570; www.shepherdhousegarden.co.uk

7m E of Edinburgh. From A1 take A6094 exit, signed to Wallyford and Dalkeith, and follow brown tourist-signs to Inveresk Lodge Gardens. House is opposite lodge at junction of main road and Crookston Road (garden entrance in Crookston Road)

Open 17th and 24th Feb for Scottish Snowdrop Festival; April to June, Tues and Thurs, 2 – 4pm. Also open for NGS and for parties by appt

Entrance: £3

Other information: Teas and plant stall on SGS open days only

Shepherd House

SCOTLAND

ST ANDREWS BOTANIC GARDEN

Fife Council

Canongate, St Andrews KY16 8RT.
Tel: (01334) 476452/477178;
www.st-andrews-botanic.org

0.5m from town centre, signed in
Canongate

Open all year, daily, 10am – 7pm
(closes 4pm Oct to April). Also open
for private tours by arrangement

Entrance: £2, concessions and children
(5–16) £1

○ WC ᠻ ⌗ ⍭

On its present site the garden dates from 1960, covering 18 acres along the Kinness Burn; in 1987 it was leased by the university to the local council. Although the botanical collections are now increasingly adapted for low maintenance, the areas of specialised planting remain excellent. Visitors will find something of interest all year; even in winter a pleasant afternoon may be spent in the greenhouses among the arid, alpine, tropical and temperate-zone plants. The pond and rock garden are particularly attractive, and the order beds are a valuable educational aid, rarely seen elsewhere. There are good collections of cotoneasters, sorbus and berberis, and stunning clumps of *Lathraea clandestina*.

STOBO CASTLE WATER GARDENS
(Historic Scotland Inventory)

Hugh and Charles Seymour

Peebles, Scottish Borders EH45 8NX.
Tel: (01721) 760245

6m SW of Peebles on B712,
12m E of Biggar

Open for SGS, and by appt, but advisable
to confirm in writing as well as
telephoning

Entrance: £3.20, children free

● ◑ ⍤ WC ᠻ ⌁ ⍭ B&B

The enduring appeal of water is exemplified in the five acreshere; the planting, although most attractive, takes second place to the visual impact of clear water flowing down a series of cascades and waterfalls. Japanese bridges and stepping stones invite frequent crossings from side to side, and peaceful rills stray from the main torrent to create one huge water garden. In fine landscape-garden tradition, man has contrived to manipulate nature – in this case a large earth dam across a steep valley – into something of classical delight. The dam was faced with stone to create a magnificent waterfall and the resulting flow is impressive even in dry summers. There are many fine mature trees, including Japanese maples.

THREAVE GARDEN AND ESTATE
(Historic Scotland Inventory)

The National Trust for Scotland

Castle Douglas, Dumfries and Galloway
DG7 1RX. Tel: (01556) 502575;
www.nts.org.uk

1m W of Castle Douglas off A75

House open

Garden open all year, daily, 9.30am – dusk
(walled garden/glasshouses close 4.30pm)

Entrance: £6, OAPs and children £5, family
£15 (2007 prices)

○ ◑ ✕ 🗄 WC ᠻ ⍭ ⊞ ⍭ ⌁

The Threave estate, which extends to 1500 acres, includes the famous 64-acre garden which has been used as a school of horticulture since 1960 and caters for trainee gardeners. For the visitor the principal interest is the working walled garden with its range of glasshouses, vegetables, orchard and wall-trained fruit. This may be contrasted with the less formal woodland and rock gardens, heath garden and arboretum. The garden is noted for its collection of daffodils, complemented in spring by rhododendrons, followed by herbaceous perennials and a good collection of flowering trees and shrubs.

TOROSAY CASTLE AND GARDENS
(Historic Scotland Inventory)

Christopher James

Craignure, Isle of Mull PA65 6AY.
Tel: (01680) 812421;
www.torosay.com

1.5m S from Craignure. Steamer 6 times
daily April to Oct (2 to 4 times daily Nov
to March) from Oban to Craignure.

The house, built in baronial castle style by Bryce (1858), is complemented by a formal Italianate main garden based on a series of descending terraces with an unusual statue walk. This features one of the richest collections of Italian Rococo

480

statuary in Britain and alone justifies the crossing from Oban to Mull. Vaguely reminiscent of Powis Castle (see entry in Wales), it makes a dramatic contrast with the rugged island scenery. The peripheral gardens around the formal terraces are also a contrast – a newly restored informal water garden and an Oriental garden looking out over Duart Bay, and a small rock garden. Rhododendrons and azaleas are a feature but less important than in other west-coast gardens, and there is a collection of Australian and New Zealand trees and shrubs. A major restoration is underway, and 2000 species and cultivars have been planted over the past five years. Outside the main garden, the owners, in conjunction with the Royal Botanic Garden Edinburgh, have created a five-acre Chilean wood and underplanted another two-acre wood with plants from the collection of the late Jim Russell.

Narrow-gauge railway from Craignure ferry. Or take Lochaline to Fishnish ferry, then travel 7m S on A849

Castle open April to Oct, 10.30am – 5pm

Garden open all year, daily, 9am – 7pm (or dusk if earlier)

Entrance: £5, children £3, family £13 (reduced rates when castle closed) (castle and gardens £6, children £3.50, family £15.50)

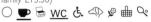

TYNINGHAME HOUSE
(Historic Scotland Inventory)

Tyninghame is renowned for the 39-acre gardens created by the late Countess of Haddington. When her husband died in 1986 the house was sold and converted into separate dwellings with great sensitivity by Kit Martin. The owners have their own private area of garden, but Lady Haddington's Secret Garden, the stunning herbaceous border and the woodland area are shared. The parterre on the upper terrace is laid out in a design of triangular beds, filled with roses that are either white or yellow, chiefly 'King's Ransom' and 'Iceberg'. The romatic and exuberant Secret Garden is an eighteenth-century French re-creation, planted with old-fashioned roses in subdued colours, clematis, philadelphus, white lilacs, peonies and geraniums. Through the gateway a path leads to woodland where many mature trees shelter azaleas, rhododendrons, shrub roses, embothriums and shrubs selected for their autumn colour. In spring the woods abound with wild primroses and bulbs. The walled garden contains a lovely apple walk and a fine arboretum, together with glasshouses and the remains of the old heating chimneys in the brick walls. The ruin of the Romanesque St Baldred's Church stands within the grounds, and there are stunning views across parkland to the Tyne estuary and the Lammemuir hills.

Tyninghame Gardens Ltd

Tyninghame, East Linton, East Lothian EH42 1XW.

25m E of Edinburgh between Haddington and Dunbar. N of A1, 2m E of A198

Open for SGS

Entrance: £3.50 OAPs £2.50, children under 12 free

TYNINGHAME WALLED GARDEN ★
(Historic Scotland Inventory)

The high brick walls, which were originally heated, and the gateways here date from 1760, making this one of the oldest walled gardens in Scotland. Within are four acres of formal gardens redesigned in 1960 by Jim Russell. The wide grass walk with its high yew hedges forms the backbone of the garden. Classical statues are set in alcoves cut in the yew, while

Mrs Charles Gwyn

Dunbar, East Lothian EH42 1XW. Tel: (01620) 860559

25m E of Edinburgh N of A1. Take turning to North Berwick and Tyninghame on A198; after 1m turn right through archway

Open for SGS, and by appt

Entrance: £3.50, children free

pedestal urns and a fine Florentine fountain stand at the intersections of two transverse paths that dissect the vista. One path, edged with nepeta, has arched supports for ornamental vines and climbing roses; the second is a beautifully planted rose walk. Extensive borders of mixed plantings, a long border of peonies and an iris border are all impeccably maintained and plant associations are often excellent. There is also a knot garden, an apple orchard, a potager and a large woodland area with mature and unusual trees underplanted with huge swathes of perennials. The famous 90-metre-long apple walk outside the walls was planted in 1891 and formed the approach to the walled garden from Tyninghame House (see entry above).

University of Dundee

Riverside Drive, Dundee DD2 1QH.
Tel: (01382) 381190;
www.dundeebotanicgardens.co.uk

2.5m from city centre on A90 Perth road.
Signposted

Open all year, daily, 10am – 4.30pm
(closes 3.30pm Nov to Feb). Closed 25th
and 26th Dec, 1st and 2nd Jan

Entrance: £3, OAPs £2, children £1, family
£7

UNIVERSITY OF DUNDEE BOTANIC GARDEN

Founded in 1971 as a source of plant material for teaching and research purposes, the garden has always been open to the public for their pleasure. The attractive planting around the glasshouse and large pond near the entrance is reminiscent of a private rather than a botanic garden. The large area beyond has plants grouped according to region or habitat, including many Scottish natives; though mainly composed of trees and shrubs, the artistic layout ensures plenty to see of interest as well as beauty. The glasshouse is brimful of fine specimens, from tropical to temperate zones, from rainforest to desert. In all, a very varied 21 acres.

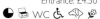

Michael and Charlotte Wemyss
(Wemyss Estate Trustees)

East Wemyss, Fife KY1 4TE.
Tel: (01592) 652181
www.wemysscastlegardens.com

2m NE of Kirkcaldy on A955. Entrance
Coaltown of Wemyss

Open 13th April, 2pm – dusk, for
erythroniums; and May to July by appt

Entrance: £4.50

WEMYSS CASTLE

The traditional six-acre walled garden dates from 1690, but gradually reverted to rough field after the 1890s. The current owners began its re-creation from scratch in 1994, retaining the original three sections and the magnificent Georgian orangery. The romantically informal garden now features long herbaceous borders planted with a large collection of roses and clematis, secret watery nooks, arches and pergolas. There is a magnificent display of erythroniums on the one-day spring opening in April.

OTHER RECOMMENDED GARDENS

ABBOTSFORD

Melrose, Scottish Borders TD6 9BQ
(www.scottsabbotsford.co.uk). Open 17th March to
Oct, daily, 9.30am – 5pm (opens 2pm Suns, March
to May and Oct)

The garden surrounding the famous house built
by Sir Walter Scott after 1817 on the banks of
the River Tweed is probably unchanged from his
time. The twin herbaceous borders in the
kitchen garden have been replanted and lead
up to the Gothick conservatory that was one
of his favourite retreats. 110 acres. (Historic
Scotland Inventory)

ACHNACLOICH

Mrs T.E. Nelson, Connel, Oban, Argyll and Bute
PA37 1PR (01631 710796). Open Easter to Oct, daily,
10am – 6pm

A fine setting for the small castellated house
sited on a rocky cliff with panoramic views to
Loch Etive and the surrounding countryside.
There are two water gardens, an oak wood and
a natural woodland of interlinked glades are
beautiful in spring with the flowering of bulbs,
magnolias, rare shrubs and rhododendrons. 35
acres. (Historic Scotland Inventory)

ARDCHATTAN PRIORY

Oban, Argyll PA37 1RQ (www.gardens-of-argyll.co.uk).
Open April to Oct, daily, 9am – 6pm

Founded by monks in 1232 and further
developed in the 19th and 20th centuries, these
charming 5-acre gardens retain the spirit of
both, with ancient buildings, mature shrubs and
trees, an excellent collection of roses, a
greenhouse with a large collection of prize
winning cacti and sweeping herbaceous borders
with views across Loch Etive to Mull and Ben
Cruachan. (Historic Scotland Inventory)

ARDKINGLAS WOODLAND GARDEN

Ardkinglas Estate, Cairndow, Argyll and Bute
PA26 8BH (01499 600261; www.ardkinglas.com).
Open all year, daily, during daylight hours

Eight champion trees are the undisputed kings
of an historic plant collection, now being
conserved and rejuvenated, in rhododendron
and bluebell woodland high above the shores of

Loch Fyne. The extensive estate nursery
specialises in unusual trees and shrubs. 25 acres.
(Historic Scotland Inventory)

ARMADALE CASTLE

Armadale, Sleat, Isle of Skye (01471 844305;
www.clandonald.com). Open April to Oct, daily,
9.30am – 5.30pm

Branching out from the well-groomed cultivated
areas – pond gardens, a long herbaceous border,
lawns with ornamental trees and a romantic
garden planted within the castle ruins – are 4
miles of nature trails set in 40 acres of woodland
and wildflower meadows. (Historic Scotland
Inventory)

BAITLAWS

Mr and Mrs M. Maxwell Stuart, Lamington, Biggar,
Lanarkshire ML12 6HR (01899 850240). Open for SGS,
and June to Aug by appt

High above sea level and encircled by hills, this
2-acre garden of clever colour-coordination and
plantsmanship includes exuberant borders of all
shapes and sizes, a sunken garden and a small
woodland glade. A raised 'bubble conservatory'
opens up views of the garden and the wider
landscape.

BARGANY

John Dalrymple-Hamilton, Girvan, South Ayrshire
KA26 9QL (01465 871249). Open May, daily,
10am – 5pm

The 18th-century park was substantially
refigured and replanted by W.S. Gilpin c. 1826,
and the impressive rockery made 100 years later
within a woodland garden densely planted with
splendid ancient rhododendrons, azaleas, fine
trees and conifers. (Historic Scotland Inventory)

BARGUILLEAN'S 'ANGUS GARDEN'

Sean Honeyman, Taynuilt, Argyll and Bute PA35 1HY
(01866 822335/822333; www.barguillean.co.uk).
Open all year, daily, dawn – dusk

A relaxed and informal 9-acre woodland garden
of native birch and oak, set on a Highland hillside
overlooking a lochan with views to Ben
Cruachan and filled with rhododendrons, azaleas,
conifers and some rare trees and shrubs.

CARNELL

Mr and Mrs J.R. Findlay and Mr and Mrs Michael Findlay, Hurlford, Kilmarnock, South Ayrshire KA1 5JS (01563 884236; www.carnellestates.com). Open for SGS, and for parties by appt

A 16th-century peel tower looks down over an estate with a long history. The 10-acre garden, however, is largely 20th-century, owing its richness and variety to the Findlay family's lavish planting of flower and shrub borders within a framework of walled, rock and water gardens. The herbaceous borders are in full bloom in July. (Historic Scotland Inventory)

EDZELL CASTLE

Edzell, Brechin, Angus DD9 7UE (01356 648631; www.historic-scotland.gov.uk). Open April to Sept, daily, 9.30am – 5pm (closes 4pm Oct to March).

In 1604, within his fortress walls, Sir David Lindsay made a uniquely curious and atmospheric 1-acre garden, with panels of alternating chequered niches and finely carved symbolic figures standing above large recesses designed for flowers. A central design of box parterres, lawns and bedding was created in the 1930s to reflect the mannered layout of the period. (Historic Scotland Inventory)

Edzell Castle

FALKLAND PALACE

Falkland, Fife KY15 7BU (01337 857397; www.nts.org.uk). Open March to Oct, daily, 10am – 5pm (opens 1pm Sun). NTS

Once the hunting lodge for the Stuart monarchs, the 3-acre grounds of the magnificent Renaissance palace were remodelled by Percy Cane in the late 1940s. His ingenious layout of generous lawn and

boldly planted island and wall borders, with a colourful formal garden and water garden thrown in for good measure, continue to pack a punch. (Historic Scotland Inventory)

GLASGOW BOTANIC GARDENS

730 Great Western Road, Glasgow G12 0UE (0141 334 2422). Open all year, daily, 7am – dusk. Glasshouses open 10am – 6pm (closes 4.15pm in winter)

Part botanic gardens, part public park, this makes for a pleasant afternoon's stroll past well-maintained borders, rose and herb gardens and an impressive range of Victorian glasshouses. The restored circular Kibble Palace, housing an important collection of tree ferns and many other exotics, is the icing on the cake. 28 acres. (Historic Scotland Inventory)

GLEN GRANT GARDEN

Rothes, Aberlour, Moray AB38 7BS (01340 832118; www.glengrant.com). Open April to Oct, daily, 10am – 5pm (opens 12 noon Sun)

A fine re-creation of the 22-acre garden developed from 1866 up the sides of the distillery's romantic glen by 'The Major' James Grant. This legendary innovator, socialiser and traveller enhanced the natural setting with a wide range of exotic plants, planted orchards, lawns and wooded glades, and built a rustic bridge and a heather-thatched dram hut.

HARMONY GARDEN

St Mary's Road, Melrose, Ettrick and Lauderdale, Scottish Borders TD6 9LT (01721 722502; www.nts.org.uk). Open April to Sept, daily, 10am – 5pm (opens 1pm Sun). Times may change – telephone to check. NTS

Located within the precincts of Melrose Abbey, this is a tranquil place to walk among generously planted borders set around a natural lawn with a mass of spring-flowering bulbs and wild and exotic flowers, and a well-stocked kitchen garden.

THE HERMITAGE

Near Dunkeld, Perthshire (01350 728641; www.nts.org.uk) Open all year, daily. NTS

The 37-acre woodland was planted with now-mighty Douglas firs as part of a contrived picturesque landscape by the 2nd Duke of Atholl. The River Braan cuts through, reaching a

The Hermitage

peak of drama with a wide and torrential waterfall, viewed from a stone pavilion beside the 18th-century bridge. A grotto deep in the woods adds to the wild and romantic effect. (Historic Scotland Inventory)

HILL OF TARVIT

Cupar, Fife KY15 5PB (0844 493 2185; www.nts.org.uk). Open all year, daily, 9.30am – sunset. NTS

The house, estate and garden created by Sir Robert Lorimer for a Dundee financier in the early 20th century were designed to impress. Grand terracing, a double staircase and miles of clipped yew hedging achieved this, with a charming rose garden to give intimacy, borders a long season of colour and woodland an overall sense of scale. 30 acres. (Historic Scotland Inventory)

THE HIRSEL

The Earl of Home, Coldstream, Berwickshire TD12 4LP (01573 224144; www.hirselcountrypark.co.uk). Open all year, daily, during daylight hours

Something here for the botanist, forester, ornithologist, zoologist, geologist, historian and archaeologist in an ancient site of woodland and picturesque landscape – peaceful and uplifting at every season of the year. (Historic Scotland Inventory)

INNES HOUSE

Mr and Mrs Mark Tennant, Elgin, Moray IV30 8NG (013443 842410; www.inneshouse.co.uk). Open for parties of 20 or more by appt

An impressive traditional garden surrounds the largely 17th-century house, dominated by an extensive ornamental walled garden divided into compartments and surrounded by a fine arboretum. The range and rarity of the trees here is echoed by the majestic survivors in the park. (Historic Scotland Inventory)

INVERESK LODGE

Musselburgh, East Lothian EH21 6TE (0131 665 1855; www.nts.org.uk). Open all year, daily, 10am – 6pm, or dusk if earlier. NTS

High and ancient stone walls protect 3 acres of gardens, semi-formal in character and with several acres of interest: azalea, white and spring borders, a rose border planted originally by Graham Stuart Thomas, a juniper terrace, and an Edwardian glasshouse housing a National Collection of tropaeolums and many other choice plants. (Historic Scotland Inventory)

LECKMELM SHRUBBERY AND ARBORETUM

Mr and Mrs Peter Troughton, Little Leckmelm House, Lochbroom, Ullapool, Ross-shire IV23 2RH. Open April to Oct, daily, 10am – 6pm

Originally planted in the1870s, the reclaimed 10-acre arboretum by the sea is filled with species rhododendrons and important trees, including a vast weeping beech and the largest *Chamaecyparis lawsoniana* 'Wisselii' and *Thujopsis dolobrata* in Europe, with ornamental shrubs and bamboos for added interest. (Historic Scotland Inventory)

LOCHALSH WOODLAND GARDEN

Lochalsh House, Balmacara, Kyle, Ross-shire IV40 8DN (01599 566325; www.nts.org.uk). Open all year, daily, 9am – sunset. NTS

The steep-sided hillside, planted with beech, larch, oak and pine in the late 19th century, is overlaid with later ornamental plantings of large-leaved rhododendrons and shrubs from China, Japan, the Himalayas and Australasia underplanted with hydrangeas, fuchsias, bamboos and ferns. There are wonderful views across the water to the mountains of Skye and Knoydart. 11 acres.

NETHERBYRES

Colonel S.J. Furness, Eyemouth, Berwickshire, Scottish Borders TD14 5SE (01890 750337). Open one day in April for charity, for SGS, and April to Sept for small parties by appt

The 1.25-acre garden is worth visiting, especially in June and July to see the unique elliptical walled garden, built before 1740. The present layout of fruit, flowers and vegetables, still fully cultivated on traditional lines, dates from the 1860s; the house and conservatory are modern. (Historic Scotland Inventory)

THE PINEAPPLE

Dunmore, nr Stirling, Stirlingshire (01628 825925; www.nts.org.uk) Open all year, daily, 10am – sunset. NTS

Anyone interested in garden buildings should visit this magnificent 1761 rendition in stone of a fruit that had been introduced into Scotland several decades earlier. Built as a banqueting house (and now available for renting from the Landmark Trust), it rises up in majesty above a pedimented portico set in one wall of the 6-acre former kitchen garden. (Historic Scotland Inventory)

PRIORWOOD GARDEN

Melrose, Ettrick and Lauderdale, Scottish Borders TD6 9PX (01896 822493; www.nts.org.uk). Open mid-April to 24th Dec, daily, 10am – 5pm (opens 1pm Sun). NTS

A unique example of a garden developed for the production of dried flowers (700 annual and herbaceous varieties in all), protected by 18th-century walls and embellished by ironwork thought to have been designed by Lutyens. (Historic Scotland Inventory)

TEVIOT WATER GARDENS

Mrs Susan Wilson, Kirkbank House, Eckford, Kelso, Scottish Borders TD5 8LE (01835 850253; www.teviotwatergardens.co.uk). Open all year, daily, 10am – 5pm

Occupying a spectacular position on a steep bank of the River Teviot, terraces linked by waterfalls display a wide range of plants giving a varied show throughout the summer. Aquatic plants are a speciality, interspersed with choice perennials, grasses, ferns and bamboos. 3 acres.

TILLYPRONIE

The Hon. Philip Astor, Tarland, Aboyne, Aberdeenshire AB34 4XX. (01339) 881238). Open for SGS, and by appt.

The overall layout of the garden and its terraces, standing on a hill high above sea level with spectacular views of the Grampians, was completed in the 1920s. Herbaceous and waterside plantings, an extensive heather garden, a rock garden and a Golden Jubilee garden provide colour throughout the summer months. (Historic Scotland Inventory)

WALES

For further information about how to use the *Guide*
and for an explanation of the symbols, see pages vi–viii.
Specific dates and times are those given to us by garden owners for 2008.
For 2009 dates, check with the individual properties.
For opening dates under the National Gardens Scheme,
readers should consult *The Yellow Book* or www.ngs.org.uk.
Maps are to be found at the end of the *Guide*.

ABER ARTRO HALL

Situated in an elevated position just a few miles from the coast, the garden benefits from the protection of a steep hillside to the west and south but has wonderful views over woodland to Rhinog Farw to the east. The attractive and quite imposing Arts-and-Crafts-style house sits perfectly in this stunning landscape and the garden is carefully designed around it. The back garden has a wide lawn leading to a steep rockery made in the 1950s; it is particularly colourful in spring and early summer with the flowering of many rhododendrons, which extend into the woodland garden above. Below the lawn, two terraced shrub borders look out over a formal and productive vegetable garden, a fruit arbour and a laburnum arch. A slightly tongue-in-cheek walled Italian garden with a Gaudi-esqe pool reveals the present owners' sense of humour, while their sense of adventure is demonstrated by the nearby garden laid out like a sheet of William Morris wallpaper, where flower shapes have been cut into an old tennis court and planted up.

Paul and Carolyn Morgan

Llanbedr, Gwynedd LL45 2PA.
Tel: (01341) 241777

From N turn right off A496 in front of Victoria Inn in Llanbedr. After 1m turn right signed Cwm Nantcol

Open for NGS, and Easter to Sept, Tues – Fri, by appt

Entrance: £3

ABERGLASNEY GARDENS ★
(Welsh Historic Garden Grade II*)

Here are gardens lost in time. Records for Aberglasney go back to the mid-fifteenth century, when mention was made of nine gardens, orchards and vineyards. Around 1600 the Bishop of St David's bought the estate to turn it into a private palace, and it was probably he who built the gatehouse and the cloister garden. To the side of the house is a rare example of a yew tunnel. After many years of neglect the 10 acres of garden are being restored. The large upper walled garden was designed by Penelope Hobhouse to complement the historic site, and the lower walled garden is home to vegetables, herbs and plants grown for cutting. The wooded area known as Bishop Rudd's Walk has collections of rare and unusual woodland plants, and Pigeon House Wood is a natural, unspoilt area with splendid beech trees. The restoration of the formal cloister garden, devoted to plants typically grown in an

Aberglasney Restoration Trust

Llangathen, Llandeilo, Carmarthenshire SA32 8QH. Tel: (01558) 668998; www.aberglasney.org

3m W of Llandeilo on A40. Turn S at Broad Oak junction

Open all year, daily except 25th Dec, 10am – 6pm (10.30am – 4pm in winter). Last entry 1 hour before closing

Entrance: £6.50, concessions £6, children £3, family £16

Other information: Holiday cottages available

Aberglasney Gardens

early-seventeenth-century garden, was completed in 2001. A new and well-designed conservatory constructed from old walls shelters tender plants.

The National Trust

Tal-y-Cafn, Colwyn Bay, Conwy
LL28 5RE.
Tel: (01492) 650460;
www.bodnantgarden.co.uk

8m S of Llandudno, just off A470

Garden open 8th March to 2nd Nov,
daily, 10am – 5pm

Entrance: £7.20, children £3.60

Other information: Parking 50 metres
from garden

◑ ☕ ✕ <u>WC</u> ⎔ ✿ ⚑ ♀ ↻

BODNANT GARDEN ★★

(Welsh Historic Garden Grade I)

One of the finest gardens in the country, not only for its magnificent collections of rhododendrons, camellias and magnolias but also for its beautiful setting above the River Conwy, with extensive views of the Snowdon range. The 80-acre garden ranks among the best-loved in Britain. The famous laburnum arch, an overwhelming mass of bloom, is matched for interest by other features, including the lily terrace, the curved and stepped pergola, the canal terrace and Pin Mill. In the dell is the tallest redwood in the country, the 45-metre *Sequoia sempervirens*. All these, together with the outstanding autumn colours, make it a garden well worth visiting at any season. The whole effect was created by four generations of the Aberconway family (who bought Bodnant in 1874), aided by three generations of the Puddle family as head gardeners; now Troy Smith has his talented hands at the helm. The walled plant centre (not National Trust) offers a good range of tender climbers and other plants seen growing in the garden.

Bodnant Garden

BODRHYDDAN
(Welsh Historic Garden Grade II*)

A historic garden of considerable interest. The box-edged parterre was laid out in 1875 by William Andrews Nesfield, who redesigned Green Park in London and was also employed at Kew, and whose equally renowned son, William Eden Nesfield, designed the 1875 alterations to the house. The paths are bordered by clipped yews and, to the north west, the two-acre Pleasance, part of a larger area known on very old maps as the Grove. This is probably because it embraces St Mary's Well, revered since pagan times and covered now by a 1612 Inigo Jones pavilion, said to have been used for clandestine marriages. The Pleasance itself, originally a Victorian shrubbery, has been restored; it has four ponds, fine mature trees and many new plantings, and an additional area has been developed as a wild garden, picnic spot and woodland walk. There is also a millennium summerhouse based architecturally on the Treasury at Petra, a building on which the present Lord Langford's great-great-grandparents inscribed their names when on honeymoon in 1835. Six acres in all.

Lord Langford

Rhuddlan, Denbighshire LL18 5SB.
Tel: (01745) 590414

4m SE of Rhyl. Take A5151 Rhuddlan – Dyserth road and turn left. Signposted

House open

Garden open June to Sept, Tues and Thurs, 2 – 5.30pm

Entrance: £2 (house and garden £5, children under 16 £2)

BODYSGALLEN HALL ★
(Welsh Historic Garden Grade I)

The Garden has written that 'there can be few better living examples of early seventeenth-century gardens anywhere in England and Wales'. Both house and gardens have been restored to a high standard. The limestone outcrops provide an interesting array of rockeries and terraces; major features include a parterre sympathetically planted with herbs and a formal walled rose garden. The fine trees and shrubs include a medlar and a mulberry, and woodland walks add a further dimension to this fine historic garden. 200 acres in all.

Historic House Hotels

Llandudno, Gwynedd LL30 1RS.
Tel: (01492) 584466; www.bodysgallen.com

2m S of Llandudno. At A55/A470 junction turn onto A470 towards Llandudno. Hall is 1m on right

Open all year, daily

Entrance: free to guests using hotel facilities

Other information: Refreshments in hotel

 B&B

CAE HIR ★

Begun in 1984, the garden was made and is still managed by just one man. Its six acres – four on one side of the road where the house is situated and two on the other – slope, very gently at first, then more steeply from a natural stream and a series of informal wildlife pools at the bottom to a summerhouse at the top with fine views of the surrounding countryside. Near the top, an 18-metre-long laburnum crescent is underplanted with late-summer-flowering yellow and orange herbaceous plants, and edged with *Geranium macrorrhizum*; immediately below, a neatly clipped yew hedge echoes the crescent shape. This formality of design occurs throughout the garden, and yet there is no formal feel to it – indeed an element of wildness is encouraged, to settle the garden into the landscape. The discreet rooms, several themed by colour, are separated by large swathes of grass

Wil Akkermans

Cribyn, Lampeter, Ceredigion SA48 7NG.
Tel: (01570) 470839;
www.caehirgardens.ws

5m NW of Lampeter off A482. Turn left onto B4337 at Temple Bar; garden is 2m on left

Open all year, daily, 1 – 6pm

Entrance: £5, OAPs £4.50, children 50p

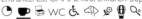

punctuated by standard trees. The owner's necessary choice of tough plants that don't need a lot of looking after has been turned to good effect: he uses them dramatically and often in masses. Trees are his passion, and he clearly enjoys trimming some of them into unusual shapes – he has a separate bonsai area. Nearby on the B4342, near Talsarn, is the *Winllan Wildlife Garden*, where several acres bordering the River Aeron are devoted to encouraging wildflowers and wildlife. [Open for NGS, June, daily, 2 – 5pm and in July and Aug by appt only – telephone (01570) 470612.]

CHIRK CASTLE ★

(Welsh Historic Garden Grade I)

The National Trust

Chirk, Wrexham LL14 5AF.
Tel: (01691) 777701; www.nationaltrust.org.uk

10m SW of Wrexham, 2m W of Chirk off A5, 1.5m up private drive

Castle open as gardens but 12 noon – 5pm (closes 4pm Oct)

Gardens open for snowdrops 3 weekends in Feb (telephone to check dates), 12 noon – 4pm; 15th March to June, Sept to 4th Nov, Wed – Sun and Bank Holiday Mons; July and Aug, Tues – Sun and Bank Holiday Mons; all 10am – 6pm (closes 5pm Oct and Nov) (last admission 1 hour before closing)

Entrance: £6.20, children £3.10, family £15.50 (castle and garden £8, children £4, family) £20

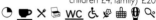

The castle, its walls now covered with climbing plants, dates from 1300 and is set in an eighteenth-century landscaped park of 12 acres. The trees and flowering shrubs, including rhododendrons and azaleas, were mostly planted by Lady Margaret Myddelton; they contrast with the yews in the formal garden, which were planted in the 1870s by Richard Biddulph. The long border has been replanted in four sections, each flowering at a different season. The addition of many herbaceous plants gives a more open feel to the border and links it to the herbaceous border planted in the 1920s. The rose garden contains mainly old cluster-flowered (floribunda) roses. From the terrace, with its fine views over Shropshire and Cheshire, the visitor passes to the classical pavilion, then along a lime tree avenue to a statue of Hercules. There is also interesting nineteenth-century topiary, a rockery and an old hawk house, and a pleasure-ground wood in which to stroll.

CLYNE GARDENS ★

(Welsh Historic Garden Grade I)

Swansea City Council

Blackpill, Swansea, West Glamorgan SA3 5BD. Tel: (01792) 401737

From Swansea take A4067 Mumbles road and turn right into car park of Woodmans Inn

Open all year, daily, 8am – dusk
Telephone for details of garden tours

Entrance: free

Other information: 'Clyne in Bloom' and rare plants sale in May

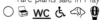

There is a combination of well-kept nineteenth-century woodland garden and open parkland with considerable botanical interest in the 48 acres here. Three National Collections are held – pieris, enkianthus and rhododendrons (Trifolia and Falconera subsections) – although they are not easy to find. Tree lovers will be well rewarded: there are many fine specimens, including the tallest recorded magnolia in Britain, *M. campbellii* Alba group. The most interesting time to visit is undoubtedly the spring, when the enormous collection of rhododendrons (over 800 varieties, some of them very rare) are at their best. These are mostly located on the banks of the stream that runs through the garden and make for a glorious walk ending up at the Japanese bridge. The nearby bog garden has extensive plantings of *Gunnera manicata*, candelabra primulas and other moisture-lovers. Pick your time right and there will also be swathes of bluebells and wood garlic.

Dewstow Grottoes

DEWSTOW GROTTOES
(Welsh Historic Garden Grade I)

The six-acre gardens and grottoes were regarded in the lifetime of its Victorian creator, Henry ('Squire') Oakley, as a unique and wondrous local landmark. Above ground were rock gardens, ponds, water features, ornamental areas, tropical glasshouses and a vast variety of plants from around the world; below ground sprawled one of the most extensive and best-preserved examples of Pulhamite rockwork in the country. A labyrinth of man-made tunnels, fern-filled caverns and artificial tufa grottoes winds its way under the house and past small pools and fountains; parts are illuminated by natural light; in others artificial light is required to negotiate them. Hardy and not-so-hardy ferns, spider plants and *Ficus pumila* thrive in the moist, frost-free conditions. This subterranean fantasy world is entered through a shady stumpery and emerges into a brightly planted bog garden ravine with a string of interconnecting lakes and small waterfalls. Next to the house a lively herbaceous border filled with strong performers has been created below a high wall as a colourful backdrop to the lawn.

John Harris

Dewstow House, Caerwent, Monmouthshire NP26 5AH.
Tel: (01291) 430444;
www.dewstow.com/gardens

5m SW of Chepstow off A48

Open April to Oct, Wed – Sun and Bank Holiday Mons, 10am – 4.30pm, and for parties by appt, Mon – Fri (advisable to telephone or check website)

Entrance: £6, concessions £5, children £3.50, under 5 free

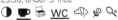

THE DINGLE NURSERIES AND GARDEN ★

Hidden in a deep Welsh valley with connecting small lakes, and making full use of the dramatic topography, the four-acre garden was planted after 1968 with a huge range of carefully chosen shrubs and trees, including a grove of acers and many other interesting specimens such as *Davidia involucrata*. Borders are sympathetically colour co-ordinated, and a large pool sets off the garden superbly. Most of the trees and shrubs in the garden can be bought from the adjoining nursery, with its extensive stock of plants ranging from herbaceous perennials to large shrubs and semi-mature trees; it is worth driving many, many miles to reach.

Jill Rock

Welshpool, Powys SY21 9JD.
Tel: (01938) 555145;
www.dinglenurseries.co.uk

3m NW of Welshpool. Take A490 for 1m to Llanfyllin then turn left signed to Dingle Nursery; after 1.5m fork left

Open all year, daily, except 25th Dec to 2nd Jan, 9am – 5pm.

Entrance: £3, children free

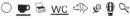

DYFFRYN FERNANT GARDENS

Christina Shand

Dyffryn Fernant, Llanychaer, Fishguard SA65 9SP. Tel: (01348) 811282; www.genuslocus.net

2m E of Fishguard off A487 Cardigan road. After long straight hill take small turning to right signed to Llanychaer (at 'Unsuitable for long vehicles' sign).

Entrance after 0.5m on left

Open 23rd March to Sept, alternate Suns and Bank Holiday Mons, 10am – 5pm. and by appt at any time

Entrance: £3, children under 16 free

Other information: self-catering cottage available

 WC

Since 1995 the owner has created an adventurous six-acre garden on an inauspicious site of boggy and stony ground surrounding her pretty house, making the most of the raw materials and applying a touch of magic to them. She is an enthusiastic plantswoman, and the courtyard garden and the house borders display a dizzy profusion of choice plants and shrubs. There is also evidence throughout of a strong grasp of design. The bog garden, formally laid out with slate paving, is dominated by a stainless steel obelisk – an inspired touch. The Rickyard (previously the nursery area) has a formal layout and strong colour plantings. At the edges of the garden things quieten down. Nicky's Tree is at the centre of a grid of 50 beds with mown paths running between them; each bed is planted with a single variety of ornamental grass. New walks are being opened up and wildflower meadows developed.

DYFFRYN GARDENS ★

Vale of Glamorgan Council

St Nicholas, Cardiff, Vale of Glamorgan CF5 6SU. Tel: (029) 2059 3328; www.dyffryngardens.org.uk

4m SW of Cardiff on A4232 turn S on A4050 and W to A48

Open all year, daily, 10am – 6pm (closes 4pm Nov to Feb)

Entrance: £6, concessions £4, children £2, family £15

Other information: No facilities in winter

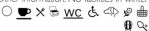

(Welsh Historic Garden Grade I)

One of Wales's largest landscape gardens and arguably one of the most important gardens of the Edwardian era, here are herbaceous borders on an heroic scale, croquet and archery lawns, flower beds laid out in a traditional pattern, rose gardens, a heather bank, a Victorian fernery, a stumpery, a rockery, an arboretum and a series of themed garden rooms, including the Pompeian Garden with a Grade-II-listed garden building. With the help of a huge lottery grant – some £6.15 million – Thomas Mawson's 1904 plans for the distinguished horticulturist Reginald Cory are being used as the basis for a full-scale restoration. Major projects include the restoration of the walled kitchen garden and its magnificent glasshouse and the reinstatement of the statue collection. 55 acres in all.

ERDDIG ★

The National Trust

Wrexham, Clwyd LL13 0YT. Tel: (01978) 355314; www.nationaltrust.org.uk

2m S of Wrexham off A525 or A483

House open as garden from 15th March, but 12 noon – 5pm

Garden open 9th Feb to 9th March, 8th Nov to 21st Dec, Sat and Sun; 15th March to 2nd Nov, Sat – Wed, plus Good Fri and Thurs in July and Aug, all 11am – 6pm (closes 4pm in winter)

Entrance: £5, children £2.50, family £12.50 (house and garden £8, children £4, family £20) (2007 prices)

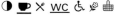

(Welsh Historic Garden Grade I)

Today there is no hint of the monumental task of restoration faced by the Trust when it acquired the almost ruinous house in 1973. The gardens, a rare example of early-eighteenth-century formal design, were almost lost along with the house, but have now been carefully restored. Thanks to Badeslade's bird's-eye view of 1739, it was possible to reconstruct the formal garden. The large walled garden contains varieties of fruit trees known to have been grown there during that period, and there is a canal garden and fish pool. South of the canal walk is a Victorian flower garden, and other Victorian additions include the parterre and yew walk. A National Collection of ivies is here, also a narcissus collection. Apple Day is celebrated in October, and the gardens are illuminated in December.

FOXBRUSH

This is a 2.5-acre plantswoman's garden, private in feel and created single-handedly from a wilderness on the site of a sixteenth-century mill; it retains its attractive wild atmosphere. Narrow paths meander through romantic plantings, incorporating rare treasures and sudden surprises, over bridges and under tunnels of laburnum and a 14-metre rose and clematis pergola, past herbaceous borders, a croquet lawn, a river and ponds. Although essentially a spring garden (despite ferocious flooding), it is much admired throughout the summer, too.

Mr and Mrs B. S. Osborne

Aber Pwll, Port Dinorwic, Gwynedd LL56 4JZ. Tel: (01248) 670463

3m SW of Bangor on B4507, N of A487. Avoiding bypass, enter village. House is on left after high estate wall

Open for NGS, and by appt

Entrance: £2, children free

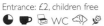

THE GARDEN HOUSE

This is a curate's egg of a garden, but one which is good in most of its parts and interesting in all of them. For a start, the tour starts rather lamely through a plant sales area and a tea room sited in a greenhouse, which lessens the undoubted impact of the ten core gardens planted round the modern house. Much of the design and planting throughout its five acres is imaginative and successful – a 'colour circle'; a golden privet hedge clipped into waves with a circle of densely planted bergenias in the centre; long paths lined with some of the hydrangeas in a National Collection held here; a striking collection of conifers tellingly grouped; a wonderful box-edged circular bed with a weeping pear underplanted with blue irises. The slate sculpture garden with its huge steel flower spikes may be an oddity too far for some visitors, but any gardener with an interest in innovation will spend a stimulating few hours here.

The Wingett family

Erbistock, Wrexham LL13 0DL. Tel: (01978) 781149; www.simonwingett.com

5m S of Wrexham off A539. Signed in village

Open March to Sept, Wed – Fri and Sun, 11am – 5pm (opens 2pm Sun), and by appt, inc. evening visits

Entrance: £4, children under 16 free

The Garden House

G. E. and M. B. Thomas

Berriew, Welshpool, Powys SY21 8AH.
Tel: (01686) 640644;
www.glansevern.co.uk

From Welshpool take A483 S. After 5m
entrance signposted on left

Open May to Sept, Thurs to Sat and Bank
Holiday Mons, 12 noon – 6pm, and for
parties by appt at other times

Entrance: £4, children free

◑ ☕ ✕ <u>WC</u> ☇ ⬦ 🐾 ⊞
                          🍶 B&B

GLANSEVERN HALL GARDENS

(Welsh Historic Garden Grade II*)

The mature 22-acre garden, set in 100 acres of parkland on the banks of the River Severn, is noted for its range of unusual trees. A four-acre lake has islands where swans, ducks and other waterfowl breed, and the streams, which form a water garden and feed the lake, are planted along the banks with moisture-loving plants and shrubs. A large area of lawn contains mature trees and herbaceous borders. Notable too are the fountain with its surround and walk festooned with wisteria, the restored rockery and the grotto. The walled garden (completely replanted in 2002), is ingeniously divided into nine separate compartments, each with its own distinctive planting.

The Hon. Christopher and Mrs McLaren

Llanrwst, Conwy LL26 0UL.
Tel: (01492) 640441

2m N of Llanrwst on E side of A470,
0.25m S of Maenan Abbey Hotel

Open for charity 27th April,
10.30am – 5pm (last admission
4.30pm), and for NGS

Entrance: £4, children £2

● ☕ WC ☇ ⬦

MAENAN HALL

Created in 1956 by the late Christabel, Lady Aberconway are formal gardens surrounding the Elizabethan and Queen Anne house, with less formal gardens in the mature woodland below. Her son and daughter-in-law, the present owners, have extended the planting of ornamental trees and shrubs in both settings. Azaleas, rhododendrons and camellias, the latter situated in a dell at the base of a cliff, make a spring visit rewarding, while roses bloom in profusion in June, and recently planted herbaceous borders carry the season on until the spectacular flowering of a large number of eucryphias in late summer. Nine acres in all.

Trustees, NBGW

Middleton Hall, Llanarthne,
Carmarthenshire SA32 8HG.
Tel: (01558) 667132/667134;
www.gardenofwales.org.uk

8m E of Carmarthen, 7m W of
Llandeilo off A48(M)

NATIONAL BOTANIC GARDEN OF WALES ★

(Welsh Historic Garden Grade II)

The first national botanic garden of the new millennium, supported by £22 million from the Millennium Commission, is located in the Regency estate of Middleton Hall, deep in the

National Botanic
Garden of Wales

beautiful Towy valley. Its scale and purpose is summed up in its centrepiece, the Great Glasshouse, a stunning 91-metre-long 'teardrop' structure designed by architects Foster and Partners. Within the world's largest single-span glasshouse, visitors can walk through and wonder at plants, landscapes and waterfalls normally found in threatened Mediterranean environments. A 300-meetre-long broadwalk of herbaceous plants and flowers leads through the middle of the garden, passing a unique restored double-walled garden and an award-winning Japanese garden; further on lie the Wallace garden, which demonstrates the history of plant genetics, the apothecaries' garden, the boulder garden and several others. The necklace of lakes is a feature of the late-eighteenth-century water park, where plants cultivated in slate beds adjoin the natural setting of gentle Welsh countryside, parkland and grassland; Paxton's View, site of the former mansion, offers a panorama down the valley.

Open all year, daily, 10am – 6pm
(closes 4.30pm Nov to Feb)
(last admission 1 hour before closing)

Entrance: £8, concessions £6, children £3, family £17 (2007 prices)

Other information: Free buggy hire for disabled

PANT-YR-HOLIAD ★

This 20-acre woodland garden, created by the owners since 1971, was started in an area of natural woodland backing onto the farmhouse. Since then hundreds of rhododendrons (species and hybrids) have been planted along the banks, and acers, eucalyptus, eucryphias and many other rare and unusual trees have now reached maturity. Paths wander in and around, and a stream runs through the middle of the garden. There is also a summer walk, along which slate-edged beds are filled with herbaceous plants, including a collection of penstemons. A small pergola has a rose-embowered seat with a fine view over the valley, and the remainder of the walk is beneath arches of climbing roses. Nearer the house is a walled garden, rose gardens, a series of pools for ornamental waterfowl and a potager-style kitchen garden. Nearby in Pontgarreg *Gwynfor Growers Nursery* has a wide range of intriguing perennials and scented shrubs for sale [open all year, Wed, Thurs and Sun, 10am – 5pm, and by appt – telephone (01239) 654151].

Mr and Mrs G. Taylor

Rhydlewis, Llandysul, Ceredigion SA44 5ST. Tel: (01239) 851493

12m NE of Cardigan. Take A487 coast road to Brynhoffnant, then B4334 towards Rhydlewis for 1m, turn left and garden is second left

Open for pre-booked parties of 10 or more by appt

Entrance: £3, children £1

PENPERGWM LODGE

This is a spacious three-acre garden, with broad south-facing terraces which command views over wide expanses of lawn well screened by mature trees and shrubs. A vine pergola makes a bold statement and provides a visual link with the house, while a formal garden of yew and box creates a delightful and effective enclosure and a folly tower adds a new dimension to the garden. Old-fashioned roses, herbaceous perennials and an imaginative vegetable garden with a new water canal contribute interest throughout the season. The nursery sells a good range of unusual plants, including herbaceous and half-hardy perennials, bulbs, shrubs and climbers.

Mrs C. Boyle

Abergavenny, Monmouthshire NP7 9AS. Tel: (01873) 840208; www.penplants.com

2.5m SE of Abergavenny off B4598 Usk road. Turn left opposite King of Prussia Inn. Entrance 300 metres on left

Open April to Sept, Thurs – Sun, 2 – 6pm

Entrance: £3.50

The National Trust

Bangor, Gwynedd LL57 4HN
Tel: (01248) 353084;
www.nationaltrust.org.uk

1m E of Bangor on A5122

Castle open

Garden open 2nd, 3rd, 9th and 10th Feb,
12 noon – 4pm; 19th March to 22nd Nov,
Wed – Mon, 11am – 5pm (opens 10am
July and Aug)

Entrance: £5.40, children £2.70 (castle and
garden £8, children £4, family £20)

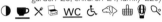

PENRHYN CASTLE

(Welsh Historic Garden Grade II*)

The large garden covers 50 acres with some fine specimen trees, shrubs and a Victorian walled garden in terraces with pools, lawns and a wild garden. Although the original house dated from the eighteenth century, the gardens are very much early-Victorian, contemporary with the present castle designed by Thomas Hopper. A giant tree fern, which will dwarf any children who visit, has been sent from Tasmania to take its place in a specialist collection that also includes another giant, gunnera, and the Australian bottle brush plant, both to be found in the spectacular bog garden beyond the walled garden.

Picton Castle Trust

Haverfordwest, Pembrokeshire SA62 4AS.
Tel: (01437) 751326;
www.pictoncastle.co.uk

4m SE of Haverfordwest off A40

Castle open

Garden open April to Oct, daily except
Mon (but open Bank Holiday Mons),
10.30am – 5pm

Entrance: £4.95, OAPs £4.75, children £2.50

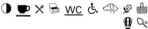

PICTON CASTLE ★

(Welsh Historic Garden Grade II*)

The castle, which has been in the hands of the Philipps family since the late fifteenth century, is late-thirteenth-century in origin, remodelled by later generations. The grounds extend over nearly 40 acres, with woodland walks among massive oaks and giant redwoods. Rarities include the biggest *Rhododendron* 'Old Port' in existence and a metasequoia, a deciduous conifer presumed extinct but rediscovered in China in 1941. In May and June all these exotic shrubs reach their full splendour. In the walled garden are herb borders, climbing roses and summer-flowering plants, with a pond and fountain creating a cool and calming atmosphere.

Llanfrothen, Penrhyndeudraeth,
Gwynedd LL48 6SW.
Tel: (07880) 766741
5m NE of Porthmadog between
Llanfrothen and Croesor

Open all year, daily, 9am – 5pm

Entrance: £3, children free (2007 prices)

○ WC &

PLAS BRONDANW ★

(Welsh Historic Garden Grade I)

This garden, in the grounds of the house given to Sir Clough Williams-Ellis by his father, is quite separate from the village of Portmeirion (see entry), and was created by the architect over a period of seventy years. His main objective was to provide a series of dramatic and romantic prospects inspired by the great gardens of Italy; it includes several architectural features, including an orangery. Visitors should walk up the avenue that leads past a dramatic chasm to the folly, from which there is a fine view of Snowdon – indeed mountains are visible from the end of every vista. Williams-Ellis made a prodigious investment in hedging and topiary (mostly yew); the hedging, if laid flat, would apparently cover four acres. Hydrangeas and ferns flourish in the damp climate.

The National Trust

Llanfairpwll, Anglesey LL61 6DQ.
Tel: (01248) 714795;
www.nationaltrust.org.uk

PLAS NEWYDD

(Welsh Historic Garden Grade I)

The eighteenth-century house by James Wyatt is worth visiting, mainly to see Rex Whistler's largest painting. Humphry Repton's suggestion of 'plantations ... to soften a bleak country and shelter the ground from violent winds' has resulted in an informal open-plan garden, with shrub plantings in the lawns and parkland, which slopes down to the Menai Strait and frames the view of the Snowdonia peaks. There is a formal Italian-style garden to the front of the house. A new arbour has replaced a conservatory on the top terrace with a tufa mound, from which water falls to a pool on the bottom terrace. The pool has acquired an Italianate fountain to add to the overall Mediterranean effect of this formal area within the parkland. The influence of the Gulf Stream enables the successful cultivation of many frost-tender shrubs, and a special rhododendron garden is open in the spring when the gardens are at their best. Major restoration of the Italianate terrace garden continues and includes the building of a deep grotto and the replanting of the mixed borders. The waterside and woodland paths along the Menai Straits have also been restored. Summer brings displays of hydrangeas, while autumn colours southern-hemisphere trees and shrubs in the ever-changing arboretum, and wild flowers appear in their seasons.

4m SW of Menai Bridge, 2m S of Llanfairpwll via A5

House with military museum open as gardens, but 12 noon – 4.30pm

Garden open March to 29th Oct, Sat – Wed, Good Friday and Bank Holiday Mons, 11am – 5.30pm (last admission 4.30pm). Rhododendron garden open 31st March to early June only. Guided tours by arrangement

Entrance: £5, children £2.50 (house and gardens £7, children £3.50, family £17.50)

Other information: Parking 0.25m from house. Complimentary minibus service between car park and house, and shuttle service available in garden

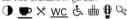

PLAS-YN-RHIW

(Welsh Historic Garden Grade II)

This is essentially a cottage garden of 0.75 acres, laid out around a partly medieval manor house perched on an exposed site on the west shore of Hell's Mouth Bay, where Atlantic rollers sweep in and the wind roars across the Lleyn Peninsula. It owes its existence to the three Keating sisters – Honora, Lorna and Eileen – who together with their mother jointly bought the house and 58 acres of land in 1938; a further 300 acres were added with the express purpose of giving the estate to the Trust. Essentially a cottage garden, thanks to the warming influence of the Gulf Stream, an array of flowering trees and shrubs, rhododendrons, camellias and magnolias flourishes in compartments framed by formal box hedges and grass paths, and on summer days scented plants infuse the air. A snowdrop wood stands on high ground above the garden. A place of romance and charm – and a characterful house which retains much of the character it must have possessed in the Keating sisters' day.

The National Trust

Pwllheli, Gwynedd LL53 8AB. Tel: (01758) 780219; www.nationaltrust.org.uk

Near tip of Lleyn Peninsular. 16m SW of Pwllheli, take A499 and B4413

House open (numbers limited)

Garden and snowdrop wood open some weekends Jan and Feb (telephone to check); 20th March to April, Oct to 2nd Nov, Thurs – Sun; May, June and Sept, Thurs – Mon; July and Aug, Wed – Mon; all 12 noon – 5pm (or dusk if earlier)

Entrance: house and garden £3.60, children £1.80, family £9

Other information: Parking 80 metres from house. No coaches

PORTMEIRION ★

(Welsh Historic Garden Grade II*)

Architect Sir Clough Williams-Ellis's wild essay into the picturesque is a triumph of eclecticism, with Gothick, Renaissance and Victorian buildings arranged as an Italianate village around a harbour and set in 70 acres of sub-tropical woodland criss-crossed by paths. This light opera is played out against the backdrop of the Cambrian mountains and the vast empty sweep of estuary sands. The gentle humour of the architecture extends to the plantings in both horizontal and

Penrhyndeudraeth, Gwynedd LL48 6ET. Tel: (01766) 770000 (Hotel Reception); www.portmeirion-village.com

2m SE of Porthmadog near A487

Open all year, daily except 25th Dec, 9.30am – 5.30pm

Entrance: £7, OAPs £5.50, children £3.60, under 5 free, family £17

Other information: Parking at top of village. Difficult for wheelchairs as steep in places

○ 🍵 ✕ 🛍 <u>WC</u> ♿ ♨ ⌕ B&B

vertical planes – in the formal gardens and in the wild luxuriance which clings to the rocky crags. Portmeirion provides one of Britain's most stimulating objects for an excursion, and during the period of the June festival in nearby Criccieth there are other good gardens open in the district. [Write for details (with s.a.e.) to Criccieth Festival Office, PO Box 3, 52 High Street, Criccieth LL52 0BW.]

POWIS CASTLE AND GARDEN ★★
(Welsh Historic Garden Grade I)

The National Trust

Welshpool, Powys SY21 8RF.
Tel: (01938) 551929;
www.nationaltrust.org.uk

0.75m S of Welshpool on A483.
Signposted

Castle open, but 1 – 5pm

Garden open 13th March to 2nd Nov,
Thurs – Mon, plus Weds, July and Aug,
11am – 5.30pm; 8th to 29th Nov, Sat and
Sun, 10am – 3pm.

Entrance: £7.50, children (5–16) £3.75,
under 5 free, family £18.75
(castle, garden and museum £10.50,
children £5.25, family £26.25)

Other information: Events programme and
guided tours of garden – telephone for
details. Picnics in park outside garden only.
Problematic for wheelchairs and
pushchairs as very steep with steps

◑ 🍵 <u>WC</u> ♿ 🐾 ♨ ⓘ

The garden was originally laid out in the 1680s, based on formal designs by William Winde, who had just finished at Cliveden (see entry in Buckinghamshire) – another cliffhanger. The most notable features are the broad cascading terraces, interestingly planted and with huge clipped yews. The terraces are inspired by those of the Palace of St Germain-en-Laye near Paris, where the 1st Marquis of Powis joined James II in exile in 1689. On the second terrace, above the orangery, are fine urns. Statuary by van Nost's workshop stands in front of the deeply recessed brick alcoves of the aviary. The late-eighteenth-century changes to the garden as a result of the English landscape style are attributed to William Emes. Advantage was taken of the many microclimates to develop the ornamental plantings during the nineteenth century, and the kitchen garden of the lower garden was transformed into a formal flower garden in 1911 by Lady Violet, wife of the 4th Earl. Unusual and tender plants and climbers now prosper in the shelter of the walls and hedges. The planting schemes are superb. The box-edged terraces have notable clematis and

Powis Castle and Garden

pittosporums; in season *Abutilon vitifolium* 'Tennant's White' matched with *Rosa banksiae* 'Lutea' and *R.* 'Gloire de Dijon' are inspiring, the collection of ceanothus cloaking the terraces magnificent; in late summer the eucryphias repeat the performance. The basket-weave terracotta pots continue to be planted with a masterly touch. The more recent gardens below, lying towards the Severn valley, are planted with old-fashioned roses and cottage-garden plants, with arches of vines continuing the formality in enclosed hedged rooms. This garden is not for the faint-hearted because it is very steep, but it is well worth the effort to enjoy the views which are as fine as any, anywhere.

ST FAGANS: NATIONAL HISTORY MUSEUM AND CASTLE ★

(Welsh Historic Garden Grade I)

National Museum of Wales

St Fagans, Cardiff CF5 6XB.
Tel: (029) 2057 3500;
www.museumwales.ac.uk

Near M4 junction 33. Signposted

Open all year, daily except 24th to 26th Dec and 1st Jan, 10am – 5pm

Entrance: free

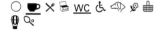

An historic garden of 100 acres with terraces, herb and knot gardens, a hornbeam tunnel, an old grove of mulberry trees and a vinery. The Rosery of 1900 has been replanted with the original varieties, and the vinery and flower house have been restored. Mature trees, both coniferous and broad-leaved, are an impresssive feature, as are the broad high terraces with massive stone walls hosting many climbing plants; beneath are large fish ponds containing carp, bream and tench, traditionally farmed over the years to feed the household. In the grounds rhododendrons are underplanted with spring bulbs. The restoration and replanting of the formal gardens, including an Arts and Crafts Italian garden, continue to reflect the Edwardian spirit of the place. Gardens attached to re-erected buildings from all over Wales are also being developed to re-create the differences in social status and period, using traditional horticultural techniques, tools and vegetable varieties.

SINGLETON BOTANIC GARDENS ★

A 4.5-acre garden with herbaceous borders, rockeries, rose beds and an interesting collection of trees and shrubs, including tapestry hedges using a variety of different shrubs. Newly erected temperate and tropical glasshouses contain an extensive range of rare and unusual plants, including orchids, bromeliads and epiphytes. While in Swansea, visit the 1600-square-metre hothouse *Plantasia*. Divided into arid, tropical and humid zones, it contains over 5000 plants and much wildlife. Signed from city centre and open all year, daily except Mondays.

Swansea City Council

Singleton Park, Swansea, West Glamorgan SA2 9DU. Tel: (01792) 298637;
www.swansea.gov.uk

In Swansea. Entrance in Gower Road

Open all year, daily, 9am – 6pm (closes 4.30pm in winter)

Entrance: free

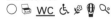

VEDDW HOUSE ★

Situated on a sheltered slope near the Wye Valley, framed by old beech woods and with views in all directions, this complex and highly individual garden has been created since 1987 by the present owners. They are fuelled by instinct and

Anne Wareham and Charles Hawes

Devauden, Monmouthshire NP16 6PH.
Tel: (01291) 650836;
www.veddw.co.uk

5m NW of Chepstow off B4293. In Devauden, signed from pub on green

Open June to Aug, Sun and Bank Holiday Mons, 2 – 5pm, and for parties of 10 or more afternoons or evenings by appt

Entrance: £5, children £1

 WC

imagination, and experimentation is key to their design philosophy. A visit to Veddw is never less than exciting. There are two acres of flower garden and meadow, where the generously planted borders include repeat plantings of many unusual varieties. Around every corner is something of interest – a philadelphus border, a purple and grey border, a bed filled with striking grey elymus grasses, a hazel coppice and a magnolia walk. The formal and wildly colourful vegetable garden has standard hollies, clematis and cardoons amidst the produce. From here an arch leads into the orchard and meadow, full of bulbs in spring and grasses and wild flowers in summer. Behind the house the ground slopes steeply upwards, with paths and steps leading to viewpoints. Yew hedges enclose a formal garden of clipped hedges and brick-paved paths, and a wonderfully dramatic enclosure has a black reflecting pool and a seat with an arching back that echoes a sinuous hedge in another part of the garden. Overlooking these spaces is an interesting parterre, where box hedges form compartments replicating the 1824 tithe map of the area. The spaces between are filled with a variety of grasses. Further up still is a hazel coppice and a two-acre wood with its superb old beeches, sorbus and hornbeams.

Veddw House

OTHER RECOMMENDED GARDENS

CENTRE FOR ALTERNATIVE TECHNOLOGY

Machynlleth, Powys SY20 9AZ (01654 705950; www.cat.org.uk). Open all year, daily except 25th Dec and mid-Jan, 10am – 5pm

High in a former slate quarry is a most interesting environmentally friendly garden, challenging every aspect of garden-making from design to planting, land reclamation to pest control. 7 eco-acres.

COLBY WOODLAND GARDEN

Amroth, Narberth, Pembrokeshire SA67 8PP (01834 811885; www.nationaltrust.org.uk). Open 15th March to 2nd Nov, daily, 10am – 5pm; walled garden 11am – 5pm. NT

Spring, when the rhododendrons, magnolias, azaleas and camellias are in flower, is a fine time to walk round the 20 acres here. Native as well as exotic trees and shrubs face each other across the valley floor, with a meadow in the distance and a walled garden planted for ornamental effect. (Listed Grade II)

DONADEA LODGE

Patrick Beaumont, Babell, Flintshire CH8 8QD (01352 720204). Open May to July by appt

This 1-acre summer garden demonstrates what creative design can achieve on a very long site. Imaginative planting, restrained and carefully thought-out colour schemes, and a great use of roses and clematis.

LLANLLYR

Mr and Mrs Robert Gee, Talsarn, Lampeter, Ceredigion SA48 8QB (01570 470900). Open for NGS, and April to Oct by appt

The 1830s layout of borders and shrubberies in this fine summer and autumn garden has been restored since 1989, and modern touches include water gardens, a parterre, a mount, a labyrinth and gravel gardens. 6 acres. (Listed Grade II)

THE NURTONS

Adrian and Elsa Wood, Tintern, Gwent NP16 7NX (01291 689253; www.thenurtons.co.uk). Open mid-April to Sept, Wed – Sun, 11am – 5pm

A sloping 3-acre plantsman's garden, with shady walks, a formal herb garden, a magnificent border surrounding a large circular lawn, and wonderful views across the Wye Valley. A wealth of summer and autumn flowers makes these some of the best times to visit.

TREDEGAR HOUSE

Newport, Gwent NP10 8YW (01633 815880; www.nationaltrust.org.uk). Garden open April to Sept, Wed – Sun, 9am – 5pm; park open all year, daily, dawn – dusk. NT

In two of the crisp early-18th-century formal gardens surrounding the splendid Restoration house are unique mineral parterres. The M4, alas, has intruded on the parkland. 90 acres. (Listed Grade II*)

WHIMBLE GARDEN AND NURSERY

Liz Taylor and Rod Lancett, Kinnerton, Presteigne, Powys LD8 2PD (01547 560413; www.whimblegardens.co.uk). Open April to Sept, Thurs – Mon, 10.30am – 5.30pm

An imaginative and richly planted garden specialising in unusual herbaceous plants and climbers, and attractive throughout the open season. 4 acres, including a meadow walk, earthworks and a toposcope. Many uncommon plants also in the small nursery.

CHANNEL ISLANDS

For further information about how to use the *Guide* and for an
explanation of the symbols, see pages vi–viii.
Maps are to be found at the end of the *Guide*.

GUERNSEY AND SARK

GRANGE COURT

Liz and Pat Johnson

The Grange, St Peter Port GY1 2QJ.
Tel: (01481) 701544

In town centre

Open for Flora Guernsey, and by appt
for parties and charities

Entrance: by donation
◐

This fine garden, set in the heart of St Peter Port, is constantly
being altered and improved by the present owners. The two-
acre site is laid out as three distinct areas. A new formal rose
garden has a folly wall; an informal garden, planted with
exotics such as bananas, stretches the whole length of the
property; and several rare plants and shrubs lead to a
beautifully restored Victorian vinery planted with a selection
of cacti. There is also a small walled garden next to a short
driveway planted with tree ferns, the August-flowering
Strelitzia reginae and an array of spider plants. This gem is really
worth several visits as it develops and the new irrigation
system and lavish composting take effect.

LA PETITE VALLÉE ★

Mrs Jennifer Monachan

Rue de Putron, St Peter Port GY1 2TE.
Tel: (01481) 238866

2m S of central St Peter Port

This is a garden full of surprises and excitement, since it
reflects the enthusiasm and passions that the owner has
lavished on her three-acre valley site leading towards the sea.
Water plays an important role: a rill flows down a staircase

La Petite Vallée

and along the lower terrace before winding around the garden to a canna-fringed lily pond. It then splashes down a waterfall to a koi pond, which is surrounded by a blue and burnt-orange garden. Elsewhere a summer bed is planted with psoraleas, *lochroma grandiflorum*, deutzias, philadelphus and daturas, and there are also wildflower meadows, shrubberies, herb, water and rose gardens, all flowing into each other with effortless ease. A sub-tropical garden has replaced the former lilac grove, and a new rock bed in front of the house includes an enticing mix of deep purple and lime-green gladioli.

Open occasionally for charity – check with local paper or tourist information office (Tel: (01481) 726611)

Entrance: charge

SAUSMAREZ MANOR EXOTIC WOODLAND GARDEN

Set around two small lakes in an ancient wood is a five-acre garden which has been crammed with the unusual and rare to give an exotic feel. It is strewn with plants from many parts of the world, particularly the sub-tropics and the Mediterranean, which enjoy Guernsey's mellow maritime climate. Collections of yuccas, ferns, camellias (over 300), bamboos, hebes, bananas, echiums, lilies, palm trees, fuchsias, as well as hydrangeas, hostas, azaleas, pittosporums, clematis, rhododendrons, cyclamens, impatiens, giant grasses etc., all jostle with indigenous wild flowers. No pesticides are used so wildlife flourishes. A poetry trail winds through the wood. Also here is an art gallery and the Art Park, showing around 200 pieces of sculpture by about 90 British, European, African, American and local artists, all for sale. A pitch-and-putt course, small children's play area and ride-on trains add to the holiday atmosphere.

Peter de Sausmarez

St Martins, Guernsey GY4 6SG.
Tel: (01481) 235571;
www.sausmarezmanor.co.uk

1.5m S of St Peter Port

Garden open all year, daily, 10.30am – 5pm (or dusk if earlier). Guided tours for parties by appt

Entrance: £5, OAPs/children £4, disabled persons and babies free

Other information: Rare plant sale 26th May. Holiday let available

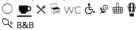

LA SEIGNEURIE

The grounds and walled garden of La Seigneurie, the residence of the Seigneurs of Sark, are beautifully maintained. Visit in spring and early summer for the camellias, azaleas and rhododendrons, later for roses, old-fashioned annuals, and in autumn for the glowing colours of dahlias and fuchsias. The walled garden contains clematis, geraniums, lapagerias, abutilons, osteospermums and many sub-tropical and tender plants. There is a potager, a wild pond area, a restored Victorian greenhouse with vines and bougainvilleas, a hedge maze for children, and a small outdoor museum with antique cannons. A Gothick *colombier* stands behind the house.

Seigneur Mr J.M. Beaumont

Sark GY9 0SF.
Tel: (01481) 832345 (Sark Tourism);
www.sark-tourism.com

0.5m NW of Creux Harbour, Sark

Open 17th March to 25th Oct, Mon – Sat, 10am – 5pm

Entrance: £2, children £1

LES VIDECLINS FARM

The 1.5-acre garden reveals itself as a surprising combination of artistry and plantsmanship, with its plethora of roses rambling over barns, a small pottery studio and old walls sheltering a relaxed and spontaneous cottage garden with a selection of interesting plants. The charming organic vegetable garden has young box hedging dividers, and there is interest

Mr and Mrs T. M. Le Pelley

Candie Road, Castel GY5 7BX.
Tel: (01481) 254788

46 metres from junction with Route des Talbots, near King's Mills

Les Videclilns Farm

Open 26th May to 28th July, Fri,
1 – 6pm, but check before travelling;
also occasionally for charity and by appt

Entrance: £2.50, children free

from spring through to autumn in the main, wild and vegetable gardens. Also surprising are the views across rolling fields to wooded hills, with scarcely a house in sight and access to the meadow in the Fauxquet Valley.

OTHER RECOMMENDED GARDENS

CANDIE GARDENS

Candie Road, St Peter Port GY1 1UG
(01481 717000). Open all year, daily, 8am – dusk

The lower garden is a rare surviving example of a Victorian public flower garden, with a splendid variety of exotic plants from all over the world revelling in the shelter of its walls. Wonderful views over the islands of Herm and Sark and a museum, art gallery and library, and exceptionally high standards of maintenance, are other good reasons to visit. 4 acres.

MILLE FLEURS

Mr and Mrs D Russell, Rue du Bordage, St Pierre du Bois GY7 9DW (01481 263911; www.millefleurs.co.uk). Open a few days a year, and for parties by appt

The charming 3-acre gardens, planted for fragrance and for wildlife, are set in a peaceful, wooded conservation valley. Plants scent the air in pots and borders around the house and holiday cottages and spill out along the paths that meander down to the valley floor, where sub-tropical plants flourish in the sheltered microclimate.

JERSEY

Mr and Mrs Marcus Binney

Rue de Bas, St Lawrence JE3 1JG.

2m N of St Helier

Open 29th June, 2 – 5pm, and for parties by appt

Entrance: £3

DOMAINE DES VAUX

Marcus Binney, architectural correspondent of *The Times*, has a passion for the preservation of architecture and landscape, and these tastes are very much reflected in his and his wife Anne's delightful 10-acre garden. It is in two completely contrasting parts. The top is a formal Italianate garden, set around and above a sunken rectangular lawn, and the borders here are a riot of unusual and familiar perennials and shrubs. This perfect formal garden was created by the previous generation, Sir George and Lady Binney, and designed by Walter Ison. Lady Binney planted with an eye for colour in foliage as much as in flowers, as is evidenced by the grey and silver borders facing the yellow, gold and bronze ones. The present generation have planted a small formal herb garden on a triangular theme and have created a *jardinière* and a pair of long flower borders. The lower garden is a semi-wild and quite steep valley with a string of ponds connected by a stream. In spring the valley and wood are at their best, with a carpet of wild Jersey narcissi under camellias, azaleas and rhododendrons. A magnificent *Magnolia campbellii* has reached maturity and flowers abundantly in March. Of particular note are the camellias in both gardens and an interesting collection of conifers, and other trees planted to give year-round foliage colour in a small arboretum. A newly created Mediterranean garden stands at the top of the valley with a collection of planted pots which reflect the colours of the south of France and Italy.

DURRELL

Over 100 rare and endangered species of animals reside within the 40 acres of parkland and water gardens. The late author and naturalist Gerald Durrell founded the Trust as a sanctuary forty years ago. Today Sumatran orang-utans, Andean bears and Montserrat orioles, rescued from beneath the smouldering volcano, live in lush, spacious environments which closely replicate their native habitats. Madagascar lemurs and tiny lion tamarins from Brazil roam free in woodland, leaping through the trees. Other exhibits include a walk-through aviary and a cloud forest inside the enclosure housing Andean bears, otters and coartis, and howler monkeys.

Durrell Wildlife Conservation Trust

Les Augres Manor, Trinity JE3 5BP.
Tel: (01534) 860000;
www.durrellwildlife.org.

2.5m NW of St Helier on B361

Open all year, daily except 25th Dec, 9.30am – 6pm (or dusk if earlier)

Entrance: £11.50, concessions £8.50, children £7.40, family £35. Favourable membership rates available

○ ☕ ✕ 🖼 WC ♿ ⊞ 🔦 ✎

ERIC YOUNG ORCHID FOUNDATION

This exquisite collection, described as 'the finest private collection of orchids in Europe, possibly the world', was built up by the late Eric Young, who came to Jersey after World War II. In 1958 he merged his own collection with that of a Sanders nursery which was closing down, and continued to acquire new plants. The purpose-built centre, which has won many awards, consists of eight growing houses and a landscaped display area where visitors may view these exotic flowers in close detail. From November to April there are cymbidiums, paphiopedilums, odontoglossums and calanthes, from May to June cattleyas, miltonias and odontoglossums and from June to October, phalaenopsis, miltonias and odontoglossums. (The beauty of these flowers is inversely proportional to the difficulty of their names.)

The Eric Young Orchid Foundation

Victoria Village, Trinity JE3 5HH.
Tel: (01534) 861963;
www.ericyoungorchidfoundation.co.uk

1.5m N of St Helier

Open all year except 25th, 26th Dec and 1st Jan, Wed – Sat, 10am – 4pm

Entrance: £3.50, concessions £3, children £1

Other information: Plants for sale when available

○ 🖼 WC ♿ 🌱 ⊞

SAMARES MANOR

The name Samares is derived from the French for salt marsh, and indeed sea salt was once extracted from marshy land nearby. It is not known who built the existing manor house, which has passed through many owners, but the 14-acre grounds have developed gradually. By 1680 they were famed for their trees. The present garden was the work of Sir James Knott, who bought the property in 1924 and had it developed, employing 40 gardeners, at a cost of £100,000. Two quite different gardens coexist here: a collection of herbs for every possible use, laid out in a partially walled

Vincent Obbard

St Clement JE2 6QW. Tel: (01534) 870551;
www.samaresmanor.com

2m E of St Helier Manor (guided tours daily except Sun, £2.80 extra) open

House open (guided tours daily except Sun, £2.90 extra)

Garden open 22nd March to 11th Oct, daily, 10am – 5pm

Entrance: £5.95, OAPs £5.55, students and children £1.95, under 5 free

Other information: self-catering accommodation available

garden leading to a lake; and a Japanese garden. Of particular note are the camellias, the *Taxodium distichum* in the lake and the rocks imported from Cumberland. There is also a specialist plant centre.

LES VAUX

Rhona, Lady Guthrie

Rozel Valley, St Martins JE3 6AJ. Tel: (01534) 861102

6m NE of St Helier

Open March to Sept by appt for parties

Entrance: £3

Other information: Garden steep in parts, so not ideal for unfit or disabled visitors

Sheltered within a steep-sided valley, the five-acre garden encompasses a variety of styles and an eclectic range of trees, shrubs, herbaceous plants and sculptures. The owner's artistry and love of unusual plants is lavished around lawns and bare rocks, on serene slopes and in richly filled shrubberies and borders. The old potato ground to the north now flowers with 30,000 bulbs, and a field at the head of the valley has been planted with 800 native trees to form a small nature reserve, with two ponds linked by a stream. Red squirrels and hedgehogs are already regular visitors, and peacocks roam the garden.

Les Vaux

OTHER RECOMMENDED GARDENS

CREUX BAILLOT COTTAGE

Judith Quérée, Le Chemin des Garennes, St Ouen JE3 2FE (01534 482191; www.judithqueree.com). Open May to Sept, Tues – Thurs, 11am or 2pm by appt for pre-booked conducted tours only

This cottage garden is a living encyclopedia of the rare and unsual packed into 0.25 acres in a secluded valley. It is a place of serious plantsmanship, lightened by nautical and humorous touches – a most enjoyable combination.

HOWARD DAVIS PARK

St Saviour, JE4 8UY. Open all year except 1st Jan, daily, from 8am (closing times vary seasonally)

The most famous of Jersey's public gardens, created in memory of a soldier-son killed in World War I. Colourful sub-tropical trees and plants flourish in its

12 acres, and the bandstand belts out an excellent variety of live entertainments during the summer months.

JERSEY LAVENDER

Alastair and Eleanor Christie, Rue du Pont Marquet, St Brelade JE3 8DS (01534 742933; www.jerseylavender.co.uk). Open mid-May to mid- Sept, Tues – Sun, 10am – 5pm

The 9 acres of lavender fields are a breathtaking sight before the start of their harvesting in late June, when visitors are invited to watch the crop being distilled and harvested. The extensive herb garden includes a National Collection of lavenders and 75 different bamboos.

NURSERIES WITH GOOD GARDENS

How often have you dithered over plants lined up in pots in your local gardening centre? Not sure how tall and wide they will grow, can't decide where to plant them or what to plant them with. Yet half the fun of shopping for plants lies in impulse-buying, not going out with a preordained list. Thankfully, there is now a growing band of nurserymen who offer gardeners the opportunity to see the plants for sale growing companionably together in a garden setting, whether it be a fine display area or their own well-designed and well-maintained private garden. The great majority of the plants in these nurseries are propagated on site or from the garden, and there are often a few treasures tucked away for discerning buyers. The gardens are often free for visitors to the nursery and the owner is usually on hand to discuss, advise and enthuse. It is no surprise that nurseries in the *Guide* have for many years featured simply as good gardens; now for the first time, we have brought them together, adding others that excel in both capacities.

The Plant Specialist, Buckinghamshire

BRISTOL

BLACKMORE AND LANGDON

Stanton Nurseries, Pensford BS39 4JL (01275 332300; www.blackmore-langdon.com). Open April to July, Mon – Fri, 9am – 5pm, Sat 10am – 4pm

The nursery specialises in begonias, on display in a 1-acre glasshouse from June to August, and delphiniums, with a first spectacular flowering in June and a secondary one in September.

BUCKINGHAMSHIRE

THE PLANT SPECIALIST

7 Whitfield Lane, Great Missenden HP16 0BH (01494 866650; www.theplantspecialist.co.uk). Open April to Oct, Wed – Sat, 10am – 6pm (Sean Walter and Keith Pounder).

The developing nursery specialises in perennials and grasses. Plants are trialled in stock beds and those for sale are grown in wide beds offset by gravel paths.

CAMBRIDGESHIRE

CAMBRIDGE GARDEN PLANTS

The Lodge, Clayhithe Road, Horningsea CB25 9JD (01223 861370). Open mid-March to Oct, Thurs – Sun, 11am – 5.30 (Chris Buchdahl).

The nursery stocks a good range of hardy perennials and roses; visitors are usually welcome to see the private 2.8-acre garden on request.

D'ARCY AND EVEREST

Pidley Sheep Lane, Somersham, Huntingdon (01480 497672; www.darcyeverest.co.uk). Open March to Sept, Wed – Fri, 10am – 4pm (advisable to telephone in advance) (Angela Whiting and Richard Oliver).

Along with herbs and selected perennials, the nursery specialises in alpines, many of them on view in a series of rock gardens, planted over 2 acres.

CHESHIRE

ARLEY HALL NURSERY

see entry

LODGE LANE NURSERIES

see entry under Bluebell Cottage Gardens

BRIDGEMERE GARDEN WORLD

see entry

DUNGE VALLEY HARDY PLANT NURSERY

see entry

NESS BOTANIC GARDENS

see entry

ONE HOUSE NURSERY

see entry

STAPELEY WATER GARDENS

see entry

STONYFORD COTTAGE GARDEN

Stonyford Lane, Cuddington, Northwich CW8 2FT (01606 888970). Open March to Sept, Tues – Sun and Bank Holiday Mons, 10am – 5.30pm, and for NGS. Evening tours of garden for parties by appt (Mr and Mrs Anthony Overland).

The nursery specialises in unusual waterside plants and perennials, and these thrive too in the 0.25-acre garden laid out with a pool, a damp garden and woodland.

CORNWALL

BOSVIGO

see entry

BREGOVER PLANTS

Middlewood, Launceston PL15 7NN (01566 782661). Open March to mid-Oct, Wed, 11am – 5pm, and most weekends, May to Sept (telephone to check). Also open by appt (Jennifer Bousfield).

A wide range of hardy plants to suit many soils and climates, some rare and unusual and all admirably displayed in the owner's appealing 'working cottage garden' on the edge of Bodmin Moor.

BURNCOOSE NURSERIES

see entry

PINE LODGE NURSERY

see entry

PINSLA GARDEN AND NURSERY

Pinsla Lodge, Glynn, Bodmin PL30 4AY
(01208 821339; www.pinslagarden.net). Open March
to Oct, daily, 10am – 6pm; in winter, please telephone
in advance (Mark and Claire Woodbine).

The nursery attached to the informal and
naturalistic 1.5-acre garden sells a huge range of
plants of all kinds, including alpines, succulents,
bamboos and ferns.

TREWITHEN NURSERIES

see entry

CUMBRIA

HALECAT

see entry

LARCH COTTAGE NURSERIES

Melkinthorpe, Penrith CA10 2DR (01931 712404;
www.larchcottage.co.uk). Open all year, daily except
Christmas period, 10am – 5.30pm (8.30am – dusk in
winter) (Joanne McCullock and Peter Stott).

The nursery stocks an exceptional range of
unusual and old-fashioned perennials, together
with conifers, rose, shrubs and Japanese maples.
The garden setting includes a Japanese garden,
a pond with a Monet bridge, a shade garden
and herbaceous borders backed by shrubs
and trees.

DERBYSHIRE

BLUEBELL ARBORETUM AND NURSERY

Annwell Lane, Smisby, Ashby de la Zouch LE65 2TA
(01530 413700; www.bluebellnursery.co.uk). Open
March to Oct, daily, 9am – 5pm (10.30am – 4.30pm
Sun); Nov to Feb, Mon – Sat, 9am – 4pm. Closed 24th
Dec to 2nd Jan and Easter Sun (Robert and Suzette
Vernon).

Make time to stroll through the display garden
and 6-acre arboretum filled with rare specimen
trees and unusual shrubs before repairing to
the extensive and well-stocked nursery.

HARDSTOFT HERB GARDEN

Hall View Cottage, Hardstoft, Pilsley, Nr Chesterfield
S45 8AH (01246 854268). Open mid-March to
mid- Sept, Wed, Thurs, Sat and Sun, 10am – 5pm
(Lynne and Steve Raynor).

A wide range of herbs to buy, and physic,
pot-pourri and lavender gardens and a scented
parterre to visit.

LEA GARDENS

see entry

DEVON

BURROW FARM GARDENS

see entry

THE GARDEN HOUSE

see entry

GLEBE COTTAGE PLANTS

Pixie Lane, Umberleigh EX37 9DH (01769 540554).
Open by appt (persevere!), and for NGS (Carol Klein).

Collected by the broadcaster and Chelsea
goldmedal winner Carol Klein, many rare and
unusual perennials are on sale and growing in
this, her own exuberant garden.

GREENWAY GARDENS NURSERY

see entry

HIGH GARDEN NURSERY

Chiverstone Lane, Kenton, Exeter EX6 8NJ
(01626 899106). Open all year except Christmas
period, Tues – Fri, 9am – 5pm (Chris and Sharon
Britton).

A wide range of unusual and interesting plants
is sold at competitive prices at the nursery. The
70-metre-long double herbaceous border
planted for vibrant colour and long-season
interest dominates the newly planted 3-acre
garden.

HILL HOUSE NURSERY

see entry

KNIGHTSHAYES NURSERY

see entry

MARWOOD HILL

see entry

PLANT WORLD GARDENS AND NURSERY

St Marychurch Road, Newton Abbot TQ12 4SE
(01803 872939; www.plant-world-seeds.com). Open
Easter to Sept, daily, 9.30am – 5pm (Ray Brown).

A wide range of rare and unusual herbaceous
plants, shrubs and alpines, and a National
Collection of primulas. The 4-acre gardens are
imaginatively laid out to represent the five
continents. The cafe has panoramic views.

ROWDEN GARDENS

Brentor, Tavistock PL19 0NG (01822 810275;
www.rowdengardens.com). Open for NGS, and by
appt April to Sept (John Carter).

The nursery specialises in aquatic and damp-
loving plants, all of them propagated in the
garden, which is set around 11 canal-like ponds
and also features bog gardens, ferns and
herbaceous borders. National Collections of
calthas and water irises (over 100 varieties.)

SAMPFORD SHRUB NURSERY

see entry for Holbrook Gardens

STONE LANE GARDENS

Stone Farm, Chagford TQ13 8JU (01647 231311;
www.mythicgarden.com). Nursery open all year,
Mon – Fri (sales area open daily), 9am – 5pm; garden
open all year, daily, 2 – 6pm, and at other times by appt
(Kenneth and June Ashburner).

The specialist nursery stocks most species of
birch and alder, plus a small selection of other
shrubs and trees grown both in pots and bare-
root. National Collections of wild-origin birches
and alders and to be seen in the attractive
5-acre woodland and water garden, where an
extensive sculpture exhibition is held during the
summer months.

WARD ALPINES

Newton Farm Nursery, Hemyock, Cullompton
EX15 3QS (01823 680410). Open frequently March
and June to Sept for NGS, and by appt (Mr and Mrs
J.F.J.M. Ward).

The nursery has a wide range of alpines and
irises and holds National Collections of *Gentiana
sino-ornata* and rhodohypoxis. The 5- acre
garden boasts a dozen herbaceous borders, a
shrub garden, a bog garden with an old
dewpond, a maze and a white hornbeam walk.

DORSET

ABBEY PLANTS

see entry under Chiffchaffs

BENNETTS WATER LILY FARM

Water Gardens, Chickerell, Weymouth DT3 4AF
(01305 785150; www.waterlily.co.uk). Open April to
Sept, Tues – Fri, Sun and Bank Holiday Mons,
10am – 5pm (J.L. and A.J. Bennett).

The nursery is an important supplier of aquatic
plants, and the ponds and lakes in the 6-acre
garden are a splendid place to see them
growing. The garden holds a National and
International Collections of water lilies. It is a
Site of Nature Conservation Interest, so wildlife
abounds, and there is also a museum and a
tropical house.

CASTLE GARDENS PLANT CENTRE

see entry under Sherborne Castle

COLD HARBOUR NURSERY

Bere Road, Wareham (01929 423520 – evenings;
www.dorset-perennials.co.uk). Open March to Oct,
Tues – Fri and most weekends (but telephone to
check), 10am – 5pm. Also open by appt (Steve
Saunders).

Unusual hardy perennials, grasses and woodland
plants are on offer in the nursery, and the
woodland garden is planted with
rhododendrons, azaleas and shade-loving
shrubs.

DOMINEYS YARD

see entry

FORDE ABBEY

see entry

KNOLL GARDENS

see entry

MORETON GARDENS

see entry

SNAPE COTTAGE

see entry

TREHANE CAMELLIA NURSERY

Staplehill Road, Hampreston, Wimborne BH21 7ND
(01202 873490; www.trehane.co.uk). Open all year
except Christmas period, Mon – Fri, 10am – 4pm;
Feb to May, Oct and Nov (telephone to check), and
most Bank Holiday Mons, 10am – 6pm (the Trehane
family).

A vast number of camellias, magnolias and
other acid-lovers displayed and sold in a
beautiful woodland setting, plus PYO
blueberries from late July.

DURHAM

EGGLESTON HALL GARDENS

see entry

ESSEX

BEECHES NURSERY

Village Centre, Ashdon, Saffron Walden CB10 2HB
(01799 584362; www.beechesnursery.co.uk) Open all
year, daily, 8.30am – 5pm (opens 10am Sun and Bank
Holiday Mons).

Over 6000 herbaceous plants, shrubs, roses,
climbers and trees on sale, plus a 4-acre
wildflower meadow and a display garden where
a good range of plants is laid out in a long
timber-framed bed.

BETH CHATTO GARDENS

see entry

GLEN CHANTRY

see entry

LANGTHORNS PLANTERY

see entry

R & R SAGGERS

see entry

GLOUCESTERSHIRE

BATSFORD GARDEN CENTRE

see entry

BROWNS BARN

Compton Lane Nurseries, Little Compton,
Moreton-in-Marsh GL56 0SJ (01608 674578). Open
all year, Thurs – Sat, 10am – 5pm, and Wed by appt
(Chris Brown).

The highly regarded nursery, which sells small
quantities of a wide range of unusual alpines,
herbaceous perennials and other garden plants,
is being expanded to include an educational
side and rare breeds of animals. The garden
setting of herbaceous and mixed borders is also
being rejuvenated.

HUNTS COURT

see entry

NATIONAL ARBORETUM, WESTONBIRT

see entry

SPECIAL PLANTS NURSERY

see entry

TINPENNY PLANTS

Tinpenny Farm, Fiddington, Tewkesbury GL20 7BJ
(01684 292668). Nursery open Feb to Oct,
Tues – Thurs, 9am – 1pm; Nov to Jan, by appt only.
Garden also open several Suns for NGS (Elaine
Horton).

Hardy plants are for sale in the small nursery,
and the garden – in a wind-swept site of heavy
clay – is filled with a riotous, not-too-tidy
collections of hellibores, irises, daylilies, Oriental
poppies, old roses, grasses; butterflies and
wildlife abound.

HAMPSHIRE

AFTON PARK NURSERY

Newport Road, Afton, Freshwater, Isle of Wight
PO40 9XR (01983 755774; www.aftonpark.co.uk).
Open all year, daily, except 25th and 26th Dec,
10am – 5pm (Paul Heathcote).

Plants for sale include everything from hedging
to grasses and Mediterranean plants, arranged
helpfully according to soil and climate; the
varied 7-acre garden is set in an area of
outstanding natural beauty.

APPLE COURT

see entry

EXBURY GARDENS PLANT CENTRE

see entry

LONGSTOCK PARK NURSERY

see entry

MACPENNYS NURSERIES

154 Burley Road, Bransgore BH23 8DB
(01425 672348; www.macpennys.co.uk). Open all year,
daily except Christmas period, 9am – 5pm (opens
10am Sun and Bank Holiday Mons) (Tim and
Vivien Lowndes).

The long-established nursery sells a good range
of shrubs, woody plants and herbaceous
perennials, some rare and unusual, and pleasant
woodland walks may be taken in the 4-acre
former gravel pit adjoining.

MRS MITCHELL'S KITCHEN AND GARDEN

2 Warren Farm Cottages, West Tytherley SP5 1LU
(01980 863101;
www.mrsmitchellskitchenandgarden.co.uk). Open April
to mid-Oct, Thurs, Fri and Sat, 10am – 5pm (but
advisable to telephone for specific dates each week).
Open by appt at other times (Louise and Julian
Mitchell).

The nursery is crowded with prairie plants and
cottage-garden favourites – Oriental poppies,
hardy geraniums, Michaelmas daisies and the
like – almost all on show in the 0.5-acre garden;
home-made preserves are also for sale.

SPINNERS GARDEN

see entry

WATER MEADOW NURSERY AND HERB FARM

Cheriton, Alresford SO24 0QB (01962 771895;
www.plantaholic.co.uk). Open March to July,
Wed – Sun; Aug to Oct, Fri and Sat; all 10am – 5pm;
and by appt at other times (Roy and Sandy Worth).

Herbs, perennials, poppies, water plants and
wild flowers are on offer in the well-stocked
nursery, and may be spotted in the herbaceous
borders, fringing a pond, and in shady walks and
a wildflower meadow. Visit in June to see a
National Collection of Oriental poppies and
Super Poppy hybrids

VENTNOR BOTANIC GARDENS

see entry

HEREFORDSHIRE

ABBEY DORE GARDENS

see entry

AULDEN FARM

Aulden, Leominster HR6 0JT (01568 720129;
www.auldenfarm.co.uk). Open April to Aug, Tues and
Thurs; March and Sept, Thurs only; all 10am – 5pm.
Also open for NGS and by appt at other times.
(Alun and Jill Whitehead).

In the 2-acre garden surrounding the charming
old farmhouse are a myriad delightful and
unusual herbaceous plants for sun, shade,
woodland and waterside. Plants for sale are all
grown on site and neatly arranged in rows
under old apple trees and on the gravel scree
of the farmyard filled with self-sown euphorbias,
cowslips, violas and *Verbena bonariensis*.

HERGEST CROFT

see entry

IVY CROFT

Ivington Green, Leominster HR6 0JN (01568 720344;
www.ivycroft.freeserve.co.uk). Nursery open Feb and
April to Sept, Thurs, 9am – 4pm. Garden open for
NGS (Sue and Roger Norman).

Roger Norman, a knowledgeable and genial
plantsman and local NCCPG treasurer, sells a
wide range of interesting, healthy and well-
grown plants. The 4-acre garden surrounding
the cottage set in rich grassland is equally
alluring, combining formal plantings and mixed
borders, a perry pear orchard and a vegetable
garden, an alpine area screened by pleached
limes and a pond fringed by willows, grasses
and ferns.

KENCHESTER WATER GARDENS

Church Road, Lyde, Hereford HR1 3AB (01432
270981). Open all year, daily except 25th Dec,
9am – 6pm (10.30am – 4.30pm Suns; closes 5.30pm
Oct to March) (Mr and Mrs M.R. Edwards).

A National Collection of water lilies is just one
of the draws to the nursery, which stocks a
wide range of other aquatic plants, many of
them well displayed in the water gardens.

KINGSTONE COTTAGE PLANTS

see entry

MOORS MEADOW

Collington, Bromyard, Hereford HR7 4LZ
(01885 410318; www.moorsmeadow.co.uk).
Open March to Sept, Fri – Tues, 11am – 5pm and by
appt at other times (Ros Bissell).

The small nursery is propagated entirely from the wide range of exotic and unusual plants to be found in the large and interesting 7-acre plantswoman's garden.

HERTFORDSHIRE

HOPLEYS PLANTS
see entry

KENT

DOWNDERRY NURSERY
Pillar Box Lane, Hadlow, Tonbridge TN11 9SW (01732 810081; www.downderry-nursery.co.uk). Open May to Oct, Tues – Sun and Bank Holiday Mons, 10am – 5pm (Dr Simon Charlesworth).

One of the most comprehensive lavender nurseries in the country (a National Collection is held here), with almost all the plants propagated on site. The display area is charmingly laid out in the old walled garden with a stylish glass water feature and a lavender maze.

EAST NORTHDOWN FARM NURSERY
Margate CT9 3TS (01843 862060; www.botanyplants.co.uk). Open all year daily except Christmas week, 10am – 5pm (opens 11am – 4pm Suns) (William and Louise Friend).

The nursery specialises in plants that thrive on chalk and in taxing seaside conditions, and these spill over into the garden surrounding the farmhouse, where the plants are encouraged to run riot and set seed.

EDENBRIDGE HOUSE
see entry

IDEN CROFT HERBS
Frittenden Road, Staplehurst TN12 0DH (01580 891432; www.herbs-uk.com). Open March to Sept, daily, 9am – 5pm (opens 11am Sun and Bank Holiday Mons); Oct to Feb, Mon – Fri, 9am – 4pm (Philip Haynes).

The perfect combination of a commercial nursery selling a wide range of herbs, perennials, grasses and native wild flowers, and a series of display gardens integrating herbs and garden plants, culminating in a well-filled Victorian walled garden. National Collections of mint, nepeta and origanum are held here.

MADRONA NURSERY
Pluckley Road, Bethersden TN26 3DD (01233 820100; www.madrona.co.uk). Open March to Oct, Sat – Tues, 10am – 5pm. Closed 2 weeks in Aug.

An unusual and interesting range of trees, shrubs, perennials, ferns and grasses in display beds laid out in a walled nursery with a charming Gothick tower.

RIVER GARDEN NURSERY
see entry

ROCK FARM NURSERY
see entry

TILE BARN NURSERY
Standen Street, Iden Green, Benenden TN17 4LB (01580 240221) www.tilebarn-cyclamen.co.uk). Open all year, Wed – Sat, 9am – 5pm, but advisable to telephone in advance (Peter and Liz Moore).

All the cyclamen and other bulbs for sale in the nursery and glasshouse are grown from home-collected seed, and vast numbers of cyclamen have colonised every conceivable patch of ground in the garden surrounding a traditional Kentish oasthouse.

LANCASHIRE

HAWTHORNES NURSERY GARDEN
see entry

LEICESTERSHIRE

GOSCOTE NURSERIES
Syston Road, Cossington LE7 4UZ (01509 812121; www.goscote.co.uk. Open all year, daily, 9am – 5pm (opens 10am Sun, closes 4.30 pm in winter). Closed over Christmas period (James Toone).

A wide range of hardy plants, including specimen trees and shrubs, conifers, fruit trees, unusual climbers and much more, and a spacious show garden laid out as island beds in grass.

THE HERB NURSERY

Thistleton, Oakham LE15 7RE (01572 767658;
www.herbnursery.co.uk). Open all year, daily except
Christmas week, 9am – 6pm (or dusk if earlier)
(Peter and Christine Bench).

A much wider range than just herbs, including
cottage-garden plants, wild flowers and scented-
leaved pelargoniums, almost all propagated in 4
acres of growing fields. Garden and sales areas
intermingle, and include a 0.5-acre walled
garden, glasshouses, an orchard and 2 acres of
woodland.

KAYES GARDEN NURSERY

1700 Melton Road, Rearsby, Leicester LE7 4YR
(01664 424578). Open March to Oct, Tues – Sun
and Bank Holiday Mons, 10am – 5pm (closes 12 noon
Sun) (Hazel Kaye).

The nursery specialises in herbaceous plants,
climbers and aquatics, and sells a good range of
grasses, all propagated on site from stock in the
garden. The 1.5-acre garden is filled with interest
through from spring in the shade garden to the
summer flowering of the double herbaceous
borders, and masses of autumn colour.

LINCOLNSHIRE

EASTON WALLED GARDEN
see entry

GARDEN HOUSE
see entry

GOLTHO HOUSE
see entry

HALL FARM AND NURSERY
see entry

HOLMDALE HOUSE
see entry

THE OLD RECTORY, SOMERBY
see entry

THE PALM FARM

Station Road, Thornton Hall Gardens, Station Road,
Thornton Curtis, nr Ulceby DN39 6XF (01469
531232; www.thepalmfarm.co.uk). Open all year, daily,
2 – 5pm (telephone in advance in winter) (W.W. Spink).

Hardy and half-hardy palms are the draw here,
but the nursery, which rings a pretty garden,
also sells unusual trees, shrubs and
conservatory plants. Palms have been planted in
the old walled garden, and the orchard is now
an arboretum with some mighty trees.

POTTERTONS NURSERY

Moortown Road, Nettleton, Caistor LN7 6HX
(01472 851714; www.pottertons.co.uk). Open all year,
daily, 9am – 4pm (Robert and Jackie Potterton).

Specialising in alpines, bulbs and rock plants –
many rare and unusual – the nursery has many
other garden plants on offer. The fine display
gardens cover a range of habitats – a rock and
water garden, troughs, raised and peat beds, and
woodland.

LONDON

HALL PLACE
see entry

THE PALM CENTRE (HAM NURSERY)

Ham Street, Ham, Richmond TW10 7HA
(020 8255 6191; www.thepalmcentre.co.uk).
Open all year, daily, 9am – 5pm (or dusk if earlier)
(Martin Gibbons).

Over 400 different species of tropical and hardy
palms, bamboos, tree ferns and exotics, housed
in topical and arid houses and planted outside
in a series of display gardens.

MANCHESTER

WYTHENSHAWE HORTICULTURAL CENTRE
see entry

NEWCASTLE UPON TYNE

BIRKHEADS SECRET GARDENS

Nr Hedley Hall Wood, Sunniside, Gateshead
NE16 5EL (01207 232262/07778 447920;
www.birkheadsnursery.co.uk). Open mid-March to
Oct, Tues – Sun and Bank Holiday Mons, 10am – 5pm,
and for groups by appt (Christine Liddle).

The nursery has a good selection of hardy
herbaceous perennials, grasses, bulbs and herbs,
and time must be allowed for a visit to the
gardens, created by a designer and plant
collector. Within the 2 acres are such delights as

an avenue of perennials, a small arboretum, a wildflower meadow, and slate, meditation, well-being and beachcomber gardens.

HALLS OF HEDDON

West Heddon Nurseries, Heddon on the Wall NE15 0JS (01661 852445; www.hallsofheddon.co.uk). Open all year, daily, 9am – 5pm (opens 10am Sun).

This is the place to come for dahlias and chrysanthemums (around 200 varieties of each for sale), and the show fields are an amazing sight when they open to visitors from the end of August until the first frosts.

NORFOLK

BRESSINGHAM GARDENS

see entry

CONGHAM HALL HERB GARDENS

see entry

EAST RUSTON OLD VICARAGE

see entry

HOECROFT PLANTS

Severals Grange, Holt Road, Wood Norton NR20 5BL (01362 684206; www.hoecraft.co.uk). Open April to Oct, Thurs – Sun, 10am – 4pm, and for NGS (Jane Lister).

The owner has assembled a nursery full of foliage plants, grasses and bamboos, together with many other garden plants; the garden itself, beautifully planted for foliage contrast, is a real bonus.

NORFOLK LAVENDER

see entry

PETER BEALES ROSES

London Road, Attleborough NR17 1AY (01953 454707; www.classicroses.co.uk). Open all year, daily: Mon to Sat, 9am – 5pm, Sun 10am – 4pm.

The famous nursery stocks some 1300 varieties of classic roses – shrub, bush, climbing, rambling and ground-cover – and holds a National Collection of species roses. There is a small display garden in which to savour a myriad flowers and scents.

P.W. PLANTS

Sunnyside, Heath Road, Kenninghall NR16 2DS (01935 888212; www.hardybamboo.com). Open April to Sept, Fri and Sat; plus Oct to March, Fri and last Sat of month; all 9am – 5pm (Paul Whittaker).

Bamboos of every size, colour and type for sale in the nursery, together with grasses and many other garden plants. In the display area, grass paths wind among plantations of bamboos, showing their versatility in a garden setting.

READS NURSERY

see entry for Hales Hall

THE ROMANTIC GARDEN NURSERY

see entry for Kettle Hill

WEST ACRE GARDENS

West Acre, King's Lynn PE32 1UJ (01760 755562). Open Feb to Nov, daily, 10am – 5pm (John and Sue Tuite).

The nursery and display gardens are attractively sited in the walled garden of an old manor house. Shrubs, alpines, ornamental grasses and herbaceous perennials – many of them rare – are grown as specimens and in mixed borders, a shade bed and a Mediterranean garden.

NORTHAMPTONSHIRE

COTON MANOR GARDEN

see entry

WOODCHIPPINGS

see entry

NORTHUMBERLAND

BIDE-A-WEE COTTAGE

see entry

CHESTERS WALLED GARDEN

Chollerford, Hexham NE46 4BQ (01434 681483; www.chesterswalledgarden.co.uk). Open end-March to Oct, daily, 10am – 5pm (telephone for winter opening times). Garden also open for NGS (Mrs S. White).

The nursery stocks over 900 herb cultivars and holds National Collections of thyme, majoram and burnet along with wild flowers, roses, herbaceous plants and grasses. In the 2-acre walled garden these mingle together in Roman, Mediterranean, dye and other themed gardens.

CHIPCHASE CASTLE NURSERY

see entry

HERTERTON HOUSE GARDE NURSERY

see entry

LONGFRAMLINGTON GARDENS

Swarland Road, Longframlington, Morpeth NE65 8BE
(01665 570382; www.longframlingtongardens.co.uk).
Open all year, daily except Christmas period, 8.30am –
5pm, and evenings by appt (Hazel Huddleston).

The nursery stocks a wide range of hardy
ornamental plants, mostly propagated on site,
and the contemporary 12-acre garden is a living
exhibition of hardy trees, shrubs, climbers and
herbaceous perennials, set in a beautiful stretch
of countryside. The varied attractions include a
garden walk (helpfully, the plants are well
labelled) and a wild meadow.

NOTTINGHAMSHIRE

FELLEY PRIORY

see entry

NATURESCAPE

Lapwing Meadows, Coach Gap Lane, Langar
NG13 9PH (01949 860592; www.naturescape.co.uk).
Open 21st March to Sept, daily, 11am – 5.30pm
(Mr and Mrs B. Scarborough and Mark Scarborough).

An important stockist of a large and varied range
of British wild plants, ravishing to behold in the
wildlife garden, with habitats including
meadowland, woodland and marshland, ponds
and cottage gardens.

NORWELL NURSERIES

Woodhouse Road, Norwell, nr Newark NG23 6JX
(01636 636337). Open Easter to Sept, daily,
11am – 5.30pm; nursery only also open Oct to March,
Mon – Fri (telephone in advance) (Dr Andrew Ward).

The nursery stocks many of the rare and unusual
plants to be found in the 0.75-acre plantsman's
garden. Orchids and erythroniums flourish in
woodland, penstemons and dieramas in a 'bell
garden' and moisture-lovers in a pond area and
bog garden; grasses, alpines, cottage-garden plants
and hardy chrysanthemums are other specialities.
There are also extensive herbaceous borders
and 'hot' and colour-themed beds.

OXFORDSHIRE

WATERPERRY GARDENS

see entry

RUTLAND

BARNSDALE GARDENS

see entry

SHROPSHIRE

DAVID AUSTIN ROSES

see entry

HALL FARM NURSERY

Vicarage Lane, Kinnerley, Oswestry SY10 8DH
(01691 682135; www.hallfarmnursery.co.uk).
Open March to Oct, Tues – Sat, 10am – 5pm, and
by appt at other times (Christine and Nick Foulkes
Jones).

A nursery to go to for unusual herbaceous
perennials, ornamental grasses and moisture-
and shade-loving plants, on show in the well-
planted and well-maintained display areas,
planted for seasonal effect.

HILLVIEW HARDY PLANTS

Worfield, Bridgnorth WV15 5NT (01746 716454;
www.hillviewhardyplants.com). Open March to
mid- Oct, Mon – Sat, 9am – 5pm, and by appt
(John, Ingrid and Sarah Millington).

Choice hardy herbaceous plants, drought-
tolerant specimens, a large range of bulbs is
for sale in the nursery, and a National
Collection of acanthus is held here. Visitors
may walk around the owners' garden
adjoining, where most of the plants in the
nursery are grown. Guided tours of nursery
and garden are available for parties by appt.

SWALLOW HAYES

see entry

SOMERSET

BROADLEIGH GARDENS

Bishops Hull, Taunton TA4 1AE (01823 286231;
www.broadleighbulbs.co.uk). Open all year, Mon – Fri,
9am – 4pm (Christine Skelmersdale).

Small bulbs, especially cyclamen and snowdrops, together with agapanthus, foliage and woodland plants, grow in the nursery beds. They are also to be found in the 3-acre display garden, which includes a dry stream, a hot bed, a pond, herbaceous borders, a parterre, many irises and a National Collection of miniature daffodils among its attractions.

EAST LAMBROOK MANOR

see entry

ELWORTHY COTTAGE PLANTS

Elworthy, Lydeard St Lawrence, Taunton TA4 3PX (01984 656427; www.elworthy-cottage. co.uk). Open mid-March to July, Thurs and Fri, 10am – 4.30pm; Feb to Oct by appt. Also open for NGS, and by appt (Mike and Jenny Spiller).

Some good and unusual perennials and clematis in the small nursery, and a charming 1-acre cottage garden planted for wildlife and blending into the scenery of the Brendon Hills on the fringe of Exmoor National Park.

JUNKER'S NURSERY LTD

Lower Mead, West Hatch, Taunton TA3 5RN (01823 481046; www.junker.co.uk). Open strictly by appt (Nick and Karan Junker).

The nursery, where everything is home-grown, is especially strong on acers, cornus, daphnes and magnolias, many of them rare and unusual. The garden, sited on heavy clay, is packed with interest, including birch and acer groves, a landscaped lake, and scree and terraced beds; wildlife abounds.

LOWER SEVERALLS

see entry

MEADOWS NURSERY

5 Rectory Cottages, Selwood Street, Mells, Frome BA11 3PN (01373 812268). Open Feb to Oct, Wed – Sun and Bank Holiday Mons, 10am – 6pm (Sue Lees and Eddie Wheatley).

The nursery which sells unusual hardy perennials, grasses, bulbs and shrubs, approached through an exuberant cottage garden, is laid out within a walled garden in the centre of an historic village. Subtle changes of level lead across the site with rich herbaceous colours among the greens and greys. Old apple trees punctuate luxurious herbaceous plantings.

MILL COTTAGE PLANTS

Henley Mill, Wookey BA5 1AW (01749 676966; www.millcottageplants.co.uk). Open March to Sept, Wed, 10am – 5.30pm, and by appt (preferable to telephone in advance, after 6pm) (Peter and Sally Gregson).

The nursery specialises in rare traditional Japanese hydrangeas, but also stocks a good range of perennials, ferns and grasses. The River Axe runs through the well-designed 2-acre garden, which has colourful beds filled with perennials, annuals and grasses, a vegetable garden and orchard, and an intriguing secret garden.

SUFFOLK

EAST BERGHOLT PLACE

see entry

HARVEYS GARDEN PLANTS

Great Green, Thurston, Bury St Edmunds IP31 3SJ (01359 233363; www.harveysgardenplants.co.uk). Open 7th Jan to 23 Dec, Tues – Sat, 9.30am – 4.30pm (Roger and Teresa Harvey).

Specialities are unusual herbaceous perennials, grasses, woodland plants and a National Collection of heleniums. It is set in a garden with a long herbaceous border planted with hot colours for summer and autumn, two mixed borders, a fine oak underplanted for winter interest, newly developed display borders and an orchard. Refreshments, talks and practical demonstrations are on offer in the new Orchard Room.

THE KITCHEN GARDEN

Church Cottage, Church Lane, Troston IP31 1EX (01359 268322; www.kitchen-garden-hens.co.uk). Open Easter to Sept, Fri and Sat, 10am – 6pm, and for groups by appt (Francine Raymond).

An unusual and enjoyable visit to a charming garden with many hens in residence and where a small and select range of unusual plants is for sale.

PARK GREEN NURSERIES

Wetheringsett, Stowmarket IP14 5QH (01728 860139; www.parkgreen.co.uk). Open March to Sept, Mon – Sat, 10am – 4pm, and by appt (Richard and Mary Ford).

NURSERIES WITH GOOD GARDENS

Hostas are the major draw, with over 200 varieties, but also a good range of perennials and grasses, many of them laid out in impressive display beds.

THE PLACE FOR PLANTS
see entry for East Bergholt Place

THE WALLED GARDEN
Park Road, Benhall, Saxmundham IP17 1JB (01728 602510; www.thewalledgarden.co.uk). Open March to Oct, Tues – Sun; Nov to Feb, Tues – Sat; all 9.30am – 5pm (Jim Mountain).

The nursery specialises in a wide range of garden plants, including climbers, tender species and hardy perennials. Yew hedges divide the 2- acre walled garden into different areas that feature a raised pond, a pergola, and yellow, mixed and perennial borders; a further 2.5 acres have been planted up outside the wall.

WOOTTENS OF WENHASTON
see entry

SURREY

CROSSWATER FARM
see entry

GREEN FARM PLANTS
see entry for Bury Court in Hampshire

HERONS BONSAI LTD
Wire Mill Lane, Newchapel, Lingfield RH7 6HJ (01342 832657; www.herons.co.uk). Open all year, daily, 10am – 5.30pm or dusk if earlier (10am – 4pm Sun) (Peter and Dawn Chan).

A must for anyone interested in the art of bonsai, with a number of gardens landscaped à la Japonaise to spur the imagination of visitors.

HYDON NURSERIES
Clock Barn Lane, Hydon Heath, Godalming GU8 4AZ (01483 860252). Open all year, Mon – Fri, 8.30am – 5pm (closes 4pm in winter); Sat 9.30am – 12.45pm; Sun by appt. Closed 12.45 – 2pm.

Rhododendrons and azaleas are the specialities here, together with camellias and magnolias and a range of fine trees, for sale in the nursery and planted out in the 25-acre grounds, where fine specimen trees and shrubs include collections of magnolias and nothofagus.

MILLAIS NURSERIES
see entry for Crosswater Farm

WISLEY PLANT CENTRE
see entry under RHS Garden Wisley

SUSSEX, EAST

GREAT DIXTER NURSERIES
see entry

KING JOHN'S LODGE
see entry

MARCHANTS HARDY PLANTS
see entry

MERRIMENTS GARDEN
see entry

PARADISE PARK
Avis Road, Newhaven BN9 0DH (01273 512123; www.paradisepark.co.uk). Open all year daily except 25th and 26th Dec, 9am – 6pm.

Attached to the garden centre, the many different displays include cactus and tropical houses, desert, oriental and seaside gardens, reproductions of famous Sussex landmarks in different garden settings.

USUAL AND UNUSUAL PLANTS
Onslow House, Magham Down, Hailsham BN27 1PL (01323 840967). Open mid-March to Oct, Wed – Sat, 9.30am – 5.30pm, and by appt at other times (Jennie Maillard).

Unusual herbaceous perennials, especially erysimums, euphorbias, hardy geraniums, salvias and grasses. Behind the house are four large raised island beds filled with bulbs, perennials and grasses, backed by woodland.

WELLINGHAM HERB GARDEN
see entry

SUSSEX, WEST

ARCHITECTURAL PLANTS
Cooks Farm, Nuthurst, Horsham RH13 6LH (01403 891772; www.architecturalplants.com). Open all year, daily except Sun, 9am – 5pm. Closed 25th and 26th Dec and 1st Jan, (Angus White).

Aptly described as 'the last outpost of empire', this exciting nursery stocks big, bold hardy exotics, set around a jungle-like garden where eucalyptus, hardy palms and bananas jostle for space. Full of inspiration for gardeners seeking a change of style.

BIG PLANT NURSERY

Hole Street, Ashington RH20 3DE (01903 891466). www.bigplantnursery.co.uk Open all year, daily, 9am – 5pm (10am – 4pm Sun and Bank Holiday Mons) (Bruce Jordan).

Another welcome nursery for hardy exotic plants, some imported but many grown and propagated on site. In the adjacent 4-acre garden are birches underplanted with grasses and herbaceous perennials, and collections of bamboos and hardy exotics.

HOLLY GATE CACTUS NURSERY

Billingshurst Road, Ashington RH20 3BB (01903 892930; www.hollygatecactus.co.uk). Open all year, daily except 25th to 27th Dec, 9am – 5pm (closes 4pm Nov to Jan) (J.M. Hewitt).

A huge range of cacti and succulents for sale. The cactus garden under glass was started in the mid-1970s and now house some 30,000 rare specimens from the Americas and Africa.

INGWERSEN'S BIRCH FARM NURSERY

Gravetye, East Grinstead RH19 4LE (01342 810236; www.ingwersen.co.uk). Open March to Sept, daily except Sun and Bank Holiday Mons; Oct to Feb, Mon – Fri; all 9am – 4pm. Closed for 2 weeks at Christmas (Paul Ingwersen).

A long-established nursery in a beautiful setting (William Robinson of Gravetye Manor was Walter Ingwersen's landlord) with an excellent range of alpines plus unusual rock plants, dwarf hardy perennials, shrubs and conifers, many of them exhibited in raised beds and troughs.

LEONARDSLEE PLANTS

see entry

WARWICKSHIRE

CHARLECOTE PLANTS AND FLOWERS

see entry for Charlecote Park

WILTSHIRE

THE BOTANIC NURSERY

Cottles Lane, Atworth, Melksham SN12 8NU (07850 328756; www.thebotanicnursery.com). Open March to Nov, Tues – Sat, 10am – 5pm, and by appt (Terence and Mary Baker).

A plantsman's nursery with many rarities and a National Collection of digitalis, plus unusual shrubs, grasses, ferns, perennials and climbers. The 1-acre display garden is planted with a good range of trees, including several variegated specimens, underplanted with sought-after varieties of hydrangea, spiraea, buddleja and other lime-tolerant shrubs.

HEALE HOUSE

see entry

THE MEAD NURSERY

Brokerswood, Westbury BA13 4EG (01373 859990; www.themeadnursery.co.uk). Open Feb to mid-Oct, Wed – Sat and Bank Holiday Mons, 9am – 5pm (open 12 noon Sun, but closed Easter Sun). (Stephen and Emma Lewis-Dale).

The nursery sells herbaceous perennials, alpines, pot-grown bulbs and grasses, and the garden is likewise full of variety and interest, with herbaceous borders, raised alpine and Mediterranean beds, a sink garden, a bog bed and a small wildlife pond.

WILTON HOUSE

see entry

WORCESTERSHIRE

EASTGROVE COTTAGE GARDEN NURSERY

see entry

PERSHORE COLLEGE

see entry

OLD COURT NURSERIES

see entry under The Picton Garden

RED HOUSE FARM GARDEN AND NURSERY

Flying Horse Lane, Bradley Green, Nr Redditch B96 6QT (01527 821269; www.redhousefarmgardenandnursery.co.uk). Open all year, daily, 9am – 5pm (opens 10am Sun and Bank Holiday Mons) (Maureen Weaver).

The small nursery specialises in shrubs and cottage-garden perennials, and also has a range of conifers, heathers and herbs. In the densely planted 0.5-acre garden (also open for NGS) gravel paths meander around a small lawn past borders planted for all-year interest with shrubs, old-fashioned roses, hardy perennials and bulbs.

STONE HOUSE COTTAGE NURSERIES

see entry

TREASURES OF TENBURY

see entry for Burford House Gardens

WEBBS OF WYCHBOLD

see entry under Riverside Gardens

YORKSHIRE, NORTH AND EAST

STILLINGFLEET LODGE NURSERIES

see entry

YORKSHIRE LAVENDER AND HOWARDIAN HERBS

see entry

NORTHERN IRELAND

BALLYROBERT COTTAGE GARDEN AND NURSERY

154 Ballyrobert Road, Ballyclare, Co. Antrim BT39 9RT (028 933 22952; www.ballyrobertcottagegarden.co.uk). Open March to 9th Oct, Mon – Sat, 10am – 5pm (opens 2pm Sun); 10th Oct to Feb by appt only.

The nursery stocks a wide range of cottage garden plants, plus shrubs, alpines and climbers, which may be seen in the display borders and in the 6-acre Robinsonian garden teeming with wildlife. The 4 acres of woodland are underplanted with many spring bulbs, and there is a small lake and other areas filled with cottage-garden plants.

SEAFORDE NURSERY

see entry

TIMPANY NURSERY AND GARDENS

77 Magheratimpany Road, Ballynahinch, Co. Down BT24 8PA (02897 562812; www.timpanynurseries.com). Nursery open all year, Tues to Sat, 10am – 5.30pm (dusk in winter). Closed over Christmas period (Susan Tindall).

The nursery stocks mainly alpines and herbaceous perennials, and the 20-acre garden is a good place to stroll, with a rock garden, herbaceous borders, 1.5 acres of woodland and a wildlife pond.

REPUBLIC OF IRELAND

ALTAMONT

see entry

ANNES GROVE

see entry

ENNISCOE

see entry

GASH GARDENS

see entry

JUNE BLAKE'S NURSERY

see entry for Hunting Brook Gardens

SCOTLAND

ABRIACHAN NURSERY

see entry

ARDKINGLAS ESTATE NURSERIES

see entry

ARDMADDY CASTLE GARDENS NURSERY

see entry

ARDTORNISH

see entry

BINNY PLANTS

West Lodge, Binny Estate, Ecclesmachan Road, nr Uphall, West Lothian EH52 6NL (01506 858931; www.binnyplants.co.uk). Open all year, daily except mid-Dec to mid-Jan, 10am – 5pm (Billy Carruthers).

The nursery carries some 2300 species and varieties, and specialises in perennials, including 300 peonies, 150 irises and many astilbes, hostas, ferns grasses and bamboos, together with an increasing range of unusual shrubs. There are show beds for peonies and irises, at their best in June and ever-developing woodland garden which reaches a peak in July and Aug.

CASTLE KENNEDY

see entry

CALLY NURSERY

see entry

CHRISTIE'S NURSERY

Downfield, Westmuir, Kirriemuir DD5 8LP (01575 572977; www.christiealpines.co.uk). Open March to Oct by appt; parties welcome (Ian and Ann Christie).

A nursery for alpines, bulbs and plants for woodland, scree and raised beds, including some rare and unusual varieties and an extensive collection of snowdrops and meconopsis. The garden is planted with trees for shelter and to encourage wildlife, with the alpines displayed in raised beds and troughs, tabletop and crevice gardens and an alpine house.

CRAIGIEBURN CLASSIC PLANTS

By Moffat, Dumfriesshire DG10 9LF (01683 221250). Open Easter to mid-Oct, Tues – Sun, 10.30am – 6pm, and by appt (Janet and Andrew Wheatcroft).

Meconopsis and herbaceous perennials are the nursery's specialities, playing a key role too in the 6-acre garden ringed by a burn, where a Nepali garden is being created near three waterfalls. Much of the garden is formal, with box-edged beds, generous twin herbaceous borders, and spring, autumn, cottage and vegetable gardens.

CRATHES CASTLE PLANT CENTRE

see entry

EAST LUGTONRIDGE GARDEN

Lochlibo Road, Burnhouse, Beith, Ayrshire KA15 1LE (01560 484800). Open daily, Easter to Oct, dawn to dusk (Jim and Joan Goldie).

Most of the rare and unusual herbaceous perennials on display in the small gem of a garden are propagated on site and for sale in the nursery, together with troughs, stones and other salvage suitable for gardens. The knowledge of the owners, the friendly advice given and the quality of the plants are all exceptional.

EDROM NURSERIES

Coldingham, Eyemouth TD14 5TZ (01890 771386; www.edromnurseries.co.uk). Open mid-March to mid- Oct, daily, 9am – 5.30pm (T. Hunt and C. Davis).

Woodland plants and alpines are the specialities here, with a fine range of trilliums, arisaemas, primulas, gentians, meconopsis and anemones. The 1-acre garden is divided into woodland, raised beds and a gentian terrace; most of the plants are labelled.

ELIZABETH MACGREGOR

Ellenbank, Tongland Road, Kirkcudbright DG6 4UU (01557 330620). Open May to Sept, Mon, Fri and Sat, 10am – 5pm (Elizabeth and Alasdair MacGregor).

The renowned nursery specialises in unusual herbaceous perennials including large collections of violas, eryngiums, anemones and thalictrums, many displayed to advantage in the walled garden adjoining.

GARDEN COTTAGE NURSERY

Tournaig, Poolewe, Achnasheen, Highland IV22 2LH (01445 781777; www.gcnursery.co.uk). Open March to Oct, daily except Sun, 10am – 6pm (Ben Rushbrooke).

Many fine plants for sale in the nursery, those that thrive in damp or boggy conditions and tough coastal plants like olearias plus a notable collection of Asiatic primulas. Many of them are to be seen growing in the small garden, and also in spectacular fashion at nearby Inverewe Gardens(see entry).

GLENDOICK GARDENS

see entry

GLENWHAN GARDENS

see entry

THE HYDROPONICUM

Achiltibuie, Ullapool IV26 2YG (01854 622202;
www.thehydroponicum.com). Open all year, daily,
11am – 4pm

The three growing houses shelter fruits and
herbs from different climate zones, all grown in a
soil-less medium that optimises nutrient uptake.
A fascinating glimpse of the future, perhaps,
and tempting to invest in the kits and systems
on sale.

JACK DRAKE

Inshriach Alpine Nursery, Aviemore, Inverness-shire
PH22 1QS (01540 651287; www.drakesalpines.com).
Open March to Oct, daily, 10am – 5pm (John and
Gunnbjørg Borrowman).

The famous alpine nursery, in a magnificent
Highland setting where only exceptionally hardy
plant survive, has been going strong since 1938.
The nursery specialises in alpines and carries a
good range of primulas, meconopsis, gentians
and heathers, while the gardens include a large
and impressive rock garden, an alpine house, a
summer garden and a wild garden with a pond.

KERRACHAR GARDENS

see entry

KIRKLANDS GARDEN

Bridge Street, Saline, Fife KY12 9TS (01383 852737;
www.kirklandshouseandgarden.co.uk). Open April to
Sept, Fri – Sun, 2.30 – 5pm, and for the SGS and by
appt (Peter and Gill Hart).

All the hardy herbaceous and woodland plants
in the small nursery come from the garden and
naturally regenerating woodland – 22 acres in all.
The 2-acre garden is traditional and charming,
with herbaceous borders, a woodland garden
and walk, a rockery and a walled garden
furnished with vegetables, fruit and flowers.

LAMBERTON NURSERY

No. 3 Lamberton, Berwickshire TD15 1XB
(01289 308515; www.lambertonnursery.co.uk).
Open April to Sept, daily except Sat, 10am – 5pm
(Ron and Susan McBeath).

A nursery to visit for rock garden and woodland
plants, and grasses. The 1-acre peat and rock
garden is filled with primulas, meconopsis and
ericaceous plants, and herbaceous borders are
planted for sun and shade.

LOGAN BOTANIC GARDEN

see entry

QUERCUS GARDEN PLANTS

Rankeilour Gardens, Rankeilour Estate, Springfield,
Cupar, Fife KY15 5RE (01337 810444). Open March,
Sat, 10am – 2pm; April to mid-Oct, Thurs – Sun,
10am – 5pm; mid-Oct to Feb, by appt only. Closed
during Christmas period (Colin McBeath).

The nursery, set in an old kitchen garden with
greenhouses and a peach house, specialises in
'easy and unusual plants for contemporary
Scottish gardens'. The walled garden has beds
planted for damp and dry conditions, a long
prairie-style border and a new hot border.

TEVIOT WATER GARDEN

see entry

WALES

ABERCONWY NURSERY

Graig, Glan Conwy, Conwy LL28 5TL (01492 580875).
Open Feb to Oct, Tues to Sun, 10am – 5pm
(Keith Lever).

The nursery offers one of the largest collection
of alpine and rock garden plants in the UK,
together with shrubs and woodland plants. The
constantly changing display area included
troughs, a limestone rockery, and ericaceous
and tufa beds.

ALED PLANTS

Tan y Graig, Mill Lane, Llannefydd Road, Henllan,
Denbigh LL16 5BD (01745 816161). Open by appt
(Jim and Barbara Buchanan).

All the plants in the small nursery are
propagated from the 0.5-acre garden dissected
by three terraced walks rising to a limestone
cliff, with a large rockery and shrub and
herbaceous beds laid out below.

BODNANT GARDEN NURSERY

see entry

CRÛG FARM PLANTS

Griffith's Crossing, Caernarfon, Gwynedd LL55 1TU
(01248 670232; www.crug-farm.co.uk). Open 8th
March to June, Thurs – Sun and Bank Holiday Mons;
July to Sept, Thurs – Sat; all 10am – 5pm. Also open
for NGS (Bleddyn and Sue Wynn-Jones).

The famous nursery excels in woodland and mountain plants, many of them rare and unusual. Plants spill out over gravel paths and luxuriate in the shade of mature trees, and the flower and foliage displays in the garden shop are spectacular.

DIBLEYS NURSERIES

Llanelidan, Ruthin LL15 2LG (01978 790677; www.dibleys.com). Open April to Sept, daily; March and Oct, Mon – Fri; all 10am – 5pm (the Dibley family).

The nursery specialises in gesneriads, especially streptocarpus, of which they hold a National Collection, and begonias. The 10-acre gardens are planted in the style of an informal arboretum.

DINGLE RETAIL NURSERY

see entry

MOORLAND COTTAGE PLANTS

Rhyd-y-Groes, Brynberian, Crymych SA41 3TT (01239 891363; www.moorlandcottageplants.co.uk). Nursery open March to Sept, Thurs – Tues, 10.30am – 5.30pm. Garden open as nursery but from mid-May (Jennifer Matthews).

The nursery stocks a wide range of favourite herbaceous perennials, plus ornamental grasses and ground-cover plants, and the charming country garden, in a fine setting with splendid views, has shady areas, grass terraces, a fernery and cottage borders.

PENPERGWM LODGE

see entry

WHIMBLE NURSERY

see entry

WORLD OF FERNS
(formerly Rickards Ferns)

Carreg y Fedwen, Lon Rallt, Pentir, Bangor, Gwynedd LL57 4RP (01248 600385; www.world-of-ferns.co.uk). Open April to Sept, daily, 10am – 5pm, and by appt (Dick Haywood, Ben Kettle and Jennie Jones).

Ferns are the nursery's speciality and feature plants for every garden situation: hardy and semi-hardy, for indoors and conservatory. The grounds, with spectacular views, show off the plants in a variety of settings that includes sheltering under a copse of trees and mingling with bulbs on a grassy bank.

CHANNEL ISLANDS

JERSEY LAVENDER

see entry

MAPS

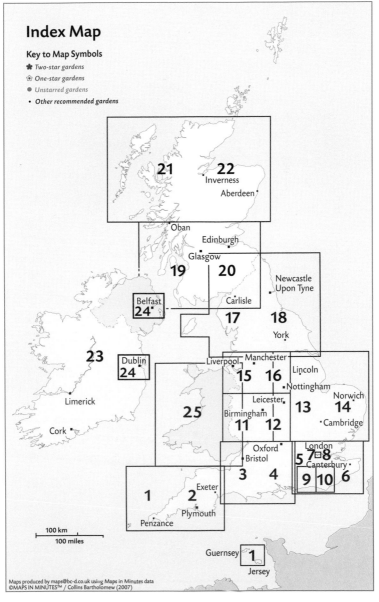

Index Map

Key to Map Symbols
- ★ *Two-star gardens*
- ✲ *One-star gardens*
- ● *Unstarred gardens*
- • *Other recommended gardens*

21
22
Inverness
Aberdeen

Oban
Edinburgh
Glasgow
19
20
Newcastle
Upon Tyne
Carlisle
17
18
York
Belfast
24
23
Dublin
24
Liverpool
Manchester
15
16
Lincoln
Nottingham
Limerick
Leicester
Norwich
25
13
14
Birmingham
Cambridge
Cork
11
12
Oxford
London
Bristol
5
7
8
Canterbury
3
4
9
10
6
Exeter
1
2
Plymouth
Penzance

100 km
100 miles

Guernsey
1
Jersey

Maps produced by maps@bc-d.co.uk using Maps in Minutes data
©MAPS IN MINUTES™ / Collins Bartholomew (2007)

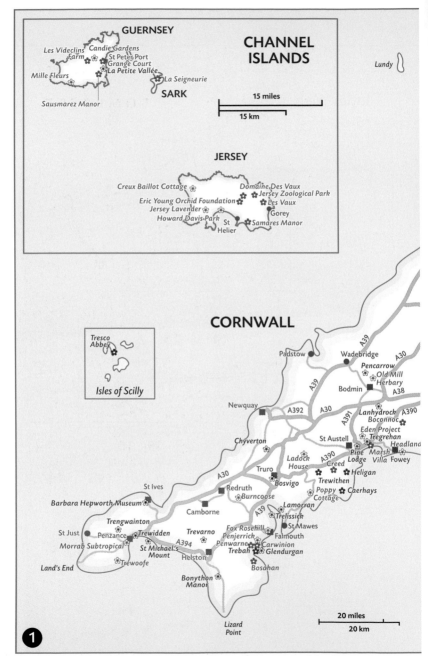

CHANNEL ISLANDS

GUERNSEY

Les Videclins Farm
Candie Gardens
St Peter Port
Grange Court
La Petite Vallée
Mille Fleurs
La Seigneurie

SARK

Sausmarez Manor

15 miles
15 km

JERSEY

Creux Baillot Cottage
Domaine Des Vaux
Jersey Zoological Park
Eric Young Orchid Foundation
Les Vaux
Jersey Lavender
Gorey
Howard Davis Park
St Helier
Samares Manor

Lundy

CORNWALL

Tresco Abbey
Isles of Scilly

Padstow
Wadebridge
Pencarrow
Old Mill
Herbary
Bodmin
A38
A39
A30
A390
Lanhydrock
A390
Boconnoc
Eden Project
Tregrehan
Headland
Pine Marsh
Lodge Villa Fowey
Creed
Heligan
Trewithen
Poppy Caerhays
Cottage

Newquay
A392
A30
A391
St Austell
Chyverton
Ladock House
A390
Truro
Bosvigo

St Ives
Redruth
Burncoose
Barbara Hepworth Museum
Camborne
Lamorran
Trelissick
St Mawes
Fox Rosehill
Trengwanton
Trevarno
Penjerrick
Falmouth
St Just
Penzance
Trewidden
Penwarne Carwinion
Morrab Subtropical
St Michael's Mount
Trebah Glendurgan
Helston
Trewoofe
Bosahan
Land's End
Bonython Manor
Bosahan

Lizard Point

20 miles
20 km

Key: ✿ Two-star gardens ✿ One-star gardens ✿ Unstarred gardens ✿ Other recommended gardens

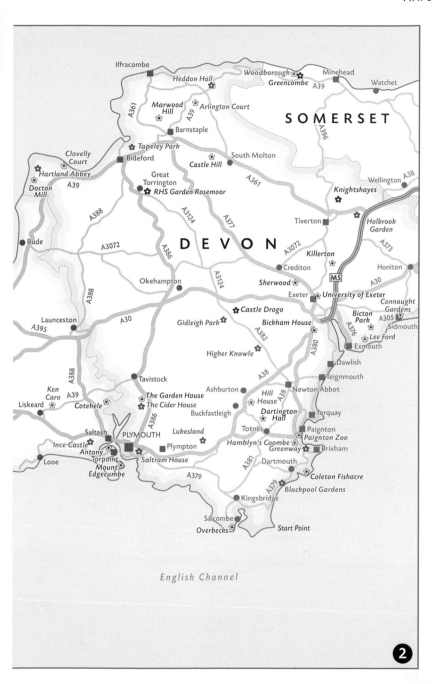

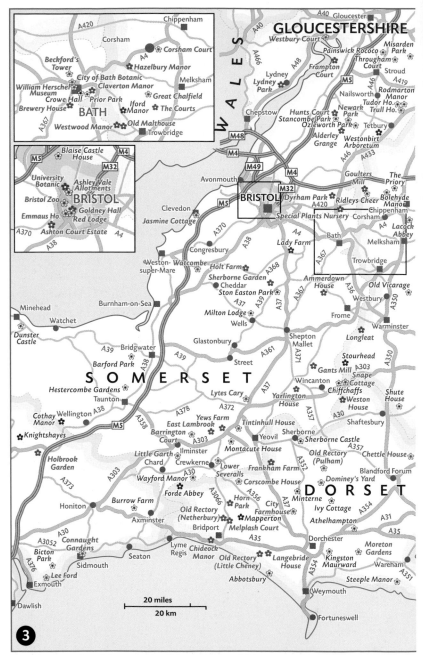

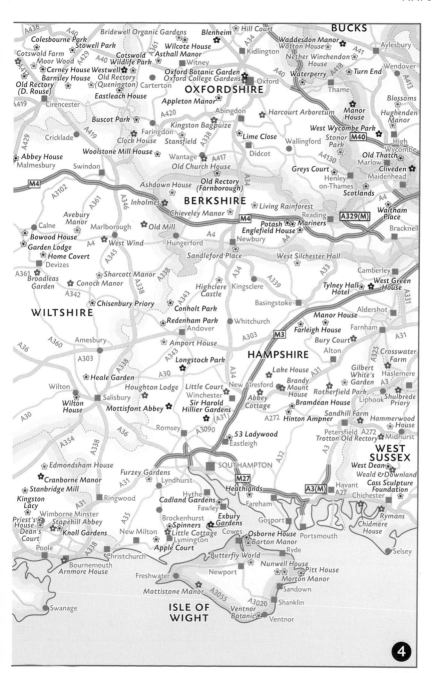

A436
A40 Bridewell Organic Gardens ❀ Blenheim ❀ Hill Court
BUCKS
Colesbourne Park ❀ Stowell Park ❀ Wilcote House ❀ Waddesdon Manor ❀ Aylesbury
Cotswold Farm Asthall Manor A361 Kidlington Wotton House A41
❀ Moor Wood A429 A40 Cotswold Wildlife Park ❀ Witney Nether Winchendon ❀ Wendover
❀ Cerney House Westwell ❀ House A418 Turn End A413
Barnsley House Old Rectory Oxford Botanic Garden A40 Waterperry ❀
Old Rectory (Quenington) Carterton Oxford College Gardens ❀ Oxford Thame Blossoms
(D. Rouse) Cirencester Eastleach House OXFORDSHIRE Hughenden
A419 Appleton Manor Harcourt Arboretum Manor Manor
Buscot Park ❀ Abingdon House West Wycombe Park ❀ High
Cricklade A419 Faringdon Kingston Bagpuize Stonor M40 Wycombe
A429 Clock House Stansfield A338 Lime Close Wallingford Park Old Thatch
A4 Woolstone Mill House Wantage ❀ A417 Didcot Marlow Cliveden ❀
❀ Abbey House Old Church House Greys Court Maidenhead
Malmesbury Swindon A4130 Henley
Ashdown House Old Rectory on-Thames A4 Waltham
M4 A3102 (Farnborough) Scotlands Place
Inholmes BERKSHIRE ❀ Living Rainforest A329(M)
Avebury Chieveley Manor ❀ Reading Bracknell
Calne Manor Marlborough ❀ Old Mill M4 Potash ❀ Mariners
Bowood House Englefield House ❀
Garden Lodge A4 ❀ West Wind Hungerford Newbury A4 Camberley
❀ Home Covert A345 Sandleford Place West Silchester Hall
Devizes A33
A361 ❀ ❀ Sharcott Manor A338 A34 West Green
Broadleas ❀ Conock Manor A339 Tylney Hall ❀ House
Garden A342 Highclere Kingsclere Hotel Aldershot
❀ Chisenbury Priory A343 Castle Basingstoke
WILTSHIRE Conholt Park Manor House
Redenham Park Whitchurch Farleigh House Farnham A31
Andover A303 M3 Bury Court ❀
Amesbury Amport House Alton Crosswater
A36 A360 A343 Longstock Park HAMPSHIRE Gilbert Farm
A303 A30 Lake House White's Haslemere
❀ Heale Garden Brandy Garden A3
Wilton Houghton Lodge Little Court New Alresford Mount ❀ Rotherfield Park Liphook Shulbrede
Wilton Salisbury Winchester Abbey House Bramdean House Priory
House Mottisfont Abbey ❀ Sir Harold Cottage Hinton Ampner Sandhill Farm Hammerwood
A36 Hillier Gardens A272 House
Romsey A3090 53 Ladywood Petersfield A272 Midhurst
A354 A338 Eastleigh Trotton Old Rectory ❀
A32 WEST
❀ Edmondsham House SOUTHAMPTON West Dean SUSSEX
❀ Cranborne Manor Furzey Gardens A3(M) Weald &Downland
❀ Stanbridge Mill A31 Lyndhurst M27 Havant Cass Sculpture
Kingston Hythe Heathlands A27 Chichester Foundation
Lacy Cadland Gardens Fareham Rymans
Wimborne Minster A35 Fawley Exbury Gosport Chidmere
Priest's Brockenhurst Gardens House
House Stapehill Abbey ❀ Spinners Cowes Portsmouth Selsey
Dean's Knoll Gardens New Milton Little Cottage Osborne House
Court Lymington Barton Manor Ryde
Poole A338 Apple Court Butterfly World
Christchurch Newport Nunwell House Pitt House
Bournemouth Freshwater Morton Manor
Armnore House Sandown
Mottistone Manor A3055 A3020 Shanklin
Swanage ISLE OF Ventnor
WIGHT Botanic ❀ Ventnor

4

529

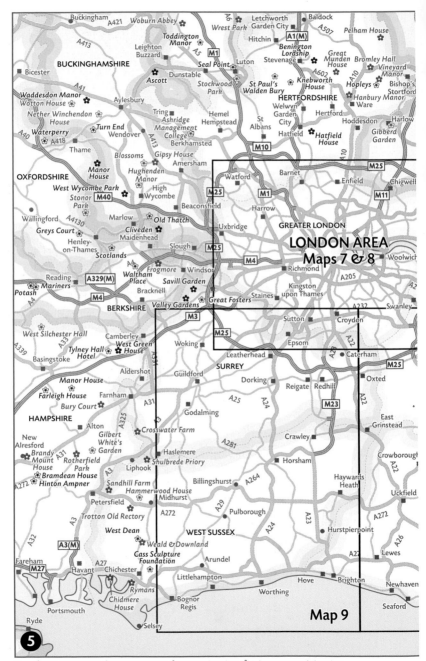

Map 9

5

Key: ✿ *Two-star gardens* ✾ *One-star gardens* ✿ *Unstarred gardens* ✾ *Other recommended gardens*

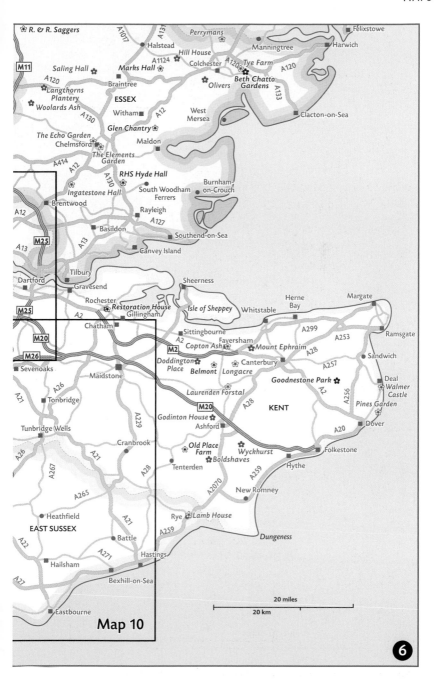

R. & R. Saggers

Felixstowe

M11

Saling Hall

A1007

A120

Langthorns
Plantery

Woolards Ash

A130

Halstead

Perrymans

Hill House

A1124

Marks Hall

Braintree

ESSEX

Witham

A12

Colchester

A120

Tye Farm

Olivers

Beth Chatto
Gardens

A120

Manningtree

Harwich

A120

A133

West
Mersea

Clacton-on-Sea

The Echo Garden

Glen Chantry

Chelmsford

A414

A12

The Elements
Garden

A130

RHS Hyde Hall

Maldon

Ingatestone Hall

Brentwood

A12

South Woodham
Ferrers

Rayleigh

Burnham-
on-Crouch

A127

Basildon

A13

A127

M25

Southend-on-Sea

A13

Canvey Island

Dartford

Tilbury

Gravesend

Sheerness

Herne
Bay

Margate

M25

Rochester

Restoration House

A2

Gillingham

Isle of Sheppey

Whitstable

A299

Ramsgate

Chatham

Sittingbourne

Faversham

A253

M20

M2

A2

Copton Ash

A28

Sandwich

M26

Doddington
Place

Mount Ephraim

A257

Sevenoaks

Maidstone

Belmont

Canterbury

Longacre

Deal
Walmer
Castle

A26

Laurenden Forstal

Goodnestone Park

A256

Pines Garden

A21

Tonbridge

A229

M20

A28

KENT

A2

Tunbridge Wells

Godinton House

Ashford

A20

Dover

A26

Cranbrook

A21

A28

Old Place
Farm

Wyckhurst

Folkestone

A267

Boldshaves

Tenterden

Hythe

A265

Heathfield

A21

Rye

Lamb House

A2070

New Romney

A259

EAST SUSSEX

A22

Battle

A271

A259

Dungeness

Hailsham

Hastings

A27

Bexhill-on-Sea

Eastbourne

Map 10

20 miles

20 km

6

531

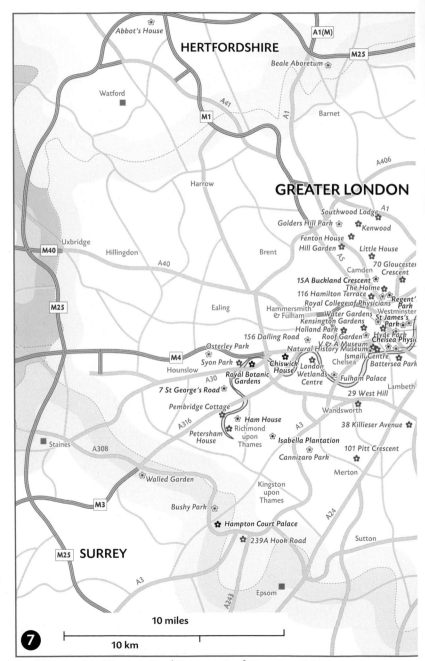

Abbot's House

HERTFORDSHIRE

A1(M)

M25

Beale Aboretum

Watford

A41

A1

Barnet

M1

A406

Harrow

GREATER LONDON

Uxbridge

Southwood Lodge

A1

Golders Hill Park

Kenwood

M40

Hillingdon

Brent

Fenton House

Hill Garden

Little House

A40

Camden

70 Gloucester
Crescent

15A Buckland Crescent

The Holme

116 Hamilton Terrace

Regent's
Park

M25

Ealing

Hammersmith
& Fulham

Royal College of Physicians

Westminster

Water Gardens

St James's
Park

Kensington Gardens

Holland Park

Roof Garden

Hyde Park

156 Dalling Road

V & A Museum

Chelsea Physic

Osterley Park

Natural History Museum

Syon Park

Chiswick
House

London
Wetlands
Centre

Ismaili Centre

Chelsea

Battersea Park

M4

Hounslow

A30

Royal Botanic
Gardens

Fulham Palace

Lambeth

7 St George's Road

29 West Hill

Pembridge Cottage

Wandsworth

A316

Ham House

38 Killieser Avenue

Petersham
House

Richmond
upon
Thames

Isabella Plantation

101 Pitt Crescent

Staines

A308

Cannizaro Park

Merton

Walled Garden

Kingston
upon
Thames

M3

Bushy Park

A24

Hampton Court Palace

Sutton

M25

SURREY

239A Hook Road

A3

Epsom

A243

10 miles

7

10 km

Key: ✿ *Two-star gardens* ❀ *One-star gardens* ✿ *Unstarred gardens* ❀ *Other recommended gardens*

532

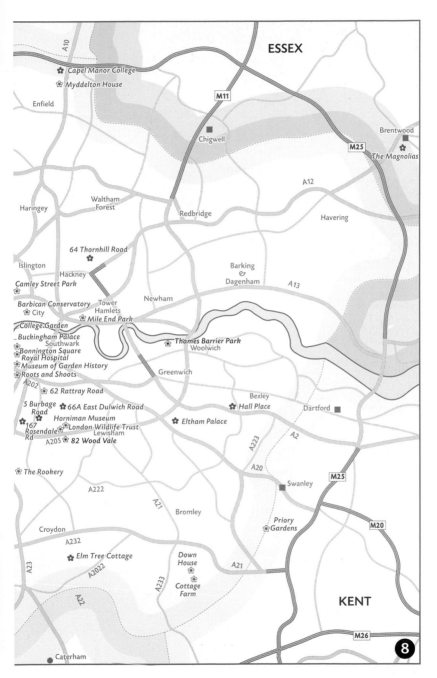

ESSEX

Capel Manor College

Myddelton House

Enfield

A10

M11

Chigwell

Brentwood

M25

The Magnolias

A12

Haringey

Waltham Forest

Redbridge

Havering

Islington

Hackney

64 Thornhill Road

Barking & Dagenham

A13

Camley Street Park

Barbican Conservatory
City

Tower Hamlets

Newham

Mile End Park

College Garden

Buckingham Palace

Southwark

Bonnington Square

Royal Hospital

Museum of Garden History

Roots and Shoots

A202

62 Rattray Road

5 Burbage Road

66A East Dulwich Road

167 Rosendale Rd

Horniman Museum

London Wildlife Trust

Lewisham

A205

82 Wood Vale

Thames Barrier Park

Woolwich

Greenwich

Bexley

Hall Place

Dartford

Eltham Palace

A223

A2

The Rookery

A222

A21

Bromley

A20

A20

Priory Gardens

Swanley

M25

M20

Croydon

A232

Elm Tree Cottage

A2022

A233

Down House

Cottage Farm

A21

KENT

A23

A22

Caterham

M26

8

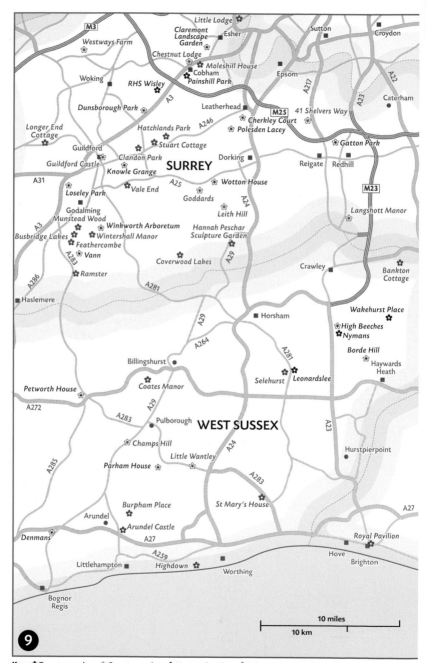

Key: ✿ *Two-star gardens* ❀ *One-star gardens* ✿ *Unstarred gardens* ❀ *Other recommended gardens*

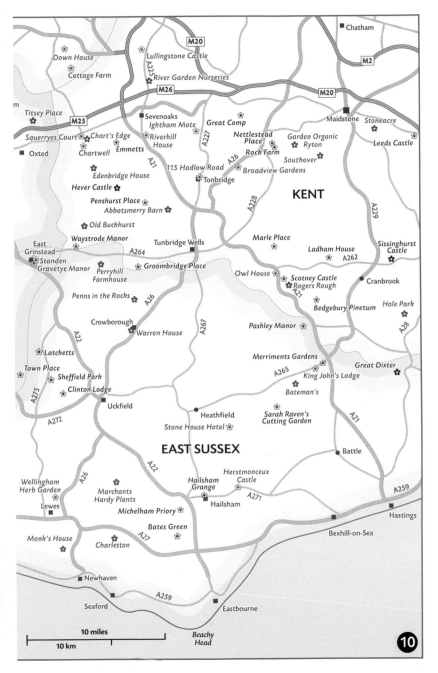

Chatham

M20

M2

Down House

Cottage Farm

Lullingstone Castle

River Garden Nurseries

A225

M26

M20

Maidstone

Stoneacre

Titsey Place

M25

Sevenoaks

Ightham Mote

Great Comp

Nettlestead Place

Garden Organic

Ryton

Leeds Castle

Squerryes Court

Chart's Edge

Riverhill House

A227

Rock Farm

Southover

Oxted

Chartwell

Emmetts

A21

115 Hadlow Road

Broadview Gardens

KENT

Edenbridge House

Tonbridge

A26

A229

Hever Castle

Penshurst Place

Abbotsmerry Barn

A228

Old Buckhurst

Marle Place

Ladham House

Sissinghurst Castle

Waystrode Manor

Tunbridge Wells

A262

East Grinstead

A264

Owl House

Scotney Castle

Cranbrook

Standen

Gravetye Manor

Groombridge Place

Rogers Rough

A21

Perryhill Farmhouse

Bedgebury Pinetum

Hole Park

Penns in the Rocks

A26

Pashley Manor

A28

Crowborough

A267

Warren House

Merriments Gardens

Great Dixter

Latchetts

A265

King John's Lodge

Town Place

Sheffield Park

Bateman's

A22

Clinton Lodge

Uckfield

Heathfield

Sarah Raven's Cutting Garden

A21

A275

A272

Stone House Hotel

Battle

EAST SUSSEX

A22

Herstmonceux Castle

Wellingham Herb Garden

A26

Hailsham Grange

A271

A259

Marchants Hardy Plants

Hailsham

Hastings

Lewes

Michelham Priory

Monk's House

Bates Green

Bexhill-on-Sea

Charleston

A27

Newhaven

A259

Seaford

Eastbourne

Beachy Head

10 miles

10 km

10

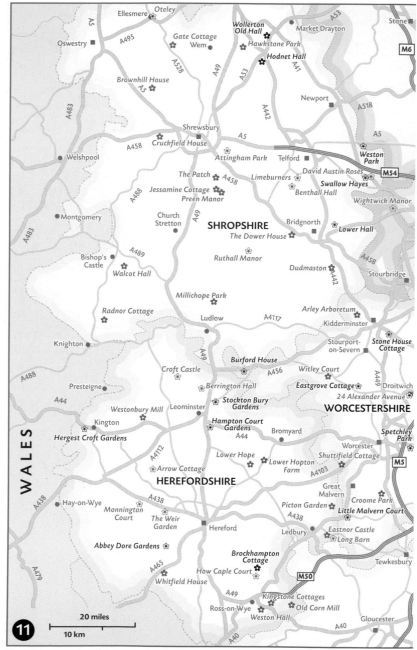

Key: ✿ *Two-star gardens* ✾ *One-star gardens* ✿ *Unstarred gardens* ✾ *Other recommended gardens*

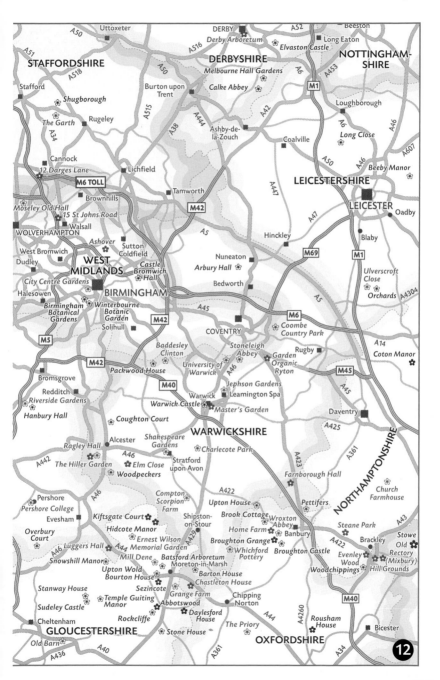

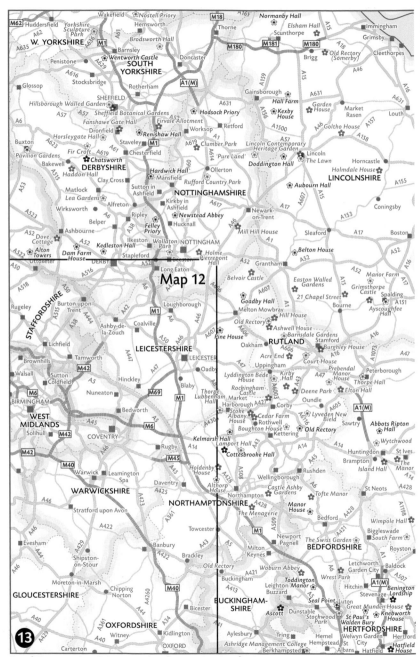

Map 12

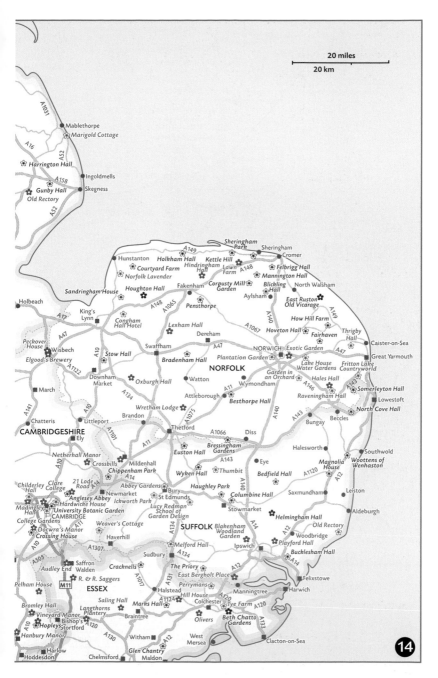

Mablethorpe
❁ Marigold Cottage
A1031
A16
A52
❁ Harrington Hall
A158
Ingoldmells
❁ Gunby Hall
Old Rectory
Skegness
A52

Sheringham
Park
Sheringham
A149
Cromer
Hunstanton Holkham Hall Kettle Hill
❁ Courtyard Farm Hindringham Lawn
Norfolk Lavender Hall Farm A148 ❁ Felbrigg Hall
❁ Mannington Hall
Houghton Hall Fakenham Corpusty Mill❁ Blickling North Walsham
Garden Hall
Aylsham East Ruston
Old Vicarage
Sandringham House A148 A1065 Penthorpe A140 How Hill Farm
Holbeach King's Congham Lexham Hall A1067 Hoveton Hall ❁ Fairhaven Thrigby
Lynn Hall Hotel Dereham Hall
A17 Peckover Stow Hall Swaffham A47 NORWICH Exotic Garden A47 Caister-on-Sea
House Wisbech A10 Bradenham Hall Plantation Garden Great Yarmouth
Elgood's Brewery Downham NORFOLK Lake House Fritton Lake
A1122 Market ❁ Oxburgh Hall ● Watton Garden in Water Gardens Countryworld
March A134 Wymondham an Orchard Hales Hall Somerleyton Hall
A141 Attleborough A11 Besthorpe Hall A146 Raveningham Hall Lowestoft
Chatteris Wretham Lodge A1075 A140 A143 Bungay North Cove Hall
Littleport Brandon Thetford Diss Beccles
CAMBRIDGESHIRE A1101 A11 A1066 Halesworth Southwold
Ely Bressingham Magnolia Woottens of
Netherhall Manor Euston Hall Gardens ● Eye House Wenhaston
Crossbills Mildenhall Wyken Hall ❁ Thumbit Bedfield Hall A1120 A12
Chippenham Park A14 Leiston
Childerley Clare 21 Lode Abbey Gardens❁ Haughley Park Saxmundham
Hall College Road Newmarket Bury A140 Columbine Hall Aldeburgh
Anglesey Abbey Ickworth Park St Edmunds Stowmarket Old Rectory
Madingley Hardwicke House Lucy Redman Helmingham Hall
Hall University Botanic Garden School of Woodbridge
College Gardens CAMBRIDGE Weaver's Cottage Garden Design SUFFOLK Blakenham Playford Hall
Docwra's Manor Haverhill Woodland Bucklesham Hall
Crossing House A1307 ❁ Melford Hall Garden A14
A505 Sudbury A134 Ipswich Felixstowe
Audley End Saffron Cracknells The Priory A12
Pelham House Walden East Bergholt Place Harwich
❁ R. & R. Saggers Perrymans Manningtree
M11 ESSEX Halstead Hill House A120 Tye Farm A120
Bromley Hall Saling Hall A1124 Colchester
Vineyard Manor Langthorns Marks Hall Olivers Beth Chatto
Hopleys Plantery Braintree A12 Gardens A133
Bishop's A120 A130 Witham A12 West Clacton-on-Sea
Hanbury Manor Stortford Mersea
A10 Glen Chantry
Harlow Chelmsford Maldon
Hoddesdon

20 miles
20 km

🖤14

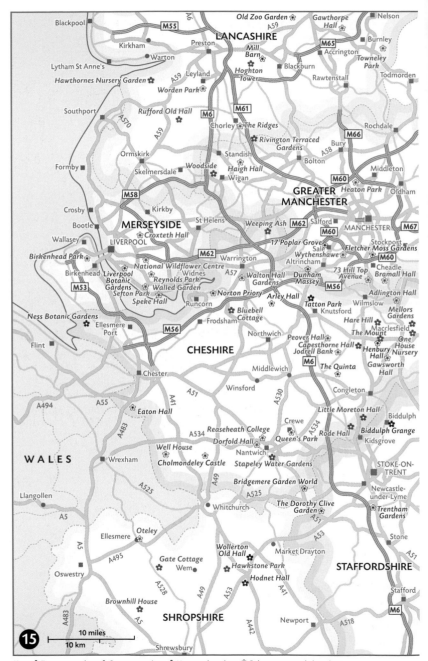

Key: ✿ Two-star gardens ⊛ One-star gardens ✿ Unstarred gardens ⊛ Other recommended gardens

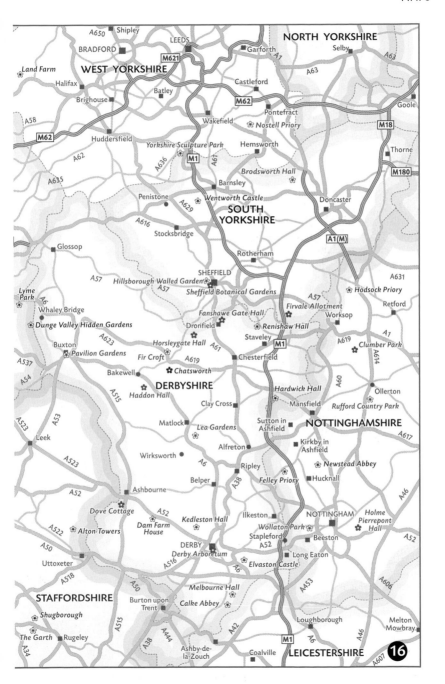

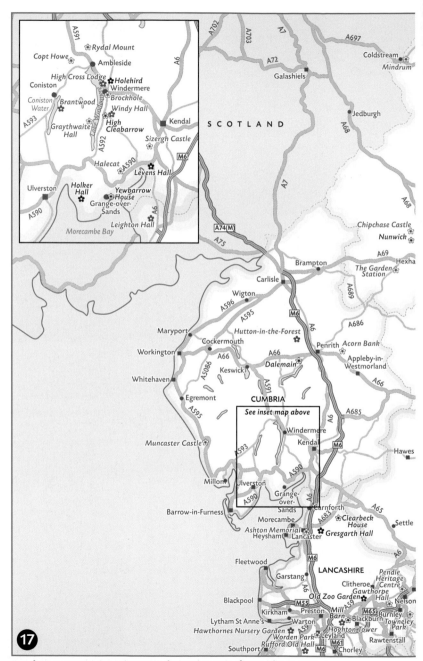

Key: ✿ *Two-star gardens* ✤ *One-star gardens* ✤ *Unstarred gardens* ✤ *Other recommended gardens*

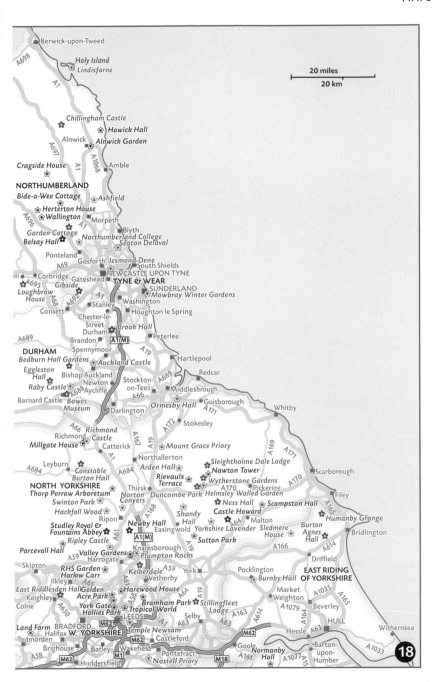

20 miles
20 km

Berwick-upon-Tweed

Holy Island
Lindisfarne

A698
A1

Chillingham Castle
Howick Hall
Alnwick Garden
Alnwick

A697
A1068
Amble

Cragside House
A1

NORTHUMBERLAND
Bide-a-Wee Cottage
Ashfield
Herterton House
Wallington
Morpeth
A696
A1
Garden Cottage
Blyth
Belsay Hall
Northumberland College
Seaton Delaval

Ponteland
A69
Gosforth
Jesmond Dene
South Shields
m
Corbridge
Gateshead
NEWCASTLE UPON TYNE
A695
Gibside
TYNE & WEAR
Loughbrow
House
A1
SUNDERLAND
A69
A692
Mowbray Winter Gardens
Stanley
Washington
Consett
Houghton le Spring
Chester-le-
Street
Crook Hall
Durham
Peterlee
A689
Brandon
A1(M)
DURHAM
Spennymoor
A19
Bedburn Hall Gardens
Auckland Castle
Hartlepool
Eggleston
Hall
Bishop Auckland
Newton
Redcar
Raby Castle
A688
Aycliffe
Stockton-
on-Tees
A689
Barnard Castle
Bowes
Museum
A66
Middlesbrough
Darlington
Ormesby Hall
Guisborough
A171
Whitby
A66
Richmond
A167
A172
Stokesley
Richmond
Castle
A19
Millgate House
Catterick
Mount Grace Priory
A169
A171

Leyburn
Northallerton
Sleightholme Dale Lodge
A684
Constable
Arden Hall
Nawton Tower
Scarborough
Burton Hall
A684
Rievaulx
Wytherstone Gardens
A170
NORTH YORKSHIRE
Thirsk
Terrace
Pickering
Filey
Thorp Perrow Arboretum
Norton
Duncombe Park Helmsley Walled Garden
Swinton Park
Conyers
A168
Ness Hall
Scampston Hall
A165
Hackfall Wood
Shandy
Castle Howard
Humanby Grange
Ripon
A64
Studley Royal &
Newby Hall
Hall
Sledmere
Burton
Fountains Abbey
A61
Easingwold
Yorkshire Lavender
House
Agnes
Bridlington
Ripley Castle
A1(M)
A19
Sutton Park
Hall
A614
Parcevall Hall
Knaresborough
A166
Skipton
A59
Valley Gardens
Plumpton Rocks
Driffield
Harrogate
EAST RIDING
RHS Garden
Kelberdale
A59
York
Pocklington
OF YORKSHIRE
Harlow Carr
Wetherby
Burnby Hall
Ilkley
A65
Harewood House
Market
A1035
A165
East Riddlesden Hall
Golden
A61
Weighton
Keighley
Acre Park
A58
Bramham Park
Stillingfleet
A1079
Beverley
Colne
A650
York Gate
Tropical World
Lodge
A163
A164
Hollies Park
LEEDS
Selby
A614
HULL
Land Farm
BRADFORD
M621
Temple Newsam
A63
A63
Hessle
A63
Withernsea
Todmorden
Halifax
W. YORKSHIRE
M62
Castleford
M62
A1033
Brighouse
Batley
M1
Wakefield
Goole
Normanby
Barton-
A58
M62
Huddersfield
Pontefract
M18
A161
Hall
A1077
upon-
Nostell Priory
Humber
A15

18

543

MAPS

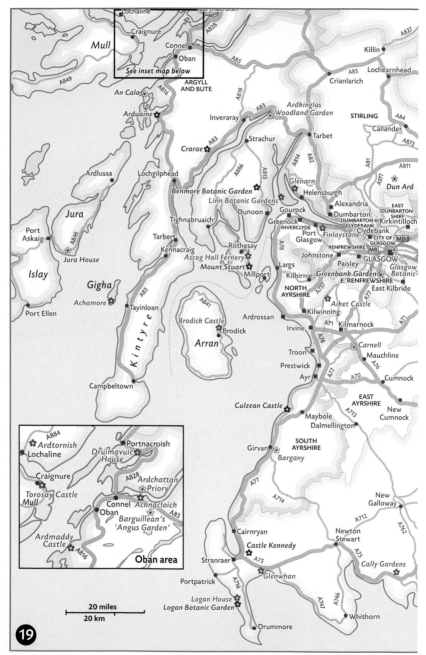

Key: ✿ *Two-star gardens* ✤ *One-star gardens* ✿ *Unstarred gardens* ✤ *Other recommended gardens*

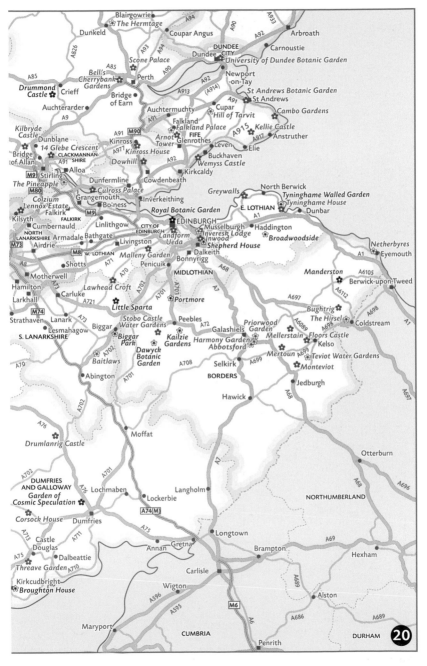

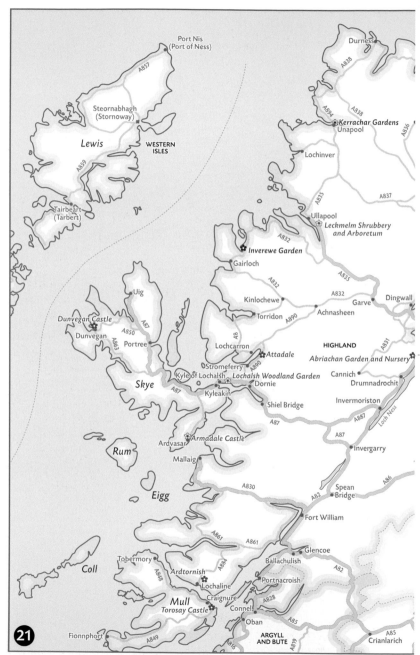

Key: ✿ Two-star gardens ❀ One-star gardens ✿ Unstarred gardens ❀ Other recommended gardens

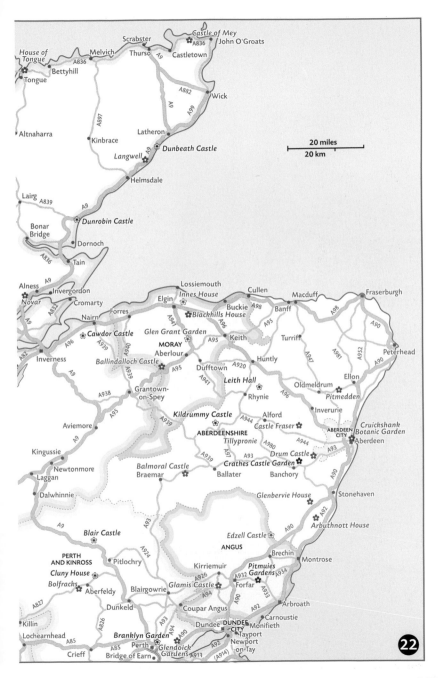

Glenveagh Castle
Buncrana Coleraine Benvarden House
Letterkenny LONDONDERRY
N13
A37
N56 A26
N13
N14
Fox Lodge Ballymena M2 Larne
Salthill Gardens N15
NORTHERN M22 M2
Omagh A505 IRELAND BELFAST
N15 A32
Enniscoe Enniskillen A4 M1
Gardens N16 Florence Court Armagh
Ballina Sligo N12
N59 N16
N26 Newry Newcastle
N17 N4 Cavan N33
Turlough Park N5 Knockabbey Castle N2
Westport N5 Loughcrew M1
Strokestown Park Dundalk
Claremorris N5 Tullynally Castle
Kylemore Abbey N3 Drogheda
N17 Mullingar N1
Ardcarraig Belvedere Navan N3
Athlone N6 N6 N51 M4 M50
Galway REPUBLIC M7 DUBLIN
An Féar Gorta OF IRELAND M9 Naas M11
N18 Birr N7 Portlaoise
Ennistymon Knappogue Birr Castle Japanese Garden Mount Usher
Ennis Castle Gash Gardens N7 Heywood Garden Wicklow
Vandeleur Walled Nenagh Carlow National Botanic Gardens,
Garden Bunratty Castle N8 Duckett's Grove Tullow Kilmacurragh
LIMERICK Kilkenny N10 Altamont
Glin Castle Georgian House N24 Kilfane Glen The Bay Garden
Tralee N21 Tipperary Woodstock Gardens New
N21 N8 Ross
Killorglin N20 Clonmel N24 John F. Kennedy Arboretum
Dunloe Castle Annes Grove N9 Kilmokea Wexford
Muckross Gardens Killarney Fermoy WATERFORD Kilmacurragh
Kenmare Lakemount Fota Lismore Castle Mount Congreve
Derreen Amergen CORK Gardens N25 Tramore
Ilnacullin Bantry Ballymaloe Youghal
Bantry House Kinsale
Glebe Gardens

20 miles
20 km

23

©Crown Copyright

Key: ✿ Two-star gardens ❀ One-star gardens ✿ Unstarred gardens ❀ Other recommended gardens

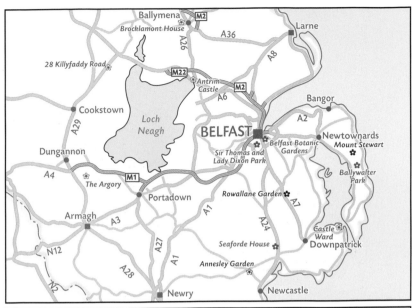

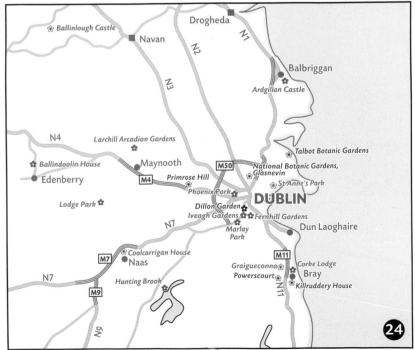

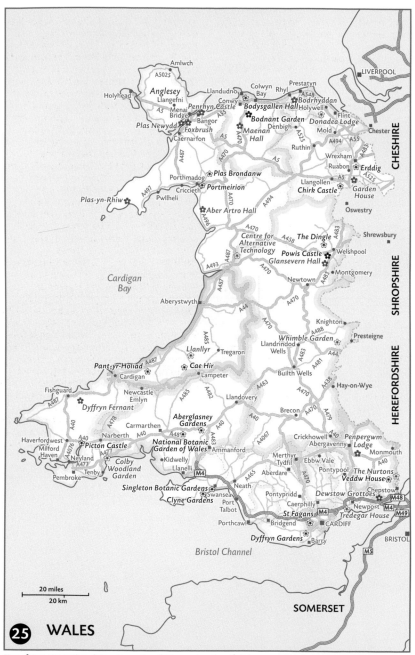

Amlwch
A5025
Anglesey
Holyhead
Llangefni
Llandudno
Colwyn Bay
Rhyl
Prestatyn
A548
Bodrhyddan
Holywell
Flint
LIVERPOOL
Conwy
Penrhyn Castle
Bodysgallen Hall
Menai Bridge
Bangor
Bodnant Garden
Donadea Lodge
Chester
CHESHIRE
Plas Newydd
Foxbrush
Maenan Hall
Denbigh
A525
Mold
Caernarfon
Ruthin
A494
A55
Wrexham
Ruabon
A5
Erddig
A525
A487
A470
Porthmadog
Plas Brondanw
Criccieth
Portmeirion
Llangollen
Chirk Castle
Garden House
Pwllheli
Plas-yn-Rhiw
A497
Aber Artro Hall
A496
A470
A494
Oswestry
Centre for Alternative Technology
A470
A458
The Dingle
Shrewsbury
A483
Welshpool
Powis Castle
Glansevern Hall
A487
A493
A470
Newtown
A483
Montgomery
Cardigan Bay
A487
Aberystwyth
A44
A470
Knighton
A488
Presteigne
SHROPSHIRE
A485
Whimble Garden
Llandrindod Wells
A483
A44
Llanllyr
Tregaron
Cae Hir
Lampeter
Builth Wells
A481
A438
Hay-on-Wye
Pant-yr-Holiad
A487
Cardigan
A485
A482
Llandovery
A483
A470
A479
Brecon
A40
HEREFORDSHIRE
Fishguard
A487
Newcastle Emlyn
Dyffryn Fernant
A40
A40
A478
Carmarthen
Aberglasney Gardens
A40
A40
Crickhowell
Abergavenny
Penpergwm Lodge
Monmouth
Haverfordwest
A4076
Narberth
A48
National Botanic Garden of Wales
A483
Ammanford
Merthyr Tydfil
Ebbw Vale
A40
Milford Haven
Picton Castle
A477
Kidwelly
A4067
A465
Pontypool
The Nurtons
Veddw House
Neyland
A477
Colby Woodland Garden
Llanelli
Aberdare
A470
Dewstow Grottoes
Pembroke
Tenby
Singleton Botanic Gardens
Swansea
Neath
Pontypridd
Caerphilly
St Fagans
Newport
M48
M4
M4
M49
Clyne Gardens
Port Talbot
Tredegar House
BRISTOL
Porthcawl
Bridgend
CARDIFF
M5
Dyffryn Gardens
Barry
Bristol Channel

20 miles
20 km

25 WALES

SOMERSET

Key: ✿ Two-star gardens ❀ One-star gardens ✿ Unstarred gardens ❀ Other recommended gardens

550

ACKNOWLEDGEMENTS

Our thanks to everyone who has helped with the preparation of the Guide – to owners, custodians, professional gardening staff, and many others. In particular, we thank our inspectors and those who advised them. Some of those who have given advice do not wish to be listed and, although anonymous, they have been every bit as valuable. We are also obliged to staff of The National Trust and The National Trust for Scotland, English Heritage, Historic Scotland, The National Gardens Scheme and Scotland's Gardens Scheme for their co–operation.

The following include inspectors (plus some past inspectors) and advisors: Barbara Abbs, Miranda Allhusen, Jane Allsopp, Gillian Archer, Diana Atkins, Rosie Atkins, Diane and Peter Baistow, David Baldwin, Jenny Baldwin, Susan Barnes, Mr and Mrs Basten, Kenneth and Gillian Beckett, Jackie Bennett, June Beveridge, Lavender Borden, Kathryn Bradley–Hole, Harry Brickwood, Hilary Bristow, Cecil Brown, Jennifer Brown, Christina Campbell, Adam Caplin, Shirley Cargill, Dr Joan Carmichael, Brian and Gillian Cassidy, Lady Cave, Liz Challen, Anne Chamberlain, Sir Jeremy and Lady Chance, Annabelle Chisholm, Timothy Clark, Sarah Coles, Anne Collins, E. Anne Colville, David Conway, Guy Cooper, Beatrice Cowan, Simon Cramp, Janet Cropley, Jo, Penelope, Rosie and Trixie Currie, Wendy Dare, Margreet Diepeveen–Bruins Slot, Marilyn Dodd, Rosemary Dodgson, Daphne Dormer, Lady Edmonstone, Matthew Fattorini, Sir Charles and Lady Fraser, Daphne Fisher, Liz Friedrich, Kate Garton, Leslie Geddes–Brown, Lucy Gent, Alison Gregory, Gwynne Griffiths, Fenja Gunn, Elizabeth Hamilton, Stuart Harding, Anne Harrison, Sunniva Harte, Charles Hawes, Jane Henson, Steve Hipkin, Judith Hitchings, Hilary Hodgson, Christopher Holliday, Mariana Hollis, Caroline Holmes, Jacky Hone, Sophie Hughes, Pam Hummer, Erica Hunningher, Jill Husselby, David and Karen Jacques, Judith Jenkins, Valerie Jinks, Vanessa Johnston, Rosemarie Johnstone, Belinda Jupp, Mary Keen, Jo Kenaghan, Margaret Knight, Shirley Lanigan, Jean Laughton, Virginia Lawlor, Andrew Lawson, Dr Elizabeth Lazenby, Anne E. Liverman, Mary-Gay Livingston, Malcolm Lyell, Charles Lyte, Rhian de Mattos, Jamie McCarter, Pat McCrostie, Anna McKane, Christopher McLaren, Deirdre McSharry, Bettine Muir, Dr Charles Nelson, Hugh Palmer, Lucinda Parry, Christine Parsons, Victoria Petrie–Hay, David Pettifer, Lady Pigot, Louisa Pink, Stephen Player, Jocelyn Poole, Jane Powers, Heather Prescott, Lorna Ramsay, Terence Reeves–Smith, Finola Reid, Anne Richards, Tim Rock, Christopher Rogers, Sara Rohling, Sue Roscoe Watts, Dorothy Rose, Jane Russell, Alison Rutherford, Sarah Rutherford, Peter de Sausmarez, Kathy Sayer, Jane Scott, Barbara Segall, Marjorie Sime, Gillian Sladen, Dr Gordon Smith, Michael Smith, Lady Smith–Ryland, Elaine Snazell, Margaret Soole, Marlene Storah, Ruth Stungo, Camilla Swift, Vera Taggart, Sally Tamplin, Gordon Taylor, Caroline Todhunter, Michael Tooley, Annetta Troth, Marie–Françoise Valery, Jackie Ward, Ian Warden, Anne Wareham, Jenifer Wates, Myra Wheeldon, Susan Whittington, Cynthia Wickham, Nigel Wilkins, John Wilks, Alice Windsor-Clive and Martin Wood. Especial thanks are due to Anita Owen, Keith Rigley, Wendy Gardner, Mala Rohling, Linda Dawes and Angie Hipkin.

PHOTOGRAPHIC CREDITS

The editors are grateful to all those who have made it possible for these images to be included. We have made every effort to trace and credit the photographer in each case, and apologise for any errors or omissions. Where no picture is credited, the image was almost always either taken by the owner or comes courtesy of the estate or institution concerned.

Half title (Easton Walled Gardens, Lincolnshire) Sir Fred Cholmeley; 4 English Heritage Photo Library; 6 John Harley; 14 (bottom) Alan Stealey; 16 NTPL/Neil Campbell-Sharp; 18 Fiona McLeod; 21 courtesy of NT, Waddesdon Manor/Hugh Palmer; 24 NTPL/Stephen Robson; 29 Fisheye Images; 44 William Pye; 46 Marcus Leith (Tate); 50 Lorna Tremayne; 52 N. Teagle; 56 Tony Hibbert; 58 Erica Hunninger; 60 Beverley Chegwidden; 63 Shirley Dean; 67 Val Corbett; 70 Matthew Bullen; 74 NTPL/Andrew Haslam; 79 Dick Cross; 88 Stephen Record; 92 Stephen Griffith; 100 Patrick Cooke; 101 Jerry Harpur; 106 Heather Edwards; 108 Keith Bell; 112 Steven Wooster; 115 Schoenaich Landscape Associates; 118 Rowan Isaac; 122 John Grimshaw; 124 NTPL/Rupert Truman; 129 Rowan Isaac; 138 Mary Best; 146 NTPL/Stephen Robson; 149 David Watson; 153 Clay Perry; 155 English Heritage Photo Library; 158 Sabina Ruber; 161 Nicola Stocken Tomkins; 165 A. F. Kersting; 167 Daniel Martin; 170 Chris Beddall; 175, 179, 185 Peter Baistow; 189 Helen Shaw, Malkin Photography; 192 Jane Sebire; 199 NTPL/Andrew Butler; 204 (top) NTPL/Andrea Jones; 206 (top) Val Corbett; 206 (bottom) Charles Rodgers; 209 Nick Johnson; 211 (top) courtesy of Liverpool City Council; 214 Dennis Firminger/Reel Film Locations; 223 Dr Henry Oakeley/Royal College of Physicians; 224 Phil Riley; 225 (top) Kim Wilkie; 225 (bottom) Ariane Severin; 231 Sarah Canet; 233 (bottom) Anne Gatti;

237 NTPL/Nick Meers; 242 Richard Bloom/Bloom Pictures; 244 Brian Chapple; 245 Louise Rout; 248 Neil Holmes; 252 Niki Bowers; 255 Michael Simon; 259 Sue Jackson; 266 Carole Drake; 268 Chris Orton; 271 Wendy Lloyd; 274 Thomas Unterdorfer; 279 Tim Miles; 283 Nicola Stocken Tomkins; 285 Timothy Walker; 286 Ray Smith; 290 Mike Peck; 297 John Glover; 300 Andrew Lawson; 303 (top and bottom) Jason Ingram; 310 NTPL/Nick Meers; 311 Jarrold Publishing, Norwich; 312 Peter Emberton; 314, 318 Jerry Harpur; 320 Carl West; 323 Andrew Lawson; 326 Kim Wilkie; 331 Troika/RHS; 333 courtesy of the Crown Estate; 341 Taryn Cook; 343 (top) Peter Baistow; 345 NTPL/Lisa Barnard; 347 Darryl Curcher; 350 Pamela Milward; 351 Edward Boscawen; 355 Charles Roe; 363 NTPL/Robert Morris; 367 NTPL/Stephen Robson; 371 Nigel White; 375 Carole Drake; 380 NTPL/Nick Meers; 381 Ros Liddington, courtesy of the Earl of Pembroke; 382 Pats Vigors; 384 Wendy Carter; 386 Mark Bolton; 398 Allison Mitchell; 400 Alexandre Bailhache; 402 NTPL/Andrew Butler; 411 John Whittaker; 412 Jonty Wild; 415 (top) Stephen Robson; 415 NTPL/Jerry Harpur; 421, 422 Jane Powers; 427 Robert Myerscough; 430 Michael White; 431 Maria Vlahos; 433 Suzanne Clarke; 442 NTS Photo Library/ Brian Chapple; 443 Geoff Stephenson; 449 NTS Photo Library/Brian Chapple; 451 Malcolm McGregor; 454, Jim Henderson; 456 (top) Deirdre Mackinnon/NTS; 456 (bottom) David Knott; 459 Ray Biggs/G&DCT; 465 NTS Photo Library/Brian Chapple; 466 (bottom), NTS Photo Library; 467 Ann Fraser; 475 Mount Stuart Trust; 484 Crown Copyright, courtesy of Historic Scotland; 485 NTS Photo Library/Brian Chapple; 493 Charles Hawes; 498 NTPL/Stephen Robson; 506 Brian Cooper; 507 Anne Gatti

INDEX

An index entry in *italic text* indicates that the garden or nursery is mentioned in the text of another garden entry. Illustrations that occur on different pages to their garden entry are indexed with *italic page numbers*. An * indicates an entry in the Nurseries with Good Gardens section.

REPORT FORM

We welcome readers' comments on gardens they have visited. Use the report form below, or send your comments on a sheet of paper to:

The Good Gardens Guide
Frances Lincoln Ltd, 4 Torriano Mews, Torriano Avenue, London NW5 2RZ

To the editors of *The Good Gardens Guide*

From my own experience the following garden should/should not be included in the *Guide*:

GARDEN NAME _____

ADDRESS _____
_____
_____

POSTCODE _____

TELEPHONE _____

NAME OF OWNER(S) _____

DESCRIPTION

1. LOCATION _____

2. GARDEN OPEN/TIMES _____

3. ENTRANCE CHARGE _____

4. HOUSE OPEN/TIMES _____

5. BRIEF DETAILS OF MAIN CHARACTERISTICS _____
_____
_____
_____
_____
_____

6. OTHER NOTES _____
_____
_____
_____

SENT IN BY (NAME AND ADDRESS) _____
_____
_____